COUNTER-TERRORISM STRATEGIES IN A FRAGMENTED INTERNATIONAL LEGAL ORDER

Few events have influenced our global order as intensely as the events of September 11, 2001. At various levels in the past twelve years, persistent attempts have been made to address the threat of terrorism, yet there is still urgent need for a joint and coherent application of a variety of regulations relating to international criminal justice cooperation, the use of force and international human rights law. In an important contribution to international discourse, Larissa van den Herik and Nico Schrijver examine the relationship between different branches of international law and their applicability to the problem of terrorism and counter-terrorism. Using a unique combination of academic perspectives, practitioners' insights and a comprehensive three-part approach, *Counter-Terrorism Strategies in a Fragmented International Legal Order* offers sound policy recommendations alongside thorough analysis of the state of international law regarding terrorism, and provides fresh insights against the backdrop of recent practice.

LARISSA VAN DEN HERIK is Professor of Public International Law at the Grotius Centre for International Legal Studies, Leiden University.

NICO SCHRIJVER is Chair of Public International Law and Academic Director at the Grotius Centre for International Legal Studies, Leiden University.

COUNTER-TERRORISM STRATEGIES IN A FRAGMENTED INTERNATIONAL LEGAL ORDER

Meeting the challenges

Edited by

LARISSA VAN DEN HERIK

and

NICO SCHRIJVER

CAMBRIDGE
UNIVERSITY PRESS

CAMBRIDGE
UNIVERSITY PRESS

University Printing House, Cambridge CB2 8BS, United Kingdom

Published in the United States of America by Cambridge University Press, New York

Cambridge University Press is part of the University of Cambridge.

It furthers the University's mission by disseminating knowledge in the pursuit of education, learning and research at the highest international levels of excellence.

www.cambridge.org
Information on this title: www.cambridge.org/9781107025387

First published 2013

Printed and bound in the United Kingdom by Clays, St Ives plc

A catalogue record for this publication is available from the British Library

Library of Congress Cataloguing in Publication data
Counter-terrorism and international law / edited by Larissa van den Herik and Nico Schrijver.
p. cm.
ISBN 978-1-107-02538-7
1. Terrorism (International law) 2. Terrorism – Prevention – Law and legislation. 3. Human rights. I. Herik, L. J. van den (Larissa J.) II. Schrijver, Nico, 1954–
KZ7220.C6775 2013
345′.02–dc23
2012028264

ISBN 978-1-107-02538-7 Hardback

Additional resources for this publication at www.cambridge.org/9781107025387

CONTENTS

NOTES ON CONTRIBUTORS

ANDREA BIANCHI, Ph.D. (Milan), LLM (Harvard) is Professor of International Law at the Graduate Institute of International and Development Studies, Geneva. His publications related to terrorism include: *International Humanitarian Law and Terrorism* (2011, co-authored with Yasmin Naqvi) *Counterterrorism: Democracy's Challenge* (2008; edited with A. Keller); *Enforcing International Law Norms against Terrorism* (2004); 'Security Council's Anti-Terror Resolutions and their Implementation by Member States: An Overview' (2006) 4 *Journal of International Criminal Justice* 1044–73; 'Assessing the Effectiveness of the UN Security Council's Anti-terrorism Measures: The Quest for Legitimacy and Cohesion' (2006) 17 *European Journal of International Law* 880–919.

KARIMA BENNOUNE is Professor of Law at the University of California, Davis School of Law. A former Amnesty International legal adviser, her human rights field missions have included Afghanistan, Egypt, Pakistan, Mali, southern Thailand and Tunisia. She has published widely on terrorism, human rights and religious fundamentalism, including the articles 'Terror/Torture' (2008) 26 *Berkeley Journal of International Law* 1–61 and 'Remembering the Other's Others: Theorizing the Approach of International Law to Muslim Fundamentalism' (2010) 41 *Columbia Human Rights Law Review* 335–98. Her topical writing has appeared in the *New York Times*, the *Guardian* and the website of Aljazeera. Bennoune's forthcoming book *Your Fatwa Does Not Apply Here: Untold Stories from the Fight against Muslim Fundamentalism*, documents popular resistance to terrorism and extremism.

TIM DANIEL is a partner in the Litigation Department of Edwards Wildman Palmer UK LLP, London. He founded his previous firm's public international law practice and has acted for a number of governments and parastatals, particularly in the developing world. This work has included representation of states before the ICJ in The Hague in boundary disputes and in international arbitration disputes. He has extensive experience of asset tracing, both in the commercial/insolvency sector and, currently, on behalf of states. He was involved in several high-profile cases in the 1980s and 1990s including the Lloyd's/PCW litigation, the Barlow Clowes liquidation and BCCI. He is currently acting for several governments and anti-corruption commissions recovering assets looted by former heads of state and high-ranking government officials, and has advised governments on anti money-laundering and proceeds of crime legislation.

CORDULA DROEGE is the legal adviser of the ICRC's delegation in Israel and the Occupied Territories. Before coming to this post, she was a legal adviser at the headquarters of the ICRC in Geneva, which she joined in 2005. Earlier positions include posts at the International Commission of Jurists in Geneva, the Inter-American Court of Human Rights and the Max Planck Institute for Comparative and International Law.

HELEN DUFFY runs an international law practice 'Human Rights in Practice' in The Hague. She has represented victims of human rights violations in the Inter-American, African and European human rights systems. For the past ten years she was Legal Director at INTERIGHTS, where she remains engaged as Senior Counsel. She was previously Legal Officer at the ICTY, Counsel to HRW, Legal Director of the Centre for Human Rights Legal Action in Guatemala, and Legal Adviser to the UK 'Arms for Iraq' Inquiry. She regularly lectures and publishes on international law and practice, including *The War on Terror and the Framework of International Law* (Cambridge University Press, 2005, 2nd edn, forthcoming 2014). Helen teaches at Leiden University and is Honorary Professor of International Law at the University of Glasgow. She serves on the advisory boards of several NGOs.

MARTIN EWI is currently a senior researcher on counter-terrorism at the Institute for Security Studies (ISS), based in Pretoria, South Africa. He joined the ISS from the headquarters of the Organisation for the Prohibition of Chemical Weapons, where he served as a political affairs officer. He was previously the African Union Commission's counter-terrorism expert, concurrently responsible for strategic security issues. He holds a master's degree in international peace studies from the University of Notre Dame and a bachelor's degree (with distinction) in peace studies and international politics from Juniata College (both USA).

CHARLES GARRAWAY served for thirty years as a legal officer in the UK Army Legal Services where he advised the Ministry of Defence (MoD) on operations in the Balkans, Sierra Leone, Afghanistan and Iraq. He has represented the MoD at a number of international conferences and was the senior Army lawyer deployed to the Gulf during the 1990/1 Gulf Conflict. More recently, he has worked for the Foreign Office on transitional justice issues in both Iraq and Afghanistan. He has taught at universities and military institutions around the world and was appointed the Stockton Chair in International Law at the United States Naval War College for 2004/5. Professor Garraway was an Associate Fellow at Chatham House, is a Fellow at the Human Rights Centre, University of Essex and has taught part-time at the LSE. His current research interests include IHL and international criminal justice.

VINCENT GLERUM is a staff lawyer at the District Court of Amsterdam. His duties include providing legal support to the extradition chamber of the District Court and acting as registrar of that chamber. The European Union Framework Decision on the European Arrest Warrant (EAW-FD), which replaced extradition between states with a much simplified procedure of surrender between judicial authorities, sparked off his interest in the transition from extradition to surrender. Since the advent of the EAW-FD, he has written a book on the Dutch act implementing the EAW-FD and, together with Klaas Rozemond, he has published on the EAW and on extradition law. He is a contributor to several commentaries on extradition law, on the EAW and on the law regarding the transfer of sentenced persons.

ROBERT K. GOLDMAN is Louis C. James Scholar; co-director, Center for Human Rights and Humanitarian Law; faculty director, the War Crimes Research Office; and professor of law. He holds expertise in international and human rights law; US foreign policy; terrorism; and the law of armed conflict. From 1996 to 2004 he was a member of the Organization of American States' Inter-American Commission on Human Rights, and was its president in 1999. From July 2004 to July 2005, Goldman was the UN Human Rights Commission's Independent Expert on the protection of human rights and fundamental freedoms while countering terrorism. In October 2005, the International

Commission of Jurists named him one of the eight jurists on the Eminent Jurists Panel on Terrorism, Counter-Terrorism and Human Rights. In 2008, he was elected Commissioner and member of the Executive Committee of the International Commission of Jurists. He is author of *The Protection of Human Rights: Past, Present and Future* (1972); co-author of Middle East Watch's book, *Needless Deaths in the Gulf War* (1991); and co-author of *The International Dimension of Human Rights: A Guide for Application in Domestic Law* (2001).

LARISSA VAN DEN HERIK is Professor of Public International Law at Leiden University. She is the editor-in-chief of the *Leiden Journal of International Law* and a member of the Advisory Committee on issues of public international law, which advises the Dutch government and parliament. Her publications related to terrorism include: 'Eroding the primacy of the UN system of collective security: The Judgment of the European Court of Justice in the cases of *Kadi* and *Al Barakaat*' (2009) 5 *International Organizations Law Review* 329; 'Addressing challenges to targeted sanctions: an Update to the Watson Report', section 3 (2009); 'The Security Council's Targeted Sanctions Regimes: In Need of Better Protection of the Individual' (2007) 20 *Leiden Journal of International Law* 797; 'Legal Aspects of Human Rights and Due Process Concerns associated with Targeted Sanctions', in T. J. Biersteker and S. E. Eckert (eds.), *Strengthening UN Targeted Sanctions by Addressing Due Process Concerns* (2006).

DAVID KRETZMER LLB, LLM (Jerusalem), Dr Jur (York, Canada), Dr Jur hc (Potsdam), is Professor Emeritus of International Law at the Hebrew University of Jerusalem, and Professor of Law at Sapir College. His books include *The Occupation of Justice: The Supreme Court of Israel and the Occupied Territories* (2002); *The Concept of Human Dignity in Human Rights Discourse* (2002, edited with E. Klein). His articles on international humanitarian, human rights and constitutional law have appeared in leading law journals, including the *American Journal of International Law, European Journal of International Law* and the *European Constitutional Law Review.*

CLAUDIA MARTIN is Co-Director of the Academy on Human Rights and Humanitarian Law, and Professorial Lecturer in residence at American University Washington College of Law. She specializes in international law, international human rights law and inter-American human rights law. Her most recent publications include 'The Inter-American Human Rights System: Selected Examples of Its Supervisory Work', in S. Joseph and A. McBeth (eds.), *Research Handbook in International Human Rights Law* (2012, co-authored with Diego Rodriguez-Pinzon). In addition, Professor Martin serves as a Contributing Editor to *Oxford Reports on International Human Rights Law* and is a member of the editorial board of *Oxford Reports on International Law in Domestic Courts.*

MICHAEL A. NEWTON is Professor of the Practice of Law at Vanderbilt University Law School. He is an expert on accountability and conduct of hostilities issues. Professor Newton is a member of the International Institute of Humanitarian Law and the IBA. He negotiated the 'Elements of Crimes' document for the ICC, and coordinated the interface between the FBI and the ICTY while deploying into Kosovo to do the forensics fieldwork in support of the Milošević indictment. As the Senior Adviser to the US Ambassador-at-Large for War Crimes Issues, US Department of State, Professor Newton implemented a wide range of policy positions relating to the law of armed conflict, including US support to accountability mechanisms worldwide. He was the senior member of the team that taught international law to the first group of Iraqis who began to think about accountability mechanisms and a constitutional structure in November 2000. He subsequently assisted in drafting the Statute of the Iraqi High Tribunal, and served as International Law Adviser to the Judicial Chambers in 2006 and 2007. Professor Newton served as the US representative on the UN Planning Mission for the Sierra Leone Special Court, and was also a member of the Special Court academic consortium. From January 1999 to August 2000, he served in the Office of War Crimes Issues, US Department of State. Professor Newton is the Senior Editor of the *Oxford International Terrorism Case Law* series.

JELENA PEJIC is Legal Adviser at the International Committee of the Red Cross's (ICRC) Legal Division in Geneva responsible, among other things, for issues related to detention policy, as well as international humanitarian law and terrorism. From 2002 to 2008 she was Head of the ICRC's Project on the Reaffirmation and Development of International Humanitarian Law. Prior to joining the ICRC, she was responsible for the Lawyers Committee for Human Rights' work in the area of international criminal justice. Ms. Pejic was also a lecturer at Belgrade University Law School. She has written and presented extensively on various issues of international humanitarian law, human rights law and criminal law.

ANTON DU PLESSIS is the Deputy Executive Director of the ISS and Head of the Transnational Threats and International Crime Division. He has worked on human security, international criminal justice and rule-of-law issues in over twenty African countries, with a focus on delivering training and technical assistance to senior law enforcement and criminal justice officials. Anton has three law degrees and is an admitted advocate of the High Court of South Africa with more than thirteen years of legal and management experience. He has worked as a consultant and expert adviser to various UN entities and other intergovernmental organisations, including the UN's Counter-Terrorism Implementation Task Force, and is a member of the World Economic Forum's Global Agenda Council on Terrorism. Before assuming his current positions, Anton was head of the International Crime in Africa Programme (ICAP) at the ISS. Prior to joining the ISS to found ICAP in early 2008, Anton was a criminal justice and counter-terrorism legal expert for the United Nations Office on Drugs and Crime (UNODC) in Vienna. Before that he was head of the Crime and Justice Programme at the ISS where he worked on a broad range of crime and criminal justice policy, research and technical assistance projects. Anton has also worked as a Senior State Advocate at the National Prosecuting Authority of South Africa where he specialized in the prosecution of serious and violent offences, including rape and gang-related crimes. Anton has published numerous articles, book chapters and training guides, and is the co-author of *Counter-Terrorism Law and Practice: A Practitioner's Handbook*.

KIMBERLY PROST graduated as a gold medallist (law) from the University of Manitoba and worked at the Canadian Department of Justice for eighteen years, including as Director of the International Assistance Group. She has negotiated over forty extradition/mutual assistance treaties and was a member of the Canadian delegation for the negotiation of several international conventions including the Rome Statute. Ms Prost has served as head of the Criminal Law Section with the Commonwealth Secretariat and as Chief, Legal Advisory Section, United Nations Office on Drugs and Crime. From July 2006 to July 2010 she served as an *ad litem* judge of the ICTY. On 3 June 2010 she was appointed as Ombudsperson for the Security Council Al Qaida/Taliban Sanctions Committee.

STEVEN R. RATNER is the Bruno Simma Collegiate Professor of Law at University of Michigan Law School. His research has focused on challenges facing new governments and international institutions after the Cold War, including ethnic conflict, territorial borders, implementation of peace agreements, accountability for human rights violations, and corporate responsibility for human rights. He has written and spoken extensively on the law of armed conflict. He served as a member of the UN Secretary-General's Group of Experts for Cambodia (1998–9) and the Secretary-General's Panel of Experts on Sri Lanka (2010–11). In 2008–9 he served in the legal division of the International Committee of the Red Cross in Geneva. Since 2009, he has served on the State Department's Advisory Committee on International Law. He holds a JD from Yale, an MA (diplôme) from the Institut Universitaire de Hautes Etudes Internationales (Geneva), and an AB from Princeton.

KLAAS ROZEMOND is associate professor at the department of Criminal Law and Criminology of the VU University Amsterdam. He is also a substitute judge at the District Court of Amsterdam, where he mainly participates in decisions of this court on extradition and the European Arrest Warrant. His main fields of research are European criminal law (especially the European Arrest Warrant), Dutch criminal law (especially criminal responsibility) and the risk society. His recent publications concern the method and the casuistry of the criminal law, surrender of nationals within the EU and judicial reasoning in the risk society.

ARVINDER SAMBEI is a director of Amicus Legal Consultants Ltd. She was, until recently, the Head of the Criminal Law Section, Legal & Constitutional Affairs Division at the Commonwealth Secretariat and was responsible for the day-to-day running of the section and ensuring design and delivery of programmes of assistance and training for member states to enhance criminal law systems and international cooperation. As a senior Crown Prosecutor within the CPS, Arvinder specialized in extradition law and international cooperation, international human rights and international humanitarian law, and counter-terrorism. In that role, she had conduct of many of the UK's high-profile extradition, counter-terrorism, transnational and war crimes cases. Prior to joining the Commonwealth Secretariat in 2005, Arvinder was employed by the Ministry of Defence as the Legal Adviser to the Permanent Joint Headquarters. Arvinder has written and spoken widely, and has provided advice and training to a wide range of states and regional bodies.

She is the co-author of the *Extradition Law Handbook* (2005), and has published, along with Martin Polaine and Anton du Plessis, *Counter-Terrorism Law and Practice* (2009).

MARGARET L. SATTERTHWAITE is a faculty director of the Center for Human Rights and Global Justice at NYU School of Law, Professor of Clinical Law, and Director of the Global Justice Clinic. She also serves as Faculty Director of the Root–Tilden–Kern programme. Satterthwaite joined the NYU faculty in 2006 after many years in the human rights field. Beginning in 2011, she has served as a consultant to the UN Special Rapporteur on the Human Rights to Water and Sanitation. Satterthwaite served as a member of the Advisory Panel of Experts to the UN Special Rapporteur on the Promotion and Protection of Human Rights While Countering Terrorism (2006–11). In 2009, she received the Pioneer of Justice and Equality for Women and the Law, and in 2011 she was awarded the Podell Distinguished Teaching Award.

NICO J. SCHRIJVER is Professor of International Law and Academic Director of the Grotius Centre for International Legal Studies, Leiden University and a member of the Senate of the Dutch house of parliament. He served as the President of the International Law Association and is a member of the Royal Netherlands Academy of Arts and Sciences, the UN Committee on Economic, Social and Cultural Rights, the Permanent Court of Arbitration and the Institut de droit international. Nico Schrijver is the author of *Sovereignty over Natural Resources: Balancing Rights and Duties* (Cambridge University Press, 1997); *The Evolution of Sustainable Development in International Law* (2008); and *Development without Destruction: The UN and Global Resource Management* (2010). He has published various articles on terrorism, including 'Responding to International Terrorism: Moving the Frontiers of International Law for "Enduring Freedom"?' (2001) 48(3) *Netherlands International Law Review* 271–91; he co-edited with N. M. Blokker *The Security Council and the Use of Force: Theory and Reality – A Need for Change?* (2005).

ELIES VAN SLIEDREGT is Dean and Professor of Criminal Law and Procedure at VU University Amsterdam and president of the International Criminal Law Network. She is a member of the editorial boards of the *Leiden Journal of International Law* and the *European Constitutional Law Review*. She has sat as a part-time judge in the extradition chamber of the District Court in Amsterdam and was a member of the Young Academy of the Royal Netherlands Academy of Arts and Sciences. Her research interests lie in the field of international, European and comparative criminal law.

CHRISTIAN J. TAMS is Professor of International Law at the University of Glasgow. After completing his legal studies in Germany, he obtained an LLM and a Ph.D. degree from the University of Cambridge (UK). His research in international law focuses on the legal rules governing the use of force, the law of state responsibility, dispute settlement and investment protection. In addition to his academic work, he has advised states in proceedings before the ICJ and the International Tribunal for the Law of the Sea (ITLOS), and serves on the German Court of Arbitration for Sport. He is a member of the ILA Committee on the Use of Force, the Royal Society of Edinburgh Young Academy, and the Research Council of the United Nations Association (Germany).

ELIZABETH S. WILMSHURST is Associate Fellow of International Law at Chatham House. She was Visiting Professor at University College, London University (2003–12), and held various posts at the British FCO (1974–2003), including as Deputy Legal Adviser, Legal Counsellor at the United Kingdom Mission to the UN in New York.

SIR MICHAEL WOOD, KCMG, is a member of the UN International Law Commission, a Senior Fellow of the Lauterpacht Centre for International Law, University of Cambridge, and a barrister at 20 Essex Street. He was Legal Adviser to the Foreign and Commonwealth Office (1999–2006). After joining the FCO in 1970, Sir Michael attended many international conferences, including most sessions of the Third United Nations Conference on the Law of the Sea. His postings included the British Embassy in Bonn as First Secretary (Legal) (1981–4); the United Kingdom Mission to the United Nations in New York as Legal Counsellor, dealing chiefly with Security Council matters (1991–4); and also with the Legal Committee of the General Assembly. He was Agent for the UK (1985–90) before the European Commission and the ECtHR, and in the *Lockerbie* and *Legality of Use of Force* cases before the ICJ, as well as in the *MOX Plant* proceedings before the International Tribunal for the Law of the Sea and two international arbitral tribunals.

FOREWORD

KAMAL HOSSAIN

Counter-terrorism strategies were not just introduced into the world as a result of the horrifying 9/11 attacks on the United States. Before 2001 many countries had to cope with acts of terrorism, often with international elements. The international community responded by adopting specific conventions, addressing terrorist acts committed on board aircraft or ships, the taking of hostages and the financing of terrorism. For long it was clear that these efforts were both insufficient and fragmented. This prompted India to launch in 1995 a proposal for drafting a comprehensive anti-terrorism convention, a project which however failed to gain widespread political support until 9/11. Although this changed markedly after 2001, negotiations floundered time and again on the definition of terrorism and some other matters.

As this volume amply demonstrates, path-breaking progress could be made in more specific fields of counter-terrorism strategies, both through enhanced traditional international criminal justice cooperation and through strengthened modern collective sanctions regimes imposed by the UN Security Council. The latter was rightly criticized for lack of conformity with fundamental human rights standards. One should never forget that the essence of the struggle against terrorism is to uphold respect for human rights; hence, only protection and not violation of human rights is the appropriate method of fighting terrorism. It is gratifying that in recent years some reparations could be made of these initial deficiencies in the UN's counter-terrorism strategies, including by the innovative establishment of the Office of the Ombudsperson and improved and more transparent listing and delisting procedures.

Reading the host of anti-terrorism conventions and UN resolutions of both the General Assembly and the Security Council examined in this

Vice-chairman of the International Law Association, former minister of foreign affairs of Bangladesh and former UN Special Rapporteur on the Human Rights Situation in Afghanistan.

book, leaves one with the impression that considerable achievements in terms of standard setting have been made towards an appropriate global normative order for the suppression of international terrorism but that enforcement completely falls below what is necessary. Here further solutions have to be found through strengthening both international criminal justice cooperation and targeted sanctions regimes which address not merely country-specific situations but transboundary terrorism as well. Furthermore, as the chapters in Part II of the book on the use of force against terrorists review, the employment of the use of force in the context of collective security or the right of self-defence can only be an ultimate resort, forming necessarily only a partial and inadequate response to international terrorism. What is most of all strikingly missing is an agenda of prevention of international terrorism. I cannot agree more with former Secretary-General Annan's observation in his report *In Larger Freedom* (2005): 'While poverty and denial of human rights may not be said to "cause" civil war, terrorism or organized crime, they all greatly increase the risk of instability and violence.' In his equally impressive report of 2006, entitled *Uniting against Terrorism*, Annan guided the member states of the United Nations to adopt the United Nations Global Counter-Terrorism Strategy (A/RES/60/288 of 8 September 2008). This document, adopted on the eve of five years after 9/11, certainly outlines a comprehensive strategy, including measures to address the conditions conducive to the spread of international terrorism, measures to prevent and combat terrorism, measures to build states' capacity to prevent and combat terrorism and to strengthen the role of the UN in this regard, and measures to ensure respect for human rights for all and the rule of law as the fundamental basis of the fight against terrorism. Subsequent resolutions of the two principal political organs of the UN have further refined elements of this global counter-terrorism strategy. This book, co-edited by professors Larissa van den Herik and Nico Schrijver of Leiden University, the Netherlands, is highly useful in mapping the state of the art in counter-terrorism strategies in three selected key fields of international law: international criminal justice cooperation in cases involving terrorism (Part I), use of force against terrorists (Part II) and the interplay between human rights law and international humanitarian law (Part III). The twenty-one chapters in this book provide an in-depth analysis of the achievements and the shortcomings of the role of international law in combating international terrorism. The collaborative efforts of this group of independent eminent international experts, facilitated by support from the Ministry of

Foreign Affairs (Netherlands), resulted in the comprehensive *Leiden Policy Recommendations on Counter-Terrorism and International Law* (annexed to this book). These provide not only ample food for thought to anyone with an interest in the subject matter of this book, but also provide politicians and policy-makers with balanced expert perspectives on areas in which more has to be done and in which greater consensus is to be pursued.

ACKNOWLEDGEMENTS

The collection of chapters in this book results from a project with the support of the Netherlands Ministry of Foreign Affairs and with the active involvement of Jean-Paul Laborde, former Chairman of the United Nations Counter-Terrorism Implementation Task Force (CTITF). First of all, we would like to record our sincere thanks to and admiration for our contributors who were with us all the way from the initial start in April 2007 at the estate Oud-Poelgeest to our Peace Palace session on 1 April 2010, during which we presented the *Leiden Policy Recommendations on Counter-Terrorism and International Law* to the Dutch Minister of Foreign Affairs Maxime Verhagen. The journey has been concluded with this book project. In particular, we express our deep appreciation to the three co-chairs of the working groups: Anton du Plessis and Michael Newton of working group 1 (in this book: Part I Improving International Cooperation in the Investigation and Prosecution of Terrorist Acts); Andrea Bianchi and Sir Michael Wood of working group 2 (in this book: Part II The Use of Force against Terrorists); and Helen Duffy and Jelena Pejic of working group 3 (in this book: Part III Intersection between International Humanitarian Law and Human Rights Law in the Fight against Terrorism). We would further like to express our gratitude for the important support we received from the Netherlands Ministry of Foreign Affairs, especially to then Minister of Foreign Affairs Maxime Verhagen, the subsequent Netherlands human rights ambassadors Piet de Klerk and Lionel Veer and their active staff, the Ministry's Legal Adviser Liesbeth Lijnzaad, Frank van Beuningen, Director of the Counter Terrorism and National Security Division in the Security Policy Department and the Directorate General of Political Affairs. Furthermore, we also thank our research and student assistants Anna Gouwenberg, Anton Fischer and Dana Burns. We have also appreciated the constructive comments from the three anonymous referees which we received through Cambridge University Press as well as the committed interest from the staff at the Press.

While many have thus contributed to the formulation of the *Leiden Policy Recommendations* and to this book project, the responsibility for errors and shortcomings rests entirely with us as the editors.

Larissa van den Herik, Nico Schrijver
Leiden, April 2012

ABBREVIATIONS

ACHPR	African Charter on Human and Peoples' Rights
ACHR	American Convention on Human Rights
AP I	Protocol Additional to the Geneva Conventions of 12 August 1949, and relating to the Protection of Victims of International Armed Conflict
AP II	Protocol Additional to the Geneva Conventions of 12 August 1949, and relating to the Protection of Victims of Non-International Armed Conflict
ASEAN	Association of Southeast Asian Nations
AU	African Union
CAT	Convention against Torture and Other Cruel, Inhuman or Degrading Treatment or Punishment
CETS	Council of Europe Treaty Series
CFI	European Court of First Instance
CoE	Council of Europe
CT	counter-terrorism
CTED	Counter-Terrorism Committee Executive Directorate
CTITF	UN Counter-Terrorism Implementation Task Force
EAW	European Arrest Warrant
EAW-FD	Framework Decision on the European Arrest Warrant
ECE	European Convention on Extradition
ECHR	European Convention on Human Rights and Fundamental Freedoms
ECJ	European Court of Justice
ECtHR	European Court of Human Rights
ETA	Euskadi Ta Askatasuna [Basque Homeland and Freedom]
FATF	Financial Action Task Force
FD	Framework Decision
GC III	Geneva Convention III Relative to the Treatment of Prisoners of War
GC IV	Geneva Convention IV Relative to the Treatment of Civilian Persons in Time of War
GWOT	global war on terror
HRC	Human Rights Committee
HRW	Human Rights Watch

IAC	international armed conflict
IACHR	Inter-American Commission on Human Rights
IACtHR	Inter-American Court of Human Rights
ICAO	International Civil Aviation Organization
ICC	International Criminal Court
ICCPR	International Covenant on Civil and Political Rights
ICJ	International Court of Justice
ICRC	International Committee of the Red Cross
ICTY	International Criminal Tribunal for the former Yugoslavia
IHL	international humanitarian law
IHRL	international human rights law
ILC	International Law Commission
IRA	Irish Republican Army
LOAC	law of armed conflict
NIAC	non-international armed conflict
OAS	Organization of American States
OAU	Organization of African Unity
OIC	Organization of the Islamic Conference
PKK	Kurdistan Workers' Party
POW	prisoner of war
RO	regional organization
SARs	Suspicious Activity Reports
TEC	Treaty Establishing the European Community
TEU	Treaty on the European Union
UNHRC	UN Human Rights Council
UNSC	United Nations Security Council
WOT	war on terror

TABLE OF CASES

Permanent Court of International Justice and ICJ

United Nations treaty bodies

International criminal courts and tribunals

Regional courts

Domestic courts

Arbitral tribunals

TABLE OF TREATIES AND UN RESOLUTIONS

Treaties

Universal

2003 United Nations Convention against Corruption, 2369 UNTS 41. Concluded in New York; entered into force 14 December 2005 101

2005 International Convention for the Suppression of Acts of Nuclear Terrorism, 2445 UNTS 89. Concluded in New York; entered into force 7 July 2007 49, 102, 590, 596, 639, 645, 663

2005 Amendment to the Convention on the Physical Protection of Nuclear Material. Available at www.iaea.org/About/Policy/GC/GC49/Documents/gc49inf-6.pdf (accessed 10 April 2012). Concluded in Vienna; not yet entered into force 49, 639

2005 Protocol to the Convention for the Suppression of Unlawful Acts against the Safety of Maritime Navigation. Available at www.imo.org/About/Conventions/ListOfConventions/Pages/SUA-Treaties.aspx (accessed 10 April 2012). Concluded in London; entered into force 28 July 2010 49

2005 Protocol to the Protocol for the Suppression of Unlawful Acts against the Safety of Fixed Platforms Located on the Continental Shelf. Available at www.imo.org/About/Conventions/ListOfConventions/Pages/SUA-Treaties.aspx (accessed 10 April 2012). Concluded in London; entered into force 28 July 2010 49, 640

2010 Convention on the Suppression of Unlawful Acts Relating to International Civil Aviation. Available at http://legacy.icao.int/DCAS2010/restr/docs/beijing_convention_multi.pdf (accessed 10 April 2012). Concluded in Beijing; not yet entered into force 49

2010 Protocol Supplementary to the Convention for the Suppression of Unlawful Seizure of Aircraft. Available at http://legacy.icao.int/DCAS2010/restr/docs/beijing_protocol_multi.pdf (accessed 10 April 2012). Concluded in Beijing; not yet entered into force 49

Regional

1950 European Convention on Human Rights and Fundamental Freedoms, CETS No. 5. Concluded in Rome; entered into force 3 September 1953 197, 201–11, 215, 220, 236–7, 454, 458–63, 487–90, 520, 536, 574–7, 582–3, 687–9, 695

Resolutions

Security Council

General Assembly

1

The fragmented international legal response to terrorism

LARISSA VAN DEN HERIK AND NICO SCHRIJVER

1 Introduction

More than any other event in the post-Cold War period, the events of 9/11 generated intensive normative activities at the international level, combined with path-breaking institutional developments. The multiplicity of responses spawned by this unusual *ouverture* of the twenty-first century involved various domains of international law. Reflecting the dynamics of the current international legal system, the normative burgeoning that followed 9/11 unsurprisingly displayed a rather disorganized and uncoordinated proliferation of possible new legal practices, principles, rules and institutions,[1] thereby potentially fragmenting the international legal response to terrorism that international society had to offer.

It is in this context, and with the hindsight of a decade of literature on the topic, that this volume addresses the challenges that combating international terrorism poses to international law. The book is premised on the idea that the main challenge to be met does not primarily pertain to the lack of applicable rules. The main challenge is arguably to ensure the coherence and unity of the application of the principles and rules originating in multiple branches of international law. This is why, instead of focusing on the applicability of rules from one specific branch of international law to the problem of terrorism, this book takes a comprehensive approach and examines the applicability as well as the interrelationship between salient branches of international law in

[1] See on the phenomenon of multilayered global governance more generally, C. Ku, 'Forging a Multilayered System of Global Governance', in R. St. J. MacDonald and D. M. Johnston (eds.), *Towards World Constitutionalism: Issues in the Legal Ordering of the World Community* (Leiden: Martinus Nijhoff, 2005), 631–51.

relation to terrorism and counter-terrorism activities. Some of these questions have already been the object of analysis in the literature. This volume however provides a rare overview of the great variety of legal issues, which arise in connection with terrorism in the twenty-first century. In combination with one another, the chapters in this volume shed light on perspectives that have sometimes been overlooked in the literature.

The collection has a threefold focus. Part I examines questions relating to law enforcement and criminal justice that are unrelated to the context of armed conflict and the need to improve international cooperation in the investigation and prosecution of terrorist acts. Part II studies operations that include the transboundary use of force, and in particular the use of force in self-defence against non-state actors. Inevitably, the use of force simultaneously raises questions regarding the applicability of international humanitarian law, including its relationship to human rights law. Part III accordingly addresses the specific relationship between international humanitarian law and human rights law. The respective parts of this book provide expert perspectives on areas in which greater consensus is needed in order to make the struggle against terrorism more effective. These perspectives are woven together in the *Leiden Policy Recommendations on Counter-Terrorism and International Law* (annexed to this book).

The specific inquiries on selected themes in the respective chapters, when taken together, expose possible instances of fragmentation and incoherence. In addition, this comprehensive study will draw attention to some implications of international counter-terrorism responses for the changing nature of international norms and international lawmaking. In this respect, the phenomenon of terrorism will be considered as particularly illustrative of the increasing pluriformity of actors on the international legal stage, both in terms of subjects of the law and international law-makers.[2] In a similar vein, the nature of terrorist threats and of counter-terrorism measures may testify to the progressive individualization of international law.[3] Or, alternatively, the record of counter-terrorism responses may overall be said to show a shift back to a more statist, power-based and security-oriented focus of international

[2] K. Annan, *We, the Peoples: The Role of the United Nations in the Twenty-First Century* (UN Doc. A/54/2000 (2000)), para. 315.

[3] A. Slaughter and W. Burke-White, 'An International Constitutional Moment' (2003) 43 *Harvard International Law Journal* 1.

society.[4] Within such a dialectic, this book examines the mark that 9/11 has effectively left on the international legal system.

This first chapter seeks to set the scene of the general overview constituted by the following chapters. It introduces some of the general issues, which arise in relation to terrorism. After these preliminary remarks, section 2 explores some of the different forms of terrorism and its transformation from a phenomenon of general international concern to one perceived as a direct threat to international peace. Subsequently, section 3 examines institutional developments in response to new terrorist threats and enquires how modern terrorism has affected approaches to international governance, in particular at the Security Council level. Section 4 introduces the fragmented response to counter-terrorism after 9/11. In section 5, an outline of the individual chapters of this volume is presented.

2 Terrorism as an international matter

It is uncontested that the epithet of terrorism has an exceptionally strong emotive value.[5] This symbolic strength of the terrorism label stands in sharp contrast to the particular weakness of the concept in terms of legal substance. Many international lawyers have already noted the elusiveness of terrorism in the legal sense. In 1974, Baxter regretted the conception of 'terrorism' as a legal term. He wrote, 'the term is imprecise; it is ambiguous; and above all, it serves no legal purpose'.[6] In 1997, Higgins also qualified terrorism as a 'term of convenience', which has 'no specific

[4] S. N. MacFarlane, 'Charter Values and the Response to Terrorism', in J. Boulden and T. G. Weiss (eds.), *Terrorism and the UN: Before and after September 11* (Bloomington: Indiana University Press, 2004), 45.

[5] There are perhaps only two epithets in international law that so directly attach an emotive stigma to a certain act: genocide and terrorism. The word 'genocide' is the linguistic embodiment of the ultimate evil whereas the 'terrorism' label is attached to acts which can under no circumstance be justified. While both terms share a strong expressive function, their significance as legal concepts varies. 'Genocide' as an international law concept is carved in stone and has become immutable as the Rome negotiations for the ICC Statute have shown. This term captures a concrete, rather narrowly defined set of acts. Apart from some legal discussion on interpretational issues and the interdisciplinary debate on the contours of the concept per se, there is general agreement on the relatively well-circumscribed phenomenon of genocide. The situation for terrorism is rather the opposite.

[6] R. R. Baxter, 'A Skeptical Look at the Concept of Terrorism' (1974) 7 *Akron Law Review* 380, 380.

legal meaning'.[7] More recently, in 2006, Saul described the term terrorism as a seductive term that serves a popular expressive function.[8]

The haziness of the concept of terrorism relates not only to its legal dimension and the lack of a clear definition, but also in social terms, the word terrorism is used in relation to a great realm of diverse acts.[9] The differentiation between domestic terrorism and international terrorism, new terrorism and old terrorism, terrorism in peacetime and terrorism in wartime, and state (-sponsored) terrorism versus terrorism committed by non-state actors, attempts to recognize this diversity. The fact that there is such a wide array of acts which are currently all captured by just one term is certainly partly responsible for the level of fragmentation of the legal response to terrorism. This section introduces the terrorism mosaic that underlies the expansion and diversification of legal responses to the terrorist threat.

2.1 *The transformation and variegation of terrorism*

Even if described as an age-old phenomenon,[10] the linguistic roots of the word 'terrorism' are relatively recent, dating back to the French Revolution and Robespierre's Reign of Terror.[11] Being coined through an incidence of state terror neatly illustrates the perplexity of the concept. After all, terrorism has predominantly been understood as a non-state actor phenomenon – perhaps sometimes state sponsored – while

[7] R. Higgins, 'The General International Law of Terrorism', in R. Higgins and M. Flory (eds.), *Terrorism and International Law* (London: Routledge, 1997) 27.

[8] B. Saul, *Defining Terrorism in International Law* (Oxford: Oxford University Press, 2006) 4.

[9] R. Kolb, 'The Exercise of Criminal Jurisdiction over International Terrorists', in A. Bianchi (ed.), *Enforcing International Law Norms against Terrorism* (Oxford: Hart, 2004), 228. Kolb also distinguishes between legal functions that the definitions fulfil, such as the freezing of assets and individual criminal prosecution.

[10] M. Lehto, *Indirect Responsibility for Terrorist Acts: Redefinition of the Concept of Terrorism beyond Violent Acts* (Leiden: Martinus Nijhoff, 2010), xxii.

[11] See, e.g., G. Guillaume, 'Terrorism and International Law' (2004) 53 *International and Comparative Law Quarterly* 537. As Guillaume explained, the term took on a new meaning in the late nineteenth century when it was used to describe the attacks by the nihilists in Russia and later the anarchists throughout Europe. Terrorism as a term then came to refer to terror against the state. The first international attempt to define terrorism responded to the assassination of King Alexander I of Yugoslavia and Louis Barthou, the president of the Council of the French Republic. The 1937 Convention for the Prevention and Punishment of Terrorism only concerned terrorist acts against a state.

the question whether it can be directly committed by states has always been one of the main bones of contention.[12] The debate on state terrorism is linked to the freedom-fighter discussion and has, to some extent, also inspired the distinction between terrorism in wartime and in peacetime.[13] The effects of the disagreements in relation to the character of the author of terrorism have mainly been felt in the context of unsuccessful attempts to arrive at a fully-fledged and general definition.

Another distinction is between domestic and international terrorism. This distinction coincides to a large extent with the traditional versus modern terrorism dichotomy. This second distinction serves a different purpose from that of the variation in the character of the perpetrator. The emergence of modern terrorism can be seen as the main driver behind the diversification of legal responses, since it brought into play new paradigms of counter-terrorism strategies. Given this immediate link to the fragmentation theme, the distinction between traditional and modern terrorism deserves some further exploration.

The concept of 'modern terrorism' has been extensively analysed in the literature and reports, and of course it is disputed by some as being a non-concept. Two key characteristics that are often mentioned as setting modern terrorism apart from traditional terrorism relate to the diffuse political agenda and the fluid organizational structures of modern terrorists.[14] In contrast to the old 'territorial' terrorist groups such as ETA in

[12] The Secretary-General tried to lay this discussion to rest in his report *Larger Freedom*, 'It is time to set aside debates on so-called "State terrorism". The use of force by States is already thoroughly regulated under international law' (para. 91). See for a critique, J. J. Paust, 'Terrorism as an International Crime', in G. Nesi (ed.), *International Cooperation in Counter-Terrorism: the United Nations and Regional Organizations in the Fight against Terrorism* (Hampshire: Ashgate, 2006), 25–32.

[13] See more elaborately H. Duffy, *The 'War on Terror' and the Framework of International Law* (Cambridge: Cambridge University Press, 2005), ch. 2. Also see Pejic who criticized the exclusion of terrorist activities carried out by state armed forces, as such an approach would disrupt the balance in international humanitarian law between the parties to a non-international armed conflict ('Armed Conflict and Terrorism: There Is a (Big) Difference', in A. M. Salinas de Friás, K. L. H. Samuel, and N. D. White (eds.), *Counter-Terrorism: International Law and Practice* (Oxford: Oxford University Press, 2012)).

[14] These characteristics are enumerated and explained in E. Muller, 'Modern Terrorism and Modern Counter-Terrorism in The Netherlands', in G. Molier, A. Ellian and D. Suurland (eds.), *Terrorism: Ideology, Law and Policy* (Dordrecht: Republic of Letters, 2010), 397–420. His analysis draws on W. Laqueur, *The New Terrorism: Fanaticism and the Arms of Mass Destruction* (Oxford: Oxford University Press, 1999) and W. Laqueur, *Voices of Terror: Manifestos, Writings and Manuals of Al Qaeda, Hamas, and other Terrorists from around the World and throughout the Ages* (New York: Reed Press, 2004). Also see Lehto, *Indirect Responsibility for Terrorist Acts*, xxii–xxxii.

Spain and the IRA in Northern Ireland, which had concrete political and territorial demands, the political agenda of new terrorist groups, with al-Qaeda as the main protagonist, is more nebulous. Even if specific objectives have at times been articulated, such as the withdrawal of US troops from Saudi Arabia, the overall ambition concentrates on more general political desires of re-establishing a worldwide caliphate.

The differences between separatist movements and al-Qaeda-type groups are significant from an operational point of view. Not only are the demands and hence the actions of the traditional terrorist groups geared towards a concrete territorial or political goal, but more importantly the actions of these groups are governed by a quest for legitimacy. The underlying political goals of traditional terrorists require a certain level of popular support, which has a pacifying effect on the nature of their acts. Traditionally, separatist terrorist movements would give warning; they would generally not commit suicide attacks; their attacks were not too gory, and mostly civilians unaffiliated to the state apparatus would be spared as much as possible. In contrast, modern terrorists intend to instil fear globally and to target the greatest number of victims possible without differentiation.[15]

The flexibility of network structures and the fluidity of financing are two other intertwined features distinguishing modern and traditional terrorism.[16] In relation to al-Qaeda, it has been observed that the successful incapacitation of the leadership of this quintessential modern terrorist group has rendered this movement particularly incongruent and scattered.[17] Additionally, there is a trend of al-Qaeda inspiring home-grown terrorists that have no or little direct connection to this movement.[18] This trend further decentralizes the already extremely loose cell structure that underlies modern terrorism. This organizational flexibility is mirrored in the ways that modern terrorist groups acquire their required financial means. Other than traditional terrorism that was frequently state sponsored in one way or another, modern terrorist groups more often turn to other forms of organized crime for financial

[15] Muller, 'Modern Terrorism'.

[16] On financing structures, see particularly Chapter 8 in this volume.

[17] E. Rosand, 'The UN-Led Multilateral Institutional Response to Jihadist Terrorism: Is a Global Counterterrorism Body Needed?' (2007) 11 *Journal of Conflict and Security Law* 399, 401.

[18] *Ibid.*

resources.[19] Direct relations with states do exist but mostly with fragile states, such as Somalia, Yemen, Afghanistan and perhaps Pakistan. Those relations generally are of a very complex and sometimes even symbiotic nature. There are thus a number of factors differentiating traditional terrorism from modern terrorism.

Some scholars have questioned the propriety or usefulness of the qualitative dimension of the distinction between traditional and modern terrorism.[20] They submit that the difference is predominantly quantitative in nature. It is the higher level of violence, also through the potential use of weapons of mass destruction and the increased geographical reach, that justify the term 'global terrorism'. However, according to this view, other than the scale of the threat, the qualitative nature of terrorist threats has not changed significantly.[21]

Lacking clear definitions, the precise boundaries between the two variations of terrorism, traditional/domestic versus modern/international, are hard to draw. Moreover, there are also hybrid situations, which are not easily identifiable as either domestic or international terrorism, but are more a mixture of the two, such as domestic terrorism that is financed through foreign channels. Furthermore, on occasion, the UN Security Council has qualified what appeared to be an act of domestic terrorism as a threat to peace and security,[22] and thereafter generally determined that any 'act of terrorism' amounted to such a threat.[23] This may further blur the conceptual differences between the two variations of terrorism. To the extent that the differentiation is accepted, it is important to realize that the two variations coexist rather than that modern terrorism has replaced traditional terrorism.[24]

Despite the divergence in characterizing the differences in terrorism as quantitative or qualitative in nature, the two schools of thought unite in the position that the mutation warrants a diversification of legal responses. The emergence of 'modern terrorism' as a variation on 'traditional terrorism' has strained the exclusive focus on the criminal law

[19] See, e.g., Outcome Document for the Special Meeting of the Counter-Terrorism Committee Commemorating the Adoption of Security Council Res. 1373 (2001) and the Establishment of the Committee (2011), para. 6.

[20] V. Lowe, 'Security Concerns and National Sovereignty in the Age of World-Wide Terrorism', in MacDonald and Johnston, *Towards World Constitutionalism*, 656–9.

[21] *Ibid.*, 659.

[22] UN Doc. S/Res./1465 (2003), regarding the bomb attack in Bogota, Colombia on 7 February 2003.

[23] E.g., UN Doc. S/Res./1516 (2003) or UN Doc. S/Res./1530 (2004).

[24] Lehto, *Indirect Responsibility for Terrorist Acts*, xxviii.

paradigm. Consequently, 9/11, as the critical expression of modern terrorism, has provoked a host of new approaches. The immediate reaction to 9/11 invoked the use of force paradigm and in its wake other coercive measures such as reinvigorated Security Council sanctions.[25] After the heat of the moment had passed, softer alternative measures gradually regained more prominence, such as preventive diplomacy, intercultural dialogue, technical assistance and the monitoring of national implementation measures.[26]

2.2 *Terrorism as a threat*

The phenomenon of terrorism has long featured on the international agenda, but it was gradually upgraded from being predominantly viewed as a matter of general international concern and perturbation[27] to being perceived as one of the most serious threats to peace and security.[28] This process was given a tremendous boost by 9/11.

The Security Council engaged in a general fashion with the terrorist phenomenon in its first-ever Heads of State meeting in 1992.[29] In a Presidential Statement, the Security Council members expressed their concern about acts of terrorism and emphasized the need for the international community to address them effectively.[30] More concretely, the Council reacted to terrorist attacks on three occasions prior to 9/11.

[25] While the sanctions under Res. 1267 had already been in existence since 1998, they were enhanced and extended to include al-Qaeda and to allow for a more intensive use. See generally, L. J. van den Herik, 'The Security Council's Targeted Sanctions Regimes: In Need of Better Protection of the Individual' (2007) 20 *Leiden Journal of International Law* 797.

[26] Lehto, *Indirect Responsibility for Terrorist Acts*, xx.

[27] See, e.g., the first General Assembly Resolution on Measures to Prevent Terrorism, UN Doc. A/Res./3034 (XXVII). In its 1994 Terrorism Declaration, the Assembly proclaimed that 'acts, methods and practices of terrorism constitute a grave violation of the purposes and principles of the United Nations, which may pose a threat to international peace and security' (Declaration on Measures to Eliminate International Terrorism, UN Doc. A/Res./49/60 (1994), para. 2). This declaration was followed by Res. 51/210 (1996). Also see the related report of the Secretary-General, UN Doc. A/51/336 (1996).

[28] *Threats to Peace and Security Caused by Terrorist Acts* (UN Doc. S/Res./1989 (2011)).

[29] The SC had dealt with terrorism sporadically on earlier occasions, e.g., in relation to the murder of Count Bernadotte in Res. 57 of 18 September 1948, and it issued Res. 286 on hijacking, on 9 September 1970. See more generally, J. Boulden, 'The Security Council and Terrorism', in V. Lowe *et al.* (eds.), *The United Nations Security Council and War: The Evolution of Thought and Practice since 1945* (Oxford: Oxford University Press, 2008), 608–23.

[30] UN Doc. S/23500 (1992).

These were the Lockerbie bombings in 1988, the assassination attempt on Mubarak in Addis Ababa in 1996, and the terrorist attacks in Kenya and Tanzania in 1998. On all these occasions, Chapter VII powers were immediately invoked.[31] Yet, the threat to peace determination mutated only gradually. Initially, the Council held in preambular paragraphs that acts of international terrorism constituted a threat to peace[32] and that the suppression of international terrorism was essential for the maintenance of international peace and security.[33] It only effectively utilized the qualification of a threat to peace in its operative paragraphs in relation to the failure of states to respond to specific requests, such as the extradition of terrorist suspects.[34] Resolution 1269 was more articulate in that it unequivocally condemned:

> all acts, methods and practices of terrorism as criminal and unjustifiable, regardless of their motivations, in all their forms and manifestations, wherever and by whomever committed, in particular those which could threaten peace and security.[35]

Yet 9/11 was the first individual terrorist attack that the Council concretely qualified as a 'threat to peace'.[36] In the resolutions addressing 9/11, the Council also made a more generalized statement that *any* act of international terrorism constituted a threat to peace.[37] With this determination that a phenomenon rather than a discrete situation constituted a threat to peace, the Security Council assumed a much debated quasi-legislative

[31] On the SC's response to terrorism, see also Chapter 2 in this volume.

[32] UN Doc. S/Res./731 (1992), 2nd preambular para.

[33] UN Doc. S/Res./748 (1992), 4th preambular para.; UN Doc. S/Res./883 (1993), 5th preambular para.; UN Doc. S/Res./1044 (1996), 5th preambular para.; UN Doc. S/Res./1054 (1996), 9th preambular para.; UN Doc. S/Res./1070 (1996), 10th preambular para.; UN Doc. S/Res./1189 (1998), 3rd preambular para.; UN Doc. S/Res./1267 (1999), 5th preambular para.

[34] UN Doc. S/Res./748 (1992), 7th preambular para.. UN Doc. S/Res./883 (1993), 6th preambular para.; UN Doc. S/Res./1054 (1996), 10th preambular para.; UN Doc. S/Res./1070 (1996), 11th preambular para.; UN Doc. S/Res./1267 (1999), 8th preambular para.

[35] UN Doc. S/Res./1269 (1999), para. 1.

[36] UN Doc. S/Res./1368 (2001), para. 1. See also B. Fassbender, 'The UN Security Council and International Terrorism', in Bianchi, *Enforcing International Law Norms against Terrorism*, 87.

[37] UN Doc. S/Res./1368 (2001), para. 1.; UN Doc. S/Res./1373 (2001), 2nd preambular para.

function as it had never exercised before.[38] In Resolution 1377, adopted at ministerial level, the Council went even one step further and declared that 'acts of international terrorism constitute[d] *one of the most serious* threats to international peace and security in the twenty-first century'.[39] It further declared that acts of international terrorism were a challenge to all states and to all of humanity.

This perception of terrorism not only as a threat to peace but also as a challenge to all of humanity persisted. According to the High Level Panel in the report entitled *A More Secure World* and the Secretary-General in his subsequent report *In Larger Freedom*, terrorism threatened and attacked:

> all that the United Nations stands for: respect for human rights, the rule of law, protection of civilians, tolerance among peoples and nations, and the peaceful resolution of conflict.[40]

Both reports stipulated that the terrorist threat had increased in urgency during the first years of the twenty-first century as a result of two dynamics. These were the global reach of transnational terrorist network groups and their desire to acquire nuclear, chemical and biological weapons.[41]

It thus seems, as some scholars have noted, that there was a certain universality in the perception of terrorism as a threat.[42] This is underscored by numerous declarations of regional organizations qualifying terrorism as a threat to peace.[43] Lack of consensus emerged more as regards the priority given to combating terrorism, the focus of responses to the threat, the identification of root causes of terrorism and the propriety of a preventive approach addressing such root causes.[44]

[38] The role of the SC as 'global legislator' has been extensively discussed in the literature, see e.g., M. Happold, 'Resolution 1373 and the Constitution of the United Nations' (2003) 16 *Leiden Journal of International Law* 593; E. Rosand, 'The Security Council as "Global Legislator": *Ultra vires* or ultra innovative?' (2004–5) 28 *Fordham International Law Journal* 542; see also note 54 below for further references.

[39] UN Doc. S/Res./1377 (2001), 2nd preambular para. This was repeated in subsequent resolutions, see, e.g., UN Doc. S/Res./1989 (2011), 2nd preambular para. Also see the *World Summit Outcome* (UN Doc. A/Res./60/1 (2005)), para. 81. The emphasis is ours.

[40] UN Doc. A/59/565 (2004), para. 145; UN Doc. A/59/2005 (2005), para. 87.

[41] *Ibid.*

[42] Boulden, 'Security Council and Terrorism', 608.

[43] AU Doc. Assembly/AU/Dec.311(XV) (2010); OAS Doc. AG/RES. 2618 (XLI-O/11) (2011); Astana Declaration for Peace, Cooperation and Development, OIC Doc. OIC/CFM-38/2011/ASTANA DEC/FINAL (28–30 June 2011); SAARC Doc. SAARC/SUMMIT.16/15 (28–9 April 2010).

[44] On the question of root causes, see more elaborately, T. Bjørgo, *The Root Causes of Terrorism: Myths, Realities and Ways Forward* (Abingdon: Routledge, 2005).

The attention to root causes started to fade in the 1980s, and this trend was consolidated in the 1994 General Assembly Declaration on Measures to Eliminate International Terrorism.[45] Whereas the immediate post-9/11 spirit followed this trend, root causes were revisited after the dust had settled.

The Secretary-General broached the disputed root causes link in his *In Larger Freedom* report. In an attempt to circumvent any discussion pertaining to causality, he observed rather neutrally:

> While poverty and denial of human rights may not be said to 'cause' civil war, terrorism or organized crime, they all greatly increase the risk of instability and violence.[46]

More concretely, in his report *Uniting against Terrorism*, the Secretary-General called for a comprehensive response that also addressed the underlying dynamics of terrorism.[47] According to the Secretary-General, conditions conducive to terrorism included extremist ideologies and dehumanization of victims, violent conflict, poor governance, lack of civil rights and human rights abuse, religious and ethnic discrimination, political exclusion and socio-economic marginalization.[48]

The General Assembly also advocated a comprehensive strategy in the World Summit Outcome that would take into account the conditions conducive to the spread of terrorism.[49] Thereupon, the UN Global Counter-Terrorism Strategy focused quite prominently on prevention and suggested various measures that would address motivating factors

45 Annex to Res. 49/6 (1994). J. Dugard, 'Terrorism and International Law Consensus at Last?', in E. Yako and T. Boumedra (eds.), *Liber Amicorum – Mohammed Bedjaoui* (Leiden: Martinus Nijhoff, 1999), 164; Higgins, 'General International Law of Terrorism', 18.

46 UN Doc. A/59/2005 (2005), para. 16.

47 Uniting against Terrorism: Recommendations for a Global Counter-Terrorism Strategy, UN Doc. A/60/825 (2006), para. 20.

48 *Ibid.*, paras. 21–38.

49 UN Doc. A/60/1 (2005), para. 82. Similarly, the G8 held in its St Petersburg Statement of 16 July 2006 on Strengthening the UN's Counter-Terrorism Program, 'A comprehensive response to the urgent threat of terrorism must be a core focus of the UN. While the Security Council should continue to play its crucial role . . . other UN organs, organizations and bodies must strengthen their efforts as well, thus, contributing to the broader counter-terrorism effort through capacity building, education, economic development and by addressing the facilitating factors that may breed terrorists. Countering terrorism, state-building and development are mutually dependent and mutually supporting. Counter-terrorism should be addressed across the UN system in a coherent and coordinated way'.

leading to terrorism.[50] This comprehensive approach takes account of the fact that, in spite of generalized claims that terrorism presents a universal threat, many developing states perceive counter-terrorism as a predominantly Western priority.[51] They see extreme poverty, underdevelopment and diseases such as HIV/AIDS and the resulting social collapse as greater threats to their society.[52] The consensus on perceiving terrorism as a threat is thus more limited in scope than is sometimes portrayed.

In light of the dynamic and complex nature of the terrorist threat, the diversity of conditions conducive to it, and the discrepancy in prioritization of counter-terrorism in different areas of the world, the institutional response could not but be multifaceted as well.

3 Terrorism and international governance

Since 9/11, international counter-terrorism activities have become more institutionalized than ever before.[53] The UN, and in particular the Security Council, took the lead in this trend towards multilateral institutionalization. The Council's (semi-)legislative activities,[54] the creation and reinvigoration of subsidiary organs, in particular the establishment of special committees, and the establishment of the Office of the Ombudsperson constituted unprecedented institutional innovations. Regional and sub-regional organizations also constitute an important thread in the institutional counter-terrorism web,[55] as do international

[50] UN Doc. A/Res./60/288 (2006), paras. 1–8. See further A. Sambeim, A. du Plessis and M. Polaine, *Counter-Terrorism Law and Practice: An International Handbook* (Oxford: Oxford University Press, 2009), 24.

[51] Rosand, 'UN-Led Multilateral Institutional Response', 404; T. Tardy, 'The Inherent Difficulties of Inter-institutional Cooperation in Fighting Terrorism', in Boulden and Weiss, *Terrorism and the UN*, 139.

[52] Boulden and Weiss, *Terrorism and the UN*, 139.

[53] P. Romaniuk, 'Institutions as Swords and Shields: Multilateral Counter-Terrorism since 9/11' (2010) 36 *Review of International Studies* 519, 593.

[54] A. Bianchi, 'Assessing the Effectiveness of the UN Security Council's Anti-terrorism Measures: The Quest for Legitimacy and Cohesion' (2007) 17 *European Journal of International Law* 881; Happold, 'Resolution 1373'; Rosand, 'Security Council'; P. Szasz, 'The Security Council Starts Legislating' (2002) 96 *American Journal of International Law* 901; S. Talmon, 'The Security Council as World Legislature' (2005) 99 *American Journal of International Law* 175; A. Boyle and C. Chinkin, *The Making of International Law* (Oxford: Oxford University Press, 2007), 3–10.

[55] As encouraged by the SC, e.g., in Res. 1805, UN Doc. S/Res./1805 (2008), para. 6.

bodies such as the IAEA,[56] ICAO,[57] IMO,[58] WCO,[59] as well as the FATF,[60] and certain specialized UN organs including the UNODC.[61] UN human rights bodies as well as regional human rights bodies have scrutinized counter-terrorism policies at various levels. In contrast, the role of international criminal courts has been limited to concrete situations.

This section first provides a succinct overview of key institutional novelties at the Security Council level, with a focus on the sanctions committees and the Ombudsperson (section 3.1). The intense use of sanctions as one of the most prominent counter-terrorism tools contrasts sharply with the much more restricted, if not quasi-non-existent role, of international criminal courts (section 3.2).

3.1 The Security Council's design of a counter-terrorism architecture

The Security Council's global counter-terrorism strategy has four components, namely condemnation of discrete terrorist acts, imposition of sanctions, the creation of universally binding counter-terrorism measures and capacity-building for counter-terrorism at the national level.[62] The Council's counter-terrorism programme effectively commenced with Resolution 1373[63] and the creation of the Counter-Terrorism Committee (CTC). This Committee coexists with the previously established targeted sanctions regime instituted by Resolution 1267 (1999) as the two principal pillars of the Security Council counter-terrorism campaign. The Council's counter-terrorism framework was later complemented by a non-proliferation committee, the 1540 Committee,[64] as well as by the 1566 Working Group which was established directly after the attacks in Beslan, Russia. This working group was given a mandate to expand the 1267 sanctions to other terrorist activities[65] and to consider the possibility of establishing a fund for victims of terrorism.[66] The

56 International Atomic Energy Administration.

57 International Civil Aviation Organization.

58 International Maritime Organization. 59 World Customs Organization.

60 Financial Action Task Force. 61 United Nations Office on Drugs and Crime.

62 E. Rosand, 'Resolution 1373 and the CTC: The Security Council's Capacity-building', in Nesi, *International Cooperation in Counter-Terrorism*, 81.

63 UN Doc. S/Res./1373 (2001).

64 UN Doc. S/Res./1540 (2004). The mandate of the 1540 committee was extended for one year on 20 April 2011, UN Doc. S/Res./1977 (2011).

65 UN Doc. S/Res./1566 (2004), para. 9. 66 *Ibid.*, para. 10.

working group has not been tremendously successful or productive. The CTC has remained the Security Council's predominant counter-terrorism organ,[67] as assisted by CTED[68] and CTITF,[69] whereas the (former) 1267 sanctions regime constitutes the most pronounced Security Council measure targeting the concrete terrorist threat posed by al-Qaeda.

The legislative character of Resolution 1373 and subsequently 1540 has been extensively discussed in scholarly writing as a new operational technique of law-making, making up for the lacuna in general international law-making to provide a prompt normative response to urgent societal demands.[70] Yet, even if these resolutions epitomized the extent and potential of the Council's powers and capacity in the current global order, they did not start a new trend. Up until now, the Council has refrained from any further legislative activity. Moreover, the political momentum of 9/11 has slowly begun to fade away.

In the context of the Taliban/al-Qaeda sanctions regime, also formerly called the 1267 sanctions regime,[71] human rights considerations have led to the creation of the Ombudsperson and the splitting up of the regime into two separate regimes, one focused on Afghanistan and another targeting al-Qaeda. The 1267 sanctions regime pre-dates 9/11 and was created in 1999 as a direct reaction to the terrorist attacks in East Africa.[72] After the attacks on the World Trade Center (WTC) and the Pentagon, the regime was reinvigorated and extended to address the terrorist threat posed by al-Qaeda directly.[73] In the heat of the moment some 200 individuals and

[67] The CTC's main task is to monitor, assess and facilitate implementation of Res. 1373, at the state, regional and international levels. In this vein, it reviews state reports, facilitates technical assistance and promotes coordination and cooperation.

[68] The Counter-Terrorism Executive Directorate assists the CTC in its monitoring task. It was established by SC Res. 1535 (2004). It has a particular responsibility to ensure that 'all human rights issues relevant to the implementation of Res. 1373 (2001) and 1624 (2005) are addressed consistently and even-handedly including, as appropriate, on country visits that are organized with the consent of the visited member State' (SC Res. 1963 (2010)).

[69] The Secretary-General established the Counter-Terrorism Implementation Task Force in June 2005 as a coordination framework. It was institutionalized through General Assembly Res. 64/235 of 14 January 2010.

[70] A. Bianchi, 'Looking Ahead: International Law's Main Challenges', in D. Armstrong (ed.), *Routledge Handbook of International Law* (Abingdon: Routledge, 2009), 396. Also see the references above n. 54.

[71] For more on this regime, see Chapter 8 in this volume.

[72] UN Doc. S/Res./1267 (1999). [73] UN Doc. S/Res./1390 (2002).

entities were listed without clear and specific listing criteria and without any procedure for delisting.[74] The intense use of targeted sanctions as a new modality in the Security Council's sanctions policy exposed some of the shortcomings of the individualization of Security Council measures. Responding to criticism from many corners,[75] the Security Council gradually introduced modest improvements into the procedure, such as notification processes, the requirement of public narrative summaries of the reasons for listing, periodic reviews and the establishment of a 'focal point' within the UN Secretariat through which an individual could communicate a request for delisting to any of the sanctions committees.[76] These measures did not satisfy elementary human rights requirements such as the right to be heard, and the European Court of Justice put the 1267 regime under the microscope in the *Kadi* judgment.[77] In direct response, the Security Council created the Office of the Ombudsperson.[78] In contrast to the focal point, which is open to persons subjected to any Security Council sanctions regime,[79] the mandate of the Ombudsperson was confined to listings under the 1267 regime.[80]

The political scene in Afghanistan spurred further institutional modifications. In one decade, the combined threat that al-Qaeda and the Taliban posed back in 2001 gradually morphed.[81] The distinctions

[74] Van den Herik, 'Security Council's Targeted Sanctions Regimes'.

[75] Political, judicial, academic and civil society voices joined forces in their criticism. See, e.g., Strengthening sanctions through fair and clear procedures (2006), at http://watsoninstitute.org/pub/Strengthening_Targeted_Sanctions.pdf; UN Doc. A/60/887-S/2006/331 (2006); *Addressing Challenges to Targeted Sanctions; An Update to the Watson Report* (2009), at www.watsoninstitute.org/pub/2009_10_targeted_sanctions.pdf.

[76] The 1267 sanctions regime was gradually modified and strengthened by the following resolutions, Res. 1333 (2000), 1390 (2002), 1455 (2003), 1526 (2004), 1617 (2005), 1735 (2006), 1822 (2008) and 1904 (2009).

[77] Joined Cases C-402/05 P and C-415/05, *Kadi and Al Barakaat International Foundation* [2008] ECR 6351, at http://curia.europa.eu.

[78] UN Doc. S/Res./1904 (2009).

[79] Upon the establishment of the Ombudsperson, the focal point ceased to exist as a point of entry for the 1267 listings as delisting requests pertaining to this regime could be addressed directly to the Ombudsperson (UN Doc. S/Res./1904 (2009), para. 21).

[80] See generally on the Ombudsperson, K. Prost, 'Fair Process and the Security Council: A Case for the Office of the Ombudsperson', in Salinas de Friás *et al.*, *Counter-Terrorism*, ch. 16.

[81] Eleventh report of the Analytical Support and Sanctions Implementation Monitoring Team established pursuant to Security Council Resolution 1526 (2004) and extended by Resolution 1904 (2009) concerning Al Qaeda and the Taliban and associated individuals and entities (UN Doc. S/2011/245 (2011), para. 16). See also the statement of the French representative on the adoption of Res. 1988 and 1989 (UN Doc. S/PV.6557 (2011)).

between the two groups became more predominant than their mutual connections, which made their grouping in one sanctions regime less obvious. Furthermore, with a view to furthering the comprehensive political process in Afghanistan, the Afghan government requested a more flexible and expedient approach to delisting requests for Taliban members that were engaged in reconciliation processes and who had severed their ties with al-Qaeda.[82] In light of these developments, the Security Council abolished the 1267 sanctions regimes on 17 June 2011. It was split up into two separate regimes, one targeting the Taliban as a nationalist movement (the 1988 sanctions regime), and the other targeting al-Qaeda as a global actor (the 1989 al-Qaeda sanctions regime).[83] The innovative features of the 1988 sanctions regime are the pronounced involvement of the Afghan government in the delisting process and the linking of this process to specific reconciliation conditions.[84] The Ombudsperson was not given any role in relation to this regime and only continues to serve a function for the al-Qaeda listings under Resolution 1989. The authority of the Ombudsperson for the al-Qaeda listings was enhanced on this occasion as she was given the express power to recommend delisting publicly.[85]

The overall picture that emerges is that 9/11 engendered significant institutional innovations at the level of the Security Council. These included the Council's legislative activities, the creation of neoteric subsidiary organs, and the establishment of an Office of the Ombudsperson with some power of scrutiny. Yet, the impact of these innovations on the overall international legal system is perhaps more limited than is sometimes suggested. One could argue that the instrument of targeted sanctions has been further developed and put to the test

82 Eleventh report of the Analytical Support and Sanctions Implementation Monitoring Team, para. 17 (n. 81 above).

83 UN Docs. S/Res./1988 and S/Res./1989 (2011).

84 The resolution expressly notes that due regard should be given to requests of the Afghan government to delist individuals who meet the reconciliation conditions (UN Doc. S/Res./1988 (2011), para. 18). The reconciliation conditions agreed to by the Afghan government and the international community include the renunciation of violence, termination of links to international terrorist organizations, including al-Qaeda, or any cell, affiliate, splinter group or derivative thereof, and respect for the Afghan Constitution, including the rights of women and persons belonging to minorities. The German representative emphasized that these novel features of Res. 1988 enabled the SC to support Afghan political dialogue constructively (UN Doc. S/PV.6557 (2011)).

85 UN Doc. S/Res./1989 (2011), para. 21. The Committee can only overrule a recommendation by the Ombudsperson by consensus, and if consensus does not exist, the matter shall be referred to the SC (see para. 23).

in counter-terrorism. Apart from this, generally the new measures have been confined to counter-terrorism-related responses and have not spilled over to other matters of concern to the Security Council or to other sanctions regimes.

3.2 *A reduced role for international criminal courts*

While the relatively new regime of international criminal law is sometimes presented as the elixir for all societal problems, its ability to address terrorism has been limited. Terrorism was not included in the ICC Statute in 1998, despite a proposal by the terrorist-affected states Algeria, India, Sri Lanka and Turkey to do so under the heading of crimes against humanity.[86] Upon an initiative by France, the Rome Conference adopted Resolution E, which recommended that *a* Review Conference, hence not necessarily the 2009–10 one, would consider the crime of terrorism. The arguments *contra* instant inclusion concerned mainly the lack of a definition, the risk of politicization of the Court, a preference for domestic prosecution as more appropriate and, interestingly, the argument that some acts of terrorism were not sufficiently serious.[87] This last trend to differentiate between acts of terrorism in terms of seriousness seems to have been overtaken by post-9/11 Security Council determinations that *any* act of terrorism constitutes a threat to peace.

In the preparatory process of the ICC Review Conference in Kampala in June 2010, the Netherlands submitted an amendment proposal to include terrorism in the ICC Statute, invoking Resolution E as integrated into the Final Act of the Statute. The Netherlands revisited the 1998 proposal to imitate the aggression construction for terrorism.[88] This

86 UN Doc. A/CONF.183/C.1/L.27 (1998). See also the more extended proposal by India, Sri Lanka and Turkey a few days later (UN Doc. A/CONF.183/C.1/L.27/Rev.1 (1998)).

87 P. Robinson, 'The Missing Crimes', in A. Cassese *et al.* (eds.), *The Rome Statute of the International Criminal Court: A Commentary* (Oxford: Oxford University Press, 2002), 517; A. Cassese, 'Terrorism Is Also Disrupting Some Crucial Legal Categories of International Law' (2001) 12 *European Journal of International Law* 993, 994. See also comments of the US on a draft Statute in an earlier stage, which expressed a strong preference for national prosecutions of terrorism and the fear that ICC prosecution would actually undermine and interfere with national investigations in *Comments of the US pursuant to paragraph 4 of General Assembly Resolution 49/53 on the Establishment of an International Criminal Court, Report of the Secretary-General* (UN Doc. A/AC.244/1/Add.2 (1995)), paras. 27–31

88 This idea was discussed in Rome, too, backed by the Netherlands; see R. Kolb, 'The Exercise of Criminal Jurisdiction over International Terrorists', in Bianchi, *Enforcing International Law Norms against Terrorism*, 279.

meant including the crime but subjecting the exercise of the Court's jurisdiction to the adoption of an adequate definition. To this end, the Netherlands further proposed that an informal working group be established to examine which statutory adaptations would be required, were terrorism to be included as a new crime. This working group would not interfere with negotiations undertaken in the context of the comprehensive terrorism convention.[89] The proposal was not presented for lack of support, and Kampala did thus not codify terrorism as a new international crime.

There has been some scholarly discussion as to whether attacks such as 9/11 could qualify as a crime against humanity under the ICC definition in its current format, i.e., without having terrorism feature as a specific criminal act.[90] From a technical perspective this discussion hinges on the interpretation of the words 'organizational policy' that must underlie the attack.[91] The question is whether al-Qaeda with its loose organizational structure would qualify as an organization within the meaning of Article 7(2)(a). Pursuant to a strict interpretation, which is most in line with the spirit of the Statute's instruction in Article 22(2),[92] the answer would have to be in the negative. According to this view, only state-like organizations that control territory or act like states in other respects would fall within the ambit of Article 7(2)(a). These are thus highly structured organizations, such as the FARC in Colombia. There are of course also voices that have advocated a more flexible approach with a view to extending the ICC's reach as far as possible.[93] The ICC has started to broach the matter in its decision to

[89] Netherlands proposal on terrorism (CN723.2009.TREATIES-5 (2009)).

[90] M. C. Bassiouni, *The Legislative History of the International Criminal Court: Introduction, Analysis and Integrated Text* (Leiden: Martinus Nijhoff, 2005), 151–2; W. A. Schabas, 'Crimes against Humanity: The State Plan or Policy Element', in L. N. Sadat and M. P. Scharf (eds.), *The Theory and Practice of International Criminal Law: Essays in Honour of M. C. Bassiouni* (Leiden: Martinus Nijhoff, 2008), 347–64; R. Arnold, 'Terrorism as a Crime against Humanity under the ICC Statute', in Nesi, *International Cooperation in Counter-Terrorism.*

[91] Art. 7(2)(a) of the ICC Statute defines the phrase 'attack directed against any civilian population' which is part of the definition of crimes against humanity. It reads: (a) 'Attack directed against any civilian population' means a course of conduct involving the multiple commission of acts referred to in para. 1 against any civilian population, pursuant to or in furtherance of a state or organizational policy to commit such attack.'

[92] Art. 22(2) on the legality principle reads: 'The definition of a crime shall be strictly construed and shall not be extended by analogy. In case of ambiguity, the definition shall be interpreted in favour of the person being investigated, prosecuted or convicted.'

[93] E.g., Arnold, 'Terrorism as a Crime'.

authorize investigations by the Prosecutor in Kenya.[94] In this decision, the majority demonstrated some inclination towards a somewhat more lenient interpretation of the term 'organizational', whereas Judge Kaul favoured a more restrictive approach in his Dissenting Opinion.[95] Scholarly commentaries on this decision have indicated that even the more lenient majority interpretation would generally not cover terrorist organizations.[96] Kaul's dissent has been widely welcomed as constituting the more compelling view.[97]

Hence, the ICC has not become the international forum for terrorism prosecution and is unlikely to be so in the near future.[98] The resistance to including terrorism in the ICC Statute and the meagre support for the Dutch proposal clearly illustrate that overall the pre-9/11 arguments against using the ICC for counter-terrorism purposes have retained their force.

In parallel with these developments at the ICC, another attempt to internationalize law enforcement was undertaken in relation to a concrete terrorist attack, namely the assassination of the former Lebanese Prime Minister Rafiq Hariri on 14 February 2005. Following this attack, the Lebanese government expressly requested the Security Council to establish an international tribunal.[99] However, in its condemnations the Security Council was careful not to characterize terrorism as an international crime,[100] and it was only after a deadlock in Lebanese politics that

94 *Situation in the Republic of Kenya*, Decision Pursuant to Article 15 of the Rome Statute on the Authorization of an Investigation into the Situation in the Republic of Kenya, ICC-01/09, 31 March 2010, paras. 115–28.

95 *Ibid.*, Dissenting Opinion of Judge Hans-Peter Kaul.

96 W. A. Schabas, 'Prosecuting Dr Strangelove, Goldfinger, and the Joker at the International Criminal Court: Closing the Loopholes' (2010) 23 *Leiden Journal of International Law* 847, 852.

97 *Ibid.*; C. Kress, 'On the Outer Limits of Crimes against Humanity: The Concept of Organization within the Policy Requirement: Some Reflections on the March 2010 ICC *Kenya* Decision' (2010) 23 *Leiden Journal of International Law* 855.

98 See also the *Leiden Policy Recommendation on Counter-Terrorism and International Law*, which observes in para. 8 that the existing framework of multilateral instruments provided sufficient legal basis for domestic prosecution of terrorist crimes and international cooperation and that inclusion of terrorism in the ICC Statute would both be unlikely and undesirable.

99 UN Doc. S/2005/783 (2005), 7th preambular para.

100 W. A. Schabas, 'The Special Tribunal for Lebanon: Is a "Tribunal of an International Character" Equivalent to an "International Criminal Court"?' (2008) 21 *Leiden Journal of International Law* 513, 521.

the *Special* Tribunal for Lebanon was established.[101] The Tribunal, which unlike the *ad hoc* Tribunals was in name not international in character,[102] had jurisdiction over the Lebanese crime of terrorism. The applicable law was thus domestic law. Earlier proposals to prosecute the Hariri assassination coupled with other attacks under the heading of crimes against humanity were rejected.[103] The spirit surrounding the establishment of the Lebanon Tribunal can therefore be understood as resisting impulses to internationalize fully the criminalization of terrorism. The 2011 attempt of the judiciary of the Lebanon Tribunal to overcome these dynamics and to unearth a definition of terrorism under customary international law[104] is probably of insufficient calibre to effectuate a change of tracks.[105]

In sum, the upgrading of terrorism from a matter of international concern to a perennial threat to peace has not been translated to a parallel acknowledgement of terrorism as an international crime on a par with genocide and crimes against humanity. The role of modern international criminal law in combating terrorism has thus remained limited, and the emphasis of counter-terrorism strategies remains on the traditional international criminal law of mutual legal assistance and international cooperation.

4 The non-existent special regime of international terrorism law

After 9/11, the exclusive focus on the traditional law enforcement paradigm to counter terrorism came under strain. The military action against

101 UN Doc. S/Res./1757 (2007). See on the particularities of the establishment process as well as on the specific features of the Special Tribunal the two symposia in (2008) 21 *Leiden Journal of International Law* 483 and the (2007) 5 *Journal of International Criminal Justice* 1061, respectively.

102 See on this point and the nature of the Tribunal more generally, Schabas, 'Prosecuting Dr Strangelove', 514.

103 N. N. Jurdi, 'The Subject-Matter Jurisdiction of the Special Tribunal for Lebanon' (2007) 5 *Journal of International Criminal Justice* 1125, 1128.

104 Interlocutory Decision on the Applicable Law: Terrorism, Conspiracy, Homicide, Perpetration, Cumulative Charging, Case No. STL-11-01/I, A.Ch., 16 February 2011.

105 The decision has been subject to quite fierce criticisms: see, e.g., B. Saul, 'Legislating from a Radical Hague: The United Nations Special Tribunal for Lebanon Invents an International Crime of Transnational Terrorism' (2011) 24 *Leiden Journal of International Law* 67; K. Ambos, 'Judicial Creativity at the Special Tribunal for Lebanon: Is There a Crime of Terrorism under International Law?' (2011) 24 *Leiden Journal of International Law* 655.

Afghanistan as well as the GWOT metaphor[106] brought in the armed conflict paradigm as a competing legal framework. This convoluted international law's approach to terrorism. At the academic level, the WTC attacks immensely increased scholarly treatment of terrorism[107] and have spawned assertions that counter-terrorism law is now a separate branch of international law.

It is well known that in her authoritative book on terrorism published before 9/11, Higgins still refused to recognize that terrorism was a discrete topic of international law. She preferred to regard terrorism as a pernicious contemporary problem to which international law had to be applied.[108] Brownlie reaffirmed this view post-9/11, in 2008:

> There is no 'law of terrorism' and the problems must be characterized in accordance with the applicable sectors of public international law: jurisdiction, international criminal justice, State responsibility, and so forth.[109]

It has been argued that the absence of a fully coherent international legal regime of terrorism is largely the result of the absence of a foundational treaty and the international community's inability to reach consensus on a general definition.[110] This rather technical explanation might not fully account for the policy considerations that underlie the jurisdictional conflicts[111] and the shift of paradigm that was advocated after 9/11. Nevertheless, it is important to note that more than a decade after 9/11 the traditional law enforcement paradigm is being reappraised as the predominant counter-terrorism response.

[106] See specifically on the use of war language, F. Megret, '"War"?, Legal Semantics and the Move to Violence' (2002) 13 *European Journal of International Law* 361.

[107] Reaffirming Hilary Charlesworth's observation that 'international lawyers revel in a good crisis'. She exposes how international lawyers tend to focus on crises as a catalyst for the development of international law ('International law: A Discipline of Crisis' (2002) 65 *Modern Law Review* 377).

[108] Higgins, 'General International Law of Terrorism', 13–14.

[109] I. Brownlie, *Principles of Public International Law* (Oxford: Oxford University Press, 2008), 745. This quote from an earlier edition was also quoted by D. Moeckli, 'Terrorism as a Distinct Category of International Law' (2008–9) 44 *Texas International Law Journal* 157, 158.

[110] World Justice Project Counter Terrorism Expert Network, *Report of Key Findings and Recommendations on the Rule of Law and Counter Terrorism* (2012), 12. The contributions for this report are published in Salinas de Frías *et al.*, *Counter-Terrorism*.

[111] Y. Shany, 'Human Rights and Humanitarian Law as Competing Legal Paradigms for Fighting Terror', in O. Ben-Naftali (ed.), *International Humanitarian Law and International Human Rights Law* (Oxford: Oxford University Press, 2011), 13–33.

This book remains informed by the perspective suggested by Higgins and Brownlie to appreciate terrorism as a contemporary problem to which an amalgam of different international rules and domains apply. The aim is not to squeeze mechanically – and somewhat naively – all these rules in one artificial so-called special regime but rather to examine the application and interface of existing rules and branches of international law.

5 The challenges – structure of the book

The interplay between the different domains of international law that are relevant to counter-terrorism is surely intricate. It is characterized by overlap, interrelatedness and fragmentation. Still, there is a certain prioritization in the invocation of different domains. This book is premised on the axiom that regular law enforcement measures should enjoy priority as a means to address international terrorism and that the use of force is a measure of last resort that is only employed when absolutely necessary. On this basis, Part I of the book examines various aspects of international criminal justice cooperation in terrorist cases.

Chapter 2 (du Plessis) revisits the post-9/11 responses to international terrorism, which consistently acknowledge the need for enhanced forms of international cooperation between intelligence, law enforcement and judicial agencies. Despite widespread acceptance of the importance of these forms of cooperation, the chapter illustrates that major challenges to effective and appropriate international criminal justice cooperation continue to exist. It provides a number of concrete recommendations to tackle existing hurdles.

Chapter 3 (Newton) explores the potential of the *aut dedere aut judicare* principle to facilitate and reinforce the criminal justice response to terrorism. It considers that this principle expresses collective moral condemnation of terrorism as a legal obligation, and, as such, this obligation captures aspirations for a unified response to terrorism. After examining the approach of the counter-terrorism conventions and the obstacles therein, the chapter provides recommendations for the principle's effective, holistic application and for a progressive development of international law in this field.

Chapter 4 (Prost) maps existing networks for mutual assistance in criminal matters, including bilateral arrangements, multilateral conventions, especially the counter-terrorism conventions, and national legislation. It analyses their content, quality and effectiveness. Drawing upon a distinction between legal and practical challenges to mutual assistance, the chapter examines the need for a multilateral cooperative framework for mutual legal assistance.

Chapter 5 (Ewi) discusses the role that regional organizations, particularly the European institutions and the African Union, play in the global war on terrorism. Arguing on the basis of each region's threat perception, the chapter highlights some of organization's main strategies for promoting regional solidarity and cooperative relations among their member states on counter-terrorism, including norm development and elucidation, coordination and promotion of a cohesive regional approach, delivery of technical assistance, promotion of human rights in counter-terrorism, and cooperation with the UN.

Chapter 6 (Glerum, Rozemond and van Sliedregt) appraises counter-terrorism cooperation within the European Union and between the EU and third states. From the perspective of the traditional requirements of extradition treaties, it analyses the strengths and weaknesses of the European Arrest Warrant in terms of interstate cooperation and human rights protection. The chapter then reviews the European Court of Human Rights' jurisprudence on extradition under the European Arrest Warrant to both EU member states and third states.

Chapter 7 (Sambei) discusses intelligence-gathering techniques. It analyses how the critical distinction between intelligence and evidence should limit powers of intelligence agencies and how this limitation may affect the relationship with investigators' intelligence agencies as well as investigating and prosecuting authorities and individual citizens, especially in terms of human rights.

Chapter 8 (Daniel) addresses international efforts to combat terrorist financing. Given the current regime's human rights challenges, it proposes a fresh approach to tackling terrorist financing on the basis of non-conviction-based forfeiture, also called civil forfeiture. Furthermore, the chapter examines the work of the Financial Action Task Force.

Part II of the book engages with the *jus ad bellum* paradigm in relation to terrorist attacks. It revisits UN Charter provisions in light of contemporary practice and explores the legal regime on self-defence against terrorists.

Chapter 9 (Bianchi) draws attention to some methodological aspects underlying the legal discourse on the use of force. Without advocating a particular normative outcome, this chapter discusses how societal consensus on the use-of-force discourse can be established or restored within the interpretative community.

Chapter 10 (Wood) examines the Security Council's evolving participation in counter-terrorism from denunciation of attacks and calls for action to sanctions, and especially the use of force. It ultimately offers proposals for the Council's enhanced role in this respect.

Chapter 11 (Ratner) revisits the notion of 'armed attack' in relation to self-defence against terrorists in terms of the source, target, scale and military nature of the attack. It addresses the related question of the permissible target of self-defence measures and so the necessity of state attribution in this context. In light of the legal questions and practical challenges of self-defence, the chapter offers recommendations to states.

Chapter 12 (Wilmshurst) deals with the controversy surrounding the right to use force in anticipation of an attack. It examines in particular the question whether international law allows a right of anticipatory self-defence in response to threats by non-state actors operating from outside the victim state and in response to cumulative attacks.

Chapter 13 (Tams) provides an assessment of the application of the principles of necessity and proportionality as restraints on the exercise of self-defence against terrorism.

Part III of the book focuses on the *jus in bello* and in particular the interrelationship between this field of international law and human rights law. It discusses the applicability of both fields of law to counter-terrorist activities as well as the interplay between the two areas on specific issues related to protected persons. It also examines intersections with other legal frameworks, specifically with criminal justice and the law on peace and security.

Chapter 14 (Garraway) revisits the notion of 'armed conflict' in relation to terrorism and discusses the question of which framework of international humanitarian law – international armed conflict or non-international armed conflict – governs transnational armed conflicts. It also highlights the distinction between application of the laws of armed conflict and extraterritorial law enforcement.

Chapter 15 (Goldman) examines the extraterritorial application of fundamental human rights during situations of armed conflict both of a non-international and an international character, including occupation. Thus it considers the relationship between international humanitarian and international human rights law. It specifically analyses the right to life, the right to liberty and the related procedural safeguard of habeas corpus based on a survey of international jurisprudence of all relevant human rights bodies and the International Court of Justice.

Chapter 16 (Duffy) addresses the relationship between international humanitarian law and human rights law in situations of armed conflict. Given that both bodies of international law protect the same underlying principles and values, it argues for a harmonious interpretation. It analyses the relevance of the notion of *lex specialis* in this respect and offers alternative approaches to the co-application of the two relevant regimes, for example as regards the lawfulness of detention, targeted killings and the investigation of violations and reparation of victims.

Chapter 17 (Pejic and Droege) focuses on the legal regime governing treatment, particularly the prohibitions against torture, cruel or inhuman treatment, and outrages upon personal dignity and procedural guarantees for persons detained in the fight against terrorism, whether in an armed conflict of an international or non-international character, and with special attention to the rules governing security detention.

Chapter 18 (Kretzmer) discusses the legal regime governing the use of lethal force in the fight against terrorism. It discusses the applicability of the competing regimes of criminal justice and armed conflict and the right to life and the rules governing detention of combatants, civilians and 'unprivileged combatants'. It provides a number of perspectives on how to clarify the borders between the two regimes.

Chapter 19 (Satterthwaite) discusses the legal regime governing the transfer of persons in the context of counter-terrorism. It maps the current legal position on formal and informal transfer and identifies the minimum standards that apply under the relevant frameworks of human rights law, international humanitarian law and refugee law.

The final two chapters of Part III discuss intersections with other legal frameworks.

Chapter 20 (Martin) considers, in the absence of a definition of an international crime of terrorism, the blurring of international terrorism and armed conflict as well as international and domestic notions of terrorism. In this context, it analyses potential tensions between counter-terrorism legislation and the human rights of freedom of expression and freedom of association.

Chapter 21 (Bennoune) addresses the Security Council's position in international law, particularly whether international human rights law binds the organ and the legal effects of non-human rights-compliant resolutions. It deals with human rights problems that have arisen in relation to Security Council resolutions and their implementation, in particular in relation to the detention of persons and the freezing of assets.

PART I

Improving international cooperation in the investigation and prosecution of terrorist acts

2

A snapshot of international criminal justice cooperation against terrorism since 9/11

ANTON DU PLESSIS

1 Introduction

Terrorism has affected communities for decades, traditionally as a domestic threat, which changed over time to become a complex form of transnational crime that exploits gaps in international and regional intelligence, law enforcement and criminal justice cooperation.[1] The attacks on the United States on 11 September 2001 (also referred to as 9/11) were the most sophisticated and deadly acts of terrorism in history.[2] These attacks forced terrorism up the list of international priorities, and spurred further multilateral responses, most notably through the United Nations Security Council (UNSC) which reconfirmed that international terrorism has become a threat to international peace and security under Chapter VII of the UN Charter. In addition to several other serious attacks across the world in the 1990s,[3] 9/11 demonstrated that terrorists have developed the capacity and infrastructure to launch attacks with the ability to cause massive destruction of life and property.

From a law enforcement and criminal justice perspective, it became clear that modern terrorist crimes could no longer be dealt with under the

1 See M. Ewi and A. du Plessis, 'Criminal Justice Responses to Terrorism in Africa: The Role of the African Union and Sub-Regional Organizations', in A. M. Salinas de Friás, K. L. H. Samuel and N. D. White (eds.), *Counter-Terrorism: International Law and Practice* (Oxford: Oxford University Press, 2011), 990–1026.

2 In total 2,974 people were killed in the 9/11 attacks (T. H. Kean *et al.*, *The 9/11 Commission Report* (New York: W.W. Norton & Company, Inc., 2004)).

3 Simultaneous attacks on the US embassies in Kenya and Tanzania in 1998; attack on the WTC in New York in 1993; Air France hijacking on 24 December 1994; bombing of the Federal building in Oklahoma City on 19 April 1995; attack on US embassy in Moscow in 1995; attack on US embassy in Athens 1996; Empire State Building sniper attack in February 1997; UN observer abductions and Somali hostage takings also in 1998.

framework of an international order defined by the nation state. Terrorist crimes are similar to complex transnational crimes in that responding to them requires a multilateral effort that, among others, depends on enhanced international cooperation in criminal matters coupled with improved criminal justice responses that uphold human rights and the rule of law.[4]

Effective international cooperation forms the cornerstone of a criminal justice response to international terrorism. This has been reiterated in numerous international and regional resolutions, instruments and declarations, most notably UNSC Resolution 1373 (2001).[5] A key element of UNSC Resolution 1373 is the imperative for all states to afford one another 'the greatest measure of assistance' in connection with criminal investigations or criminal proceedings relating to the financing or support of terrorist acts, including assistance in obtaining evidence in their possession necessary for the proceedings.[6] More recently, the UN General Assembly adopted the UN Global Counter-Terrorism Strategy (UNGCTS),[7] which resonates with the recognition by states of the centrality of international cooperation to successful counter-terrorism efforts.

To comply with UNSC Resolution 1373, several regional and sub-regional organizations introduced new and enhanced international cooperation provisions into their respective legal regimes, mostly through conventions and protocols. In Africa, for example, the African Union (AU) reinvigorated the Organization of African Unity (OAU) Convention on the Prevention and Combating of Terrorism[8] by adopting an additional Protocol,[9] which includes several elements aimed at enhancing the sharing of information and formal cooperation in criminal matters. The AU also adopted a Plan of Action[10] to guide the implementation of the Protocol. At the sub-regional level in Africa, the Southern African Development Community (SADC) adopted two Protocols aimed at enhancing international cooperation in criminal matters.[11] Although not designed to respond only to terrorist crimes,

[4] For the purposes of this chapter, 'criminal justice responses' include the activities of intelligence (collecting and analysing intelligence for law enforcement and prosecution purposes), law enforcement and judicial (prosecution and judiciary) officials.

[5] UN Doc. S/Res./1373 (2001). [6] *Ibid.*, para. 2.

[7] UN Doc. A/Res./288/60 (2006).

[8] 1999 OAU Convention on the Prevention and Combating of Terrorism, 2219 UNTS 179.

[9] 2004 Protocol to the OAU Convention on the Prevention and Combating of Terrorism.

[10] 'The Plan of Action of the African Union on the Prevention and Combating of Terrorism in Africa' (2002), section E.

[11] 2002 Protocol on Extradition, www.sadc.int/english/key-documents/protocols/protocol-on-extradition/; 2002 Protocol Mutual Legal Assistance in Criminal Matters,

the SADC Protocols on Extradition[12] and Mutual Legal Assistance[13] provide additional sub-regional tools to assist law enforcement and criminal justice officials to cooperate more effectively when dealing with transnational terrorist crimes as well. Similar initiatives have been developed in other regions of the world.[14]

At the national level, most governments demonstrated unprecedented support for the new global counter-terrorism regime spearheaded by UNSC Resolution 1373. Although this support began to wane with time, several governments took steps to sign and ratify relevant international counter-terrorism instruments and adopted or amended laws and policies to domesticate these instruments and comply with UNSC Resolution 1373. At a practical level, national responses also included additional mechanisms to enhance international cooperation in terrorism cases.

However, despite this recognition of the importance of international cooperation in countering terrorism, and the subsequent enhancement of international and regional legal regimes in this regard, cooperation between intelligence, law enforcement and judicial agencies has been far from ideal. For a variety of reasons national action has not matched the rhetoric, and levels of information sharing and formal criminal justice cooperation has remained limited in many respects. This reflects the political challenges and technical difficulties associated with international cooperation in highly sensitive and complex terrorism cases.[15]

In addition to the limited levels of law enforcement and criminal justice cooperation in terrorism cases, there have been a number of well-publicized extrajudicial and unlawful counter-terrorism cooperation practices that have fallen short of key international human rights, rule of law and due process protections.[16] For example, the practice of extraordinary rendition, which is the transportation of suspected foreign terrorists or other individuals suspected of crimes, to third countries for interrogation and imprisonment without due process. In this regard, the US-led programme of extraordinary rendition was supported by a

www.sadc.int/english/key-documents/protocols/protocol-on-mutual-legal-assistance-in-criminal-matters/ (accessed 15 March 2012).

12 SADC Heads of States Meeting, Luanda, 3 October 2002. 13 *Ibid.*

14 See section 4 below for more details.

15 UNODC, Digest of Terrorist Cases, www.unodc.org/documents/terrorism/09-86635_Ebook_English.pdf (accessed 17 January 2012).

16 E. Rosand, A. Millar and J. Ipe, *Implementing the UN Global-Counter Terrorism Strategy in East Africa*, at: www.globalct.org/images/content/pdf/reports/eastafrica/pdf (accessed 17 January 2012).

number of countries, and was often accompanied by other serious human rights violations, including indefinite and secret detention and torture.[17] This practice hindered cooperation between several states and contributed to the negative reputation of global counter-terrorism efforts. It has thrown into sharp focus the importance of upholding human rights and legal protections when countering terrorism, even in the name of state security.

This chapter does not attempt to analyse all forms of counter-terrorism cooperation since 9/11, which would also include military and diplomatic cooperation efforts. The chapter focuses on cooperation aimed at enhancing criminal justice responses to terrorism, including intelligence, law enforcement and judicial cooperation mechanisms, at international, regional and national levels. The chapter summarizes the main developments in these areas of cooperation since 9/11 and highlights the key challenges that have hindered effective and appropriate cooperation.

The chapter works from the premise that the international community has entered a new era of counter-terrorism. An era that is shaped not so much by the post-9/11 discourse that favoured a military and state security approach, as by an era that is increasingly built on the foundations of human rights, due process and the rule of law. Counter-terrorism success in this era will depend heavily on the ability of national criminal justice processes to ensure fair, efficient and effective justice for perpetrators of terrorist crimes. The chapter's main conclusion is that counter-terrorist responses that are not rule of law based, whatever their perceived short-term benefits, not only lack legality and legitimacy but are also ultimately counter-productive.[18]

2 The importance of criminal justice responses to terrorism

Military-based responses to terrorist attacks could be appropriate in narrowly defined circumstances. However, for the most part terrorism will amount to a crime requiring national-level law enforcement and

[17] American Civil Liberties Union, Factsheet: Extraordinary Rendition (2005), at: www.aclu.org/safefree/extraordinaryrendition/22203res20051206.html; A. Cohen, 'Extraordinary rendition', CBS News, 11 February 2009, at: www.cbsnews.com/stories/2005/02/18/opinion/courtwatch/main674973.shtml.

[18] See also above n. 1.

criminal justice responses, which include the investigation, prosecution and adjudication of terrorist crimes. National-level criminal justice responses are the cornerstone of any sustainable global counter-terrorism effort that respects the principles of rule of law and human rights, and which offers a peaceful, accountable and legitimate response to terrorism. International or transnational terrorist attacks could make an impact on a number of jurisdictions. Consequently successful investigation and prosecution would depend heavily on effective cooperation between several countries.

The important role of criminal justice responses to terrorism is recognized in UNSC Resolution 1373. The UN's Counter-Terrorism Executive Directorate[19] has explained that the intent behind the Resolution is that states establish:

> a clear, complete and consistent legal framework that specifies terrorist acts as serious criminal offences, penalizes such acts according to their seriousness and helps the courts bring terrorists to justice. This framework should in turn provide the basis for the development of a domestic counter-terrorism strategy that is rooted in a legal approach, ensures due process of law in the prosecution of terrorists and appropriately protects human rights, while combating terrorism as effectively as possible.[20]

Despite the fact that there exists no broad internationally accepted definition of terrorism, a number of clear rules exist already. These rules range from rules governing the use of force against suspected terrorists, to their capture, detention and treatment, and ultimately to the trial of suspected terrorists. Many of these rules derive from international human rights law. The overarching legal and policy framework of international and regional counter-terrorism instruments[21] and the universal validity of fundamental human rights standards provide the normative guidelines to national criminal justice systems. Understandably national criminal justice systems will approach these challenges somewhat differently, depending on their legal tradition, their level of development, their relative institutional sophistication and their own circumstances.

[19] See section 3.1 below for more information on the CTED.

[20] Survey of the implementation of Security Council Resolution 1373 (2001), UN Doc. S/2008/379 (2008) [hereafter CTED 2008].

[21] See section 3 below.

2.1 *Terrorism: a global problem requiring domestic criminal justice responses*

Although regarded by the UNSC as a threat to international peace and security,[22] acts of international terrorism are not, bar in exceptional circumstances, regarded as 'core international crimes' such as genocide, crimes against humanity and war crimes.[23] There are no international criminal tribunals (except for the Lebanon tribunal)[24] with jurisdiction over terrorist acts.[25]

The duty to bring terrorists to justice therefore depends almost entirely on national criminal justice systems. In practice, most countries have criminalized terrorism under existing common law or statutory laws, which often incorporate the treaty crimes defined in the international counter-terrorism instruments. However, without adequate capacity to engage effectively in international cooperation with other states, these counter-terrorism efforts will fail.

Moreover, the UNSC has, in particular through Resolution 1373, 'put unprecedented obligations on Member States to implement its decisions through their national criminal justice systems'. States are

[22] UN Docs. S/Res./1267 (1999) and S/Res./1373 (2001).

[23] Several commentators highlight that serious terrorist attacks (like those perpetrated on 9/11) could constitute crimes under customary international law, including war crimes and crimes against humanity. See M. A. Newton and M. P. Scharf, 'Terrorism and Crimes against Humanity', in L. N. Sadat (ed.), *Forging a Convention for Crimes Against Humanity* (Cambridge: Cambridge University Press, 2011), 268. This discussion, however, falls beyond the scope of this chapter.

[24] The Special Tribunal for Lebanon came about at the request of the government of the Republic of Lebanon on 13 December 2005, following the attack in Beirut on 14 February 2005 that killed the former Lebanese Prime Minister Rafiq Hariri and twenty-two others. Pursuant to SC Res. 1664 (2006) and further to SC Res. 1757 (2007) the Tribunal was negotiated into existence and its Statute entered into force on 10 June 2007. The mandate of the Special Tribunal for Lebanon is to prosecute persons responsible for the attack on 14 February 2005 and other attacks in Lebanon spanning 1 October 2004 and 12 December 2005, which are connected with the February attack whether in motive, purpose, target, *modus operandi* or perpetrators. Because of its very mandate, Daniel Bellemare, the Tribunal's Chief Prosecutor, declared it the world's first counter-terrorism tribunal.

[25] Unlike other specific areas of international law, such as international humanitarian law applicable in armed conflict, or international criminal law applicable to grave violations of international law, there is as yet no fully coherent international legal regime governing terrorism and responses to terrorism. This is largely attributable to the continued inability of the international community to reach agreement on a universal definition of terrorism, and therefore to adopt a consistent approach to terrorism and counter-terrorism.

under a legal obligation to ensure that their national criminal laws enable them lawfully to prevent and/or prosecute or extradite in relation to terrorist activity.

There are a number of persuasive reasons supporting criminal justice responses to terrorism. These can be summarized as follows.

First, a criminal justice approach assists in the prevention of terrorist acts. By ensuring clear national laws that criminalize conduct preparatory to terrorist attacks, such as conspiracy (in the civil law countries, *association de malfaiteurs*), incitement, recruitment and financing, prosecutions can be brought against suspected persons. This allows officials to intervene at early stages in the planning of attacks. Early intervention often produces vital intelligence and evidence capable of disrupting and revealing related activities, as well as exposing other members of the criminal enterprise. However, criminal justice systems in many countries are geared more towards responses to acts after the fact than towards ensuring proactively that laws and procedures exist to convict persons of incidental conduct prior to their ability to carry out the overt act. Proactive law enforcement emphasizes the prevention and interruption of crime, rather than reacting to crimes already committed. Additional awareness raising and specialized training in this regard may be required, as many countries do not make proper use of the criminal justice system for purposes of preventing terrorist attacks.[26]

Second, by affording suspects due process in the criminal proceedings from investigation to conviction, the state complies with its international and national legal and constitutional duties. Importantly, the state also retains the long-term strategic advantage of moral supremacy. If states abandon human rights and due process safeguards this may lead to them using methods that are indistinguishable from their enemy, thereby depriving the state of legitimacy and elevating the claims of terrorists groups to some further degree of moral equivalency. The state can thus be open to accusations of brutality that could give terrorist propaganda unmerited significance. National responses that do not comply with constitutional and legal protections and civilian court systems can indicate when the state is acting irrationally, by using criminal methods such as torture to respond 'assertively' to crime and terrorism.

Third, a predominantly military-based counter-terrorism strategy can have unintended consequences enabling terrorists to cast themselves as

[26] J. Ford, *Beyond the War on Terror: Criminal Justice Responses to Terrorism in the Maghreb* (2009), ISS Monograph Series, No. 165.

'warriors', justifiably engaged in some form of noble enterprise. Prosecuting alleged terrorists as criminals deprives them of this undeserved badge of honour. There is even a case for prosecuting such persons, where possible, for ordinary criminal offences which relate to their conduct such as murder, arson, conspiracy to murder, etc., rather than attaching the 'terrorist offence' label, which may be seen by some suspects as a form of political statement or victory.

Fourth, national criminal justice responses to terrorism help to strengthen the social contract with the community. History has shown that neglecting or undermining ordinary criminal justice systems and undisciplined pursuit of terrorists at any cost can lead to wider disillusionment in society, mistrust of the government and even (in extreme cases of frustration with an unjust state), sympathy or collaboration with those pursuing violent terrorism. A human rights-compliant strategy to law enforcement treats citizens with respect and ensures that the community is available for cooperation, including as a source for vital information about possible nascent terrorist activity. Citizens can see justice being done in their national courts, even against supposedly 'undeserving' suspects. Unjust or unfair policing and prosecutions undermine this possibility.[27]

The conduct of a transparent and public (where possible) trial affords victims a voice in the process, whereas secretive, non-legal channels of dealing with terrorist cases denies this opportunity to them. It also denies the possibility that offenders, faced with victims or with society as represented by the court, might denounce their criminal past and contribute to society, including to national counter-terrorism efforts.

The definitive test of effective and appropriate criminal justice responses to terrorism is whether state authorities can, within an ordinary law enforcement and prosecution paradigm, lawfully deal with terrorist threats while complying with constitutional and international standards. Care must be taken to curb 'overzealous' responses couched within the criminal justice framework. National responses that are 'too strong' with overly broad definitions of crimes, unreviewable conduct of officials and minimal safeguards are likely only to weaken the rule of law and respect for the law in the society at large. In addition, such national responses could further isolate the government from its population over time, and perhaps provide a grievance issue for terrorist organizations to

[27] *Ibid.*

mobilize around, including for recruitment purposes. An important source of potential weakness is where governments seek to derogate from their obligations under international human rights law on the basis of the terrorist threat being exceptional and justifying a state of emergency.

Enhanced and appropriate criminal justice responses require relevant laws, policies and specialized capacity. Like other forms of transnational crime, the successful investigation and prosecution of acts of international terrorism is not easy. Success will depend on levels of international cooperation between intelligence, law enforcement and judicial agencies, as well as their ability to deal with complex issues relating to conspiracy, incitement and financing of terrorism, often involving several jurisdictions at once.

2.2 *International cooperation is central to any effective criminal justice approach*

As highlighted above, international cooperation is a key element of any effective law enforcement and criminal justice response to terrorism. International cooperation in this context comprises a broad spectrum of activities and agencies, ranging from sharing of intelligence to cooperation on prisoner exchange programmes. In the context of national criminal justice counter-terrorism efforts, the following key areas of cooperation exist.

Intelligence and law enforcement cooperation: the transnational nature of terrorism means that intelligence agencies increasingly cooperate with their foreign counterparts, especially considering that many terrorist cells and networks are based in several jurisdictions. The secret nature of intelligence cooperation creates additional challenges to effective oversight and protection of human rights and due process. In this regard, it is important to clearly distinguish between the role of law enforcement and intelligence agencies. The latter should not operate as law enforcement officials and should not have the powers of arrest and detention.

Mutual assistance and *mutual legal assistance* (*MLA*): transnational counter-terrorism operations, like other forms of globalized crime, often require investigators and prosecutors to gather evidence across borders. Against that background, the framework and procedures within which both formal assistance (referred to as 'mutual legal assistance' (MLA)) and informal cooperation (referred to as 'mutual assistance') are obtained are often complex and frequently depend on the attitude and opinions of those on the ground to whom the request is made.[28]

To facilitate this form of cooperation, states often make use of bilateral and multilateral treaties on MLA in criminal matters, in addition to informal cooperation mechanisms. MLA can take several forms, ranging from obtaining evidence from abroad to summoning witnesses for the purposes of giving testimony.[29] The current trend in international cooperation is to promote, wherever possible, informal mechanisms that allow for direct transmission between national authorities, including central authorities[30] without the use of diplomatic channels, in order to expedite proceedings. Other trends in international cooperation in criminal (and terrorism) matters include: lowering of evidential formalities and procedures; authorization of controlled deliveries to allow covert investigations to take place across borders; the development of joint investigation teams; the admissibility of witness testimony by video or telephone link; and the permission to transfer persons in custody to assist with investigations.

The extent to which countries are willing to enhance cooperation in these ways does, of course, vary greatly. In many cases, it depends on a particular country's own domestic laws, on the state of the relationship between that country and the requesting state and the attitude and helpfulness of those on the ground to whom the request is made. Consequently, the importance of excellent working relationships being built and maintained at the transnational level cannot be overstressed.

The international counter-terrorism legal regime described in section 3 of this chapter introduces a number of mechanisms to enhance international cooperation in the form of MLA.[31] In addition to the binding obligation to cooperate under UNSC Resolution 1373, many of the international and regional counter-terrorism instruments provide additional legal bases for requesting and providing MLA, even in the absence of a bilateral or other agreement between the states. Moreover, offences

[28] A. Sambei, A. du Plessis and M. Polaine, *Counter-Terrorism Law and Practice: An International Handbook* (Oxford: Oxford University Press, 2009), 393.

[29] *Ibid.*; UNODC, Mutual Legal Assistance checklist www.unodc.org/pdf/lap_mlaeg_report_final.pdf.

[30] 2000 United Nations Convention against Transnational Organized Crime, 2225 UNTS 209, Art. 18(13).

[31] UNODC, International Cooperation in Criminal Matters, www.unodc.org/documents/terrorism/Publications/Training_Curriculum_Module3/Module3_EN.pdf.

defined in the international counter-terrorism instruments may not, for the purposes of MLA, be regarded as political offences.

Regional MLA treaties and schemes have the advantage of reducing the resources necessary to negotiate individual agreements with states. Moreover, their regional scope allows for the development of fairly effective instruments that take regional specificities into account. While not an exhaustive list, the following regional MLA agreements are currently in existence:

- Inter-American Convention on Mutual Assistance in Criminal Matters[32] (OAS Convention);
- Economic Community of West African States Convention on Mutual Assistance in Criminal Matters[33] (ECOWAS Convention);
- Intergovernmental Authority on Development Conventions on Extradition and Mutual Legal Assistance (IGAD Conventions)[34]
- Caribbean Mutual Legal Assistance Treaty in Serious Criminal Matters[35] (Caribbean Convention);
- Minsk Convention on Legal Assistance and Legal Relations in Civil, Family, and Criminal Matters[36] and the Kishinev Convention[37] (CIS Conventions);
- Southern African Development Community Protocol on Mutual Legal Assistance in Criminal Matters[38] (SADC Protocol);
- Association of Southeast Asian Nations Treaty on Mutual Legal Assistance in Criminal Matters (ASEAN Treaty);[39]

[32] Inter-American Convention on Mutual Assistance in Criminal Matters (adopted 23 May 1992, entered into force 14 April 1996) OAS Treaty Series No. 75 (OAS Convention).

[33] Economic Community of West African States Convention on Mutual Assistance in Criminal Matters (adopted 29 July 1992, entered into force provisionally 29 July 1992 and definitively 28 October 1998) 2329 UNTS 301 (ECOWAS Convention).

[34] Intergovernmental Authority on Development Conventions on Extradition and Mutual Legal Assistance (adopted 7–8 December 2009) www.igad.org (IGAD Conventions).

[35] Caribbean Mutual Legal Assistance Treaty in Serious Criminal Matters (adopted 6 July 2005) www.caricomlaw.org (Caribbean Convention).

[36] Convention on Legal Assistance and Legal Relations in Civil, Family, and Criminal Matters (adopted 22 January 1993, entered into force 19 May 1994, amended 28 March 1997) (Minsk Convention).

[37] Convention on Legal Assistance and Legal Relations in Civil, Family and Criminal Matters (adopted 7 October 2002, entered into force 2004) (Kishinev – Chishinau Convention).

[38] Southern African Development Community Protocol on Mutual Legal Assistance in Criminal Matters (adopted 3 October 2002, entered into force 1 March 2007) www.sadc.int (SADC Protocol).

[39] Association of Southeast Asian Nations Treaty on Mutual Legal Assistance in Criminal Matters (adopted 29 November 2004) www.aseansec.org/17363.pdf (ASEAN Treaty).

- South Asian Association for Regional Cooperation Convention on Mutual Assistance on Criminal Matters[40] (SAARC Convention);.

At the operational level, it has become common practice for states to designate central authorities to deal with all incoming and outgoing requests for MLA and extradition. This has assisted states better to coordinate their ability to engage in international cooperation in criminal matters. Several international treaties dealing with transnational crime, including the Organized Crime Convention and Convention against Corruption,[41] require that states parties designate a central authority (often the Ministry of Justice) to which requests for assistance can be sent.

Extradition: this is the process by which states seek the return of fugitives, meaning the surrender of persons either accused or convicted of crimes to the state where those crimes were allegedly committed. The practice of extradition has its roots in the idea of territorial jurisdiction; that is, a state could not prosecute or imprison a fugitive who had committed a crime in the territory of another state, as the courts of the state where the fugitive was found did not have jurisdiction over his conduct.

Historically, states entered into bilateral treaties in order to secure the surrender of fugitives. This however had a limited effect since only parties to the treaty were bound by its terms. With the advent of crime of a more international nature and easier travel, the international community adopted a number of multilateral treaties. Multilateral treaties have the advantage of being open to ratification by several countries. Furthermore, every state party is then fully aware of the obligations of each party and any reservations/declarations they may enter. A classic example of a multilateral treaty is the 1957 European Convention on Extradition (the ECE),[42] which is a regional arrangement.

The UN counter-terrorism instruments discussed in section 3.2 of this chapter have at their core the idea of extending jurisdiction so that states may assert jurisdiction over crimes which were neither committed on, nor necessarily had any direct effect upon, their territory. These arrangements apply particularly to crimes which affect the international community, for example, hostage taking, torture, drug trafficking and hijacking aircraft.

[40] South Asian Association for Regional Cooperation Convention on Mutual Assistance on Criminal Matters (adopted 3 August 2008) http://saarc-sec.org/SAARC-Conventions/63/ (SAARC Convention).

[41] UN Doc. A/Res./55/25 (2001). [42] Council of Europe Treaty Series No. 024.

These UN counter-terrorism instruments invariably contain 'prosecute or extradite'[43] clauses, i.e. the state is obliged either to extradite the offender or to prosecute him itself. The basic idea is that criminals should not escape trial and punishment simply by absconding to another country.

Extradition is an act of the state. A state may choose, in the absence of any arrangement between the requesting and requested state, to enter into an *ad hoc* arrangement or simply surrender the fugitives. Extradition proceedings generally involve both the executive and judiciary. The involvement of the executive is largely dependent on domestic law and arrangements. Certain countries have no executive involvement in such requests because extradition is regarded as a matter for the judiciary. However, most Commonwealth states engage both elements.

Other forms of cooperation: there are several other forms of international cooperation in criminal matters, including the execution of foreign penal judgments, the transfer of prisoners, transfer of criminal proceedings, international cooperation for the purposes of confiscation of criminal proceeds and asset recovery, and cooperation in witness protection.

3 International developments in counter-terrorism cooperation

Multilateral counter-terrorism efforts have substantially evolved since 9/11. The threats posed by terrorism, the awareness of those threats, and the norms and institutions in place to tackle them around the world have changed significantly, partly due to the extensive efforts undertaken through the UN and other international and regional organizations.[44]

These efforts originated with the drafting of the Convention for the Prevention and Suppression of Terrorism by the League of Nations in 1937.[45] Terrorism has been an item on the agenda of the international community since. However, in the 1970s, it started to receive greater attention following a number of serious terrorist incidents, including the hijackings of several transnational airliners and the assault on the Olympic Games in Munich, Germany, in 1972. Efforts to counter terrorism

[43] Latin: *aut dedere aut judicare.*

[44] J. Cockayne *et al.*, 'Reshaping United Nations Counterterrorism Efforts: Blue Sky Thinking for Global Counterterrorism Cooperation 10 Years After 9/11', Center for Global Counter-Terrorism (2012).

[45] 1937 Convention for the Prevention and Punishment of Terrorism (League of Nations Doc.C.546M.383 V (1937)).

culminated with the adoption of the UNGCTS[46] by the General Assembly on 6 September 2006.

The UN and its numerous specialized agencies played a pivotal role in the global effort to counter terrorism. Initially the General Assembly was at the forefront of the UN's counter-terrorism programme until the 1990s, when the issue was taken up on the agenda of the UNSC after the UNSC declared terrorism a threat to international security.[47] Like all UN counter-terrorism efforts, the progress in the General Assembly was shaped by the political realities of the day. Political divisions on essential points, such as the question of state terrorism, coupled with the existence of several recognized wars of national liberation against former colonial powers in the 1970s and 1980s, fuelled disagreements on the scope of application of any possible definition of terrorism. Therefore attempts to reach consensus were abandoned.[48] Instead, it was considered more effective to develop many international treaties to suppress specific acts of terrorism on which there was some consensus reached. These treaties were often drafted following tragic events in which the specific acts of terrorism were committed.

The end of the Cold War in 1989 and apartheid in 1990, as well as the achievement of independence from colonialism for several African countries saw a shift in global politics. This global shift in politics created space for the General Assembly to make progress towards gaining global consensus on how to respond to terrorism. In 1999, the General Assembly entrusted an ad hoc Committee with the difficult task of resuming efforts towards the elaboration of a comprehensive convention on international terrorism. Negotiations within the *ad hoc* Committee on this convention started in 2000 and despite important progress being made, the Working Group encountered serious difficulties in finding solutions to three seemingly intractable points of contention among member states. The first related to the definition of terrorism, including its scope of application. The second intractable point was the relationship between the comprehensive convention and existing as well as future counter-terrorism legal instruments. The final issue was that of

[46] See above n. 5. UN Global Counter-Terrorism Strategy, UN Doc. A/Res./288/60 (2006); subsequently reviewed by the UNGA biennially in A/Res./62/272 (2008) and A/Res./64/297 (2010).

[47] A. Bianchi, 'Security Council's Anti-terror Resolutions and their Implementation by Member States' (2006) 4 *Journal of International Criminal Justice* 1044.

[48] S. Makinda, 'Terrorism, Counter-Terrorism and Norms in Africa' (2006) 15 *African Security Review* 19.

differentiating between acts of terrorism and the right of peoples to self-determination and to combat foreign occupation.[49]

However, despite the lack of consensus on a comprehensive convention against terrorism or a definition of terrorism, a wide variety of act-specific UN counter-terrorism instruments, General Assembly and UNSC resolutions, and a universally accepted Global Counter-Terrorism Strategy have evolved over time to provide a global framework. These instruments, resolutions and the strategy to a large extent fill the normative and legal gaps created by the lack of a comprehensive convention or agreement on the definition of terrorism. In addition, several regional counter-terrorism instruments have also been adopted to supplement the universal legal regime.[50]

As highlighted above, 9/11 was a catalyst that ensured a significant increase in multilateral activities to combat terrorism. The number of signatories to these instruments and domestic efforts of implementation increased notably after 9/11. Furthermore, there have been a vast number of pronouncements against terrorism in global and regional fora. New areas of cooperation have emerged in the important fields of maritime security, aviation, combating the financing of terrorism, border control, and the regulation and control of weapons of mass destruction.

3.1 UNSC resolutions dealing with terrorism

On 31 January 1992, the UNSC held its first meeting of Heads of State and Government. At this inaugural meeting, the members of the UNSC expressed 'deep concern over acts of international terrorism and emphasized the need for the international community to deal effectively with such acts'. Prior to 9/11, the UNSC's approach to terrorism was mostly reactive. The UNSC's responses to three particular cases are worth highlighting. First, the UNSC responded to the downing of Pan AM and UTA flights in 1988. Second, the UNSC responded to the attempted assassination of Egypt's president in 1991. Third, the UNSC responded

[49] Sambei *et al.*, *Counter-Terrorism Law and Practice.*

[50] Some examples of these regional instruments are: Arab Convention on the Suppression of Terrorism (1998), Convention of the Organization of the Islamic Conference on Combating International Terrorism (1999), European Convention on the Suppression of Terrorism (1977), OAS Convention to Prevent and Punish Acts of Terrorism (1971), OAU Convention on the Prevention and Combating of Terrorism (1999), SAARC Regional Convention on the Suppression of Terrorism (1987).

to the bombing of the United States' embassies in Dar es Salaam, Tanzania and Nairobi, Kenya, in 1998. These events led to sanctions against Libya and Sudan for refusing to extradite the suspects and against the Taliban in Afghanistan for supporting terrorist groups and refusing to extradite al-Qaeda leader Osama bin Laden.[51] Several commentators have characterized the 1998 bombings of the US embassies in Tanzania and Kenya as the forerunners to the attacks on the US on 11 September 2001.[52] It is worth noting that prior to 9/11, in 1999, the UNSC recognized international terrorism as a threat to international peace and security and strongly condemned all such acts in Resolution 1269.[53]

The 9/11 attacks sparked immediate, unprecedented and unified international action and political cohesion against terrorism, epitomized by the rapid adoption of UNSC Resolution 1373 just two weeks after the attack. Adopted on 28 September 2001, UNSC Resolution 1373 heralded a new and relatively controversial quasi-legislative role for the UNSC. UNSC Resolution 1373 imposed legally binding obligations on all states to undertake wide-ranging legal reforms and introduced several new counter-terrorism measures. UNSC Resolution 1373 focused heavily on prevention through the targeting of persons and entities that support and finance terrorism. Furthermore, UNSC Resolution 1373 recognized, in its preamble, the 'inherent right of individual or collective self defense' as a legitimate response to terrorism.

Notably, UNSC Resolution 1373 requires every country to freeze the financial assets of terrorists and their supporters, deny them travel or safe haven, prevent terrorist recruitment and weapons supply, and cooperate with other countries in information sharing and criminal prosecution. Member states are also called upon to sign and ratify the UN conventions and protocols against terrorism. In addition, member states must afford one another 'the greatest measure of assistance' in investigating terrorist acts. Unlike previous UNSC resolutions on terrorism, UNSC Resolution 1373 is not temporal or limited in application to a specific group or territory. UNSC Resolution 1373 is open-ended and far-reaching, particularly in that it

[51] Sanctions against the Taliban were imposed under the well-known SC Res. 1267 (1999). This resolution (together with its related successor resolutions) imposed sanctions in the form of travel bans, asset freezing and arms embargoes against individuals and entities listed by the SC pursuant to these resolutions.

[52] J. Cilliers, 'Africa, Root Causes, and the "War on Terror"' (2006) 15 *African Security Review* 58.

[53] UN Doc. S/Res./1269 (1999).

imposes extensive counter-terrorism legal obligations on all UN member states.[54]

UNSC Resolution 1373 gave an impetus never before seen to counter-terrorism measures, generally, and to international cooperation, in particular. As highlighted above, UNSC Resolution 1373 obliges states to afford one another the greatest measure of assistance in connection with criminal investigations or criminal proceedings relating to the financing or support of terrorist acts, including assistance in obtaining evidence in their possession necessary for the proceedings, and calls upon all states to cooperate, particularly through bilateral and multilateral arrangements and agreements, to prevent and suppress terrorist attacks and take action against perpetrators of such acts.

UNSC Resolution 1373 also created the Counter-Terrorism Committee (CTC),[55] which consists of all fifteen members of the UNSC. The CTC received priority attention within the UN and was described by then UN Secretary-General Kofi Annan as the 'centre of global efforts to fight terrorism'.[56] The CTC's main function has been to strengthen the counter-terrorism capacity of UN member states. Its mission is to 'raise the average level of government performance against terrorism across the globe'.[57]

The CTC aims to facilitate the provision of technical assistance to countries needing assistance in implementing counter-terrorism mandates. The CTC has also attempted to coordinate the counter-terrorism efforts of a wide range of international, regional and subregional organizations inside and outside the UN system. To reinforce the CTC's efforts towards more effective collaboration and state capacity building, the CTC established the Counter-Terrorism Committee Executive

[54] Res. 1373 was passed under Chapter VII of the UN Charter, which permits the SC to take legally binding decisions under Art. 25 directing member states to impose economic sanctions or to use force to maintain international peace. Because of the serious consequences of such action, the permanent members of the Council have not hesitated to use their veto power to obstruct action of this kind where their interests have been involved. Most recently, through S/Res./1963 (2010), the UNSC further extended the mandate of Counter-Terrorism Committee Executive Directorate (CTED) as special political mission under the policy guidance of Counter-Terrorism Committee (CTC).

[55] The CTC website is available online at www.un.org.

[56] Statement at Ministerial Level Meeting of the UN Security Council (UN Doc. S/PV.4688 (2003)).

[57] E. Rosand, 'Security Council Resolution 1373 and the Counter-Terrorism Committee: The Cornerstone of the United Nations Contribution to the Fight against Terrorism', in C. Fijnaut, J. Wouters and F. Naerts (eds.), *Legal Instruments in the Fight against International Terrorism* (Leiden: Martinus Nijhoff, 2004), 606.

Directorate (CTC/CTED), which became fully operational in 2005. CTED also enhances the CTC's capacity to identify and prioritize the technical assistance needs of member states. As part of its core function, CTED is tasked with reviewing states' reports in order to identify priority areas for assistance and then liaise with donor states and other partners who may be willing and able to provide the necessary resources.

CTED also has the mandate to facilitate the provision of rule of law-based technical assistance to member states, which should be based on international human rights, refugee and humanitarian law, in connection with the identification and implementation of effective measures to implement UNSC Resolution 1373. CTED's focus on rule of law issues was enhanced following the adoption of UNSC Resolution 1963,[58] which appears to signify the beginning of a convergence between the international counter-terrorist framework and the broader global effort to promote development, rule of law and human rights such that counter-terrorist responses may no longer be considered in isolation.

UNSC Resolution 1373 succeeded and was followed up by several other Chapter VII UNSC resolutions. The most important elements of these resolutions are summarized below.

Prior to UNSC Resolution 1373, UNSC *Resolution 1267* was passed on 15 October 1999 for the purpose of overseeing the implementation of sanctions (including the freezing of assets, an arms embargo and a travel ban) on Taliban-controlled Afghanistan for its support of Osama bin Laden following the 1998 simultaneous bombings of US embassies in Nairobi, Kenya and Dar es Salaam, Tanzania, that killed 257 people and wounded over 4,000. The sanctions regime contained in UNSC Resolution 1267 received added impetus, however, after the 9/11 attacks in the United States due to the involvement of al-Qaeda and the Taliban in the planning and execution of the attacks.

Since then, it has been modified and strengthened by resolutions 1390,[59] 1455,[60] 1526,[61] 1617,[62] 1730,[63] 1735[64] and 1820.[65] On 17 December 2009, the UNSC passed the innovative UNSC Resolution 1904[66] that established the Office of the Ombudsperson to assist the CTC when it considers

[58] UN Doc. S/Res./1963 (2010). In particular, the resolution recognizes that 'development, peace and security, and human rights are interlinked and mutually reinforcing' (preamble). See also para. 10.

[59] UN Doc. S/Res./1390 (2002).
[60] UN Doc. S/Res./1455 (2003).
[61] UN Doc. S/Res./1526 (2004).
[62] UN Doc. S/Res./1617 (2005).
[63] UN Doc. S/Res./1730 (2006).
[64] UN Doc. S/Res./1735 (2006).
[65] UN Doc. S/Res./1820 (2008).
[66] UN Doc. S/Res./1904 (2009).

delisting requests. The establishment of the Office of the Ombudsperson represented a success for states and organizations that had lobbied for the CTC to be more responsive to due process concerns regarding the listing and delisting process and requests by individuals to petition the CTC. Judge Kimberley Prost of Canada was appointed as the Ombudsperson in June 2010.[67] On 17 June 2011, in UNSC Resolution 1989[68] the UNSC reaffirmed the assets freeze, travel ban and arms embargo affecting all individuals and entities on the CTC's al-Qaeda Sanctions List. In doing so the UNSC decided to split the Consolidated List, thereby separating the al-Qaeda and Taliban lists. The UNSC also extended the mandate of the Analytical Support and Sanctions Monitoring Team, as well as the mandate of the Office of the Ombudsperson for a further period of eighteen months.

UNSC Resolution 1456[69] was passed on 20 January 2003. Its operative paragraph six declares that '[s]tates must ensure that any measure taken to combat terrorism comply with all their obligations under international law, and should adopt such measures in accordance with international law, in particular international human rights, refugee, and humanitarian law.'[70] UNSC Resolution 1456 is often regarded by many human rights non-governmental organizations (NGOs) as a flagship resolution for safeguarding human rights in the fight against terrorism. It reminds states that 'terrorism can only be defeated, in accordance with the Charter of the United Nations and international law, by a sustained comprehensive approach involving the active participation and collaboration of all States, international and regional organizations, and by redoubled efforts at the national level'.

UNSC Resolution 1540[71] on non-proliferation of nuclear weapons was unanimously adopted on 28 April 2004, following the confession by Dr Abdul Qadeer Khan that he had shared nuclear technology with Iran, Libya and North Korea. The UNSC adopted the non-proliferation resolution in which it decided that all states shall refrain from supporting by any means non-state actors that attempt to acquire, use or transfer nuclear, chemical or biological weapons and their delivery systems. The UNSC also decided that all states should establish domestic controls to prevent the proliferation of such weapons and means of delivery, in particular for terrorist purposes, including by establishing appropriate controls over

[67] Press Conference to Present Ombudsperson of Security Council's 1267 Committee, 15 July 2010, www.un.org/News/briefings/docs/2010/100715_1267.doc.htm.

[68] UN Doc. S/Res./1989 (2011). [69] UN Doc. S/Res./1456 (2003). [70] My emphasis.

[71] UN Doc. S/Res./1540 (2004).

related materials, and adopt legislative measures in that respect. UNSC Resolution 1540 also established a committee to monitor state implementation of its provisions relating to domestic controls to prevent the proliferation of nuclear, chemical or biological weapons and their means of delivery.

UNSC Resolution 1566[72] was passed in October 2004, following the school massacre at Beslan in North Ossetia. This Russian-drafted resolution urged greater cooperation in the fight against terrorism and established a working group to consider additional counter-terrorism measures. Unfortunately, implementation of this resolution has been lax. The working group established by UNSC Resolution 1566 has not met regularly, and little progress is foreseen in the near future.[73]

These new resolutions demonstrated the UNSC's resolve in countering terrorism, but they also created potential overlap with the mission of the CTC and generated uncertainty about how the new bodies would work together.

3.2 UN counter-terrorism instruments

Another important component of the global legal and normative regime against terrorism are the international counter-terrorism instruments, in the form of conventions, protocols and related amendments that have been developed under the auspices of the UN General Assembly and various UN specialized agencies. Since 1963, the international community has developed eighteen legal instruments that deal with specific acts of terrorism, ranging from aircraft hijacking to nuclear terrorism.[74]

[72] UN Doc. S/Res./1566 (2004).

[73] V. Comras, 'The United Nations and the Fight Against Terrorism and Nonproliferation' (statement, Committee on International Relations, US House of Representatives, Washington, DC, 17 March 2005), 4.

[74] These eighteen instruments are: 1963 Convention on Offences and Certain Other Acts Committed on Board Aircraft, 704 United Nation Treaty Series 220; 1970 Convention for the Suppression of Unlawful Seizure of Aircraft, 704 United Nation Treaty Series 106; 1971 Convention for the Suppression of Unlawful Acts against the Safety of Civil Aviation, 974 UNTS 178; 1973 Convention on the Prevention and Punishment of Crimes against Internationally Protected Persons, Including Diplomatic Agents, 1035 UNTS 168; 1979 International Convention against the Taking of Hostages, 1316 UNTS 206; 1979 Convention on the Physical Protection of Nuclear, 1456 Material UNTS 125; 1988 Protocol for the Suppression of Unlawful Acts of Violence at Airports Serving International Civil Aviation, Supplementary to the Convention for the Suppression of Unlawful Acts against the Safety of Civil Aviation, 1589 UNTS 474; 1988 Convention for the Suppression of Unlawful Acts against the Safety of Maritime Navigation, 1678 UNTS 222; 1988 Protocol for the Suppression of Unlawful Acts against the Safety of Fixed

These instruments create, *inter alia*, the obligation on state parties to adopt criminal and procedural criminal law measures to counter these various acts of terrorism. Together with the relevant UNSC resolutions referred to above, these instruments create what is commonly referred to as the universal legal regime against terrorism.

The overall objective of the universal scheme is to harmonize all national laws to create a seamless web of preventive, punitive and cooperative legal measures that can constitute the primary resource or asset in counter-terrorism strategies. The eighteen instruments cover the following terrorist acts:

- acts of aircraft hijacking;
- acts of aviation sabotage;
- acts of violence at airports;
- acts against the safety of maritime navigation;
- acts against the safety of fixed platforms located on the continental shelf;
- acts against internationally protected persons;
- acts of unlawful taking and possession of nuclear material;
- acts of hostage taking;
- terrorist bombings;
- acts of funding of the commission of terrorist acts and terrorist organizations; and
- acts of nuclear terrorism.

Underlying the universal legal regime is the basic notion that the state should bring terrorist suspects to criminal trial, or should be able and willing to extradite the suspects lawfully to another state with jurisdiction over the offences that will try them. This 'extradite or prosecute' principle is intended to deprive those who intend to engage in, finance or support terrorist conduct of any safe haven in the world.

Platforms Located on the Continental Shelf, 1678 UNTS 304; 1991 Convention on the Marking of Plastic Explosives for the Purpose of Identification, 2122 UNTS 374; 1997 International Convention for the Suppression of Terrorist Bombings, 2149 UNTS 256; 1999 International Convention for the Suppression of the Financing of Terrorism, 2178 UNTS 179; 2005 International Convention for the Suppression of Acts of Nuclear Terrorism, 2445 UNTS 89; 2005 Amendment to the Convention on the Physical Protection of Nuclear Material; 2005 Protocol to the Convention for the Suppression of Unlawful Acts against the Safety of Maritime Navigation; 2005 Protocol to the Protocol for the Suppression of Unlawful Acts against the Safety of Fixed Platforms Located on the Continental Shelf; 2010 Convention on the Suppression of Unlawful Acts Relating to International Civil Aviation; 2010 Protocol Supplementary to the Convention for the Suppression of Unlawful Seizure of Aircraft.

This scheme requires national-level measures and actions in order to fulfil this objective. Most of the instruments contain detailed provisions on international cooperation, and provide important tools for extradition and MLA that enable national authorities to cooperate with each other to ensure that there are not safe havens for terrorist suspects protecting them from prosecution or extradition. A typical example of this international cooperation clause as contained in Article 8 of the Terrorist Bombings Convention,[75] which reads as follows:

> 1. The offence shall be deemed to be included as an extraditable offence in any extradition treaty existing between Contracting States. Contracting States undertake to include the offence as an extraditable offence in every extradition treaty to be concluded between them.
> 2. If a Contracting State, which makes extradition conditional on the existence of a treaty, receives a request for extradition from another Contracting State with which it has no extradition treaty, it may at its option consider this Convention as the legal basis for extradition in respect of the offence. Extradition shall be subject to the other conditions provided by the law of the requested State.
> 3. Contracting States, which do not make extradition conditional on the existence of a treaty, shall recognize the offence as an extraditable offence between themselves subject to the conditions provided by the law of the requested State.
> 4. The offence shall be treated, for the purpose of extradition between Contracting States, as if it had been committed not only in the place in which it occurred but also in the territories of the States required to establish their jurisdiction in accordance with Article 4, paragraph 1.

The international legal instruments thus provide the basis for national-level criminal justice initiatives. This is in line with the understanding that global problems require buy-in from all countries by ensuring that their criminal justice systems are capable of preventing terrorist acts and dealing with terrorism suspects. Although most of these instruments were developed before 9/11, the attacks served as a catalyst to speed up the global ratification and implementation of these instruments. This was largely as a result of the increased pressure imposed on states by UNSC Resolution 1373 to ratify and implement the UN counter-terrorism instruments, and its obligation on states to enhance international cooperation in countering terrorism.

Currently, most instruments have been ratified by a significant number of states, ranging from 115 to over 180 Contracting Parties per

[75] Bombings Convention.

instrument. Assessing the effectiveness of these instruments, however, does not depend merely on their high ratification levels. More important is the extent of national-level implementation through the domestication of the criminalization and international cooperation provisions into workable legal provisions, policies and practices.

Unfortunately, unlike a number of other international and regional penal law conventions, none of the articles in the UN counter-terrorism conventions are detailed enough to provide practical guidance for the rendering of comprehensive criminal justice cooperation. To rectify this shortcoming (which is an understandable element of international agreements), the three most recent conventions – the Terrorist Bombings Convention (1997), the Financing of Terrorism Convention (1999) and the Nuclear Terrorism Convention (2005) – include some additional provisions related to criminal justice cooperation, and to MLA in particular. These conventions contain separate articles on a specific form of assistance – the temporary transfer of witnesses.[76] The Financing Convention also contains provisions on non-refusal of requests on the basis of bank secrecy[77] and a 'limitation of use' clause,[78] which would prevent the use of evidence, received for matters other than that for which it was requested. In summary, the majority of the counter-terrorism treaties create a binding obligation to render mutual assistance, the terms of which, however, will need to be worked out as between the relevant parties in an individual case.

4 Regional developments in counter-terrorism cooperation

Terrorism has afflicted various regions in different ways for many years. Regional and subregional responses to terrorism have understandably been shaped by these individual experiences to reflect regional priorities and specificities. However, the 9/11 attacks created a new impetus on the part of regional and subregional bodies to enhance international cooperation in the fight against terrorism. Several of these bodies amended their respective conventions and protocols to comply with the broad obligations imposed by UNSC Resolution 1373, particularly in the area of international cooperation.

Despite these noble efforts, the practical realities, which often include limited resources, narrow mandates and higher priorities than dealing

[76] *Ibid.*, Art. 13; Financing Convention, Art. 16; and Nuclear Convention, Art. 17.
[77] Art. 12(2). [78] See Art. 12(3).

with terrorism, have resulted in uneven contributions from the various regional organizations. Many of these regional initiatives are discussed in detail in the other chapters of this volume. The section below merely summarizes some of key developments in selected regions.

4.1 Europe

Europe has the most developed regional counter-terrorism architecture. The Council of Europe (CoE), the European Union (EU) and the Organization for Security and Cooperation in Europe (OSCE) all play an important role in pursuing a regionally coordinated counter-terrorism response. Europe's counter-terrorism framework encompasses a wide range of programmes, activities and initiatives that substantially mirror similar global efforts developed by the UN. In 2004, the EU made a declaration on combating terrorism.[79] This declaration was followed in 2005 by a comprehensive counter-terrorism strategy and action plan.[80] The EU has also adopted, among others, the EU Strategy for combating radicalization and recruitment to terrorism,[81] an EU strategy to combat the financing of terrorism,[82] a framework decision on terrorism that provides a definition of terrorism and an EU terrorist list. Furthermore, the EU attempts to improve coordination and sharing of sensitive information and intelligence among member states.

Europe also has two counter-terrorism conventions, the 1977 Convention on the Suppression of Terrorism[83] and the European Convention on the Prevention of Terrorism,[84] which came into force on 1 June 2007. Negotiated under the auspices of the CoE, both conventions provide a broad framework for the criminalization of terrorist and related conduct and the enhanced cooperation between member states.

[79] Council of the European Union, Declaration on Combating Terrorism (2004), www.consilium.europa.eu/uedocs/cmsUpload/DECL-25.3.pdf.

[80] *European Union Counter Terrorism Strategy* (Doc.14469/4/05 REV 4 (2005)).

[81] *European Union Strategy for Combating Radicalization and Recruitment to Terrorism* (Doc. 14781/1/05 REV 1 (2005)).

[82] *Council of the European Union, Fighting against Terrorist Financing: Six Months Report* (Doc. 11948/2/07 REV 2 (2007)).

[83] 1977 European Convention on the Suppression of Terrorism, Council of Europe Treaty Series No. 090.

[84] 2005 European Convention on the Prevention of Terrorism, Council of Europe Treaty Series No. 196.

An important initiative aimed at promoting cooperation in criminal matters was the creation of the European Arrest Warrant (EAW) that facilitates extradition among EU members. The EAW replaced the previous extradition system by requiring each national judicial authority (the executing judicial authority) to recognize *ipso facto* and with a minimum of formalities, requests for the surrender of a person made by the judicial authority of another member state (the issuing judicial authority).

At an operational level, Europe has established both Eurojust,[85] to facilitate coordinated criminal investigations, and Europol,[86] to improve coordination in the exchange of intelligence and to provide investigative support. It has also developed a robust counter-terrorism capacity-building fund to assist developing countries to enhance their counter-terrorism responses and has appointed a counter-terrorism 'czar' to coordinate the activities of the European Commission and EU members.[87]

Eurojust's main aim is to support national investigations and prosecutions by member states of serious forms of crime, including terrorism. Traditional instruments of judicial cooperation were simplified or replaced by new instruments, which addressed some fundamental impediments to cooperation such as those attributable to the principles of sovereignty and territoriality. Eurojust has four principal functions. First, Eurojust facilitates the exchange of information between the judicial authorities of the different member states involved in investigations and prosecutions against the same terrorist organization. Second, Eurojust must provide support to the judicial authorities of member states in the issuing and execution of EAWs. Third, Eurojust must facilitate investigative measures and the gathering of evidence necessary for prosecuting the suspects of terrorism offences at trial stage (specifically, witnesses' testimony, scientific evidence, searches and seizures, the interception of telecommunications). Fourth, Eurojust facilitates the freezing and confiscation of the benefits from

[85] Eurojust was established by Council Decision 2002/187/JHA of 28 February 2002 setting up Eurojust with a view to reinforcing the fight against serious crime [2002] OJ L63; as amended subsequently by Council Decision 2009/426/JHA of 16 December 2008 on the strengthening of Eurojust and amending Decision 2002/187/JHA setting up Eurojust with a view to reinforcing the fight against serious crime [2009] OJ L138.

[86] Europol www.europol.europa.eu/.

[87] Rosand, 'Security Council Resolution 1373 and the Counter-Terrorism Committee'.

other criminal offences that are suspected as being used for terrorist financing.[88]

All of Eurojust's activities have the objective of strengthening interstate cooperation by providing a forum where practitioners and decision-makers from all relevant disciplines and perspectives may exchange views on how best to coordinate their counter-terrorist efforts, ranging from bringing a particular terrorist suspect before a national court to wider anti-terrorism policy and legislative matters. Each of these functions aims 'to support and strengthen' cooperation and coordination between practitioners.

4.2 *Africa*

The development of counter-terrorism responses in Africa has taken place within the context of the broader debate that emerged after 9/11 as to whether terrorism, in its current manifestations, represents a serious threat to the continent on the same scale as poverty, the ongoing health crises, climate change and internal conflicts. Despite this context, African subregional organizations, and its continental body, the AU, have taken a number of additional steps to strengthen their counter-terrorism capacity. Many of these new initiatives built on the existing legal and normative infrastructure that existed before 9/11.

Since its inception in July 2002, the AU has made countering terrorism a regular agendum of Africa's peace and security vision. Counter-terrorism also became one of the priorities in the strategic framework document of the New Partnership for Africa's Development (NEPAD), adopted by the AU in July 2002. A high-level meeting of the AU in Algiers in September 2002 endorsed the UN universal legal instruments against terrorism and developed a plan of action on the prevention and combating of terrorism in Africa. The AU Peace and Security Council (PSC), launched in May 2004, also sought to coordinate continental efforts in the prevention and combating of international terrorism in all its aspects, including enhancing the criminal justice counter-terrorism capacity of African countries.

Notably, the attacks in Kenya and Tanzania in 1998 introduced a new dimension of terrorism. These attacks demonstrated that terrorism could no longer be seen as merely a local or domestic problem, but rather as an

[88] M. Coninsx, 'Strengthening Interstate Cooperation: The Eurojust Experience', in A. M. Salinas de Friás, K. L. H. Samuel and N. D. White (eds.), *Counter-Terrorism: International Law and Practice* (Oxford: Oxford University Press, 2011), 965–89.

international threat with global reach. Thus Africa had to be part of the global response to counter this new threat. These concerns culminated in the adoption of the OAU Convention on the Prevention and Combating of Terrorism (Algiers Convention) by the 35th Ordinary Session of Heads of State and Government in Algiers, Algeria in July 1999.[89] The Algiers Convention was the first instrument on preventing and combating terrorism in Africa and provided an African definition of terrorism.

The Algiers Convention came into force in December 2002, following ratification by 30 of the then 53 AU member states. The coming into force of the Algiers Convention was a crucial step in the development of Africa's counter-terrorism efforts, which could henceforth be guided by a local multilateral legal instrument. Several subregions also developed their own counter-terrorism-related legal instruments, including a number of conventions and protocols on extradition and mutual legal assistance such as the SADC Protocols on Extradition and Mutual Legal Assistance, IGAD's Convention on Mutual Legal Assistance and Extradition and the ECOWAS Convention on Extradition.

In addition to these policy developments, the AU established the Algiers Centre on the Study and Research on Terrorism (ACSRT) to provide counter-terrorism training and technical assistance support to AU member states, and provide for a network of national and regional counter-terrorism focal points that envisions a highly integrated network of state and regional focal points that could share information and good practice. Furthermore, a number of subregional organizations have established capacity within their secretariats to support various forms of subregional counter-terrorism capacity and cooperation. Examples include the IGAD that in 2004 launched the IGAD Capacity Building Programme against Terrorism (ICPAT),[90] the Eastern Africa Police Chiefs' Cooperation Organization (EAPCCO),[91] the Southern African

89 See above n. 33.

90 ICPAT is an initiative of the Intergovernmental Authority on Development (IGAD), which is implemented by the Institute for Security Studies (ISS). Launched on 14 June, ICPAT has the following key components: enhancement of judicial measures, optimization of interdepartmental cooperation, enhancement of border control, training, sharing of information and best practices, and promotion of strategic cooperation.

91 The Eastern Africa Police Chiefs Cooperation Organization (EAPCCO) was created in 1998, in Kampala, Uganda, as a regional practical response to the need for joint police effort against transnational and organized crime. Its priority crime areas include anti-terrorism, motor vehicle thefts, anti-drugs, economic crimes and corruption, illegal firearms, cattle rustling, environmental and wildlife crime and trafficking in human beings and illegal immigrants.

Regional Police Chiefs' Cooperation Organization (SARPCCO),[92] and the Eastern and Southern African Anti-Money Laundering Organization (ESAAMLG).[93]

In 2010 the AU adopted a Comprehensive African Anti-terrorism Model Law[94] to assist member states with the implementation of the OAU Convention and other international and UN counter-terrorist instruments. Although not intended to be formally binding on states, the Model Law creates a 'blueprint' for states' effective domestication of regional and international legal obligations, providing guidance and a template reflecting an African perspective and concrete mechanisms to enhance international cooperation in terrorism matters. Novel aspects of the Model Law include provision for a new 'African arrest warrant', and the drawing up of a 'blacklist' of terrorist entities in Africa.

Despite these positive developments and efforts by the AU to augment the criminal justice regimes and their effective implementation, the AU's legal framework suffers from a number of significant weaknesses. One of them arises from the wording of the definition of terrorist acts in Article 3 of the OAU Convention. Although a regional definition is normally to be welcomed, not least for the purpose of achieving increased harmonization between national criminal justice systems, the definition in the OAU Convention has raised a number of concerns. One of the most important is its potential to create impunity gaps for any terrorists who seek to justify their activities within the scope of its exemptions, for example violence committed as part of a struggle against any occupation, aggression or domination by foreign forces.[95]

[92] SARPCCO is the Southern African Regional Police Chiefs Cooperation Organisation, set up on 23 September 1994 in Swaziland, whose main objective is to promote, strengthen and perpetuate cooperation and foster joint strategies for the management of all forms of cross-border and related crimes with regional implications.

[93] ESAAMLG was launched at a meeting of Ministers and high-level representatives in Arusha, Tanzania, on 26–7 August 1999. The purpose of ESAAMLG is to combat money laundering by implementing the FATF Forty Recommendations. This effort includes coordinating with other international organizations concerned with combating money laundering, studying emerging regional typologies, developing institutional and human resource capacities to deal with these issues, and coordinating technical assistance where necessary. ESAAMLG enables regional factors to be taken into account in the implementation of anti-money-laundering measures.

[94] Adopted by the AU Assembly (Malabo, 30 June–1 July 2011).

[95] Ewi and du Plessis, 'Criminal Justice Responses to Terrorism in Africa'.

4.3 Central Asia

The three main regional organizations in Central Asia, the Commonwealth of Independent States (CIS),[96] the Collective Security Treaty Organization (CSTO)[97] and the Shanghai Cooperation Organization (SCO)[98] have focused largely on improving joint military operations aimed at preventing drug trafficking, arms smuggling and terrorism.[99] Regional political divisions have prevented agreement on a number of issues. However, recently there have been some positive developments in counter-terrorism cooperation in Central Asia. For example, the SCO established a Regional Anti-Terrorism Structure in 2004, which, among others, aims to enhance cooperation between member states in countering terrorism. In addition, the CSTO and CIS have made a number of statements supporting the UN as an important instrument to promote international cooperation in countering

[96] Commonwealth of Independent States (CIS) was created in December 1991. In the adopted Declaration the participants of the Commonwealth declared their interaction on the basis of sovereign equality. The CIS currently unites Azerbaijan, Armenia, Belarus, Georgia, Kazakhstan, Kyrgyzstan, Moldova, Russia, Tajikistan, Turkmenistan, Uzbekistan and Ukraine and seeks to promote and facilitate integration among these states. Integration of the countries in the framework of the CIS is executed through its coordinating institutions (charter bodies, executive bodies and the bodies of branch cooperation of the CIS).

[97] The Collective Security Treaty Organization grew out of the framework of the CIS, and first began as the CIS Collective Security Treaty (CST), which was signed on 15 May 1992, by Armenia, Kazakhstan, Kyrgyzstan, Russian Federation, Tajikistan and Uzbekistan, in the city of Tashkent. Azerbaijan signed the treaty on 24 September 1993, Georgia on 9 December 1993 and Belarus on 31 December 1993. The Treaty came into effect on 20 April 1994.The purposes of the Organization are to strengthen peace and international and regional security and stability and to ensure the collective defence of the independence, territorial integrity and sovereignty of the member states, in the attainment of which the member states shall give priority to political measures.

[98] The Shanghai Cooperation Organization (SCO) is an intergovernmental international organization founded in Shanghai on 15 June 2001 by six countries: China, Russia, Kazakhstan, Kyrgyzstan, Tajikistan and Uzbekistan. According to the SCO Charter and the Declaration on the Establishment of the SCO, the main purposes of SCO are: strengthening mutual trust and good-neighbourliness and friendship among member states; developing their effective cooperation in political affairs, the economy and trade, science and technology, culture, education, energy, transportation, environmental protection and other fields; working together to maintain regional peace, security and stability; and promoting the creation of a new international political and economic order featuring democracy, justice and rationality.

[99] E. Rosand *et al.*, 'The UN Global Counter-Terrorism Strategy and Regional and Subregional Bodies: Strengthening a Critical Partnership' (2008) Centre on Global Counterterrorism Cooperation.

terrorism.[100] Furthermore, the CIS's Counter-Terrorism Centre is compiling a list of terrorist organizations operating in a number of states. The Counter-Terrorism Centre is also working towards promoting joint activities among its eleven member states.

4.4 Middle East and North Africa (MENA)

The primary organizations promoting counter-terrorism cooperation in the MENA are the Organization of the Islamic Conference (OIC)[101] and the League of Arab States (LAS).[102] In addition to a number of important declarations and resolutions on counter-terrorism taken at regional meetings, the OIC also adopted the 1999 Islamic Convention on Combating Terrorism, which entered into force in 2002. The Convention includes a rather controversial definition of terrorism that includes state terrorism and excludes acts committed in the course of opposing a foreign occupation.

After 9/11, the OIC developed a proactive counter-terrorism plan of action to combat international terrorism. The plan of action gives a ministerial committee the authority to prepare guidelines and recommendations for member states on a broad range of counter-terrorism areas, including ways to enhance international cooperation in terrorism cases.

The LAS adopted the Arab Convention for the Suppression of Terrorism that contains a broad definition of terrorism that excludes wars of national liberation and struggles against foreign occupation. The

[100] http://cis.misk.by/main.aspx?uid=11350.

[101] The Organization of the Islamic Conference (OIC) is the second-largest intergovernmental organization after the UN, which has membership of fifty-seven states spread over four continents. The Organization is the collective voice of the Muslim world, to safeguard and protect the interests of the Muslim world in the spirit of promoting international peace and harmony among various peoples of the world. The Organization was established upon a decision of the historical summit, which took place in Rabat, Kingdom of Morocco on 12th Rajab 1389 Hijra (25 September 1969) as a result of criminal arson of the Al-Aqsa Mosque in occupied Jerusalem.

[102] The League of Arab States is a regional organization of Arab states in South-West Asia, and North and North-East Africa. It was formed in Cairo on 22 March 1945 with six members: Egypt, Iraq, Transjordan (renamed Jordan after 1946), Lebanon, Saudi Arabia and Syria. Yemen joined as a member on 5 May 1945. The Arab League currently has twenty-two members. The main goal of the League is to 'draw closer the relations between member States and co-ordinate collaboration between them, to safeguard their independence and sovereignty, and to consider in a general way the affairs and interests of the Arab countries'.

Convention also prioritizes the promotion of mutual cooperation in the suppression of terrorist offences, and has entrusted the Council of Arab Ministers of the Interior to monitor its implementation. This Council has convened meetings of ministers and experts from member states to explore ways to enhance cooperation among them and improve national responses to terrorism.

4.5 *South-East Asia*

Countries in South-East Asia have taken seriously their obligations to respond effectively to international terrorism. The key subregional structures in this regard include the Asia-Pacific Economic Cooperation Forum (APEC),[103] the Association of Southeast Asian Nations (ASEAN)[104] and the ASEAN Regional Forum (ARF).[105] A notable regional counter-terrorism development was the adoption in January 2007 of the regional legally binding counter-terrorism instrument – the ASEAN Convention on Counter-Terrorism. This Convention, together with the signing of the ASEAN Charter in November 2007, may significantly enhance ASEAN's institutional capacity and ability for autonomous action, including in the field of countering terrorism. The Convention contains significant sections aimed at promoting international cooperation in terrorist cases. Specific countries in ASEAN, such as Pakistan and Indonesia, have made notable developments in countering terrorism.

At the national level, Pakistan reviewed its National Security Strategy, and in October 2008 passed a fourteen-point Anti-Terrorism

[103] APEC is the premier forum for facilitating economic growth, cooperation, trade and investment in the Asia-Pacific region, and was founded in 1989. APEC's twenty-one member economies are Australia, Brunei Darussalam, Canada, Chile, People's Republic of China, Hong Kong, China, Indonesia, Japan, Republic of Korea, Malaysia, Mexico, New Zealand, Papua New Guinea, Peru, Republic of the Philippines, the Russian Federation, Singapore, Chinese Taipei Thailand, United States of America, Vietnam.

[104] ASEAN was established on 8 August 1967 in Bangkok. The ASEAN Declaration states that the aims and purposes of the Association are: (1) to accelerate economic growth, social progress and cultural development in the region and (2) to promote regional peace and stability through abiding respect for justice and the rule of law in the relationship among countries in the region and adherence to the principles of the UN Charter.

[105] ARF was inaugurated on 25 July 1994 with two objectives: (1) to foster constructive dialogue and consultation on political and security issues of common interest and concern; and (2) to make significant contributions to efforts towards confidence-building and preventive diplomacy in the Asia-Pacific region.

Resolution[106] aimed at solidifying the government's position on counter-terrorism in policy and in principle. Pakistan plays a crucial and critical role in the region as it holds strong linkages with the Taliban.[107] Similarly, Indonesia launched an Interdepartmental National Anti-terrorism Agency (BNPT),[108] which has made significant progress in countering terrorism in the country and the region. The Indonesian government also developed a framework on combating terrorism based on six principles, which outline the supremacy of the law, indiscrimination, independence, democracy and participation.[109]

4.6 *The Western Hemisphere*

The thirty-four-member state Organization of American States (OAS), which represents states from the Western Hemisphere beyond Europe, is the most developed and effective regional organization, specifically in relation to its programmes aimed at promoting coherent and cooperative counter-terrorism between its member states. The work of the OAS is complemented by a number of subregional bodies, including the Caribbean Financial Action Task Force (GFATF), the South American Financial Action Task Force (GAFISUD), the Caribbean Community (CARICOM) and the Southern Common Market (Mercosur).

OAS's counter-terrorism work is led by the Inter-American Community against Terrorism (CICTE), which is supported by a small secretariat. CICTE has facilitated a number of counter-terrorism technical assistance and training workshops for all OAS member states, including specialized training for relevant law enforcement and criminal justice officials on international cooperation in countering terrorism.

Taken together, the international and regional counter-terrorism legal regimes provide a solid normative guide to member states to build coherent and streamlined national responses to international terrorism.

106 See K. Kronstadt, 'Pakistan–US Anti-Terrorism Cooperation' (2003) Congressional Research Service.

107 S. D'Souza, 'US–Pakistan Counter-Terrorism Cooperation: Dynamics and Challenges' (2006) 30 *Strategic Analysis* 525.

108 D. Christano, 'Indonesia Launches its First Counterterrorism Agency', *Jakarta Post*, 9 August 2010, www.thejakartapost.com/news/2010/09/08/indonesia-launches-first-counterterrorism-agency.html.

109 R. E. Tumanggor, 'Indonesia's Counter-terrorism Policy' (2007) 15 UNISCI Discussion Paper 87, www.ucm.es/info/unisci/revistas/UNISCI15_Tumanggor.pdf.

Key to the success of global counter-terrorism efforts will be the ability of national governments to investigate and prosecute international terrorist crimes as defined in the respective UN and regional instruments described above and in compliance with the legally binding obligations imposed by the various counter-terrorism UNSC resolutions, most notably 1373. To provide this effective criminal justice response to terrorism, states need adequately functioning counter-terrorism legal regimes and criminal justice systems, as well as the related capacity to deal with potentially complex criminal cases, while engaging in effective international cooperation in criminal matters. This requires a firm commitment from member states to pursue common objectives at national, subregional and regional levels.[110]

4.7 Interpol

Interpol is another important international organization that works to enhance international cooperation among law enforcement agencies and officials. Interpol was created in 1946 with the primary role of preventing and combating ordinary law crimes through facilitating the widest possible mutual assistance between all criminal police authorities. This must be done within the limits of the law and includes the establishment of any necessary institutions. Interpol has expanded its mandate in response to the subsequent development of international law and the increase in terrorist activities. Interpol is now actively involved in processing cooperation requests concerning terrorist cases, albeit under certain conditions.[111]

In relation to countering terrorism, Interpol has developed a number of important tools and best practices aimed at strengthening international cooperation. One is I-24/7, a secure global police communications system, which enables Interpol to collect, store, analyse and exchange information about suspected individuals and terrorist groups with its member countries.[112] Moreover, Interpol coordinates the circulation of alerts and warnings by means of specific tools such as its colour-coded international notices system. Key as regards its counter-terrorist

[110] UNODC, *Handbook on Criminal Justice Responses to Terrorism* (UN Office on Drugs and Crime, 2009), 3.
[111] Res. AGN/53/Res./7 (1984).
[112] Interpol's Global Police Communication System I-24/7 www.interpol.int/Public/NCB/I247.

activities is the Fusion Task Force.[113] Created in 2002, the Task Force's primary objectives are to identify members of groups involved in international terrorist activities and to provide a searchable database of wanted or suspected terrorists. To assist in the subsequent locating of suspected or convicted individuals is Interpol's 'Red notice' system which is aimed at facilitating the provisional arrest of a person wanted by its member countries with a view to extradition based on an arrest warrant or a court decision; in doing so, the notice also benefits non-member countries by alerting them to an individual's suspected activities. Finally, the Interpol–UNSC Special Notice was created in 2005 to alert member countries of individuals and entities associated with al-Qaeda and the Taliban,[114] as listed by the Security Council's 1267 Committee, and to help countries to implement the freezing of assets, travel bans and arms embargoes.[115]

5 Major challenges to effective and appropriate international cooperation in criminal matters

Few practitioners, policy-makers and criminal justice experts would dispute that international cooperation in law enforcement and criminal justice matters is an indispensable element of any effective response to transnational crimes, including terrorism. Almost all transnational terrorist acts will trigger more than one jurisdiction, involve suspects and witnesses from more than one country, and therefore require a broad range of cross-border cooperation between intelligence, law enforcement and criminal justice officials.

However, despite this widespread acceptance of the importance of these various forms of international cooperation, in reality the pursuit of effective and appropriate counter-terrorism cooperation still has hurdles to overcome. This concluding section summarizes some of the key challenges in this regard.

5.1 Intelligence cooperation

The nature of terrorism necessitates the gathering, sharing and analysis of information and intelligence, often in several jurisdictions at the same

113 'Best Practices' in Combating Terrorism www.un.org/en/sc/ctc/docs/bestprac-interpol.pdf.

114 Implemented through the adoption of Interpol Res. AG-2005-RES-05 (2005).

115 Interpol, www.asil.org/rio/interpol.html.

time. Intelligence plays a crucial role in identifying and analysing terrorist threats. It also provides important leads for criminal investigations and in the development of effective strategies to counter terrorism. With the transnationalization of terrorism, and especially after 9/11, the work of intelligence agencies has moved centre stage in the broad spectrum of counter-terrorism measures available to governments. This centrality is reflected in the expanded powers of intelligence agencies, the increased focus on intelligence sharing and international cooperation.

Although improved use of intelligence, and enhanced cooperation between intelligence agencies is a seemingly positive development, intelligence gathering and sharing carries a number of inherent risks, often associated with the secret and covert nature of intelligence work. Secrecy, while of course necessary, can also lead to a lack of transparency, accountability and oversight. This lack of transparency has the potential to undermine the rule of law, due process and human rights. A second potential for abuse arises when intelligence agencies are given too much executive power, with too little parliamentary or judicial scrutiny. Finally, and rather ironically, when one considers the context of this chapter, the risk for abuse actually increases with greater cooperation among intelligence agencies as a result of weakened domestic oversight and accountability mechanisms.

These challenges are not merely academic. Intelligence services in various parts of the world have overstepped the mark drawn by accepted international human rights, rule of law and due process standards. The recent International Commission of Jurists (ICJ) report by the Eminent Jurists' Panel on Terrorism, Counter-Terrorism and Human Rights[116] identified a number of concerns relating to intelligence cooperation and recommended the development of a clear regulatory framework and international safeguards to enhance due process and the rule of law in intelligence cooperation.[117] The ICJ report singled out the following key concerns:

- Extraordinary rendition was identified as one of the most worrying developments arising from increased intelligence cooperation. The practice violates a number of human rights, including the rights protecting individuals against arbitrary arrest, enforced disappearance, forcible transfer, subjection to torture and other forms of cruel

[116] Eminent Jurists' Panel on Terrorism, Counter-terrorism and Human Rights: Assessing Damage, Urging Action [hereafter ICJ Report].

[117] *Ibid.*, 79.

and inhuman treatment. The frequent use of secret and unacknowledged detention associated with this practice was also a violation of international law norms.[118]

- Complicity of several countries in human rights violations in the name of enhanced intelligence cooperation to counter terrorism. The report named a number of countries that have actively participated in extrajudicial renditions as well as examples of subregional cooperation structures that have been utilized in this regard.
- Impunity and lack of accountability have prevailed in far too many cases, often as a result of countries relying on state secrecy laws to block investigations and efforts to ensure accountability for government officials involved in alleged human rights violations. The unwillingness on the part of individual states to ensure effective accountability, and to address alleged human rights violations in intelligence cooperation, is replicated at the regional level. As an example, the CoE failed to respond to the findings and conclusions of the EU parliamentary inquiry into cooperation with extraordinary renditions. Moreover, the Committee of Ministers of the CoE failed to implement the proposals of the regional organization's Secretary-General to draw up standards to protect against renditions and secret detentions.[119]

The ICJ report contains a number of useful recommendations aimed at addressing the concerns raised above. The most relevant of these are summarized below:

- States should recognize the clear distinction between the role of intelligence and law enforcement, with the former having no powers to detain or arrest people.
- States should ensure that data gathering and storage is handled with due respect for their human rights obligations. Judicial authorities should exercise oversight in respect of these activities.
- States should recognize that they are responsible under international law for the actions of their intelligence agencies and that they need to ensure effective oversight and control mechanisms to prevent abuse of human rights, impunity and lack of redress.

[118] For more information on extraordinary rendition, see Chapter 19 in this volume.

[119] *Pace* Recommendation 1801 (2007), *Secret Detentions and Illegal Transfers of Detainees Involving Council of Europe Member States: Second Report* (Doc. CDL(2007)082). See ICJ Report, 88.

5.2 *Preventive counter-terrorism practices and the abuse of the principle of non-refoulement*

Many governments have since 9/11 prioritized the practice of early intervention aimed at preventing terrorist attacks. This is understandable. Unfortunately, a number of preventive actions have resulted in the serious flouting of human rights and due process protections. The areas of cooperation between states, practices of extrajudicial removals, disguised extraditions and the abuse of the principle of *non-refoulement* in particular give cause for concern.

The principle of *non-refoulement* (which is firmly established under a number of regional and international human rights instruments and customary international law) prohibits governments from returning, deporting, extraditing, expelling or otherwise sending someone to a country where that person might face a real risk of serious human rights violations.[120] However, this principle has been under attack in recent years because of the increased reliance by some states on deportation and expulsion as part of their preventive counter-terrorism strategy.[121]

5.3 *Challenges in MLA and extradition in counter-terrorism cases*

Effective MLA and extradition between law enforcement authorities of different jurisdictions is often a prerequisite for successful criminal justice responses to international terrorism. However, despite this reality, and the significant focus that has been placed on international cooperation in terrorism cases, levels of cooperation, especially MLA and extradition, are still not what they need to be.

There are a number of reasons for this. Most notably, if an investigation involves an influential or powerful figure in the requested country, the requested assistance may never be provided. The requested authority might even cite 'national interest' or immunities enjoyed by certain sections of the community to refuse cooperation. In relation to terrorist-financing investigations, the person in respect of whom the request for

[120] The scope of violations that trigger the *non-refoulement* principle has expanded over time. It has its origins in refugee law (1951 Convention Relating to the Status of Refugees, Art. 31). Similar protections are included in international regulations on extradition.

[121] ICJ Report, 102. For more information on the principle of *non-refoulement*, see Chapter 19 in this volume.

MLA is made is, in certain countries, able to appeal against the sharing of evidence with the requesting country. These kinds of appeals can cause lengthy delays in investigations and prosecution and could also alert the suspect of the investigation into his alleged involvement. Moreover, in countries that have traditionally enjoyed favourable tax and banking conditions (such as Liechtenstein and Switzerland) an appeal avenue is available in relation to the disclosure of information about a person's financial position. In those countries, in addition, institutions such as banks may have similar rights of appeal. The last reason relates to the lack of specialized capacity and expertise required to engage in specific forms of cooperation such as complicated search-and-seizure operations, asset tracing, forfeiture and freezing.

6 Conclusion

An effective and sustainable global response to terrorism must be built on several pillars, aimed at addressing the underlying causes of the problem, respecting human rights and building specialized capacity to respond to the threat, including through enhanced international cooperation in criminal matters. UN member states recognized this when they unanimously adopted the UN Global Counter-Terrorism Strategy at the end of 2006. The Global Strategy reiterated what was contained in numerous preceding UN Security Council and General Assembly resolutions – that states must do more to improve levels of law enforcement and criminal justice cooperation in their efforts to respond effectively and appropriately to terrorism.

Much progress has been made since 9/11. But despite this progress and the improved normative legal regimes to support cooperation in criminal matters, political factors and policy and capacity gaps still hinder effective and appropriate cooperation between officials trying to ensure fair and transparent prosecution of terrorist suspects and the prevention of future terrorist attacks. States, supported by their regional organizations and international actors, need to do more to close the gaps in international criminal justice cooperation. Too few states have updated and comprehensive laws that deal with all modalities of international cooperation. Many countries have no international cooperation legislation at all, and most countries still rely on bilateral treaties. This insistence on bilateralism over multilaterism is linked to the fact that states view international cooperation in criminal matters as an extension of their political relations, which often means they only cooperate with friendly states that they trust. Unfortunately this relegates international cooperation to the political realm, as opposed to a legal process and obligation as it should be.

A new approach is needed to overcome the political hurdles that too often scupper much-needed international cooperation in terrorism cases. New regional and international treaties (including a multilateral treaty on international cooperation) will help, but will not deal with the political challenges and trust deficits that lie at the heart of the problem. States, working with international partners and technical assistance providers, should develop initiatives that enhance political will and build trust among countries and relevant law enforcement agencies. Adopting human rights-compliant international cooperation practices will contribute greatly to this effort.

3

Terrorist crimes and the *aut dedere aut judicare* obligation

MICHAEL A. NEWTON

1 Introduction

The transnational transfer of terrorist suspects remains one of the most controversial and politically charged dimensions of state cooperative efforts in response to increasingly effective terrorist organizations. Terrorism in all its forms and manifestations constitutes a continuing and serious threat to international peace and security. Transnational terrorism, in particular, represents perhaps the most pernicious threat to the fundamental human rights of private peace-loving citizens. The security, stability, economic vitality, sovereignty, political independence and citizen safety of all sovereign states are accordingly protected against terrorist acts, irrespective of the democratic aspects or governing structure of the state in question. The obligation of states to use their domestic judicial processes to punish terrorist crimes or to transfer custody of suspects to another state for such punishment is therefore an essential cornerstone of the modern framework for confronting transnational terrorist acts. Because terrorist acts undermine the quintessential function of a state by endangering the core human rights of its citizens, the correlative legal duty either to surrender a suspect to another state with the jurisdiction and willingness to prosecute or to adjudicate the case in its own national courts (termed *aut dedere aut judicare*) encompasses a grave responsibility even as it exemplifies the solemn duty to join in common purpose to combat terrorism.

Extradition battles are fought at the confluence of competing legal domains, conflicting human rights obligations and politically charged

The author wishes to thank the Grotius Center, and in particular Nico Schrijver and Larissa van den Herik for their insights and improvements to this work. The inevitable omissions, errors and oversights contained herein are solely attributable to the author.

contexts. Indeed, some of the most compelling revelations from the public release of diplomatic correspondence by WikiLeaks involve politically embarrassing details of discussions among allies over the extradition of terrorist suspects.[1] Extradition battles are often extended jurisprudential proxy fronts that force officials to navigate between the Scylla of state-sanctioned human rights violations[2] for persons subject to the authority of state actors and the Charybdis of paralysis and overly politicized prosecutions.

International law currently embodies universal and strongly articulated support for the positivist premise that 'any acts of terrorism are criminal and unjustifiable, regardless of their motivation, whenever and by whomsoever committed and are to be unequivocally condemned'.[3] The UN General Assembly reaffirms that 'no terrorist act can be justified in any circumstances',[4] and regional instruments adhere to the same legal premise.[5] Therefore, the precept that states must use their domestic processes to cooperate together in the investigation and punishment of terrorist acts

[1] At the time of this writing, Indian officials are rebutting the American ambassador's report over the extradition of LeT operative David Headley. According to WikiLeaks, in a cable to the US State Department on 17 December 2009, then US Ambassador to India Timothy J. Roemer reported that the Indian National Security Adviser M. K. Narayanan had told him on the issue of Headley's extradition that it was 'difficult not to be seen making the effort', but that the government was not seeking extradition 'at this time'. The government countered this report: 'There is no question about the fact that we are serious about his extradition. We are interested about information about him', the West Bengal Governor told reporters here when asked about leaked US communication on whistle-blower WikiLeaks. The former NSA declined to comment on the communication between US officials and said any questions and doubts on this issue should be addressed to the US officials. 'How can I comment on what communication has been made by American officials to his government. Why don't you ask the American Ambassador', he shot back. Press Trust of India, 'We are Serious about Headley's Extradition says Narayanan', *Oman Daily Observer*, 5 September 2011, 11.

[2] See, e.g., *Khadr* v. *Canada (Attorney General) (FC)*, 2008 FC 46 (holding that Khadr's interest in obtaining sensitive information needed to fight his extradition to the United States outweighed that of Canadian officials in the possession of the information notwithstanding the established risk of disclosure to Canada's reputation and international relations), reprinted in M. Newton (ed.), *Terrorism International Case Law Reporter 2008* (Oxford: Oxford University Press, 2010), vol. I, 371.

[3] UN Doc. S/Res./1456 (2003). The United Nations Global Counter-Terrorism Strategy reiterates the 'strong condemnation' of the international community and states that 'terrorism in all its forms and manifestations, committed by whomever, wherever and for whatever purposes'.

[4] General Assembly, Draft Resolution Measures to eliminate international terrorism, UN Doc. A/C.6/62/L.14 (2007).

[5] Council Framework Decision 2002/475/JHA of 13 June 2002 on combating terrorism [2002] OJ L 164/3, preamble (1)–(2); 1999 Convention of the Organisation of the Islamic Conference on Combating International Terrorism, 1999-1420H, preamble; OAU

reflects the terrible truth that terrorist acts violate the essential precepts of civilization. Private efforts to wage war fall outside the structure of law that binds sovereign states together on the basis of reciprocity and shared community interests. In the modern vernacular, those who commit acts in contravention of the applicable conventions are termed terrorists, regardless of their ideological or religious motivations.[6]

As a qualitative matter of modern international law, terrorist offences are on substantive par with the grave breach provisions of the 1949 Geneva Conventions, the 1948 Genocide Convention and the provisions of the Torture Convention precisely because of the *aut dedere aut judicare* obligation. The lofty status of these categories of criminality as the core *jus cogens* violations proscribed by the express language of almost universally binding international treaty obligations makes *aut dedere aut judicare* really nothing more than a common-sense obligation rooted in community morality that morphed into international obligation. Indeed, the roots of the concept can be traced to philosophical thinking as early as the fourteenth century.[7] As a matter of legal conception, the principle that states are obligated to use domestic forums to punish violations of international law has roots that go back to the ideas of Hugo Grotius.[8] Grotius described the concept of *aut dedere aut punire* (either extradite or punish) in his epochal 1625 work *On the Law of War and Peace*.[9] The 'Father of International Law' opined that a general obligation to extradite or punish exists with respect to 'crimes which in

Ministerial Communiqué on Terrorism, 11 November 2001; OAS Declaration of Lima to Prevent, Combat, and Eliminate Terrorism, 26 April 1996, preamble.

6 See, e.g., 1999 International Convention for the Suppression of the Financing of Terrorism, 2178 UNTS 197, Art. 6 (requiring acceding states to 'adopt such measures as may be necessary, including, where appropriate, domestic legislation, to ensure that criminal acts within the scope of this Convention are under no circumstances justifiable by considerations of a political, philosophical, ideological, racial, ethnic, religious or other similar nature') [hereafter Terrorist Financing Convention].

7 M. C. Bassiouni, *Introduction to International Criminal Law* (Ardsley, NY: Transnational, 2003), 337.

8 R. Tuck, *The Rights of War and Peace: Political Thought and the International Order from Grotius to Kant* (Oxford: Oxford University Press, 1999).

9 H. Grotius, *de Jure Belli Ac Pacis* (1625), Bk. II, ch. XXI, secs. III and IV ('Since as a matter of fact states are not accustomed to permit other states to cross their borders with an armed force for the purpose of exacting punishment, and since such course is inexpedient, it follows that the state in which he who has been found guilty dwells ought to do one of two things. When appealed to it should either punish the guilty person as he deserves, or it should entrust him to the discretion of the party making the appeal. This latter course is rendition, a procedure most frequently mentioned in historical narratives'), at www.lonang.com/exlibris/grotius/gro-221.htm.

some way affect human society'; states particularly aggrieved by a criminal act enjoyed in his view a 'natural right to exact punishment' with the consequence that 'the state in which the guilty person dwells, or its ruler, ought not to interfere with this right'.[10]

To analogize from the preamble of the Rome Statute of the International Criminal Court, terrorism rightfully belongs in the small core of criminal acts that represent the 'crimes of most serious concern to the international community as a whole'.[11] If a terrorist is found on the territory of a state party, that state has an affirmative duty arising from the modern multilateral framework, as well as customary international law,[12] to extradite that terrorist suspect to another state which itself has the motivation and jurisdictional basis to adjudicate the offender; in the alternative it agrees a priori 'without exception whatsoever and whether or not that offense was committed in its territory, to submit the case without undue delay to its competent authorities for the purpose of prosecution through proceedings in accordance with the laws of that state'.[13] This *aut dedere aut judicare* implementation of an obligation to treat terrorist offences as crimes universally recognized and proscribed flows from the moral and legal moral commitment of states to each other and to the demands of sovereignty itself. Phrased another way, states are obligated to preserve the human rights of those citizens under their jurisdiction and the judicial response to terrorist acts is accordingly at the very heart of the treaty regime designed to address multinational terrorist acts on a cooperative community basis.

Aut dedere aut judicare therefore reflects the very essence of an international legal regime in which states share a common purpose to effectively respond to terrorist acts in the defence of shared sovereign interests in a sustainable peace and economic integration. At the same time, the conventional scaffolding for addressing transnational terrorism preserves sovereign interests by reserving exclusive domestic

[10] M. C. Bassiouni and E. M. Wise, *Aut Dedere Aut Judicare: The Duty to Extradite or Prosecute in International Law* (Leiden: Martinus Nijhoff, 1995), 5.

[11] 1998 Rome Statute of the International Criminal Court, 2187 UNTS 3 [hereafter Rome Statute].

[12] See Interlocutory Decision on the Applicable Law: Terrorism, Conspiracy, Homicide, Perpetration, Cumulative Charging, STL-11-01/I, A.Ch., 16 February 2011, paras. 83–113, at www.stl-tsl.org/en/the-cases/stl-11-01/rule-176bis/filings/orders-and-decisions/appeals-chamber/interlocutory-decision-on-the-applicable-law-terrorism-conspiracy-homicide-perpetration-cumulative-charging (accessed 23 March 2012).

[13] 1997 International Convention for the Suppression of Terrorist Bombings, 2149 UNTS 256, Art. 8.1 [hereafter Terrorist Bombing Convention].

jurisdiction over offences committed within a single state, in cases where the victims are nationals of that state, the offender is also a national of that state and is present on its territory, and in which no other state has a colourable claim to jurisdiction.[14]

The import of these provisions has been demonstrated many times over by the phenomenon of globalized and coordinated terrorist cells that seek to wage asymmetric warfare across continents and cultures. The Canadian case against Mohammed Momin Khawaja perfectly illustrates the necessity for these provisions. Khawaja's involvement in an al-Qaeda-inspired plot that spanned three continents to build and detonate ammonium nitrate-rich fertilizer bombs surfaced during an investigation by the British Security Services, and the day after his arrest in Ottawa, his co-conspirators were arrested in London.[15] While Khawaja was convicted in Canada, his seven co-conspirators were sentenced to life imprisonment by British authorities. In this, and in many other similar cases, the *aut dedere aut judicare* principle reflects basic common sense and fairness, as well as enduring principles of justice and equal application of the law. An individual's personal freedom and concomitant ability to plan additional terrorist acts, either in isolation or in coordination with a larger group of colleagues across international boundaries, should not depend on successfully reaching a state of safe haven or the fortuity of finding a state whose criminal justice system is inadequately equipped to address the nature of the offences.

Breaking down the macro problem of terrorism into its identifiable manifestations, nation states have negotiated and ratified a web of multilateral anti-terrorism conventions built on the cornerstone of sovereign enforcement of applicable norms. Terrorist attacks endanger the whole range of human rights otherwise enjoyed by the victims of such attacks. The *aut dedere aut judicare* obligation as applied to terrorist cases thus reflects an entirely logical extension of the paramount state obligation to protect the basic human rights of all persons within their scope of lawful authority. Hence, the duty to prosecute terrorist crimes in some sense represents an extension of state authority to protect the human rights of its own citizens, as well as those from other states. This chapter examines the scope of the present obligation to cooperate in the investigation and

[14] *Ibid.*, Art. 3.

[15] *Her Majesty the Queen* v. *Mohammed Momin Khawaja* [2008] Ontario Superior Court of Justice, Court File 04-G30282, reprinted in M. Newton (ed.), *Terrorism International Case Law Reporter 2008* (Oxford: Oxford University Press, 2010), vol. I, 319.

prosecution of terrorist acts. The integrated aspect of the cooperative framework must be fully appreciated and consistently applied by states. The inherent obstacles of these complex and often emotionally and politically charged cases often prevent a uniform realization of the textual aspiration for a holistic response to terrorist acts relying on the *aut dedere aut judicare* obligation. This chapter concludes by making three specific recommendations that would constitute progressive developments in the framework of international law.

2 The approach in the current anti-terrorism conventions

The persistence of transnational terrorism as a feature of the international community shows that the plethora of multilateral conventions is no panacea.[16] The attacks of September 11, 2001 highlighted this striking systematic failure and prompted renewed interest in the possibility of an internationally accepted general definition of terrorism and an international forum to prosecute terrorist offenders. However, the current framework that defines and criminalizes the distinctive manifestations of terrorism remains as the only viable judicial mechanism for responding to terrorist acts. This means that the integrated efforts of sovereign states to interdict and address the various forms of terrorist acts must be more than a chimera. International cooperation in the investigation and adjudication of transnational terrorism is an essential aspect of defending civilization and may literally be regarded as defending the rule of law against those organizations and individuals who simply disregard international norms as constraining principles. Domestic officials of all nations should share a determination to reduce the delays and difficulties that inevitably arise in the course of protecting the citizens of all nations from ongoing transnational terrorism.

2.1 The 1937 Convention

The desire to reach international consensus on appropriate venues for prosecuting terrorists dates back to the League of Nations era.[17] The

[16] M. C. Bassiouni, 'Legal Control of International Terrorism: A Policy Oriented Assessment' (2002) 43 *Harvard Journal of International Law* 83, 90.

[17] *Vœau of the International Congress of Penal Law Concerning an International Criminal Court* (1926), reprinted in *Historical Survey of the Question of International Criminal Jurisdiction, Memorandum Submitted by the Secretary-General* (UN Doc. A/CN.4/

roots of the modern normative priority placed on domestic enforcement are easily recognizable from the beginning of those international discussions. In 1926, the International Congress of Penal Law recommended that the Permanent Court of International Justice 'be competent to judge individual liabilities' incurred as a result of crimes considered as international offences 'which constitute a threat to world peace'.[18] This proposal died on the vine of international diplomacy. The assassination of King Alexander of Yugoslavia in Marseilles on 9 October 1934 prompted the French government to propose an international convention for the suppression of terrorism in a letter to the Secretary-General of the League of Nations.[19] The core of the French proposal was a suggestion that an international criminal court would be the most feasible forum for addressing political crimes of an international character, and the Council of the League responded by establishing a Committee of Experts to prepare a preliminary draft of 'an international convention to assure the repression of conspiracies or crimes committed with a political and terrorist purpose'.[20] From 1–16 November 1937, the International Conference for the Repression of Terrorism met in Geneva and adopted a Convention for the Creation of an International Criminal Court.[21] This effort at an international forum to respond to terrorism was implicitly rejected by the international community after only one state (Italy) ratified the multilateral treaty.

Although the proposed 1937 Convention never entered into force, it remains highly relevant in the current context for two reasons. First, the jurisdiction of the international court proposed in the treaty text derived solely from the consent of the affected states[22] and the court was limited

7Rev.1 (1949)), 74 (translating the original French text found in *Premier congrès international de droit pénal*, 634).

18 *Ibid.* This strain of thought eventually led to the development of a draft statute for a criminal chamber of the Permanent International Court of Justice, International Law Association, *Report of the 34th Conference*, Vienna, 5–11 August 1926 (1927), 113–25.

19 *Historical Survey* (UN Doc. A/CN.4/7Rev.1 (1949)).

20 *Ibid.* See also 15 League of Nations OJ 1760 (1934) (containing the text of the full resolution passed by the Council).

21 1937 Convention for the Prevention and Punishment of Terrorism, League of Nations Doc. C.546(I).M.383(I)1937.V (1938), reprinted in M. C. Bassiouni, *International Terrorism: Multilateral Conventions (1837–2001)* (Ardsley, NY: Transnational, 2001), 71 [hereafter 1937 Convention].

22 1937 Convention, Art. 21 (referring to the obligation of the domestic states to enact criminal legislation to punish the acts defined in the underlying multilateral treaty and empowering those same states to 'commit the accused to trial' before the ICC). This provision is in stark contrast to the defined and prescribed jurisdictional provisions of

to applying the 'least severe' domestic law of either the state in which the crimes were committed or the state of the offender's nationality.[23] In effect, the 1937 Convention created an internationalized process for applying the substantive law of different domestic systems, which is the antithesis for modern arguments that an international forum is essential for applying the international norms against terrorism. This model of the 1937 Convention is really the precursor for the *Lockerbie* Bombing Court[24] and stands in sharp contrast to the efforts of some pundits in the wake of September 11 to portray transnational terrorism as an international problem necessitating a generalized international definition and an accompanying supranational jurisdiction. In a more modern vein, the 1998 Rome Statute of the ICC does not contain a substantive offence of terrorism *stricto sensu* due to the difficulty of reaching consensus agreement on its incorporation into the fabric of a permanent international criminal court.[25] The high degree of domestic motivation and the existence of a complex framework for the effective investigation and prosecution of transnational terrorist acts in sovereign forums caused a counterproductive drag on the negotiations for the ICC. Despite the presence of a definition for terrorism in the text proffered during the Preparatory Committee preceding the Rome negotiations,[26] terrorism was not included in the Final Act in order to achieve agreement during the available time frame for negotiations.[27]

the Rome Statute which allow the ICC to bypass non-consenting states in establishing personal jurisdiction over their citizens. Rome Statute, Arts. 12–19.

23 1937 Convention, Art. 21.

24 The Scottish Court in the Netherlands was an internationalized process applying Scots law to prosecute the Libyan nationals responsible for the 1988 bombing of Pan Am Flight 103. The case arose from the specific treaty obligations found in the 1971 Convention for the Suppression of Unlawful Acts against the Safety of Civil Aviation (Montreal Hijacking Convention), 10 ILM 1151.

25 L. Martinez, 'Prosecuting Terrorists at the International Criminal Court: Possibilities and Problems' (2002) 34 *Rutgers Law Journal* 1, 18.

26 *Report of the Preparatory Committee on the Establishment of an International Criminal Court* (UN Doc. A/CONF.183/2/Add.1 (1998)), 27 (defining terrorism as: undertaking, organizing, sponsoring, ordering, facilitating, financing, encouraging, or tolerating acts of violence against another state directed at persons or property and of such a nature as to create terror, fear, or insecurity in the minds of public figures, groups of persons, or the general public or populations, for whatever considerations and purposes of a political, philosophical, ideological, racial, ethnic, religious, or other such nature that may be invoked to justify them).

27 M. H. Arsanjani, 'The Rome Statute of the International Criminal Court' (1999) 93 *American Journal of International Law* 22, 31.

Second, it is important to note that every one of the multilateral conventions in the years of international dialogue since the 1937 Convention have adhered to its pattern by defining specific terrorist acts as substantive violations of international law and specifically requiring sovereign states to enact domestic criminal legislation for the purpose of punishing those acts. This uniform historical pattern undercuts arguments that the very nature of transnational terrorism requires articulation of terrorism as a crime against humanity or mandates an overarching supranational framework for adjudication that is independent of the cooperative framework of sovereign states. The implication of this truism is that states must be vigilant to improve international cooperation or risk terrorist acts that are committed beyond the reach of applicable punitive forums. The *aut dedere aut judicare* obligation is the linchpin for actualizing this aspiration.

2.2 *The definitional dilemma*

The clarity with which international law categorizes and condemns discrete manifestations of terrorism actually masks the indeterminacy of the underlying definitional framework. One scholar, who neatly captured the sentiments of many in the international community and many more private citizens around the world, has noted that terrorism 'is not only a phenomenon, it is also an invective, and there are many examples of States using this invective in a most subjective manner to delegitimize and demonize political opponents, associations, or other States'.[28] Some scholars have expressed scepticism that a comprehensive definition of terrorism is even possible given the inherent complexity of a clean delineation between terrorism and other points on the spectrum of political violence that becomes manifest in seemingly unending ways in the context of human society.[29] The claim that 'what looks, smells and kills like terrorism is terrorism'[30] belies the reality that the international community has unsuccessfully sought to reach agreement on a comprehensive definition of the term for more than a century.[31] No single

[28] C. Much, 'The International Criminal Court (ICC) and Terrorism as an International Crime' (2006) 14 *Michigan State University College of Law Journal of International Law* 121, 133.

[29] A. Roberts, 'Can We Define Terrorism?' (2002) 14 *Oxford Today* 18.

[30] UN Doc. A/56/PV.12 (2001).

[31] T. M. Franck and B. Lockwood, Jr., 'Preliminary Thoughts towards an International Convention on Terrorism' (1974) 68 *American Journal of International Law* 69.

definition has achieved universal acceptance, whether approached from a moral,[32] psychological[33] or historical[34] perspective.

Nevertheless, the potency and persistence of terrorism sustained diplomatic efforts to pinpoint its legal boundaries and precise scope. Echoing the language of the 1937 League of Nations Convention, the 1994 General Assembly Resolution 'Measures to Eliminate International Terrorism' provided a general definition of terrorism that provides a useful, if dated, juxtaposition to the more modern multilateral conventions by proscribing:

> [c]riminal acts intended or calculated to provoke a state of terror in the general public, a group of persons or particular persons for political purposes are in any circumstance unjustifiable, whatever the considerations of a political, philosophical, ideological, racial, ethnic, religious or any other nature that may be invoked to justify them.[35]

The focus of effort in the General Assembly context was the politicized inclusion of state terrorism alongside the clear intent to disallow any exceptions. Despite the fact that non-state participants in a non-international armed conflict are fully subject to prosecution for their warlike acts,[36] and will often be simultaneously subject to the jurisdiction of courts with substantive authority over terrorism, the inequality of power between the state and sub-state actors can create the

[32] C. A. J. Coady, 'The Morality of Terrorism' (1985) 60 *Philosophy* 47, 52.
As amended then, the definition of a terrorist act would go as follows: 'A political act, ordinarily committed by an organized group, which involves the intentional killing or other severe harming of non-combatants or the threat of the same or intentional severe damage to the property of non-combatants or the threat of the same.' The term 'terrorism' can then be defined as the tactic or policy of engaging in terrorist acts.

[33] M. Crenshaw, 'The Psychology of Terrorism: An Agenda for the 21st Century' (2000) 21 *Political Psychology* 405, 406.

[34] G. Guillaume, 'Terrorism and International Law' (2004) 53 *International & Comparative Law Quarterly* 537, 540 ('In the context of international law, it would appear to me that the adjective terrorist may be applied to any criminal activity involving the use of violence in circumstances likely to cause bodily harm or a threat to human life, in connection with an enterprise whose aim is to provoke terror').

[35] UN Doc. A/Res./49/60 (1994), para. 1.3.

[36] Y. Dinstein, *The Conduct of Hostilities under the Law of International Armed Conflict* (Cambridge: Cambridge University Press, 2004), 31 (clarifying that *jus in bello* merely prescribes the offences under which lawful combatants can be brought to trial. With regard to unlawful combatants, *jus in bello* 'merely takes off the mantle of immunity from the defendant, who is therefore accessible to penal charges for any offense committed against the domestic legal system').

perception that prosecutions are merely another front in an ongoing conflict. Defendants have often attempted to project an image that the courtroom is itself intimately linked to an armed struggle. Some have even argued that applying the label 'terrorist' to a non-state actor in a non-international armed conflict carries a pejorative taint that creates an undesirable disincentive to abide by the laws and customs of war.[37] This position obscures the reality that the very essence of terrorist crimes is to deny the applicability of established reciprocal duties in favour of tactics that kill, maim or destroy property to achieve ideological or political objectives. The failure to repress or respond to such acts risks undermining adherence to the very basic rule of law that links the institutions of society, both in the national and supranational sense.

The paradox in a post-September 11 world is that the United Nations Security Council *requires* nations to 'accept and carry out'[38] resolutions that oblige them to act against 'terrorists' and 'terrorism' but has not itself reached binding consensus on what those terms mean. Giving operative legal significance to vaguely defined terms could be seen as undermining the world's 'normative and moral stance against terrorism'.[39] Rather than relying on an overarching definitional framework couched as a generalized crime of 'terrorism' or creatively packaged as a crime against humanity with uncertain pedigree and feigned international acceptance, the international community developed a patchwork of norms and conventions designed to prevent and punish specific manifestations of terrorist activities.[40] This approach has significant merit because the template of specific prohibitions can be readily replicated in domestic codes around the world, which in turn generates a regularity of enforcement and an accompanying universal condemnation of the act that penetrates the consciousness of citizens. The *aut dedere aut judicare* obligation serves as the capstone of this regime to ensure that there is no lawful sanctuary for the acts that are universally condemned and proscribed.

[37] M. C. Bassiouni, 'The New Wars and the Crisis of Compliance with the Law of Armed Conflict by Non-State Actors' (2008) 98 *Journal of Criminal Law & Criminology* 711.

[38] UN Charter, Art. 25.

[39] UN High Level Panel on Threats, Challenges and Change, *A More Secure World: Our Shared Responsibility* (UN Doc. A/59/565 (2004)), para. 159.

[40] B. Saul, *Defining Terrorism in International Law* (Oxford: Oxford University Press, 2006), 129–90.

2.3 The framework of modern multilateral prohibitions

Though they nowhere use the word 'terrorism', the three ICAO conventions[41] defining offences against plane and passenger safety are widely acknowledged to represent the first true anti-terrorism conventions. Modern anti-terrorism conventions eschew overarching and generalized condemnations in favour of particularized and specific descriptions of prohibited acts. Thus, 'terrorist acts' are detailed with sufficient particularity using language that can be readily adapted into domestic criminal codes to gain acceptance as a criminal prohibition in accordance with basic notions of fairness in criminal proceedings and the specific mandates of international human rights norms.

While the preambles of most anti-terrorism conventions restate generalized condemnations of terrorism in view of the costs it inflicts in human suffering and the sense of lingering societal vulnerability, or refer to the broader subjective purposes that are at the heart of a layperson's understanding of 'terrorism', the core substantive prohibitions are narrowly tailored in terms of *actus reus* requirements and an accompanying mental element if required. The 1999 Terrorist Financing Convention, for example, specifies that any person violates its provisions if he/she by 'any means, directly or indirectly, unlawfully and wilfully, provides or collects funds with the intention that they should be used or in the knowledge that they are to be used, in full or in part' to commit an act of terror defined in an enumerated multilateral convention[42] or any other act:

> intended to cause death or serious bodily injury to a civilian, or to any other person not taking an active part in the hostilities in a situation of armed conflict, when the purpose of such act, by its nature or context, is to intimidate a population, or to compel a government or an international organization to do or to abstain from doing any act.[43]

The gravamen of the offence is the specific act of collecting or disseminating funding with the requisite intention, and this approach mirrors

[41] 1963 Convention on Offences and Certain Other Acts Committed on Board Aircraft, 1969 UNTS 220; 1970 Convention for the Suppression of Unlawful Seizure of Aircraft, 1973 UNTS 106; and 1970 Convention for the Suppression of Unlawful Acts against the Safety of Civil Aviation, 1975 UNTS 178 [hereafter Montreal Convention].

[42] The Annex to the Terrorist Financing Convention lists nine different treaties that specify terrorist acts, thereby linking its core prohibition of providing financial support to terrorist activities to the concrete offences found in the treaty regime.

[43] Terrorist Financing Convention, Art. 2(1)(b).

criminal statutes around the planet. By extension, the modern framework of multilateral conventions obligates states to cooperate in eradicating the specific acts deemed to be the most representative of the broader phenomenon of transnational terrorism and to use their domestic legal systems to the fullest extent possible in the detection and prosecution of persons involved with the perpetration or support of terrorist activities. For example, the 2005 Council of Europe Convention on the Prevention of Terrorism required states parties to adopt three new criminal offences (along with penalties commensurate with their severity): 'public provocation to commit a terrorist offence', recruitment for terrorism, and training for terrorism.[44]

Employing the recurring formula that typifies the multilateral regime, the modern conventions seeking to prevent and punish terrorist acts embody the broadest possible jurisdictional authority for domestic courts.[45] Nevertheless, the universalized prohibition of terrorist acts and the expansion of both substantive and personal jurisdiction in domestic criminal forums should not be regarded as simply creating a preconceived inequality that always leads to convictions. In fact, similar

[44] Opened for Signature 16 May 2005, ETS No. 196, Arts. 5–7.

[45] Terrorist Financing Convention, Art. 7.

1. Each State Party shall take such measures as may be necessary to establish its jurisdiction over the offences set forth in article 2 when:
   (a) The offence is committed in the territory of that State;
   (b) The offence is committed on board a vessel flying the flag of that State or an aircraft registered under the laws of that State at the time the offence is committed;
   (c) The offence is committed by a national of that State.
2. A State Party may also establish its jurisdiction over any such offence when:
   (a) The offence was directed towards or resulted in the carrying out of an offence referred to in article 2, paragraph 1, subparagraph (a) or (b), in the territory of or against a national of that State;
   (b) The offence was directed towards or resulted in the carrying out of an offence referred to in article 2, paragraph 1, subparagraph (a) or (b), against a State or government facility of that State abroad, including diplomatic or consular premises of that State;
   (c) The offence was directed towards or resulted in an offence referred to in article 2, paragraph 1, subparagraph (a) or (b), committed in an attempt to compel that State to do or abstain from doing any act;
   (d) The offence is committed by a stateless person who has his or her habitual residence in the territory of that State;
   (e) The offence is committed on board an aircraft which is operated by the Government of that State.

to the decisions in other nations turning on the evidentiary difficulties of proving a causal relationship between a particular terrorist organization and a specific criminal act,[46] the 2009 trial of Khalid al-Yousef in Sweden on charges that he funnelled funding to Hamas using his charity al-Aqsa Spannmål Stiftelse (the al-Aqsa Grain Foundation) resulted in his acquittal due to insufficient evidence adduced by the prosecution.[47] There is solid international consensus that the substantive framework of treaty norms should not be corrupted to subvert due process rights or spawn tacit acceptance of human rights violations in the context of trial proceedings. Indeed, the participating states in the OSCE Ministerial Council pledged to 'fully respect international law and human rights'[48] while defending individual liberties from terrorist acts based in part on the desire to prevent a climate of alienation and mistrust that would in turn exacerbate the potential for radicalization and recruitment to terrorism. *Aut dedere aut judicare* helps to ensure that the system of justice functions as intended to incentivize regularity of process and efficient prosecutions that in turn minimizes the inclination of state officials to bypass established avenues for cooperation.

3 The benefits of an integrated framework

Aut dedere aut judicare operates as the essential pinnacle of an interlocking normative framework. The effect of each multilateral convention is not only to proscribe the specific manifestations of terrorism, but to create an effective and holistic approach for addressing the resulting criminality. The crimes should be investigated and prosecuted by the sovereign authorities that are best prepared for trial, and other states should share that jurisprudential burden. States 'shall afford one another the greatest measure of assistance in connection with criminal investigations or extradition proceedings . . . including assistance in obtaining evidence in their possession necessary for the proceedings'.[49] The

46 See *Boim* v. *Holy Land Foundation for Relief and Development et al.*, 511 F.3d 707 (7th Cir. 18 Dec. 2007).

47 Swedish al-Aqsa case, Court Transcript, Mål No. B 8056-06 Malmö Tinsgrätt, Sweden (17 February 2009).

48 Decision No. 1 on Combating Terrorism, OSCE MC(9).DEC/1 (4 December 2001).

49 Terrorist Financing Convention, Art. 12, para. 1. This provision operates in tandem with a separate requirement that states 'coordinate their actions appropriately, in particular concerning the conditions for prosecution and the modalities for mutual legal assistance' (Art. 7(5)).

community interest in an effective and efficient judicial proceeding is reinforced by the commonly replicated textual requirement that states 'immediately notify' other states that have established jurisdiction over a particular offender, as well as 'any other interested States Parties, of the fact that such person is in custody and of the circumstances that warrant that person's detention'.[50] Following an investigation, the custodial state must 'promptly notify' other relevant states of 'its findings and shall indicate whether it intends to exercise jurisdiction'.[51]

Each of the relevant conventions specifies that states shall either extradite the offender following sufficient investigation, or 'be obliged, without exception whatsoever and whether or not the offence was committed on its territory, to submit the case to its competent authorities for the purpose of prosecution, through proceedings in accordance with the laws of that State'.[52] Furthermore, the treaty regime effectively incorporates the substantive crimes into any existing extradition agreements by automatically modifying pre-existing agreements 'to the extent that they are incompatible' with the treaty obligation, and even replaces a separate formal agreement for states that may extradite by law do not require a specific bilateral treaty for the purposes of extradition.[53]

Against this backdrop of procedural regularity and prescribed international cooperation, the modern conventions strive to eliminate the taint of subjective ideological motivations that commonly spawn terrorist acts by requiring acceding states to 'adopt such measures as may be necessary, including, where appropriate, domestic legislation, to ensure that criminal acts within the scope of this Convention are under no circumstances justifiable by considerations of a political, philosophical, ideological, racial, ethnic, religious or other similar nature'.[54] This normative principle is replicated in every major multilateral terrorism convention.

When incorporated into domestic statutes, this textual language preempts the most common affirmative defence raised by terrorist perpetrators, but serves a very important expressive function as well. In sentencing the shoe bomber Richard Reid, a US federal judge discounted his attempted invocation of political ideology as follows:

> Here in this court, where we deal with individuals as individuals, and care for individuals as individuals, as human beings we reach out for justice, you are not an enemy combatant. You are a terrorist. You are not a soldier in any war. You are a terrorist. To give you that reference, to call

[50] *Ibid.*, Art. 9(6). [51] *Ibid.* [52] *Ibid.*, Art. 10(1). [53] *Ibid.*, Art. 11. [54] *Ibid.*, Art. 6.

> you a soldier gives you far too much stature. Whether it is the officers of government who do it or your attorney who does it, or that happens to be your view, you are a terrorist. And we do not negotiate with terrorists. We do not treat with terrorists. We do not sign documents with terrorists. We hunt them down one by one and bring them to justice So war talk is way out of line in this court. You are a big fellow. But you are not that big. You're no warrior. I know warriors. You are a terrorist. A species of criminal guilty of multiple attempted murders.[55]

Similarly, the judge in *Her Majesty the Queen* v. *Mohammed Momin Khawaja* rejected the defence of combatant immunity for a defendant describing himself as a 'wanna be' front-line mujahedin on the grounds that the armed conflict exclusion in Canadian law

> should not be non-combatant activity. To extend it to what they were doing would shelter from the reach of our terrorism legislation, the very kind of support of terrorism that Security Council Resolution 1390 (2002) called on Member Nations, including Canada, to interdict.[56]

Thus, the specific eradication of subjective motivations and ideology from the context of a particular criminal case serves to give the proceedings an unemotional, apolitical majesty appropriate to a rule-based process based on law and regularity. Such a process is based on rationality and procedural particularity rather than the shrill invocation of political passions. As a logical extension of this principle, the international treaties and their implementing statutes around the world expressly remove terrorist acts from the class of political offences that might otherwise hinder extradition or requests for mutual legal assistance.[57] Conversely, the obligation to extradite a particular offender is subject to the specific caveat domestic courts should retain jurisdiction if there are 'substantial grounds' for believing that an extradition or mutual legal assistance request sought to prosecute or punish a suspect 'on account of that person's race, religion, nationality, ethnic origin or political opinion or that compliance with the request would cause prejudice to that person's position for any of these reasons'.

The implementation of the *aut dedere aut judicare* principle binds nations together despite linguistic and legal barriers. Hugo Grotius's

[55] Available at www.nacic.gov/news/2003/april/SENTENCING_OF_RICHARD_REID.pdf Termed the 'shoe bomber', Mr Reid pled guilty to attempted multiple murders for his attempt to blow up a civilian airliner in flight using a bomb built into the sole of his shoe. His attempt was foiled by alert fellow passengers.

[56] *Her Majesty the Queen* v. *Mohammed Momin Khawaja*.

[57] Terrorist Financing Convention, Art. 14; Terrorist Bombing Convention, Art. 9(1).

argument from nearly four hundred years ago yet has the ring of truth with respect to the modern prohibitions on terrorist acts; states must affirmatively endeavour to seek justice 'in the case of crimes by which another state or its ruler is in a special sense injured, and on account of which that ruler or state, for the sake of dignity or security, has the right to exact punishment'. *Aut dedere aut judicare* can effectuate the sovereign rights of states only when it operates to ensure efficient adjudication of terrorist acts in the forum best situated to serve the interests of justice and the larger needs of civilized society. As noted in other chapters in this volume, terrorist crimes involve cases that raise issues of inherent complexity and political sensitivity, and a viable system of *aut dedere aut judicare* helps to prevent the irregular renditions that have become prevalent in some parts of the world.[58] This chapter concludes with three specific recommendations that portend progressive development towards regularity of process and transparent adjudication built on the foundation of the *aut dedere aut judicare* obligation.

4 Recommendations for reinforcing *aut dedere aut judicare*

4.1 Recommitment to unqualified universal state jurisdiction

The object and purpose of the modern framework of multilateral conventions is to establish a substantive framework for efficient domestic prosecution of terrorist acts. Phrased another way, the very *raison d'être* of the multilateral treaty regime is to embody the expressive condemnation of states that ratify those agreements, which in turn symbolizes the commitment of civilized states to stand firm in upholding the rule of law against threats to the established legal order. In that vein, the *aut dedere aut judicare* principle should be implemented as broadly as possible in practice, particularly when measured against the broad statements of personal jurisdiction reflected in the treaty regime. The very broad right of states to prosecute suspected terrorist actors should be mirrored by statutory authority that permits an unqualified extension of universal jurisdiction.

To that end, the Kingdom of the Netherlands re-examined its reservations and declarations to an entire series of terrorism treaties[59] and

[58] Amnesty International, *Kenya/Ethiopia/Somalia Unlawful Transfers in the 'War on Terror'* (AFR 25/006/2007 (June 2007)).

[59] E.g., *inter alia*, 1973 Convention on the Prevention and Punishment of Crimes against Internationally Protected Persons, Including Diplomatic Agents, 1035 UNTS 168; 1979 International Convention against the Taking of Hostages, 1316 UNTS 206; Montreal

decided to shift towards an unqualified secondary universal jurisdiction. Secondary universal jurisdiction entails prosecution of cases where an offence falling under one of the relevant conventions or protocols was committed outside its sovereign territory, but the alleged perpetrator is located within its territory and the affected state elects not to extradite the individual. Under its previous diplomatic statements, the obligation to prosecute a perpetrator on the basis of secondary universal jurisdiction would only arise in situations where extradition had been specifically requested by another state and rejected by the appropriate authorities.[60] The original intent of the reservations was to impose restraint on the principle of universal jurisdiction, excepting cases in which the 'gravity and international character of the acts covered by the convention in question gave adequate cause' for exercising jurisdiction based only on the presence of the perpetrator on territory within the Kingdom's judicial authority.[61]

In a sense, the previous limitations on secondary universal jurisdiction reflect a pragmatic recognition that evidence may be lacking in certain cases. Several states could in theory attempt to establish jurisdiction over one perpetrator on the basis of differing jurisdictional claims, which could in turn lead to disputes between sovereign authorities. Lastly, the declarations to the Terrorist Bombing Convention and the Terrorist Financing Convention were intended to preserve the discretion of prosecuting authorities in cases where significant factors of a procedural nature made prosecution difficult.[62] The shift in official policy nevertheless reflects an assessment that the text of the Conventions provides sufficient latitude for official determinations regarding the efficacy of particular cases. In any event, it must be borne in mind that the normative fabric of the international treaty regime relies on swift prosecution in the state best positioned in which jurisdiction is warranted. These changes may facilitate that goal.

Despite the countervailing interests that prevailed at the time of ratification, the virtues of consistency and efficiency in counter-terrorism prosecutions have led to the shift described above. To that end, the elimination of any domestic barriers or reservations regarding

Convention; 1988 Protocol for the Suppression of Unlawful Acts against the Safety of Fixed Platforms Located on the Continental Shelf, 1678 UNTS 304.

60 M. A. van der Harst, 'Treaties and other International Agreements to which the Kingdom of the Netherlands Is a Party: Conclusions and Developments 2008' (2009) 40 *Netherlands Yearbook of International Law* 299.

61 *Ibid.* 62 *Ibid.*, 300.

the *aut dedere aut judicare* obligation is wholly desirable. Even if the policy shift does not effectuate a statistically significant shift in cases prosecuted, it has value in expressing the universal condemnation of civilized states of the acts prohibited in the multilateral treaty regime. It is only to be hoped that such self-imposed barriers to prosecutions will be eliminated in more states in the near future, which in turn validates the object and purpose of the Conventions, i.e. the effective and efficient use of criminal forums to prevent and punish the range of terrorist acts proscribed in the treaty regime.

4.2 *Resisting efforts to commingle criminal regimes*

As a related matter, states should continue to strongly resist recurring efforts to commingle the criminal regime applicable to the conduct of hostilities with that embodied in the normal domestic criminal codes around the world. Non-state participants in a non-international armed conflict are fully subject to prosecution for their warlike acts, and a parallel creation of a form of combatant immunity applicable to terrorist acts would erode the *aut dedere aut judicare* obligation nearly to its vanishing point. For example, the object and purpose of the Terrorist Bombing Convention is to regulate terrorist bombings, *not* to provide a basis for invoking a moral equivalency between terrorist acts and the conduct of operations by armed forces. The Terrorist Bombing Convention sought to fill lacunae in the normative structure, but even in its preambular language reinforces the dichotomous approach to the prevention and prosecution of terrorist acts. It specifically notes 'that the activities of military forces of States are governed by rules of international law outside the framework of this Convention and that the exclusion of certain actions from the coverage of this Convention does not condone or make lawful otherwise unlawful acts, or preclude prosecution under other laws'. Indeed, a subjective assessment by one state that particular perpetrators are entitled to immunity from prosecution because of the warlike character of their acts would subvert the entire framework of anti-terrorism criminal law by sheltering them from prosecution in every state with an ostensible jurisdiction claim.

One of the most important and widely agreed upon provisions addresses precisely this dilemma. Article 19(2) of the Terrorist Bombing Convention (which is replicated verbatim in the Convention for the Suppression of Acts of Nuclear Terrorism) reinforces the division between the law of terrorism and the *jus in bello* applicable to armed conflicts:

> activities of armed forces during an armed conflict, as those terms are understood under international humanitarian law, which are governed by that law, are not governed by this Convention, and the activities undertaken by military forces of a State in the exercise of their official duties, inasmuch as they are governed by other rules of international law, are not governed by this Convention.

Recent practice has reinforced the jurisprudential value of these prohibitions in that the deliberate use of terror as a military tactic cannot constitute a viable basis for legalized violence. In convicting one perpetrator, the International Criminal Tribunal for the former Yugoslavia opined that 'the prohibition against terror is a specific prohibition within the general prohibition of attack on civilians, the latter of which constitutes a peremptory norm of international law'.[63] In other words, there can never be a lawful attack that is expressly intended to provoke terror in the civilian population or political structure that comports with the laws and customs of war. Indeed, the ICRC Commentary notes that military operations that seek to inflict terror 'are particularly reprehensible, occur frequently, and inflict particularly cruel suffering on the civilian population'.[64] In upholding the convictions in the AFRC Case, the Appeals Chamber of the Special Court for Sierra Leone accepted that convictions for 'acts of terrorism' could lie for the three appellants who engaged in a 'common plan to carry out a campaign of terrorising and collectively punishing the civilian population of Sierra Leone . . . in order to achieve the ultimate objective of gaining and exercising political power and control over the territory of Sierra Leone'.[65] The case against Radovan Karadžić is proceeding at the time of this writing based, *inter alia*, on the charge of unlawfully inflicting terror upon civilians.[66]

Though some states have attempted to blur the lines between differing legal regimes, they have met a uniform response based on a teleological

[63] *Prosecutor* v. *Stanislav Galic*, Judgment and Opinion, Case No. IT-98-29-T, T.Ch.I, 5 December 2003, paras. 66, 94–100, at www.icty.org/x/cases/galic/tjug/en/gal-tj031205e.pdf

[64] C. Pillout *et al.*, *Commentary on the Additional Protocols of 8 June 1977 to the Geneva Conventions of 12 August 1949* (Leiden: Martinus Nijhoff, 1987), para. 4785, fn. 195.

[65] *Prosecutor* v. *Alex Tamba Brima et al.* (*AFRC Case*), Appeal Judgment of 22 February 2008, Case No. SCSL-2004-16-A, A.Ch , para. 70 (see Trial Judgment of 20 June 2007, T. Ch.II., paras. 1633, 2113, 2117, 2121) at www.sc-sl.org/CASES/ArmedForcesRevolutionaryCouncilAFRCComplete/AFRCJudgment/tabid/173/Default.aspx (accessed 1 March 2009).

[66] *Prosecutor* v. *Radovan Karadžić*, Amended Indictment of 28 April 2000, Case No. IT-95-5/18-I, paras. 44–52, at www.un.org/icty/indictment/english/kar-ai000428e.htm.

approach to the anti-terrorism conventions. For example, in reserving to the Terrorist Bombing Convention, 'The Government of the Arab Republic of Egypt declares that it is bound by Article 19, paragraph 2, of the Convention insofar as the military forces of the State, in the exercise of their duties, do not violate the rules and principles of international law.'[67] The response of the United Kingdom[68] exemplifies the language and approach taken by the other states in opposition to the Egyptian effort (which included Canada, France, Germany, Italy, the Netherlands, the Russian Federation, Spain and the United States):

> With regard to the reservation made by Egypt upon ratification:
>
> > The Government of the United Kingdom of Great Britain and Northern Ireland have examined the declaration, described as a reservation, relating to article 19, paragraph 2 of the International Convention for the Suppression of Terrorist Bombings made by the Government of the Arab Republic of Egypt at the time of its ratification of the Convention.
> >
> > The declaration appears to purport to extend the scope of application of the Convention to include the armed forces of a State to the extent that they fail to meet the test that they 'do not violate the rules and principles of international law'. Such activities would otherwise be excluded from the application of the Convention by virtue of article 19, paragraph 2. It is the opinion of the United Kingdom that the Government of Egypt is entitled to make such a declaration only insofar as the declaration constitutes a unilateral declaration by the Government of Egypt that Egypt will apply the terms of the Convention in circumstances going beyond those required by the Convention to their own armed forces on a unilateral basis. The United Kingdom considers this to be the effect of the declaration made by Egypt.

The French added that 'the effect of the reservation made by the Government of the Arab Republic of Egypt is to bring within the scope of the Convention activities undertaken by a State's armed forces which do not belong there because they are covered by other provisions of international law. As a result, the reservation substantially alters the meaning and scope of article 19, paragraph 2 of the Convention.'[69]

[67] CN 634.2005.TREATIES-11 of 16 August 2005.
[68] CN 655.2006.TREATIES-11 of 3 August 2006.
[69] CN 667.2006.TREATIES-13 of 15 August 2006.

The net effect of these consular notifications is to reinforce the bright-line distinction between the relevant bodies of law. The military forces representing sovereign states are subject to the limitations of the laws and customs of war – they cannot be demeaned as terrorists because they are not operationally or legally equivalent to terrorists. This principle in no way undermines the right of states to prosecute as war criminals those combatants who transgress the boundaries of the law of war. Terrorists, on the other hand, are subject to the criminal sanctions of domestic laws, especially those deriving from the definitions and condemnations enshrined in the plethora of multilateral conventions that proscribe their tactics. States are, and ought to remain, absolutely united in opposing any efforts to erode the core prohibition that all acts of terrorism are, and ought to be, criminalized. Any attendant claim to shelter terrorist acts under the rubric of combatant immunity is unfounded and ill-advised. As the Special Tribunal for Lebanon noted in its landmark ruling regarding the definition of transnational terrorism, 'the very few states still insisting on an exception for freedom fighters and therefore objecting to the coalescing definition of terrorism could, at most, be considered persistent objectors thereof', which in turn would make them in violation of their duty to abide by the Chapter VII mandate from the Security Council to prevent terrorist acts and to ensure that such acts are punished consistent with their gravity and their implications for peace and stability.[70] The unconstrained application of the *aut dedere aut judicare* obligation ensures that most appropriate judicial authorities will handle each specific case concerning the criminal acts of any other person or entity.

4.3 *Drafting of a new diplomatic protocol to ensure due process protections*

Erosion of the *aut dedere aut judicare* regime leads to a paralysed and impotent system of transnational accountability. Systematic disregard for human rights in the larger struggle to preserve human rights from the threat of continuing terrorist acts has the paradoxical effect of impeding international cooperation, which in turn allows culpable terrorists to remain unpunished. Courts have been unmistakably clear that there is no rule of expediency that can be superimposed on the treaty regime for

[70] Interlocutory Decision on the Applicable Law: Terrorism, Conspiracy, Homicide, Perpetration, Cumulative Charging, para. 110.

regulating terrorism. The European Court of Human Rights punctuated this trend in the watershed case of *Saadi* v. *Italy*.[71] In *Saadi*, the Grand Chamber firmly restated its position that the prohibition against torture is absolute and may not be the subject of derogation whatever the motivation of particular states, even as against convicted terrorist perpetrators. In doing so, the Chamber rejected appeals to accept a balancing test that would duly consider the threat posed to the security interests of European Union states in assessing the reasonableness of risk posed by removal to another nation. Although there may be instances in which diplomatic assurances are sufficient to satisfy the human rights obligations of the deporting state, the circumstances of Saadi's conviction led the Chamber to conclude that the indications of maltreatment in Tunisian detention facilities led to an unwarranted risk of removal on the part of Italy.

From these cases, and many others, it is clear that the very integrity of the *aut dedere aut judicare* principle depends upon a framework of trust in which the preservation of human rights of perpetrators, i.e. pending defendants, is better managed in the context of transfers as well as prosecutions. To that end, states should negotiate a binding protocol regulating a range of matters that need to be specifically addressed to facilitate transfers of terrorist actors, particularly those of a trans-regional nature. Trans-regional transfers are precisely those most likely to involve difficult facts and emotive cries for revenge that potentially undermine human rights and thereby hinder efficient transfers to face trial.

A new protocol on terrorist transfers would readily be incorporated by reference into an array of existing treaties and could augment efforts to negotiate a Comprehensive Convention in coming years. A new Framework Agreement on Terrorist Extradition should specifically address such issues as the provision of intelligence information between states, particularly as that issue arises in the context of extended extradition proceedings which impairs timely prosecution of terrorist acts. Similarly, a binding agreement based on consensus should address gaps in domestic implementation of the authoritative UN list of prohibited terrorist entities. This provision would overcome the issue raised by the Thai trial chamber in *Attorney General* v. *Bout*,[72] which refused a US extradition request involving a Russian citizen on charges of selling arms

[71] *Saadi* v. *Italy*, Judgment of 28 February 2008 [2008] ECHR.

[72] *Attorney General* v. *Bout*, Black Case No. Por. 3/255: Thailand Judgment Bangkok Criminal Court (11 August 2009).

to insurgents in Colombia. Thai officials did not recognize the authoritative listing of the terrorist group under the authority of UN Resolution 1267. The *aut dedere aut judicare* principle must operate on an authoritative basis that overcomes technical barriers such as these.

An authoritative protocol would facilitate more comprehensive and efficient implementation of the extradition regime by ensuring uniform compliance. For example, the Framework Agreement on Terrorist Extradition would strengthen the regime of diplomatic assurances by requiring a priori agreement of domestic officials to unimpeded rights of access to the perpetrator with no prior notice to authorities. It could go so far as to designate one international actor as the authoritative monitor for the conditions under which terrorists are held and prosecuted pursuant to the *aut dedere aut judicare* principle. The High Commissioner for Human Rights could be entrusted with this duty, or a Special Ombudsman representing the Security Council, or even the International Committee of the Red Cross. The state surrendering custody of a terrorist perpetrator would remain responsible for the treatment of that suspect in the hands of the detaining state. Such a Framework provision would be modelled on that found in the Geneva Convention for the Protection of Prisoners of War which incentivizes the protection implemented by detaining states in the context of international armed conflicts. By extension, it is entirely conceivable that the agency or official responsible for authorizing the transfer of a terrorist should be made expressly liable for the treatment of that suspect in foreign custody, which would in turn create the expectation of affirmative oversight following transfer. The most powerful words in the diplomat's vocabulary should be 'we'll be back'.

The essential point remains that identifying and addressing the major barriers to extraditions would help to ensure swift and fair criminal trials, with the foreseeable benefits to the common struggle against terrorism. It is far beyond the scope of this chapter to fully recount the scope of a new Framework Agreement on Terrorist Extradition, and such an effort would likely be mooted in any event following international negotiations on the matter. A comprehensive agreement that addresses the obstacles to efficient extraditions in express language could be the most important element in protecting private citizens over the coming decades because it would signal a strengthening of international resolve and procedural uniformity. Given the demonstrated faults in the existing regime, systematic improvements are desperately needed to achieve the efficiency and certainty needed to ensure that transnational terrorists face accountability for their acts in the forum that is best suited to try the case.

5 Conclusion

The stark experience in recent years has demonstrated that the textual clarity and unambiguous authority of the *aut dedere aut judicare* precept has run aground on the shoals of sovereign interests and recurrent resistance. In her classic text recounting the dynamics of the Adolf Eichmann trial, Hannah Arendt wrote:

> The focus of every trial is upon the person of the defendant, a man of flesh and blood with an individual history, with an always unique set of qualities, peculiarities, behavior patterns, circumstances. All the things that go beyond that ... affect the trial only insofar as they form the background and the conditions under which the defendant committed his acts.[73]

Through the lens of each specific trial, that sentiment has the ring of truth even after more than four decades, yet it is only in contradistinction to the larger constellation of cases that the evolution of a particular field or issue can be reasonably measured. It is not unreasonable to extrapolate from the increasing ossification of the extradition processes around the globe that *aut dedere aut judicare* may actually be endangered in practice. This presents the possibility of moral hazard as states subvert human rights in order to protect and defend the human rights of their citizenry. States should reinforce the extradition regime with the urgency appropriate to the values it protects: security, stability, economic vitality, sovereignty, political independence and the human rights of peace-loving citizens. Because terrorist acts undermine the instruments of the modern sovereign state and endanger the human rights of her citizens, the *aut dedere aut judicare* obligation encompasses a grave responsibility even as it exemplifies the solemn duty to join in common purpose to combat terrorism. If the international community continues to disregard the clear warning signs that the *aut dedere aut judicare* does not ineluctably produce efficient and fair justice for terrorist perpetrators, then the peace and stability of society remains at risk.

[73] H. Arendt, *Eichmann in Jerusalem: A Report on the Banality of Evil* (New York: Penguin, 1994), 285.

4

The need for a multilateral cooperative framework for mutual legal assistance

KIMBERLY PROST

1 The 'status quo' for international cooperation in information and evidence gathering

1.1 Introduction

Mutual assistance[1] in criminal matters is a process by which states seek and provide assistance in gathering evidence for use in criminal cases or in the restraint and confiscation of proceeds of crime. Today, this particular form of international cooperation is receiving considerable attention, given its central role in effectively combating transnational and international crime, including organized crime, corruption and terrorism.

Despite significant advances in mutual assistance within the past fifteen years, it remains difficult for countries to receive and provide assistance in criminal cases in a timely manner. The reasons for these challenges to effective mutual assistance are multiple and varied. This chapter will focus on one particular issue – the basis for the rendering of mutual assistance – with a view to determining if there is a need for a new multilateral cooperative framework. While the chapter is not intended to give an overview of other impediments to the mutual assistance process, some consideration of the overall challenges is necessary to properly assess whether a multilateral instrument is a priority concern for improved international cooperation in evidence gathering.

With a contribution from Håkan Friman, Director and Head of the Division for Criminal Cases and International Legal Cooperation, albeit views expressed are personal and not attributable to any organization.

1 Also referred to as mutual legal assistance, but for the purpose of this chapter the term 'mutual assistance' or 'mutual assistance in criminal matters' will be used as a term of art.

This chapter focuses on international cooperation in combating terrorism. While this specific context is considered in the course of the discussion below, the chapter takes a broad approach and considers the question whether a multilateral instrument on mutual assistance is needed to facilitate international cooperation in criminal matters generally.

1.2 Mechanisms for gathering evidence and information in criminal cases

Countries have long assisted each other in gathering information and evidence for criminal investigations and prosecutions through a broad range of mechanisms. In assessing the need for a multilateral convention, it is relevant to put mutual assistance into the broader context of the various measures available for cross-border investigations. Some key considerations in that respect are outlined below.

1.2.1 Police-to-police channels

There are well-established police-to-police/agency-to-agency channels through which much essential information has been and continues to be shared. These channels include direct relationships between police officers and police forces, agency-to-agency networks, the posting of police/magistrate liaison personnel in foreign states and formalized organizations such as Europol and Interpol. All of these measures remain critical to cooperation in evidence gathering and have not been replaced by the more formal process of mutual assistance.

An extension of this form of cooperation which is being applied with favourable results is that of joint investigations/operations between police forces and other investigative agencies of different countries. Through these cooperative ventures, on a bilateral or multilateral basis, operations can be aimed at crime or criminal organizations of a transnational nature. In the course of the investigation, each of the police or investigative agencies involved can legitimately and lawfully employ domestic powers to gather evidence, which can be shared ultimately for the purpose of prosecuting any resulting cases. This mechanism of cooperation is of particular value in instances where there is urgency to the measure that must be taken. Increasingly, the use of joint operations is being seen as an effective alternative to mutual assistance, particularly in complex international cases. There are however limitations to this form of cooperation. Notably, it is unlikely to function effectively unless there is a close underlying relationship between the participating states to ensure a sufficient level of confidence and trust. In addition, the varying legal constraints within the relevant countries may restrict the nature and extent of any such operations. Therefore, while it is an important and useful mechanism for criminal investigations, it is not a form of assistance which can ever replace mutual assistance on a general level.

1.2.2 Prosecutorial and judicial cooperation

Recently there has been an increased focus on judicial and prosecutorial cooperative arrangements, which can be used to facilitate evidence gathering in transnational cases. Given the scope of this contribution, no attempt will be made to canvass those arrangements in an exhaustive manner. One example of a very successful endeavour in this respect is Eurojust.[2] It is a European body which is designed to stimulate and improve coordination with respect to investigations and prosecutions. Each of the twenty-seven member countries appoints a national member, who is a prosecutor, judge or investigator. These national members work together with relevant competent authorities within the states to facilitate cooperation and effective mutual assistance on an operational, case-by-case basis. Eurojust is an example of a very successful support mechanism for improving international cooperation in criminal cases. However, despite its successes, Eurojust is not a model which is easily replicated in other parts of the world. It is clearly an organization which functions effectively, in no small part, due to the underlying relationship geographically, politically and legally between the participant countries and through its association with the structures of the European Union. Thus, while it remains an important initiative to consider in terms of improving international cooperation in other regions of the world, it is unlikely that other such models will be created in the short term.

All of these informal and formalized means for pursuing criminal matters across national borders are important. They generate significant results in terms of evidence gathering and information sharing. Equally, to the extent that these measures are employed as much as is lawfully permissible, the drain on formal mutual assistance resources can be reduced. So in considering the broader question of improving the effectiveness of mutual assistance, consideration should be given to encouraging the development of these types of contacts, networks and

[2] See Eurojust website: www.eurojust.europa.eu.

organizations with a view to reducing the need for law enforcement to resort to formal mutual assistance.

1.3 *Limitations and the need for formal mutual assistance*

However, whatever the innovations or developments in cooperation in evidence gathering, there will remain many instances where the type of assistance sought can only be obtained through the use of formal mutual assistance. In particular, this will be the case where police or informal channels cannot be used because the measure sought will require resort to the legal process within the requested state; where some type of judicial order or compulsory measure must be applied to produce the desired information or evidence, in an acceptable form. In these circumstances and in the absence of the possibility of a joint investigation, resort to the more formal mechanism of mutual assistance will be necessary.

It is this necessity which has led to the development of a myriad of instruments for seeking and providing assistance in evidence gathering and with the restraint and confiscation of proceeds of crime. Any consideration of the need for a multilateral convention must begin with a review and analysis of this existing network for mutual assistance.

2 The existing network for mutual assistance in criminal matters

2.1 *The European Convention*

It is helpful to consider the existing network of mutual assistance instruments and regimes in the context of some historic milestones and the general evolution of this measure of cooperation.

The development of mutual assistance can best be described as a haphazard process. Driven by necessity and influenced by the long-standing practices in extradition, the basis for and content of mutual assistance have changed considerably over time. The first significant instrument for mutual assistance was the European Convention on Mutual Assistance in Criminal Matters.[3] It was an important achievement of its time in its recognition of the necessity for specific instruments for cooperation in evidence gathering. And

[3] 1959 European Convention on Mutual Assistance in Criminal Matters, Council of Europe Treaty Series No. 30 (1959 European Convention).

it remains a significant instrument to date with forty-eight state parties.[4] While there are ongoing changes in the practice of mutual assistance within the European Union, which will be described in more detail below, this instrument remains of importance, particularly in the wider European context. The original treaty has since been augmented by protocols and there are related treaties of relevance to the European Union and beyond.[5]

2.2 *Bilateral treaties*

In the 1970s, countries with a significant interest in gaining access to evidence on an international basis – notably the United States – began to negotiate bilateral agreements which would regulate the mutual assistance process and overcome the specific challenges as between individual states. The often cited example of the first 'breakthrough instrument' is the treaty between the United States and Switzerland which came into force in January 1977.[6] It is referred to as the seminal mutual legal assistance instrument because of its innovative measures aimed at bridging the differences between common law and civil law states. Following this breakthrough, many countries began developing and entering into bilateral arrangements for mutual assistance.[7] Today a multiplicity of such arrangements exists and the import of this base for mutual assistance must be stressed. Because bilateral treaties are specially crafted to overcome any particular problems between two states, countries will tend to rely on these instruments in preference to any form of regional or

[4] This includes Israel as a non-member state of the Council of Europe.

[5] See 1978 Additional Protocol to the European Convention on Mutual Assistance in Criminal Matters, Council of Europe Treaty Series No. 99 (forty states parties); 1990 Convention Applying the Schengen Agreement (see: http://eur-ex.europa.eu/LexUriServ/LexUriServ.do?uri=CELEX:42000A0922(02):EN:NOT); Second Additional Protocol, Council of Europe Treaty Series 182; 1958 Benelux Treaty, at: www.benelux.be/en/rgm/rgm_unieverdrag.asp.

[6] L. Frei and S. Freschal, 'Origins and Application of the United States – Switzerland Treaty on Mutual Assistance in Criminal Matters' (1990) 31 *Harvard International Law Journal* 77–9, 77.

[7] For example the United States has 61 mutual legal assistance treaties in force (http://travel.state.gov/law/info/judicial/judicial_690.html); the United Kingdom has 35 treaties for mutual legal assistance (www.fco.gov.uk/en/about-the-fco/publications/treaties/lists-treaties/bilateral-mutual-legal); South Africa has 9 mutual legal assistance in criminal matters treaties in force (www.doj.gov.za); Australia has 25 mutual assistance in criminal matters treaties in force (www.ag.gov.au/www/agd/agd.nsf/Page/Extraditionandmutualassistance_Relationshipwithothercountries_Australianbilateralmutualassistanceagreements). See also the hybrid bilateral–multilateral Agreement on Mutual Legal Assistance between the European Union and the United States of America (2003) OJL 181, 34–42.

multilateral scheme. In addition, such bilateral agreements will most often be created in the context of the relationships which generate the most situations where mutual assistance will be required. While not constituting a basis for mutual assistance per se it is relevant to note the adoption by the General Assembly of the United Nations of the Model Treaty on Mutual Assistance.[8] The Model Treaty is intended to assist countries with the drafting and negotiation of bilateral mutual assistance treaties. The fact that such an instrument was elaborated and agreed upon by member states of the United Nations evidences the import of these particular instruments in the mutual assistance process. One further advantage of bilateral treaties is that the negotiation process itself is a form of training and capacity building for the relevant countries. Even if the officials involved in the negotiation move on to other responsibilities, the record of the negotiations and the contacts forged will be used in the future to facilitate the practice of mutual assistance under the treaty. In assessing, the need for and role of, a multilateral instrument, these advantages of the bilateral approach must be borne in mind.

2.3 Regional schemes

At the same time, the use of bilateral instruments for mutual assistance has inherent and obvious limitations. With globalization and the rise of various forms of transnational and international crime, mutual assistance has become of increasing importance for many states. However, the vast majority of these states do not have the resources necessary to negotiate bilateral instruments for cooperation on the wide scale which is now needed. Because of this dilemma, various multilateral instruments – particularly regional treaties and schemes – for the rendering of mutual assistance have been elaborated. These have the advantage of reducing the resources necessary to negotiate individual agreements with states and their regional scope still allows for the crafting of fairly effective instruments responsive to the particular context of the relevant region. In addition, as with bilateral instruments, regional agreements with the countries which are most geographically proximate are likely to cover the relationships with the most 'traffic' in terms of mutual assistance. More so than any other form of instrument, regional agreements are also the most likely to have a 'harmonization' effect on the laws and practice of mutual assistance depending on the strength of the particular regional grouping. For example, as will be discussed below, the European Union

[8] UN Doc. A/45/49 (1990).

arrangements have had the most significant impact on the practice of mutual assistance among member states than any other multilateral or bilateral instrument.

While not intended as an exhaustive list, the following is an overview of key regional schemes for mutual assistance which illustrates the reach of such arrangements:

- Inter-American Convention on Mutual Assistance in Criminal Matters[9] (OAS Convention);
- Economic Community of West African States Convention on Mutual Assistance in Criminal Matters[10] (ECOWAS Convention);
- Intergovernmental Authority on Development Conventions on Extradition and Mutual Legal Assistance[11] (IGAD Conventions);
- Caribbean Mutual Legal Assistance Treaty in Serious Criminal Matters[12] (Caribbean Convention);
- Minsk Convention on Legal Assistance and Legal Relations in Civil, Family, and Criminal Matters[13] and the Kishinev Convention[14] (CIS Conventions);
- Southern African Development Community Protocol on Mutual Legal Assistance in Criminal Matters[15] (SADC Protocol);
- Association of Southeast Asian Nations Treaty on Mutual Legal Assistance in Criminal Matters (ASEAN Treaty);[16]

9 Inter-American Convention on Mutual Assistance in Criminal Matters (adopted 23 May 1992, entered into force 14 April 1996) OAS Treaty Series No. 75 (OAS Convention).

10 Economic Community of West African States Convention on Mutual Assistance in Criminal Matters (adopted 29 July 1992, entered into force provisionally 29 July 1992 and definitively 28 October 1998) 2329 UNTS 301 (ECOWAS Convention).

11 Intergovernmental Authority on Development Conventions on Extradition and Mutual Legal Assistance (adopted 7–8 December 2009) www.igad.org (IGAD Conventions).

12 Caribbean Mutual Legal Assistance Treaty in Serious Criminal Matters (adopted 6 July 2005) www.caricomlaw.org (Caribbean Convention).

13 Convention on Legal Assistance and Legal Relations in Civil, Family, and Criminal Matters (adopted 22 January 1993, entered into force 19 May 1994, amended 28 March 1997) (Minsk Convention).

14 Convention on Legal Assistance and Legal Relations in Civil, Family and Criminal Matters (adopted 7 October 2002, entered into force 2004) (Kishinev – Chishinau Convention).

15 Southern African Development Community Protocol on Mutual Legal Assistance in Criminal Matters (adopted 3 October 2002, entered into force 1 March 2007) www.sadc.int (SADC Protocol).

16 Association of Southeast Asian Nations Treaty on Mutual Legal Assistance in Criminal Matters (adopted 29 November 2004) www.aseansec.org/17363.pdf (ASEAN Treaty).

- South Asian Association for Regional Cooperation Convention on Mutual Assistance on Criminal Matters[17] (SAARC Convention);.

2.4 The Commonwealth Scheme

Another distinct instrument of relevance is the Commonwealth Scheme for Mutual Assistance (Harare Scheme). Adopted by Commonwealth Law Ministers in Harare, Zimbabwe in 1986[18] the scheme is not a treaty, though its content mirrors the provisions found in such treaties. The Harare Scheme is a set of agreed recommendations, intended to guide Commonwealth governments in regulating mutual assistance with other Commonwealth countries. The adoption of the Harare Scheme by Law Ministers represents a commitment on the part of the member countries to have national legislation and administrative measures that will allow for the rendering of mutual assistance in accordance with the content of the Harare Scheme. The goal of the Harare Scheme is not to prescribe uniform legislation but rather to encourage the adoption of national legislation and practices among member countries which will afford a high level of cooperation.[19] If properly implemented, the Harare Scheme would operate as a basis for mutual assistance to be rendered between the fifty-four member countries of the Commonwealth.

2.5 The penal law conventions

What has been described so far is the network of treaties and schemes which have mutual assistance as their sole subject matter. However, of equal importance, are various multilateral instruments which focus on particular criminal subject areas and include a specific article or articles related to mutual assistance. The first of these – a seminal treaty in the development of mutual legal assistance on a global basis – is the 1988 Vienna Convention against the Illicit Traffic in Narcotic Drugs and Psychotropic Substances (1988 Drug Convention).[20] The inclusion of this 'stand-alone' provision on

[17] South Asian Association for Regional Cooperation Convention on Mutual Assistance on Criminal Matters (adopted 3 August 2008) http://saarc-sec.org/SAARC-Conventions/63/ (SAARC Convention).

[18] Scheme Relating to Mutual Assistance in Criminal Matters within the Commonwealth, Commonwealth Secretariat, London, LMN (86) 13 (at: www.thecommonwealth.org).

[19] Commonwealth Schemes on Mutual Assistance in the Administration of Justice, June 1991, Commonwealth Secretariat.

[20] 1988 United Nations Convention against the Illicit Traffic in Narcotic Drugs and Psychotropic Substances, 1582 UNTS 95 (1988 Drug Convention).

mutual assistance has often been referred to as the adoption of a 'mini-treaty' within a treaty. Article 7 of the 1988 Drug Convention includes all of the fundamental provisions necessary for the rendering of mutual assistance albeit limited by the context to drug cases. Similar articles, with some additions and improvements,[21] were incorporated into the subsequently adopted United Nations Convention against Transnational Organized Crime (TOC Convention)[22] and the United Nations Convention against Corruption (Corruption Convention).[23] Importantly the Corruption Convention significantly improves upon the provisions relating to mutual assistance in asset confiscation by the addition of further cooperation measures and a chapter relating specifically to asset recovery.[24]

Interestingly, these three penal law conventions contain articles relating to mutual assistance and extradition which provide that the convention forms a basis for the rendering of these forms of cooperation. However, while states have discretion as to whether to use the convention as a basis for extradition, there is an obligation associated with the mutual assistance articles. That is, unless there is a bilateral agreement between the two parties, parties to these conventions are obligated to render mutual assistance in respect of the relevant treaty offences on the basis of the convention provisions. In addition, if it will be beneficial, the parties can also agree to use the convention in place of an existing bilateral instrument. The effect is that among the parties to three conventions – the 1988 Drug Convention (184 Parties), the TOC Convention (148 Parties)[25] and the Corruption Convention (136 Parties) there exists a binding mutual assistance relationship with reference to three of the most significant areas of international crime – drugs, corruption and transnational organized crime as it may manifest itself.

[21] 2000 United Nations Convention against Transnational Organized Crime, 2225 UNTS 209. Paras. 4 and 5 of Art. 18 of the TOC Convention contains a new provision on spontaneous disclosure and para. 13 on authorities for the transmission of requests has been modified from its predecessor (para. 8 of Art. 7 of the 1988 Drug Convention) notably by requiring the identification of a single central authority as opposed to competent authorities.

[22] UN Doc. A/Res./55/25 (2000).

[23] UN Doc. A/Res./58/4 (2003), 2003 United Nations Convention against Corruption, 2369 UNTS 41.

[24] *Ibid.*, Chapter V on asset recovery.

[25] 2000 Protocol to Prevent, Suppress and Punish Trafficking in Persons Especially Women and Children, 2237 UNTS 319, 129 parties; 2000 Protocol against the Smuggling of Migrants by Land, Sea and Air, 2241 UNTS 507, 110 parties; and 2001 Protocol against the Illicit Manufacturing of and Trafficking in Firearms, Their Parts and Components and Ammunition, 2326 UNTS 208, 79 parties.

2.6 The counter-terrorism conventions

The majority of the international anti-terrorism instruments include provisions related to mutual assistance.[26] These articles place a general obligation on state parties to afford each other the greatest measure of assistance in connection with criminal proceedings, including assistance in obtaining evidence. Unfortunately, unlike the penal law conventions, none of the articles in the counter-terrorism conventions are particularly detailed so as to provide practical guidance for the rendering of such assistance. Still, each of the conventions does create an obligation on states to cooperate in this respect. Such an obligation is sufficient to classify the instruments as a 'base' for mutual assistance in relation to the offences outlined in the individual conventions. The three most recent conventions – the International Convention for the Suppression of Terrorist Bombings (1997) (Bombing Convention), the International Convention for the Suppression of the Financing of Terrorism (1999) (Financing Convention) and the International Convention for the Suppression of Acts of Nuclear Terrorism (Nuclear Convention) – include some additional provisions relating to mutual assistance. All of them contain separate articles on a specific form of mutual assistance – the temporary transfer of witnesses.[27] The Financing Convention, because of its relationship to financial matters, also contains provisions on non-refusal of requests on the basis of bank secrecy[28] and a 'limitation of use' clause[29] which would prevent the use of evidence received for matters other than that for which it was requested. In summary, the majority of the counter-terrorism treaties create a binding obligation to

[26] See 1970 Convention for the Suppression of Unlawful Seizure of Aircraft, 704 UNTS 106, Art. 10; 1971 Convention for the Suppression of Unlawful Acts against the Safety of Civil Aviation, 974 UNTS 178, Art. 11; 1973 Convention on the Prevention and Punishment of Crimes against Internationally Protected Persons, Including Diplomatic Agents, 1035 UNTS 168, Art. 10; 1979 International Convention against the Taking of Hostages, 1316 UNTS 206, Art. 11; 1979 Convention on the Physical Protection of Nuclear, Material 1456 UNTS 125, Art. 13; 1988 Convention for the Suppression of Unlawful Acts against the Safety of Maritime Navigation, 1678 UNTS 222, Art. 12; 1997 International Convention for the Suppression of Terrorist Bombings, 2149 UNTS 256, Art. 10; 1999 International Convention for the Suppression of the Financing of Terrorism, 2178 UNTS 179, Art. 12; 2005 International Convention for the Suppression of Acts of Nuclear Terrorism, 2445 UNTS 89, Art. 14.

[27] See Bombing Convention, Art. 13; Financing Convention, Art. 16; and Nuclear Convention, Art. 17.

[28] See Art. 12(2). [29] See Art. 12(3).

render mutual assistance, the terms of which however will need to be worked out as between the relevant parties in an individual case.

2.7 UN Security Council Resolution 1373

In the context of counter-terrorism investigations and prosecutions there is a school of thought which advances Security Council Resolution 1373[30] as a legal basis for mutual assistance. That position however is by no means universally accepted. For the purposes of this chapter, it is unnecessary to come to any conclusion on the point. From a practical perspective, the resolution contains no detailed provisions which would assist states on a practical level in rendering mutual assistance. So again, at best it can be considered that the resolution places an obligation on member states to cooperate in terrorism investigations, without providing any concrete mechanism for that cooperation.

2.8 Mutual recognition in the European Union

Since the programme adopted by the European Council in Tampere in 1999, the traditional form of international criminal cooperation – whereby one state requests another state to assist with certain measures or to achieve a certain result – is being replaced within the European Union. The cooperation is instead increasingly based upon the principle of mutual recognition of decisions and judgments handed down in another member state. National judicial authorities in different member states are to cooperate directly with each other and the foreign decisions to be recognized and enforced as such with a minimum of formalities. Standard forms are to be used and time limits apply. The intention, at least in the longer term, is to reduce the grounds for refusal, such as the double criminality requirement, to an absolute minimum.

The principle of mutual recognition is a way to increase the efficiency of the cooperation without necessarily requiring harmonization of the substantive penal and procedural law of the cooperating states. On the other hand, in order to operate well, the principle requires a high level of mutual trust, which in turn depends upon reducing the differences

Section 2.8 of the chapter was prepared by Håkan Friman of the Swedish Ministry of Justice.

[30] UN Doc. S/Res/1373 (2001).

between the national systems. Indeed, a degree of harmonization, or as it is called in the EU 'approximation', of penal and procedural law is taking place as part of the development process.

A number of new instruments, so-called framework decisions, based on the principle of mutual recognition, have been adopted within the EU in recent years. Most of them, so far, will replace the traditional form and extend the scope of criminal cooperation, in the field of extradition[31] and international enforcement of penalties.[32]

In the field of mutual assistance, however, the developments have not progressed that far and only certain areas of cooperation are covered by instruments based upon the principle of mutual recognition. For most parts, the cooperation follows the traditional scheme as set out in bilateral agreements and in the 1959 Council of Europe Convention on Mutual Assistance in Criminal Matters, as amended by a modernized regime through the 2000 EU Convention on mutual assistance in criminal matters[33] and an Additional Protocol of 2001.[34]

The only mutual recognition instrument that is operational so far is one on execution of freezing orders.[35] However, it is very seldom utilized

[31] The primary example is the Council Framework Decision 2002/584/JHA of 13 June 2002 on the European Arrest Warrant and the surrender procedures between member states [2002] OJ L 190/1. A further step was taken in December 2008 when the Council reached a political agreement concerning a European supervision order, which provides for cooperation concerning alternatives to deprivation of liberty (i.e., bail conditions, reporting obligations, travel restrictions, etc.); the framework decision can be adopted once some member states have lifted their parliamentary scrutiny reservations.

[32] Council Framework Decision 2005/214/JHA of 24 February 2005 on the application of the principle of mutual recognition to financial penalties [2005] OJ L76/16; Council Framework Decision 2006/783/JHA of 6 October 2006 on the application of the principle of mutual recognition to confiscation orders [2006] OJ L328/59; Council Framework Decision 2008/909/JHA of 27 November 2008 on the application of the principle of mutual recognition to judgments in criminal matters imposing custodial sentences or measures involving deprivation of liberty for the purpose of their enforcement in the EU [2008] OJ L327/27; Council Framework Decision 2008/947/JHA of 27 November 2008 on the application of the principle of mutual recognition to judgments and probation decisions with a view to the supervision of probation measures and alternative sanctions [2008] OJ L337/102.

[33] Convention established by the Council in accordance with Article 34 of the Treaty on European Union, on Mutual Assistance in Criminal Matters between the Member States of the European Union [2000] OJ C197/3.

[34] Protocol established by the Council in accordance with Article 34 of the Treaty on European Union to the Convention on Mutual Assistance in Criminal Matters between the Member States of the European Union [2001] OJ C326/2.

[35] Council Framework Decision 2003/577/JHA of 22 July 2003 on the execution in the European Union of orders freezing property or evidence [2003] OJ L196/45.

in practice, one reason being that the execution of a freezing order must be followed up by a traditional request for legal assistance in order to secure the transfer of the assets or evidence involved. Another instrument, creating a European Evidence Warrant, was adopted in December 2008[36] and is meant to remedy this, but the scheme is much less far-reaching than initially suggested and it will only in part meet the expectations. Moreover, in its current form the Evidence Warrant will not entirely replace traditional requests; the two schemes will thus run in parallel. In addition, a framework decision concerning the exchange of criminal records has been adopted.[37]

2.9 National law

Left until last is one of the most important developments in mutual assistance practice: the use of national legislation for the rendering of assistance without a requirement for treaty. Several countries have now adopted an approach to mutual assistance which obviates the need for any underlying international agreement as a precondition to cooperation. Instead they have adopted national laws which allow for assistance to be rendered to any state in accordance with that law with or without a requirement for reciprocity.[38]

3 Analysis of existing network

3.1 Scope of existing network

The existing inventory of mutual assistance instruments, as illustrated above, might best be described as an extensive "patchwork" of instruments for cooperation. Some further consideration of the actual reach of these agreements, in terms of practice, is warranted.

[36] Council Framework Decision 2008/978/JHA of 18 December 2008 on the European Evidence Warrant for the purpose of obtaining objects, documents and data for use in proceedings in criminal matters, OJ L350/72.

[37] Council Framework Decision 2009/315/JHA of 26 February 2009 on the organization and content of the exchange of information extracted from criminal records between member states [2009] OJ L93/23.

[38] See for example Swiss Federal Act on Mutual Assistance in Criminal Matters of 20 March 1981; Thailand Act on Mutual Assistance in Criminal Matters 1992; UK Mutual Assistance in Criminal Matters Act; Act on International Judicial Cooperation in Criminal Matters, Sweden, 2000.

3.1.1 The 'regional' instruments

The existing regional instruments[39] for mutual assistance provide for a fairly extensive network of cooperation between countries within the relevant regional groupings. This is important since, as mentioned above, in practice a large percentage of mutual assistance work will be with the most proximate geographic neighbours. However, obviously the very nature of these agreements limits the scope of application to a particular geographic sphere. There are two important aspects to that geographic restriction. First, it limits quantitatively the number of mutual assistance relationships created. Additionally, while the agreements may cover the most numerous situations, they do not address cooperation between countries of different regions, which will often involve relationships which are the most difficult to manage in practice because of the differing cultural and legal traditions involved.

There are two notable exceptions to the network of 'regional agreements' for which the scope of application is broader than a particular geographic area. Mirroring the membership of the organization, the Harare Scheme stretches across several regions of the world and thus does not constitute a strictly 'regional' agreement. In this respect, it does have an impact on some cross-regional relationships that would otherwise be without a base for cooperation. However, its scope is still far from universal – limited to fifty-four member countries – most of which come from the same common law legal tradition. As a result, the Harare Scheme does not address many of the difficult challenges which arise primarily from the procedural differences between the major legal systems.

Similarly, the 1959 European Convention is open to both member and non-member states of the Council and Israel is a party to the 1959 European Convention as a 'non-member'. However, despite this principle, in reality the vast majority of the parties are European and most come from a 'civil law' tradition. Again there is the limitation in so far as the Convention has not proved an attractive instrument for most common law countries because its provisions are more suitable to the civil law tradition that predominates in continental Europe.

[39] See Chapter 5 in this volume.

3.1.2 The penal law conventions

Of overlapping application are the subject-specific multilateral instruments – in particular the drug and crime conventions. These have the benefit of a broader geographic scope and provisions which are designed to allow for the rendering of mutual assistance between states of different legal traditions. In addition, the 1988 Drug Convention has attained almost universal adherence and the TOC Convention and the Corruption Convention also have a very significant record of acceptance. However, the obvious limitation is the restriction to specific crime, albeit the treaties do address some of the most prominent forms of international crime.

3.1.3 The terrorism conventions

Similarly, the counter-terrorism conventions provide a basis for cooperation among most countries in the world. However, scope is again limited to particular types of terrorist crime and the instruments lack the detailed measures that can facilitate mutual assistance in practice.

3.1.4 Bilateral instruments and national law

And finally there are the bilateral cooperation instruments and the provisions of national law which are the most precise in terms of content and which have the potential to allow for the most effective mutual assistance. The limitation however is that while the number of bilateral instruments continues to increase only a handful of countries have an extensive network of such treaties.

To date the number of countries with national laws which permit mutual assistance without treaty is somewhat limited. Yet in terms of the effectiveness of mutual assistance, it is the basis that has the most future potential. It is in fact the only measure available whereby a state can take unilateral action to improve its ability to provide mutual assistance and thus it is also the most flexible measure in so far as amendments to it would not require any international process.

3.1.5 Summary

The existing network for mutual assistance is quite extensive in terms of its scope. In fact, one of the practical problems flowing from the 'patchwork' is that it can create confusion as to the appropriate instrument to apply when more than one may be applicable to any given situation. While it is not possible to say that a basis for mutual legal assistance exists for every country in every case, the existing combination of instruments spans a good portion of the globe, most significantly in relation to serious crime that is likely to have a transnational component. In addition, the growing reliance of states on national law, without the need for a treaty, means that the absence of laws and treaties in one country may be compensated for in another, with the result that mutual assistance will be possible despite the limitations in a particular country.

In addition, in the particular context of terrorism, post-9/11 and Security Council Resolution 1373, most countries are now parties to the vast majority of the counter-terrorism conventions. Thus, as between the parties to those conventions, there is a treaty base for mutual assistance and an obligation to render that assistance. What remains lacking, of course, is any procedural provisions for the actual practice of mutual assistance but that falls to be considered later. Importantly, the existing network for mutual assistance in counter-terrorism cases is the most expansive in relation to any specific form of crime save perhaps for drug cases.

3.2 *Effectiveness of existing network*

What has been described above must be qualified as the 'optimum' in terms of a network for cooperation. For there is a reality applicable to all treaties and conventions; they are nothing but paper in the absence of effective implementation. And, sadly, the international instruments for cooperation, like many other international instruments, suffer from chronic problems in terms of effective implementation.

Using the term broadly there are three components to effective implementation – ratification or accession, adoption of necessary national law and subsequent use of the convention or treaty in practice. A brief consideration of all three issues with reference to the various cooperation instruments is helpful.

3.2.1 Ratification and accession

International cooperation instruments have a mixed rate of success in terms of ratification or accession.

The most successful in this regard are bilateral treaties. Generally, given the resources involved, bilateral instruments will be negotiated in response to a particular need or, at the least, on a priority basis. As a result, necessity will drive the negotiation process and the subsequent ratification procedures. Yet, there are certainly instances where treaties are neglected post-negotiation, either because of resource constraints or a change of priorities or because obstacles may arise in the course of the domestic implementation process. But overall the challenges to ratification of bilateral instruments are not particularly significant.

The rate of success with respect to regional agreements can vary significantly. Some have gained a fairly high level of support, albeit it tends to be incremental progress. For example, 24 of the 34 state parties of the Organization of American States are parties to the OAS Convention and all 47 members of the Council of Europe (plus one non-member) are parties to the 1959 European Convention. At the same time, the ECOWAS Convention has yet to achieve sufficient ratifications to bring it into force. The IGAD Convention has only recently been adopted (2009) and thus it is too soon to consider and analyse ratification and accession efforts.

The penal law and counter-terrorism conventions have garnered an exceptionally high number of parties over a relatively short period of time. However, it is important to understand that the political pressure driving ratification has been the underlying subject of these conventions and not necessarily the issue of international cooperation. It remains to be seen if international cooperation as a stand-alone subject area would garner sufficient political 'gravitas' to support the necessary ratifications to bring such an international convention into force.

Thus, in assessing the need for a multilateral convention on mutual assistance it is necessary to bear in mind that adoption of such a convention does not mean that it will gather sufficient ratifications to come into force or that it will have such a reach so as to constitute a 'global' convention for mutual legal assistance.

3.2.2 Adoption of national laws

In terms of national law, there are distinct principles which apply in different states as to the necessity for national implementing law once a treaty has been ratified. However, even in states where ratified treaties become a part of domestic law, some legislation and procedural changes may be needed to ensure that the treaty can be fully implemented. This is particularly the case with treaties on cooperation which are closely tied to national criminal law and procedure and which directly affect the rights of individuals. The problem is more acute when it comes to states where treaties do not form part of domestic law and the implementation of the instrument is dependent entirely on national law. The reality is that there are far too many examples where adoption of, or amendments to, national law are slow to follow ratification of an international instrument. The instruments providing for international cooperation in criminal matters have suffered from this problem.

In the case of bilateral treaties, because of the one-to-one relationship involved, it is rare for a country to embark on such a negotiation without already having an implementing law in place or the intention to adopt one swiftly.

Implementation of regional agreements varies considerably. For example, most, though certainly not all, of the countries within the OAS, which have ratified the OAS Convention, have adopted implementing laws as necessary. The same is true with respect to the relevant European conventions, to the extent that national law is required to implement the instruments.

In contrast, the Harare Scheme – which has the potential to serve as a cooperation instrument between fifty-four countries – suffers from a lack of implementation. As the scheme is dependent upon the enactment of national laws to allow for assistance to be sought and rendered between member countries, the absence of such implementing legislation restricts the effectiveness of the Scheme in practice. However, over the past few years, the Harare Scheme has seen incremental progress in implementation with the adoption of more mutual assistance legislation in the member countries.

The challenges are significant with the international penal law and, to a lesser degree, the counter-terrorism conventions. Here the political drive to become parties to the conventions often results in a ratification or accession process which is far speedier than the measures for effective implementation. The TOC Convention provides a good illustration of the problem. For the third session of the Conference of the Parties to the Convention, the Secretariat issued an analytical report on implementation of the Convention.[40] The paper reported that only roughly 50 per cent of the parties to the Convention had responded to the questionnaire submitted, as of the summer of 2006. Of that 50 per cent, ten states reported not having mutual assistance legislation in place and eight different states indicated that they could not rely on the Convention as a basis for mutual assistance in the absence of a bilateral treaty, despite

[40] Analytical Report by the Secretariat on Implementation of the United Nations Convention against Transnational Organized Crime, UN Doc. CTOC/COP/2005/2/Rev. 1 (2005).

the Convention obligation to the contrary.[41] Various states reported an inability to provide certain types of assistance mandated by the Convention.[42] Paragraph 8 of Article 18 provides as follows: 'States Parties shall not decline to render mutual legal assistance pursuant to this Article on the ground of bank secrecy.' Five states reported that bank secrecy was a ground for refusal of assistance under their domestic legal framework. While these numbers may not seem high in isolation, considering they are taken from the 50 per cent of countries which even responded, it is not unreasonable to assume an equal, if not more significant, lack of implementation among all the parties to the Convention. Similar challenges arise with the 1988 Drug Convention and the Corruption Convention particularly as the provisions are similar in each convention and there is considerable overlap in terms of the state parties.

National legislation to implement mutual assistance obligations in the counter-terrorism context has been more favourable in the post-9/11 era. This is largely as a result of UN Security Council Resolution 1373 (SCR 1373) and the obligation to afford assistance reflected in paragraph 2(f). This requirement has motivated some states to include abbreviated mutual assistance provisions within counter-terrorism legislation, albeit limited to those types of investigations and prosecutions.[43] While not necessarily aimed at implementation of the conventions the effect has been to do so.

3.2.3 Use in practice

Use of the various treaties in practice is the hardest area to measure, especially in relation to multilateral instruments, because of the lack of oversight or statistics relating to their operation. Again, while there are bilateral instruments which are sometimes negotiated for political, as opposed to practical reasons, and thus may remain gathering dust on a shelf, overall these instruments are the most commonly used in mutual assistance practice.

The practice in relation to the regional agreements is once more uneven. The 1959 European Convention is probably the most used multilateral instrument and the Inter-American Convention, according to the available information, is increasingly applied quite successfully as a basis for assistance in that region, at least among the states which do not have supervening bilateral relationships. In contrast, while the CIS Conventions are widely

[41] *Ibid.*, 21, paras. 87–9. [42] *Ibid.*, 21–2, paras. 90–1.
[43] See, for example, Prevention of Terrorism Act, Act 2 of 2002 (Mauritius).

employed for cooperation much of the work is in the realm of extradition. There is little evidence of any use being made of the Caribbean and SADC agreements, and, as mentioned, the ECOWAS Treaty does not seem to have the drive of practical necessity which would bring it into force and make it available for use in practice. It is too soon to evaluate the effectiveness of the recently adopted ASEAN and SAARC Conventions.

What remains most puzzling is the slow application of the crime-specific conventions in practice. With respect to the 1988 Drug Convention and the counter-terrorism conventions, the absence of any 'review' or 'monitoring' mechanism makes it difficult to assess the use which has been made of the conventions for the purpose of mutual assistance over the years. The only data available are anecdotal information from relevant authorities which suggests limited, if any, use of these multilateral instruments for mutual assistance.

Slightly more information is available in terms of the two newest crime conventions because of the existence of the bodies[44] which consider the implementation of these instruments – regular conferences of the states which are parties to the conventions. Here again a recent Secretariat report on the TOC Convention highlights the challenges with gathering information on the use of the conventions:

> The secretariat, in the course of workshops and other training activities it organized, endeavoured to collect from competent authorities and practitioners information on cases where the Organized Crime Convention had been used as a basis for cooperation. It appeared that such specific information on cases was scattered among the many practitioners involved in international cooperation and that even the central authorities seldom had centralized data available on that matter.[45]

From the information that could be gathered, a slightly better picture was depicted with respect to the TOC Convention than historically has been the case, at least with regard to the 1988 Drug Convention. The report highlighted some examples of countries which had used the Convention for the purpose of mutual assistance.[46] While this is

[44] Conference of the Parties for the TOC; Conference of the States Parties for Corruption.

[45] UN Doc. CTOC/COP/2008/5 (2008), para. 28.

[46] Brazil provided detailed information on nine selected cases (from among many) where the Convention had been used successfully; the United States reported five cases for mutual assistance and Canada indicated that generally it had been used. Research indicated that Venezuela had used the Convention for cooperation as well (*ibid.*, 9–10 paras. 29–30).

encouraging, even if a part of the problem lies in the inaccessibility of data, the number of countries where evidence of practical use can be found – which is four – is not particularly significant in the face of the 149 state parties to the Convention.

3.2.4 Conclusions

It is not possible to reach any general conclusion as to the overall effectiveness of 'implementation' of the existing network of mutual assistance instruments as there is significant variation in terms of ratification, legal and practical implementation. But broad trends can be identified which are of relevance to the question of the practical effect of, and thus the need for, a multilateral mutual assistance convention.

First, excluding national law, bilateral instruments remain the most effective instruments in terms of implementation and use in practice.

In the context of regional agreements, it can be said that there is room for optimism, as there is increasing success. The 1959 European Convention, OAS Convention and to a lesser extent the Harare Scheme, are notable examples of the successful use of regional schemes for mutual assistance. It is interesting that these are the oldest of the regional instruments and the organizations associated to them have carried out intensive information and training programmes in support of implementation/use of the convention or scheme and in relation to mutual assistance practice.

For example, the OAS has an ongoing intensive programme in support of mutual assistance practice. Since 2003, meetings of Central Authorities and other Experts on Mutual Assistance and Extradition have convened every two years to discuss the practical challenges in practice in the region. Since 2000 a Hemispheric Information Exchange Network for Mutual Assistance in Criminal Matters and Extradition has been in development consisting of public and private websites and a secure communication network.[47] A review of the reports generated from the meetings indicates that these measures have had a positive effect on mutual assistance practice in the region and under the OAS Convention. This is an important consideration to keep in mind in assessing the most useful steps towards more effective mutual assistance.

At the same time, regional agreements in other regions have been much less successful or are too recent to assess. One particularly

[47] See: www.oas.org/juridico/mla/en/index.html.

disturbing phenomena is the lack of ratifications of instruments which have been adopted in order to bring them into force.

The problem is somewhat reversed in the case of the crime-specific treaties. All have entered into force in a relatively short period and have garnered significant support in terms of state parties. And yet they remain perhaps the least successful of the range of instruments in terms of practical application, at least to date. This lack of implementation and use is puzzling and a dearth of available information and survey-weary authorities makes it even more difficult to assess. It may be attributable to the speed of ratification which precludes effective implementation or to a lack of resources, knowledge and training. It is also possible that 'global' conventions do not have the immediacy of bilateral and regional instruments and thus the imperatives which drive domestic process are not present.

However, for the purpose of this chapter, the central issue is whether an international convention on mutual assistance would be more likely to suffer the fate of the crime-specific treaties because of its global nature or it would fare better, as in the case of some regional conventions, because it is an instrument dedicated to international cooperation.

3.3 *The quality of the content of existing instruments*

3.3.1 General content

An examination of existing instruments for mutual assistance – bilateral and multilateral – reveals a consistency in content that perhaps may be surprising to some. Generally, each of the instruments will cover – to a greater or lesser degree – the following:

- the scope of application (types of crimes or widest measure of assistance);
- the types of assistance;
- identification of authorities for the transmission and receipt of requests;
- content of requests;
- grounds of refusal;
- postponement of requests;
- execution of requests;
- limitation of use (MLA form of speciality protection);
- confidentiality; and
- specific provisions for the different types of assistance.

The details in each article will vary depending on when the instrument was drafted and the legal tradition of the states to which the instrument applies. However, even older instruments will still contain the basic framework for the rendering of assistance, in terms of the most common types of measures sought such as the taking of testimony or statements, search and seizure and the production of documents.

Where there is significant variation – especially as between multilateral and bilateral instruments – is in the applicable grounds of refusal – including whether dual criminality is a requirement for assistance or a ground of refusal – and in the nature of the procedures mandated for the specific types of assistance. These are understandable deviations which flow from the differing nature of bilateral and multilateral relationships.[48]

Thus, it can be expected that any global mutual assistance framework would follow the general practice in terms of the content. In addition, it is unlikely that any of the more specific provisions found in bilateral treaties would achieve sufficient consensus to be incorporated into such a multilateral instrument.

3.3.2 Developments in the content

Over the past twenty to thirty years the process of globalization has spurred developments in the area of international cooperation which has manifested itself most significantly in changes to extradition practice. Considerable improvements have been made, in particular as to the definition of 'extradition crime', the reduction of evidentiary requirements, redefining principles on the extradition of nationals and provisions for temporary extradition. As a result, the framework of an effective extradition treaty has changed considerably and the use of outdated instruments does significantly hamper extradition in practice.

In contrast, while clearly the most recent instruments relating to mutual assistance contain provisions which are more 'state of the art', the advancements in mutual assistance are not as dramatic in terms of the content of the treaties or instruments. The improvements have been much more with respect to the underlying practices, without the necessity for significant changes to the instruments upon which assistance is

[48] In general terms, multilateral instruments will tend to incorporate broader grounds of refusal given the application to potentially hundreds of treaty partners. Bilateral instruments also afford the opportunity to craft more specific procedural provisions designed for the two states involved in the agreement.

grounded. Generally, the most prominent differences in the more recent mutual assistance treaties are the entrenchment of some 'best practices' and the addition of some forms of assistance. Little, if any, variation appears in the existing measures of assistance or the general requirements or procedures.

The nature of the changes in terms of mutual assistance instruments is probably best illustrated by comparing the oldest of the crime-specific treaties – the 1988 Drug Convention and the most recent – the Corruption Convention. The main substantive additions in Article 46 of the latter convention are the new provisions on spontaneous transmission, temporary transfer and video conferencing as a means of hearing witnesses. While these are useful additions, they do not alter significantly the practice in mutual assistance where the most common types of compulsory measures employed remain those for the production of documents, search and seizure and the taking of statements and testimony. While the specific mention of video/satellite evidence is an enhancement with respect to the last of these measures, it is something which generally can be used by states without the necessity of mentioning it in the underlying instrument.

This point is further illustrated when one examines perhaps the most 'modern' multilateral mutual assistance instrument – the 2000 EU Convention on mutual assistance in criminal matters. Again the major developments in the Convention relate to measures such as spontaneous transmission and video conferencing and the inclusion of assistance with the interception of communications. While the last provision would be useful, it is unlikely to be accepted in any 'global' convention given the controversy which surrounds assistance with this most invasive of compulsory measures.

As mentioned, an important improvement in mutual assistance over the past several years has been the enhancement of the practice itself. For example, one of the most significant problems is ensuring that the evidence which is gathered is obtained in a form which is admissible in the proceedings in the requesting state. In the early days of mutual assistance, it was common for evidence to be gathered in a manner consistent with the procedures and practices of the requested state without regard to the requirements of the requesting state. As a result, the request would be technically fulfilled but the evidence was not useable. Over time, practices have developed to overcome these challenges. This principle has long been reflected in instruments for mutual assistance – with articles which call for the evidence to be gathered 'in accordance with the procedures specified in the request unless such procedures are contrary to the fundamental principles of the law of the requested state'.[49] However, the real change has come in the attitude of the officials executing the requests and the pragmatic compromises which have been achieved in practice.[50] While it is certainly helpful to have clear provisions in the relevant instruments which emphasize the importance of this principle, what is most essential is the practice which is adopted under the instrument.

In summary, a new multilateral instrument on mutual assistance would present an opportunity to expand the forms of assistance available and to enshrine best practices. However, it is unlikely that the convention would introduce any radical changes or additions which would make the instrument significantly more effective in terms of practice.

3.3.3 Specific forms of cooperation

There are two aspects of mutual assistance where there have been substantial advancements in the past few years which are not adequately captured in most bilateral or multilateral instruments; cooperation in the restraint, confiscation and repatriation of proceeds and instruments of crime and cooperation in relation to computer and computer-related crime.

On cooperation in asset confiscation, again the contrast between the 1988 Drug Convention and the Corruption Convention provides an apposite example. The 1988 Drug Convention is a seminal instrument in the field of proceeds of crime as it was the first to incorporate an obligation not only for mutual assistance but also for restraint and confiscation of proceeds of crime and international cooperation in that context. The 1988 Drug Convention places an obligation on parties to:

- Create an offence for money laundering and, subject to constitutional provisions, for the possession of proceeds of crime;
- Adopt provisions for the restraint and confiscation of proceeds and, subject to constitutional provisions, instruments of crime;
- Provide measures for restraining and confiscating proceeds and instruments of crime in response to a request for assistance from another state. (See in particular Articles 3, 5 and 7.)

[49] See, for example, Second Additional Protocol to the European Convention.

[50] For example, in the hearing of a witness, where it is important for representatives of the requesting state court and counsel to be present, arrangements are made to have the relevant authorities from both states present and the procedure is worked out among them.

It is of course the latter which is of most importance in the context of mutual assistance. At the time, the reference to asset confiscation was an important milestone in terms of advancing practices aimed at 'taking the profit' out of crime. However, the difficulty was that the practice was of such limited scope in the mid-1980s when the Convention was being negotiated, very little was included in terms of detailed provisions or procedures. Similarly bilateral and regional mutual assistance treaties adopted in the same era or shortly thereafter may contain a reference to assistance with asset confiscation but will not contain much in terms of detailed procedures.

In contrast, asset confiscation and more importantly asset recovery, forms a much more significant component of the Corruption Convention. The expansion of these provisions in the Convention was of course driven by the subject matter; it was a direct result of cases of 'grand corruption' where governments had been defrauded of significant sums of money by corrupt officials and leaders and the funds had been moved to another jurisdiction. There were enormous challenges to tracking the funds and obtaining restraint and confiscation, and even more difficulties in repatriation of the assets. In many instances recovery of the funds has been painfully slow – taking years – or impossible. Thus, considerable attention was paid to the subject in the context of the Corruption Convention with the result that, *inter alia*, provisions on cooperation in asset confiscation, incorporated into a separate section on international cooperation in asset confiscation and a chapter dedicated to asset recovery, are much enhanced. While the asset recovery provisions may to a large extent be of most relevance in the context of corruption crimes and thus this convention, many of the general additions in terms of mutual assistance in asset confiscation are of more general application and use. Such provisions generally cannot be found in treaties which pre-date the Corruption Convention.

Similarly, one of the significant challenges in mutual assistance arises when the crime involves use of the technology and particularly the internet. When information from internet service providers is required, invariably most countries will have to seek assistance from a foreign state. And given the speed at which such information can be lost, 'normal' mutual assistance is of limited value. As a direct result of these challenges, new measures are needed for such cases. The best example of the kind of comprehensive regime required is the Council of Europe Convention on Cyber Crime (Cyber Crime

Convention).[51] As is the case with asset confiscation, very few mutual assistance instruments contain provisions of this nature although interestingly the Harare Scheme was updated recently to incorporate measures relating to computer data.[52]

In these two specific areas therefore, a new multilateral instrument on mutual assistance would be advantageous in terms of the additional provisions which could be inserted for asset confiscation and freezing and accessing evidence generated by computer and computer-related technology.

3.3.4 Counter-terrorism

One final point is worth reiterating, albeit it has been highlighted previously. For counter-terrorism investigations and prosecutions, there is room for significant improvement in the content of the mutual assistance components of the existing conventions as these instruments contain little, if any, detail regarding the content or modalities of mutual assistance. While the inclusion of a specific reference to mutual assistance in SCR 1373 has had an impact on the practice of states in this area, the resolution similarly creates, at best, an obligation on states to cooperate without providing any further practical assistance. A multilateral mutual assistance convention of general application, including with respect to terrorism investigations, could have the advantage of supplementing the existing regime for mutual assistance in the case of those specific types of investigation.

4 Lack of treaty basis as an impediment to cooperation

While the analysis above of the existing instruments is important to the question of a multilateral convention, an equally imperative issue is whether a lack of instruments is a significant impediment to mutual assistance.

It is trite to state that there are currently significant problems with mutual assistance. Practitioners repeatedly describe a process which is

[51] 2001 Council of Europe Convention on Cyber Crime, Council of Europe Treaty Series No. 185, twenty-six parties.

[52] See Scheme Relating to Mutual Assistance in Criminal Matters within the Commonwealth including amendments made by Law Ministers in April 1990, November 2002 and October 2005.

impossibly slow, replete with delay and non-responsiveness. These challenges are the *raison d'être* of this book project and this chapter.

It is beyond the scope of this chapter to consider in detail the reasons for the difficulties in mutual assistance practice. However, to the extent possible, it is necessary to touch upon the primary challenges, in order to determine the relative importance to attach to the development of a new multilateral instrument.

There is little documentation available to assist in assessing the key problems in mutual assistance practice. Again, as noted above, it is the practitioners who are best placed to identify the key issues and it is often difficult to retrieve that data from them. However some insight can be garnered from a consideration of various expert and other reports which have considered international cooperation, in particular, mutual assistance.

By way of example, in the recent report generated by the Conference of the States Parties to the Corruption Convention, some key issues identified in international cooperation were the practical problems such as 'the absence of direct channels of communication for the transmission of information needed for the execution of a request, differences in the legal systems of the requesting and requested states and the need to translate documentation supporting the request'.[53]

In 1993 an expert working group was convened by UNODC on mutual assistance in respect of the 1988 Drug Convention.[54] Four key problem areas identified were as follows:

1. problems with identification of, and communication between, the authorities responsible for handling requests;
2. problems with infrastructure, roles and resources for these authorities;
3. procedural and substantive constraints in the requested state which prevent full execution of requests;
4. form and contents of requests, particularly lack of critical information.[55]

[53] UN Doc. CAC/COSP/2008/15 (2008), at www.unodc.org/documents/treaties/UNCAC/COSP/session2/V0851339e.pdf.

[54] UNODC, Report of the Expert Working Group on Mutual Legal Assistance and Related International Confiscation (1993), at www.unodc.org/pdf/lap_maewg_1993_final.pdf.

[55] *Ibid.*, para. 1.5.

Eight years later, in 2001, a second expert group was convened on the subject of mutual assistance. The recommendations of that group on 'best practices' centred on strengthening the effectiveness of central authorities, improving communication as to requests and legal system information, improving the quality of the requests and reducing impediments – legal and practical – to effective execution. The two reports illustrate that despite progress, the general themes as to problem areas and recommended 'best practice' have remained strikingly similar.

A review of the reports and recommendations of the OAS meetings on mutual assistance reveals a similar focus on establishing functional central authorities, reduction of practical impediments and improving networks and information exchange on legal system requirements.

Admittedly, all of the reports above were generated in a context where there was an existing framework for cooperation at issue.[56] Still the discussions therein are extremely relevant in so far as they highlight a consistent pattern of problems and best practice recommendations which are identified regardless of the existence of a treaty base for assistance.

Repeatedly, experience and anecdotal information reinforces the point that the key problems in mutual assistance are lack of effective authorities, problems with communication, legal and practical impediments to execution and incomplete or incomprehensible requests.

In summary, there is at least some evidence to suggest that the most significant challenges to mutual assistance lie in these problems in practice and not in an absence of a basis for cooperation.

5 The necessity for treaty-based assistance

One final issue to be addressed is whether there is a need for a treaty base for mutual legal assistance at all.

Mutual assistance is a creature of evolution as opposed to development. It is not the product of considered discussion and debate but rather a means of cooperation between states which has been driven by necessity and moulded by practice. Its features have been crafted using extradition practice as a model, since it is the oldest and most well-known form of international cooperation in criminal matters. Because extradition has been, and is still, conducted for the most part on the basis

[56] Corruption Convention, 1988 Drug Convention, and Inter-American Convention, respectively.

of treaty, mutual assistance has been viewed traditionally as requiring a treaty base. However, as indicated above, some states now render assistance solely on the basis of national law. The time has thus arrived to challenge the hypothesis that a treaty is necessary for effective mutual assistance.

To begin with, it is difficult to determine what added benefit is generated by a treaty-based process for this form of cooperation.

Perhaps the most fundamental point is that a treaty creates a binding obligation between states to render the assistance in accordance with the terms set out therein. In the absence of a treaty, it is the principle of international comity which must be relied upon, providing no certainty and no 'leverage' to a requesting state. But advocating the necessity for treaty-based assistance on the basis of this principle mixes two important concepts – ability to assist and obligation to assist. While it is helpful for states to have the latter, it is essential for states to have the former. And ability or capacity to render assistance is best advanced and regulated through national law.

As to the obligation between states, it is of course important, particularly for states with 'high traffic' between them. For this reason, bilateral instruments remain a central component of mutual assistance practice. Yet, unlike other subject areas, mutual assistance does not involve competing interests; it is a matter of mutual benefit to states. The underlying premise for international cooperation in criminal matters is the commitment of both states to combating crime – in particular transnational and international crime. It is not evident, therefore, that the existence of a treaty obligation will enhance assistance on a practical level. In essence, if the common interest in combating crime is not present already or there are political problems in the relations between the states generally, no cooperation framework can create it or overcome those hurdles.

It is also important to understand that mutual assistance, even rendered pursuant to treaty, is of an inherently discretionary nature. Whether the treaty contains a single broad ground of refusal or a detailed list, if a state is not willing to cooperate in a particular case, a basis for refusal will always be found. Even with that reality, those instances of refusal are extremely rare. Practitioners consistently recount that the number of times requests for assistance are refused through invocation of a formal 'ground of refusal' are minimal. The most common reason for failure of a request is the inadequacies of the request itself and a lack of sufficient information. Thus, it does not appear that the creation of an 'obligation to assist' is a particularly strong argument in favour of maintaining a treaty-based approach to assistance.

A treaty of course can also play a significant role in enshrining protections for individuals. In the process of extradition for example, where an individual can be forced exceptionally across a national border into another state, one of the functions of a treaty is to provide those protections. However, unlike extradition, mutual assistance does not affect directly the liberty of an individual. While evidence obtained may be used to detain a person for trial and, perhaps ultimately, lead to imprisonment, the restriction on liberty will flow from the judicial process in the requesting state and not from the transmission of evidence gathered in the requested state. In this context, there is not a similar need to enshrine protections in an international instrument. Rather, what needs to be regulated in mutual assistance is the process by which evidence is gathered or assets are frozen or confiscated, to ensure that the procedures employed are consistent with the fundamental rights of those affected by these compulsory measures in the requested state. For the most part, such protections are not dependent on assurances from the requesting state but rather constitute essential concerns which are best addressed by national law. To the extent that some assurances are required – such as limiting the use to be made of the evidence provided or addressing questions related to the ultimate penalty arising from any prosecution in which the evidence is used – those can be obtained on a case-by-case basis without the necessity for an underlying treaty.

Given the absence of a strong motivation for retaining treaty-based assistance there is, on the other hand, much to commend mutual assistance premised on national law. It opens up the possibility of seeking and providing assistance from and to any country in the world with respect to a broad range of crimes. At the same time, the requested state is protected from any potential abuses as the process is regulated by national law and will invariably have built in discretion. In so far as there are certain types of criminality which the international community considers sufficiently grave as to require the broadest measure of mutual assistance, it is most likely already covered by existing international agreements. Assistance based on national law is also much less resource intensive than the negotiation of multiple treaties or a multilateral initiative. While of course there are problems with the use of national laws – if they are designed in an inflexible manner – this goes more to the content of the law than the underlying principle of assistance premised on national law.

On balance, there is a good case for moving away from a treaty-based approach to mutual assistance to the more flexible process of reliance on national law.

6 General conclusions and recommendations

6.1 Scope

A multilateral instrument on mutual assistance in criminal matters would create, in principle, a global scope for such assistance. However, the reach of the existing network of instruments is already such that for most serious crime there is a base upon which a state could seek or provide mutual assistance. In terms of existing gaps that states face, two measures would be more effective to address those lacunae than the resource-intensive undertaking of a new convention:

1. to increase efforts towards ratification and effective implementation of all the existing instruments; and
2. to encourage states to adopt or amend their national laws to allow for mutual assistance to be sought and rendered without the requirement for a treaty.

In the specific context of terrorism, if a state has ratified and implemented all of the counter-terrorism conventions, it is difficult to envisage a terrorism offence for which assistance could not be sought, except with respect to another state which is not a party to one of the relevant conventions. But a general multilateral convention on mutual assistance would have minimal practical effect in that scenario as there would be no guarantee that any convention adopted would meet with better success in terms of ratification. And, in relation to terrorism, a state would probably have better results citing SCR 1373 as a means to 'persuade' another state towards cooperation. Again, in the specific context of terrorism, the solutions outlined above would be far more efficient in terms of extending the basis for mutual assistance.

6.2 Effectiveness in practice

As to effectiveness in practice, nothing in the history of mutual assistance instruments would suggest that a general multilateral convention would meet with greater success in terms of implementation and use in practice than the existing instruments. The broad lessons of history in this field are:

- the most effective tools are bilateral instruments;
- multilateral instruments have varying success rates and considerable time and effort is required to achieve effective practice under them; and
- regional instruments appear to be more useful in practice than global crime-specific conventions as a basis for cooperation.[57]

In terms of increasing effectiveness in practice, time and effort would be better allocated to measures designed to increase the use that is made of the existing counter-terrorism conventions as a basis for cooperation, than in negotiating a new instrument.

6.3 *Quality of assistance*

The negotiation of a multilateral convention for mutual assistance would provide an opportunity to craft an instrument which reflects the current best practice and contains 'modernized' provisions. However, the gains from a 'modern' convention would be minimal in terms of enhancing practice. Much more can be accomplished by focusing on flexible national laws, better communication, trained authorities and the reduction of practical and legal impediments to execution. In other words emphasis on best practices will produce much better results than the adoption of a multilateral framework. On balance, it is difficult to justify the deployment of efforts and resources towards the negotiation of a convention when urgent attention is required on the actual practice of mutual assistance.

As for mutual assistance in the restraint and confiscation of proceeds and instruments of crime, there is little doubt that the current regime lacks sufficient provisions to address this new and complex form of international cooperation. However, the best solution to this problem is not an international convention. The most effective regimes for asset confiscation require the introduction of concepts which would be highly controversial in a broad multilateral context.[58] The provisions of the Corruption Convention represent perhaps the best progress that can be made on the issue at this stage and only time will tell if those are sufficiently advanced. Therefore, efforts towards effective

[57] Though this may change over time, particularly with reference to the most recent of the penal conventions.

[58] See, for example, Recommendations of the Commonwealth Working Group on Asset Confiscation (at: www.thecommonwealth.org).

implementation of that Convention and the development of national laws relating to confiscation should be given priority.

A similar concern exists with respect to a global instrument to address the complex issues in mutual assistance involving technology. Here the dangers are perhaps more significant given that there is already the high-quality Cyber Crime Convention in place, which is open to accession by non-member states of the Council of Europe. This too is an issue which is probably best resolved through pursuing changes to national law and should be left for further consideration in that context, particularly given the broad range of capacity in this particular field as between states. There would be a significant danger of creating an instrument which would be regressive, as opposed to progressive, in this context.

This leaves the issue of the current regime for mutual assistance in the terrorism conventions which admittedly is woefully inadequate in terms of the practical guidance provided. However, the solution to that particular deficiency is not a simple one. One option would be to create a multilateral instrument specific to counter-terrorism. However, there are many problems associated with any proposal to create a crime-specific multilateral regime for mutual assistance.

Already, significant practical problems in having separate 'crime-specific' regimes for mutual assistance have been identified. The penal conventions provide a good example in this regard in that a multiplication of instruments has led to problems with responsible authorities, channels for requests and the variation in standards between the relevant instruments.

In addition, if a stand-alone instrument were contemplated, the starting point would be a definition of the crime of 'terrorism', which would immediately bring into play the same political reality which surrounds the draft comprehensive convention on terrorism. While one theoretical possibility would be to incorporate more detailed provisions on mutual assistance into that draft convention, the practical chances for such amendment are minimal and the problems with finalization and adoption of that draft convention would remain in any event.

An alternative would be to consider protocols to the existing crime-specific counter-terrorism conventions. Again one would need to consider whether that is a realistic or even sensible option when the central issue with all of these conventions is effective implementation and use in national systems.

And, finally, on the point which is at the core of the issue – enhancing mutual assistance on the ground – among the problems most often identified with mutual assistance, absence of a treaty base does not appear to be among the priority concerns. And particularly in the context of terrorism – where states can rely on various instruments to evoke an obligation to assist – there is no indication that the absence of a multilateral instrument constitutes a major impediment to effective mutual assistance in practice.

On balance, a consideration of the factors outlined above leads to the conclusion that although there would be some benefits, there is no significant need for a multilateral convention to enhance the practice of mutual assistance generally or in the context of counter-terrorism investigation and prosecutions.

Instead, the challenge in mutual assistance lies in ensuring that the existing instruments live up to their potential in terms of implementation. Efforts must be dedicated to improving the practice of mutual assistance and the entrenchment of best practices that can lead to effective international cooperation 'on the ground'.

5

The role of regional organizations in promoting cooperation on counter-terrorism matters: the European and the African institutions in a comparative perspective

MARTIN EWI

1 Introduction

Counter-terrorism (CT)[1] has been a pre-eminent focus of the past decade following the herculean and devastating terrorist attacks against the United States of America on 11 September 2001, or what was codenamed '9/11'. In the words of Magdalena Grajny, '9/11 was a turning point in world history. Events of that day not only shook the whole world, but also ushered in a new era of terrorism.'[2] As the most prevalent if not preponderant issue of the decade, counter-terrorism did not only emerge as the topmost priority of international politics, it also attracted a multitude of actors, each claiming a specific niche. Among them are regional organizations (ROs),[3] which, in the international hierarchy, are often placed in the space between the United Nations (UN) and states. The involvement of ROs in CT matters revived

[1] In this chapter, the term 'counter-terrorism' (CT) refers to all the means and measures taken by states, regional and international organizations and other actors to combat and prevent terrorism. See for example Thomas Mockaitis's definition in T. Mockaitis (ed.), *The 'New' Terrorism: Myths and Reality* (Stanford, CA: Stanford University Press, 2008), 100.

[2] M. Grajny, 'The European Union Counterterrorism Policy before and after the 9/11 Attacks: To What Extent Does the European Union Have an Integrated Policy towards Terrorism?', *terroryzm!com* papers (2009), www.terroryzm.com/the-european-union-counterterrorism.htm.

[3] Regional organizations have been defined variously by different scholars. For the purpose of this chapter, we are concerned here with organizations whose membership is restricted to states occupying a specific geographic space and/or sharing a common historical, cultural, political and economic heritage. These include, for example, the AU, EU, ASEAN (Association of South East Asian Nations), SAARC (South Asian Association for Regional Cooperation), LAS (League of Arab States) and the OAS. A common trait of such organizations is that they bear the names of the regions that they represent.

the debate among scholars as to what role such organizations play in international relations, not least on an issue that had traditionally been the high prerogative of states.

The previous militarization of CT, particularly in the period prior to 9/11, further strengthened scepticism about the significance of ROs' contribution to what was described in colloquial terms as the 'global war on terrorism (GWOT)'[4] in the aftermath of 9/11. ROs' active participation in the GWOT in the first post-9/11 decade, however, demonstrates a solid record of achievements that have firmly established them as key actors that shape the GWOT.

ROs offer a wide range of services to their member states but the promotion of cooperation remains their principal and defining task.[5] How this cooperation is achieved is itself a complex undertaking, influenced by a variety of factors including historical kinship, political constellations, nature of the issue and the institutional design of each RO. Just as ROs are designed differently and operate in different political, socio-economic and cultural milieus, their counter-terrorism cooperation activities in the post-9/11 decade have also varied significantly across geographic regions. This variation may further be explained by differences in terrorism threat perceptions among states and across regions. ROs tend to be more active where the threat of terrorism is perceived to be high. As a result, ROs' CT cooperation has been wide-ranging, encompassing military, political and economic activities. While some ROs such as NATO and the EU have played a more prominent international role, others such as the African Union, Association of South East Asian Nations (ASEAN), and the Organization of American States have confined their CT activities to their respective geographic spaces.

Despite certain inherent and reputed weaknesses, ROs' major contribution to the GWOT resonates in five salient areas: (1) norms and standards setting; (2) coordination and the promotion of a cohesive regional approach; (3) delivery or the facilitation of technical assistance; (4) advocating human

[4] The term, 'global war on terrorism' refers to various efforts and initiatives taken by states, international and regional organizations, and other actors in the international system to prevent and combat terrorism in all its forms and manifestations. The term has evolved from its first use by the then US President, George W. Bush, who declared a 'global war on terror' in response to 9/11. From its inception in 2001, it has been used to denote the ensuing US military campaign against al-Qaeda and other terrorist networks. See, for example, 'War on Terror', *Wikipedia*, at http://en.wikipedia.org/wiki/War_on_Terror.

[5] According to Barbara Koremenos, Charles Lipson and Duncan Snidal, 'states devise institutions to promote cooperation and make it more resilient' ('The Rational Design of International Institutions' (2001) 55 *International Organization* 766).

rights protection in states' CT activities; and (5) cooperation with the UN in the implementation of international CT norms. The main thrust of this chapter is to illuminate and assess the CT responses of European and African regional organizations in these five areas. In doing so, the chapter seeks to compare and contrast the different schemes and strategies used by the Council of Europe (CoE) and the EU and the AU to craft and consolidate cooperation on CT matters. It is argued that though not originally designed as specialized anti-terrorism mechanisms, ROs have, however, played an instrumental and catalytic role in promoting cooperation and consolidating multilateralism in the GWOT, and that their mere involvement has helped to strengthen the moral imperative of the GWOT. Eric Rosand makes a forceful case for the utility of ROs in the GWOT in his assertion that 'they offer an ideal forum for building trust, information sharing, developing strategies that can take into account cultural and other contextual issues, and undertaking region-specific initiatives or other actions that complement and build upon global counterterrorism objectives'.[6] Their mastery of regional dynamics, including geography, culture and politics, as well as their proximity to states arguably give them a competitive advantage over other competitive multilateral institutions in addressing localized security problems, particularly at an early stage, whereby most states would otherwise not bring to the United Nations. Sudan for example, insisted on the AU-led mediation at the early stages of the conflict in Darfur.

This chapter is divided into five main sections. Following section 1, which sets out the introduction, section 2 examines the terrorism threat perceptions in Europe and Africa, which is often used to explain differences in prioritization and responses to terrorism, based on the axiom that the higher the perceived threat, the higher the priority and the more robust the CT actions states are likely to take. Section 3 compares and contrasts the actions of European and African organizations in the above-mentioned five salient areas, with a view to illustrating variation in strategies aimed at building cooperation among states. Through the discussion on norms and standards setting, the paper highlights the key elements of regional definitions of terrorism, the main legal frameworks and the CT positions of the main European and African organizations including the Council of Europe, the EU and the AU. The main observation is that, while there exists no consensus on a common definition of terrorism at the global level, it is a less

[6] E. Rosand, 'Global Terrorism: Multilateral Responses to an Extraordinary Threat' (2007) *Coping with Crisis*, Working Paper Series 9, www.globalct.org/images/content/pdf/articles/coping_with_crisis.pdf.

serious issue at the regional level, where most regional CT instruments contain for consensus regional definitions of terrorism. It is as a consequence of the proliferation of regional definitions that has hindered efforts to adopt a common international definition. In section 4, the chapter provides an appraisal of the role of ROs in promoting cooperation on CT matters in order to assess their strengths and challenges. This is followed by a conclusion and some recommendations for strengthening the role of ROs in promoting cooperation on CT matters in section 5.

2 Terrorism threat perceptions in Europe and Africa

The intensity of counter-terrorism cooperation and actions or how ROs prioritize counter-terrorism is largely a function of how states perceive the threat of terrorism. If states perceive the threat to be high, they are likely to accord a high priority to counter-terrorism. This perception is often influenced by the pattern and intensity of terrorist incidents as well as peer pressure. For example, after 9/11, the United States and a number of European countries exerted political pressure on other states to treat terrorism as a serious security threat deserving appropriate national measures. A common perception or shared understanding of the nature and gravity of the threat is important, or as Oldřich Bureš puts it, 'a key prerequisite for the design and execution of any security policy'.[7] It is also a key requirement for states to cooperate on CT matters. Europe and Africa have both been plagued by terrorism to different degrees. Though the two regions have their peculiar threats and vulnerability patterns, there are increasing links between terrorism in both regions largely due to globalization, the global jihad networks, geographical and historical affinities as well as emigration. For example, terrorists in Africa have targeted European interests including citizens, businesses and diplomatic infrastructures. For example, since 2010, Europeans have been the main victims of a series of kidnappings in the Sahel, particularly in southern Algeria, Mali, Niger and Mauritania. In one of the largest hostage crisis incident in Africa, a break-away faction of Al-Qaeda in the land of Islamic Maghreb (AQIM) led by an Algerian fugitive Mokhtar Belmokhtar, took over 800 people hostage including foreigners – among them were citizens from France, the UK, Norway, Romania, and Ireland, at the Tigantourine gas facility in the Algerian South-eastern city of In Amenas.

[7] O. Bureš, 'Perceptions of the Terrorist Threat among EU Member States' (2010) 4 *Central European Journal of International and Security Studies* 51. See electronic version www.cejiss.org/issue/2010-volume-4-issue-1/bures (accessed 10 November 2011).

The four-day crisis that began on 16 January 2013, cost the lives of at least 39 foreign hostages including Europeans. Furthermore, Africans living in Europe have been implicated in terrorist attacks against European states such as the 2004 Madrid train bombings and the 2005 London bombings.[8] Some studies have emphasized these links in terms of the use of Europe for the [cross]radicalization or what may be termed 'jihadization' of Africans born or living in Europe.[9] In spite of these links, terrorism threat perceptions in Europe and Africa differ in many respects. This section aims to explain the trends in the terrorism perceptions of Europe and Africa, in order to understand differences in European and African responses to terrorism.

2.1 European perceptions

Terrorism as a concept is believed to have emerged in Europe, and the continent has remained under its spell for more than two hundred years since it first rose to the fore in the late 1790s during the French Revolution.[10] In 1893, Auguste Vaillant, a French anarchist, bombed the Chamber of Deputies in France, injuring twenty deputies,[11] in what represented a classic act of the modern phenomenon of terrorism. Scholars such as Michael Burleigh have traced the roots of the phenomenon of modern terrorism to the emergence of 'Fenians' or the Irish Republican Brotherhood in Dublin in the mid-nineteenth century.[12] The resurgence of terrorism in Europe in the 1960s and 1970s, culminating in the 1972 Munich Olympics massacre, and the storming of OPEC Ministerial meeting in Vienna are often identified as the beginning of the contemporary trend in Europe.[13]

Arguably, Europe as a geographic entity has been seriously affected by terrorism, accounting for a high number of terrorist incidents,

[8] See K. Archick, 'Muslims in Europe: Promoting Integration and Countering Extremism', Congressional Research Service (2011), 1–2.

[9] See, for example, M. D. Silber and A. Bhatt, 'Radicalization in the West: The Homegrown Threat', New York City Police Department Intelligence Division (2007), 22. For a better appreciation of radicalization in Europe, see L. Vidino, 'Radicalization, Linkage, and Diversity: Current Trends in Terrorism in Europe', *RAND Occasional Paper* (2011).

[10] For a comprehensive discussion on the origins of terrorism in Europe, see P. Bobbitt, *Terror and Consent: The Wars for the Twenty-First Century* (New York: Anchor, 2009).

[11] See 'List of terrorist incidents', *Wikipedia*: http://en.wikipedia.org/wiki/List_of_terrorist_incidents&action.htm.

[12] M. Burleigh, *Blood and Rage: A Cultural History of Terrorism* (2009), 2–26.

[13] See for example, V. Grammatikas, 'EU Counter-Terrorist Policies: Security vs. Human Rights' (2006) 2, at www.humsec.eu/cms/index.php?id=341.

though more terrorist attacks have been directed against Americans outside America. The current threat of terrorism to Europe is both domestic[14] or home-grown and international or transnational,[15] but until 9/11 most CT focus in Europe was on domestic terrorism.[16] According to the TWEED dataset, about 2,938 internal terrorist attacks occurred in eighteen West European countries from 1950 to 2004.[17] The causes of the threats and vulnerabilities in Europe are often identified with the global jihad led by al-Qaeda and its affiliates in Europe and around the world that often prey on Islamic radicalization and extremism; ideologically motivated groups such as the Baader Meinhof gang or the Rote Armée Faktion,[18] Red Brigades;[19] as well as nationalist or separatist groups such as the IRA,[20] ETA[21] and ELA (Basque Workers' Solidarity).[22] Despite this seeming widespread threat, EU members, as

[14] See for example recent attacks in Sweden (in December 2010) and Norway (in July 2011). For detail, see www.bbc.co.uk/news/world-europe-11978389 and www.bbc.co.uk/news/world-europe-14256712.

[15] Domestic or home-grown terrorism refers to the threat of terrorism which is caused by internal factors and perpetrated by citizens of the same country. This may include the lone-wolf phenomenon. International or transnational terrorism refers to the threat of terrorism caused by external or global factors such as the notion of global Islamic jihad or the global al-Qaeda ideology. The perpetrators may be foreign or citizens of the same country who are acting on the instructions or call from a supranational terrorist organization or movement such as al-Qaeda. For more on domestic and international terrorism, see K. Kis-Katos, H. Liebert and G. G. Schulze, 'On the Origin of Domestic and International Terrorism' (2010) University of Freiburg Department of International Economic Policy Discussion Paper Series No.12, 1–3. See, for more information on the different forms of terrorism, the Introduction to this volume.

[16] See M. Den Boer, '9/11 and the Europeanisation of Anti-Terrorism Policy: A Critical Assessment' (2003) Groupement d'Études et de Recherches Notre Europe Policy Papers Series No. 6, 1–2.

[17] See J. Eugene, 'Terrorism in Western Europe: Event Data (TWEED)', at http://folk.uib.no/sspje/tweed.htm.

[18] See complete profile and history, www.baader-meinhof.com/. See also http://news.bbc.co.uk/2/hi/6314559.stm.

[19] For detail, see www.historyofwar.org/articles/weapons_red_brigades.html. See also http://en.wikipedia.org/wiki/Red_Brigades.

[20] See profile www.fas.org/irp/world/para/ira.htm. See also http://en.wikipedia.org/wiki/Irish_Republican_Army.

[21] For detail, see brief history and timeline, see www.guardian.co.uk/world/2011/oct/21/eta-timeline-history-short. See also http://en.wikipedia.org/wiki/ETA.

[22] For detail on ELA, see http://en.wikipedia.org/wiki/Basque_Workers%27_Solidarity. For a complete list of terrorist groups in Europe see Wikipedia http://en.wikipedia.org/wiki/List_of_designated_terrorist_organizations. See also, M. Levitt, *'Islamic Extremism in Europe Beyond al Qaeda: Hamas and Hezbollah in Europe'* (Statement, Subcommittee on Europe and Emerging Threats, Committee on International Relations, United States House of Representatives, 2005).

Oldřich Bureš finds in a study, still differ in their analyses of both the nature and salience of the threats posed by contemporary terrorism.[23] According to Bureš, 'before 9/11, only six EU members had perceived terrorism as a threat to the extent that they actually defined it as a serious crime and/or national security threat'.[24] Similarly, Edwin Bakker[25] and Konstantinos Drakos and Catherine Müller[26] demonstrate in their studies key differences in terrorist threat perceptions among European countries. These differences mainly exist between countries that regularly experience terrorism and those that rarely do. While the former consider counter-terrorism a priority, the latter do not consider terrorism or counter-terrorism a national priority. Despite these differences among member states, counter-terrorism, particularly after 9/11 and following the Madrid and London bombings, emerged as one of the key priority issues for Europe as more members perceived the threat to be high.[27] This is evident in the resources allocated by the EU to fight terrorism as well as the counter-terrorism instruments adopted by the Union. In addition, the EU has defined the threat far beyond its borders and has taken a prominent international role in the promotion of counter-terrorism cooperation.[28] Counter-terrorism has therefore become an important part of European cooperation although it was not a self-defined function in the different incarnations of the EU prior to the 1970s. It is indeed the high vulnerabilities of individual European countries and the acknowledgement of the fact that no country is capable of preventing and combating the threat of terrorism single-handedly that has triggered the unconditional cooperation among EU members. It should also be noted that the debate among scholars about the differences in threat perception is only important for understanding the internal or micro-political dynamics of counter-terrorism. At the macro-level, however, there seems to be a general consensus among CoE and EU members about the gravity of the threat of terrorism.

[23] Bureš, 'Perceptions of the Terrorist Threat'. [24] *Ibid.*, 52.

[25] E. Bakker, 'Differences in Terrorist Threat Perceptions in Europe', in D. Mahncke and J. Monar (eds.), *International Terrorism: A European Response to a Global Threat?* (Brussels: Peter Lang, 2006), vol. III, 47–62.

[26] K. Drakos and C. Müller, 'Terrorism Risk Concern in Europe' (2010) Economics of Security Working Paper Series No. 37.

[27] See the Introduction to this volume.

[28] For details on EU counter-terrorism actions abroad, see P. Wennerholm, E. Brattberg and M. Rhinard, 'The EU as a Counter-Terrorism Actor Abroad: Finding Opportunities, Overcoming Constraints' (2010) EPC Issue Paper No. 60.

2.2 African perceptions

In April 2012, a rebel movement calling itself the National Movement for the Liberation of Azawad (MNLA) joined forces with Islamist and terrorist organizations; flaunting their newly acquired weapons from the Libyan black market, they defeated the Malian government and occupied northern Mali, or two thirds of the country. The eruption of the Malian crisis and the rapidity with which the Malian government fell was symptomatic of the fragility of the African states and the gravity of the threat of terrorism. It triggered a French-led intervention, followed by a West African-led intervention – Marking the second African intervention forces to fight terrorism (after the African mission in Somalia).

Collective action against terrorism at the continental level in Africa is fairly new since terrorism first became a concern in 1992. The 'Africanization' of counter-terrorism has, however, been slow. Even with the tragic terrorist bombings in Kenya and Tanzania in 1998 still fresh in the minds of many Africans, counter-terrorism never truly attracted attention and many saw the GWOT not of the continent's making but as a Western-imposed agenda. The different dimensions of terrorism and the scope of vulnerabilities in Africa have been well appraised by a number of experts and scholars.[29] Andre Le Sage, for example, investigates the variation of the threat of terrorism in the five subregions in Africa and offers compelling findings – with 35 of the 53 countries surveyed described as 'low level' threat with little or no terrorist presence, 11 countries with 'moderate' threat level and 7 countries with 'significant' threat level.[30]

These figures are indicative of the differences in terrorism threat perceptions among African countries, with North Africa having the largest concentration of states with a significant level threat, joined by East Africa, while two regions – the Indian Ocean and Central Africa – are generally perceived to have a low-level threat. Since the publication of *African Counterterrorism Cooperation: Assessing Regional and Subregional Initiatives* in 2007, new trends in terrorism have emerged. The epicentre of terrorism on the continent has shifted from North

[29] See for example, S. Makinda, 'History and Root Causes of Terrorism in Africa', in W. Okumu and A. Botha (eds.), *Understanding Terrorism in Africa: In Search of an African Voice* (Pretoria: Institute for Security Studies, 2006), 15–21; A. Botha, 'Africa's Vulnerability to Terrorism and Its Ability to Combat It', in Okumu and Botha, *Understanding Terrorism in Africa*, 23–41.

[30] A. Le Sage, 'Terrorism Threats and Vulnerabilities in Africa', in A. Le Sage (ed.), *African Counterterrorism Cooperation: Assessing Regional and Subregional Initiatives* (Washington, DC: Potomac, 2007), 1–38.

Africa to East Africa and recently to Nigeria in West Africa. Since 2006, Nigeria has been confronted by deadly trends of terrorism, perpetrated by militant groups in the Niger Delta region (between 2006 and 2009) and by the Islamic sect known locally as 'Boko Haram', which means Western education is profane or sinful.[31] The group seeks the imposition and strict application of Islamic law or shariah throughout Nigeria, the release of its members detained in prisons and the return of exiled members.[32]

Boko Haram has become notorious for its gruesome and rampant daily attacks on civilians and military installations in predominantly Muslim northern Nigeria.[33] By the end of 2011, Boko Haram represented the most dangerous and rapacious terrorist group in Africa, responsible for nearly 70 per cent of all terrorist attacks on the continent between July 2010 and December 2011. Of the 196 attacks that occurred during that period, about 130 attacks occurred in Nigeria.[34] Boko Haram claimed responsibility for 115 attacks including a suicide attack on the UN Headquarters in Abuja in August 2011 that killed 23 UN staff. Similarly in 2012 over 130 attacks were linked to Boko Haram, which killed nearly 1,000 people. Security forces also uncovered evidence that Boko Haram had established working links with the global al-Qaeda network, transforming itself from a local or domestic to an international terrorist group. Of the 66 incidents that occurred outside Nigeria, only 6 of these occurred in other West African countries (Niger, Mali, Côte d'Ivoire), 14 in North Africa (Algeria, Egypt, Mauritania, Morocco and Tunisia), 4 in Central Africa (Cameroon) and 42 in East Africa (Uganda, Sudan, Burundi, Rwanda and Kenya). A majority of the East African attacks occurred in clashes between the Somali terrorist group – al-Shabaab[35] – and Kenyan and African Union forces. Another notorious terrorist group is the Algeria-based AQIM,[36] which has evolved from Armed Islamic Group (GIA) or the latter version of the Salafi Group for Preaching and Combat (GSPC). Indeed the activities of AQIM and its knack for

[31] See M. Ewi, 'A New Phase for Boko Haram as UN Deplores Attacks in Abuja', *Allafrica.com*, 29 August 2011, at http://allafrica.com/stories/201108292162.html.

[32] A. Adegbamigbe, 'Osama's Nigerian Agents' (2001) 36 *News* 17.

[33] See Boko Haram's profile www.bbc.co.uk/news/world-africa-13809501.

[34] These figures are based on all reported major terrorist attacks in Africa between July 2010 and December 2011.

[35] See al-Shabaab's profile http://news.bbc.co.uk/2/hi/7307521.stm. See also http://news.bbc.co.uk/2/hi/7307521.stm.

[36] For detail, see AQIM's profile www.adl.org/terrorism/symbols/al_qaeda_maghreb.asp or http://en.wikipedia.org/wiki/Al-Qaeda_Organization_in_the_Islamic_Maghreb.

kidnapping for ransom payment, as well as the formation of like-minded Islamist groups such as Ansar-al Dine and the Movement for Unity of Jihad in West Africa (MUJAO) in northern Mali, have rendered the Sahel one of the 'unsafest' regions in Africa. Because of the prevalent lawlessness in the region, a unique brand of terrorism has emerged in the Sahel, the so-called narco terrorism, evincing a toxic mix of religion, cross-border criminality and a sophisticated transatlantic drug trade, which allows for heroin and cocaine shipment from South America via the Sahel to Europe.[37]

Unlike Europe, and despite the growing threat of terrorism in different parts of the continent, there is no consensus among African countries about the gravity of the threat of terrorism, not least whether it should be considered a continental priority. The vast majority of African countries do not consider terrorism a high national priority. Indeed, as Ernest Harsch contends, this is 'because the continent confronts so many pressing problems, tackling terrorism has so far not taken a high profile, despite calls to wage "war on terror" that have been so prominent internationally since the 11 September 2001 attacks in New York and Washington'.[38] Similarly, Fernanda Faria and Alvaro Vasconcelos note that the governments of Morocco, Tunisia and Egypt, which are fighting Islamic fundamentalism that threatens their survival, are giving priority to development.[39] Indeed, this developmental approach to counter-terrorism or the view that counter-terrorism should not distract from the priority focus on development became the nexus. The threat of terrorism to Africa is much more complex and not limited to attacks or suicide terrorism or kidnapping and hijacking, but includes the use of African territories by terrorist groups as safe havens where they recruit, train and plan attacks, as well as mobilize resources. As Princeton Lyman and J. Stephen Morrison point out, 'Al Qaeda has used the region less to foment terrorism than to protect and expand its finances'.[40] The region suffers from various debilitating factors such as failing or weak states, extreme poverty in the face of skyrocketing prices, chronic youth unemployment, cancerous corruption, conflict and political instability, all of which provide propitious conditions for radicalization and participation in terrorist activities. The disparity in threat perception,

[37] See for example www.unodc.org/unodc/en/press/releases/2008-04-15.html

[38] E. Harsch, 'Africa Looks Beyond "War on Terror" for Long-Term Solutions Rooted in Development, Human Rights' (2009) 23 *Africa Renewal* 16.

[39] F. Faria and A. Vasconcelos, 'Security in Northern Africa: Ambiguity and Reality', Chaillot Paper 25 (1996), 7 at www.iss-eu.org/chaillot/chai25e.html.

[40] P. Lyman and J. S. Morrison, 'The Terrorist Threat in Africa' (2004) 83 *Foreign Affairs* 83.

particularly the dominant view that terrorism is not the region's topmost priority, coupled with the endemic lack of resources have marginalized the terrorism agenda in the AU and crippled the Union's efforts to promote CT cooperation on the continent.

3 Salient activities of ROs in promoting counter-terrorism cooperation

3.1 Norms and standards setting

One of the main preoccupations of ROs in the GWOT has been to put in place the necessary normative frameworks against terrorism. Through their legislative powers, ROs serve as a clearing house for regional norms and for the dissemination and regionalization of international norms. Most ROs such as the EU, AU, OAS and LAS already had conventions and protocols pre-dating 9/11, which criminalized acts of terrorism. Nonetheless, 9/11 generated a new impetus for ROs to review and update their CT measures in light of new developments. The increasing use of electronic and sophisticated technologies introduced a new form of terrorism, which may be referred to as 'smart terrorism', that relies on the exploitation of modern science and technology for the commission of terrorist acts. One of these new electronic tools is the internet, used increasingly by al-Qaeda and other terrorist groups for recruitment, training, planning and for operating without much external support, through which they have been able to evade government censorship and prevent leaks. ROs responded by creating tougher comprehensive regulations and exhorted states to exercise more vigilance. The key challenge to ROs after 9/11 has been to scrupulously enforce both international and regional CT instruments. This section reviews the salient norms and standards set out in the CT legislative frameworks of the EU and the AU.

3.1.1 Development of European counter-terrorism norms[41]

The theoretical and legal basis for European ROs' involvement in CT matters owe their origins to Article 2 of the Maastricht Treaty (outlining the objectives of the EU), which *inter alia*, states that the 'Union shall set itself the objective to maintain and develop the Union as an area of freedom, security and justice, in which the free movement of persons is assured in conjunction with appropriate measures with respect to

[41] See Chapter 6 in this volume.

external border controls, asylum, immigration and the prevention and combating of crime'.[42]

Contemporary counter-terrorism cooperation within Europe is believed to have begun as far back as in the 1970s, culminating in the establishment of the Terrorism, Radicalism, Extremism, and International Violence group (TREVI) in 1975.[43] It is therefore evident that initial EU response was to address the root causes of terrorism in member states. This was later followed by a legal instrument, the 1977 Convention on the Suppression of Terrorism, which was aimed at regulating states' conduct and criminalizing terrorist-related offences in Europe.

In response to 9/11, the Council of Europe adopted an additional protocol to the Convention in 2003, in order to bring the latter up to date and to strengthen its provisions in light of new developments ushered in by 9/11. Furthermore, in 2005, the Council adopted the Convention on the Prevention of Terrorism.[44] These instruments constitute the principal European legal framework and criminal justice response to terrorism. Until the adoption of the two Conventions, CT activities were solely the responsibility of states, some of which already had penal legislations or some form of constitutional criminalization of terrorism. Cooperation and mutual legal assistance on criminal matters including terrorism had a much longer history in Europe, dating back to 1923, and was fostered through Interpol. With respect to the development of the body of law against terrorism at the European institutional level, most scholars refer to the 1957 Convention on Extradition and the 1959 Convention on Mutual Legal Assistance as laying the foundation pillars of Europe's ability to seriously fight organized crime as well as terrorism.[45]

The European institutions' main role in the fight against terrorism has been essentially aimed at achieving 'greater unity' among their

[42] 1992 Treaty on European Union [1992] OJ C 191/01, Art. 2 [hereafter TEU]. See electronic version http://eur-lex.europa.eu/en/treaties/dat/11992M/htm/11992M.html#0001000001.

[43] See D. Casale, 'EU Institutional and Legal Counter-Terrorism Framework' (2008) 1 *Defence against Terrorism Review* 50.

[44] In addition to these two principal legislative instruments, the European institutions have adopted the Convention on laundering, search, seizure, and confiscation of the proceeds from crime and on the financing of terrorism in 2005; Framework Decision on combating terrorism in 2002; European Arrest Warrant in 2002; Plan of action to combat terrorism in 2004; EU declaration on combating terrorism in 2004.

[45] H. Nilsson, 'The EU Action Plan on Combating Terrorism: Assessment and Perspectives', in Mahncke and Monar, *International Terrorism*, vol. III, 76.

members.[46] With the entry into force of the 1977 Convention, two key anti-terrorism norms became firmly established among European countries. The first was the de-linking or separation of terrorist offences from political crimes. Under Article 1 of the Convention, offences involving the seizure of aircrafts, hijacking, kidnapping, the taking of hostages, attacks on diplomatic personnel, unlawful detention as well as offences involving the use of bombs and other explosives could not be considered as political crimes for the purposes of extradition.[47] The 1977 Convention focuses mainly on extradition, which according to its drafters, constitutes an effective measure to ensure that the perpetrators of terrorist acts do not escape prosecution and punishment for their crimes.[48] Though the Convention does not define terrorist offences per se, states parties are to implement the provisions of Article 1 of the Convention in accordance with the relevant international law, particularly the four main international anti-terrorism treaties existing at the time.[49]

By separating terrorist offences from political crimes, states parties to the Convention could no longer deny extradition for offences identified in Articles 1 and 2 of the Convention on the basis that the offence is politically motivated or connected with political motives.[50] The status quo *ante bellum* was that extradition could not be guaranteed in cases of political crimes, and terrorist offences were generally regarded as a category of political crimes.[51] This hindered effective cooperation on CT matters especially with respect to extradition as states often invoked political motives to deny extradition. Although the Convention does

[46] See the preamble to the 1977 European Convention on the Suppression of Terrorism.

[47] See 1977 European Convention on the Suppression of Terrorism, Council of Europe Treaty Series No. 090, Art. 1(a–f).

[48] *Ibid.*, preamble.

[49] The lack of a definition on the terrorist offences mentioned in Art. 1 meant that for states parties to implement the Convention effectively, they must also be parties to the four international anti-terrorism treaties at the time. The four main international treaties that were in existence in 1977 included the 1963 Convention on Offences and Certain Other Acts Committed on Board Aircraft, 704 UNTS 220; 1970 Convention for the Suppression of Unlawful Seizure of Aircraft, 704 UNTS 106; 1971 Convention for the Suppression of Unlawful Acts against the Safety of Civil Aviation, 974 UNTS 178; and 1973 Convention on the Prevention and Punishment of Crimes against Internationally Protected Persons, Including Diplomatic Agents, 1035 UNTS 168.

[50] See 1977 Convention, Art. 2.

[51] 1957 European Convention on Extradition, Council of Europe Treaty Series No. 24, Art. 3 states that: 'Extradition shall not be granted if the offence in respect of which it is requested is regarded by the requested Party as a political offence or as an offence connected with a political offence.'

not specifically list terrorism per se as a political crime, it provides in its Article 3(3) that, '[t]he taking or attempted taking of the life of a Head of State or a member of his family shall not be deemed to be a political offence'.

The second norm established by the Convention also connected with the first is the requirement that states extend to one another the widest measure of mutual assistance in criminal matters related to proceedings brought in respect of offences mentioned in Articles 1 and 2, and that such mutual assistance cannot be refused on the sole ground that it concerns a political offence or an offence connected with political motives.[52]

What constitutes terrorism or a terrorist offence has always been an issue of strenuous debate among EU members. The need for a common definition was considered a *sine qua non* for effective implementation and coordination of CT activities in Europe. Until 9/11, there was no consensus on a common definition of terrorism, despite what was provided in the 1977 convention, partly due to the heterogeneous causes of terrorism in the region and also due to differences in terrorism threat perception among EU countries. Edwin Bakker identifies six main factors that influence differences in terrorism threat perception among the twenty-five EU member states surveyed. He argues that recent and past experiences with terrorist incidents, presence of sizeable Muslim communities, active participation in the US-led war against terrorism, the way in which countries deal with security threats, and other major issues (such as social, economic or political issues) affect the way a country perceives the threat of terrorism.[53]

After 9/11, and particularly following the Madrid and London bombings in 2004 and 2005, respectively, the terrorism threat perception in Europe was elevated to its all time high, and in some countries such as the United Kingdom, terrorism amounted to a 'public emergency threatening the life of the nation'.[54] This provided a new impetus for the European ROs to strengthen their roles.[55] The lack of a single definition, however, meant that each European country could adopt its own national definition, hence giving rise to a variety of conceptual approaches to terrorism among members, which in effect hampered coordination of CT activities. The need for a

[52] See 1977 Convention, Art. 8.

[53] E. Bakker, 'Differences in Terrorist Threat Perception in Europe', in Mahncke and Monar, *International Terrorism*, vol. III, 47–62.

[54] Lord Phillips, 'Impact of Terrorism on the Rule of Law', 15, at www.judiciary.gov.uk/Resources/JCO/Documents/Speeches/lcj_american_bar_assoc_031007.pdf.

[55] In addition, the European institutions have adopted at least seven related framework decisions and about eight related decisions on terrorism matters post-9/11.

common European definition was therefore crucial if the organizations were to be successful in promoting cooperation and in creating a unified European framework for combating and preventing terrorism. This definitional problem was resolved in a Framework Decision on combating terrorism adopted by the Council of Europe in response to 9/11 in 2002. Article 1 of this decision defines terrorism as follows:

> Each Member State shall take the necessary measures to ensure that the intentional acts referred to below in points (a) to (i), as defined as offences under national law, which, given their nature or context, may seriously damage a country or an international organization where committed with the aim of:
>
> - seriously intimidating a population, or
> - unduly compelling a Government or international organization to perform or abstain from performing any act, or
> - seriously destabilising or destroying the fundamental political, constitutional, economic or social structures of a country or an international organization,
>
> shall be deemed to be terrorist offences:
>
> (a) attacks upon a person's life which may cause death;
> (b) attacks upon the physical integrity of a person;
> (c) kidnapping or hostage taking;
> (d) causing extensive destruction to a Government or public facility, a transport system, an infrastructure facility, including an information system, a fixed platform located on the continental shelf, a public place or private property likely to endanger human life or result in major economic loss;
> (e) seizure of aircraft, ships or other means of public or goods transport;
> (f) manufacture, possession, acquisition, transport, supply or use of weapons, explosives or of nuclear, biological or chemical weapons, as well as research into, and development of, biological and chemical weapons;
> (g) release of dangerous substances, or causing fires, floods or explosions the effect of which is to endanger human life;
> (h) interfering with or disrupting the supply of water, power or any other fundamental natural resource the effect of which is to endanger human life;
> (i) threatening to commit any of the acts listed in (a) to (h).

The definition provided a broad concept of terrorism and terrorist offences. For example, offenders could be prosecuted for merely possessing or researching on materials and explosives that could be used to carry out an attack aimed at intimidating or compelling a government or organization, or seriously destabilizing national order. The Framework Decision further defined, in its Article 2, offences that relate to a terrorist group and also set out those offences related to terrorism. Article 4 obliges member states to criminalize inchoate offences such as inciting, aiding, abetting or attempting to commit any terrorist offence or an act connected with a terrorist offence.[56]

The 2005 Council of Europe Convention on the Prevention of Terrorism further expanded the scope of European norms against terrorism and set out comprehensive standards or measures that states parties must take in the fields of training, law enforcement, education, culture, information, media and public awareness raising, in order to prevent terrorist acts or tensions and conditions that contribute to the commission of terrorist offences.[57] The purpose of the Convention was, in the words of Erling Husabø, to 'consider the need for supplementary regulation of terrorism at the European level'.[58] The Convention does not define terrorism as such but in its Article 1(1), a terrorist offence is, in generic terms, referred to as any of the offences within the scope of and as defined in one of the ten international conventions listed in its appendix.

In the framework of this Convention, the Council of Europe imposed on its member states the obligation to put in place at the national level specific measures to combat and prevent training, recruitment and acts that provoke the commission of terrorist offences, as well as measures to address what the Convention refers to in its Article 9 as 'ancillary offences'.[59] The Convention has also perpetuated the norm that obliges members to extradite or prosecute (wherever they have jurisdiction) an offender of the Convention. Under Article 18 of the Convention, it is compulsory for a state party to prosecute without undue delay, an offender who for justifiable reasons cannot be extradited even if the crime was not committed on the territory of the state party concerned. In this case, the state party shall take its decision in the same manner as in the case of any other

[56] For a detailed analysis of the 2002 Council of Europe Framework Decision, see S. Peers, 'EU Responses to Terrorism' (2003) 52 *International & Comparative Law Quarterly* 227.

[57] See 2005 European Convention on the Prevention of Terrorism, Council of Europe Treaty Series No. 196, Art. 3.

[58] E. Husabø, 'The Interaction between Global, Regional, and National Regulation in the Definition of Terrorism', in A. Follesdal, R. Wessel and J. Wouters (eds.), *Multilevel Regulation and the EU: The Interplay between Global, European and National Normative Processes* (Leiden: Martinis Nijhoff, 2008), 175.

[59] The use of 'ancillary offences' in Art. 9 is interpreted to mean the role of second and third parties who may have been directly or indirectly involved in the commission of a terrorist act either by participating as an accomplice or organizing, directing, inciting, directing or contributing in any form to the commission of any of the offences listed in Arts. 5–7 of the Convention.

offence of a serious nature under its national law. This norm ensures that there are no unnecessary delays in the legal process or the prosecution of alleged offenders as a result of lapses in extradition.

The European definition of terrorism and, indeed, the development of anti-terrorism norms in Europe as evident in the Framework Decision and the 2005 Council of Europe Convention is deeply rooted in relevant international treaties, conventions and protocols. Erling Johannes Husabø, for example, has rightly pointed out that the definition in the framework decision was greatly influenced by the 1999 International Convention for the Suppression of the Financing of Terrorism and previous UN conventions.[60] This interplay between the regional and global CT regimes, particularly its support for and recognition of the primacy role of the UN in the GWOT, constitutes an important dimension of understanding Europe's CT regimes. It also reveals the role of ROs as important building blocks in the wider UN regimes. Furthermore it helps to shed more light on the hierarchy that exists between ROs and international actors (such as the UN) in terms of their roles in the GWOT, which is often blurred.

3.1.2 Development of African counter-terrorism norms

The pre-9/11 CT cooperation in Africa was led by the Organization of African Unity (OAU), which existed from 1963 until its demise in 2002. The post-9/11 CT cooperation has taken place under the aegis of the African Union that formally replaced the OAU in July 2002. The discussion on the post-9/11 CT measures in Africa therefore takes place in the context of the measures that the AU has taken. The AU's post-9/11 CT agenda has shown both continuity and transformation. On the one hand, the Union has continued with the implementation of the decisions and CT instruments adopted by the OAU. On the other hand, it has moved away from the OAU's policy of indifference and slow reaction, to one that emphasizes non-indifference, and robust and proactive CT measures. Unlike its predecessor, CT has been a self-defined function of the AU. The Constitutive Act of the Union identifies terrorism as a threat to peace and security, which all member states are required to confront both individually and collectively within the AU framework.

The theoretical and legal basis of AU's involvement in the fight against terrorism are anchored on Article 4(o) of the Constitutive Act of the African Union, which enunciates, *inter alia*, the principle of the 'respect for the sanctity of human life, condemnation and rejection of impunity and political

[60] Husabø, 'Interaction between Global, Regional, and National', 174.

assassination, acts of terrorism and subversive activities',[61] and Article 3(d) of the Protocol relating to the establishment of the Peace and Security Council (PSC) of the African Union, which enjoins the PSC to 'coordinate and harmonize continental efforts in the prevention and combating of international terrorism in all its aspects'.[62] The AU's responses to terrorism and the impetus to promote continental unity on the matter have been predicated on the need for security as a prerequisite for development.[63]

The current legal framework of the AU was inherited from the OAU, which despite the lack of political will among its members adopted a number of key decisions and instruments at a time when terrorism was considered a low-key issue. One of the early norms adopted by the OAU was the total rejection of the use of violent and religious extremism against African states.[64] It constituted the organization's first attempt to address the root causes of terrorism and the rising problem of violent jihadism perpetrated by radical Islamic movements which were becoming increasingly political and violent.[65] The resolution, as its title signified, was aimed at enhancing cooperation and friendly relations among African states.[66] In particular, the drafters were concerned about the growing problem of some African

[61] 2000 Constitutive Act of the African Union, 2158 UNTS 3, Art. 4(o), at www.africa-union.org/root/au/AboutAU/Constitutive_Act_en.htm.

[62] 2002 Protocol Relating to the Establishment of the Peace and Security Council of the African Union, Art. 3(d), at www.africa-union.org/root/au/Documents/Treaties/Text/Protocol_peace%20and%20security.pdf.

[63] See for example the Dakar Declaration against terrorism adopted by the Summit of African Heads of State and Government held in Dakar, Senegal, on 17 October 2001, which in its para. 8 recommended that the 'OAU convene an extraordinary summit to discuss the progress so far made in Africa in the fight against terrorism and to ensure that the post September 11, 2001 events and their consequences have the least possible adverse impact on the development of Africa, in particular on the implementation of the New African Initiative'.

[64] See the OAU decision, AHG/Res. 213 (XXVIII) on the strengthening of cooperation and coordination among African states, adopted by the 28th ordinary session of the OAU Summit held in Dakar, Senegal, in 1992. In that resolution, the OAU Assembly urged member states not to allow 'any movement using religion, ethnic or other social or cultural differences to indulge in hostile activities against Member States as well as to refrain from lending any support to any group that could disrupt the stability and the territorial integrity of Member States by violent means, and to strengthen cooperation and coordination among the African countries in order to circumstances the phenomenon of extremism and terrorism' (see para. 2).

[65] In Egypt, for example, the Egyptian Islamic Group assassinated Egyptian president Anwar Sadat in 1981; in Algeria, the Armed Islamic Movement (MIA) massacred ten soldiers in Guemmar in November 1991; and in Tunisia, an-Nahda was suspected of a plot to overthrow the government.

[66] The resolution was inspired by various UN resolutions on the elimination of all forms of religious intolerance. See for example GA Res. 45/136 adopted on 14 December 1990 and 47/129 adopted on 18 December 1992.

governments and leaders fomenting rebellions, civil wars and insurgencies in other states by funding, arming, equipping and providing safe havens to militant groups, either on an ethnic, religious or political basis.[67] The drafters avoided any attempt to legislate on the matter and merely established a political principle to guide inter-African relations. The ban on violent extremism was further strengthened with the adoption of a declaration on a code of conduct on inter-African relations on 15 June 1994, which *inter alia*, unequivocally condemned as criminal all terrorist acts, methods and practices, and resolved to set up cooperation among African states in order to erase terrorism, whose threat to Africa was compared to 'arms racketeering and drug peddling'.[68] It is evident that the declaration was an attempt to build on Resolution AHG/Res. 213 (XXVIII), of 1 July 1992 with a view to establishing certain benchmarks or what its drafters called a code of conduct. In its paragraph 15, the declaration committed OAU member states, for the first time at the continental level, as far as CT is concerned, to comply with their obligations under international law and to:

> refrain from organizing, instigating, facilitating, financing, encouraging or tolerating activities that are terrorist in nature or intent, and from participating in such activities in whatsoever manner, and to take necessary operational measures to ensure that Member States' territories do not serve as training camps or indoctrination centres for terrorist elements and movements and as sanctuaries for planning and organization of terrorist and destabilization activities directed against the territorial integrity and security of Member States or other states or their nationals.

The declaration drew inspiration from the United Nations General Assembly resolutions on measures to prevent international terrorism and from the Code of Conduct adopted by the Organization of Islamic Conference (OIC), at its ministerial meeting in Tunis, Tunisia in 1994.[69] Like the Resolution AHG/Res. 213 (XXVIII), the declaration was purely a political statement. It lacked the legal force to compel OAU members to implement its provisions. Second, it failed to go into any substantive details to spell out the specific measures, such as the enactment of national CT legislations, ratification of international treaties and extradition measures expected of member states. Third, there was no institutional framework to

[67] See Res. on AIDS and Africa: An Agenda for Action, Doc. AHG/Res. 213 (XXVIII) (1992), paras. 1–2.

[68] See Declaration on a Code of Conduct for Inter-African Relations, Doc. AHG/Decl. 2 (XXX) (1994), para. 10.

[69] See for example, UN Doc. A/Res./44/29 (1989).

monitor and ensure states' compliance with its decisions, which meant that implementation was based on states' volition. Fourth, the declaration failed to define terrorism and therefore left it open to member states' interpretations. As such, the term became convoluted and political opponents including legitimate political parties were rebranded as 'terrorists'.

Despite the adoption of the above-mentioned decision and declaration, the OAU had no binding legal framework for fighting terrorism. This also meant that cooperation on such matters was limited and largely so, because for most of Africa, terrorism during that period was viewed as a North African issue. Furthermore, there existed little or no extradition and mutual legal assistance practices in Africa, particularly on criminal matters. The first legal codification of extradition and mutual legal assistance at the continental level came in 1977 with the adoption of the OAU Convention for the Elimination of Mercenarism in Africa (in Libreville, Gabon), which entered into force on 22 April 1985.[70] Article 10 of that Convention obliged contracting parties to afford to one another 'the greatest measures of assistance in connection with the investigation and criminal proceedings brought in respect of the offence and other acts connected with the activities of the offender'. Under Article 8 of the Convention, political offences are exempted from extradition and a contracting state that refuses to extradite has an obligation to prosecute and punish the offender in accordance with Article 7 of the Convention, which obliges contracting states to make offences committed under the Convention (as listed in Article 1) punishable by the severest penalties including capital punishment.[71]

For the most part of its colonial and post-colonial history, the OAU considered terrorism a term of the colonial powers to reject and undermine the activities of 'freedom fighters' including those of the OAU itself.[72] This was evidenced in a number of major terrorist incidents that occurred in the years prior to the 1990s. For example, the OAU remained indifferent to the attacks at the Embassy of Saudi Arabia in Khartoum in March 1973, which resulted in the assassination of three diplomats including an American ambassador visiting the embassy; the hijacking of a school bus carrying thirty pupils of mostly foreign

[70] See 1977 OAU Convention on the Elimination of Mercenarism, Doc. CM/817 (XXIX), Annex II Rev. 1, at www.africa-union.org/root/au/Documents/Treaties/Text/Convention_on_Mercenaries.pdf.

[71] Art. 9 of the Convention outlines the conditions for extradition whereby a contracting state may claim jurisdiction over extraditable offences under the Convention.

[72] See for example, E. Efrat, 'Terrorism in South Africa', in Y. Alexander (ed.), *International Terrorism: National, Regional and Global Perspectives* (New York: Praeger, 1976), 194.

background in Djibouti, on 3 February 1976; the Entebbe hijacking/hostage crisis from 27 June to 2 July 1976; the hijacking of a Lufthansa Flight 181 bound for Frankfurt from Palma, Majorca, to Mogadishu, Somalia on 13 October 1977; the deadly hijacking of an Egypt Air Flight 648 on 23 November 1985; and the mid-air bombing of a French UTA flight near Bilma, Niger, killing all 171 on board on 19 September 1989.[73]

The 1992 decision and the 1994 declaration therefore represented a shift in OAU policy and also signalled the Organization's formal acknowledgement of the threat of terrorism to Africa. The spread of violent jihadism around the continent at the wake of the 1990s, particularly in North Africa, West Africa (Nigeria), East Africa (Somalia) and Southern Africa (South Africa) presented a serious threat to the fragile peace and security of the continent, which was also already mired in a sea of armed conflict and political instability. The bombing of US embassies in Nairobi, Kenya and Dar es Salaam, Tanzania in August 1998, killing over 250 people and leaving more than 5,000 others injured by al-Qaeda cells in East Africa, represented the deadliest terrorist incidents to occur in Africa and demonstrated the magnitude of the danger that terrorism posed to the continent.

In response to those attacks, the OAU, at its 35th ordinary summit, held in Algiers, Algeria, in July 1999 adopted the OAU Convention on the Prevention and Combating of Terrorism (hereafter the 1999 Algiers Convention).[74] The Algiers Convention responded to the needs for legalization of the emerging CT norms in Africa and for a binding framework for cooperation and states' commitments to anti-terrorism. Drafted by an Algerian expert under the auspices of a Committee of the OAU Central Organ of the Mechanism for Conflict Prevention, Management and Resolution, the draft Convention received a swift and unanimous approval by the 70th ordinary session of the Council of Ministers and the 35th session of the Assembly of Heads of State and Government, although it would take three years for the Algiers

[73] Jo-Ansie van Wyk has observed that since '1970, a number of planes were either hijacked on the continent or, after a hijack, rerouted to an African country'. For example, following the Entebbe hostage crisis, a Lufthansa plane en route to Spain was hijacked to Somalia in 1977. See J. van Wyk, 'Africa and the War on Terror: from Kalashnikovs to Qurans to Cooperation', in M. Miller and B. Stefanova (eds.), *The War on Terror in Comparative Perspective: US Security and Foreign Policy after 9/11* (Basingstoke: Palgrave Macmillan, 2007), 125–6.

[74] 1999 Convention on the Prevention and Combating of Terrorism, at www.africa-union.org/root/au/Documents/Treaties/Text/Algiers_convention%20on%20Terrorism.pdf.

Convention to obtain the fifteen instruments of ratification required under its Article 20 for it to enter into force.

Algeria played an instrumental role in the negotiations and adoption of the Algiers Convention. As a state that has experienced terrorism for most of its independent history, perhaps far more than any other African country, terrorism has always been a passionate subject for Algerians, many of whom regard the fight against terrorism as the second liberation struggle. Algeria's determination to root out terrorism in the Sahelian Sahara, a vast desert and hostile region, which, according to American and Algerian intelligence sources, is 'a conduit for potential terrorists',[75] has been the major drive for Algeria's quest for a viable and robust continental CT framework. The dominant role played by Algeria in the development of the AU CT is an important dimension for assessing the effectiveness and challenges to the OAU/AU CT regimes. To a larger extent, Algeria's leadership has helped to advance the African CT agenda. To another extent it has negatively impacted on effective CT cooperation on the continent, particularly among critics who view the OAU/AU CT regimes as an extension of the Algerian national interest.

The 1999 Algiers Convention drew largely, in terms of its substantial provisions, from international and similar regional conventions, particularly those adopted by the League of Arab States and the OIC (Organization for the Islamic Conference), in 1998 and 1999, respectively.[76] The Algiers Convention helped to codify into law Africa's common position and the continent's stringent rejection of terrorism.[77] It also firmly established various norms against terrorism, including a common African definition of terrorism. In its Article 1(3), the Algiers Convention defines a terrorist act as:

> (a) any act which is a violation of the criminal laws of a State Party and which may endanger the life, physical integrity or freedom of, or cause serious injury or death to, any person, any number or group of

[75] J. Keenan, 'Terror in the Sahara: the Implications of US Imperialism for North and West Africa' (2004) 31 *Review of African Political Economy* 475, 480.

[76] There is a great deal of similarity in the counter-terrorism regimes of the League of Arab States (LAS), the Organization for Islamic Conference (OIC) and the OAU/AU. The three organizations also share common membership. At the time, Egypt, Libya and Algeria, which were among the most influential members of the OAU, were also the most influential members in the LAS and OIC.

[77] Some observers described the OAU Convention as part of a pact between the Arab world and Africa to wage war against Islamic activism aimed at stemming the growing tide of Islamic revivalism. See, for example, Muslimedia, 'Arab League and OAU mobilize against Islamic movements' (1999), available electronically: www.muslimedia.com/archives/oaw99/arab-oau.htm (17 August 2009).

persons or causes or may cause damage to public or private property, natural resources, environmental or cultural heritage and is calculated or intended to:

(i) intimidate, put in fear, force, coerce or induce any government, body, institution, the general public or any segment thereof, to do or abstain from doing any act, or to adopt or abandon a particular standpoint, or to act according to certain principles; or

(ii) disrupt any public service, the delivery of any essential service to the public or to create a public emergency; or

(iii) create general insurrection in a State.

(b) any promotion, sponsoring, contribution to, command, aid, incitement, encouragement, attempt, threat, conspiracy, organizing, or procurement of any person, with the intent to commit any act referred to in paragraph (a) (i) to (iii).

Most scholars agree that the definition in Article 1 is all-encompassing as it contains some of the key elements for an objective definition of a terrorist act.[78] It should be noted that the definition does not criminalize terrorism but rather a 'terrorist act'. In this context, it is the act that defines terrorism and not vice versa. The challenge with such a broad definition is that it provides states parties with a blanket for a selective or perceptive application of acts that may qualify as offences under the Convention and to label political opponents and their activities as terrorist.

Although the concept of a 'terrorist act' as defined in Article 1 is broad enough to include various forms of terrorism, its scope of applicability in the African context is limited. This limitation is provided in Article 3 of the Algiers Convention, promulgating into law the norm that acts of people fighting against occupation and colonialism cannot qualify as terrorist acts under the Algiers Convention. As Article 3(1) states:

> Notwithstanding the provisions of Article 1, the struggle waged by peoples in accordance with the principles of international law for their liberation or self-determination, including armed struggle against colonialism, occupation, aggression and domination by foreign forces shall not be considered as terrorist acts.[79]

[78] See for example, A. Cassese, 'The Multifaceted Criminal Notion of Terrorism in International Law' (2006) 4 *Journal of International Criminal Justice* 935. In the same vein, Fergal Davis identifies key elements for an objective definition of terrorism, namely: should identify the essence of the activity; should recognize that the aim of the activity is political; and explicitly note that the targets of the activity are civilians (see 'The Fight against Global Terrorism – How Can the Law Respond to "New" Terrorism?', in D. Lewis (ed.), *Global Governance and the Quest for Justice* (Oxford: Hart, 2006), vol. I, 21–38).

[79] 1999 Algiers Convention, Art. 3(1).

This is arguably the most controversial if not contentious provision in the Algiers Convention. Critics argue that such an exemption provides unfettered freedom to 'freedom fighters' to use whatever means including those acts considered as offences (as defined in Article 1) for their 'legitimate causes'. As a consequence, the US did not have any meaningful CT cooperation with the OAU. It was only in 2005 that the US State Department for the first time initiated a dialogue with the African Union on a broad array of issues including CT, but here too, the discussion did not lead to any substantial cooperation or support.[80]

The exemption in Article 3(1) was not new, nor was it a peculiar African position when it was introduced into the OAU Convention. The issue of 'freedom fighters' and terrorism has been and remains one of the most contentious issues in the terrorism discourse and is the thrust of the division in UN efforts to define the crime of terrorism. It has become in recent years the imaginary line that divides the South and the North. Proponents of the African position have argued that, for Africa, the inclusion of Article 3 in the definition of terrorism was not only a legitimate thing to do, but that it would, otherwise, have been self-incriminating for many of the African leaders, who, during their campaign for independence, had been labelled terrorists by their Western colonial masters.[81] Historical experience has therefore been a key factor for the definition.

In order to prevent terrorists from exploiting this conceptual ambiguity, Article 3(2) of the Convention enjoins states parties not to recognize political, philosophical, ideological, racial, ethnic, religious or other motives as justifications for terrorist acts. Other salient norms promulgated under the Convention include extradition and state jurisdiction on terrorism matters.[82] In view of the lack of a single continental instrument on extradition and mutual legal assistance in Africa, the provisions in parts III, IV and V of the Convention established a solid basis for

[80] Prior to this meeting, AU–US counter-terrorism cooperation mostly took place within the folds of the US Washington-based Africa Centre for Strategic Studies (ACSS), which organizes a range of events on defence and security matters in cooperation with African states and relevant institutions.

[81] See for example, M. Ewi and K. Aning, 'Assessing the Role of the African Union in Preventing and Combating Terrorism in Africa' (2006) 15 *African Security Review* 32, 36–7, for a detailed discussion on the origin and implication of the 1999 OAU Convention's definition of terrorism.

[82] Art. 9 of the 1999 OAU Convention obliges states parties to include, as an extraditable offence, any terrorist act as defined in Art. 1.

anti-terrorism norms on extradition and mutual legal assistance. The rules and guidelines for state jurisdiction in Articles 6 and 7, and the terms of extradition in Articles 8 to 13, as well as the provisions for extra-territorial investigations and mutual legal assistance in Articles 14 to 18 are all in congruence with relevant international treaties. In practice, however, the limits of the provisions of the OAU Convention have not been tested. So far, there have been no legal challenges to or even a conflict of interpretation over the Convention's provisions brought to the AU.

Like the 2005 Council of Europe Convention on the Prevention of Terrorism, the 1999 OAU Convention does not regard terrorism as a political offence. The two treaties also oblige their states parties to prosecute or extradite offenders. Under Article 8 of the OAU Convention, a state party in whose territory an alleged offender is present is obliged, whether or not the offence was committed in its territory, to submit the case without undue delay to its competent authorities for the purpose of prosecution if it does not extradite that person.[83] Article 18 of the Council of Europe Convention takes this provision further by emphasizing that '[t]hose authorities (in the state party which has opted to prosecute an offender) shall take their decision in the same manner as in the same case of any other offence of a serious nature under the law of that Party'.[84]

3.2 Coordination and the promotion of a cohesive regional approach

As a catalyst of regional cooperation and integration, ROs' fundamental approach to counter-terrorism is premised on the need to promote a common regional response, to ensure unity of purpose and that states are on the same wavelength in terms of policies and strategies. Cooperation among states eliminates safe havens, hideouts or terrorist sanctuaries and facilitates the application of criminal justice and prosecution of perpetrators of terrorist acts. Coordination is therefore a crucial aspect of cooperation and an indispensable function of ROs. Coordination here refers to the efforts and strategies of regional organizations aimed at harmonizing and streamlining the CT policies and activities of states in order to enhance synergies and consolidate a common regional position.

[83] Art. 8(4).

[84] Council of Europe Convention on the Prevention of Terrorism, Art. 18(1).

Even when states recognize a security threat as a common problem, their knowledge of and capabilities to deal with such a threat often vary. There is also a tendency for such variations to lead to mistrust and oscillation in regional cooperation, thus, becoming an even greater threat to regional security. In this context, states seek ROs not only to provide a forum for information sharing and transparency in their actions but also to serve as a point of convergence for the various national CT legacies. In performing this core function, ROs are able to regularly assess progress made, determine measures remaining to be taken by states and the specific challenges to states' CT efforts.

The tools adopted by ROs to coordinate states' CT actions vary across regions. The most common strategies include the adoption of plans of action and common strategies; organization of regional summits, conferences, seminars and other forums; establishment and/or designation of specific regional institutions and mechanisms for that purpose; as well as periodic reporting. These measures are often helpful in sustaining awareness, mobilizing political support for concrete actions at the national level, sharing CT best practices and critical information about terrorist groups and activities, as well as promoting ratification and effective implementation of regional and international CT instruments.

3.2.1 Counter-terrorism coordination within Europe

The EU is considered the most successful regional organization,[85] not only for the unprecedented degree of integration in the region, but also for its aggressive and intrusive CT policies. The Union has adopted a myriad of rules, decisions, laws and policies, which in most respects cross over traditional lines of sovereignty, in favour of a rigorous and coordinated European approach to counter-terrorism. Initially, practical cooperation on counter-terrorism matters within the EU was limited. Patrizia de Cesari identifies two main levels: 'The first was at the level of cooperation between Ministers of the Interior and, more specifically, between

[85] See for example, B. Møller, 'European Security: The role of the European Union' (2008) Crisis States Working Papers Series No. 2, 1, at www.crisisstates.com/download/wp/wpSeries2/wp29.2.pdf. In the same vein, Richard Higgott argues that the EU is still 'the most institutionalised regional policy community exhibiting a complex system of governance beyond the territorial state' ('The Theory and Practice of Global and Regional Governance: Accommodating American Exceptionalism and European Pluralism' (2005) GARNET Working Paper No 01/05, 3, at www.garnet-eu.org/fileadmin/documents/working_papers/0105.pdf).

the police forces and intelligence services of the various member states. The second level took place in the area of political cooperation at the meetings of the European Council.'[86]

Currently, EU member states are required to cooperate with one another in all areas of CT including the following: EU blacklists of terrorists and terrorist groups; legislative and judicial cooperation; counter-terrorism services cooperation (police and intelligence services); passport checks and the Schengen Information System (SIS); terrorist financing and border controls and terrorist victims' assistance. The specific measures to be taken in these areas are provided in the EU Action Plan on Combating Terrorism and the EU CT Strategy, which identifies four strategic action areas, or the so-called four pillars for combating terrorism, namely, prevention, protection, pursuit and response to acts of terrorism.[87]

The EU institutional framework for countering terrorism could, in broad terms, be divided into four different institutions or groupings: the Council of the European Union and the European Parliament with all their bodies, working groups and the secretariat; the Commission of the European Communities; independent agencies of the EU; and member state cooperation outside the formal Council structure.[88] While the Council of the European Union is responsible for the formal adoption of policies including legislation and decisions at the highest level, practical coordination and implementation of European norms are carried out by agencies such as Eurojust. Eurojust provides a framework for magistrates, investigators, prosecutors and other judicial entities from EU member states dealing with crimes related to terrorism to cooperate and share information. For example, ministers of justice from EU member states meet at least twice a year or at least once during each EU presidency. The EU has also established the European Judicial Network (EJN) to further improve judicial cooperation between the member states in combating serious crimes such as corruption, drug trafficking and terrorism. Another important body for CT coordination is Europol,

[86] P. de Cesari, 'The European Union', in G. Nesi (ed.), *International Cooperation in Counterterrorism: The United Nations and Regional Organizations in the Fight Against Terrorism* (Farnham: Ashgate, 2006), 207.

[87] See Report 115358/09 of the EU Counterterrorism Coordinator on the Implementation of the Action Plan for Combating Terrorism of 26 November 2009, at http://register.consilium.europa.eu/pdf/en/09/st15/st15358.en09.pdf.

[88] L. Lugna, 'Institutional Framework of the European Union Counterterrorism Policy Setting' (2006) 8 *Baltic Security and Defence Review* 1.

which enables national police and other law enforcement forces from member states to exchange intelligence and critical information on terrorism-related crimes and criminals.

In order to focalize its coordination activities, the EU, in 2004, decided to set up a specific body called the Counterterrorism Coordinator. According to the Council of the European Union declaration of March 2004, 'the Coordinator works within the Council Secretariat, coordinates the work of the Council in combating terrorism and, with due regard to the responsibilities of the Commission, maintains an overview of all the instruments at the Union's disposal with a view to ensure regular reporting to the Council and effective follow-up of Council's decisions.'[89]

The EU has also established various working groups devoted to the prevention and combat of terrorism and to ensure practical coordination among member states. One of these working groups is the Terrorism Working Group (TWG), composed of representatives of the member states' ministries of the interior and/or law enforcement agencies, which meets three to five times per EU presidency and deals with internal threat assessments, practical cooperation and coordination among EU bodies.[90] Another working group devoted to terrorism is the Working Party on Terrorism (International Aspects) (COTER), which is mainly composed of representatives of the member states' ministries of foreign affairs and meets once a month to deal with issues related to external matters, threat assessments and policy recommendations as regards third countries and regions, implementation of the United Nations conventions and the coordination of work, particularly in the United Nations, as well as handling seminars on the financing of terrorism.

3.2.2 Counter-terrorism coordination within Africa

Counter-terrorism has been incorporated into the African Union Peace and Security Architecture (APSA), which provides the political impetus and a larger legal framework for coordination and implementation of counter-terrorism norms in Africa. For example, the Solemn Declaration on a Common African Defence and Security Policy identifies international terrorism and terrorist activities as factors engendering

[89] The Council of the European Union in that declaration also appointed Mr Gijs M. de Vries, a former Dutch deputy minister, who since 19 September 2007 has been replaced by Mr Gilles de Kerchove, a Belgian diplomat, as the Counterterrorism Coordinator (see *ibid.*, 111).

[90] *Ibid.*, 109.

insecurity in Africa and requiring coordination and collective responses by AU member states.[91] In addition, AU member states further commit themselves to intensify collaboration and cooperation in all aspects related to combating international terrorism and any other form of organized transnational crime or destabilization efforts directed against any member state.[92] This means that the obligation to implement the AU CT norms is not limited only to those states that have ratified or acceded to specific relevant AU treaties, but extended to all AU member states. In fact, as a matter of AU legal practice, activities of the AU Commission aimed at ensuring coordination within the framework of the AU CT instruments do not distinguish between states parties and states not parties to AU treaties. All the Commission's CT activities are intended for all member states.

The African Union Plan of Action on the prevention and combat of terrorism underscores the importance of joint action and a concerted response to eradicate terrorism and notes also that given the severe conditions of poverty and deprivation experienced by large section of the African population, few countries on the continent are in a position on their own to marshal the requisite resources to combat terrorism. The Plan of Action adumbrates a wide range of measures to be taken in the areas of police and border control, legislation and judiciary, suppression of financing for terrorism, and exchange of information as well as the ratification and accession to regional and international CT treaties. It also specifically identifies measures for ensuring coordination at the national, regional, continental and international levels.

The need to enhance and harmonize continental efforts in the prevention and combat of terrorism in all its aspects is further underlined by the Protocol to the OAU Convention on the prevention and combating of terrorism, which obligates states parties to 'establish national contact points in order to facilitate the timely exchange and sharing of information on terrorist groups and activities at the regional, continental and

[91] See paras. 9(d) and 13(a) of the Solemn Declaration on a Common African Defence and Security Policy, adopted in Sirte, Libya, by the Second extraordinary session of the AU summit, 27–8 February 2004. See: www.africa-union.org/News_Events/2ND%20EX%20ASSEMBLY/Declaration%20on%20a%20Comm.Af%20Def%20Sec.pdf.

[92] See Art. 5(a) of the African Union Non-Aggression and Common Defence Pact, adopted by the Fourth ordinary session of the AU summit, held in Abuja, Nigeria, January 2005. See: www.africa-union.org/root/au/Documents/Treaties/text/Non%20Aggression%20Common%20Defence%20Pact.pdf.

international levels, including the cooperation of States for suppressing the financing of terrorism'.[93] In addition, states parties are required to strengthen coordination in the areas of smart terrorism, or the use of sophisticated technology including the internet and/or the possible acquisition of weapons of mass destruction by terrorists.[94]

Operational coordination is maintained at the level of the Assembly of Heads of State and Government of the African Union, which periodically reviews the issue, particularly through the biannual reports of the Peace and Security Council of the African Union on its activities and the state of peace and security in Africa. The Assembly is also the highest decision-making body, which adopts legally binding instruments and determines policy directions for the Union. Other policy organs are the Executive Council and the Committee of Ambassadors (Permanent Representative Committee), which review and recommend policies on a more regular basis.

The PSC has the primary responsibility for the day-to-day harmonization and coordination of AU counter-terrorism efforts. Under the Protocol to the OAU Convention, the PSC is expected to establish the operating procedures for information gathering, processing and dissemination, as well as the mechanisms to facilitate the exchange of information on patterns and trends in terrorist activities.[95] Counter-terrorism, however, has become the weakest link of the PSC's agenda, which, since its inauguration in 2004 has dedicated less than 1 per cent of its time to the issue. As such, many aspects of the AU counter-terrorism regimes, particularly those related to coordination, remain unimplemented. The AU Commission is also entrusted with the task of coordinating, monitoring and evaluating progress on the implementation of AU counter-terrorism norms. Subregional mechanisms such as the Economic Community of West African States (ECOWAS) and the Intergovernmental Authority on Development (IGAD) are also recognized as institutions to promote AU counter-terrorism coordination both at the subregional level among states and at the level of interaction with relevant continental institutions including the AU.

[93] Art. 3(d) of the Protocol to the OAU Convention on the prevention and combating of terrorism, adopted by the Third ordinary session of the AU summit, held in Addis Ababa, Ethiopia, July 2004. See: www.africa-union.org/root/au/Documents/Treaties/Text/The%20Protocol%20on%20Terrorism%2026July2004.pdf.

[94] Protocol to the OAU Convention, Art. 3(f). [95] *Ibid.*, Art. 4(a–b).

Technical coordination is carried out by the African Centre for the Study and Research on Terrorism (ACSRT), which was established in October 2004, specifically to serve as an AU mechanism to centralize, collect and disseminate information, studies and analysis on terrorism and terrorist groups; provide technical expertise and promote the coordination and standardization of efforts aimed at enhancing the capacity of member states to prevent and combat terrorism.[96] In spite of a number of challenges including inadequate resources, the ACSRT has, with funding support from the United States, EU member states and the government of Algeria, organized seminars, regional workshops and other capacity-building activities for African states on critical topics related to the prevention and combating of terrorism including law enforcement training, critical infrastructure protection, combating the financing of terrorism and the terrorist use of the internet.[97] These seminars have also served as forums for reassessing vulnerabilities of each region, taking stock of counter-terrorism measures and existing capacities of states, facilitating information-sharing and counter-terrorism best practices, as well as enhancing synergies among national, regional and continental counter-terrorism initiatives.

Prior to the establishment of the ACSRT, practical counter-terrorism coordination within the AU was sustained through the high-level intergovernmental meetings, which brought together experts and governmental authorities including intelligence officials from AU member states,[98] international partners, the United Nations and other international organizations to review and discuss the continued threat posed by international terrorism, the state of preparedness in Africa and areas to strengthen coordination. The first high-level meeting, which was held in Algiers in September 2002, adopted the AU Plan of Action, containing a

[96] See Parts IV and V of the Modalities for the Functioning of the African Centre for Studies and Research on Terrorism (ACSRT). See: www.caert.org.dz/en/index.

[97] Center on Global Counterterrorism Cooperation, 'Building Capacity in the Area of Counterterrorism in West Africa in the Framework of the UN Global Counterterrorism Strategy', Workshop Discussion Paper (17 September 2009), 1. See: www.globalct.org/images/content/pdf/discussion/09Sept17_discussion_paper.pdf.

[98] In 2005, the AU established the Committee of Intelligence and Security Services of Africa (CISSA), to strengthen coordination among intelligence agencies in Africa. See AU decision, Assembly/AU/Dec.62 (IV) adopted in Abuja, Nigeria in January 2005. See: www.africa-union.org/root/au/Documents/Decisions/hog/Decisions_Abuja_Jan_2005.pdf.

comprehensive set of recommendations on measures to be taken including the establishment of the ACSRT to prevent and combat terrorism in Africa. The second high-level meeting also held in Algiers, in October 2004, identified existing gaps in the implementation of regional and international instruments and adopted a declaration, containing recommendations for bridging those gaps and for quelling the terrorist threat in Africa.[99]

Despite these measures, practical CT coordination within the AU is weak. This is not peculiar to CT, though it is certainly more acute given the low terrorism threat perception in Africa. The history of Pan-Africanism and regional integration in Africa, from which the AU emerged, did not give priority to collective security, and therefore cooperation among African countries on security issues, particularly transnational threats such as terrorism, is only emerging.

3.3 *Delivery of technical assistance*

Technical assistance here refers to goods and/or services including financial support provided to states to enable them to acquire or enhance their capabilities individually or collectively to prevent and combat terrorism. The delivery of technical assistance has become an important tool for promoting regional cooperation in the implementation of counter-terrorism agreements. According to the United Nations Security Council Counter-Terrorism Committee (CTC) established pursuant to the Security Council Resolution 1373, technical assistance contributes to help states to build their capacities to combat terrorism, facilitates in-state cooperation and improves states' protection against terrorism.[100]

While international and regional agreements provide for the same obligations for all states, there is, however, a big disparity among states in their capacities to fulfil these obligations. Since international law does not require that states demonstrate technical and resource fitness to implement a treaty prior to joining it, many states, especially those from the developing world, lack the technical skills and equipment to

[99] See the Declaration of the Second High-Level Intergovernmental Meeting on the prevention and combating of terrorism in Africa, held in Algiers, 13–14 October 2004 (Mtg/HLIG/Conv.Terror/Decl. (II) Rev. 2).

[100] See report by the Chair of the Counterterrorism Committee on the problems encountered in the implementation of Security Council Res. 1373 (2001) (UN Doc. S/2004/70 (2004)), 4.

implement regional and international agreements effectively. ROs therefore serve as regional hubs for identifying, pooling and redistributing appropriate resources to states to build or enhance their capabilities and to ensure a uniform and effective application of regional and international counter-terrorism agreements. The common ROs' methodology for delivery of assistance comprise needs assessment of member states, tailor-made training programmes, and assistance workshops and seminars.[101] It also indicates that ROs are not alone in the task of delivering counter-terrorism technical assistance, as they do so together with other international organizations and institutions such as the United Nations, United Nations Office on Drugs and Crime (UNODC), Financial Action Task Force (FATF), World Bank, International Monetary Fund (IMF), Interpol and NATO. ROs, however, still hold the comparative advantage because of their proximity and ability to identify needs and technical assistance resources.

There are various forms of counter-terrorism technical assistance. These include assistance in legal matters such as drafting and/or reviewing and commenting on national legislations, advising states on best practices or on what strategy or measures to take to prevent and combat terrorism, helping states to join and implement regional and relevant UN counter-terrorism instruments dealing with different aspects of terrorism (currently sixteen treaties), and providing financial support and counter-terrorism equipment. Assistance is often delivered through national, subregional and regional workshops and seminars on specific counter-terrorism topics.

3.3.1 European counter-terrorism technical assistance delivery

The delivery of technical assistance is an integral part of the EU counter-terrorism strategy. Since 9/11, the EU has prioritized on security as a precondition for development,[102] which has allowed it to include counter-terrorism as a condition for official development assistance. This nexus between development and terrorism has helped to broaden the scope for technical assistance on terrorism matters. Technical assistance coordination takes place at two main levels. First is at the level of

[101] See, for example, the CTC's technical assistance database at: www.un.org/sc/ctc/directory/dindex.html.

[102] A Secure Europe in a Better World: European Security Strategy (2009) at: www.consilium.europa.eu/uedocs/cmsUpload/78367.pdf.

the EU and member states. Objective 5 of the EU Plan of Action on combating terrorism emphasizes the need 'to enhance the capability of the European Union and of Member States to deal with the consequences of a terrorist attack'. Such assistance should be channelled to strengthen states' capabilities in the areas such as emergency response, protection of critical infrastructure, protection of citizens, detection and identification of threats, as well as support to terrorist victims. The second level of technical assistance is support to external entities or countries and organizations outside the European Union. Objective 7 of the EU Plan of Action on combating terrorism requires the Union to 'target actions under EU external relations towards priority Third Countries where counter-terrorist capacity or commitment to combating terrorism needs to be enhanced'. Member states and the EU are required to carry out a range of measures, including measures to develop and implement technical assistance strategies and programmes aimed at enhancing the counter-terrorist capacity of priority countries, in coordination with other international organizations (including the United Nations) and donor states.

This new EU post-9/11, development–terrorism nexus finds practical expression in the Partnership Agreement between the members of the African, Caribbean and Pacific Group of States and the European Community and its Member States, signed in Cotonou, Benin, on 23 June 2000 (commonly referred to as the EU–ACP Cotonou Partnership Agreement), which remains the largest EU overseas development support programme involving over one hundred countries. After 9/11, the Agreement was revised in 2005 to explicitly provide, *inter alia*, for counter-terrorism measures.[103] Indeed as Niagalé Bagoyoko and Marie Gibert[104] and Kwesi Aning[105] have illustrated in their papers, development aid is increasingly being used for a wider variety of donor objectives including for combating terrorism. In this context, EU development assistance has served as extended counter-terrorism technical assistance.

[103] See Art. 11(a) of the revised Partnership Agreement between the Members of the African, Caribbean and Pacific Group States of the One Part, and the European Community and its Member States, of the Other Part, signed in Lomé, Togo, 2005.

[104] N. Bagoyoko and M. Gibert, 'The European Union in Africa: The Linkage Between Security, Governance and Development from an Institutional Perspective' (2007) IDS Working Paper 284.

[105] K. Aning, 'Security, the War on Terror and Official Development Assistance', Kofi Annan International Peacekeeping Training Centre, at www.nsi-ins.ca/english/pdf/Theme_paper_Three.pdf.

The Cotonou Agreement, for example, states that 'Financial and technical assistance in the area of cooperation in the fight against terrorism will be financed by resources other than those intended for the financing of ACP–EC development cooperation.'[106]

Funding for counter-terrorism-related activities is provided through the EU regular external assistance programmes. Such financial assistance covers eight main areas as identified by the UN Counter-Terrorism Committee (CTC) established pursuant to the UN Security Council Resolution 1373, namely, drafting of counter-terrorism legislation; financial law and practice; customs law and practice; immigration law and practice; extradition law and practice; police and law enforcement work; illegal arms trafficking and capacity building for the judiciary. Currently, the EU is providing around €400 million to ongoing counter-terrorism programmes in about eighty countries.[107] It is also providing a modest degree of assistance to the African Union Centre for Study and Research on Terrorism.[108] In 2007, the EU pledged to provide technical assistance support to the ACSRT amounting to €665 million for CT programmes relating to information technology, the development of a database system, the setting up of a documentation centre and for the organization of training programmes for AU member states.[109]

Another important aspect of EU counter-terrorism technical assistance delivery is the Atlas Network – an informal cooperation structure among special intervention units in member states, through which the EU has been able to provide technical training by organizing joint CT exercises and seminars, studies and the exchange of materials on operational procedures and techniques.[110] The success of such exercises as in Germany (2003) and the Netherlands (2004) has made the Atlas Network a critical CT tool.

[106] Declaration XI of the Agreement amending the Partnership Agreement between the Members of the African, Caribbean and Pacific Group States of the One Part, and the European Community and its Member States, of the Other Part, signed in Lomé, Togo, in 2005.

[107] See EU website: http://ec.europa.eu/justice_home/fsj/terrorism/international/fsj_terrorism_international_en.htm#technical_assistance.

[108] See G. de Vries, 'The Nexus between EU Crisis Management and Counterterrorism', in S. Blockmans (ed.), *The European Union and Crisis Management: Policy and Legal Aspects* (The Hague: TMC Asser Press, 2008), 355.

[109] Noted in E. Rosand, A. Millar, J. Ipe and M. Healey, 'The UN Global Counterterrorism Strategy and Regional and Subregional Bodies: Strengthening a Critical Partnership' (2008) Center on Global Counterterrorism Cooperation, 11, at www.globalct.org/images/content/pdf/reports/strengthening_a_critical_partnership.pdf.

[110] L. Block, 'Europe's Emerging Counterterrorism Elite: The Atlas Network' (2007) 5 *Terrorism Monitor* 10.

3.2.2 African counter-terrorism technical assistance delivery

The AU does not directly provide technical assistance to states; the need for such assistance is, however, well enshrined in AU counter-terrorism instruments. The main role of the AU is to assess the needs of states, identify sources and providers of technical assistance, and facilitate access of states to technical assistance resources. In this context, the AU cooperates with relevant international organizations including the UNODC, IMF, World Bank, UN and the EU in the delivery of assistance programmes to African States. The AU, however, may also deliver its own limited technical assistance to states. Under the AU Plan of Action for the prevention and combating of terrorism and the Protocol to the OAU Convention on the prevention and combating of terrorism, the AU Commission is required to take a range of measures including the provision of technical assistance covering legal and law enforcement matters, combating the financing of terrorism, the preparation of model laws and guidelines to help member states to formulate legislation and related measures for the prevention and combating of terrorism.[111]

A blueprint of the AU technical assistance delivery in the African Model Anti-Terrorism Law, adopted by the 17th summit held in Malabo, Equatorial Guinea in July 2011. The Model Law is a ready-made technical assistance or an aide to African states to bring their CT legislation up to date and to provide guidance in the effective implementation of international and regional CT instruments. The establishment of the ACSRT was an attempt by the AU to endow itself with a capacity to deliver, in a more systematic manner, technical assistance to its members. Currently, the Centre provides assistance on threat and readiness assessment and analysis; assessment and analysis of domestic legislation and CT measures; identification of gaps, priority needs, problems and challenges associated with the implementation of Resolutions 1373 (2001) and 1624 (2005); assistance in preparing country reports, and advice concerning best technical assistance and expertise available on the continent.[112]

The ACSRT's main methodology for the delivery of technical assistance has been through regional workshops held in all the five subregions in

[111] See for example, Protocol to the OAU Convention on the Prevention and Combating of Terrorism, Art. 5(2a).

[112] See details on the CTC website: www.un.org/sc/ctc/directory/doa/ACSRT.html.

Africa, addressing specific regional and individual states' counter-terrorism challenges. To further facilitate the provision of technical assistance to AU states, the ACSRT is developing a database of CT experts in Africa. It also has plans to institute a blacklist of terrorists and terrorist groups and their activities in Africa. Since 9/11, 46 of the 53 AU African states have received technical assistance in one form or another, with the majority of countries receiving assistance in the areas of CT law and practice, police and law enforcement, extradition law and practice and financial law and practice from both international and regional technical assistance providers.[113] Since its inauguration in October 2004, the ACSRT has yet to reach its full functional capacities. As already discussed above, the Centre suffers from a perennial lack of sustainable funding and inadequate human resources, further compounded by internal bureaucratic bottlenecks, lengthy and cumbersome recruitment procedures at the AU Commission, geopolitical factors within the AU, as well as the structural design of the Centre.

The Centre was initially envisaged to have a capacity of fifty-one personnel (including experts and general service staff), but the final structure approved by the Executive Council and the Assembly of the African Union, in Khartoum, Sudan, in January 2006, provides for just half of that. The fact that the issue of terrorism does not rank high among the AU's priorities has further aggravated the funding chances of the Centre. Indeed, the first AU budget allocation to the Centre in 2005 was just a little below US$700,000, an amount that fell well short of what is needed to cover the annual running cost of the Centre. The Algerian government, however, provided the Centre's headquarters free of charge and also a lump sum of US$2 million as seed money for running the Centre.

3.4 Promoting human rights in counter-terrorism

ROs have been the strongest defendants of human rights in counter-terrorism. The question of human rights is one of the most controversial issues and the weakest link in the global fight against terrorism. In the view of Joan Fitzpatrick, the implications for human rights fall into two categories – the first relates to the control measures against individuals suspected of terrorist involvement, and the second relates to the intervening states, which frequently commit human rights violations against

[113] See CTC index for Africa: www.un.org/sc/ctc/matrix/mindex.html.

terrorist suspects and collaterally affect civilians.[114] The commission of a terrorist act is in itself an infringement against the human rights of individuals.[115] To borrow Fitzpatrick's words, 'Acts of terrorism such as the attacks of September 11 are obviously antithetical to human rights values, not least the right to life and the inherent dignity of the human person.'[116] Terrorists take advantage of human rights values such as the right to freedom of movement, freedom of speech and the right to privacy in order to commit terrorist acts. These values are often the first casualties in states' responses to terrorism. States have a high tendency to respond to terrorist acts with impunity, and national counter-terrorism strategies are heavily reliant on military actions and draconian anti-terrorist legislations, which often contravene international law and human rights values. As Justice Goldstone and Janine Simpson aver, 'states cannot be allowed to subvert fundamental human rights and freedoms such as those guaranteed in the key international human rights instruments'.[117] Reconciling the dichotomy between the exigencies of national security and the necessity to protect human rights values is crucial to winning the global war on terrorism.

As the clearing house for regional norms, ROs have a specific mandate to ensure that states' counter-terrorism activities are conducted in conformity with the relevant regional and international human rights law. There are a range of measures that ROs could take to promote human rights. These include: making respect for human right in counter-terrorism actions a regional norm by incorporating human rights concerns into regional counter-terrorism instruments; scrutinizing states' counter-terrorism activities; promoting awareness and strategies for protecting human rights in counter-terrorism efforts; commenting on states' counter-terrorism legislation and providing advice on human rights best practices; and establishing regional human rights courts and other mechanisms to coordinate and harmonize states' counter-terrorism actions and policies with human rights.

114 J. Fitzpatrick, 'Speaking Law to Power: The War against Terrorism and Human Rights' (2003) 14 *European Journal of International Law* 241, 247.

115 These human rights are enunciated in the 1948 Universal Declaration of Human Rights. For a complete list of international human rights law treaties, see Office of the United Nations High Commissioner for Human Rights, 'Human Rights, Terrorism and Counterterrorism', Fact Sheet No. 32, 3.

116 Fitzpatrick, 'Speaking Law to Power', 243.

117 R. Goldstone and J. Simpson, 'Evaluating the Role of the International Criminal Court as a Legal Response to Terrorism' (2003) 16 *Harvard Human Rights Journal* 13, 14.

3.4.1 Measures taken in Europe to ensure human rights in counter-terrorism

The legal framework for the protection of the human rights of European citizens is the European Convention for the Protection of Human Rights and Fundamental Freedoms, adopted in Rome in 1950, and which has been supplemented by several protocols.[118] The Convention obligates all contracting parties to secure to everyone within their jurisdiction fundamental rights and freedoms such as the rights to life, liberty and security, fair trial; no punishment without law; respect for private and family life; freedom of expression and of thoughts, conscience and religion; and the prohibition of discrimination.[119] It is beyond the scope of this chapter to discuss in detail the European human rights regimes and the scope of their application. It is however necessary to point out at this juncture that human rights instruments both regional and international are not antithetical to the fight against terrorism; rather, they are the central pillar for winning the war on terrorism.

The requirement to respect human rights in counter-terrorism activities is a well-established norm of the European institutions, which have incorporated human rights concerns into their counter-terrorism arsenal including decisions, common positions and strategies. As early as 2002, the Committee of Ministers of the Council of Europe adopted 'Guidelines on Human Rights and the Fight against Terrorism' in which member states reaffirmed their obligations to respect human rights (as provided under international and regional instruments including the ECHR) in all measures taken to fight terrorism.[120] The Guidelines also enumerated measures that states cannot take in the fight against terrorism which were viewed to trample on human rights. For example, states cannot use torture and other degrading treatment or punishment against a terrorist suspect.[121] The Guidelines also prevent states from using unlawful measures such as

[118] Other fundamental human rights instruments include the 1997 Treaty of Amsterdam amending the Treaty on European Union, the Treaties establishing the European Communities [2008] OJ C 340; 1961 European Social Charter, Council of Europe Treaty Series No. 35; 1989 Community Charter of the Fundamental Social Rights of Workers.

[119] See 1950 Convention for the Protection of Human Rights and Fundamental Freedoms, Council of Europe Treaty Series No. 5, Art. 1(1), at www.echr.coe.int/nr/rdonlyres/d5cc24a7-dc13-4318-b457-5c9014916d7a/0/englishanglais.pdf.

[120] See 2002 Guidelines on Human Rights and the Fight against Terrorism, preamble, at www.coe.int/T/E/Human_rights/h-inf(2002)8eng.pdf.

[121] See Guidelines, Art. IV.

espionage, body searches, house searches, bugging, telephone tapping, surveillance, which are not provided by law.[122]

The European Union complements the organs of the Council of Europe in relation to counter-terrorism measures. In November 2004, the European Council approved The Hague Programme on strengthening freedom, security and justice in the European Union. The Programme has contributed to strengthening the coordination and the capability of the EU and its member states in guaranteeing fundamental rights, minimum procedural safeguards, more freedom of movement, and access to justice, as well as protection to persons in need. It also identified common actions such as availability of information to regulate migration flows and to control the external borders of the Union in order to fight organized cross-border crimes including the threat of terrorism, by introducing a Common European Asylum System.[123]

The norm against human rights violation in counter-terrorism was codified into law through adoption and ratification of the Council of Europe's 2005 Convention on the Prevention of Terrorism.[124] The Convention reiterates the principles enunciated in the ECHR and obligates states to protect those rights in their activities aimed at combating terrorism, particularly in the areas relating to the training of law enforcement authorities and other bodies, and in the field of education, culture, information, media and public awareness raising.[125] There are three main categories of persons protected under European counter-terrorism human rights, namely, individual citizens (general public), whose rights need to be guaranteed and protected; the victims of terrorist acts, who need to be cared for and compensated; and terrorist suspects, whose rights to dignity, due process of law and fair trial are to be respected.

Through its case law, the European Court of Human Rights plays an instrumental role in strengthening the fight against terrorism, as well as streamlining states' human rights practices. In *Öcalan* v. *Turkey*,[126] for

[122] *Ibid.*, Art. VI.

[123] See 'The Hague Programme: Strengthening Freedom, Security and Justice in the European Union', approved by the Council of the European Union on 5 November 2004. See: www.libertysecurity.org/IMG/pdf/hague_programme_en.pdf.

[124] 2005 Convention on the Prevention of Terrorism, Council of Europe Treaty Series No.196.

[125] See Art. 3 of the Council of Europe Convention on the Prevention of Terrorism, adopted in Warsaw, 16 May 2005.

[126] *Öcalan* v. *Turkey*, Judgment of 12 May 2005 [2005] ECHR IV.

example, the Court emphasized that terrorist suspects must be given a fair trial. The applicant of the case, Mr Öcalan, the leader of the Kurdistan Workers' Party, considered a terrorist group, was convicted in 1999 by the Turkish court for his alleged role in various crimes committed by his party and was given a death penalty, at a time when capital punishment had not been abolished in Turkey. In its judgment, the Court reasoned that with respect to the death penalty, Articles 2 (right to life) and 3 (prohibition of torture), regarded as core rights of the ECHR, had not been violated. It, however, found that the imposition of the death sentence following an unfair trial that had not been in compliance with Article 6 (right to a fair trial) of the Convention amounted to inhuman treatment and thus constituted a violation of Article 3.[127]

In another case, *Ramirez Sanchez* v. *France*,[128] the Court considered it necessary for a state to take some extraordinary security measures to keep a high-profile terrorist away from the society, given the danger that such a person may pose to the society. In this case, the applicant, Mr Ramirez Sanchez, popularly known as 'Carlos', was convicted by the French government on terrorist charges. Mr Sanchez complained that he had been kept in solitary confinement for over eight years and that this amounted to both mental and physical torture or that his Article 3 rights under the ECHR had been violated. The Court accepted that Mr Sanchez, 'one of the world's most dangerous terrorists', posed serious problems for the French authorities and found it understandable that the French government had considered it necessary to take extraordinary security measures.[129] The Court also noted the fact that the applicant had not been kept in complete solitary confinement or total social isolation as he had claimed. With this reasoning, the Court ruled (in a close vote of four to three) that Article 3 had not been violated or that the confinement of Mr Sanchez did not amount to torture. Here the Court failed to uphold the principle it had established in a similar case, *Mathew* v. *the Netherlands*[130] (though not related to terrorism) – that solitary confinement for an excessive and unnecessarily protracted period, detention 'for at least seven months in a cell that failed to offer adequate protection against the elements, and detention in a location whereby the

[127] *Ibid.*, para. 169.
[128] *Ramirez Sanchez* v. *France*, Judgment of 4 July 2006 [2006] ECHR IX.
[129] *Ibid.*, para. 125.
[130] *Mathew* v. *the Netherlands*, Judgment of 29 September 2005 [2005] ECHR IX.

applicant could not gain access to outdoor exercise and fresh air without unnecessary and avoidable physical suffering', constituted a violation of Article 3.[131]

Similarly, in a landmark case, *Saadi* v. *Italy*,[132] the Court in February 2008 ruled unanimously that under no circumstances, including the threat of terrorism or national security concerns, should an individual be exposed to the real risk of torture and other serious human rights abuses. The applicant, Mr Nassim Saadi, a Tunisian national lawfully residing in Italy, had been convicted in absentia in Tunisia of terrorism-related offences and sentenced to twenty years' imprisonment. The Italian government had authorized the deportation of Mr Saadi on grounds that he posed a high security risk to Italy. Mr Saadi claimed that he would be at risk of torture and ill-treatment if deported to Tunisia, where mistreatment of alleged terrorists is routine and well documented. In its judgment, the Grand Chamber, as in a previous decision in *Chahal* v. *United Kingdom*,[133] reaffirmed the absolute nature of Article 3 of the Convention, making the prohibition of torture a peremptory international norm that European states cannot derogate even on serious matters of national security such as terrorism. The issues of deportation, human rights and national security considerations remain contentious; and many European governments are not at ease with the rulings of the European Human Rights Court at Strasbourg.

3.4.2 Measures taken in Africa to promote human rights in counter-terrorism

The legal foundation for human rights protection in Africa is the African Charter on Human and Peoples' Rights (ACHPR), which has been ratified by all fifty-three AU member states and entered into force on 21 October 1986.[134] The Charter postulates a complex notion of human rights, which go beyond the rights and freedoms of the individual to include the obligation of the individual to his/her society or community. It also weaves together political, cultural, social and economic rights of

[131] *Ibid.*, para. 217. [132] *Saadi* v. *Italy*, Judgment of 28 February 2008 [2008] ECHR.

[133] *Chahal* v. *the United Kingdom*, Judgment of 15 November 1996 [1996] ECHR V.

[134] 1988 African Charter on Human and Peoples' Rights, 1520 UNTS 217. The Charter is supplemented by two protocols – 2003 Protocol to the African Charter on Human and Peoples' Rights on the Rights of Women in Africa, and the 1998 Protocol to the African Charter on Human and Peoples' Rights on the Establishment of the African Court on Human and Peoples' Rights; as well as the 1990 Charter on the Rights and Welfare of the Child, OAU Doc. CAB/LEG/24.9/49 (1990).

the individual, as well as the rights of the community over an individual, as constituting human and peoples' rights. The Charter promulgates the principle that human beings are inviolable and that every human being is entitled to respect for his life and the integrity of his person and that no one may be arbitrarily deprived of either.[135] Article 5 of the Charter obligates states parties to protect the rights of every individual, to respect the dignity inherent in a human being and to recognize his legal status. It also prohibits all forms of exploitation and degradation of man particularly slavery, the slave trade, torture, cruel, inhuman or degrading punishment and treatment.

The OAU/AU has long espoused the need to ensure human rights protection in efforts to promote peace and security in Africa. African states committed themselves to the 'unhindered exercise of individual rights as enshrined in the African Charter on Human and Peoples' Rights and those of the Universal Declaration of Human Rights as a prerequisite for sustainable peace and security in Africa, as well as a necessary condition for economic development, cooperation and integration'.[136] This has been further institutionalized in the new African Peace and Security Architecture (APSA), which includes among its objectives for the prevention of conflicts, the need to protect human rights and fundamental freedoms and respect for the sanctity of human life.[137]

In the area of counter-terrorism, the preamble to the 1999 OAU Convention states that 'terrorism constitutes a serious violation of human rights and, in particular, the rights to physical integrity, life, freedom and security, and impedes socio-economic development through destabilization of states'. Indeed, the Protocol to the 1999 OAU Convention obligates states to take all necessary measures to protect the fundamental human rights of their populations against all acts of terrorism[138] and to outlaw torture and other degrading and inhumane treatment, including discriminatory and racist treatment of terrorist suspects, which are inconsistent with international law.[139]

The AU counter-terrorism human rights regimes still have gaps, particularly in the area of states' accountability for human rights abuses in their actions aimed at preventing and combating terrorism. Another

135 See African Charter, Art. 3.

136 See Memorandum of Understanding on Security, Stability, Development and Cooperation in Africa, Doc. OAU/Civil Society.3 (II), Core Objective I(h).

137 See Protocol Relating to the Establishment of the Peace and Security Council of the African Union, Art. 3(f).

138 Protocol to the 1999 OAU Convention, Art. 3(1)(a).

139 *Ibid.*, Art. 3(1)(k).

major pitfall is the lack of a stringent enforcement of both AU human rights and counter-terrorism regimes. This is even more alarming as there is no single body that can hold states accountable for their human rights violations. As Paul Tiyambe Zeleza has rightly observed:

> Many African governments have rushed to pass broadly, badly or cynically worded anti-terrorism laws and other draconian procedural measures, and to set up special courts or allow special rules of evidence that violate fair trial rights, which they use to limit civil rights and freedoms, and to harass, intimidate, and imprison and crackdown on political opponents.[140]

The most disturbing fact is that the African Union is kept completely outside the loop on counter-terrorism developments in member states, especially on matters relating to legislation, investigation, police enforcement and the judiciary. The failure of many states to report regularly to the African Union on their counter-terrorism activities, as provided under the Protocol and the AU Plan of Action, has meant that many states' legislation has gone unnoticed, and the AU is unable to tell which country is actually in full or partial compliance with continental counter-terrorism instruments. Take for example, the famous anti-terrorism bills of South Africa, Kenya and Ethiopia, which have drawn widespread criticisms from their own citizens and human rights groups such as Amnesty International and Human Rights Watch. The AU never commented on these bills to determine if they were consistent with regional and international instruments. And, indeed, these bills do define terrorism in ways that are inconsistent with the 1999 OAU Convention.

The AU's inability to effectively monitor states' compliance of human and peoples' rights in counter-terrorism is essentially due to the absence of an enforcement mechanism such as a human rights court, as is the case of Europe. The African Commission for Human and Peoples' Rights established pursuant to Article 30 of ACHPR, which is responsible for solving legal problems relating to human rights and fundamental freedoms arising from the Charter, has no clout to enforce the provisions of the Charter. The Commission can only make recommendations to the AU Assembly about its findings as to which state is not in compliance with the Charter. Members of the Commission are often bullied by government executives, and critical reports of the Commission are treated with

[140] P. Zeleza, 'The Causes and Cost of War in Africa: From Liberation Struggles to the "War on Terror"', in A. Nhema and P. Zeleza (eds.), *The Roots of African Conflicts: The Causes and Costs* (Oxford: James Currey, 2008), 14.

disdain, which sometimes leads to such reports not being published. Another reason for the Commission's inability to address the issue of human rights in counter-terrorism is the fact that terrorism is not mentioned in the ACHPR and that the issue was never featured in the agenda of the Commission until after 9/11. Thus, the Commission has not been able to examine the anti-terrorism activities of member states in terms of their compliance with the Charter. It has, however, recently included the issue on its agenda and indicated its desire to lay out guidelines on the respect for human rights in counter-terrorism activities.

The recent operationalization of the African Court on Human and Peoples' Rights and its emergence with the African Court of Justice is a positive development in efforts towards ensuring the day-to-day protection of human rights in Africa. Although it has not been given a specific mandate to deal with counter-terrorism matters, it is expected that the Court will, through jurisprudence, extend its jurisdiction to matters relating to human rights protection in states' counter-terrorism actions.[141] The issue of human rights and international criminal justice in Africa once again came to the fore, following tension between the AU and the ICC over the latter's indictment of President al Bashir of Sudan and the late Colonel Muammar Gaddafi of Libya, for their roles in atrocities committed in Darfur and Libya, respectively. A positive development, if one could call it so, has been the decision to enlarge the jurisdiction of the African Court to include various international crimes, such as war crimes, crimes against humanity, genocide and terrorism. It may therefore be expected that the new court will contribute to the prosecution of terrorist cases in Africa and human rights regimes.

3.5 Cooperation with the United Nations

The theoretical framework for ROs–UN cooperation on counter-terrorism can be traced to Chapter VIII of the UN Charter, which although it does not make specific reference to terrorism, does provide for cooperation between the UNSC and regional arrangements and agencies.[142] Chapters V (Article 24), VII and VIII established a hierarchical order that accords to the UNSC the primacy role for the

[141] Art. 3 of the Protocol to the African Charter on Human and Peoples' Rights on the Establishment of the African Court of Human and Peoples' Rights, states that the jurisdiction of the Court shall extend to all cases and disputes submitted to it concerning the interpretation and application of the Charter, this Protocol and any other relevant Human Rights instrument ratified by the States concerned.

[142] See UN Charter, Ch. VIII, Arts. 52–4.

maintenance of international peace, while ROs or 'regional arrangements' are conceived as building blocks or complementary mechanisms with the requirement to coordinate their activities with the UNSC as long as such activities are consistent with the purposes and principles of the UN Charter. But to what extent are ROs important to the UN in the prevention and combating of terrorism?

The nature of the relationship between the UN and ROs is not clear, at least within the context of the Charter. Indeed, the absence of details in Chapter VIII, as Ademola Abass argues, meant an uncertain relationship between the UN and regional organizations.[143] This is more of a theoretical problem. In reality, however, the ambiguity in Chapter VIII has enabled the UN to be flexible in its relations with ROs, adapting to the challenges in each region. The way the UN relates to the Council of Europe is different from how the Organization relates to the AU. For example, in the case of the latter, the UN has used the AU to deploy peacekeeping missions in complex cases such as Darfur and Somalia where the UN itself is unable to do so directly. In the area of counter-terrorism, operational cooperation between the UN and ROs is relatively recent. In the 105 resolutions adopted between 1972 and 2011 by the Security Council (since 1989) and the General Assembly (since 1972) on matters relating to terrorism, few of them make references to ROs. The UN therefore preferred direct cooperation with states on matters relating to the prevention and combating of terrorism. This was also a consequence of the fact that until the end of the Cold War, ROs played a small role in matters of peace and security. It was only after 9/11 that the UN decidedly gave significant attention to cooperation with ROs on counter-terrorism matters. First, counter-terrorism was included in UN bilateral cooperation with regional and subregional organizations. And, second, the Security Council Counter-terrorism Committee organized for the first time, in March 2003, a special meeting (that later became a series) with international, regional and subregional organizations with a view to strengthening international cooperation on counter-terrorism. That meeting helped to define the role that ROs should play in the GWOT vis-à-vis the UN and its agencies, international bodies and subregional organizations.

ROs were deemed to be particularly suited for sustaining a broad-based international cooperation and for providing a platform for states

[143] A. Abass, 'The Security Council and the Challenges of Collective Security in the Twenty-First Century: What Role for African Regional Organisations?', in Lewis, *Global Governance*, vol. I, 91–2.

to share information on terrorist groups and activities, in consonance with Resolution 1373 (September 2001). They were also expected to promote ratification of and adherence to UN CT treaties including their implementation. Cooperation between the UN and ROs on CT matters was also highlighted in the UNSC first ever resolution on cooperation between the two sides. In that resolution, the UNSC, *inter alia*, urged all relevant ROs and subregional organizations to enhance the effectiveness of their counter-terrorism efforts within their respective mandates and to improve coordination with the United Nations.[144]

The goal of UN–ROs cooperation on CT matters has been to promote and sustain multilateral cooperation on counter-terrorism matters. The UN has used ROs' geographic, political, technical and financial leverage to ensure effective implementation of both UN and international CT instruments. The adoption of Resolution 1373 (2001) under Chapter VII of the Charter with sweeping and far-reaching legal obligations on states, as well as the General Assembly Global Counter-Terrorism Strategy (2006) have orchestrated a new era of cooperation between the UN and ROs. These resolutions explicitly request states to intensify their cooperation at all levels and for international, regional and subregional organizations to support them in that endeavour.

As part of cooperation with the UN, ROs have taken broad measures to promote implementation of UN norms. Most regional counter-terrorism norms emanate directly from the UN measures. Both the European institutions and the AU have incorporated into their legal regimes the obligations of states to ratify all UN counter-terrorism conventions and protocols, enact relevant legislations, intensify cooperation on border security, police, extradition, mutual legal assistance, investigation and prosecution of terrorists, suppression of financing of terrorism, respect for human rights in counter-terrorism and a host of other requirements provided for under UN instruments and resolutions. All organizations have also adopted plans of actions and established mechanisms to coordinate and provide counter-terrorism assistance to states.

4 An appraisal of ROs' efforts to promote cooperation on counter-terrorism matters

How one assesses the role of ROs depends on one's theoretical affiliation. A realist would tend to emphasize the centrality of the state in the fight

[144] See UN Doc. S/Res./1631 (2005), para. 6.

against terrorism. This is consistent with the realist–theoretical paradigm, which has always treated the state as the alpha and omega of international relations, whereby intergovernmental institutions such as ROs play a minimal role. As John Mearsheimar states it bluntly, '[intergovernmental] institutions are not the important cause of peace. They matter only on the margins.'[145] In reality, the realist theorem fails to recognize the increasing powers of non-state actors including multinational corporations, and that there are certain issues over which states do not always have choices. With the exception of a few powerful states such as the US and a couple of European countries, the GWOT was driven by institutions such as the UN and ROs. States were at the receiving end.

On the other hand, a liberal institutionalist would stress the utility of ROs as an important force for combating terrorism, premised on the liberal-institutionalist view that intergovernmental organizations (IGOs) do significantly influence states' behaviour in ways that limit tendencies towards realpolitik and conflicts.[146] In their article, 'Do Intergovernmental Organizations Promote Peace?', Charles Boehmer, Erik Gartzke and Timothy Nordstrom capture the main tenet of the institutionalist argument: 'global politics is increasingly organized around regimes and institutions that foster cooperation by providing information and organizational structure, promoting norms and common belief systems, and reducing transaction costs.'[147]

The direct relevance of this debate to the current GWOT has been challenged by some scholars on the grounds that the GWOT is predominantly between states and non-state actors or 'a handful of fanatics scattered across the globe', to borrow Fareed Zakaria's words[148] as opposed to the interstate wars of the past that provided the theatrical cushion for the realist–liberal institutionalist theoretical war.[149] In practice, however, the two theoretical paradigms continue to dominate policy directions and how roles are apportioned to actors in international

145 J. Mearsheimar, 'False Promise of International Institutions' (1994–5) 19 *International Security* 5, 7.

146 This debate is by no means limited to realists and liberal institutionalists. Other theoretical paradigms such as functionalism, the English School and social constructivism, though marginal, have contributed to the debate.

147 C. Boehmer, E. Gartzke and T. Nordstrom, 'Do Intergovernmental Organizations Promote Peace?' (2004) 57 *World Politics* 1, 3.

148 See F. Zakaria, 'The Jihad against the Jihadis: how modern Muslim leaders wage war on extremists – and won', *Newsweek*, 22 February 2010, 23.

149 See for example, A. Cronin, 'Behind the Curve: Globalization and International Terrorism' (2002) 27 *International Security* 30.

relations. A realist would typically respond to terrorism with military force, while a liberal institutionalist will emphasize the need for far more comprehensive and multifaceted measures that combine enduring military and non-military strategies for combating contemporary terrorism.[150] The US initial response to 9/11 evinced President George W. Bush's realist inclination.[151] As such, the US's CT strategy of 2002 was premised on military solutions and never articulated a role for ROs. Consistent with this realist logic, many CT experts and practitioners alike in the administration were dismissive of the utility of ROs, on grounds that they were characterized by weak institutional design, including bureaucratic bottlenecks and consensus-based decision-making approaches that render them slow and ineffectual in responding to complex security emergencies of the magnitude of 9/11.

Notwithstanding this, the fact that most of today's ROs were set up mainly to promote integration and economic development and that security, not least CT for that matter, was not initially a central part of their mandate, many ROs, such as the EU, NATO, OSCE, AU, ASEAN, SAARC and the OAS have evolved significantly in performing this function. Despite insurmountable economic and developmental challenges, many of these organizations have made CT one of the core issues for regional cooperation and have also allocated needed resources for that purpose. In their book, *Uniting against Terror: Cooperative Nonmilitary Responses to the Global Terrorist Threat*, David Cortright and George Lopez have fully discerned the significance of ROs' contribution to the GWOT and recommended their inclusion in any holistic, global and sustainable strategies to prevent and combat terrorism.[152] In the same vein, Douglas Lewis argues in favour of greater status for ROs in the governance of the current global order.[153]

Through their more frequent summits and other policy meetings, ROs provide a platform for enforcement by generating pressure on their

[150] See, for example, R. Gunaratna, 'Military and Non-Military Strategies for Combating Terrorism', in R. Gunaratna (ed.), *Combating Terrorism* (Singapore: Marshall Cavendish Academic, 2005), 1–36.

[151] Robert Singh for example, describes the Bush doctrine as representing 'an intellectually coherent amalgam of traditional realist approaches to international relations and an expansively muscular Wilsonianism' ('The Bush Doctrine', in M. Buckley and R. Singh (eds.), *The Bush Doctrine and the War on Terrorism: Global Responses, Global Consequences* (Abingdon: Routledge, 2006), 13).

[152] See D. Cortright and G. Lopez, 'Strategic Counterterrorism', in D. Cortright and G. Lopez (eds.), *Uniting against Terror: Cooperative Nonmilitary Responses to the Global Terrorist Threat* (Cambridge, MA: MIT Press, 2007), 169–88.

[153] D. Lewis, 'Global Governance and the Search for Justice', in Lewis, *Global Governance*, vol. I.

members to implement their regional and international CT obligations. ROs such as the EU also regularly publish data and checklists showing which member states have done what. This helps to generate peer pressure for those states lagging behind to catch up with other states in the community. In addition, ROs provide incentives to states by offering technical assistance, equipment and other forms of CT support. In Africa, for example, nearly all the fifty-three members of the AU have benefited from some form of assistance. ROs therefore play a catalytic role in the efforts of states aimed at deterring terrorism. They help to empower states and regulate their CT activities. ROs such as NATO have contributed militarily to the GWOT. For example, NATO declared the 9/11 terrorist attacks to constitute an attack on all its then nineteen members, invoking its Article 5, thereby equating terrorism to the crime of aggression. In response to 9/11, the Alliance deployed its military aircraft to help to guard the airspace of the United States and eventually took on the fight against terrorism in Afghanistan,[154] and subsequently in Libya (though this operation was not undertaken as a CT venture).

As discussed, the extent to which ROs are successful in mitigating terrorism and in strengthening regional cohesion varies among regions. While this variation is not peculiar to the field of terrorism, it is arguably the weakest link in ROs' CT performance. Regionalism scholars have attributed this discrepancy in ROs' ability to create a common security community to a range of political, economic, social and cultural variables.[155] In the specific area of counter-terrorism, the main factors influencing differences in ROs' performance include structural design (including mandate), nature of states in the region, how local actors perceive terrorism, availability of resources and geopolitical factors, as well as the history of regional cooperation and/or integration on political and security matters.

The European and African CT regimes bear certain resemblances. For example, they both have conventions, protocols, plans of action, decisions and institutions for coordinating a common action. They also reflect developments at the larger international level including the UN. There are also visible differences. For example, the European regimes apply both to states (governments) and to individuals (citizens in

[154] See 'NATO Response to terrorism', *NATO Briefing* (March 2005), 1.

[155] See for example, A. Acharya and A. Johnston, 'Comparing Regional Institutions: An Introduction', in A. Acharya and A. Johnston (eds.), *Crafting Cooperation: Regional International Institutions in Comparative Perspective* (Cambridge: Cambridge University Press, 2007), 7.

member states). European regimes put much emphasis on cooperative law enforcement through mechanisms such as the European Arrest Warrant, Europol and Eurojust. According to David Cortright and George Lopez, this 'institutionalised rule-based approach' is a major distinguishing factor between CT in Europe and what they refer to as the 'extralegal efforts' employed by the United States.[156] The European institutions also have a comprehensive strategy, which determines member states' priorities and harmonizes their approach to combating terrorism. In this case, AU regimes are narrower and regulate only the activities of states without much emphasis on enforcement.

The most serious challenge to ROs' contribution to the GWOT is enforcement of regional and international norms. With the exception of Europe, which has successfully integrated Europol, the European Arrest Warrant and Eurojust into its CT enforcement apparatus, there remain huge gaps in ROs' enforcement efforts. Many ROs lack the structural mechanisms and resource capacity to monitor implementation and enforce CT measures at the national level. ROs such as the AU, ASEAN, SAARC and the OAS prefer a consultative and/or consensus-based approach to a legalistic and institutionalized one to conflict resolution, which has also been applied to counter-terrorism. Enforcement through this approach is based on states' volition or goodwill, and therefore CT has become a victim of states' priorities.

Another challenge resides in the area of cooperation. Despite elevating counter-terrorism cooperation to a fundamental international norm for combating terrorism, there remain barriers to regional CT cooperation. Some of these barriers, as John McFarlane has identified, include corruption, sovereignty, economic considerations, nationalism, technology, national interagency rivalries and state complicity.[157] In Europe, the barrier has been more visible in the area of police and intelligence cooperation. As Paul Wilkinson puts it, 'the reality is that national governments are unwilling to allow other governments' intelligence services and police anything more than a limited access to their secret intelligence on terrorism [or indeed on other key security issues]'.[158]

[156] Cortright and Lopez, 'Strategic Counterterrorism', 7.

[157] J. McFarlane, 'Regional and International Cooperation in Tackling Transnational Crime, Terrorism and the Problems of Disrupted States' (2005) 12 *Journal of Financial Crime* 1, 2.

[158] P. Wilkinson, 'International Terrorism: The Changing Threat and the EU's Response' (2005) Chaillot Paper 84, 34–5.

A common dilemma for both Europe and Africa is the role of more powerful states that tend to act alone outside the framework.

The challenges faced by the AU are even more complex and daunting. Countries in the region lack a history of cooperation on mutual legal assistance, judicial, intelligence and security matters. Collective security in Africa has been a colossal failure. As Jeffrey Herbst put it blatantly, 'Numerous attempts at creating formal regional organizations have failed in Africa, leaving a veritable organizational junkyard of unsuccessful attempts to reduce the continent's balkanization.'[159] Indeed, the shifting of loyalties by European states that enabled the creation of the EU is yet to take hold in Africa. For example, states in the region have consistently rejected the idea of creating 'an African Army', or 'an African High Command', including in 2005 during the adoption of an African Non-Aggression and Common Defence Pact. As a consequence, there is a disconnection between the regulations established at the AU headquarters in Addis Ababa and what is happening at the national level.

5 Conclusion and recommendations for strengthening ROs' capacity

5.1 Recommendations

The following is a set of recommendations for strengthening the role of ROs in the promotion of cooperation on CT matters:

- There should be more regular bilateral and multilateral inter-regional forums on counter-terrorism to allow for information sharing and exchange of views and to address disparity in ROs' CT capacities. CT should be made an important component of the African–European dialogue.
- Regional and central banks such as the African Development Bank and its subregional versions, Banque Centrale des États de l'Afrique Centrale (BEAC) and Banque Central des États de l'Afrique de l'Ouest (BCEAO), should establish CT programmes and focal points to streamline their activities with international CT standards, particularly with respect to the suppression of terrorist financing.
- ROs, particularly the AU, should be given technical and financial assistance to address inadequacies in equipment, expertise and

[159] J. Herbst, 'Crafting Regional Cooperation in Africa', in Acharya and Johnston, *Crafting Cooperation*, 129.

human resources. EU support to ROs, particularly the AU, should focus on building capacity through CT training programmes.

- ROs, particularly the AU, should establish a roster or checklist of regional and international CT measures and a regularly updated status of implementation by each member state.
- The EU should assist the AU in encouraging and strengthening practical cooperation among African states on CT matters, particularly on criminal justice matters involving investigation, intelligence gathering and prosecution of terrorist cases.
- Strengthen UN–ROs' practical cooperation through regular meetings and develop a guide for ROs' CT best practices.
- Expand the mandate and/or jurisdiction of regional courts of justice and human rights courts to include terrorism, in particular, the AU Court on Human and Peoples' Rights.
- The second CT decade should be dedicated to practical enforcement of existing CT instruments and norms. In this respect, ROs should be encouraged to establish arrest warrants, common passport standards and a blacklist of terrorist elements independently from the UN.

5.2 Conclusion

The complex nature of terrorist crimes, including their transnational character, underscores the importance of CT cooperation, which must constitute a central part of the global efforts to outlaw and eliminate terrorism. ROs are instrumental actors in enhancing such cooperation, promoting coordination and coherency of states' actions. Their institutional limitations and ability to effectively perform this duty should be addressed. ROs have been successful where the UN has failed, for example, in adopting common regional definitions. As mechanisms for cooperation, their accomplishments include regional norms, various assistance programmes to states, engendering human rights and adapting UN norms to regional dynamics. Notwithstanding the dilemmas that they face such as the backlash in the fight against terrorism and human rights, the invisible hand of state sovereignty and resource constraints, which often impair their efforts, they, nonetheless, remain instrumental actors for the global governance of the GWOT.

6

Lessons of the European Arrest Warrant

VINCENT GLERUM, KLAAS ROZEMOND,
ELIES VAN SLIEDREGT

1 Introduction

Paragraph 10 of the preamble to the Framework Decision (FD) on the European Arrest Warrant (EAW) reads: 'The mechanism of the European arrest warrant is based on a high level of confidence between member states. Its implementation may be suspended only in the event of a serious and persistent breach by one of the Member States of the principles set out in Section 6(1) of the Treaty of the European Union.'

International cooperation in criminal matters requires trust in another state's criminal justice system. Such trust is often presumed when an extradition treaty exists. In the words of Justice Holmes in the *Glucksman* v. *Henkel* case: 'we are bound by the existence of an extradition treaty to assume that the trial will be fair'. However, no rule of international law obliges states to trust another state blindly and to cooperate with it unconditionally. In fact, many states have limited their cooperation under extradition treaties by adopting declarations, reservations and refusal grounds, so they can demand guarantees and safeguards before deciding on extradition requests. *Ne bis in idem*, *in absentia* trials, prosecution of minors, these are all grounds upon which to base a refusal to cooperate. This widespread practice of reservations and refusal grounds indicates that parties to an extradition treaty to a certain extent retain their sovereignty. Moreover, such practice wrongs the idea that concluding an extradition treaty implies unlimited trust in another state's criminal justice system.

Mutual trust, or 'a high level of confidence', has been a key notion underlying the system of cooperation in criminal matters in the EU. Mutual trust was referred to by the Council of the European Union as the 'bedrock' of the Framework Decision on the EAW. It provides the basis for mutual recognition which in turn is considered to be the 'cornerstone' of EU judicial cooperation in criminal matters. In the context of the EAW mutual trust has been the reason for abolishing the dual (double) criminality rule for a number of crimes and for removing the executive from the decision-making process, all on the assumption that the EU member states share common values and rights. However, it has not resulted in eliminating refusal grounds, as will become apparent.

The EAW-FD entered into force on 7 August 2002. The member states had to comply with the provisions of the EAW-FD by 31 December 2003. Since the adoption of the Italian law transposing the Decision on 22 April 2005, it has been operational throughout the EU. In its evaluation report of April 2011 the European Commission welcomes the Arrest Warrant as an 'operational success', as it provides for an efficient mechanism to ensure that open borders are not exploited by those seeking to evade justice. National evaluation reports, such as the 30th report of the House of Lords Select Committee on the European Union, go to show that the European Arrest Warrant is widely used to secure the arrest and surrender across the Union. The EAW seems to have largely taken over traditional extradition procedures. After almost ten years of EAW practice it is time to take a step back and to see if, and how, the European Arrest Warrant has changed the landscape of interstate transfer of accused and convicted persons in the EU.

In the following, we will appraise EAW practice with regard to issues that specifically surface or play a role when interstate cooperation is sought with regard to terrorism. Refusal grounds such as the political offence exception and the discrimination and human rights clauses will be examined, as well as the speciality rule. We will start, however, with discussing the dual criminality requirement. Dual criminality features as a requirement in most forms of interstate cooperation in criminal matters. Yet, the EAW-FD abolishes the dual criminality requirement for thirty-two (categories of) offences in Article 2(2). Discussing dual criminality in the context of the EAW serves to illustrate how the EAW does (and does not) differ from classic extradition. Moreover, since the EAW scheme lists terrorism as one of the offences for which dual criminality is no longer required, it is opportune to examine how this abolition came about and how it has worked out in practice.

2 Dual criminality

Pursuant to Article 2(1) EAW-FD the act in relation to which an EAW is issued must be punishable under the law of the issuing state – to use

This section draws on E. van Sliedregt, 'The Dual Criminality Requirement', in N. Keijzer and E. van Sliedregt (eds.), *The European Arrest Warrant in Practice* (The Hague: TMC Asser Press, 2009), 51.

EAW-FD terminology – with a custodial sentence or detention order of a maximum of at least twelve months, or when the EAW concerns the execution of a sentence, the imposed sentence must be for a period of at least four months. In the latter case the offence does not have to carry a maximum of at least twelve months. Here the EAW-FD differs from the European Convention on Extradition (ECE), which provides for the twelve months (length of the potential punishment) and four months (length of the actual/imposed punishment) threshold as cumulative requirements. In Article 2(1) EAW-FD, the twelve-month limit features as an alternative rather than a cumulative condition. Dutch, as well as (former) Austrian legislation implementing the Framework Decision maintained the classic extradition regime; the twelve-month threshold is made a cumulative condition.[1] The Commission in its Evaluation Report of 2007 has found these provisions to be 'contrary to the Framework Decision'.[2] The Austrian legislator subsequently changed the implementing legislation; as of 1 January 2008 the twelve-month requirement has been removed.[3]

2.1 *Non-list offences*

Article 2(4) EAW-FD retains the dual criminality test for offences not covered by Article 2(2). It stipulates that the executing state *may* subject

[1] See Art. 7(1)(b) Dutch Surrender Act (*Overleveringswet*) and para. 4(2) Austrian EAW Act (*Bundesgesetz über die justizielle Zusammenarbeit in Strafsachen mit den Mitgliedstaaten der Europäischen Union*).

[2] Annex to the Report from the Commission on Art. 34 SEC (2007) 979 final, 11 July 2007; see comments regarding Art. 2 EAW-FD.

[3] The old para. 4(2) stipulates that 'Ein Europäischer Haftbefehl kann zur Vollstreckung einer Freiheitsstrafe oder einer mit Freiheitsentziehung verbundenen vorbeugenden Maßnahme erlassen oder vollstreckt werden, *wenn das Urteil wegen einer der in Abs. 1 angeführten mit Strafe bedrohten Handlungen* [i.e. acts punishable with a custodial sentence or detention order of a maximum of at least twelve months] *ergangen ist und noch mindestens vier Monate zu vollstrecken sind.*' The new text that replaced the clause in italics reads: '[w]enn noch mindestens vier Monate zu vollstrecken sind und die zugrunde liegende Handlung unabhängig von ihrer gesetzlichen Bezeichnung auch nach dem Recht des Vollstreckungsstaats eine mit gerichtlicher Strafe bedrohte Handlung darstellt' [unofficial translation: 'A European Arrest Warrant may be issued for the execution of a sentence or for a preventive measure, which is combined with deprivation of liberty where the sentence has been rendered on the basis of an act punishable under para. 1 [i.e. of an act punishable with a custodial sentence or detention order of a maximum of at least twelve months] and may be executed for at least four months.' The new text that replaced the clause in italics reads: 'where the sentence may be executed for at least four months and where the underlying act constitutes also an act punishable under the law of the executing state, irrespective of its legal designation'].

the execution of an EAW to the condition that the act is also punishable under its own law. In other words, a dual criminality test can be applied. As the Commission reports in its evaluation of EAW practice, sixteen member states have made lack of incrimination under 2(4) EAW a mandatory ground of refusal with nine member states maintaining it as an optional ground.[4] Article 2(4) does not allow the qualification that the act carries a certain minimal maximum penalty,[5] or that the act is a crime and not a misdemeanour. The Dutch Surrender Act (*Overleveringswet*) is not in line with the Framework Decision, since it requires that the act is punishable by a maximum sentence of at least twelve months under the law of the issuing state *and* under Dutch law. With this requirement the Dutch legislature embraced the doubly required minimal maximum penalty of Article 2(1) ECE.

2.2 List offences

The descriptions of the offences listed in Article 2(2) EAW-FD are rather vague and are categories of crimes rather than crime definitions. This can be partly explained by the fact that the list was copied from the Europol Convention where the list merely has a 'task-allocating' function, i.e. it triggers certain Europol powers. Another explanation is the 'enumerative method'.[6] One has to allow for a certain laxity in definition to prevent the list from being outdated and in need of constant amendment. Moreover, the categories of crimes cannot be too narrow since the list needs to accommodate the crime definitions of twenty-seven member states.

Some terms used in the list refer to other international or European instruments, for instance: 'crimes within the jurisdiction of the International Criminal Court' or 'sexual exploitation of children and child pornography' which is defined in and the subject of a Council Framework Decision. However, difficulties remain, especially with those acts that have a discrepancy in wording or translation (computer-related crime) or for which there is a discrepancy in meaning among the member states (rape).[7]

[4] Annex to the Report from the Commission on Art. 34 SEC (2007) 979 final, 11 July 2007, comments regarding Art. 4 EAW-FD.

[5] As one often finds in extradition treaties.

[6] See section 3.3.

[7] For discussion of the list *per category/crime*, see N. Keijzer, 'The Double Criminality Requirement', in N. Keijzer and E. van Sliedregt (eds.), *The European Arrest Warrant in Practice* (The Hague: TMC Asser Press, 2009), 137.

The Council of Ministers accepts that '[t]here is no completely harmonised definition at Union level'.[8] In draft minutes of a meeting the Council defined (1) racism and xenophobia (2) sabotage and (3) racketeering and extortion.[9] Member states were requested to be guided by these definitions. However, this did not prevent Germany from declaring that it would verify dual criminality with regard to list offences in another context: that of the Framework Decision on the European Evidence Warrant (EEW).[10] Like the EAW Framework Decision, the EEW Framework Decision abolished the dual criminality verification while employing the same list of offences as the EAW Framework Decision. Germany retained the right to verify dual criminality with regard to terrorism, computer-related crime, racism and xenophobia, sabotage, racketeering and extortion or swindling when executing an EEW.[11] These offences were thought to be lacking in specificity and in need of further definition.

On 3 May 2007 the ECJ ruled on the first preliminary reference on the EAW.[12] The preliminary ruling was requested by the Belgian Court of Arbitration upon a complaint by the organization Advocaten voor de

[8] Council of the European Union, Proposal for a Council Framework Decision on the European Arrest Warrant and the surrender procedures between Member States, 14867/1/01.

[9] Revised Addendum to the Draft Minutes, 2436th meeting of the Council (Justice and Home Affairs and Civil Protection) held in Luxemburg on 13 June 2002, 9958/02, Add 1/Rev 1, 16 July 2002, 6. Racism and xenophobia should be interpreted according to the Joint Action of 15 July 1996 (96/443JAI); sabotage as 'Any person who unlawfully and intentionally causes large-scale damage to a government installation, another public installation, a public transport system or other infrastructure which entails or is likely to entail considerable economic loss'; racketeering and extortion as: 'Demanding by threats, use of force or by any other form of intimidation goods, promises, receipts or the signing of any document containing or resulting in an obligation, alienation or discharge'. As the EAW-FD does not refer to these definitions, it can be argued that they 'cannot therefore be given any legal significance or be used in the interpretation' of the EAW-FD. Compare Case C-35/04 P *Segi and others* v. *Council* [2007] ECR I-1657, para. 60.

[10] EU Council Framework Decision 2008/978/JHA of 18 December 2008 on the European Evidence Warrant for the purpose of obtaining objects, documents and data for use in proceedings in criminal matters [2008] OJ L 350/72.

[11] Declaration of the Federal Republic of Germany [2008] OJ L 350/92.

[12] Case C-303/05 *Advocaten voor de Wereld* v. *Leden van de Ministerraad* [2007] ECR I-3672. See for a commentary, F. Geyer, 'European Arrest Warrant, Court of Justice of the European Communities' (2008) 4 *European Constitutional Law Review* 149; G. Gattinara, 'Il mandato d'arresto europeo supera l'esame della Corte di Giustizia' (2008) 13 *Il Diritto dell'Unione Europea* 183, also at http://ssrn.com/abstract=1152332; M. J. Borgers, 'Commentary to Case C-303/05, 3 May 2007' (2007) 619 *Nederlandse Jurisprudentie* 1458.

Wereld. In this case the Court – among other things – ruled on the interpretation of the categories of offences in Article 2(2) by holding that:

> [e]ven if the Member States reproduce word-for-word the list of the categories of offences set out in Article 2(2) of the Framework Decision for the purposes of its implementation, the actual definition of those offences and the penalties applicable are those which follow from the law of 'the issuing Member State'. The Framework Decision does not seek to harmonise the criminal offences in question in respect of their constituent elements or of the penalties which they attract.[13]

The Court thus endorsed a non-uniform interpretation of list offences. This is a somewhat different approach to that which the Council of Ministers adopted when it decided to clarify and define the meaning of certain list offences at Union level. It further stands in contrast to the ECJ's more recent ruling in *Kozłowski*.[14] In the latter case the Court was asked to clarify the meaning of the optional refusal ground of Article 4(6) EAW-FD, relating to the execution of sentences of nationals and/or residents.[15] It held that:

> Since the objective of the Framework Decision, as indicated in paragraph 31 of this judgment, is to put in place a system of surrender, as between judicial authorities, of convicted persons or suspects for the purpose of enforcing judgments or of criminal proceedings, based on the principle of mutual recognition – a surrender which the executing judicial authority can oppose only on one of the grounds for refusal provided for by the Framework Decision – the terms 'staying' and 'resident', which determine the scope of Article 4(6), must be defined *uniformly*, since they concern *autonomous concepts* of Union law.[16]

Thus, in *Kozłowski* the ECJ requires a uniform and autonomous interpretation of EAW terms. It is not yet clear how the list offences should be interpreted; in a uniform and autonomous manner, or by relying on the law of the issuing state. It has been argued that Article 2(2) and the list offences qualify as the exception referred to in the *Kozłowski* ruling; 'non-uniform interpretation' is acceptable in situations where there is 'express reference to the law of the Member States'.[17] The clause 'the following offences ... as they are defined by the law of the issuing

[13] *Advocaten voor de Wereld*, para. 52.

[14] Case C-66/08 *Kozłowski* [2008] ECR I-6041.

[15] See for a more elaborate analysis of the *Kozłowski* case, V. Glerum and K. Rozemond, 'Surrender of Nationals', in Keijzer and van Sliedregt, *European Arrest Warrant*, 71.

[16] *Kozłowski*, para. 43; the emphasis is ours.

[17] *Ibid.*, para. 42.

Member State in Article 2(2) can be regarded as such an "express reference"'.[18]

What is clear by now is that (solely) interpreting list offences according to the law of the executing member state is contrary to the EAW system. This would essentially bring back the dual criminality test.[19]

2.3 *State practice*

According to the 2007 Commission report, the majority of member states have implemented/transposed the list in complete conformity with the wording of Article 2(2) EAW-FD.[20] However, some member states omitted some categories of offences; these offences were thought to be covered by other categories.[21] Other member states have transposed the list using different wording, sometimes widening the meaning of a list offence: 'illicit trading and trafficking in drugs'[22] for 'illicit trafficking in narcotic drugs and psychotropic substances', sometimes narrowing the meaning, e.g. qualifying the list offence of racketeering or extortion by adding 'committed as part of a group or using weapons or dangerous instruments'.[23] Italy disregards the list contained in the Framework Decision altogether, and has replaced it with its own list of corresponding offences under national law.[24] According to the Commission this means that Italy has effectively reintroduced the dual criminality verification.[25] Strictly speaking, this is true. However, a closer look at EAW practice goes to show that within the EAW context, to a greater or lesser extent, there is still some form of dual criminality

[18] See N. Rozemond, 'De geldigheid van het Kaderbesluit betreffende het Europees aanhoudingsbevel en de legaliteit van de regeling van de "lijstfeiten"' (2008) 14 *Nederlands Tijdschrift voor Europees Recht* 285.

[19] See also section 2.3.

[20] Annex to the Report from the Commission on Art. 34 SEC(2007) 979 final, 11 July 2007; see comments regarding Art. 2 EAW-FD, 4.

[21] This concerns the following offences: racketeering and extortion (Greece, Estonia, and France), bribery and corruption (Finland); see Annex to the Report from the Commission on Art. 34 SEC(2007) 979 final, 11 November 2007; see comments regarding Art. 2 EAW-FD, 4.

[22] Greek EAW Act; see Annex to the Report from the Commission on Art. 34 SEC(2007) 979 final, 11 November 2007, see comments regarding Art. 2 EAW-FD, 4.

[23] See Art. 11(2) Slovenian EAW Act (at www.eurowarrant.net).

[24] See Art. 8(1)(a)(mm). For background to the EAW codification process in Italy, see L. Marin, 'The European Arrest Warrant in the Italian republic' (2008) 4 *EuConst* 251.

[25] Annex to the Report from the Commission on Art. 34 SEC(2007) 979 final, 11 November 2007, see comments regarding Art. 2 EAW-FD, 4.

assessment with regard to list offences. As is discussed below, examining the classification of a list offence will very often involve a reflection on corresponding provisions in domestic law. The process of subsumation that takes place when deciding whether the issuing state reasonably ticked the box of one of the list offences, is in essence a marginal dual criminality verification. Italy is making explicit what many member states do when they decide on the admissibility of an EAW request.

Both the United Kingdom and Dutch implementing legislation violate the EAW Framework Decision, since the dual criminality verification is retained with regard to list offences. The dual criminality test with regard to list offences in the UK Extradition Act 2003 seems 'unintended'; it is the result of bad drafting. In a way the same can be said about the Dutch Surrender Act (*Overleveringswet*). By applying by analogy classic extradition practice with regard to the transfer of sentenced Dutch nationals, a dual criminality test is applied 'through the back door' and the foreign sentence is converted to Dutch standards. Although the Framework Decision on mutual recognition of custodial sentences should have led to an amendment, Dutch legislation still provides for conversions of foreign sentences.[26] In the latter Framework Decision it is no longer possible to convert to domestic standards the sentence of a transferred person.[27] However, this Framework Decision does make it possible to check dual criminality before enforcing a custodial sentence of another member state.[28]

The dual criminality requirement may have been abolished, but this does not mean that the legal classification of a list offence goes unexamined. The Commission writes that the 'overall view' is that such an examination may not go further than a 'prima facie examination'.[29] What does that mean? Šugman, on the basis of her experience as national reporter for the Euro warrant project,[30] suggests that there are three ways of scrutinizing and checking an EAW: (1) a formal check; (2) a prima facie examination; and (3) an in-depth examination.[31]

The first EAW assessment is nothing more than checking formal requirements: has the EAW been issued by the proper judicial authority?

[26] Council Framework Decision 2008/909/JHA of 27 November 2008 on the application of the principle of mutual recognition to judgments in criminal matters imposing custodial sentences or measures involving deprivation of liberty for the purpose of their enforcement in the European Union, OJ L 327/27.

[27] Art. 8. See Glerum & Rozemond, 'Surrender of Nationals', 87. [28] Art. 7(4).

[29] *Ibid.* [30] Coordinated by the TMC Asser Institute (at www.eurowarrant.net).

[31] See K. Šugman Stubbs and P. Gorkič, 'Abuse of the European Arrest Warrant System', in Keijzer and van Sliedregt, *European Arrest Warrant*, 245.

Is the maximum length of the custodial sentence at least three years? Does the warrant contain the requisite supplementary information? The second assessment type is more in-depth; the judicial authority will ask him/herself whether the described act can reasonably be qualified as a list offence. As Šugman points out, answering the latter question already means engaging in a process of subsumation, or legal qualification, of the facts. The third type of EAW assessment is an in-depth examination of the EAW, for instance by examining the evidence produced in the EAW. The latter test would seem impermissible under the EAW scheme. After all, it would defy the purpose of mutual recognition and mutual trust, and complicate and delay the EAW procedure. As such it is inappropriate with regard to both list offences and non-list offences.

Most judicial authorities seem to occupy the middle ground: they go no further than a prima facie assessment. The Belgian EAW Act stipulates in Article 16 (1)–(3) that, on the basis of the circumstances described in the EAW, the judicial authority examines the list to see whether the offence for which the EAW has been issued features on the list. When that is the case, the description of the facts and the elements of the crime as defined in the law of the issuing state are no longer contestable, nor can they be subject to further examination.[32] This approach was endorsed in a decision by the Belgian Supreme Court (*Hof van Cassatie*).[33] Thus, the legal classification of the offence is a matter of the issuing judicial authority. As the UK European Scrutiny Committee observed: '[c]lassification must be accepted by the executing State'.[34] A similar conclusion was drawn by the French Cour de cassation on 21 November 2007 when it held: 'il n'appartient pas à la chambre de l'instruction, sauf inadéquation manifeste entre les faits et la qualification retenue, d'apprécier le bien fondé de la qualification donnée par l'autorité judiciaire de l'État d'émission'.[35] Also the German legislature, in the Explanatory Memorandum to Article 81 of the German EAW Act (*Europäisches Haftbefehlsgesetz*), emphasizes that classification as a '*Listentat*' is a matter for the issuing judicial authority. This does not preclude an '*Überprüfung*' of the description of the circumstances in

[32] Parliamentary paper 51 279/001, 14, third col. [33] 10 April 2007.

[34] European Scrutiny Committee, 33rd Report of Session 2005–6 (HC 2005–6, 33–4), para. 7.4 (see www.parliament.uk).

[35] Cour de cassation, No. de pourvoi 07-87540. [Unofficial translation: 'It is not within the competence of the Chambre d'Instruction to evaluate the merits of the determination made by the judicial authority of the state of emission, unless in case of a manifest discrepancy between the facts and such a determination.']

which the offence was committed. However, as the *Oberlandesgericht* in Karlsruhe held, such circumstances should be concrete enough to enable such an examination/*Überprüfung*.[36]

This brings us to the issue of the legal context of an EAW. Does the issuing member state have to supply the executing member state with (a translation of) the text of the relevant provisions? This question was at the heart of an EAW case before the Dutch Supreme Court. The District Court in Amsterdam had refused to execute a Spanish EAW because the EAW did not contain the text of the applicable criminal law provisions. Sending the provisions (in Spanish) separately at a later stage did not cure this defect since it was impossible to determine whether these provisions applied at the time of the offence. The District Court justified its decision by referring to the Explanatory Memorandum to the Dutch Surrender Act (*Overleveringswet*) in which the minister of justice held that an EAW would need to contain the text of the criminal law provisions. However, on 8 July 2008 the Dutch Supreme Court declared the District Court's decision null and void.[37] It ruled that, interpreting the Surrender Act in light of the wording and purpose of the EAW Framework Decision[38] and in conformity with the surrender procedures of other EU member states,[39] the District Court's decision could not stand. The fact that the minister of justice had changed his position may have played an important role in the Supreme Court's decision. In a letter dated 1 July 2005 and addressed to the Public Prosecutor in Amsterdam, the minister explained that his earlier view was based on classic extradition practice and as such was not, or no longer, relevant for surrender proceedings. For an EAW, it suffices to mention the relevant provisions, which substantially restricts the scope for assessing the legal classification of a list offence.

[36] *OLG Karlsruhe*, 10 February 2005, 1 AK 4/05, para. 9. In another case the Oberlandesgericht in *Karslruhe* held that a 'Schlüssigkeitsprüfung' (literal translation: conclusiveness test) should be applied to determine whether a list offence could be qualified as such. *OLG Karslruhe*, 10 August 2006, 1 AK 30/06, paras. 2 and 11.

[37] (2008) 594 *Nederlandse Jurisprudentie*.

[38] In accordance with C-105/03 *Pupino* v. *Italy* [2005] ECR I-5309.

[39] Here the Supreme Court refers to paras. 23–5 of the submission of the 'Procureur-Generaal' who issued the appeal and who relies on German, UK, French, Austrian and Belgian legislation. The following case law is cited: *Dabas* v. *High Court of Justice, Madrid* [2007] UKHL 6, para. 55 *per* Lord Hope of Craighead; OLG Stuttgart Beschl., 26 October 2006, 3 Ausl 52/06, para. II.5; OLG Köln, Beschl. 8 March 2005, Ausl 22/05 – 14/05, para. II.3.b; Cour de cassation, 5 August 2004, No. 04-84.511 (2004) 187 Bull. Crim. 2004, 681, 682.

3 The speciality rule

The speciality rule is a traditional feature of extradition law. Since the sovereignty of states prohibits one state from enforcing its criminal law on the territory of another state, they are dependent on international cooperation in criminal matters. To this end, states have signed treaties whereby they undertake to cooperate with one another, e.g. in the field of extradition, under certain conditions (such as dual criminality) and with certain exceptions (such as the political offence exception). The obligation to extradite if the conditions of the treaty are met and no exception applies is a limitation on the sovereignty of the requested state. The requesting state must, however, respect this limitation by only proceeding against the extradited person for the offence for which extradition was granted. Otherwise, the treaty conditions and exceptions would be meaningless. In this respect, the sovereignty of the requesting state must also suffer a limitation. The speciality rule is, therefore, founded upon the treaty conditions and exceptions, which in turn are expressions of the sovereignty of the parties to the treaty. Inasmuch as the conditions for and exceptions to extradition protect the interests of the requested person, the speciality rule also affords protection to the requested person.[40]

3.1 The speciality rule and the EAW

The speciality rule is included in the Framework Decision on the European Arrest Warrant in Articles 27 and 28.[41] At first blush, this is somewhat surprising. In contrast to extradition, surrender does not take place between sovereign states, but between judicial authorities, on the basis of the principle of mutual recognition. This principle requires recognition of judicial decisions. One might, therefore, wonder why the execution of an EAW should entail any limitation on the *jus puniendi* of the authorities of the issuing member state. Recognition, however, is not automatic, but 'pratiquement automatique'.[42] The EAW-FD

[40] According to some authors the speciality rule only protects the interests of states. See, e.g., T. Vogler, 'Der rechtshilferechtliche Grundsatz der Spezialität', in Manfred Seebode (Hrsg.) *Festschrift für Günter Spendel zum 70. Geburtstag am 11. Juli 1992* (Berlin: Walter der Gruyter, 1992), 871, 881.

[41] See O. Lagodny and C. Rosbaud, 'Speciality Rule', in Keijzer and van Sliedregt, *European Arrest Warrant*, 265.

[42] *Monedero Angora contre l'Espagne* App. No. 41138/05 (ECtHR, 7 October 2008) (decision on admissibility).

contains conditions for surrender (Article 2), mandatory and optional grounds for refusal (Articles 3, 4 and 4a) and provides for particular situations where surrender may be made dependent upon guarantees (Article 5). The executing judicial authority must or may refuse to execute the EAW, if these conditions are not met, if a ground for refusal applies, or if the authorities of the issuing member state have not given the relevant guarantee. This context of conditions and exceptions explains the inclusion of the speciality rule in the EAW-FD. In fact, the ECJ has held that the speciality rule is linked to the sovereignty of the executing member state and confers a right on the surrendered requested person.[43] Although the Court did not explain this, its reference to the sovereignty of the executing member state and to the right of the requested person seems to suggest a reasoning along the lines of extradition law as outlined above.

Articles 27(2) and 28(2) of the EAW-FD lay down the principal rules. The issuing member state must refrain from prosecuting, sentencing and depriving of his liberty the person surrendered for an offence committed prior to his surrender other[44] than that for which he was surrendered. Likewise, the issuing member state may not surrender to another member state the person surrendered for an offence committed prior to his surrender. These rules are subject to a number of exceptions.

First, member states may make a notification that, in relation to member states which have made a similar notification, consent is presumed to have been given for the prosecution, sentencing or detention for a prior offence, unless in a given case the executing judicial authority decides otherwise (Article 27(1)). The same goes for surrender to another member state (Article 28(1)). This exception only applies on a reciprocal basis. Where the executing member state has not made such a notification, the issuing member state is bound by the speciality rule, even if the latter has made a notification, and vice versa. This exception is a 'reversal of the rule of specialty by consent', based on the mutual confidence between member states.[45] Only three member states, however, have availed themselves of the opportunity afforded by

[43] Case C-388/08 PPU, *Artur Leymann and Aleksei Pustovarov* [2008] ECR I-8993, para. 44.

[44] For the criteria determining whether the offence in question is an offence other than that for which the person concerned was surrendered, see *Leymann and Pustovarov*, para. 57.

[45] *Minister for Justice, Equality and Law Reform* v. *Gotszlik* [2009] IESC 13, para. 14.

Article 27(1)[46] and only one member state has made a notification under Article 28(1).[47]

Second, in a number of cases the principal rule does not apply (Articles 27(3) and 28(2)). These exceptions may be categorized as follows. A number of exceptions concern the consent of the authorities of the executing member state or of the requested person. Another set of exceptions is based on the relatively minor seriousness of the offence or the relatively minor consequences for the requested person. Lastly, one of the exceptions places a temporal restriction on the speciality rule: it does not apply when the surrendered person has not left the issuing member state within forty-five days after his final discharge, having had the opportunity to do so, or when he has returned to that state after having left it.

The EAW-FD treats the speciality rule not as a condition to surrender or as a bar to surrender, but rather as a rule regarding the consequences of surrender. The speciality rule in the context of an EAW is, therefore, not a 'proper' refusal ground.[48] As a result, as far as the *execution* of an EAW is concerned, member states need not implement the speciality rule at the national level.[49] Still, some member states have integrated the absence of speciality arrangements with the issuing member state as grounds for refusal.[50] In the Netherlands, moreover, the executing judicial authority may only execute an EAW on the general condition that the authorities of the issuing member state will not prosecute, etc. for another offence. In applying these domestic provisions, however, the executing judicial authorities seem to rely heavily on the presumption that the issuing member state will honour its commitments under the EAW-FD.[51] Indeed, the Irish legislation contains an explicit

46 Austria, Estonia and Romania: *Annex to the Report from the Commission on the implementation since 2005 of the Council Framework Decision of 13 June 2002 on the European Arrest Warrant and the surrender procedures between Member States* (SEC (2007) 979 final), 34.

47 Romania, *ibid.*, 35.

48 See Lagodny and Rosbaud, 'Speciality Rule', 276–7.

49 As regards the *issuing* of an EAW, however, member states are required to implement the speciality rule, at least for those instances in which the executing member state has not made the notification of Art. 27(1) or Art. 28(1) EAW-FD.

50 Malta and the UK: *Annex to Report from Commission* (n. 47 above), 34.

51 See, e.g., *Hilali* v. *Central Court of Criminal Proceedings No. 5 of the National Court, Madrid* [2006] EWHC 1239 (Admin.), para. 52 and District Court of Amsterdam (*Rechtbank Amsterdam*), 13 May 2009, *LJN* BI3787. The District Court held that, as the EAW-FD is based on a high level of confidence between member states, it had to be presumed that the issuing judicial authority would act in accordance with the speciality rule as laid down in the EAW-FD and its national implementing legislation. The Court refused to make surrender dependent on the express condition that the authorities of the

presumption that the issuing member state will abide by the speciality rule; the burden of proof is on the requested person to show that the law of the issuing member state does not provide for the speciality rule and that the authorities of that state intend to proceed against the requested person for another offence.[52]

4 Refusal grounds

4.1 The political offence exception

Traditionally three reasons are given for mandatory refusal of extradition for political offences.[53] The first reason originates in the nineteenth century with its emerging liberal democracies, and relates to sympathy for those who resisted autocratic and oppressive regimes. Second, refusal affords the requested state the possibility of refraining from taking sides in the political troubles in the requesting state. The political offence exception thus enables the requested state to uphold its neutrality. Third, the fear/presumption that political offenders will not receive a fair trial in the state against which their actions were directed, or will receive disproportionate sentences.

It is left to the competent authority of the requested state to determine the political character of the offence. Because there is no generally recognized definition of what constitutes a political offence, the requested state has considerable latitude in determining the nature of the offence. However, if the requested state holds that the offence is political, then refusal is mandatory. In effect, mandatory refusal for political offences means that the presumptions which lie at the heart of the exception are non-rebuttable.

Going back to the three reasons that underlie a refusal because of the political offence exception, for the first rationale it is not necessarily so that a political offender seeks to overthrow an oppressive regime which leaves no room for non-violent opposition. He may well seek to overthrow a perfectly democratic system of government and replace it with an autocratic and oppressive one. As regards the second rationale, the requesting state may well view a refusal to extradite an offender whom it

issuing member state would abide by the speciality rule, even though Art. 14(2) Dutch Act on Surrender (*Overleveringswet*) requires that such a general condition be made.

52 *Minister for Justice, Equality and Law Reform* v. *Pùta and Šulej* [2008] IESC 30.

53 See C. Van den Wyngaert, *The Political Offence Exception to Extradition: The Delicate Problem of Balancing the Rights of the Individual and the International Public Order* (Deventer: Kluwer, 1980), 2–4.

considers to be a common criminal on the grounds of the political character as a partisan act. In other words, alleged neutrality may be interpreted as bias nevertheless. As to the third rationale, the prosecution of a political offender does not, in itself, infringe fundamental human rights.

Taken together, the political offence exception may result in a political offender escaping prosecution and punishment – especially if the requested state has no jurisdiction to prosecute the offence itself – regardless of whether his acts merit sympathy from a democratic point of view, and regardless of whether his trial and punishment in the requesting state would contravene human rights law. As a result and over time a number of solutions have been developed to deal with some of the problems the political offence exception entails. One solution is the introduction by the courts of restrictive tests when dealing with politically motivated acts of violence. Another solution is to implement the principle of *aut dedere aut judicare*: if the requested state refuses extradition on the grounds of the political nature of the offence, it should then itself prosecute the offender. Lastly, certain acts of violence have been 'depoliticized'. This technique consists in declaring that, for the purposes of extradition, those acts shall not be regarded as political offences.[54]

4.1.1 Political offence exception and the EAW

The EAW-FD altogether abolishes the political offence exception. As the EAW-FD does not contain an explicit provision pertaining to political offences and as the grounds for refusal to execute an EAW are limited to those mentioned in Articles 3, 4 and 4a EAW-FD,[55] it follows that the political character of the offence or the offender's political motivation

[54] Quite early in the history of the exception the so-called *attentat clause*, which depoliticized attempts on the life of the head of state or his family members, was introduced. See Van den Wyngaert, *Political Offence Exception to Extradition*, 136–9. Art. 3(3) European Convention on Extradition contains an *attentat clause*. After the horrors of the Second World War it was felt that some crimes were so abominable that no immunity from extradition could be granted. The Genocide Convention depoliticized genocide. The Additional Protocol to European Convention on Extradition added other crimes against humanity, grave breaches of the Red Cross Conventions and comparable violations of the laws of war (see *ibid.*, 140–6). The European Convention on the Suppression of Terrorism created the obligation to regard certain serious offences as non-political offences and authorized parties not to regard as political offences other serious offences involving acts of violence against the life, physical integrity or liberty of a person or acts against property creating collective dangers for persons (*ibid.*, 149–58).

[55] *Leymann and Pustovarov*, para. 51; Case C-123/08 *Dominic Wolzenburg* [2009] ECR I-9621, para. 57; Case C-261/09 *Gaetano Mantello* [2010] ECR I-11477, para. 37, Case C-396/11 *Ciprian Vasile Radu*, para. 36.

does not bar surrender.[56] Despite the abolition of the exception, Italy has implemented the political offence exception as a mandatory ground for refusal, because the Italian Constitution prohibits extradition for political offences.[57] The Polish Constitution prohibits extradition for non-violent offences which are committed for political reasons. As a result of the Polish Constitutional Tribunal's ruling that surrender is a form of extradition, the implementing legislation was amended to include a mandatory ground for refusal in case the EAW concerns a non-violent offence committed for political reasons.[58]

Apparently, the member states were of the opinion that the three rationales legitimizing the political offence exception no longer apply within the context of the EU. After all, recognition of a right to unlawful opposition would be incongruous with the principles and values on which the EU is based and which are shared by all member states.[59] Within the EU there is only room for lawful political opposition. In view of these principles and because the member states are striving to establish an ever closer union,[60] there is no reason why one member state would want to stay aloof from unlawful political strife in another member state. Unlawful attacks on the democratic system of government of

[56] See V. Murschetz, *Auslieferung und Europäischer Haftbefehl. Kontinentaleuropäische und anglo-amerikanische materielle Prinzipien des Auslieferungsrechts im Vergleich zum Europäischen Haftbefehl und dessen Umsetzung in Österreich* (Vienna: Springer, 2007), 385.

[57] However, the Italian exception excludes genocide, terrorist bombing and the offences mentioned in Art. 1 European Convention on the Suppression of Terrorism. See F. Impalà, 'The European Arrest Warrant in the Italian Legal System: Between Mutual Recognition and Mutual Fear within the European Area of Freedom, Security and Justice' (2005) 1 *Utrecht Law Review* 56, 67, 75. The Evaluation Report on Italy recommends that Italy delete the political offence exception. See Council Document 5832/2/09 of 18 March 2009, Evaluation report on the fourth round of mutual evaluations 'The practical application of the European arrest warrant and corresponding surrender procedures between member states': Report on Italy [2009], 76.

[58] *Annex to Report from Commission* (n. 47 above), 10. See P. Nalewajko, 'Der Europäische Haftbefehl: aktuelle Entwicklungen in Polen' (2007) 3 *Zeitschrift für Internationale Strafrechtsdogmatik* 113, 115–16. According to the Evaluation Report on Poland the political offence exception is 'in complete opposition to the principle of mutual recognition and, more generally, to the setting up of an area of freedom, security and justice'. See Council Document 14240/2/07 of 7 February 2008, Evaluation report on the fourth round of mutual evaluations 'The practical application of the European arrest warrant and corresponding surrender procedures between member states': Report on Poland [2008], 35.

[59] For instance, the values of respect for democracy and for the rule of law. See Art. 2 TEU.

[60] *Ibid.*, Art. 1.

one member state, therefore, do concern the other member states. Moreover, in essence the first two rationales are based on considerations of national interest and national policy. In the system of extradition such considerations play an important role, which is why in most states the final decision on a request for extradition is left to the government. The principle of mutual recognition, however, limits the role of the central authorities to administrative and practical assistance, thereby excluding political discretion and policy considerations.[61] Lastly, the presumption underlying the political offence exception that a political offender might not receive a fair trial in the requesting state, seems at odds with the duty of the EU and the member states to respects the human rights and fundamental freedoms of the European Convention on Human Rights and Fundamental Freedoms and with the high degree of confidence between the member states. Having said that, even EU member states sometimes violate the Convention. Nevertheless, surrender for a politically motivated offence should only be refused if, in a given case, there are substantial grounds for believing that the issuing member state would not respect the requested person's human rights.

4.2 *The anti-discrimination clause*

Paragraph 12 of the preamble is aimed at protecting human rights. This paragraph states, *inter alia*, that nothing in the EAW-FD may be interpreted as prohibiting a refusal to execute a EAW when there are substantial grounds for believing that the requested person is being prosecuted or punished on account of his 'sex, race, religion, ethnic origin, nationality, language, political opinions or sexual orientation' or that his position may be prejudiced for any of those reasons. The overall wording is reminiscent of Article 3(2) European Convention on Extradition (ECE), which contains the so-called anti-discrimination clause. This clause protects the requested person from discriminatory prosecution, punishment or prejudicial treatment, i.e. persecution. The clause is closely connected to the principle of *non-refoulement* of refugees. Indeed, it has been said that the anti-discrimination clause is the 'the legal embodiment of the principle of *non-refoulement* in extradition

[61] See Opinion of Advocate General Ruiz-Jarabo Colomer in Case C-303/05 (ECJ), paras. 42–4.

law'.[62] The list of non-discrimination grounds draws on Article 21(1) of the Charter of Fundamental Rights of the European Union and Article 1(1) of Protocol nr. 12 to the ECHR, although there are some differences.[63] The grounds mentioned in paragraph 12, however, are exhaustive, while the grounds mentioned in the Charter and in Protocol 12 ECHR are not. Paragraph 12 of the EAW-FD preamble is both broader and narrower than Article 3(2) ECE. It is broader in that the list of non-discrimination grounds is more extensive. It is narrower because of its optional – and not as in 3(2), mandatory – wording.

Of the twenty-seven member states thirteen have either partly or fully integrated the anti-discrimination clause into their domestic legislation as grounds for refusal.[64] However, since paragraph 12 does not form part of the operative provisions of the EAW-FD, the question arises whether or not an executing judicial authority may rely on the anti-discrimination clause as grounds for refusal to execute an EAW. The ECJ has held that the executing judicial authority may only refuse to execute an EAW on the grounds mentioned in Articles 3, 4 and 4a EAW-FD.[65] Some member states, however, are of the opinion that the EAW-FD cannot detract from the obligations to respect human rights arising from international treaties to which the member states are parties and from EU law itself. According to this view an explicit provision permitting or requiring refusal on human rights grounds is therefore not necessary, although such a provision would have been preferable from the point of view of legal certainty.[66] The ECJ's ruling in the case of *Maria Pupino*

[62] See Van den Wyngaert, *Political Offence Exception to Extradition*, 80–93. The English High Court of Justice has held that refugee status under the Convention on the Status of Refugees constitutes a bar to surrendering the requested person to his country of nationality: *District Court in Ostroleka, Second Criminal Division (A Polish Judicial Authority)* v. *Dytlow and another* [2009] EWHC 1009 (Admin.). Refugee status does not bar surrender to a member state which is not the country of the requested person's nationality: Cour de cassation (France) 26 September 2007, *Bulletin criminel* 2007, No. 229. However, the executing judicial authority must make sure that the issuing member state will not expel or return the refugee to his country of nationality: Cour de cassation (France) 21 November 2007, *Bulletin criminel* 2007, No. 292. A mere application for asylum or for the grant of refugee status does not constitute grounds for refusal: Case C-306/09 IB [2009] OJ C 346/16, para. 43.

[63] Para. 12, e.g., does not mention colour as a non-discrimination ground.

[64] *Annex to Report from Commission* (n. 47 above), 5.

[65] *Leymann and Pustovarov*, para. 51; *Wolzenburg*, para, 57; *Mantello*, para. 37; *Radu*, para. 36.

[66] See S. Peers, *EU Justice and Home Affairs Law* (2nd edn, Oxford: Oxford University Press, 2006), 472–3. See also J. Wouters and F. Naert, 'Of Arrest Warrants, Terrorist Offences and Extradition Deals: An Appraisal of the EU's Main Criminal Law Measures

could be cited in support of this view. The ECJ held that in accordance with Article 6(2) EU, framework decisions should be interpreted in such a way that fundamental rights are respected.[67] In essence, Article 1(3) EAW-FD, which states that the EAW-FD does not modify the obligation to respect those fundamental rights and fundamental legal principles, says the same.[68] Moreover, in implementing EU law the member states are subject to review of the conformity of their acts with fundamental rights and fundamental legal principles as general principles of law.[69] Lastly, as the Charter of Fundamental Rights of the European Union has become binding on the member states when implementing Union law,[70] it could be said that member states are under a duty to refrain from surrendering a requested person where surrender would clearly expose the requested person to treatment contrary to Article 21 of the Charter. It can, therefore, be argued[71] that, irrespective of whether or not the EAW-FD contains a specific provision to that effect, an executing judicial authority may in a given case rely on the discrimination clause when refusing to execute an EAW, if the particulars of the case so warrant.

Moreover, while a ground for refusal based on a gross abuse of trust by the authorities of a member state seems at odds with the high degree of confidence between the member states, it cannot be denied that offences directed against the political organization of some member states are still being committed within the EU. Since the political offence exception is no longer legitimate as such, a safety valve against politically motivated prosecution or punishment is not superfluous.[72] It should also be noted that some member states' constitutional principles

against Terrorism after "11 September"' (2004) 41 *Common Market Law Review* 909, 923–5.

[67] *Pupino*, paras. 58–9.

[68] Even the European Commission recognizes that an executing judicial authority 'is, of course, always entitled to refuse to execute an Arrest Warrant, if it finds that the proceedings have been vitiated by infringement of Article 6 of the Treaty on European Union and the constitutional principles common to the Member States' (*Report from the Commission based on Article 34 of the Council Framework Decision of 13 June 2002 on the European Arrest Warrant and the surrender procedures between Member States*, COM(2006) 8 final, 6).

[69] *Advocaten voor de Wereld*, para. 45.

[70] See Art. 6(1) TEU, as amended by the Treaty of Lisbon, and Art. 51(1) of the Charter.

[71] As the Advocate General Y. Bot does in his Opinion in the *Wolzenburg* case (Case C-123/08). See paras. 147–9 of the Opinion. See also S. Bot, *Le mandat d'arrêt européen* (Brussels: Larcier, 2009), 412–15.

[72] See Murschetz, *Auslieferung und Europäischer Haftbefehl*, 386.

require them to refuse extradition in case of discriminatory prosecution or punishment.[73]

Still, the importance of the anti-discrimination clause as ground for refusal should not be overestimated. Given the high degree of confidence between the member states it seems likely that an executing judicial authority will only rely on it in exceptional cases. The requested person would have to show a causal link between the EAW and prosecution/punishment, on the one hand, and discrimination, on the other hand.[74] The mere fact that a German judicial authority has issued an EAW on suspicion of belonging to a criminal organization (the Kurdish PKK) against a Turkish Kurd, who was accorded refugee status by France because of the risks he might face in Turkey on account of his PKK activities, does not establish 'le caractère politique de la demande'.[75]

5 Human rights protection

The preamble to the EAW-FD contains two clauses that can be termed human rights refusal grounds in paragraphs 12 (the anti-discrimination clause) and 13, which declares that no person shall be removed, expelled or extradited to a state where there is a serious risk that he or she would be subjected to the death penalty, torture or other inhuman or degrading treatment or punishment. Indeed, these paragraphs show a tension between the principles that underlie the EAW-FD. On the one hand, the principle of mutual recognition of judicial decisions and the principle of mutual trust, which were the basis for abolishing, e.g., the dual criminality requirement and the political offence exception. On the other hand, the classic grounds for refusing interstate cooperation in

[73] For France, see R. Errera, 'The Relationship of Extradition Law in International Treaties with the European Arrest Warrant and Its Application in France', in E. Guild (ed.), *Constitutional Challenges to the European Arrest Warrant* (Nijmegen: Wolf, 2006), 141, 149, 155. For Finland, see T. Ojanen, 'The European Arrest Warrant in Finland – Taking Fundamental and Human Rights Seriously' (*ibid.*, 89, 96–8).

[74] *Hilali*, para. 62.

[75] Cour de cassation (France) 26 September 2007, *Bulletin criminel* 2007, No. 229. However, in one case an English District judge did rule that the requested persons, who were of Roma origin, might be prejudiced in Hungary by reason of their race. The appeal against this ruling was dismissed: *Szombathely City Court and others* v. *Fenyvesi and another* [2009] EWHC 231 (Admin.).

criminal matters: human rights protection in general and the anti-discrimination clause (a specific human rights clause).[76]

The EAW-FD itself does not contain a general ground of refusal for non-execution in cases of (possible) human rights violations. Article 1(3) EAW-FD states that this Framework Decision shall not have the effect of modifying the obligation to respect fundamental rights and fundamental legal principles as enshrined in Article 6 of the Treaty on European Union (TEU) (which refers to the human rights protected under the ECHR and the principles and fundamental rights underlying the EU). While there are no – general or specific[77] – refusal grounds premised on human rights protection in the EAW-FD, Articles 3 and 4 do contain refusal grounds that can be regarded as protecting the rights of the requested person. The EAW-FD provides for a mandatory refusal ground (under certain conditions) of *ne bis in idem* (double jeopardy) where the executing judicial authority is informed that the requested person has been finally judged by a member state in respect of the same acts (Article 3(2) EAW-FD)[78] and an optional ground of refusal if it concerns a judgment by a third state in respect of the same acts (Article 4(5) EAW-FD). Moreover, Article 4a EAW-FD provides for the possibility of refusing surrender by the executing judicial authority in cases of verdicts *in absentia*, unless the EAW states information on the way the requested person (1) was summoned in court; (2) was represented by a legal counsellor; (3) was informed of his right to a retrial; or (4) will be given a right to a retrial after surrender to the issuing member state.[79]

The absence of a general human rights refusal ground did not prevent a number of member states from adopting such a general ground in their national law implementing the EAW-FD. Eleven member states

[76] The text of para. 12 is based on Art. 21(1) Charter of Fundamental Rights of the European Union. See also Art. 14 ECHR and Protocol 12 ECHR, Art. 1.

[77] Compare the European Convention on Extradition (ECE): Art. 3(2) ECE (refusal of extradition in relation to discriminatory prosecution or punishment) or Art. 11 ECE (refusal of extradition in relation to the death penalty).

[78] This principle is formulated as a fundamental right in Art. 50 Charter of Fundamental Rights of the European Union. See also Art. 4 Protocol 7 ECHR, which is restricted to judgments by the same state, whereas Art. 50 of the Charter contains a broader right in respect of judgments within the EU. The *ne bis in idem* rule is a ground for refusal of extradition under Art. 9 ECE.

[79] Council Framework Decision 2009/299/JHA of 26 February 2009 amending Framework Decisions 2002/584/JHA, 2005/214/JHA, 2006/783/JHA, 2008/909/JHA and 2008/947/JHA, thereby enhancing the procedural rights of persons and fostering the application of the principle of mutual recognition to decisions rendered in the absence of the person concerned at the trial [2009] OJ L 81/24.

implemented a mandatory human rights refusal ground (relating to the rights referred to in Article 6 TEU), thirteen member states have codified paragraph 12 (discrimination clause) in their national law, while another eleven member states have either partially or fully implemented paragraph 13 (death penalty, torture and inhuman or degrading treatment).[80] It seems that not all member states view Article 1(3) and paragraphs 12 and 13 of the preamble as compelling reasons to implement a general human rights refusal ground. It is not clear how member states that do not provide for a human rights refusal ground in their national law deal with violations of human rights in the issuing member state. It could be argued that the principles of mutual recognition and mutual trust prohibit refusal for 'human rights reasons'. According to one commentator, the more human rights are used as a ground for non-execution of a warrant, the less one can legitimately presume that the EAW fosters mutual trust.[81] Moreover, a high number of refusals can be viewed as a serious compromise to the building of trust within the EU.[82] It could also be argued that the European Convention on Human Rights provides the ground for refusing execution of an EAW in case of (possible) human rights violations.[83]

At this point we need to explore the case law of the European Court of Human Rights, which can be used to argue in two opposite ways: a party to the European Convention on Human Rights has an obligation to refuse surrender in cases of serious violations of human rights in the issuing state, or a party to the ECHR has no such obligation because the issuing state itself is party to the ECHR and can therefore be trusted.

5.1 *The* Soering *and* Cenaj *decisions*

In the *Soering* case the ECtHR held that a requested state which is party to the ECHR has an obligation to protect the requested person against violations of human rights in the requesting state after extradition.[84] The

80 *Annex to Report from Commission* (n. 47 above), 5–6.

81 M. Fichera, 'The European Arrest Warrant and the Sovereign State: A Marriage of Convenience?' (2009) 15 *European Law Journal* 81.

82 *Ibid.*

83 P. Garlick, 'The European Arrest Warrant and the ECHR', in R. Blekxtoon and W. van Ballegooij (eds.), *Handbook on the European Arrest Warrant* (The Hague: TMC Asser Press, 2005), 173; M. Mackerel, 'Human Rights as a Barrier to Surrender', in Keijzer and van Sliedregt, *European Arrest Warrant*, 140, 145, 153, 155.

84 *Soering* v. *the United Kingdom*, Judgment of 7 July 1989 [1989] ECHR (Ser. A) No. 161.

ECtHR found that the decision by a contracting state to extradite a fugitive may give rise to an issue under Article 3 ECHR where substantial grounds have been shown for believing that the person concerned, if extradited, faces a real risk of being subjected to torture or to inhuman or degrading treatment or punishment in the requesting state. In the *Soering* case the United States had requested the extradition from the United Kingdom of Jens Soering, a German citizen suspected of a double murder in Virginia. Soering feared that he would be sentenced to death in Virginia and that his stay on death row awaiting execution would constitute inhuman or degrading treatment. According to the Court, a death sentence as such is not a violation of Articles 2 or 3 ECHR,[85] but the stay on death row would be inhuman or degrading treatment in this case in relation to the youth and mental state of Soering at the time of the murders.

In the *Soering* case the requesting state was not party to the ECHR. In later cases the Court affirmed the *Soering* ruling in, e.g., the *Einhorn* case[86] and the case of *Al-Moayad*.[87] Both cases concerned extradition to the US, in the case of Einhorn in relation to a conviction *in absentia* for murder, and in the case of Al-Moayad in relation to the suspicion of terrorist activities for which Al-Moayad could be sent to Guantánamo Bay. The American authorities guaranteed that Einhorn could ask for a new trial after extradition and that Al-Moayad would get a trial within the US. Because of these guarantees, the ECtHR did not consider the decisions to extradite Einhorn and Al-Moayad by the French and German authorities, respectively, as violation of Arts. 6 or 3 ECHR.

In the case of *Cenaj* v. *Greece and Albania* the requesting state (Albania) was (and still is) party to the ECHR.[88] Albania requested the extradition of Lefter Cenaj from Greece for the execution of a conviction *in absentia*. Cenaj complained that his conviction *in absentia* constituted

[85] See also *Shamayev and others* v. *Georgia and Russia*, Judgment of 12 April 2005 [2005] ECHR III, para. 333, and *Öcalan* v. *Turkey*, Judgment of 12 May 2005 [2005] ECHR IV, paras. 162–5, where the Court speculates on possible violation of Arts. 2 and 3 ECHR in relation to the death penalty, but does not draw a definite conclusion on this issue. Art. 19(2) Charter of Fundamental Rights of the European Union states that extradition is forbidden in cases where there is a serious risk that the extradited person would be subjected to the death penalty.

[86] *Einhorn* v. *France*, Decision on Admissibility of 16 October 2001 [2001] ECHR XI.

[87] *Al-Moayad* v. *Germany*, Decision on Admissibility of 20 February 2007, App. No. 35865/03.

[88] *Cenaj* v. *Greece and Albania*, Decision on Admissibility of 4 October 2007, App. No. 12049/06.

a violation of Article 6 ECHR. He also submitted that his conviction violated Article 7 ECHR, because the maximum penalty was increased after he committed the offence. He filed his complaints against his conviction in Albania, and also against the decision of the Greek authorities to extradite him to Albania. The ECtHR found that his complaints against Albania were inadmissible because of procedural errors; he had not filed his complaint within six months after the conviction was final (Articles 4 and 35(2) ECHR). The Court further found that his complaints against Greece were inadmissible because the conviction *in absentia* did not fall under the responsibility of Greece. Albania is party to the Convention and therefore has to give procedural guarantees and effective remedies to Cenaj in relation to violations of the ECHR. In its decision the Court made a clear distinction between the case of *Cenaj* and the earlier cases of *Soering*, *Einhorn* and *Al-Moayad*, which concerned extraditions to a third state (US). The acts of the US remain outside the control of the ECHR, whereas Cenaj can file a complaint with the ECtHR against Albania when it does not comply with its obligations under the Convention.

It is not yet clear whether the *Cenaj* decision marks a fundamental distinction between extradition cases to third states and ECHR member states in respect of all the relevant rights of the ECHR. It is possible that the Court will only make such a distinction in cases concerning the right to a fair trial (Article 6) and not in cases where substantial grounds have been shown for believing that the person concerned faces a real risk of being subjected to torture or to inhuman or degrading treatment or punishment in the requesting state. In the case of *Shamayev and others* v. *Georgia and Russia* the Court did not dwell on the fact that both Georgia and Russia are contracting states. In this case, the Court found that the execution of an extradition decision by Georgia would be a violation of Article 3 ECHR, because of the real risk that a Chechen suspect would be subjected to torture or inhuman or degrading treatment after extradition to Russia.[89] In the case of *Gasayev* v. *Russia*, however, the ECtHR did take into account that Russia is a party to the ECHR. In this case the Russian authorities had given the guarantee that Gasayev would not be subjected to torture or inhuman or degrading treatment after his extradition to Russia and that he could be visited by representatives of the Spanish embassy and members of the European Committee for the Prevention of Torture.[90]

[89] See *Shamayev and others* v. *Georgia and Russia*, paras. 358–68.

[90] *Gasayev* v. *Spain*, Decision on Admissibility of 14 February 2009, App. No. 48514/06.

5.2 *The* Stapleton *decision*

In the *Stapleton*[91] case the ECtHR for the first time had to decide on the surrender of a requested person on the basis of an EAW. In this case the United Kingdom had issued an EAW for the arrest of Robert Stapleton. The warrant concerned thirty charges of fraud allegedly committed by Stapleton between 1978 and 1982. The EAW was issued on 29 July 2005 and Stapleton was arrested in Ireland on 14 September 2005. Before the ECtHR Stapleton contested the decision of the Irish courts to surrender him to the UK since his trial in the latter jurisdiction would violate Article 6 of the Convention and, notably, the right to a fair trial within a reasonable time.

The ECtHR found Stapleton's complaints inadmissible on the ground that 'the UK is a Contracting Party and that, as such, it has undertaken to abide by its Convention obligations and to secure to everyone within its jurisdiction the rights and freedoms defined therein, including those guaranteed by Article 6. It has incorporated the Convention's provisions into domestic law by virtue of the Human Rights Act, 1998.' The Court also rejected Stapleton's suggestion that an executing state should go beyond the examination of a 'flagrant denial' and determine whether there has been established a real risk of unfairness in the criminal proceedings in the issuing state. According to the ECtHR such an approach would run counter to the principles established in *Soering* and confirmed by its subsequent jurisprudence. The ECtHR was of the opinion that it would be more appropriate for the courts within the UK to hear and determine the applicant's complaints in relation to the alleged unfairness caused by delay. The ECtHR also rejected the applicant's submission that he is entitled to protection of Convention rights on the first occasion when it becomes relevant (in this case before the Irish courts). The Court found this submission misplaced in view of the status of the UK as a contracting party to the Convention.

In its *Stapleton* decision the ECtHR makes clear that the principles established in *Soering* and in subsequent jurisprudence are applicable to the EAW. The ECtHR also applies its distinction between third states and ECHR contracting parties in relation to alleged violations of Article 6 ECHR. The reasoning of the Court in relation to Article 6 seems to be that the responsibility to guarantee the right to a fair trial primarily lies

91 See Chapter 19 in this volume.

with the trial judge in the issuing member state and not with the judicial authority in the executing member state.

5.3 *Convictions in absentia*

Both *Einhorn* and *Cenaj* concerned extradition in relation to convictions *in absentia*. In the *Einhorn* case the US was asked to give a guarantee to the French authorities that the requested person could ask for a new trial after extradition. In the *Cenaj* case Greece did not demand such a guarantee from Albania and the ECtHR found that the right to retrial did not fall under the responsibility of Greece because Albania is party to the ECHR. However, within the Council of Europe it is possible to refuse extradition if the decision to impose a sentence was rendered *in absentia*. The possibility to refuse extradition in such a case can be based on Article 3(1) of the Second Additional Protocol to the ECE. Article 3(1) of the Second Additional Protocol prohibits refusal when the requesting state gives an assurance considered sufficient to guarantee that the person can claim the right to a retrial safeguarding the rights of defence. Albania is party to this Protocol, but Greece is not, and therefore Greece could not refuse extradition on the basis of this Protocol in the *Cenaj* case. The EAW-FD contains a similar provision. Article 4a EAW-FD states that a judicial authority may refuse to execute an EAW issued for the purpose of executing a custodial sentence or detention order if the requested person did not appear in person at the trial resulting in the decision unless the EAW provides information on the way the requested person was summoned in court, was represented by legal counsel, was informed by his right to a retrial or will be given a right to a retrial after surrender to the issuing member state.

The *Cenaj* case, however, raises the question why extradition or surrender should be subject to such conditions. After all, according to the Court's ruling the protection of the right to a fair trial is primarily the responsibility of the requesting/issuing state which is a party to the ECHR. Therefore, the Convention does not imply the obligation for the requested state or the executing state to ask such a guarantee. Article 3(1) of the Second Additional Protocol is based on the defence rights of Article 6(3c) ECHR.[92] In the *Soering* case the ECtHR stated that a flagrant denial of the right to a fair trial may raise an issue under Article

[92] See Explanatory Report to the Second Additional Protocol to the European Convention on Extradition, para. 24.

6 ECHR in an extradition case. In the *Einhorn* case the ECtHR made it clear that extradition with the purpose of the execution of a judgment *in absentia* may lead to such a flagrant denial, but in the *Cenaj* case the ECtHR absolved the requested state of the responsibility to prevent such a flagrant denial in cases where the requesting state is party to the ECHR and the ECtHR made a similar decision in the *Stapleton* case concerning the right to a fair trial within a reasonable time. This could lead to the conclusion that the evolution in the decisions of the Court from *Soering* to *Cenaj* and *Stapleton* makes the Second Additional Protocol to the European Convention on Extradition superfluous. The same conclusion could be drawn in relation to Article 4a EAW-FD.

One could, however, reason differently. Within the Council of Europe and the European Union special rules concerning extradition and surrender in relation to judgments *in absentia* are currently subject to streamlining. On 26 February 2009 the Framework Decision enhancing the procedural rights of persons and the application of the principle of mutual recognition to decisions rendered in the absence of the person concerned at the trial came into force.[93] This Framework Decision shows the concern of the Council of the EU to protect the right to a fair trial provided for in Article 6 ECHR.[94] The Framework Decision added Article 4a to the Framework Decision on the European Arrest Warrant. It can be deduced from this new provision that the EU member states are of the view that the protection of fair trial rights not only falls within the responsibility of the issuing state, but also within the responsibility of the executing state. When a member state implements the new Article 4a EAW-FD *literally* into its national legislation, this implementation must be given an autonomous and uniform interpretation in the light of the principle of equality and the need for uniform application of Union law, as the ECJ has held earlier with regard to Article 4(6) EAW-FD.[95] In the light of the *Wolzenburg* judgment of the ECJ, however, member states do not seem to have an obligation to implement the new Article 4a EAW-FD. A member state may choose to refrain from implementing this new provision in order to facilitate the

93 Council Framework Decision 2009/299/JHA of 26 February 2009 amending Framework Decisions 2002/584/JHA, 2005/214/JHA, 2006/783/JHA, 2008/909/JHA and 2008/947/JHA, thereby enhancing the procedural rights of persons and fostering the application of the principle of mutual recognition to decisions rendered in the absence of the person concerned at the trial [2009] OJ L 81/24.

94 See preamble to the new Framework Decision, para. 1.

95 See *Kozłowski*, paras. 42–3.

surrender of requested persons, in accordance with the principle of mutual recognition.[96]

6 Legal challenges and outstanding legal issues

6.1 *Speciality rule*

Although the EAW-FD is based on mutual trust, the member states apparently were not prepared to jettison the speciality rule. Moreover, only a few member states have availed themselves of the possibility of reversing the speciality rule. Most likely, this reluctance on the part of the member states is connected to the existence of conditions for and exceptions to surrender. The suggestion, however, that the authorities of the issuing member state might not respect the speciality rule is frequently met with the presumption that the issuing member state will live up to its international obligations.

A recent evaluation of the EAW-FD has shown that the application of the speciality rule has given rise to a number of practical problems, mainly arising from a lack of information on the conditions for the previous surrender to the issuing member state. More importantly, during this evaluation some have questioned the continued application of the speciality rule within a European area of freedom, security and justice,[97] which, after all, is based on a high degree of confidence between member states. As a result, the Council of the European Union proposes to conclude that 'reflection should continue both at EU and bilateral level as to the advantages of moving gradually towards abolishing the application of that rule'.[98]

[96] *Wolzenburg*, paras. 57–9.

[97] See Council Document 8302/4/09 REV 4 of 28 May 2009 *Final Report on the fourth round of mutual evaluations – The practical application of the European Arrest Warrant and the corresponding surrender proceedings between Member States* [2009], 16–17.

[98] See Council Document 8436/10, of 12 April 2010 *Follow-up to the recommendations in the final report on the fourth round of mutual evaluations, concerning the European Arrest Warrant, during the Spanish Presidency of the Council of the European Union – Draft Council Conclusions*, 5. Interestingly, Denmark, Finland, Iceland, Norway and Sweden (three of which are EU member states) have concluded the Convention on the Nordic Arrest Warrant, which, although based on the EAW-FD, does as a rule permit prosecution for offences committed prior to surrender, subject to a limited number of narrow exceptions. Apparently, this Convention reflects a higher degree of mutual confidence between the Nordic countries than between EU member states. See G. Mathisen, 'Nordic Cooperation and the European Arrest Warrant: Intra-Nordic Extradition, the Nordic Arrest Warrant and Beyond' (2010) 79 *Nordic Journal of International Law* 1, 22–3, 33.

6.2 *Political offence and anti-discrimination clause*

The EAW-FD and its implementation by the member states show considerable tension between, on the hand, a high degree of mutual confidence, and concern for human rights on the other. Apparently, the member states did trust one another sufficiently to dispense with the political offence exception altogether, apart from two member states who, for constitutional reasons, have included the political offence exception in their implementing legislation. One might be tempted to say, however, that the member states did harbour some residual distrust: why else would they have included the anti-discrimination clause in the EAW-FD, albeit in a paragraph of the preamble, and why else would thirteen of them have included it in their domestic legislation? But the anti-discrimination clause does not necessarily imply distrust. It can also be seen as recognition by the member states of the fact that, despite their trust in one another, they're not above human rights violations and that they, therefore, have a right and – depending on the case law of the ECtHR – a duty to protect requested persons from such violations when they have good reasons for believing that such violations have occurred or will occur.

6.3 *Human rights*

Paragraph 13 of the preamble to the EAW-FD and Article 19(2) Charter of Fundamental Rights of the European Union clearly state that extradition is prohibited in cases where there is a serious risk that the requested person would be subjected to the death penalty, torture or other inhuman or degrading treatment or punishment. This statement confirms the judgment of the ECtHR in the *Soering* case in respect of torture and inhuman and degrading treatment or punishment. It adds to the *Soering* judgment the prohibition on extradition where there is a serious risk that the requested person would be subjected to the death penalty. There is no indication in the preamble and the Charter that Article 3 ECHR does not apply to surrender cases based on EAWs. Paragraph 12 of the preamble permits refusal of surrender in cases of discriminatory prosecution or punishment. Article 1(3) EAW-FD generally confirms the obligation of member states to respect the fundamental rights of Article 6 TEU. Article 4a EAW-FD protects the right to a fair trial in cases where the requested person is convicted *in absentia*.

These paragraphs and rules seem to indicate a general agreement between the member states of the European Union that fundamental rights of the requested person should be protected in cases where an EAW has been issued. The *Cenaj* and *Stapleton* decisions of the ECtHR seem to be exceptional decisions that do not have a firm basis in the rights, rules and principles of the European Union. It could be argued that in those cases the criteria from *Soering* and *Einhorn* should be applied in surrender cases. This does not mean that the principles of mutual recognition and mutual trust do not play any role in surrender cases where fundamental rights are at stake. Those principles can be used to argue that only in very exceptional cases there exists a serious risk that the requested person will be subjected to torture or inhuman or degrading treatment or that this person will suffer a flagrant denial of the right to a fair trial. But when that risk is serious surrender must be refused.

6.4 *Dual criminality*

An issue that arose in the context of *Advocaten voor de Wereld* concerns dual criminality and the principle of legality. *Advocaten voor de Wereld* argued that the Framework Decision violated the principle of legality – encapsulated in Article 7 ECHR – by abolishing the requirement of dual criminality with regard to the offences listed in Article 2(2) EAW-FD and by listing vague categories of crimes in the latter provision. The Court rejected the complaint. It held that Article 2(2) only provides for *categories* of offences while 'the definition of those offences and of the penalties applicable continue to be matters determined by the law of the issuing member state'.[99] In other words, it is only at state level that the principle of legality can be infringed. The ECJ's ruling sides with the 'classic' view that extradition proceedings do not amount to criminal proceedings per se,[100] which entails that the legality principle does not apply to extradition/surrender proceedings.

There is another school of thought that seems to have gained support in recent years, certainly since the introduction of the EAW system, and that holds that extradition is more than mere assistance to criminal

[99] Para. 53.

[100] See *X* v. *Netherlands* (1976) 6 DR 184 where it was held that 'the concept of "guilty" in Article 7, although autonomous, cannot cover the decision on extradition which may lead to a conviction'. See also *Mamatkulov and Askarov* v. *Turkey*, Judgment of 4 February 2005 [2005] ECHR I, paras. 82–3. Art. 6(1) ECHR does not apply to extradition.

proceedings.[101] Extradition authorizes infringement on human rights, namely the right to liberty (Article 5 ECHR), namely foreign criminal law provisions serve as a basis for arrest and extradition (surrender). Against that background, characterizing extradition proceedings as mere assistance to foreign proceedings would undermine material principles of constitutional and criminal law. Instead it can be viewed as part of the (foreign) criminal process and should be treated as such. The ECJ, however, did not follow the reasoning of this school of thought in the case of *Advocaten voor de Wereld*. The ECtHR likewise held that Article 7(1) ECHR does not apply to surrender proceedings (concerning an EAW issued for the purpose of executing a custodial sentence or a detention order): 'la remise . . . n'étant pas une peine infligée à l'intéressé pour la commission d'un délit, mais une procédure destinée à permettre l'exécution d'un jugement rendu en France'.[102]

[101] See for instance Peers, *EU Justice*, 442; B. S. Braum, 'Das Prinzip der gegenseitigen Anerkunnung – Historische Grundlagen und Perspektiven europäischer Strafrechtsentwicklung' (2005) 152 *Goltdammer's Archiv für Strafrecht* 690.

[102] *Monedero Angora*. The Belgian Supreme Court (Hof van Cassatie) has also held that Art. 6 ECHR does not apply to surrender proceedings: Hof van Cassatie 21 September 2005, AR P.05.1270.F. The French Supreme Court has ruled that surrender does not fall within the scope of Art. 7 ECHR: Cour de cassation 23 November 2004, *Bulletin criminel* 2004, No. 293, 1099. [Unofficial translation: 'the surrender of the applicant to the French authorities was not a penalty inflicted on him for committing an offence, but a procedure intended to permit the execution of a judgment given in France'.]

7

Intelligence cooperation versus evidence collection and dissemination

ARVINDER SAMBEI

1 Introduction

One of the key roles of a government is the protection of its citizens from the threat of terrorism. This threat has become more prominent over recent years, and has been highlighted by a number of attacks, notably: United States (2001), the Madrid train bombings (2004), the Bali night club bombings (2002), Kula tourist district (2002), the London Underground bombs (2005) followed by the failed bombings on the London transport system (2007), the attacks on Glasgow International Airport (2007), the concurrent failed bomb explosion in the Haymarket, West End of London (2007), Mumbai (2008), and the more recent events in Kampala (2010). These events bring into sharp relief the importance of intelligence and intelligence-gathering techniques.

The function of intelligence handling and development is critical to detecting, and ultimately preventing, terrorism both at the national and international level. At the same time it plays a critical role in intelligence-led operations and proactive investigations. Since the early 1990s there has, worldwide, been ever-increasing reliance on intelligence-led and proactive criminal investigations not just in relation to acts of terrorism, but serious and organized crime generally.

It is important at the outset to highlight the critical distinction between intelligence and evidence. Evidence is that which is capable of being adduced in any criminal trial and must be relevant and admissible in proceedings; by contrast, intelligence may, or may not, be relevant or admissible or be capable of being admitted in the format it is gathered. Investigators must therefore exercise great care when reliance is placed on intelligence-led investigations to ensure that the product gathered is capable of being relied upon as evidence in any future proceedings, or risk discontinuance.

2 Development of intelligence

Intelligence is more commonly described as information about plans, activities and information secured from both open and closed sources. In the context of terrorism it is information about terrorist groups, their associates, supporters, individual members and their financial supporters.

Intelligence can be developed using a number of techniques (discussed below), many of which exploit the terrorist needs to communicate with others and engage in the transfer of money, both nationally and internationally. The information gathered in this manner is more commonly referred to as intelligence 'product'. Once the product is collected, it is usually analysed and if it supports an investigation, the product and the analysis is handed to the law enforcement agencies.

Intelligence gathering, therefore, involves the collection,[1] assessment (analysis), gauging, balancing and dissemination of the material to determine its use, that is to say, either as intelligence only (prevention or deterrence), or as material that can support an investigation (pursuit and prosecution).

Intelligence functions, therefore, operate at three distinct and separate levels:

- First, it aims to provide reliable information to deter and prevent an act of terrorism from taking place.
- Second, where an act of terrorism has come to fruition, intelligence can, if handled correctly and sensitively, pave the way for the gathering of evidence, identity of the suspects, and background information on the group or cell held responsible for the attack, etc. (reactive investigation).
- Third, and increasingly, it is at the heart of proactive investigations and plays a critical role. In such instances, intelligence should drive all activity and a failure of that function leaves a government and its citizens open to the very real and credible threat that terrorism poses today.

The handling of intelligence product and its development is critical to detecting, and ultimately preventing, terrorism both at the national and international level; at the same time it plays a critical role in

[1] It must be gathered and held without caveat until assessed.

intelligence-led operations and proactive investigations.[2] In some instances a proactive investigation based on covert methodologies may be the only way of progressing enquiries. Covert deployment may form the basis of intelligence gathering, obtaining evidence or both. This may involve the use of information from a source, intelligence and/or evidence from the deployment of an undercover agent or participating source, and surveillance or telecommunications product. Recent experience has shown that use of intelligence in a timely manner is a more economical way of preventing a terrorist atrocity or a serious and organized crime.[3] A subsequent investigation can be very time-consuming in personnel hours and costly.

This overarching responsibility is to ensure that the product gathered is capable of being relied upon, and can be used through conversion into evidence, or could be used in the creation of an opportunity to obtain evidence. Any deviation from this may compromise an investigation or any subsequent legal proceedings.

[2] At any given time the UK MI5 monitors about 2,000 people in Britain who form an estimated 200 networks suspected of links to violent extremism. Each individual is subjected to a range of monitoring on a sliding scale depending on the agency's assessment of the threat they pose and how close they are thought to be to 'attack planning'.

[3] Operation Pathway, a UK proactive investigation: searches were undertaken of addresses in Liverpool, Manchester and Clitheroe, Lancashire by the Metropolitan Police, Counter-Terrorism Command, the North-West Counter Terrorism Unit and West Yorkshire and Lancashire Constabularies. Police arrested eleven adult male Pakistanis (originally from the Peshawar region) in the United Kingdom under the guise of being students and on visas; among them was one British subject. Motor vehicles believed to have been used by them or held under their control were seized and searched. This intelligence-led operation commenced some months earlier in December 2008, following the arrests of fourteen males in Belgium. It was believed that these two groups were 'terrorist cells' and had the potential aspiration to mount a suicide-bombing plot against European leaders at a summit meeting. (The UK hosted the G8 meeting in March 2009.) One suspect in Belgium had apparently given details in interview of the AQ–Pakistan leadership agreeing to the plan and granting the operation support. The Belgian suspect was interviewed by an MI5, British Security Service agent and revealed details of a pseudonym of the leader of a UK cell. The leader and director of the operational cells was believed to be Rashid Rauf, a key and former conspirator of the failed 21/7 attack in London involved in its planning and training. Rauf was allegedly killed by a US Predator Drone in Alikhel Village, North Waziristan during 2008. (Rauf had been arrested after the Airline Liquid bomb plot of 2006 was discovered, but he later escaped during transit while detained by the Pakistani authorities.) It is believed the UK and Belgian arrests have uncovered, and so far prevented, several planned attacks by similarly sized cells. Despite in-depth searches and lengthy periods of interrogation, no incriminating terrorist-related paraphernalia has been recovered.

The work of the intelligence agencies (both civilian and military) is, more often than not, undertaken in a covert and discrete manner. However, this does not mean that they operate in a legal vacuum. It is vital that their activities are subject to some form of scrutiny whether by an oversight committee or a similar body, such as a commissioner or ombudsperson to ensure the methods used are necessary, proportional, human rights compliant and ethical.[4] At the heart of intelligence gathering lies the need to ensure its compliance with human rights, particularly if reliance is then to be placed on the product in any subsequent legal proceedings; such a need becomes more significant where intelligence is gathered through a human source (discussed below).

The formation and operations of an intelligence agency is usually carried out with the consent of the government of the day with some oversight and legal scrutiny. Intelligence agencies must not only adhere to national law, but must also be fully conversant with the norms under international law and regional human rights instruments. In the case of European states they are bound by the European Convention on Human Rights which reflects the obligations under the International Covenant on Civil and Political Rights as well as other international instruments such as the Torture Convention. Therefore, to ensure integrity in the intelligence process there must be accountability throughout the whole process with in-built controls and systems that do not permit abuse.

Although the work of an intelligence agency is predominantly covert and not in the public domain, it is critical that the executive is satisfied that the activities of intelligence agencies are undertaken for the benefit of society at large and it creates or promotes a safer environment. Intelligence agencies often come under criticism as the process of gathering intelligence may well violate the right to privacy of individuals, and is seen as a 'fishing expedition', as illustrated by a recent case in the US.[5] Niazi has been indicted in California in respect of immigration charges. It is alleged that he provided false information on his application for naturalization in the US and failed to disclose his links to terrorist organizations. It is further alleged that Niazi's brother-in-law, Amin al-Haq, was closely associated with Osama bin Laden and has in fact

[4] The UK Intelligence and Security Committee (ISC) was established by the Intelligence Services Act 1994 to examine the policy, administration and expenditure of the Security Services.

[5] *USA* v. *Ahmadullah Niazi* (US District Court for the Central District of California, Southern Division. October 2008).

worked for him. At a hearing in early 2009, it became apparent that the investigation had cultivated and received information from a source implicating Niazi. The Council on American–Islamic Relations (CAIR) has challenged the right of the FBI to collect information in a clandestine manner on the basis that such deployment is an attack on the civil liberties of all Muslim Americans.

3 Sources of intelligence

Sources can vary dramatically but typically intelligence will be from:

- communications intelligence;
- covert surveillance;
- human intelligence;
- financial intelligence;
- other sister agencies, national and foreign;
- open sources; and
- members of the public alerted to abnormal behavioural patterns or changes; in essence a 'sixth sense' feeling of impropriety.[6]

The chapter will briefly examine each of these sources.

3.1 Communications intelligence

Communications intelligence includes both the interception of telephonic and internet systems, as well as information acquired through the routine monitoring and analysis of communications traffic. It is also the resultant product from any other method of communication, and as telephones can be used for many varied activities and the internet can be used to carry speech, whether encrypted or not, it would capture all modes of communication.

It is a tool used by governments to protect their economic stability or to maintain public safety. While sister agencies may use the captured data, the interception facilities are more usually separately funded and staffed. Most intelligence agencies have a separate dedicated collection capability as the capture of communications intelligence is specialized.

Data capture and communication interception agencies, like their sister agencies, create an evidence-gathering opportunity for law

[6] A key part of the UK 21/7 investigation commenced, following a member of the public simply 'ringing the police' with concerns about a neighbour's behaviour.

enforcement provided the information is passed using a sensitive and safe method, that does not reveal the technique or method of capture. Many jurisdictions rely heavily on the product of telephone interception to detect and to prosecute cases; however in the UK there is significant restriction on the use to which such product can be put.

For such a system to work there must be a continuous monitoring system in place. This can be either through full time coverage or to have the opportunity to direct appropriate technical resources as and when required 'on demand'. As this is a highly specialized and sensitive field in which specific technical expertise is employed, the staffing of such facilities is more commonly split between those engaged in the technical capture of 'traffic' and those who are involved in the subsequent analysis of the material/product.

The routine monitoring of electronic traffic creates as many problems as it seeks to solve. Not all information captured is relevant. Analysis by sister agencies in the domestic arena may dictate a need to verify intelligence received; while the seizing agency may wish to sanitize a report or retain the details it has seized as it may reveal a technique used to capture the product.

Equally, the revelation of the entire intelligence product, which may be used for other purposes elsewhere during an operation, may reveal a time line of activity undertaken by the intelligence community or indeed law enforcement agencies. It is therefore critical that there is sanitization of any intelligence material captured electronically in order to progress an investigation. For example, an interviewer later questioning a suspect may need to refer to information created or obtained by colleagues at the intercept stage, which could, in turn, alert the suspect that he was the target of a data-capturing operation.

One of the challenges to the intelligence agencies is the need to retain data for longer than that provided by the industry. Given that most communication today is transmitted electronically, this places a heavy burden on the intelligence community to decipher and analyse the information gathered. To that end, dialogue commenced with the mobile telephone, internet and telephonic/radio and other providers in order to require them to retain all data and location communication traffic far in excess of their desired period of time.[7] This has caused considerable difficulty, as it initially conflicted with EU directives concerning the retention of communication data.

[7] Initially set at one year for mobile and fixed line telephony and six months for internet data.

Of very serious concern to the intelligence community is the internet communication product Skype, a voice over Internet Protocol (VoIP). It provides cheap, often free, telephone access through a dedicated handset or a computer terminal and requires both caller and called to use a Skype-enabled handset.[8] The use of a compatible device is directly related to the encryption process used by Skype. As Skype is a spoken communication, uses an internet portal and can be saved as a message in a similar manner to traditional email it is caught by the same time period of twelve months. Another facet to this communications capture is the ability of law enforcement and intelligence agencies to reveal historical account and contract details of telephone and Internet Service Provider (ISP) ownership.

The Data Retention (EC Directive) Regulations[9] require service providers to retain details of user internet access, email and internet telephony for twelve months. ISPs must also be able to respond to access requests by law enforcement and other designated authorities. The details of UK citizens' communications to be retained include which IP address people have been assigned, plus log-in and log-off times; the sender, recipient, date and time of emails; and the caller and recipient of internet telephone calls. In addition, the Regulations state that telecommunications companies must also retain details of all fixed and mobile telephony usage, including the geographical location of the caller.

In the UK an application to a communication provider, whether for intelligence or evidence, must be processed, reviewed and subject to quality assurance by a dedicated unit.[10] This unit, more commonly known as a Single Point of Contact (SPOC), can be one or several people

[8] A new term called 'vishing' which is essentially phishing (tricking people into giving up personal and financial details) by telephone, has been credited as being enabled by VoIP.

[9] Directive 2006/24/EC of the European Parliament and of the Council of 15 March 2006 on the retention of data generated or processed in connection with the provision of publicly available electronic communications services or of public communications networks and amending Directive 2002/58/EC [2006] OJ L 105/54.

[10] The UK Regulation of Investigatory Powers Act 2000 (RIPA) provides a statutory regulatory framework for covert law enforcement techniques. The Act provides a regime of primary legislation and Codes of Practice that divide covert techniques into categories distinguished by the degree of intrusion involved with the aim of regulating the following investigatory powers: the interception of communications; the acquisition of communications related data (e.g. telephone billing data); 'intrusive' surveillance on residential premises or in private vehicles; 'directed' surveillance (i.e. surveillance in the course of a specific operation); the use and conduct of 'covert human intelligence sources' (agents, informants, undercover officers); the power to seize electronic keys giving access to encrypted computer material. The Act aims to ensure the powers are used lawfully and in a way that is compatible with the ECHR. It also requires, in

who work within this dedicated unit that the telephonic and data creation industry are satisfied will apply for, receive and hold their data in a secure way. This unit is pivotal when data acquisition is required in a proactive and intelligence-led investigation.

The benefit of such a unit is enhanced when the initial intelligence-led investigation of a case progresses, as the unit will ensure that the relevant protocols with the industry are adhered to: this helps to build confidence and trust between the intelligence/investigation agencies on the one hand and the communications industry on the other. If the initial intelligence-gathering applications for the communication product are made correctly, in the correct time frame and are deemed to be of evidential use, the subsequent applications usually become more of a transition than an inconvenience.

Urgent applications for data are similarly obtained through this unit 'out of hours', for example in instances where there is an immediate threat to life or state security and when the necessary application process and correspondence will be submitted subsequent to the data being furnished.

3.2 *Covert surveillance*

Covert surveillance has long been recognized as an intelligence-gathering technique, and is, increasingly, used as a means of evidence gathering, given the need in some circumstances for the initiation of a proactive rather than a reactive investigation.

The use of covert surveillance in counter-terrorism operations has raised concerns in the US[11] and, more recently, in the House

particular, those authorizing the use of covert techniques to give proper consideration as to whether their use is necessary and proportionate.

11 *American Civil Liberties et al.* v. *National Security Agency et al.*, Judgment of 6 July 2007, United States District Court Eastern District of Michigan Southern division, Case No. 06-CV-10204. Following the events of 11 September 2001, President Bush authorized NSA to deploy a counter-terrorism operation which is referred to as the 'Terrorist Surveillance Program' (TSP). The details of the operation have never been disclosed save to say that it is commonly known that NSA does intercept communications (telephone and email) without a warrant where one party to the communication is outside the US and the NSA has a 'reasonable basis to conclude that one of the parties to the communication is a member of Al Qaeda, affiliated with Al Qaeda or a member of an organization affiliated with Al Qaeda or working in support of Al Qaeda' (press briefing by Attorney General Alberto Gonzales and General Michael Hayden, Principal Deputy Director for National Intelligence, White House, 19 December 2005).

of Lords' decision *In re McE, In re M and In re C (AP) and another.*[12]

The appellants, who were in custody for offences relating to terrorism, sought assurances from the officers that they would not be the subject of monitoring during consultations with their solicitors, and, in the case of one of them, with his consultant psychiatrist. The police officers refused to give any assurances. The appellants commenced judicial review proceedings seeking declarations that their consultations would not be monitored and that the refusal by the officers to provide assurances was in violation of the European Convention on Human Rights.

The Divisional Court, in granting the relief sought, found that Part II of RIPA[13] extended to consultations between lawyers and clients but that such surveillance, in the present cases, was not proportionate. The court gave leave and certified the question of the impact of RIPA on the common law right to legal professional privilege (LPP) and on the right accorded by statutory provisions for a person to consult a lawyer privately.

In dismissing the appeal, the majority (Lord Phillips dissenting) found that the common law right to LPP, and the right accorded by other statutory provisions, were capable of being subject to covert surveillance. However, surveillance of legal consultations should fall within the category of intrusive surveillance (Part II RIPA) rather than directed surveillance,[14] and in

A group comprising lawyers, academics and journalists brought an action in the Eastern District of Michigan seeking a permanent injunction against NSA for actions taken by them under the TSP and a declaration that the warrantless wiretapping and data mining by the NSA violated provisions of the Constitution and other legislation.

The NSA invoked the state secrets doctrine to bar the discovery of any material on the grounds of national security. They claimed that in the absence of such material, the group had no *locus standi*.

The District Court rejected the claim for the data mining but granted the relief sought for the warrantless wiretapping. NSA appealed. The Court of Appeal, in granting the appeal concluded that the group had no *locus standi*, vacated the order of the District court and remanded the matter to the district court for dismissal.

12 *In re McE, In re M and In re C (AP) and another* [2009] UKHL 15.

13 On the UK's Regulation of Investigatory Powers Act 2000 (RIPA), see n. 10 above.

14 When the matter was heard before the courts, surveillance of legal consultations fell within the category of 'directed surveillance' rather than intrusive surveillance which has its own safeguards. The House of Lords criticized the Secretary of State issue for failing to take any action in ensuring that surveillance of private consultations fell in the category of intrusive surveillance since the decision of the Divisional Court, nearly a year earlier. Lord Neuberger commented that this failure 'strongly suggests that the Government has been knowingly sanctioning illegal surveillance for more than a year. If that is indeed so, to describe such a state of affairs as "regrettable" strikes me as an understatement.' The Home Office is now engaged in consultation on the Codes of Practice after which they will be amended.

relation to the impact of RIPA on express statutory provisions, their Lordships found that RIPA permitted covert surveillance even in those instances on the grounds that:

> It was inevitable that covert surveillance of the kind that RIPA was intended to provide for would intrude on conversations that were intended to be private. Privacy under a right given by statute is no exception. To conclude that consultations that were being conducted in private under a statutory right are immune from covert surveillance under RIPA would be wholly at variance with the obvious intention that RIPA should be general in its application, subject to the strict conditions that it lays down. (*per* Lord Hope)

3.3 *Human intelligence*

Human intelligence involves the recruitment, tasking and handling of covert human intelligence sources known more commonly as CHIS. It is essential that the use and deployment of CHIS is strictly regulated and employs a rigorous regime of source management.[15] The system and oversight must be robust and able to withstand scrutiny. All dealings with CHIS and decisions as to their employment and tasking should be recorded. Any intelligence or potential evidential product disclosed by a CHIS should be recorded and graded as to its potential use and disseminated. The interaction between intelligence agents and law enforcement officers should be undertaken by dedicated and specifically trained 'handlers', who in turn should be overseen by a 'controller' who is responsible for regulating the relationship between the handlers and the source. A controller will also be able to quality-control the reports of handlers and dictate the dissemination strategy for the reports compiled by handlers. The timely release of information gained by a CHIS is of paramount importance. The intelligence product may be revealed to an intelligence agency for assessment, but may be retained by the law enforcement agency as it has created an evidence-gathering opportunity.

[15] Covert human intelligence sources (CHISs) can operate in a number of ways: (1) someone who establishes or maintains a relationship, under their own or an assumed identity, with the express intent of using that relationship to obtain information; (2) covert disclosure of information obtained by virtue of a relationship, whether or not the initial purpose of establishing or maintaining the relationship was to obtain such information; (3) the use of a relationship to gain or provide access to another person for the purpose of anything within (1) or (2).

Both the intelligence agency and law enforcement agencies can either separately handle CHIS subjects or they may co-handle a subject which may take some substantial agreement as to who may ultimately own or take primacy over the use of the resultant product.

An operation to accumulate intelligence or discover the proposed plans involving a major crime syndicate or an intelligence group is considerably cheaper in personnel hours and monetary value if a CHIS is used. A CHIS can describe a criminal, a reformed criminal, a person in industry who comes by information in sensitive circumstances, or a covert placement of someone. The well-placed or situated CHIS, or a CHIS with unique access to a group of suspects, is able to report 'live' on their activity. If used appropriately, a CHIS is more advantageous as he/she is able to report much more quickly than a communication interception, particularly in the event of a terrorist attack. This is because the information is released in its most raw format where a communication interception product will need to be assessed and sanitized before release.

There are also unique challenges presented when using a CHIS.[16] Handlers and controllers will need to satisfy themselves of the motive of the CHIS in providing the information. They will need to address the following: is the CHIS motivated by greed, monetary reward, public goodwill, releasing information to remove a competitor or a disenchanted former criminal or cell member.

Information and intelligence would need to be uniquely graded on reliability of the source, the information itself and attendant factors. Nonetheless, whatever is imparted to a handler would still need to be corroborated. The United Kingdom uses a scheme known as a 5 x 5 x 5 system. This uniquely grades the intelligence or CHIS product so that all readers and authors of reports can understand the use and reliability of the detail.[17] The corroboration might be through traditional monitoring by surveillance or by watching the suspect complete some activity that was reported by the CHIS.

In the context of terrorism, the use of intelligence through human intelligence (HUMINT), both civilian and military, has been the subject of considerable concern and judicial comment, in particular in relation

[16] See UK HM Revenue and Customs advice at www.inspectorates.homeoffice.gov.uk/hmic/inspections/

[17] See for example courses for 5 x 5 x 5 training www.toddington.com/westyorkshirepolice/ Intel and analysis training schedule.

to the techniques of interrogation. It is well known that the US, under the Bush administration, sanctioned the use of waterboarding, the use of dogs (particularly offensive to Muslims), and hooding, etc.[18] Although such techniques were considered legally unacceptable under international norms and condemned, the US was of the view that they did not amount to torture as it did not result in 'severe pain and suffering' as required by the Convention against Torture (1984),[19] and were considered necessary in order to secure intelligence or information from those subject to interrogation by a US agency. The reliability of intelligence secured in such a manner must be questionable, and little or no reliance can be placed upon it in any subsequent legal proceedings. However, the use or authorization of such techniques does expose the individual to criminal responsibility, as illustrated by the US prosecution of the personnel deployed in Abu Ghraib. In Spain, Judge Baltasar Garźon, on 17 April 2009, decided to consider criminal charges against six former Bush administration officials for alleged torture of Spanish nationals who were held in the Guantánamo facility, although the Spanish attorney general opposed the action on the basis that it was for the US to try its own officials.

In the UK the House of Lords in the cases of *A and others*[20] considered the question of admissibility of evidence obtained by torture by the Special Immigration Appeals Commission (SIAC).

On the question of inhuman or degrading treatment and whether the treatment of evidence obtained through inhuman or degrading treatment follows that obtained through torture, Lords Bingham and Hope concluded that based on existing European Court jurisprudence, there is a distinction between the two. Where evidence is obtained through

[18] Upon taking office, President Obama issued four Executive Orders on Detention and Interrogation. Executive Order 3 'Ensuring Lawful Interrogations' sets the standards and practices for interrogation and lists methods which must never be used – waterboarding, use of extreme cold, use of dogs, stripping persons naked and hooding. The methods are considered to amount to torture, cruel and inhuman treatment.

[19] Art. 1 1984 Convention against Torture and other Cruel, Inhuman or Degrading Treatment or Punishment, states 'For the purposes of this Convention, the term "torture" means any act by which severe pain or suffering, whether physical or mental, is intentionally inflicted on a person for such purposes as obtaining from him or a third person information or a confession.' Torture Convention, 1465 UNTS 85.

[20] *A (FC) and others (FC) (Appellants)* v. *Secretary of State for the Home Department (Respondent)* [2004] UKHL 56 [2005] 2 AC 68; *A (FC) and others (FC) (Appellants)* v. *Secretary of State for the Home Department (Respondent) (Conjoined Appeals)* [2005] UKHL 71 [2006] 2 AC 221.

torture it is inadmissible in judicial proceedings per se, while evidence that is said to have been obtained as a result of inhuman or degrading treatment, such evidence in English proceedings may be rendered inadmissible by virtue of section 78 Police and Criminal Evidence Act 1984, and, in other common law jurisdictions, by the common law discretion to exclude evidence on the grounds that unfairness outweighs the probative value.[21]

The speeches also examine the issue of under which circumstances the executive may consider material that could be a product of torture when making operational decisions (for instance in the 'ticking-time bomb' scenario), and, in this case, whether the Secretary of State can rely upon material that may be tainted when considering whether or not to issue a certificate in respect of the detention of an individual (Lord Nicholls expressed some reservation in respect of any reliance being placed by the Secretary of State on such tainted information).[22]

Their Lordships unanimously found that the executive is able to rely on such information and acknowledged the inevitable 'mismatch' that arises particularly in the context of counter-terrorism when conflicting interests must be balanced.[23]

The need to gather and develop the intelligence picture of those engaged in terrorism also led to the creation of 'ghost' prisoners and the removal of individuals, so-called extraordinary renditions, to sites or countries in order to 'extract' intelligence from those suspected of being engaged in terrorist activities. Such deportations or removals were based on initial intelligence about the individual without verification of the information and without sufficient safeguards or oversight. This was amply illustrated in the case of *Maher Arar*.[24] Maher Arar, a 34-year-old wireless technology consultant, was born in Syria, and went to Canada with his family at the age of 17. He became a Canadian citizen in 1991, but retained dual citizenship.

On 26 September 2002, while in transit through New York's JFK airport when returning home from a holiday, Arar was detained by US officials and interrogated about alleged links to al-Qaeda. The US authorities detained and questioned him for twelve days during which he alleged he was tortured. He was first sent to Jordan and then to Syria.

[21] Conjoined Appeals [2005] UKHL 71, para. 53.

[22] *Ibid.*, paras. 68 (Nicholls) and 160 (Brown).

[23] *Ibid.*, paras. 71–2 and 92–3.

[24] D. O'Connor, *Commission of Inquiry into the Actions of Canadian Officials in Relation to Maher Arar* (*Arar Commission*) (2006).

In Syria he was held in a tiny 'grave-like' cell for over ten months before he was moved to a better cell in a different prison. While in Syria, he was beaten, tortured and forced to make a false confession. Syria subsequently concluded that he had no terrorist association and he was released. Upon his release he returned to Canada.

In Canada an inquiry was held in relation to the actions of the Canadian, Syrian and US authorities in the handing over of Maher Arar. The report in condemning the actions of the officers found that the Canadian intelligence officials were under pressure to find terrorists following the events of 11 September 2001 and had provided incorrect information regarding Arar. The deportation on intelligence only in the absence of sufficient safeguards was condemned by the inquiry.[25]

The US has made no comment on the case, nor offered any apology.

Recently, the Kenyan government came under criticism[26] for its part in the handing over of some one hundred individuals (between 2 to 31 January 2007), without due process, to either neighbouring countries or to the US. In South Africa, the Constitutional Court criticized the handing over of *Khalfan Mohammed*[27] to the US authorities in violation of its Constitution and without essential safeguards in place.

In Italy, Abu Omar, an Egyptian national with Italian residency, was abducted from a Milan street on 17 February 2003. He was taken to a US military base in northern Italy and then flown, via another US base in Germany, to Cairo, where he was secretly detained for fourteen months and allegedly tortured. The 'extraordinary rendition' was based entirely on an intelligence-led operation between the CIA and the Italian intelligence services. Prosecution proceedings were commenced against twenty-six CIA agents (*in absentia*) and seven Italians. This was the first prosecution in Europe in respect of 'extraordinary rendition'. During the course of the trial, the Italian authorities appealed to the Constitutional Court. On 11 March 2009, the Constitutional Court, Italy's highest court, ruled that some of the evidence relied upon at the trial by the prosecutors violated state secrecy laws and excluded some of

25 *Report of the Events Relating to Maher Arar: Analysis and Recommendations*, vol. III (at www.pch.gc.ca/cs-kc/arar/Arar_e.pdf).

26 Al-Amin Kimathi and Altan Butt, 'Horn of Terror: Report of US-Led Mass Extra-Ordinary Rendition from Kenya to Somalia, Ethiopia, and Guantánamo Bay' (Muslim Human Rights Forum, 6 July 2007), 10.

27 *Khalfan Khamis Mohammed, Abdururahman Dalvie* v. *President of the Republic of South Africa and six others and the Society for the Abolition of the Death Penalty in South Africa*, Constitutional Court of South Africa, Judgment of 28 May 2001, CCT 17/01.

the evidence from the public domain, namely use of classified documents found following a search of premises said to be under the control of the SISMI (Italian military intelligence service), and evidence provided by a military police officer.

3.4 *Financial intelligence*

Preventing terrorists and terrorist organizations from funding their activities and planned attacks is an essential component of any successful global counter-terrorism campaign. Targeting the finances of terrorists and terrorist organizations can provide vital intelligence information concerning their activities and insight on how to formulate policies that deny terrorists access to funds and restrict their ability to function. However, there have been relatively few prosecutions of terrorist financing worldwide.[28] Most prosecutions tend to focus on other substantive offences such as conspiracy to murder, etc. and charges relating to the financing of the operation may or may not be included in the indictment. This is largely due to the fact that it is difficult to prove a charge of financing, particularly where a group may rely on alternative remittance systems to finance the terrorist act. The focus is therefore on developing financial intelligence.

By using methods of financial investigation, it has become possible to identify and profile suspects, link addresses, storage facilities and methods of communication. Furthermore, financial investigations can reveal travel and spending patterns, provide valuable information on recruitment methods and operational strategies as well as areas of vulnerability in terrorist organizations.

Much intelligence can be obtained through tracing the financial footprint of a person the subject of an intelligence report. In these days of e-commerce, automatic teller machines (ATMs) and banking/credit agencies, it is difficult not to leave a trail of transfer of monies and goods. Skilled intelligence analysts and investigators can trace suspects'

[28] A recent case on financing of terrorism is the US case *Holy Land Foundation and five others*. On 24 November 2008 the Holy Land Foundation for Relief and Development and five defendants, were convicted of a number of charges, including providing material support to a foreign terrorist organization, being engaged in prohibited financial transactions with a Specially Designated Global Terrorist, money laundering, conspiracy and filing false tax returns. The organization and its leaders were accused of channelling some US$12 million to Hamas, which was declared by the US in 1995 to be a terrorist group.

activities covertly and provide invaluable information to both intelligence and investigating agencies.

The international community, in recognition of the importance of tracing finance, has encouraged the work of the Financial Action Task Force (FATF) in developing the intelligence picture. The FATF was established at the G-7 Summit in 1989 in direct response to growing international concerns with money laundering. The organization is an intergovernmental body that prescribes both domestic and international anti-money laundering policy standards. It also conducts evaluations of states' current anti-money laundering procedures, and examines the techniques of money launderers and terrorist organizations, developing annual typologies reports on money-laundering trends and techniques. It is important to note that the FATF does not conduct criminal investigations either domestically or internationally, but analyses the information it receives.

In 1990, FATF[29] issued forty recommendations designed to assist the fight against money laundering. These were thoroughly revised in 2003. In 2002, FATF also produced 'Guidance for Financial Institutions in Detecting Terrorist Financing Activities'[30] which seeks to ensure that financial institutions do not unwittingly move or hide terrorist funds. The document acknowledges that banks and other financial institutions will find it difficult to detect terrorist financing transactions, unless a known terrorist or terrorist organization directly opens an account. As such, financial institutions are guided to be alert to suspicious transactions which could be indicative of criminal activity.

In response to the attacks of 11 September, FATF issued eight Special Recommendations on Terrorist Financing, later followed by a ninth Recommendation on cash couriers in 2004.[31] To clarify provisions and assist with implementation, FATF produces a series of Interpretive Notes and International Best Practice papers that contain specific guidance on several of the Special Recommendations for states, relevant organizations and departments.

By creating a monitoring and reporting requirement on the international financial community to file reports of suspicious financial

[29] See also Chapter 8 in this volume.

[30] FATF, 'Guidance for Financial Institutions in Detecting Terrorist Financing Activities' (2002), at www.fatf-gafi.org/dataoecd/39/21/34033955.pdf.

[31] FATF, 'FATF IX Special Recommendations' (2001), at www.fatf-gafi.org/dataoecd/8/17/34849466.pdf.

activity,[32] it assists in the analysis of typologies which in turn informs the best practices to counter the financing of terrorism. Suspicion however varies, what may be suspicious to one person may not be so to another. Any report released to a central nominated point is done so on an 'intelligence only' basis and acts as a catalyst for further and more detailed enquiry.

All financial material obtained by specialist Financial Investigation Units (FIUs)[33] presents the immediate opportunity of being gathered in an evidential format. It can be released to an intelligence agency for use as intelligence product. Due to the sensitive nature of the information held by banks and financial institutions details are only released to an FIU following the service of an appropriate court order. An application for an order in the UK is *ex parte* and the judge must be satisfied that the application is necessary, proportionate and complies with the Human Rights Act 1998. However, where there is a threat to life, details that would assist an investigation can be released to an FIU by the financial institution on the basis that a court order will be served retrospectively.

Following the service of a court order in urgent cases financial companies can, and do, contact an FIU and provide limited information. The applicant can serve court orders personally on a company, but it is more usual for such orders to either be faxed or posted. If a fax service has been used a copy of the original will be provided subsequently. Any verbal communication should be treated with a degree of sensitivity as the company advising may not understand the significance of the material 'in hand'. It is always preferable to receive any financial material accompanied by a witness statement and/or deposition with the documents produced as exhibits.

The provision of statements and exhibits enables an investigator the opportunity of reviewing the items for relevance and suitability for any court proceedings. It must not be forgotten that what may seem urgent and of pivotal importance during an intelligence phase of an operation may subsequently be of negligible use in a later prosecution.[34]

Another international initiative in developing financial intelligence is the Egmont Group formed in 1995, when a group of national financial

[32] Suspicious activity reports are more commonly known as SARs or suspicious transaction reports STRs.

[33] FIU in this context is the Financial Investigation Units and must not be confused with the more widely used acronym for Financial Intelligence Units.

[34] See World-Check report Open Source www.world-check.com/media/d/content_whitepaper_reference/Integration.

intelligence units (FIUs) began to informally work together. While other organizations have provided good practical guidance and developed legislation in areas of money laundering and terrorist financing, the Egmont Group recognized that in practice, countries needed to be able to cooperate with each other in making financial enquiries in order to have any real advancement in this field. As such, one of the stated objectives of the Egmont Group is to create a global network of FIUs able to communicate with one another on an 'intelligence basis only' on issues such as money laundering and terrorist financing and possess the ability to analyse raw data to provide financial intelligence which is key when dealing with money laundering or the financing of terrorism.

There are currently 108 members in the Egmont Group, each is required to have a recognized FIU and must satisfy set criteria in order to be recognized as a member. First and foremost an applicant must be an established and nationally recognized FIU. They must be efficient, secure and effective. They must routinely handle suspicious activity reports (SARs).[35] An SAR/STR (suspicious transaction report) is a set of forms that contain a certain amount of financial information that identifies and refers to a person, business entity, financial business transaction or a company. They are completed initially by a staff member of a financial institution and submitted to a company official known as the Money Laundering Reporting Officer (MLRO). The MLRO reviews the information brought to their attention, and may choose to conduct a limited amount of research to determine if the activity is suspicious. If the MLRO concludes that the activity is suspicious, they advise their domestic FIU. An FIU will accept the report and issue a 'case number'. An FIU will then research the matter further and either disseminate the report in a sanitized format to law enforcement or an intelligence agency. Conversely, an FIU may be aware of other factors unknown to a disclosing institution and they may choose to store the data rather than disseminate it.[36]

Second, an established member must sponsor an aspirant to the Egmont Group. This may seem quite straightforward but the sponsor must undertake some wide-ranging activity at its own expense. Sponsorship, while notional, must also include ongoing reviews of all

[35] Such reports are also commonly known and referred to as Suspicious Transaction Reports (STRs) in some jurisdictions.

[36] Egmont Group of Financial Intelligence Units, 'About', www.egmontgroup.org/about.

activity from data storage to staff employment, training and effectiveness. One of the key principles of Egmont is to enhance bilateral and multilateral cooperation in strategic analysis. Each member must also have the ability to submit enquiries through a secure network.

Access to the network is via the designated contact point in a state. The information released following an application by a state is released on an 'intelligence only' basis, but the information is still owned by the disclosing state/FIU. It is important to note that an intelligence agency cannot task this group. Any subsequent request for fuller details will be transmitted through a request for mutual legal assistance in the usual way.

One of the key challenges to the sharing of financial intelligence is where a host country does not have an effective and functioning FIU or where countries are signatories to international and regional agreements on mutual assistance and mutual legal assistance. There is a critical need for FIUs to have the capability to exchange information and release evidence on a more informal basis. However, care must be exercised in the release of information on an informal basis, for example the Belgium Privacy Commission ruled (September 2006) that the US surveillance programme from the Belgium-based Society for Worldwide Interbank Financial Telecommunication (SWIFT) was illegal and criticized the handing over of information without due regard to the principle of proportionality, transparency and requirement for independent control and adequate protection.

3.5 *Intelligence held by other agencies, national or foreign*

Intelligence is gathered by several agencies in a state set up to perform a duty, role or activity on behalf of central government. Such a body does not change following a general election or a change of political leadership. It may however change its business portfolio or method of delivering its product, message or service.

As an example, in the UK, there are in excess of thirty databases controlled and maintained for and on behalf of government agencies. Some require compliance through the submission of personal data,[37] while others require the submission of data to obtain a service, product and social payment/benefit in compliance with a state requirement.[38] All these agencies retain raw data without analysis and it is held indefinitely.

[37] For example the Internal Revenue Collection.

[38] Passport, welfare benefit, driver's licence or registration of a motor vehicle.

Clearly an intelligence agency would expect to have ready and regular access to such data on an unrestricted basis. However, their use of such data can only ever be used as a catalyst to greater and more detailed analysis. It provides helpful information that could assist in the location of family members or cell members of a terrorist group.

Law enforcement nominates as best practice a single point of contact (SPOC) and subscribes to a memorandum of understanding when seeking to obtain data. Of particular importance to both law enforcement and the intelligence agencies is data held on a government 'licence' by a third party which requires it to maintain and be responsible for updating a database, for example in the case of the UK the payment of social and welfare benefits. An initial enquiry of one database may reveal a social payment but the further more urgently required detail is controlled, administered and owned by a third party[39] which can lead to additional and unnecessary work on the part of the investigation team.

Therefore, although the state ultimately controls the database and requires its existence, access to the databases can be problematical as agencies are not coordinated and more often than not are reluctant to share the information with the other government agencies without relevant court orders. Other frustrations when dealing with such state-held databases is that the information sought is not fully revealed to an investigator, intelligence agent/analyst thereby hindering any meaningful analysis of the information.

A further practical difficulty arises when seeking information from other government agencies. It is sometimes essential to the sanctity of an investigation that a requesting unit does not divulge fully the use it intends to make of the data held by another agency. However, the person or department requested to reveal data is best placed to advise what they hold, but is unable to act as it does not have sufficient information to assess what data should properly be disclosed. A possible solution is for the investigating agency to provide sufficient details to permit the agency to ensure that the information held by the agency is of any assistance to the enquiry.

The key to a successful investigation lies in a coordinated approach among domestic agencies as well as relevant foreign agencies. Such coordination and sharing of information is of particular significance given the transnational reach of terrorist or organized crime operations.

[39] Social payments are routinely authorized by the Benefit Agency, paid by them into an account held by the subject and administered by a financial factoring company.

3.6 *Open source*

Material held by open sources is often overlooked and a great deal of time, effort and resources can be saved by using information sources that are already in the public domain, for example reports, documents, news items and other reliable sources of information.

One such information source is the internet where a check on a name or address may reveal details which can be of use to intelligence development; however, the effective use of the internet in this way is a specialist area of work and secure methods of searching must be employed so as not to compromise operations. Although research of the internet does not reveal provenance or ownership of the information retrieved, its use reveals a footprint each time it is accessed. While this form of enquiry and investigation should not be missed, its use has to be risk assessed and should be conducted by a stand-alone computer to avoid contamination.

4 Handling of intelligence

A key requirement in the gathering of intelligence is the handling, storage and dissemination of the product. A failure to carefully handle any intelligence product can compromise an operation,[40] particularly where an investigation has components of both a proactive and reactive investigation and is likely to lead to the arrest of other suspects or prevent second or further attacks.

Once intelligence is collected, it remains quite simply intelligence until it can be analysed and assessed to ascertain if the original intelligence product could be true or relied upon. To that end, a degree of corroboration may assist if the product is to be acted upon, for example, a suspect may reveal details of his proposed travel which may then be corroborated by physical surveillance of the suspect, which could then be relied upon as evidence in any subsequent proceedings. This information could also help to build the financial intelligence, as the purchase of an airline or railway ticket can be traced. The purchase of a ticket would reveal the sum spent. A law enforcement agency could obtain an appropriate court

[40] On 8 April 2009 the Assistant Commissioner of the Metropolitan Police, Bob Quick, was photographed holding sensitive documents as he arrived in Downing Street for a meeting with the Prime Minister and the Home Secretary during an intelligence-led operation. The documents were clearly visible and showed top-secret details of a major anti-terror operation in north-west England. The error meant a police operation to arrest the suspects had to be expedited and led to the resignation of the officer.

order and serve it on the financial institution that handled the transaction and the material obtained by the law enforcement agency from the financial institution as well as the surveillance is now obtained as evidence. In this way it helps to build the blocks of an investigation and gather evidence and/or provide further intelligence-capturing opportunity. It can lead to another deployment of a surveillance unit or the monitoring of CCTV on the day that a suspect is expected to travel. This activity may reveal whether the suspect is travelling on his own or with an associate(s), and more data and intelligence-capturing opportunities are created. Therefore, although the initial intelligence product still remains as intelligence, its correct handling enables and assists in the crucial identification of suspects, the analysing of trends and in the understanding of mindsets of terrorists as well as permitting an investigation and possible prosecution to take place.

While intelligence affords the agencies an opportunity to view the conduct of an individual or a cell, it is vital that there is proper handling and accountability for retaining the product. When first received, the content of any report must be prioritized for assessment. Assessments vary considerably but one must be undertaken. A decision must be made to determine whether the product should be stored, catalogued, retained or allocated or passed on for dissemination to a third party or even disregarded. It can be retained by the agency that collected the data for further action or released to a partner intelligence agency. However, agencies must guard against speculative intelligence gathering as it can lead to innocent information being misunderstood or wrongly assessed. Unnecessary intrusive methods deployed and used during a gathering and accumulation phase can lead to collateral intrusion[41] and infringe the right to privacy.

Another facet of handling of intelligence is that it must be assessed at regular intervals to ascertain if it is, and remains, relevant. Crucial considerations include questioning whether the information is known to be a fact or not. Part of any assessment process will include the veracity of the original source and to determine if the information was 'created or revealed' to misinform or mislead.

Critical to a successful counter-terrorism operation is the need and requirement for agencies to operate in a coordinated manner as well as sharing the information both in domestic and foreign cases. The

[41] Collateral intrusion is unwarranted or unauthorized intrusion into the privacy of innocent third parties.

domestic sharing of intelligence is undertaken more routinely for the benefit of law enforcement. It is to assist in the prosecution of offenders or prevent atrocities or major crimes that could not be discovered or revealed using more traditional methods of police investigation.

Where intelligence is shared with international partners, there must be strict compliance with a code of ethics. International cooperation could quite simply be the revelation of intelligence product that prevents the travel of a suspect or the revelation of a suspect. While operational sharing of intelligence is crucial, the release process must be handled very carefully. It would be very easy for a 'rogue' agency to request intelligence product from a partner fully intending to use it for purposes other than those for which it has been requested. Quite often data shared is very personal and sensitive in nature and may be used to locate a citizen rather than to prevent a crime or a terrorist atrocity. Trust is, therefore, paramount if there is to be an open exchange of intelligence.

Where joint operations are conducted, the agencies must have agreed work plans, and decisions that can dictate further intelligence gathering should be set. Some data acquisition effort can overlap, but, subject to caveats on the handling and use of the product, it must be shared between analysts and investigators. Where there is no actual primacy established in an operation, it is necessary that any product gathered is shared promptly. Both or all organizations involved may retain data in different ways for different use.

For intelligence product to be of ongoing use to an intelligence operation, or even a reactive law enforcement investigation, it has to be understood that there must be an opportunity for evidence to either be drawn from that product, or at least an evidence-capturing opportunity created.

5 Human rights considerations

The deployment of covert, intrusive techniques is not new and is not unique to counter-terrorism investigations. However, it should be remembered that the gathering of intelligence in counter-terrorism operations, through any of the sources discussed above, often intrudes into the private lives of persons and their personal information. The right to privacy is a fundamental tenet of international human rights law and aims to protect a person, within the jurisdiction of a state, from any unlawful interference by the state. As with interference with liberty, clear legal justification must exist for interfering with the privacy of individuals, by whatever means, technological or otherwise.

The right to a personal or private life can be subject to restrictions or limitations and such rights are often referred to as restrictive or derogable rights.[42]

Restrictive/derogable rights are those rights which a state may be permitted to restrict or limit in accordance with the criteria laid down in the relevant convention. Broadly speaking, the restriction is generally for public order/safety. However such limitations must be: lawful, necessary, and proportionate.

The requirement of lawful, necessary and proportionate limitations essentially means:

- All measures taken by states must be lawful. That is, they must be by reference to and within prescribed laws duly passed in the constitutional manner.
- Measures and actions should not be 'arbitrary' and based only on an official's discretion or whim. For the law enforcement official, this means acting only where certain that one's actions are 'covered' or authorized by a valid law.
- Measures should be necessary and proportionate to the aim that is sought to be achieved.

There must, therefore, be a basis in domestic law or legislation which provides for the deployment of the covert activity or technique. Such legislation must be accessible to those liable to be affected and must have sufficient clarity to give a person an indication as to the circumstances and conditions in which covert methods by a public authority may be used. However, practice varies and where such powers are vested in the executive, the essential safeguards may not follow. In other countries, such as Uganda,[43] the counter-terrorism legislation permits interception and covert surveillance, but does not provide for a proper framework or safeguards for such deployment.

[42] The ICCPR and general international human rights law jurisprudence draw a distinction between those rights which are: absolute–non-derivable and restrictive–derivable. This in effect means that despite any declaration of derogation, the rights which are determined as absolute may never be derogated. The two most significant absolute rights which are common to all IHRL/IHL instruments and which give rise to individual criminal responsibility are the right to life (which implicitly prohibits murder, crimes against humanity and genocide); and the prohibition on torture (ICCPR 1966, 999 UNTS 171).

[43] Uganda Anti-Terrorism Act 2002.

The practical effect of the regional initiatives[44] is an expectation that there should be a regime of independent supervision of the use of covert, intrusive powers.[45] Interference with an individual's right to a private life must fulfil a pressing social need, be in pursuit of an aim which can be justified in law (e.g. to prevent or detect crime) and any covert deployment must be only that which is necessary to achieve what is sought to be achieved (i.e. the detection of a particular crime). In addition, safeguards must be in place to prevent abuse by intrusive techniques and remedies must be available in the event of such abuse.

The European Court of Human Rights has, in a number of cases, emphasized the need for legality, necessity and proportionality when a right is restricted. It has elaborated the principles and reiterated them in *Association for European Integration and Human Rights and Ekimdzhiev* v. *Bulgaria*:[46]

> The expression 'in accordance with the law', as used in Article 8 § 2, does not only require that the impugned measure should have some basis in domestic law. It also refers to the quality of this law, demanding that it should be accessible to the person concerned, who must moreover be able to foresee its consequences for him or her, and compatible with the rule of law.
>
> In the context of covert measures of surveillance, the law must be sufficiently clear in its terms to give citizens an adequate indication of the conditions and circumstances in which the authorities are empowered to resort to this secret and potentially dangerous interference with the right to respect for private life and correspondence ... In view of the risk of abuse intrinsic to any system of secret surveillance, such measures must be based on a law that is particularly precise. It is essential to have clear, detailed rules on the subject, especially as the technology available for use is continually becoming more sophisticated.
>
> To ensure the effective implementation of the above principles, the Court has developed the following minimum safeguards that should be set out in statute law to avoid abuses: the nature of the offences which may give rise to an interception order; a definition of the categories of

44 The regional instruments are as follows: 1950 European Convention on Human Rights, Council of Europe Treaty Series, No. 5; 1969 American Convention on Human Rights, 1144 UNTS 123; 1981 African (Banjul) Charter on Human and Peoples' Rights, 1520 UNTS 217.

45 See, for example, the ECtHR case of *Malone* v. *UK*, Judgment of 2 August 1984 [1984] ECHR (Ser. A).

46 Judgment of 28 June 2007, App. No. 62540/00. The application was lodged by the Association for European Integration and Human Rights, a non-profit body. It alleged that the Bulgarian legislation allowing the use of secret surveillance measures infringed rights under Arts. 6(1), 8 and 13 of the Convention, as it fell short of the standards set out in the Court's jurisprudence under these provisions.

> people liable to have their communications monitored; a limit on the duration of such monitoring; the procedure to be followed for examining, using and storing the data obtained; the precautions to be taken when communicating the data to other parties; and the circumstances in which data obtained may or must be erased or the records destroyed.[47]

6 Conclusion and recommendations

Traditionally those states that had some regulation of the use of covert means relied on codes of practice or guidelines (in common law jurisdictions) and often a disparate range of laws (in civil law states). However, an increase in human rights challenges and the passing of specific, human rights-compliant legislation in many states, has led to recognition that covert activity must have an explicit and workable framework in domestic law.

The intrusive nature of any form of covert investigation has to be considered in the light of international human rights instruments and, in particular, with the qualified, or restricted, right to a personal/private life which will invariably be found therein.[48]

The international community is correct to encourage and openly request mutual cooperation between intelligence agencies, and it is right that intelligence agencies should seek out fresh and new partners in their counter-terrorism operations. While the desire to enable wider intelligence-gathering opportunities is commendable, there must be a very distinct line drawn where it is known that the rights and safety of the wider populace are compromised, or violence and torture are used during that acquisition process.

Law enforcement has also built up unique and trusted contacts within its community and should be encouraged to exchange information on an 'intelligence only' basis, but the sensitivity of the information may prevent it being acted upon, or used in evidence.

[47] *Ibid.*, paras. 71–6.

[48] For states who are parties to the ECHR, Art. 8 addresses privacy, and provides that: '(1) Everyone has the right to respect for his private and family life, his home and correspondence. (2) There shall be no interference by a public authority with the exercise of this right, except such as is in accordance with the law and is necessary in a democratic society in the interests of national security, public safety, or the economic well-being of the country, for the prevention of disorder or crime, for the protection of health or morals, or for the protection of the rights and freedoms of others.' Art. 8, then, guarantees a right to private and family life, home and correspondence. However, it is a qualified, not an absolute right.

The release of information must be risk assessed in order to ensure that the receiving institution will not use it in an illegal or improper way which would undermine the spirit in which it was revealed. Equally, the information received should be scrutinized, in particular where the information is from a human source and there could be any danger of placing reliance on 'evidence' obtained through torture, or suspected to be obtained through torture.

The Egmont Group has shown that on the financial side of investigations, subject to caveats, there can be a quick, ready and reliable exchange of information.

The handling and use of intelligence has caused very deep concerns to the international community, in particular where the intelligence has been received from those subject to extraordinary rendition (discussed above). Due to the manner in which individuals have been removed from various states by complicit agencies, the general public has lost all confidence in the methodologies deployed by states.

One of the key challenges to the intelligence community is the gathering of intelligence or evidence in those parts of the world where there is little or no state control. This has the effect of creating safe havens for both terrorists and organized crime generally in for example, the North-West Frontier Province in Pakistan. Similarly, the escalation of piracy and the general threat to maritime security in the Horn of Africa due to the lack of an effective government in the Somali Republic, means there is little prospect of gathering any meaningful information about suspects, their organizations and their finance. The reluctance of the community to be involved in providing assistance to the intelligence community for fear of reprisals or corruption means that vital information may be lost.

States should be urged to take steps to ensure that:

- There is a framework for the exchange of information and the need for effective regional and international cooperation.
- The use and dissemination of intelligence product is undertaken in a timely and robust manner.
- A request for intelligence product is appropriate and will not be used in a disproportionate way, and/or lead to torture or human rights abuse.
- Intelligence agencies remain a separate entity to law enforcement and although they may assist and complement some activities, the powers of arrest and detention should rest with law enforcement agencies as it permits judicial scrutiny.

- Regular reviews are undertaken to ensure the relevance of data stored and data being captured is not routinely intrusive.
- Intelligence agencies continue to widen their accumulation efforts in ways that an oversight committee or ombudsperson can be satisfied are reasonable, productive and in the public interest.
- There is a review of the practice whereby intelligence agents are afforded the opportunity to conduct interviews of detained suspects in a third state.
- While protecting the secrecy and sanctity of their methods, review the receipt of intelligence product from a state which is known to use torture, excessive detention methods or has a very poor human rights record.

8

International cooperation in counteracting terrorist financing

TIM DANIEL

1 Questions of finance

There were many who took issue with George W. Bush's characterization of the post-9/11 era as being dominated by 'the war on terror'. How could a war be fought against an emotion? Who was the enemy? Who would fight this 'war'? What would constitute victory? And how to define 'defeat'? To fight a war you need money, that much was known: 'Point d'argent, point de Suisse',[1] medieval monarchs were told. The American taxpayer was to discover just how expensive the assault on this shadowy enemy was to be. But in this war, the casualties were not military personnel: they were ordinary unsuspecting citizens, going about their daily business. And that is just how the perpetrators also endeavour to appear. So, how on earth do you go about trying to track down how these people finance themselves? Especially when, as it turns out, their financial needs are modest in the extreme?[2] A great deal of effort, on a global scale, has

[1] 'No money, no Swiss' – Swiss mercenaries were highly regarded at the end of the fifteenth and the early sixteenth centuries: they struck terror into their enemies because of their ruthlessness, and were used by, among others, the Pope and Henry VIII. Their absolute requirement to be paid however contrasts sharply with today's terrorists who are motivated by idealism, not money.

[2] The National Commission on Terrorist Attacks upon the United States, *Monograph on Terrorist Financing* (at http://govinfo.library.unt.edu/911/staff_statements/911_TerrFin_Monograph.pdf) estimates that the 9/11 attacks cost no more than $500,000 to plan and execute: see in particular Appendix A to the monograph which sets out in minute detail all that is known about the financing of the 9/11 plot. The first report of the Analytical Support and Sanctions Monitoring Team appointed under UN SC Res. 1526 (2004) states that the bombings of the US embassies in Kenya and Tanzania in 1998 cost less than $50,000; the 2000 attack on the *USS Cole* cost less than $10,000; the Bali bombings in 2002, less than $50,000; and the Madrid bombings in 2004 less than $10,000 (letter dated 18 August 2004 from Chairman of the Security Council Committee

been directed at trying to find answers to these questions, in order, if at all possible, to discover the trails that may lead to the planners of the next atrocity. But, realistically, can it be done, or will 'the authorities' always be boxing shadows?[3]

2 An existing infrastructure

Faced with an unprecedented challenge, one way of proceeding is to ask what resembles that challenge most closely in the known world? The answer appeared to lie in financing crime, and, especially, in dealing with its proceeds. And which criminal activity needed the highest levels of continuous financing, networks of ordinary people, very competent organization, and the ability to make the profits 'disappear' back into the everyday economy? Which activity was carried out across continents, frequently required instantaneous access to cash, and had always to be carried out under the noses of conventional players, such as banks? The answer was, of course, the drug trade. Combating that trade has given birth to a range of tools which have become the daily instruments of law enforcement, and the creation of international networks and institutions to facilitate the cooperation needed to deal with hugely complex international operations. Some of these will be examined, at least in outline, below. Yet there remains a nagging question: does all the paraphernalia which has grown up deliver the results which are sought when it comes to combating terrorist financing? This chapter will look at that paraphernalia and endeavour to analyse whether it is, or can be, of real practical assistance in the fight against terrorism, and what obstacles stand in the way of achieving that goal. It will endeavour also to identify action which might be taken to heighten the effectiveness of the fight against what is, by any standard, one of the most elusive prey at large in our society.

established pursuant to Res. 1373 (2001) concerning counter-terrorism addressed to the President of the Security Council, UN Doc. S/2004/670 (2004), 12); M. Buchanan, 'The London bombs cost just hundreds', BBC News, 3 January 2006, at http://news.bbc.co.uk/1/hi/uk/4576346.stm.

3 Although it is extremely difficult in practice to 'predict' purely from banking transactions, freezing of accounts and using financial leads 'after the event' can be extremely helpful in identifying parties involved. This was demonstrated in the aftermath of the '7/7' bombings in London.

3 A personal experience

In August 2003, just one year after the further Kenyan terrorist attack in August 2002 targeted at an Israeli-owned hotel in Mombasa, and the failed attack on an Israeli-owned airliner taking off from Mombasa,[4] the author was asked to be the UK representative on a US Financial Systems Assessment Team (FSAT), which had been detailed to carry out a brief survey of financial institutions in Nairobi in order to try to get an idea of the state of Kenya's financial services sector. FSATs were originally conceived as a tool to fight money laundering, but their remit came to encompass terrorist financing as well. The Nairobi and Dar es Salaam bombings had occurred five years previously, and Kenya was perceived by the US, and the UK, as being a country particularly vulnerable to terrorist activity.[5]

In the course of a week the team called on, among others, the Central Bank, the stock exchange, the Kenya Bankers' Association, which represented Kenya's forty-odd commercial banks, the body responsible for licensing NGOs, the Gaming Commission, the Revenue service, the Attorney General's office, the DPP's office, the police section responsible for dealing with financial crime, and the National Security and Intelligence Service, an embryonic financial intelligence unit.[6]

One of the main purposes of the exercise was to ascertain the extent to which financial activity in Kenya could be said to be regulated. In particular the team was interested in finding out how easy or difficult it would be for anyone, including terrorists, to launder funds through Kenya's financial sector. The answer, perhaps unsurprisingly, was, with no difficulty at all. The concept of 'know your customer' (KYC) was certainly known about, and procedures were in place to send suspicious activity reports (SARs) to the Central Bank. As far as KYC was

[4] See M. Hammock, 'Hotel bomb threatens Kenya's economy', BBC News, 28 November 2002, at http://news.bbc.co.uk/1/hi/business/2523253.stm.

[5] In March 2009 the Interpol website set up under UNSC Res. 1267, UN Doc. S/Res./1267 (1999), showed on the 1267 Committee website the top-ten wanted terrorists on the 1267 List (as to which, see further below). Four were Kenyan by birth, or claimed Kenyan nationality. See poster at www.interpol.int/Public/NoticesUN/poster.asp.

[6] The full list was the: Anti-Money Laundering Task Force; Central Bank of Kenya; Bank Fraud Investigation Department; Kenya Revenue Authority; Attorney General, DPP and Principal State Counsel; Kenya Bankers' Association; Capital Markets Authority; Department of Immigration; Betting Control and Licensing board; NGO Coordination Board; Commissioner General; National Security and Intelligence Service (NSIS); Anti-Terrorism Police Unit (ATPU); Kenya Commercial Bank, and Transparency International.

concerned, the top ten or so banks operating out of Nairobi, part of global groups, had procedures in place, and staff trained to use them. The remainder of the banking sector, some thirty-odd local banks, either paid lip-service to KYC or ignored it in their scramble to attract clients in a fiercely competitive market. The managements of these banks were notorious for not allowing their staff to attend training courses, on the grounds that they could not be spared from their work. Although banking qualifications could be obtained at a college in Nairobi, many working in the sector were unqualified.

At the time of our visit the number of SARs filed was fewer than a dozen. The first ones filed had ended up in the courts, with the customer claiming that reporting him to the Central Bank was a gross breach of the confidentiality of the customer–banker relationship. Heavy damages were claimed, and awarded. The need for comprehensive legislation was starkly underlined.

The FSAT found that there were virtually no regulations in place to check sources of funds being used to purchase shares on the stock exchange. No checks were made at casinos, or for that matter bureaux de change, on the legitimacy of funds being used. Over 2,000 NGOs were 'licensed' by the NGO Coordination Bureau. Minimal checks were carried out, and it was said that there were, in addition, about 200,000 community based self-help organizations. Many NGOs chose to register as societies, companies or trusts: there was no requirement to register with the Coordination Bureau. Achieving NGO status in Kenya is all too often the first step on the road to amassing a fortune from overseas aid and 'charitable' donations.

One result of the FSAT was to provide donor-aided assistance to Kenya in drafting effective anti-money laundering and proceeds of crime legislation. That draft legislation went through extensive stakeholder consultation and, five years on, finally passed through parliament in December 2009.[7] When the FSAT visited Kenya draft anti-terrorism

[7] In the intervening period the international spotlight has focused on corruption in Kenya. See M. Wrong, *It's Our Turn to Eat: The Story of a Kenyan Whistleblower* (Hammersmith: Fourth Estate, 2009), in which former *Financial Times* journalist, Michela Wrong, describes the work of John Githongo, the former Permanent Secretary in Charge of Governance and Ethics, in trying to expose the notorious 'Anglo-Leasing' corruption affair, and concludes that the bloodshed following the December 2007 elections was largely the result of corrupt political parties clinging to power. Politicians in such parties will have little incentive to pass legislation which might facilitate the pursuit of the proceeds of crime and money laundering: legislation which might also be used to combat terrorist financing.

legislation had just been rejected as being in breach of fundamental human rights. In fact, it was probably too closely modelled on the rigorous legislation developed over the years by the United Kingdom in its fight against the IRA.

The author relates these matters in an effort to demonstrate the myriad difficulties that may face an international effort to coordinate a response to all facets of financial crime–corruption, fraud, money laundering and terrorist financing. These myriad difficulties point to a solution based on holistic responses of the type envisaged by the UN in its Global Counter-Terrorism Strategy.[8]

4 The two strands

Two distinct objectives may be discerned in the international effort to combat terrorist financing. One has to do with removing the means whereby the terrorists can recruit, train and arm their operatives, and, possibly, provide support to their families. Although it seems inherently unlikely that any of the 45 terrorist organizations proscribed under the UK's Terrorism Act of 2000, which included al-Qaeda, the Tamil Tigers, the military wing of Hezbollah, Hamas and many organizations of which the majority of the UK population would never have heard, but did not include the Taliban, could be counted as wealthy,[9] the fact is that they all recruit, many run training camps, they purchase arms and they travel. Even though much of the recruiting is done over the internet, and very often local cells will take care of everyday needs, certain minimum levels of expenditure are likely to be incurred. The expenditure itself will always be difficult to identify, and efforts tend to concentrate on identifying sources of income. This also may not be straightforward. Consider this list of ways in which terrorist organizations have raised funds:[10]

[8] See UN Doc. A/Res./60/288 (2006), referred to further below.

[9] The Taliban in Afghanistan would in fact be the exception: recent press reports suggest that the UN estimates that the total export value of the poppy crop in 2008 approached US$3.5bn, and that the Taliban are major beneficiaries of the illegal drug trade. See 'Opium production decreases', VOA News, 18 February 2010, at www.voanews.com/uspolicy/2009-03-06-voa1.cfm.

[10] T. Parkman, 'Terrorist Finance – Staying out of Trouble', *Finance Director Europe*, 4 February 2008, at www.the-financedirector.com/features/feature1594/.

- Cash donations from local and expatriate sympathizers.
- Donations collected by religious leaders and clergy.
- The use of cells or moles to divert funds and resources from legitimate charities and not-for-profit organizations.
- The creation or acquisition of legitimate businesses.
- The extortion of money/forced donations from individuals and businesses from within the terrorists' local community.
- Funds from fraudulent schemes, such as credit card fraud, insurance fraud and government subsidy fraud.
- Funds derived from the trading of so-called 'blood diamonds' and other precious metals and stones.
- Cash and profits from prostitution, people trafficking, smuggling, narcotics and other forms of organized crime.

Links with charities, particularly Muslim ones, and organized crime – particularly in the narcotics trade, are probably the more straightforward to tackle. There is, however, the difficulty that the usual money-laundering process is typically turned on its head when dealing with terrorist financing. Instead of illicit monies needing to be laundered to become 'clean', it will very often be the case that the process starts with clean money that only becomes 'dirty' at the moment that it is used for a criminal purpose.[11] Even that may be difficult to determine: as Parkman points out, purchasing flying lessons, hiring cars, renting accommodation, travelling to the place where the terrorist act is to be carried out, are all legitimate acts, so when does the actual criminal act take place? The reality may be that the best chance of detection rests with the investigation of laundering the proceeds of crime: FARC, the IRA, LTTE and the Taliban have all derived large parts of their funding from organized crime and the drugs trade.

Some terrorism is said to be state financed:[12] that will present a wholly different set of challenges, and one that will almost certainly necessitate

[11] A helpful diagram: 'The Processes of Money Laundering and Financing of Terrorism', contrasting the two, appears in the World Bank publication: P. A. Schott, *Reference Guide to Anti-Money Laundering and Combating the Financing of Terrorism* (Washington, DC: World Bank Group, 2004), 1–8.

[12] See 'Seven Nations Cited as Sponsors of Terror in State Department Report', at www.iwar.org.uk/news-archive/2003/04-30-9.htm, citing United States Department of State, 'Patterns of Global Terrorism 2002' (2003), at www.state.gov/j/ct/rls/crt/2002/. The seven states cited were: Cuba, Iran, Iraq, Libya, North Korea, Syria and Sudan.

state action, in the form of sanctions, travel bans or, in extreme cases, the freezing of all of a state's assets by the affected country.[13]

This strand is susceptible, in theory, to being dealt with through mechanisms similar to those built up and deployed over the years in the fight against the drugs trade and other forms of organized crime. Yet there are differences. A major objective in dealing with the drugs trade is to confiscate the profits. Smashing the drug-dealing organization is desirable also, but eliminating the trade is an illusory goal unless the whole methodology is rethought. One such route that is often discussed but seldom acted upon is the legalization of drugs and licensing of dealers. Switzerland has had some success with such initiatives, but concerted international action would be needed to make a real difference. Interestingly, a similar realization is now affecting the whole UN approach to dealing with terrorism, as attention swings to addressing the conditions conducive to the spread of terrorism.[14] There may be a parallel here with the overall objective of the legislation to fight against the drugs trade, i.e. removing both the incentives and the involvement of organized crime.

The other distinct strand in attempting to counteract terrorist financing is the acquisition of intelligence through pursuing financial 'leads'. If it were only possible to identify in time transfers of funds to individual operatives before attacks took place the world could be made a safer place. That is the wishful thought. The reality, as we have seen, is that the sums involved in mounting attacks are, by accepted money-laundering 'standards', minimal.[15] The panoply of international initiatives and instruments in place, which increased exponentially in the aftermath of 9/11 seem in this context to form a classic sledgehammer–nut scenario. Again, it is apparent that this is a problem which is not going to be solved by the use of traditional tools. Far wider-ranging, and, at first sight, less obvious, steps will need to be taken. The Kenyan example cited above is instructive in a number of ways: ultimately, work and training of the type undertaken by the FATF which leads to an all-round tightening of financial discipline, and heightened levels of awareness at a grass-roots

[13] See, e.g., the work of the Iran–United States Claims Tribunal, arising out of the detention of fifty-two US nationals at the US embassy in Teheran in 1979, concerned with the subsequent freeze of Iranian assets by the US, see Background Information Iran–United States Claims Tribunal, at www.iusct.org/background-english.html.

[14] See 'Pillar One' of the *United Nations Global Counter-Terrorism Strategy*, UN Doc. A/Res./60/288 (2006), referred to below.

[15] See n. 2 above.

level, leading to meaningful reporting, will be the only way to achieve the kind of results looked for.[16]

5 The response of the international community

Having identified some of the problems presented by terrorist financing, what efforts have been made by the international community to deal with them? In order to fight an international phenomenon such as terrorism it was imperative to reach some kind of consensus between states acknowledging the rule of law. International instruments were needed, and they arrived thick and fast. No other activity in the modern world has had quite the same unifying and bonding force.

The first UN Convention directed specifically at tackling terrorism was in fact concluded in Tokyo in 1963.[17] The second was also directed at aircraft, specifically hijacking.[18] Since then some sixteen conventions[19] on terrorism have come into existence, of which thirteen are in force. The various conventions and protocols are aimed at providing for enhanced international cooperation mechanisms and grounds for establishing jurisdiction. A key aim is to provide a seamless international criminal law regime that reduces the existence of safe havens for those committing or attempting to commit terrorist acts. The cornerstone of virtually all the instruments is the *aut dedere aut judicare* (states must either extradite or prosecute) obligation regarding those accused of terrorist acts.[20]

In 1972 the General Assembly established the first Ad Hoc Committee on International Terrorism, to consider:

> Measures to prevent international terrorism which endangers or takes innocent human lives or jeopardises fundamental freedoms and study of the underlying causes of those forms of terrorism and acts of violence which lie in misery, frustration, grievance and despair and which cause

[16] The role of FATF is examined in more detail below, but the banks are critical of the effectiveness of the reporting obligations in a counter-terrorism context: detailed financial record-keeping has proved more effective in bringing terrorists to justice.

[17] 1963 Convention on Offences and Certain Other Acts Committed on Board Aircraft, 704 UNTS 220.

[18] 1970 Convention for the Suppression of Unlawful Seizure of Aircraft, 704 UNTS 106.

[19] See list at http://treaties.un.org/Pages/DB.aspx?path=DB/studies/page2_en.xml.

[20] See, generally, A. Sambei, A. du Plessis and M. Polaine, *Counter-Terrorism Law and Practice: An International Handbook* (Oxford: Oxford University Press, 2009), 1.29ff. and 2.23ff. See also Chapter 2 in this volume.

> some people to sacrifice human lives, including their own, in an attempt to effect radical changes.[21]

It is interesting to note that even at this early stage there was implicit recognition of the deep-seated causes of terrorism: tackling those causes has however only recently become a priority.[22]

In 1994 the General Assembly adopted a Declaration on Measures to Eliminate International Terrorism,[23] and in 1996 a new ad hoc committee was formed to elaborate international conventions on terrorism.[24] This Committee provided the genesis of the Convention on the Suppression of the Financing of Terrorism ('the Convention'), adopted by the General Assembly on 9 December 1999.[25] The Convention was originally signed by 132 states, and, as at August 2012, there were 179 parties:[26] thus, only 14 states are not parties. And, yet, astonishingly, before 9/11, the only states which had ratified were the UK, Botswana, Sri Lanka and Uzbekistan. It was in fact only in April 2002 that there were sufficient accessions for the Convention to become law. In large part this was due to Security Council Resolution 1373,[27] which required member states of the UN to implement various measures within ninety days, including becoming parties to relevant international conventions and protocols relating to terrorism. Legislators were shocked into action,[28] and, between 11 September 2001 and 19 February 2002, 90 countries signed, and 13 more ratified the Convention.

The Convention itself was the result of a French initiative which was supported by the G8, the prevention of terrorist financing having been identified by their foreign ministers at their meeting in May

[21] UN Doc. A/Res./3034 (XXVII); passed following the terrorist attack on the Munich Olympic Games in 1972.

[22] Nearly thirty-five years later, in fact: as will be seen below, it was not until 2006 that the UN Global Counter-Terrorism Strategy was adopted: its first priority is to address the conditions conducive to the spread of terrorism. The UK government published, on 24 March 2009, *The United Kingdom's Strategy for Countering International Terrorism*, Cm 7547, entitled *Pursue Prevent Protect Prepare-'the Four P's'*. 'Prevent' is recognized as a key objective. At: www.tsoshop.co.uk. See also Chapter 1 in this volume.

[23] UN Doc. A/Res./49/60 (1994). [24] UN Doc. A/Res./51/210 (1997).

[25] UN Doc. A/Res./54/109 (1999).

[26] United Nations Treaty Collection, at http://treaties.un.org/Pages/ViewDetails.aspx?src=IND&mtdsg_no=XVIII-11&chapter=18&lang=en.

[27] UN Doc. S/Res./1373 (2001).

[28] M. Pieth 'The Financing of Terrorism: Following the Money' (2002) 2 *European Journal of Law Reform* 374.

1998 as a 'priority [area] for further action'.[29] Later in 1998, France tabled a draft at the UN. In December the General Assembly put the Ad Hoc Committee established by Resolution 51/210[30] in charge of developing the draft. The text was adopted by the General Assembly on 9 December 1999.

In the Convention there are three main obligations for states parties:

(1) they must establish an offence of financing of terrorist acts in their domestic criminal legislation;
(2) wide-ranging cooperation between them must be given and legal assistance provided in all matters covered by the Convention; and
(3) certain requirements concerning the role of financial institutions in the detection and reporting of evidence of financing of terrorist acts were to be enacted by each state.

Thus, the burden imposed on each state party was not inconsiderable, and it would certainly have been true to say that some states, such as the UK, were far better prepared to introduce such legislation than others. Indeed, the UK, having had the experience of dealing with the activities of the IRA over a long period of time, already had a series of Acts directed at terrorist activity on the statute book. Helpfully, however, the UNODC produced in 1999 model legislation to provide guidance to states parties. Draft legislation for civil law countries, and a draft for common law countries have been publicized by the IMF.[31]

6 Criminalization of financing of terrorist acts

This provision is at the heart of the Convention, and was unique when it was introduced. It was the first counter-terrorism legislation to 'take a proactive and preventive approach by criminalizing the financing of terrorism as a stand-alone preparatory offence and requiring states to freeze and forfeit funds used for or derived from the commission of terrorist acts'.[32]

[29] Conclusions of G8 Foreign Ministers, 9 May 1998, para. 28, at www.dfait-maeci.gc.ca./g8fmm-g8rmae/bir_g8concl-en.asp.

[30] Measures to Eliminate International Terrorism, UN Doc. A/Res./53/108 (1999).

[31] G. Gottselig and P. Gleason (eds.), *Suppressing the Financing of Terrorism: A Handbook for Legislative Drafting* (Washington, DC: IMF, 2003): Appendix VII for civil law jurisdiction, and Appendix VIII for common law jurisdictions (based on legislation enacted in Barbados).

[32] Sambei *et al.*, *Counter-Terrorism Law and Practice*, 6.10.

Article 1(1) of the Convention broke new ground by defining, albeit in quite general terms, the meaning of 'funds':

> assets of every kind, whether tangible or intangible, movable or immovable, however acquired, and legal documents or instruments in any form, including electronic or digital, evidencing title to, or interest in, such assets, including, but not limited to, bank credits, travellers cheques, money orders, shares, securities, bonds, drafts, letters of credit.

The main problem with this definition is that it is couched very much in what might be termed 'bankerese'. It targets transfers of assets by a conventional, Western-based banking system, with tangible transfer instruments operating within an environment susceptible to regulation. It does not here, nor anywhere else in the Convention, even begin to attempt to define what is probably the single most effective, and elusive, form of transfer – that carried out under what are referred to generically as 'alternative remittance systems'. No international instrument, nor, so far as is known, any state-based legislation has yet come up with effective means to monitor, let alone regulate, trust-based systems based on messages.[33] The messages may be telephoned, texted, faxed or emailed, but no documentation which would be familiar to a Western banker comes into existence.[34]

Immediately, therefore, one has a potential problem with the Convention: does it even cover what is probably the most frequently used method of financing terrorism? The only words in the definition that seem applicable in a *hawala* transaction may be: 'tangible ... movable ... assets ... however acquired'. That puts something of a premium on finding the cash. This problem is not unique to terrorist financing; it is a phenomenon which is familiar to drug enforcement authorities.[35] All of the 'legal documents or instruments' mentioned in the Article 1 definition, while expressed to include, but 'not [be] limited to', the traditional instruments described therein, make no mention of prepaid cards, sometimes described as 'stored value cards'. These are

[33] This is however now being actively worked on by the bodies described in n. 38 below. In 2010 the World Bank published 'Alternative Remittance and Terrorist Financing', which gives guidance on tackling this issue.

[34] For a detailed description of how *hawala*, the best-known informal system, works, see M. El Qorchi *et al.*, 'Informal Funds Transfer Systems' (2003) International Monetary Fund Occasional Paper 222.

[35] See, for example, J. Simser, 'Money Laundering and Asset Cloaking Techniques' (2008) 11 *Journal of Money Laundering Control* 123, which 'explores the various typologies and methods used to cloak assets following the placement stage of money laundering'.

now probably the single most common method for terrorists to acquire funds 'on the street'.[36]

Stored value cards are not, however, by any means the only 'new game in town'. Digital currencies, mobile payments, internet gambling and online games are all now available technologies[37] for making illicit payments. As the US Department of Justice admits, none of these are as yet fully addressed by anti-money laundering regulations, and they enable financial transactions to be made internationally with very little oversight, and a high degree of anonymity.[38]

The Convention envisages, under Article 8(1), that 'Each State Party shall take appropriate measures, in accordance with its domestic legal principles, for the identification, detection and freezing or seizure of any funds used or allocated for the purpose of committing the offences set forth in Article 2 *as well as the proceeds derived from such offences*'.[39] This is obligatory for all states parties: the number that will, in reality, have the capacity to comply with this obligation is almost certainly very small – despite the large number of signatories to the Convention, the number of prosecutions relating to terrorist financing remains very low. Many will have signed up on the basis of reciprocity. Under Article 9 states parties are obliged to take action on intelligence provided to them regarding the presence in their territory of a person who has or is alleged to have committed an Article 2 offence, and to investigate. They must then either prosecute the offender themselves or make the alleged

[36] Private conversation between the author and an officer in the counter-terrorist section of SOCA, February 2009. However in 2009 the Counter-Terrorism Implementation Task Force (CTITF) was set up in the US: it is a coordinating and information-sharing body consisting of twenty-five entities drawn from within the UN system and other international organizations. It has set up a Working Group on Tackling the Financing of Terrorism to assist states in this regard. The Working Group is led by the IMF, the World Bank and UNODC. The first report of the CTITF is to be found at: www.un.org/terrorism/pdfs/CTITF_financing_ENG_final.pdf. It found no evidence of widespread use of stored value cards. See also the following recently published World Bank working papers: http://siteresources.worldbank.org/FINANCIALSECTOR/Resources/Alternative_Remittance_Systems.pdf and http://siteresources.worldbank.org/FINANCIALSECTOR/Resources/New_Technogies.pdf.

[37] An overview of all these 'cyber methods' is available at: www.usdoj.gov/ndic/pubs31/31379/finance.htm.

[38] National Drug Threat Assessment 2009, US National Drug Intelligence Center (2008), at www.justice.gov/ndic/topics/ndtas.htm#y2009.

[39] Emphasis added. This wording seems more appropriate to classic money-laundering legislation aimed at capturing drug-dealing proceeds: it is difficult to imagine the circumstances in which an Art. 2 offence would generate 'proceeds'. It is, however, also included as an obligation under SC Res. 1373, Art. 1(c).

offender available for extradition. A number of human rights safeguards are written into the Article, but as will become apparent below, the number of human rights challenges is increasing.

Just supposing that the intelligence services of a state party to the Convention are sufficiently equipped, or sufficiently lucky, to identify funds 'used or allocated for the purpose of committing the offences set forth in Article 2 [of the Convention]',[40] what does it have to do? It has to 'take appropriate measures, in accordance with its domestic legal principles, for the forfeiture of [such] funds'.[41] This presupposes that the state party has in place legislation which will give it those powers.[42] Such has been the cumulative effect of signing up to the Convention and the UN Resolutions referred to below, that it is estimated by the UNODC that nearly 180 states have now ratified the first twelve international instruments and many have taken significant steps towards implementation.[43] But the question must still be asked, how many have effective legislation in place, and how effective is that legislation likely to be against innovative technologies of the kind described above? That gives rise to the further question: is it not likely that the legislation will always be at least one step behind the latest technical innovation? These are matters for concern, but the reality will probably continue to be that 'cash is king': the use of sophisticated technology still tends to leave some form of audit trail, which can be of enormous assistance in post-event investigations.[44]

7 The 'offence'

Under Article 2 of the Convention the offence is committed if a person 'by any means, directly, or indirectly, unlawfully and wilfully, provides or

[40] As to which, see further below; Art. 8(1). [41] Art. 8(2).

[42] For Kenya, proceeds of crime legislation, of the type envisaged, and provisionally drafted after the FSAT report (above), would make this task relatively straightforward. Six years after the provisional draft was prepared, the legislation has only just made its way to the statute book. Why is this? It remains to be seen when it will actually take effect. Note 7, above, gives a hint of the difficulties faced in the implementation of such legislation in Kenya.

[43] The UNODC Global Project on Strengthening the Legal Regime against Terrorism states that 69 countries have new or revised counter-terrorism legislation in different stages of development, but, in addition, some 9,600 criminal justice officers in 168 countries have undergone UNODC capacity-building exercises: www.unodc.org/unodc/en/terrorism/unodcs-taas.html.

[44] Above nn. 2 and 3.

collects funds with the intention that they should be used *or in the knowledge that they are to be used*, in full or in part, in order to carry out [the proscribed acts]'. (Emphasis added: these words go beyond specific intent to commit the offence, which is the normal subjective component of *mens rea* – knowledge in the context of the Convention is a form of direct intent.)[45] The proscribed acts are either one which constitutes an offence under one of the previous international counter-terrorism instruments listed in the Annex to the Convention;[46] or:

> any other act intended to cause death or serious bodily injury to a civilian, or to any other person not taking an active part in the hostilities in a situation of armed conflict, when the purpose of such act, by its nature or context, is to intimidate a population, or to compel a government or an international organization to do or to abstain from doing any act.[47]

This was the radical provision in the Act. It went beyond previous definitions of terrorist crimes and introduces a so-called 'mini-definition' of terrorism, concentrating on the protection of civilians: it represents an important advance in the use of anti-terrorism measures to prevent, rather than merely react to, terrorist violence.[48] Non-violent logistical preparation and support that make terrorist groups and operations possible are caught, and under Article 2(3) it is provided that the prohibited provision or collection of funds which does not result in a violent act is nevertheless punishable. This is an important element of the offence – 'one often misunderstood by policymakers and criminal justice officials',[49] but not those involved with FATF, where there is much discussion on the necessity for this provision; it being argued,

[45] Sambei *et al.*, *Counter-Terrorism Law and Practice*, 6.15.

[46] These treaties are (1) the Unlawful Seizure of Aircraft Convention; (2) 1971 Convention for the Suppression of Unlawful Acts against the Safety of Civil Aviation, 974 UNTS 178; (3) 1973 Convention on the Prevention and Punishment of Crimes against Internationally Protected Persons, Including Diplomatic Agents, 1035 UNTS 168; (4) 1979 International Convention against the Taking of Hostages, 1316 UNTS 206; (5) 1979 Convention on the Physical Protection of Nuclear Material, 1456 UNTS 125; (6) 1988 Protocol for the Suppression of Unlawful Acts of Violence at Airports Serving International Civil Aviation, Supplementary to the Convention for the Suppression of Unlawful Acts against the Safety of Civil Aviation, 1589 UNTS 474; (7) 1988 Convention for the Suppression of Unlawful Acts against the Safety of Maritime Navigation, 1678 UNTS 222; (8) 1988 Protocol for the Suppression of Unlawful Acts against the Safety of Fixed Platforms Located on the Continental Shelf, 1678 UNTS 304; and (9) 1997 International Convention for the Suppression of Terrorist Bombings, 2149 UNTS 256.

[47] Art. 2.1.(b) [48] Sambei *et al.*, *Counter-Terrorism Law and Practice*, 6.13 [49] *Ibid.*

particularly by civil law nations, that ancillary offences and preparatory acts are already caught by existing terrorist legislation.

With regard to the offence under Art 2.1 (a), there are, as has been mentioned, nine counter-terrorism instruments listed in the Annex.[50] It does seem somewhat anomalous that a provision which is as ground-breaking as Art 2.1 (b) should be linked in with instruments whose dates stretch back as far as 1970. Some of those instruments came about as the result of specific terrorist events – each was a classic example of the reactive, piecemeal approach to outlawing terrorist acts which had prevailed prior to 1999. Several have to do with the hijacking of aircraft – most notably the successful 'skyjack' of El Al Flight 707 by the Popular Front for the Liberation of Palestine (PFLP) en route to Lod in Israel from Rome[51] in 1968, the bombing of Air Cubana Flight 455 killing 73 people in 1976 – or the hijacking of a ship and the taking of hostages – the *Achille Lauro* by the Palestine Liberation Front in 1985. However, some were, as it were, anticipatory – the protection of nuclear material, oil platforms and airports – all high-priority potential targets. Indeed, the Convention itself was reactive, resulting in part from the simultaneous attacks on the US embassies in Nairobi and Dar es Salaam in 1998. Given the diversity of targets, objectives and ideals of the perpetrators, it is perhaps not surprising that none of these instruments actually sought to define terrorism or terrorist acts. Apart from anything else, there was always the lurking point that one man's terrorist is another man's freedom fighter.[52] At the end of the day, the one identifiable linking factor could be said to be money, as noted above.

Once that link was in place, it became possible to build on the whole international instrument edifice which had grown up around the drugs trade: most notably the UN Convention Against Illicit Traffic in Narcotic Drugs and Psychotropic Substances 1988 ('the Vienna Convention'), and the United Nations Convention against Transnational Organized Crime 2000 (the 'Palermo Convention'). Possibly even more important, however, was the adaptation of the FATF 40 Recommendations by the addition of a further nine specifically directed at financing terrorism.[53] All this was good, but more was needed.

[50] See above n. 47. [51] See www.skyjack.co.il/chronology.htm.

[52] B. Ganor, 'Defining Terrorism: Is One Man's Terrorist Another's Freedom Fighter?', in B. Ganor (ed.), *ICT Papers on Terrorism* (Herzliya: International Institute for Counter-Terrorism, 2002), 3–21.

[53] See section on FATF, below.

8 Security Council resolutions

That 'more' was provided by the United Nations Security Council, and the catalyst was 9/11. As mentioned above, the take-up by states parties to the Convention was initially very slow. No doubt many saw it as a good thing in principle, but were perhaps concerned at the burden to legislate and implement that would be placed on them.

The events of 9/11 sent an unprecedented shockwave through the entire world, and not least the Security Council. Within a month it had passed Resolution 1373.[54] Using hitherto unused powers under Chapter VII of its Charter, the Security Council actively required members of the UN to sign up to the Convention and to introduce the legislation required under the Convention. States suddenly started signing up, the Convention entered into force on 10 April 2002,[55] and legislators were galvanized into action. There was no doubt that the US was the driving force behind this frenetic activity, all done in the name of the UN. The US was, after all, the immediately injured party, and it already had a certain amount of intelligence in place which was now deployed. Much of that intelligence amounted only to suspicion, but distinctions tend to get lost in a frenzy, particularly a frenzy of rushed lawmaking, and, ultimately, invasion plans. Legislation which comes about as a reaction to a one-off crisis (and nobody could be certain at the time that it was going to be one-off) is bound to be far from ideal, particularly when individual liberties and human rights threaten to get in the way. And so it has proved. But, on the other hand, the slow take-up of the Convention – of which the US was no less guilty than the majority of other states[56] – was testimony to the inertia that had surrounded these measures: an inertia which could no longer be tolerated in the eyes of the White House, and, to be fair, many within the UN.

To a large extent, Resolution 1373 was based on a restatement of the Convention. An analysis carried out by the IMF[57] reduced the obligations placed on states to two groups for presentational purposes. One was headed 'Setting international norms on combating the financing of terrorism', the other, 'Freezing assets of terrorists and terrorist organizations'.

[54] See n. 27 above.

[55] Thirty days after the 22nd ratification was lodged with the Secretary General of the UN.

[56] The US did not in fact ratify until 2002.

[57] Gottselig and Gleason, *Suppressing the Financing of Terrorism*, 17.

Under the 'norms' heading, two requirements are identified, one relating to the financing of terrorist acts, the other to the financing of terrorists. As far as the financing of terrorist acts is concerned, the requirements are virtually identical to those set out in the Convention, in particular the elements of criminalization set out in Article 2. States are required to ensure that terrorist acts are established as serious offences under domestic laws, and that punishment for these offences reflects the seriousness of the crimes. These provisions are all in the Convention.

What is different under 1373 is the requirement placed on states to:

> prohibit their nationals or any persons or entities within their territories from making any funds, financial assets or economic resources or financial or other related services available, directly, or indirectly, for the benefit of persons who commit or attempt to commit or facilitate or participate in the commission of terrorist acts, of entities owned or controlled, directly or indirectly, by such persons and of persons and entities acting on behalf of or at the direction of such persons.[58]

The hire of a taxi to a terrorist, albeit unwittingly, could thus become an arrestable offence, to say nothing of the potential exposure of individuals who donate to charities which are subsequently found to have been providing terrorist finance. This is an autonomous obligation imposed under 1373, which is not contained in the Convention, which does not deal with financial support to terrorists or terrorist entities.[59]

In addition to being enjoined to refrain from giving support to terrorists, states were required to take steps to prevent terrorist acts, deny safe haven to terrorists, and those who finance terrorist acts, bring such persons to justice, and afford other states the greatest measure of assistance in respect of criminal investigations or proceedings. States were also required to prevent the movement of terrorists or terrorist entities by effective border controls and other measures; a requirement the

[58] Res. 1373, para. 1(d).

[59] Various anomalies arise in respect of freezing of terrorist assets which stem from the fact that this is an administrative measure, not a criminal one – for a long discussion of this point see the third report of the Analytical Support and Sanctions Monitoring Team appointed pursuant to Res. 1526 (2004) concerning Al-Qaida and the Taliban and associated individuals and entities (UN Doc. S/2005/572 (2005), para. 41). Uncertainty exists as to whether it was in fact intended to criminalize the unwitting provision of funds to designated entities: one can have a situation where the funds of a designated terrorist are frozen – an administrative act – but anyone who gives money to that person is committing a criminal act.

effects of which can be experienced at first-hand by anyone taking an international flight from almost anywhere in the world.

SCR 1373 also lashed out at asylum seekers; enjoining states to ensure that they are not planning, facilitating or participating in terrorist attacks (the paranoia was really showing through). States were also to ensure that refugee status was not abused by terrorists and that claims of political motivation were not recognized as grounds for refusing requests for extradition of alleged terrorists.[60]

There followed a host of 'wake-up' injunctions, all aimed at getting states to participate as fully as possible in the global 'war on terror'. States were to intensify and accelerate exchanges of information on terrorist movements and actions, to prevent the commission of terrorist acts through appropriate administrative and judicial action,[61] to cooperate through bilateral and multilateral arrangements and agreements to prevent, suppress and prosecute terrorist acts, and to become parties to the 'relevant' global conventions against terrorism (including the Convention).[62]

Becoming a party was not, however, of itself, sufficient. States were already expected fully to implement these instruments: Security Council Resolutions 1269 (1999)[63] and 1368 (2001)[64] had contained strong exhortatory provisions, likely to be acted upon by those sympathetic to the US cause, but not necessarily by those states which the US might really have liked to bring on board – in particular, the so-called 'axis of evil', Iran, Iraq and North Korea. As commentators have pointed out, however, designation by the State Department as a state sponsoring terrorism,[65] is not going to promote ratification, or, if it does, then that ratification may be simply a cynical ploy to try to secure a positive international reaction, there being no real intention to comply.[66] There

60 Res. 1373, para. 3(a–g).

61 Situations in which judicial action is likely to be required occur where, e.g., problems arise in connection with requests made for mutual legal assistance, or extradition, see Sambei *et al.*, *Counter-Terrorism Law and Practice*, 9.99.

62 'Relevant' is not defined, but this is a reference to the nine other instruments annexed to the Convention, and any subsequent relevant conventions.

63 UN Doc. S/Res./1269 (1999), calling upon states to cooperate in the prevention and suppression of terrorist acts.

64 UN Doc. S/Res./1368 (2001), calling upon states to redouble their efforts to prevent and suppress acts of terrorism.

65 See n. 12 above.

66 See, e.g., R. Ehrenfeld, *Terror Financing. Myth and Reality* (Jerusalem: American Center for Democracy, 2004).

is also the matter of the US's own policy of 'de facto exceptionalism', under which the US only signs up to international instruments when it suits it to do so.[67] The US failures can be regarded as a serious undermining of the moral authority of the world's only superpower. China delayed ratification of the Convention until 2006, and Pakistan, a key country in the fight against terrorism, has yet to ratify it.

9 Freezing the assets of terrorists and terrorist organizations

Resolution 1373 was also the latest in a series of UN resolutions aimed at freezing the assets of designated individuals and organizations. By the time it was passed there were in existence not only a series of previous resolutions but a whole mechanism at the UN directed to implementation. Resolutions 1267 (1999) and 1333 (2000) were aimed at freezing the assets of the Taliban and of Osama bin Laden respectively, and entities owned or controlled by them. Under Resolution 1267 a Committee, known as the 'Al-Qaida and Taliban Sanctions Committee' (also dubbed the '1267 Committee'), was established.[68] These resolutions established autonomous asset-freezing regimes under which lists[69] of persons and entities whose funds and assets are to be frozen are issued and modified from time to time under the full authority of the Security Council: 'full authority' because the 1267 Committee is in reality the entire Council, but, when it sits, it sits in closed session. The Committee's Guidelines[70] contain detailed provisions regarding the manner in which additions and deletions may be made.[71]

[67] Examples of unratified treaties include: 1982 Law of the Sea Convention (UNCLOS), 1833 UNTS 3; 1997 Kyoto Protocol to the United Nations Convention on Climate Change, 2303 UNTS 148; 1992 Convention on Biological Diversity (CBD), 1760 UNTS 79; Comprehensive Nuclear Test Ban Treaty (CTBT); 1966 International Covenant on Economic, Social and Cultural Rights, 993 UNTS 3; 2003 United Nations Convention against Transnational Organized Crime, 2225 UNTS 209; 1989 Convention on the Rights of the Child, 1577 UNTS 3; 1979 Convention on the Elimination of all Forms of Discrimination against Women (CEDAW), 1249 UNTS 13; and 1998 Rome Statute for the International Criminal Court, 2187 UNTS 3.

[68] Guidelines of the Committee for the Conduct of Its Work (2002), para. 1 refers to the Security Council Committee Established Pursuant to Res. 1267 (1999).

[69] The first such list appeared in January 2001: there were slightly fewer than 100 names on it: see press release at www.un.org/News/Press/docs/2001/afg124.htm-old.

[70] Note 68 above.

[71] It has been estimated that by the beginning of April 2006 some US$140 million contained in 1,400 bank accounts had been frozen: the Council on Foreign Relations: www.cfr.org/publication/10356/tracking_down_terrorist_financing.html.

It is stipulated that proposed additions should include 'a narrative description of the information that forms the basis or justification for taking action'. The proposed names of individuals or entities are circulated among members of the Committee, and the designation is considered accepted if no state objects to it within forty-eight hours – in other words, it is a kind of default process, but that, no doubt, is merely to recognize the realities of the situation.[72] If, after circulation, states were to have a longer period within which to consider the denominations one could foresee endless delay. This is why the mechanism for removals from the list become extremely important.

A person or entity seeking to be removed from the list must first petition the government of residence or citizenship to request a review of the case. If the petitioned government endorses the petition, it must first try to reach an agreement for de-listing with the original designating government, which must refer the case to the 1267 Committee (and, later, to the Security Council, in open session).[73] Unanimity is required to give effect to a de-listing request. Updated lists, including the names of those removed from the list, are sent to UN members without delay, and posted on the website of the 1267 Committee. It is not difficult to envisage that a system such as this will be challenged in the courts, and so it has proved. Some of those challenges will be examined below.

The general obligation to freeze assets under the Resolution is similar to that under the Convention, but the Convention is more specific regarding the steps to be taken. Article 8(1), it will be recalled, provides for a state to take steps *in accordance with its domestic legal principles*, for 'the identification, detection and freezing or seizure of . . . funds'. The Resolution requires only the *freezing* of assets. Both the Resolution and the Convention give considerable latitude to states in the design of appropriate freezing, seizure and confiscation regimes.

On the basis of Resolution 1390,[74] the Consolidated List came into being, combining the Taliban and al-Qaeda lists: listing by the Security Council might now be thought to be the effective listing procedure,

[72] In April 2010, 137 individuals associated with the Taliban were listed, and 258 associated with al-Qaeda; 103 entities, other groups and undertakings associated with al-Qaeda were listed, and none such associated with the Taliban. See www.un.org/sc/committees/1267/consolist.shtml.

[73] In 2006 however a focal point was established in the UN to receive delisting requests: UN Doc. S/Res./1730 (2006).

[74] UN Doc. S/Res./1390 (2002).

with states responding to freezing decisions of the Council under 1373, rather than the earlier resolutions. However, 1373 mandates that states themselves should have in place mechanisms to freeze the assets of terrorists, which implies that states themselves should have a mechanism for designating terrorists. Thus there are two separate obligations – one for the state to have a procedure for determining who is a terrorist, and then freezing the assets of that person, as well as freezing the funds of those designated by the 1267 Committee.[75] Thus, the US Treasury Department, for example, runs its own designation scheme through the Office of Terrorism and Financial Intelligence (TFI).[76]

It is said that the reasons for this lie in the lack of uniformity in the definition of terrorism among states, and the varying degrees of legal protection given to those whose names appear on the lists. States are also often reluctant to provide full factual information on which their suspicions are based.[77] This led almost immediately to questions being raised regarding the efficacy of the state-based asset freezing regime.[78] Those questions have now extended to the whole basis on which listing and de-listing takes place, and the right of individuals and entities to challenge their listing at law. So serious are these challenges that some question whether the authority of the UN itself is at stake in this area. Predictably, as will be seen below, the major challenges have been fought through the European courts.

10 The United Nations Global Counter-Terrorism Strategy

Although, as has been seen, the events of 9/11 galvanized the US, and then the UN, into frenetic action, there would always have been a danger that, after all the initial activity, the world would move on, and counter-terrorism measures would fade into the background of the UN agenda. That did not happen, however, as an increasing number of states suffered from terrorist activity, and came to realize that it would only be through

[75] The requirement for states to carry out their own designations raises important questions regarding the mechanisms to be used – should it be through the judicial system, or can it be done by administrative procedures (e.g. a determination by a minister of justice)? For more discussion on these points, see paras. 5 and 6 of the Interpretative Note to FATF Special Recommendation III, at: www.fatf-gafi.org/document/53/0,3343,en_32250379_32236947_34261877_1_1_1_1,00.html-INSRIII.

[76] The TFI website provides a continuous update on designated individuals and entities: www.treas.gov/offices/enforcement/.

[77] This reluctance will now have to be overcome – see below.

[78] See, e.g., K. Alexander, 'International Legal Developments' (2003) 6 *Journal of Money Laundering Control* 201, 212–13.

concerted world action that gains would be made, as the terrorists spread their net more and more widely. On 6 September 2006, the General Assembly adopted the United Nations Global Counter-Terrorism Strategy,[79] uniting all 192 member states behind a common strategic framework. Four 'pillars of action' were identified:

1. Measures to address the conditions conducive to the spread of terrorism;
2. Measures to prevent and combat terrorism;
3. Measures to build States' capacity to prevent and combat terrorism and to strengthen the role of the United Nations in that regard; and
4. Measures to ensure respect for human rights for all and the rule of law as the fundamental basis for the fight against terrorism.

Two years later, in September 2008, all 192 states confirmed their full commitment to the principles of the Strategy, and pledged to pursue its vigorous implementation. The Strategy was said by the Secretary General, in the Introduction to his 2008 Report,[80] to have outlined more than fifty practical recommendations and provisions, setting what he identified as 'an ambitious agenda for at least the next decade'. His Report goes on to highlight action taken by UN departments, programmes, funds and agencies in a whole range of areas stated to be within the framework of the Counter-Terrorism Implementation Task Force (CTITF). The CTITF had come into being in 2005 at the instigation of the Secretary General, in an effort to provide overall coherence and cohesion between all the UN entities involved in counter-terrorism efforts. It was much needed: by that time there were some twenty-four separate UN entities involved, and no less than nine separate Task Forces comprising representatives from selected entities.[81]

The Working Group on tackling the financing of terrorism is one of the two smallest groups, with just six members. They are the:

- International Monetary Fund;
- UN Office on Drugs and Crime;
- World Bank;
- Counter-Terrorism Committee Executive Directorate;

[79] UN Doc. A/Res./60/288 (2006). [80] UN Doc. A/62/898 (2008).

[81] The entities and the Task Force members are listed in the Annex to A/Res./62/898, above. A helpful organigram entitled Main Actors of the UN System in Counter-Terrorism Efforts can be downloaded from www.un.org/terrorism.

- International Criminal Police Organization (Interpol); and
- Monitoring Team of the Security Council Committee established pursuant to Resolution 1267 (1999).

The IMF, UNODC, World Bank and the Monitoring Team are described as 'lead' organizations within the Group.[82] The 1267 Monitoring Team is one of the CTITF-listed groups, and produces very regular updates on its work.[83] Anyone wishing to 'feel the pulse' of the UN's anti-terrorist financial sanctions activity is advised to visit their website.

In 2008 the Security Council directed that the Committee, with the help of the Monitoring Team, and in coordination with the relevant designating states, make available on the 1267 Committee website a narrative summary of reasons for listing for each entry on the Consolidated List.[84] That has now been done and these summaries have been placed on the website.[85] In addition, the Security Council directed that the Committee conduct a review of all 489 names on the Consolidated List as at 30 June 2008, to be completed by 30 June 2010, 'in order to ensure the Consolidated List is as updated and accurate as possible and to confirm that listing remains appropriate'.[86] There can be little doubt that this belated recognition of the need for transparency in listing arose in part from criticism of the topicality of the List, but, even more pressingly, as the result of the legal action taken in Europe which is described below. Recognition of the need to deal with these issues has led to the creation of the Office of the Ombudsperson.[87]

11 The United Kingdom's strategy

The UK's *Pursue Prevent Protect Prepare* strategy has been mentioned above.[88] That strategy is now commonly referred to as the 'Prevent' strategy which, in its latest manifestation,[89] sets out the following three main objectives, which are to:

[82] Although the Monitoring Team does a lot for the working group, in practice it is actually the UNODC (together with the IMF and World Bank) that provides the 'lead', rather than the 1267 Monitoring Team.

[83] See: www.un.org/sc/committees/1267/latest.shtml.

[84] See UN Doc. S/Res./1822 (2008), para. 13.

[85] See: www.un.org/sc/committees/1267/narrative.shtml.

[86] UN Doc. S/Res./1822 (2008), para. 25.

[87] See section 13 below.

[88] See n. 22 above.

[89] Prevent Strategy (2011), at www.homeoffice.gov.uk/publications/counter-terrorism/prevent/prevent-strategy/.

- respond to the ideological challenge of terrorism and the threat from those who promote it
- prevent people from being drawn into terrorism and ensure that they are given appropriate advice and support
- work with sectors and institutions where there are risks of radicalisation that we need to address.

The methodology for carrying these objectives into effect is all-important. The co-director of the European Muslim Research Centre, based at Exeter University, warned in scathing terms of the dangers of the government linking the fight against terrorism with issues of 'identity, assimilation and "rootlessness"', especially in a Britain beset with economic cuts, many of which effectively withdraw funding from Muslim support groups. Instead, the tried-and-tested policies already being pursued by the Home Office should continue to be adhered to: 'evidence, not emotion', should be the guiding principle.[90]

12 The challenge in Europe to the SCR regime

These challenges focus on the workings and enforceability of the listing procedures in light of the human rights of those affected. On 7 November 2001 the US Treasury Department's Office of Foreign Assets Control (OFAC) blocked assets held by US persons or US-controlled persons throughout the world within the Al-Barakaat International Foundation, a legal business entity established in Sweden, which comprised a global network of money-remitting companies. The grounds for the US freeze order were that Al-Barakaat was controlled by Osama bin Laden to support terrorist activities. Interestingly, although the operations of Al-Barakaat in the USA relied on the formal banking system, it operated internationally through a *hawala* network which channelled funds into Somalia through Dubai. According to OFAC, the *hawala* network was used not only to fund al-Qaeda and other bin Laden organizations, but also provided logistical support to his networks. Al-Barakaat denied any involvement with bin Laden or any other terrorist groups, but OFAC claimed that its freezing orders had put Al-Barakaat out of business.[91]

[90] J. Githens-Mazer, 'Club Britain: access denied', Aljazeera, 10 February 2011, at http://english.aljazeera.net/indepth/opinion/2011/02/201128114625731221.html#.

[91] The legal battle which arose was something of a disaster for the US government – see the Al-Barakaat Case Study in *Monograph on Terrorist Financing*; I. Warde, *The Price of*

In order to facilitate the implementation of Resolution 1267 (1999) in Europe, the Council of the European Union had adopted European Regulation 881/2002,[92] which contains the list of individuals and entities whose assets must be frozen, in particular because of their alleged relationship with the Taliban, al-Qaeda or bin Laden. Ahmed Ali Yusuf, together with Al-Barakaat and others, filed a petition to the European Court of First Instance (CFI) in 2001,[93] seeking annulment of Regulation 881 under Article 230 of the European Communities Treaty. Their case was that the insertion of their names in the list was inaccurate and that the mechanism of listing breached their fundamental human rights. The petitioners' names had been designated by the 1267 Committee and, without any further procedure, their names were simply incorporated by the EC Regulation (which was undoubtedly the intention behind the whole apparatus). They were originally listed on 17 October and 9 November 2001 pursuant to Resolution 1267, and had their names published under Resolution 1333.

In order to challenge their listing at that time,[94] they had, as has been seen above, to petition their home states to get them to 'espouse' their cause to challenge the listing decisions. This process fell some way short of international human rights standards which demand access to a court and the right to a judicial remedy. Thus, before the CFI, they argued that the EC lacked the power to adopt targeted sanctions, and that the imposition of the sanctions violated their fundamental rights of due process, and respect for property – hence the request for annulment of the regulation under Article 230 of the Treaty Establishing the European Community (TEC). This important provision provides that '[t]he Court of Justice shall review the legality of acts adopted [by the Community institutions]'.[95] If it is found that a Community act is vitiated by any of the annulment grounds listed in Article 230 (2) TEC, such as 'lack of competence, infringement of this Treaty or of any rule of law relating to

Fear: The Truth Behind the Financial War on Terror (London: IB Tauris, 2007), which gives a good description of the whole affair.

92 This Regulation also implements UN Doc. S/Res./1390 and UN Doc. S/Res./1455: Regulation 2580/2001 implements S/Res./1373.

93 Case T-306/01, *Ahmed Ali Yusuf, Al Barakaat International Foundation* v. *Council and Commission* [2005] ECR II-3533.

94 The de-listing procedures have subsequently been modified by UN Doc. S/Res./ 1730 (2006).

95 Art. 230(1) Treaty Establishing the European Community.

its application, or misuse of powers' the 'Court of Justice shall declare the act concerned to be void'.[96]

A similar application had been made by Yassin Abdullah Kadi, a Saudi Arabian national[97] who had also been listed. Judgment was given by the CFI in both cases in September 2005. The CFI rejected both challenges. Its reasoning was of considerable interest. It held that, as a matter of principle, under public international law, it had no jurisdiction to review the legality of the EC Regulation, because it resulted from a binding UNSCR, which, according to the UN Charter (Chapter VII) prevailed over any other law, including Community law. The only way in which the Resolution could be challenged would be if it could be shown that the Resolution violated a norm of *jus cogens*. *Jus cogens* was stated by the court in the *Kadi* case to be 'a body of higher rules of public international law binding on all subjects of international law, including the bodies of the United Nations ... from which no derogation is possible'[98] under which the court had the power to check 'indirectly' the lawfulness of resolutions of the Security Council. Having identified this principle, the Court did find that rights to be heard, to have access to courts, and to property, all possessed a *jus cogens* character, but, somewhat perversely, refused to find a *jus cogens* violation by the Security Council, on the ground that the right to judicial review can be derogated in certain prescribed circumstances, of which this was one.

This judgment was criticized by the EU Advocate-General, Miguel Poiares Maduro, who issued an Opinion in January 2008 arguing that there is no basis in community law for according supra-constitutional status to measures adopted by the EU Commission that are necessary for the implementation of resolutions adopted by the Security Council.[99]

Kadi and the Al Barakaat International Foundation joined cases and lodged appeals with the European Court of Justice (ECJ) on 17 and 21

[96] Treaty Establishing the European Community, 25 March 1957, 298 UNTS 11, amended by Treaty of Amsterdam, 2 October 1997 OJ (C 350) 1, amended by Treaty of Nice, 26 February 2001 OJ (C 80) 1, consolidated version reprinted in 2002 OJ (C 325) 33.

[97] Case T-315/01, *Kadi* v. *Council and Commission* [2005] ECRII-3649.

[98] *Ibid.*, 226.

[99] Case C-402/05 P, *Yassin Abdullah Kadi* v. *Council of the European Union and Commission of the European Communities, Opinion of Advocate-General Poiares Maduro* delivered on 16 January 2008, 1; see http://curia.europa.eu/en/actu/communiques/cp08/aff/cp080002en,pdf.

November 2005, respectively,[100] seeking to set aside the CFI judgments. On 3 September 2008, the Grand Chamber (i.e., full court) of the ECJ did, in a landmark judgment,[101] largely set aside the judgments of the CFI, and introduced a completely new legal framework within which to review UN sanctions within the Community, and quite possibly, beyond.

The ECJ affirmed the CFI's decision to the effect that the Community had the power to adopt targeted sanctions legislation. This was on the basis that, although the TEC only provided for traditional interstate sanctions, the Community's implied powers under Article 308 TEC could form the legal basis for financial sanctions against individual non-state actors.[102] Having established that the Community could impose such sanctions, they then fell for full review under Community law. In the view of the ECJ there was no commingling of UN resolutions and EC regulations. In a key passage of the judgment, the Court stated:

> the community judicature must, in accordance with the powers conferred upon it by the EC Treaty, ensure the review, in principle the full review, of the lawfulness of all Community acts in the light of the fundamental rights forming an integral part of the general principles of Community law, including review of Community measures which, like the contested regulation, are designed to give effect to the resolutions adopted by the Security Council under Chapter VII of the Charter of the United Nations.[103]

The ECJ explicitly rejected the idea that Community courts would have jurisdiction 'to review the lawfulness of [UN resolutions], even if that review were to be limited to examination of the compatibility of that resolution with *jus cogens*'.[104]

On the basis of these pronouncements, the Court proceeded to scrutinize the actual listing procedure and asset freezing process for their conformity with human rights values. It found that the inclusion of the appellants' names in the list led to a situation in which 'the rights of the defence, in particular the right to be heard and the right to effective judicial review of those rights, were patently not respected.'[105] The Court further held that a Community organ imposing restrictive measures against individuals on security grounds must communicate to that

[100] *Kadi*; *Al-Barakaat*.

[101] Cases C-402/05 P and C-415/05 P, *Yassin Abdullah Kadi and Al-Barakaat International Foundation* v. *Council of the European Union and Commission of the European Communities* [2008] ECR 285, 2.

[102] *Ibid.*, paras. 224–230. [103] *Ibid.*, para. 326. [104] *Ibid.*, para. 287.

[105] *Ibid.* para. 334.

individual or entity the grounds on which the restriction is being made, either at the time of making it, or as soon as possible thereafter, in order to give the individual or entity the opportunity to bring legal action to challenge those grounds.[106] The Court did acknowledge that fashioning an appropriate system of human rights protection in this area will require a balancing of 'legitimate security concerns about the nature and sources of information taken into account in [imposing the restriction]'.[107] But the failure to provide any procedure for challenge was an infringement of the basic human right of defence, and to an effective legal remedy.[108]

The Court also dismissed the Commission's argument that there existed an effective administrative review procedure for targeted individuals within the UN legal system. Such re-examination did not offer guarantees of judicial protection, being 'in essence diplomatic and intergovernmental, the persons or entities concerned having no real opportunity of asserting their rights [before a] committee taking its decisions by consensus, each of its members having a right of veto'.[109]

In the actual cases of Mr Kadi and Al-Barakaat, the Court further found that there had been a fundamental infringement of their right to enjoy their property, and annulled EC Regulation 881/2002 in so far as it concerned both parties. However, since such action could seriously and irrevocably affect the effectiveness of the freezing orders, the Court imposed a stay of three months from the date of judgment in order to allow the Council to remedy the infringements found, if it could.

The implications of the ECJ's decision in these cases are profound. Although not denying the primacy of UN resolutions, the clear possibility exists that the EU/EC and its member states may not act in accordance with UN resolutions. This may have considerable repercussions for individual member states in terms of state responsibility, since, in practice, the powers of implementation of UN resolutions now lies with the EU/EC, and member states may thus not be able to act in conformity with their international obligations.

The decision in Kadi and Al-Barakaat by the Grand Chamber of the ECJ is the most resonant challenge to the UN designation procedures to date, but it does not stand in isolation. According to the UN, al-Qaeda Committee's own monitoring team, there were at the end of 2008 no

[106] *Ibid.*, para. 336. [107] *Ibid.*, para. 344 [108] *Ibid.*, paras. 345–51.
[109] *Ibid.*, paras. 322–3.

fewer than fifteen major cases ongoing, in at least seven countries.[110] These included the US, Italy, the Netherlands, Pakistan, Switzerland and Turkey. These challenges questioned the legal effect of designation and the equity and fairness of the procedures used by the UN Al-Qaida and Taliban Sanctions Committee both in making designations and considering petitions for de-listing. Political challenges are being debated in the European Parliament, the Council of Europe, and national parliaments around the world.[111]

In April 2008, in the UK case of *A, K, M, Q and G* v. *Her Majesty's Treasury*,[112] a UK freezing order against the five claimants, all designated by the UN Al-Qaida and Taliban Sanctions Committee, were overturned as being *ultra vires*. The UK terrorist asset-freezing measures are contained in the Terrorism (United Nations Measures) Order 2006, and the Al-Qaida and Taliban (United Nations Measures) Orders 2002 and 2006. These measures were introduced directly by the government through Orders in Council to implement the UN Security Council resolutions in order to strengthen domestic controls on financing terrorism and to comply with the British government's obligations under the Convention and UNSCR 1373. As a result of using the Order in Council route, the measures were never properly scrutinized, debated or approved by Parliament. The judge, Mr Justice Collins, condemned as impermissible this ousting of Parliament: 'in deciding the appropriate way in which the obligation should be applied and in particular in creating the criminal offences set out in the Orders it was necessary that Parliamentary approval should be obtained' he stated in his judgment.[113]

The Treasury appealed, and on 30 October 2008, the Court of Appeal[114] held that the Orders would be valid, provided that the words 'or may be' were excised from Article 4 (2) of the Order in

[110] Letter dated 13 May 2008 from Chairman of the Security Council Committee established pursuant to Res. 1267 (1999) concerning Al-Qaida and the Taliban and associated individuals and entities addressed to the President of the Security Council (UN Doc. S/2008/324 (2008), Annex 1).

[111] Annex 1, n. 30 above.

[112] *A, K, M, Q and G* v. *H.M. Treasury*, Judgment of 24 April 2008, High Court of Justice Queen's Bench Division Administrative Court [2008] EWHC 869 (Admin.), mentioned in Annex 1 above n. 30.

[113] *Ibid.*, 37.

[114] *A, K, M, Q and G* v. *HM Treasury*, Judgment the Supreme Court of Judicature Court of Appeal (Civil Division) on Appeal, Case No.: T1/2008/1080 [2008] EWCA Civ. 1187, 2008 WL 4698916.

Council.[115] The result was that the Treasury had to show that there were 'reasonable grounds for suspecting the involvement of the designated person in committing or facilitating terrorism and not simply suspecting that he might be involved'. The Court also ruled that a designated person should always be entitled to a merits-based review. In this way the decisions of the UN Committees might appear, in the UK, now to be subject to judicial review, but as 1267 determinations are implemented by the European Union this may be open to some doubt, particularly as the Court held that, once revised in the manner suggested, the Orders would be compliant with the ECHR, and that they would not be unlawful at common law.

In January 2010, the first case to come before the UK's newly constituted Supreme Court was the appeal from the Court of Appeal's decision.[116] The Supreme Court decided that section 1(1) United Nations Act 1946 did not provide sufficient powers to implement Resolution 1267 as amended and extended by subsequent resolutions. Accordingly on 4 February 2010 the Supreme Court ordered that the 2002 and 2006 Orders in Council be quashed. Assets frozen under the 2006 Order remained frozen however under Council regulation (EC) 881/2002. Thus the Court held that the EC Regulation was directly applicable to the UK, but that secondary legislation was required to provide for penalties for failing to comply with the Regulation. This was not achieved by the use of Orders in Council. As a result of this decision the government hastily passed the Al-Qaida and Taliban (Asset Freezing) Regulations 2010 on 5 February, the day after the judgment was handed down. The intention was to remedy the gaps exposed by the Supreme Court's judgment. The new Act also provides a national framework for gathering and sharing information and granting licences,[117] including providing penalties for providing false information, obstructing the Treasury's exercise of its information-gathering powers, or failing to comply with licensing conditions. It remains to be seen whether this legislation will itself be challenged in its turn, but the case and its consequences demonstrate very clearly the need for national

[115] United Kingdom, the Terrorism (United Nations Measures) Order 2006, No. 2657, at: www.legislation.gov.uk/uksi/2006/2657/contents/made.

[116] Cited in the Supreme Court as *HM Treasury* v. *Ahmed and others* [2010] UKSC 2 (Ahmed No. 1 [2010] All ER (D) 179 (Jan.)) and *HM Treasury* v. *Ahmed and others* [2010] UKSC 5 (Ahmed No. 2 [2010] All ER (D) 40 (Feb.)).

[117] Licences can be granted to disapply prohibitions imposed under the Act on dealing with or making available funds or economic resources for the benefit of designated persons.

governments to take the greatest care when legislating to implement these UN resolutions in order to ensure that they are effective under their own jurisdictions.

The far-reaching implications of the wording used in the Convention and UNSCR 1373, as adopted in Council Regulation 2580/2001, to the effect that '[n]o economic resources shall be made available, directly or indirectly, to, or for the benefit of a listed person so as to enable that person, group or entity to obtain funds, goods or services' was considered by the ECJ in the case of *Möllendorf*,[118] where the Court held that a land transaction in which a listed person had sold land to innocent purchasers could not be registered. As the purchasers had already paid for the land, the case has the potential to cause them a considerable injustice. The ECJ has referred back to the German national court the question of whether a requirement under national law that the sellers refund the purchase price for such an incomplete sale has disproportionately infringed their right to disposal of property.[119]

It was inevitable that measures introduced nationally under such far-reaching instruments as Resolutions 1267 and 1373 should provoke widespread debate and legal challenges, once the international outrage sparked by the events of 9/11 had died down.[120] At the time a number of commentators queried the UN's ability to impose upon states the obligation to give effect to 1373 – effectively purporting to give the resolution the status of a norm under public international law,[121] even using its Chapter VII powers. The resolution was, understandably, very much driven by US sentiment, but, then, so was the setting up of the detention camp at Guantánamo Bay, the policy of so-called extraordinary rendition, and the invasion of Iraq. It is totally understandable that the US wanted the toughest possible measures taken internationally in order to suppress the financing of terrorism, but the definition of terrorism, as has been seen,[122] itself causes great debate in different jurisdictions. Its own Supreme Court has now given the US a number of sharp reminders regarding the rule of law and the values enshrined not only in its own

[118] Case C-117/06 [2007] ECR I-8361, see paras. 11, 60 and 80 in particular.

[119] *Ibid.*, paras. 60, 74 –80.

[120] As at 2 April 2008, there were twenty-six legal challenges known to the Monitoring Team (see Annex 1 to UN Doc. S/2008/324).

[121] See, e.g., L. M. H. Martinez, 'The Legislative Role of the Security Council in Its Fight against Terrorism: Legal, Political and Practical Limits', *International & Comparative Law Quarterly* 52 (2008), 333.

[122] See n. 52 above.

Constitution, but also in the common law.[123] It is also worth pointing out that the Commonwealth, representing fifty-four states, and nearly two billion people, filed *amicus* briefs in the Guantánamo Bay cases before the Supreme Court, citing the long history of habeas corpus in the common law. The Supreme Court, in its decisions, noted those authorities, and now a significant body of both common and civil law authorities is building up in relation to the human rights aspects of the whole listing and de-listing procedures.

At the same time, it has to be recognized that there are formidable difficulties facing those who gather, and act upon, the evidence that leads to listing. By its very nature the gathering of that evidence has for much of the time to be carried out by covert means. In the UK it is still not permissible to use telecommunications-intercepted evidence. To do so, say the authorities, in this case MI5 and MI6, would be to risk having to disclose methodologies used, and put operatives at risk, as well as alerting criminals, in this case, terrorists, to what is being done and facilitating avoidance techniques.[124] At the same time, it is difficult to see how, for example, the use of *hawala*-type remittance systems can at this time be otherwise effectively monitored: the only realistic course, and it is bound to be long drawn out and controversial, would seem to be some form of regulation of alternative remittance systems.

13 Creation of the Office of Ombudsperson

On 17 December 2009 the Security Council sought to find a solution to the increasing number of delisting challenges being mounted in different jurisdictions by creating the Office of Ombudsperson.[125] Its mandate was extended on 17 June 2011, and at the same time the Security Council decided to split the al-Qaeda and Taliban sanctions regime, so that the 1267 List would become the 'Al-Qaida Sanctions List', and include only names of those individuals, groups, undertakings and entities associated

[123] See, e.g., *Rasul* v. *Bush*, Supreme Court of the United States of America, Judgment of 28 June 2004, No. 03-334; *Al Odah* v. *United States*, Supreme Court of the United States of America, Judgment of 30 June 2010, No. 09-5331.

[124] There is a considerable body of authoritative support for a change in the law, backed by the former Prime Minister, Gordon Brown, but a report published in July 2009 rejected such a change. See: 'Gordon Brown's plans to use phone-tapping evidence in court thrown into chaos', *The Times*, 22 July 2009, at www.timesonline.co.uk/tol/news/uk/crime/article6722429.ece. It remains to be seen whether the new coalition government will take this issue up.

[125] UN Doc. S/Res./1904 (2009): its mandate was extended by S/Res./1989 (2011).

with al-Qaeda.[126] The first Ombudsperson, appointed by the Secretary-General on 3 June 2010, was Kimberly Prost.[127]

The Ombudsperson is mandated to gather information and to interact with the petitioner for de-listing, and relevant states and organizations with regard to any request.[128] The Ombudsperson's first report was submitted to the Security Council on 24 January 2011,[129] and on 18 March 2011 Ms Prost gave a presentation to the 41st meeting of the Council of Europe Committee of Legal Advisers on Public International Law (CAHDI) at Strasbourg.[130] In that presentation, Ms Prost noted that the creation of the Office was the product of a compromise between those who believed that the introduction of a review process was contrary to the fundamental nature and clear powers of the Security Council, and those individuals and entities subject to the sanctions to whom the procedure 'felt like' a measure which was the product of a judicial or administrative process. As such, the process raised expectations that there would be the types of protections and recourse which normally surround such proceedings. The talk goes on to describe how she has endeavoured to achieve procedural fair process in her first year in office. The matters raised in Ms Prost's first report gave rise to discussion within the 1267 Committee on a large number of issues, including the proposal (on which a letter was sent to the Security Council) that a de-listing recommendation by the Ombudsperson should become final unless challenged within thirty days.[131] On the question of effectiveness of the Ombudsperson's Office, Ms Prost acknowledges that it will only be once some cases have proceeded through to the end of the process that a full assessment can be made, but cautions that the process which leads to the outcome is arguably as important as the outcome itself.[132]

[126] A summary of the changes effected and other relevant information can be found at www.un.org/sc/committees/1267.
[127] See Chapter 4 in this volume.
[128] The Office and its functions are described at www.un.org/en/sc/ombudsperson.
[129] UN Doc. S/2011/29.
[130] Her speaking notes are at www.un.org/en/sc/ombudsperson/pdfs/CAHDI_remarks_18.03.2011_E.pdf.
[131] The topics covered and steps taken are contained in a press release: www.securitycouncilreport.org/site/c.glKWLeMTIsG/b.7497325/k.C720/June_2011brCounterterrorism_1267_Committee.htm.
[132] *Ibid.*

14 The Financial Action Task Force

The final part of this chapter reviews what is arguably the most effective focus for the international effort to suppress terrorist financing; the work of FATF, the Financial Action Task Force. Alongside FATF, there is MONEYVAL, which is the organization having specific responsibility for setting standards for, and monitoring, some twenty-nine states under Council of Europe Conventions,[133] MONEYVAL is itself a member of the FATF.[134] Following the review of the work of FATF below a suggestion is made regarding a hitherto largely neglected route to tackling terrorist financing.

The FATF was established in 1989 at a G7 Summit. At that time international concerns with criminal financial activity were focused on money laundering. FATF currently has thirty-three member states, but its reach is far wider. It is an intergovernmental policy-making body that prescribes both domestic and international anti-money laundering policy standards.[135] Most importantly, however, it also conducts evaluations of states' current anti-money-laundering procedures, and examines techniques used by money launderers and terrorist organizations. Annual typology reports are prepared and distributed to governments. In 1990 FATF issued 40 Recommendations developed to assist the fight against money laundering. The 40 recommendations were updated in 1996 and 2003 because of the need to reflect developments in global money-laundering trends and methodologies.

After the 9/11 attacks FATF expanded its remit to deal specifically with terrorist financing, and in October 2001 it published a list of Eight Special Recommendations on Terrorist Financing.[136] These had the specific aim of assisting private, rather than national authorities, detect the movement of terrorist funds. In October 2004 a ninth Recommendation was added specifically to deal with the issue of cash couriers.

[133] Information regarding the background and work of MONEYVAL can be found at www.coe.int/t/dghl/monitoring/moneyval/About/MONEYVAL_in_brief_en.asp.

[134] It became an Associate Member in 2006 as an FSRB (see below). This allows MONEYVAL members to participate actively in the work of the FATF and provide input on policy-making.

[135] Note however that the commitments made by states to adhere to FATF standards are typically made by treasury and/or justice departments – the penalty for non-compliance is to be blacklisted: an interesting example of a 'soft law' approach producing a regime which is arguably harsher than a treaty-based one.

[136] For the role of FATF regarding terrorist financing generally, see: www.fatf-gafi.org.

Although the 9 FATF Special Recommendations cover much of the same ground as 1267 and 1373, there is in fact much more to them than simply a reiteration of the call to member states to ratify and implement the international legal instruments against terrorism.[137] The great value of FATF is that, through regional FATFs, it has been able to export its model to regions of concern. These FSRBs (FATF-style regional bodies)[138] effectively extend FATF's reach beyond its 33 members to over 130 states, all of whom are subject to reporting obligations and peer review. Having this widespread network enables FATF to suggest effective responses to the various manifestations of terrorism wherever they occur, and they do differ quite markedly from region to region. Where necessary, FATF will impose counter-measures on non-compliant members, as well as non-members.[139]

The first part of the first Special Recommendation enjoins states to ratify and fully implement the 1999 Convention and the second part urges full implementation of SCR 1373.

The second Recommendation is also in two parts. The first requires states to criminalize the financing of terrorism, terrorist acts and terrorist organizations. The second recommends that such offences are designated money-laundering offences.

The third Recommendation deals with the freezing and confiscation of terrorist assets in accordance with the UN resolutions and the Convention.

The fourth Recommendation tracks Recommendations in the original 40 Recommendations, putting them in a specifically terrorist-financing context. It requires certain financial institutions, particularly banks, to report activities to the state's competent authorities where there is a 'suspicion' of those activities being linked to terrorist financing. In practice, however, this Recommendation is almost impossible for banks to implement: many banks have indicated that it is impossible to identify a terrorist finance-related transaction based purely on the

[137] SC Res. 1617 (2005) reinforces the 9 FATF Special Recommendations and specifically obliges states to implement them (UN Doc. S/Res./1617, New York, 29 July 2005).

[138] The bodies are: Asia/Pacific Group on Money Laundering (APG); Caribbean Financial Action Task Force (CFATF); Council of Europe MONEYVAL (previously PC-R-EV) Committee; Eastern and Southern African Anti-Money Laundering Group (ESAAMLG); and Financial Action Task Force on Money Laundering in South America (GAFISUD).

[139] A visit to the ESAAMLG website reveals, however, that the last entry posted in relation to Kenya is dated 2003, and no peer review of legislation has been carried out. This may be an indicator that the FSRBs are lagging behind in achieving their objectives.

characteristics/pattern of financial behaviour of an account holder. The identity of the customer may be cause for concern, but that, of itself, is not the type of 'red flag' encountered in money-laundering situations, where an attempt is being made to move large amounts of money through the system without being detected.

The fifth Recommendation provides that each state shall afford other states, on the basis of treaties, arrangements or other mechanisms for mutual legal assistance or information exchange, the greatest possible measure of assistance in connection with criminal and civil enforcement, and administrative investigations, inquiries and proceedings relating to the financing of terrorism, terrorist acts and terrorist organizations.

The sixth Recommendation tackles the phenomenon of alternative remittance systems in the context of terrorist-financing referred to above. It requires states to take measures to ensure that persons or legal entities, including agents, that provide a service for the transmission of funds through an informal money or value transfer network, should be licensed or registered and subject to all the FATF Recommendations that apply to banks and non-bank financial institutions.

The seventh Special Recommendation deals with the highly practical question of monitoring wire transfers. The idea behind it is that every financial institution, including money remitters, should take steps to ensure that meaningful originator information, including name, address and account number, should accompany every transfer of funds, and that that information should remain with the transfer throughout the payment chain. The eighth Recommendation has to do with regulating non-profit organizations, such as NGOs and charities.[140]

The final Special Recommendation, 9, which was added after the original eight, requires states to have in place measures to detect the physical cross-border transportation of money and bearer negotiable instruments.[141]

One of the most interesting Mutual Evaluation Reports posted on the FATF website is one carried out by the Asia Pacific Group on Money Laundering (APG) – the FSRB for the region, on Indonesia.[142] Indonesia

140 See, above, the Kenyan FSAT findings on the NGO sector: this is clearly an important area on which to focus.

141 Experience in dealing with the transmission of drug-related cash, and the use of stored cards, emphasize the importance of this recommendation.

142 Asia Pacific Group on Money Laundering, *APG 2nd Mutual Evaluation Report on Indonesia*, 9 July 2008. Available at: www.apgml.org/documents/docs/17/Indonesia%20MER2_FINAL.pdf.

has suffered approximately 450 terrorist attacks in the past five years. The Report refers to a World Bank Study carried out in September 2007 which noted that Indonesia had total remittance inflows from all countries of US$ 5.6 billion in 2006, while formal inflows into Indonesia from all countries were only US$ 1.96 billion in 2005. Thus, approximately 80 per cent of the total remittance flow into Indonesia is through informal channels.[143] Faced with such daunting figures it comes as little surprise to learn that the counter-terrorism focus is on apprehending/killing the terrorists, not pursuing their finances.[144] Nevertheless, the report contains detailed recommendations regarding improvements to existing Indonesian regulations and how registration and licensing procedures can be improved.

15 A possible fresh approach to tackling terrorist financing?

In July 2009 the European Union Committee of the House of Lords published its report entitled *Money Laundering and the Financing of Terrorism.*[145] The report contains a detailed critique of the international effort to combat terrorist financing from the UK's point of view. It is particularly critical of the failures by states to sign up to some of the basic measures drawn up by the EU to combat financial crime and facilitate the giving of mutual legal assistance.[146] Startlingly, the report reveals that an EU–US Agreement on mutual legal assistance which includes important provisions on access to bank accounts, the negotiations for which were launched 'the day after 9/11', has yet to be brought into force.[147] One of the most egregious failures highlighted in the report[148] is the UK's continued failure to sign and ratify the 2005 Warsaw Convention on Money Laundering and Terrorist Financing.[149]

143 *Ibid.*, para. 733.

144 Source: one of the experts who carried out the mutual evaluation in a private conversation with the author in April 2009.

145 House of Lords, European Union Committee, *Money Laundering and the Financing of Terrorism*, vol. I (London: TSO, 2009).

146 See, *ibid.*, e.g., para. 36 of the report which deplores the failure of five EU member states to sign the Protocol to the Convention on Mutual Legal Assistance in Criminal Matters of 2000 which enables full cross-border cooperation on obtaining details of bank accounts – a vital component in combating money laundering.

147 *Ibid.*, paras. 38–40. 148 *Ibid.*, paras. 43–8.

149 *Council of Europe Convention on Laundering, Search, Seizure and Confiscation of the Proceeds of Crime and on the Financing of Terrorism*, Warsaw, 16 May 2005, CETS No. 198, entry into force, 1 May 2008. The full text and Explanatory Report are to

This failure leads the Committee to consider in some depth an aspect of dealing with terrorist financing which has hitherto been largely ignored, namely civil recovery. The report devotes a whole section to it.[150] The Committee begins by reverting to Recommendation 3 of the original FATF 40 Recommendations, which reads in part:

> Countries may consider adopting measures that allow [proceeds of crime] to be confiscated without requiring a criminal conviction, or which require an offender to demonstrate the lawful origin of the property alleged to be liable to confiscation, to the extent that such a requirement is consistent with the principles of their domestic law.

The Committee then produces a masterly summary of the attributes of civil recovery which is worth reproducing in full:

> This hesitant language [contained in Recommendation 3] demonstrates at once the importance of civil recovery and some of the obstacles to it. In many countries civil recovery is not consistent with domestic law; in some it is unconstitutional, since it involves an adjustment to the burden of proof. A confiscation order made in criminal proceedings of course follows a conviction made on proof beyond reasonable doubt. Civil recovery may arise when there is only a suspicion that assets are the proceeds of serious crime, based on their being disproportionate to the declared income of their owner. The suspicion may be reinforced by other facts, such as contacts between the owner and known criminals. A case may be brought before a civil court based on an assumption, on the balance of probabilities, that the assets may be proceeds of crime. In some countries the burden of proof may then be reversed, and it is for the owner of the assets to prove that their origin is legitimate.[151]

The Committee then goes on to note that civil forfeiture in criminal matters has long been available in the US, and that it was first introduced in the United Kingdom by Part 5 Proceeds of Crime Act 2002 (POCA).[152] However, the Committee then identifies Article 23(5) Warsaw Convention as being potentially highly significant as far as civil recovery in a terrorist finance context is concerned. It reads as follows:

> The Parties shall co-operate to the widest extent possible under their domestic law with those Parties which request the execution of measures equivalent to confiscation leading to the deprivation of property, which are not criminal sanctions, in so far as such measures are ordered by a

be found at: http://conventions.coe.int/Treaty/Commun/QueVoulezVous.asp?NT=198&CM=8&DF=&CL=ENG.

150 HL, European Union Committee, *Money Laundering*, paras. 81–95.

151 *Ibid.*, para. 82. 152 *Ibid.*, para. 83.

> judicial authority of the requesting Party in relation to a criminal offence, provided that it has been established that the property constitutes proceeds or other property in the meaning of Article 5 of this Convention.

The Committee points out that this is a mandatory provision to which no reservation is allowed, and that it is a broad provision, given the wide definition of 'property' in Article 5, and that cooperation has to be provided 'to the widest extent possible'.[153]

One of the witnesses who appeared before the Committee, Mr Ringguth, who is the Executive Secretary of MONEYVAL, stated that the United Kingdom would have many more opportunities to enforce civil confiscation orders in other countries if more countries would ratify the Warsaw Convention.[154] The same would of course apply to all those other countries.

It is interesting to note that the World Bank, as part of its StAR (Stolen Asset Recovery) Initiative, produced in 2009 *A Good Practices Guide for Non-Conviction Based Asset Forfeiture*.[155] As the World Bank states in its Guide: 'Criminal forfeiture is an *in personam* order ... it requires a criminal trial and conviction', whereas 'NCB (non-conviction based) forfeiture, also referred to as "civil forfeiture", "*in rem* forfeiture", or "objective forfeiture" in some jurisdictions, is an action against the asset itself ... not against an individual'.[156] While the StAR Initiative was conceived primarily as a means of facilitating the recovery of the proceeds of grand corruption, where for example heads of state and those holding high office have looted their own treasuries, there is no reason in principle why *in rem* forfeiture should not be deployed in the fight against terrorist financing.[157] However, figures recently released by the UK Treasury reveal that there are only thirty-three persons in the United Kingdom currently subject to asset freezes under the various Terrorism (United Nations) Orders and just £150,000 is frozen. These figures are testimony to the comparatively small sums involved in terrorist

153 *Ibid.*, para. 88.

154 See Mr Ringguth's answer to Q 493 in HL, European Union Committee, *Money Laundering*, vol. II, *Evidence*.

155 Stolen Asset Recovery, T. S. Greenberg *et al.*, *A Good Practices Guide for Non-Conviction Based Asset Forfeiture* (Washington, DC: World Bank Group, 2009), available at: http://siteresources.worldbank.org/EXTSARI/Resources/NCBGuideFinalEBook.pdf.

156 *Ibid.*, 13–14.

157 Civil recovery has been used to considerable effect in a Nigerian context: to date US$2.5bn of the estimated US$3–5bn looted by the former Head of State, Sani Abacha, has been recovered by a combination of criminal and civil procedures.

financing and call into question the effectiveness of the asset-freezing regime. Financial information regarding terrorist activity is very important for the intelligence it provides when conducting investigations, but, on these figures, seems unlikely to prevent or to halt terrorist activity.

16 Conclusions

It is thought that there have been remarkably few prosecutions under legislation emanating from the Convention. It is significant that the majority of the litigation which has taken place to date has had to do with the alleged violations of human rights occurring under the UN listing regime. These cases underline the huge importance of obtaining accurate intelligence, which is, in itself, a major task, and, once obtained, there are still problems in many jurisdictions, as in the UK, relating to its use in court. There is also the growing problem, referred to above, of advances in technology providing ever more anonymous methods of effecting funds transfers.

The political will to engage terrorism financing remains a major issue, and one that can only be resolved at a political and diplomatic level. The effectiveness of targeted sanctions in this field remains highly questionable. Threats to withdraw aid are hardly an appropriate response to failure to implement FATF Recommendations.

What is needed ultimately is the holistic approach referred to above,[158] and there are signs that this is taking place. It was not long before the new administration in the US indicated fresh approaches in Syria and Iran: President Obama's Nowruz[159] message to Iran was particularly encouraging in this regard. The events of the 'Arab Spring' have, however, rather overtaken this type of initiative, for as long as the ultimate outcome of those events remains unknown. There was early recognition of the problem that needed to be addressed,[160] and the whole tenor of the recent UN Strategy[161] is, again, encouraging, as is the UK's 'Prevent' initiative.[162] However, there are those that sound a loud note of caution in this regard.[163]

[158] See section 10 above on UN Global Counter-Terrorism Strategy.

[159] Persian New Year; alternative message broadcast with Farsi subtitles on Middle Eastern satellite channels beamed illegally into 4 million Iranian homes: see *The Times*, 21 March 2009: 'You have a choice, Obama tells Iran'.

[160] See n. 21 above. [161] See above n. 79. [162] See section 11 above.

[163] See S. Maher and M. Frampton, *Choosing Our Friends Wisely: Criteria for Engagement with Muslim Groups* (London: Policy Exchange, 2009), at www.policyexchange.org.uk/assets/Choosing_Our_Friends_Wisely.pdf.

Efforts to suppress terrorist financing are rightly perceived as a legitimate part of the fight against terrorism and the loss of innocent lives, but they can only ever be holding measures. An end to terrorism in Northern Ireland was negotiated through engagement. Removing the incentive to engage in terrorism is, ultimately, the only realistic path forward, but, in the meantime, determined implementation of the Recommendations contained in FATF Mutual Evaluation reports must continue to play an important role. On the technological front it is clear that major effort needs to be invested in finding means of controlling and regulating 'cyber-finance' remittance systems.

International cooperation to counteract terrorist financing has happened, and is happening, and is a vital part of the fight against terrorism, but action at a national level remains a vital pre-requisite: the possibility of action through civil procedures should not be overlooked.

PART II

The use of force against terrorists

9

The international regulation of the use of force: the politics of interpretative method

ANDREA BIANCHI

1 How method bears on normative outcomes: a divided interpretative community

The international legal regulation of the use of force is often referred to as one of the most controversial and politically charged areas of international law, or as the domain in which the hiatus between theory and practice is most prominent. While these statements may well be an accurate representation of widespread convictions, they fail to capture the reasons that inspire such a perception. In particular, the descriptive elements underlying these propositions are unlikely to constitute a reasonable explanation of the phenomena they are meant to shed light on. To say that the use of force is controversial is tantamount to stating the obvious and does not make this area any different from others in which the substance or the scope of application of international regulatory standards is disputed. Nor is the contention that the subject at hand is highly political sufficient to explain its allegedly peculiar character. Most of international law is influenced by political (and other) considerations.[1] To believe that the law is distinct from its underlying social realities is either illusory or mystifying.

An advance version of this chapter was published in *Leiden Journal of International Law* 22 (2009) 651–76. The author would like to thank Lorenzo Gradoni, Clauss Kress, Steven Ratner, Christian Tams, Elizabeth Wilmhurst, Michael Wood, Fouad Zarbiev and the two anonymous reviewers of the *Leiden Journal* for their useful comments on earlier drafts of the chapter.

[1] See R. Higgins, *Problems and Process: International Law and How We Use It* (2nd edn, Oxford: Oxford University Press, 2004): 'I believe there is no avoiding the essential relationship between law and policy. I also believe that it is desirable that the policy factors are dealt with systematically and openly' (5). See also by the same author: 'Integrations of Authority and Control: Trends in the Literature of International Law and Relations', in B. Weston and M. Reisman (eds.), *Towards World Order and Human*

This chapter submits that the current difficulties in determining the exact contours of the international legal regulation of the use of force would greatly benefit from a reflexive consideration, by all relevant actors, of some methodological aspects underlying the legal discourse on the use of force. The fundamental contention is that to agree on *method* could cure much of the current divergence of views about the content and scope of application of some of the international rules regulating the use of force. For the limited purpose of this chapter, method is taken to mean the intellectual matrix that provides the paradigms (legal categories and interpretative techniques) used to identify the state of the law on the use of force. The importance of paradigms in any given discipline can hardly be underestimated, as they are the tools by which reality is constructed. The paradigm provides all the relevant players 'with the rules of the game, describes the pieces with which it must be played, and indicates the nature of the required outcome'.[2] An explicit reflection on method, meant as the way in which a set of relevant normative and interpretative paradigms are used to analyse, explain and justify legal and social realities, is all the more compelling at a time when the capacity of international law to provide satisfactory regulation of the use of force is increasingly called into question.[3]

The interpretative presuppositions that inspire doctrinal analysis or diplomatic stances taken by states are rarely revealed and yet there is always an implicit set of methodological assumptions that directs the normative outcome. Despite the abundant writing on the use of force, only episodic

Dignity: Essays in Honor of Myres S. McDougal (New York: Free Press, 1976): 'Policy considerations … are an integral part of that decision making process which we call international law; the assessment of so-called extralegal considerations is *part of the legal process* … A refusal to acknowledge political and social factors cannot keep law "neutral", for even such a refusal is not without political and social consequences. There is no avoiding the essential relationship between law and politics' (85).

[2] See T. Kuhn, 'The Function of Dogma in Scientific Research', in A. C. Crombie (ed.), *Scientific Change: Historical Studies in the Intellectual, Social and Technical Conditions for Scientific Discovery and Technical Invention, from Antiquity to the Present* (Oxford: Oxford University Press, 1963), 362. See also T. Kuhn, *The Structure of Scientific Revolutions* (Chicago, IL: University of Chicago Press, 1996): 'a paradigm is prerequisite to perception itself. What a man sees depends both upon what he looks at and also upon what his previous visual–conceptual experience has taught him to see' (113).

[3] In particular, claims are often made that the changing circumstances of the use of force warrant a reconsideration of a legal regime that was largely designed in the aftermath of the Second World War. Such allegations are oblivious of the fact that law possesses tools of analysis and interpretation that may ensure the adjustment of its rules to the changing demands of international society (see below, especially sections 2–5), if only can one agree on how to use them.

attention is paid to the methodology of the discourse. Exceptions exist,[4] but they tend to simplify the debate by contrasting European and American approaches or conservative and progressive scholarly stances.[5] The problem, however, is not one of taxonomy, but rather of lack of social consensus on the use of methods of legal analysis and interpretation.

If the way in which legal categories and interpretation techniques are used is determinant of the normative outcome, one may wonder why issues of method have attracted so little interest. In fact, neglect for method may be partly due to the attitude of considering methodological issues as a purely theoretical preoccupation and of regarding theory and practice as the two opposite poles of the legal spectrum, which are doomed never to meet. This simplistic attitude, which inspires many a practitioner's disbelief as to the relevance of the theoretical/doctrinal debate carried out in academic circles to the practice of the use of force, hides the simple fact that theory and practice are complementary and mutually constructive. Despite some attempts at 'armchair theorizing' that certain strands of academic work indulge,[6] most of the time theory provides the framework for justifying practice. Sometimes its role consists in opening up a range of possible avenues, in which practice can be channelled. At the same time, the widely spread belief that the practitioners do the job on the ground without bothering too much with the theoretical aspects of the matter is simply false. Practitioners, even when not conscious of it, always presuppose 'a theory' or 'a method'. It is against the backdrop of theory and method, whatever they may be, that they provide their choices with the necessary level of credibility and persuasiveness required by the players of the game, which are no longer exclusively states.

[4] See the introductory remarks by C. Gray to her *International Law and the Use of Force* (Oxford: Oxford University Press, 2008), 1–29.

[5] See for instance O. Corten, 'The Controversies over the Customary Prohibition on the Use of Force: A Methodological Debate' (2005) 16 *European Journal of International Law* 803 and, more extensively, by the same author, *Le droit contre la guerre: l'interdiction du recours à la force en droit international contemporain* (Paris: Pedone, 2008), especially 9–62.

[6] Admittedly, a certain strand of literature has favoured the emergence of such a bias, particularly by projecting into the practice the ideal of an absolute, rational coherence, detached from reality and removed from the actual practices of the agents. According to Pierre Bourdieu this amounts to a most serious epistemological error, that of 'putting a scholar inside the machine', with the undesirable effect of 'picturing all social agents in the image of the scientist, or, more precisely, to place the models that the scientist must construct to account for practices into the consciousness of agents, to operate as if the constructions that the scientist must produce to understand practices, to account for them, were the main determinants, the actual cause of the practices' ('The Scholastic Point of View' (1999) 5 *Cultural Anthropology* 384).

Furthermore, the attitude of distinguishing sharply between theory and practice is oblivious to the modalities by which the legal discourse is formed. The *interpretative community*[7] that shapes the common understanding of legal rules on the use of force is much wider than that of national governments and their legal advisers or the judges of the International Court of Justice (ICJ). It includes also the handful of academics that have made the use of force their specialty or occasionally write about it, non-governmental organizations, lobbies and pressure groups that may have an interest in particular instances as well as intellectuals and opinion-makers who influence public opinion by publicly voicing their position on any given matter. The concept of interpretative community is key to understanding that the discourse about the legal aspects of the use of force is a single one, in which different societal forces are at work and several actors interact at different levels and with a varying degree of influence and responsibility with a view to imposing their own way of interpreting legal rules. The complexity of this interpretative community hardly allows differentiating between the theory and practice of the international regulation of the use of force. The problem rather lies in the fact that the interpretative community is currently divided and is no longer able to agree on the method that must be used for interpreting the law.

The tendency to obfuscate the terms of the discussion by using different interpretative methods, the presuppositions of which are often hidden or merely implied, has found fertile ground in international law where, as aptly noted some time ago by Sir Gerald Fitzmaurice, lawyers must often confront themselves not just with the question of 'what is the

[7] On the concept of 'interpretative community', see S. Fish, *Is There a Text in This Class? The Authority of Interpretive Communities* (Cambridge, MA: Harvard University Press, 1980), and, by the same author, *Doing What Comes Naturally: Change, Rhetoric, and the Practice of Theory in Literary and Legal Studies* (Oxford: Clarendon, 1989). As is known, the notion of 'interpretative community' was developed by Fish in connection with literary studies, to explain the question of the source of interpretative authority (see *Doing What Comes Naturally*, 141). Fish describes an interpretative community as 'not so much a group of individuals who shared a point of view, but a point of view or way of organizing experience that shared individuals in the sense that its assumed distinctions, categories of understanding, and stipulations of relevance and irrelevance were the content of the consciousness of community members who were therefore no longer individuals, but, in so far as they were embedded in the community's enterprise, community property. It followed that such community-constituted interpreters would, in their turn, constitute, more or less in agreement, the same text, although the sameness would not be attributable to the self-identity of the text, but to the communal nature of the interpretive act' (*ibid.*).

law?' but also with the much more challenging one of determining 'what the law is'.[8] While, traditionally, in case of disputed issues, the international lawyerly instinct is to revert to the case law of the ICJ to find guidance,[9] the exercise risks being futile at this time. Despite the strong influence of the *Nicaragua* case,[10] the ICJ, certainly an important actor in the interpretative community, has failed to convincingly address the issues related to the use of force recently submitted to it. After the cautious and narrow approach taken in the *Oil Platforms* case,[11] with Judge Simma complaining of a missed chance for shedding light on the more fundamental aspects of the regime, the Court had two more chances to provide the much needed interpretative guidance on the regulation of the use of force. In a fairly convoluted paragraph in its Advisory Opinion on the *Israeli Wall*, the ICJ interpreted narrowly Article 51 of the Charter, by postulating the requirement that an armed attack must be carried out by a state in order to trigger the right to self-defence, and distinguished, not without ambiguities, the case of terrorist attacks, to which SC Resolutions 1368 and 1373 would

8 G. Fitzmaurice, 'The Future of Public International Law and of the International Legal System in the Circumstances of Today', Special Report, *Annuaire IDI*, Livre du Centenaire (1973), 251.

9 Such an instinct is curious indeed, given that in the international legal system the judicial function remains minimal. It can probably be explained by the inferiority complex that international lawyers have long suffered vis-à-vis their fellow domestic lawyers, to whom they were in desperate need to demonstrate that international law was like domestic law, including the function of the judiciary. Occasionally, the almost religious deference shown by some commentators towards the ICJ judgments borders on the ridiculous (see the remarks by R. Jennings, 'The Role of the International Court of Justice' (1997) 68 *British Yearbook of International Law* 41, describing the way in which some international lawyers scrutinize the tiniest detail of a judgment as if it were a religious text). This attitude is by no means peculiar to international lawyers. Pierre Schlag has qualified many domestic law scholars as 'journalists of case law' (*The Enchantment of Reason* (Durham, NC: Duke University Press, 1998), 109). The irony is that even some distinguished (former) judges of the Court reject such deferential attitude and invite paying more attention to what the actors, rather than the Court, think to be normative. See R. Higgins, 'International Law and the Avoidance, Containment and Resolution of Disputes: General Course on Public International Law' (1991) 230 *Recueil des cours Académie de Droit International* 9, 43.

10 *Military and Paramilitary Activities in and against Nicaragua* (*Nicaragua* v. *United States of America*), Jurisdiction and Admissibility, Judgment of 26 November 1984 [1984] ICJ Rep. 392; *Military and Paramilitary Activities in and against Nicaragua* (*Nicaragua* v. *United States of America*), Merits, Judgment of 27 June 1986 [1986] ICJ Rep. 14.

11 *Oil Platforms* (*Islamic Republic of Iran* v. *United States*), Judgment of 6 November 2003 [2003] ICJ Rep. 161 and 324 (Judge Simma, Separate Opinion).

apply.[12] Finally, in *Congo* v. *Uganda* the Court held it unnecessary to pronounce on the very aspect which would have been most relevant to the current debate on self-defence and terrorist activities, namely the determination of whether or not self-defence can be relied on against large-scale attacks by irregular forces.[13]

Interestingly enough, the individual opinions attached by some judges to the above-mentioned cases indirectly provide the reasons for the lacunal and laconic treatment of the subject. Judges Kooijmans and Simma's views on self-defence and defensive actions more properly amount to a dissent rather than to a concurring opinion.[14] In other words, the Court itself reflects the difference in opinion that

[12] *Legal Consequences of the Construction of a Wall in the Occupied Palestinian Territory*, Advisory Opinion [2004] ICJ Rep. 136, para. 139. It is interesting to note that Judge Higgins rightly pointed out that what the Court says in §139 of its judgment, namely that 'Article 51 of the Charter recognizes the existence of an inherent right of self-defence in the case of armed attack by one State against another State', is erroneous, as Art. 51 states nothing of the kind. Judge Higgins underscores that the requirement that the prior armed attack be carried out by a state was stipulated by the Court itself in the *Nicaragua* case (Separate Opinion of Judge Higgins [2004] ICJ Rep. 215, para. 33).

[13] *Armed Activities on the Territory of the Congo* (*Democratic Republic of the Congo* v. *Uganda*), Judgment of 19 December 2005, ICJ Rep. 168:'[T]he Court finds that the legal and factual circumstances for the exercise of a right of self-defence by Uganda against the DRC were not present. Accordingly, the Court has no need to respond to the contentions of the Parties as to whether and under what conditions contemporary international law provides for a right of self-defence against large-scale attacks by irregular forces' (para. 147).

[14] *Ibid.* (Judge Kooijmans, Separate Opinion): '[T]he Court refrains from taking a position with regard to the question whether the threshold set out in the *Nicaragua* Judgment is still in conformity with contemporary international law in spite of the fact that that threshold has been subject to increasingly severe criticism ever since it was established in 1986 ... Even if one assumes (as I am inclined to do) that mere failure to control the activities of armed bands cannot in itself be attributed to the territorial State as an unlawful act, that in my view does not necessarily mean that the victim State is under such circumstances not entitled to exercise the right of self-defence under Article 51 ... If the activities of armed bands present on a State's territory cannot be attributed to that State, the victim State is not the object of an armed attack by it. But if the attacks by the irregulars would, because of their scale and effects, have had to be classified as an armed attack had they been carried out by regular armed forces, there is nothing in the language of Article 51 of the Charter that prevents the victim State from exercising its *inherent* right of self-defence' (paras. 25–9, internal references omitted). (*Ibid.* Judge Simma, Separate Opinion): 'I fully agree with his [Judge Kooijmans] conclusions that, if armed attacks are carried out by irregular forces from such territory against a neighbouring State, these activities are still armed attacks even if they cannot be attributed to the territorial State, and, further, that it "would be unreasonable to deny the attacked State the right to self-defence merely because there is no attacker State and the Charter does not so require" ... I also subscribe to Judge Kooijmans' opinion that the lawfulness of the conduct of the attacked State in the face of such an armed attack by a non-State group must be put to the

characterizes the debate on the use of force and pays little attention to interpretative and methodological issues.[15] The lack of social consensus on some fundamental interpretative tenets of the regime of the use of force is thus unlikely to be reconstituted by the piecemeal and inconsistent approach of the Court after *Nicaragua*.

The ambition of the following remarks is a limited one. They are not meant to advocate any particular normative outcome, although personal preferences might occasionally come to the surface. They rather attempt to draw attention on some methodological issues that should be carefully assessed with a view to establishing (or restoring, as the case may be) societal consensus, within the interpretative community that generates the discourse on the use of force, on *how* certain legal categories and interpretative techniques should be used in relation to the use of force.

2 The UN Charter as beginning and end of inquiry?

Nobody would seriously contest that the UN Charter provides the basic legal framework for the international regulation of the use of force. The history and purpose of the Charter's regime are often analysed in detail to provide further support to the proposition that the only source of the rules on the use of force is the UN Charter. Indeed, to many states and scholars alike the Charter ought to be the starting and ending point of any inquiry on the regulation of the use of force. This stance is not without merit. The Charter was intended to provide a comprehensive and exclusive system of collective security where the unilateral use of force was outlawed. Whatever the customary international law that existed before with respect to the use of force, the Charter clearly laid down rules for the purpose of establishing a special regime. Nowadays, the Charter being ratified by virtually all states, its regulatory framework

same test as that applied in the case of a claim of self-defence against a State, namely, does the scale of the armed action by the irregulars amount to an armed attack and, if so, is the defensive action by the attacked State in conformity with the requirements of necessity and proportionality?' (paras. 12–13, internal references omitted).

[15] Besides Judge Higgins' critical remarks, see also the statement by Judge Kooijmans in his Separate Opinion, *Armed Activities* case (Judge Kooijmans, Separate Opinion). Kooijmans states in strong terms his conviction that the use of force against terrorist groups in the territory of another state is lawful under international law, regardless of which particular legal justification one is prone to use (self-defence, necessity or legality of extraterritorial law enforcement operations against terrorists, as advocated by Dinstein) (para. 31).

can be deemed to be generally applicable as treaty law, regardless of any other considerations related to customary law.

Furthermore, to many the UN Charter would enjoy a quasi-constitutional status, given that it contains the 'fundamental rules' of the post-Second World War international order. This strand of international constitutionalism, developed primarily by European (and most notably German) scholars projects at the international level the structural mode of domestic legal orders, importing into international law a vertical or hierarchical element of organization which would find in the Charter its centre of gravity.[16] However reassuring one might find this intellectual construct, the approach is far from universally shared, particularly in terms of its potentially far-fetched consequences. To give quasi-constitutional status to some of the Charter provisions may have non-negligible systemic effects, which the international legal order is not particularly prepared to absorb. As acknowledged by some of its most fervent proponents, the choice of the Charter as 'Constitution' is somewhat compelled by the very simple fact that the Charter is the one international law instrument that resembles most a Constitution,[17] which – of course – is not dispositive of the issue of whether there is or there should be anything like a Constitution in the international legal system.

Be that as it may, there are good reasons for considering the provisions of the Charter as the starting point of the inquiry on the international legal regulation of the use of force. The first obvious reason is that there is widespread social consensus on this proposition. In most of the debates before the Security Council, in which issues of use of force are discussed, reference is primarily made to the law of the Charter. Also in other fora

[16] See for instance, A. Verdross and B. Simma, *Universelles Völkerrecht: Theorie und Praxis* (Berlin: Duncker & Humblot, 1984); commented also by B. Simma, 'The Contribution of Alfred Verdross to the Theory of International Law' (1995) 6 *European Journal of International Law* 33. Earlier European contributions to the constitutionalism strand include A. Verdross, *Die Verfassung der Völkerrechtsgemeinschaft* (Vienna: Spring, 1926); G. Scelle, 'Le droit constitutionnel international', in *Mélanges Carré de Malberg* (1933), 501ff; W. Friedman, *The Changing Structure of International Law* (New York: Colombia University Press, 1964), 293ff. An overview of the constitutionalism debate can be found in the recent collection of essays: R. St. J. Macdonald and D. Johnston (eds.), *Towards World Constitutionalism: Issues in the Legal Ordering of the World Community* (Leiden: Martinus Nijhoff, 2005).

[17] B. Fassbender, 'The United Nations Charter as World Constitution' (1998) 36 *Columbia Journal of Transnational Law* 529; see also P.-M. Dupuy, 'The Constitutional Dimension of the Charter of the United Nations Revisited', in A. von Bogdandy and R. Wolfrum (eds.), *Max Planck Yearbook of UN Law* (1997), vol. I, 261–328.

the official discourse on the use of force heavily relies on the central character of the Charter provisions. It is obvious that most states would consider it risky to depart from the Charter. A good illustration of this attitude is the justification provided by the United Kingdom for the war against Iraq.[18] The UK found it wise to justify its decision to participate in the military intervention by resorting to a 'creative' interpretation of Resolution 1441. By acknowledging that in the very words of the Resolution Iraq was found by the Security Council to be in 'material breach' of its previous resolutions, including the so-called 'truce resolution' 687 of 1991, in which the cessation of hostilities was made dependent on Iraq's pledge fully to disarm, the argument was made that the failure by Iraq to honour its pledge would entitle the parties to the conflict to suspend the application of Resolution 687 and to revive the authorization to use force under Resolution 678. Whatever one may think of this legal reasoning, which draws the decisive argument by way of analogy from the law of treaties (in particular Article 60 of the Vienna Convention on suspension and termination of the operation of a treaty as a consequence of its breach) by equating an SC resolution to a treaty, the attitude of the UK is quite telling of its willingness not to venture into the slippery slope of justifications grounded outside the law of the Charter. It is of note that even the United States addressed to the Security Council a letter of almost identical content to that sent by the UK,[19] even if the legal justification used by the US government for the war in Iraq heavily relied on the notion of pre-emptive self-defence.[20]

The instinct of giving priority to the UN Charter provisions is also understandable in light of the allegedly more secure character of a

[18] See letter dated 20 March 2003 from the Permanent Representative of the United Kingdom of Great Britain and Northern Ireland to the United Nations addressed to the Security Council (UN Doc. S/2003/350 (2003)). See also 'Statement by the Attorney General, Lord Goldsmith, in answer to a parliamentary question, Tuesday 18 March 2003', at www.fco.gov.uk. For further comments on Britain's and similar positions, see: T. Franck, 'What Happens Now? The United Nations after Iraq' (2003) 97 *American Journal of International Law* 607; V. Lowe, 'The Iraq Crisis: What Now?' (2003) 52 *International and Comparative Law Quarterly* 859; J. Yoo, 'International Law and the War in Iraq' (2003) 97 *American Journal of International Law* 563; C. Stahn, 'Enforcement of the Collective Will after Iraq' (2003) 97 *American Journal of International Law* 804.

[19] See letter dated 20 March 2003 from the Permanent Representative of the United States of America to the United Nations addressed to the Security Council (UN Doc. S/2003/351 (2003)).

[20] For an accurate reconstruction of the justifications used by the US for the war in Iraq see Gray, *International Law and the Use of Force*, 216ff.

written text, particularly as compared to the uncertain process of ascertaining the existence as well as the content of unwritten rules of customary law. To be able to rely on written provisions traditionally gives lawyers an argumentative advantage over claims based on unwritten rules. This remains the case regardless of any technical consideration on the relationship between treaty and customary law. It is also a basic finding of hermeneutics that 'the sheer fact that something is written down gives it special authority. It is not altogether easy to realize that what is written down can be untrue. The written word has the tangible quality of something that can be demonstrated and is like a proof.'[21]

As is well known the problem with the Charter is twofold. On the one hand, the collective security system has proved over time that it is flawed or, if one were to use a euphemism, unduly selective and inefficient. This is particularly true as regards situations concerning the use of force by one of the five permanent members or one of its allies. In such instances the collective security system is doomed not to work. Certainly, at least in theory, there is the possibility that the General Assembly may take over as it did by adopting the 'Uniting for Peace' resolution, a development recently sanctioned by the ICJ in its Advisory Opinion on the *Israeli Wall*.[22] However, such scant practice hardly amounts to convincing evidence that this option will be often resorted to. The point is reinforced if one considers the projects of Security Council reform, which all acknowledge the continuing central role of the organ for the maintenance of international peace and security.[23]

[21] H. G. Gadamer, *Truth and Method* (London: Continuum, 2004), 274. Gadamer concluded that: 'It requires a special critical effort to free oneself from the prejudice in favor of what is written down and to distinguish here also . . . between opinion and truth'.

[22] *Israeli Wall*, paras. 28–32.

[23] The High-level Panel on Threats, Challenges and Changes stated: 'The Security Council is fully empowered under Chapter VII of the Charter of the United Nations to address the full range of security threats with which States are concerned. The task is not to find alternatives to the Security Council as a source of authority but to make the Council work better than it has' (*A More Secure World: Our Shared Responsibility* (UN Doc. A/59/565 (2004)), paras. 198, 193–8; 244ff.). In the same vein, the UNSG: 'The Council must be not only more representative but also more able and willing to take action when action is needed. Reconciling these two imperatives is the hard test that any reform proposal must pass' (*In Larger Freedom: Towards Development, Security and Human Rights for All* (UN Doc. A/59/2005 (2005)), para. 168). Finally, the 2005 World Summit Outcome stated: 'We also reaffirm that the Security Council has primary responsibility in the maintenance of international peace and security. We also note the role of the General Assembly relating to the maintenance of international peace and security in accordance with the relevant provisions of the Charter' (UN Doc. A/Res./60/1 (2005),

On the other hand, despite the rhetorical commitment to the Charter, the interpretation of its provisions, particularly Article 2(4) and Article 51, has become highly controversial. In other words, the social consensus on the centrality of the Charter regulatory framework to the use of force evaporates when it comes to interpreting the content and scope of application of its most fundamental provisions. If this is evidence that textual determinacy is but a myth, also as regards legal texts, the problem remains of how to reconstruct the necessary societal consensus on the interpretation of such provisions.

Be that as it may, to assume that the Charter is the central normative reference for reconstructing the international regime of the use of force presupposes some constraints on the interpreter. In particular, the main challenge lies in the interpretation of the text as it currently stands. Just to give an example, the 'prior armed attack' requirement of Article 51 would make it difficult, in the absence of any accepted modification via the development of customary law, or other theories that may allow departing from the text, to justify the doctrine of preventive self-defence. To go against the letter of the provision may turn out to be a difficult (albeit not impossible)[24] task, if one starts from the assumption that self-defence is regulated only, or at least primarily, by Article 51. Textual constraints might appear less compelling as regards the interpretation of Article 2(4), where threats or uses of force that are not directed against the territorial integrity and political independence of a state might be considered not to be within the purview of the prohibition. However, the subsequent requirement prohibiting the threat or use of force 'in any other manner inconsistent with the Purposes of the United Nations' might actually reintroduce further constraints on possible justifications and contribute, together with a contextual and teleological interpretation of Article 2(4), to making the margin for manoeuvring a very narrow one indeed.

paras. 80, 79, 152–4). See also: *Strengthening of the United Nations: An Agenda for Further Change* (UN Doc. A/57/387 (2002)), paras. 20–2.

[24] An often neglected interpretative instrument to depart from the ordinary meaning of the text is Art. 31.4 VCLT, which stipulates that: 'A special meaning shall be given to a term if it is established that the parties so intended.' The intention of the parties as to the interpretation of any treaty provision is also a way to secure the latter's adjustment to new societal demands. The parties' intention should not be taken to mean an immutable stance taken at the time of negotiating the treaty. If it can be established that the parties to the agreement intend to give new meaning to a term of the treaty, departure from ordinary meaning is a perfectly admissible process. What matters is that the parties' intent be rigorously established.

The above considerations have been advanced with the sole purpose of showing that to take the Charter as the starting point of analysis creates interpretative constraints and directs the discourse on the use of force towards issues of treaty interpretation. Therefore, from this perspective, any attempt to justify threats or uses of force should be carried out at the level of interpretation of the Charter provisions. The textual constraints notwithstanding, it would still be possible to maintain that the Charter provisions have been amended via subsequent practice. Modification of a treaty by a subsequent 'consistent practice, establishing the common consent of the parties to the application of the treaty in a manner different from that laid down in certain of its provisions' was thought by the ILC as a perfectly admissible process.[25] The notorious Article 38, elaborated by the ILC draft articles on the law of treaties and eventually not included in the Vienna Convention, envisaged this process as a different one from that of interpreting a treaty provision in light of the subsequent practice of the parties. For this finding the ILC relied on the *Air transport services agreement* arbitration.[26] Although claims of modification of a treaty by way of subsequent practice remain scant,[27] this is a theoretical possibility under the law of treaties. Certainly, the proponent would bear the burden of proving that such subsequent practice exists, and given the high number of parties to the UN Charter, the argument would need to rely on a substantial and coherent body of practice of states and, arguably, UN organs. Whether modification of a treaty by subsequent practice is coterminous with the issue of modification of treaties by custom is no easy question to answer.[28] The

[25] See 1966 *Yearbook of the International Law Commission*, vol. II, 236.

[26] *Ibid.* In the arbitration award rendered in Geneva on 22 December 1963, the arbitrators (R. Ago, P. Reuter and H. P. de Vries) held that subsequent practice by the parties of a treaty was not only relevant for the purpose of treaty interpretation but could also be 'a possible source of a subsequent modification, arising out of certain actions or certain attitudes, having a bearing on the juridical situation of the parties and on the rights that each of them could properly claim'.

[27] See, for instance *Öcalan* v. *Turkey*, Grand Chamber Judgment of 12 May 2005 [2005] ECHR IV, paras. 162–3, quoting with approval paras. 190–6 of the Trial Chamber Judgment of 12 March 2003, where subsequent practice by the parties to the European Convention was deemed to justify the abrogation of Art. 2(1), second sentence, allowing for the death penalty in certain circumstances.

[28] The question has arisen also as regards the interpretation of Art. 27(3) UN Charter. In this respect, see the interesting remarks by the representative of the Secretary-General of the UN, Mr Stavropoulos, 'The constant practice of the Security Council of not treating the voluntary abstention of a permanent member of the Security Council as a vote against a substantive draft resolution before the Council is customary law . . . Even if the

issue was set aside by the ILC as too complex to be broached in isolation from the more general topic of the relationship between treaty and custom and was thought to depend in any given case on the particular circumstances and intentions of the parties to the treaty.[29]

3 Is there a customary law on the use of force?

The answer to the rhetorical question of whether there is a customary law on the use of force ought to be in the affirmative if one takes the findings of the ICJ in the *Nicaragua* case as an authoritative determination of the state of international law on the matter.[30] The ICJ held then that not only is there a customary international law on the use of force which is distinct from the law of the Charter, but also that that body of law has a separate existence and can be applied separately to states.[31] Contrary to the US allegations that existing customary law rules had been incorporated into the Charter or had been 'subsumed and supervened' by the Charter[32] – quite an ironic stance in light of subsequent US practice! – the Court maintained that the two regimes do not have an identical content and 'do not exactly overlap'.[33] Interestingly enough, the Court added that the UN Charter 'by no means covers the whole area of the regulation of the use of force in international relations'.[34] Emphasizing the use of the adjective 'inherent', attached to the right of self-defence in Article 51, which, in the Court's view, clearly hints at the

development relating to voluntary abstentions is looked upon as an interpretation of the Charter by subsequent practice, the result cannot be different and the practice must be recognized as being authoritative' (Oral Statement of Mr Stavropoulos, *Legal Consequences for States of the Continued Presence of South Africa in Namibia (South West Africa) notwithstanding Security Council Resolution 276 (1970)*, ICJ, *Pleadings, Oral Arguments, Documents*, vol. II, 39).

[29] See 1966 *Yearbook of the International Law Commission*, vol. II, 236.

[30] 'The fact that the above-mentioned principles, recognized as such, have been codified or embodied in multilateral conventions does not mean that they cease to exist and to apply as principles of customary law, even as regards countries that are parties to such conventions. Principles such as those on the non-use of force, non-intervention, respect for the independence and territorial integrity of States, and freedom of navigation, continue to be binding as part of international customary law, despite the operation of provisions of conventional law in which they have been incorporated' (*Nicaragua* 1984, para. 73; *Nicaragua* 1986, para. 174). Generally, on this issue, see H. Charlesworth, 'Customary International Law and the *Nicaragua* case' (1991) 11 *Australian Yearbook of International Law* 1.

[31] *Nicaragua* 1986, paras. 175–6. [32] *Ibid.*, paras. 46 and 14. [33] *Ibid.*, para. 175.

[34] *Ibid.*, para. 176.

existence of a pre-existing customary law, the Court concluded that 'customary international law continues to exist alongside treaty law'.[35]

It matters little that the ICJ's findings might have been prompted by the need to circumvent the difficulty posed by the Connelly's reservation to the jurisdiction of the Court. The Connelly's reservation, attached by the US to the unilateral declaration of acceptance of the Court's jurisdiction, prevented the Court from applying the Charter to the case at hand. Therefore, in order to decide the case on the merit, the Court was compelled to find rules of customary international law applicable to the conduct of the United States, regardless of the UN Charter provisions. The systemic consequences of admitting of the separate existence of a customary international law on the use of force might have escaped the Court's attention at the time.

To conceive of a separate and distinctly applicable customary law on the use of force has allowed states to invoke and rely on customary international law rules justifying intervention on humanitarian grounds and anticipatory self-defence. Unlike in *Nicaragua*, where customary law was used to complement the law of the Charter by specifying the requirements of necessity and proportionality for the exercise of self-defence and by demanding that the victim of an armed attack expressly ask others to intervene in collective self-defence, arguments based on customary international law have gone as far as to admit the existence of further exceptions not included in the Charter. These arguments allege the existence of contemporary rules on humanitarian intervention, or draw on those customary rules that pre-date the Charter and would remain unaffected by it, as is the case with anticipatory self-defence, whose existence in pre-Charter customary law is asserted with reference to the *Caroline* case. One may or may not agree with any specific justification for the use of force advanced by states at different occasions, but it is undoubtedly true that the ICJ itself favoured, by its findings in *Nicaragua*, the use of customary law rules on the use of force, which might not necessarily be identical to those of the Charter.

If the idea of the distinct existence and separate applicability of the international customary law regime on the use of force was expedient to overcome the jurisdictional objections and provide the applicable law in the *Nicaragua* case, to conceive of two distinct lives for the same societal body (virtually all states are parties to the UN Charter) may be difficult. In other words, it is puzzling to see how there can be state practice on the

[35] *Ibid.*

use of force outside the UN Charter.[36] It is enlightening that the ICJ in Nicaragua stated that not all the issues of use of force in international relations are regulated by the UN Charter,[37] but it would have been useful had the Court sketched out where these unchartered waters lie and how a UN member state could freely sail in them without colliding with the 'cornerstone' of the prohibition of the use of force.[38]

4 The old controversy: words or deeds?

To admit that there may be rules of customary law on the use of force that do not coincide with those of the Charter is not tantamount to saying that the customary rules invoked by states in recent practice actually exist. Their existence needs to be established. Ascertaining whether customary rules have emerged, allowing states to act in preventive self-defence, on grounds of humanitarian intervention or to resort to force against a military intervention short of an armed attack, is a matter of interpretative method. The ICJ has invariably upheld the dual element theory of custom, whereby the generality of practice must be accompanied by *opinio juris*. A certain relaxation of the element of *usus* has already taken place in certain areas of international law. By way of example, one may quote the jurisprudence of the ICTY, which seems to attribute more importance to states' official pronouncements than to other elements. The reasons for giving priority to 'words' rather than 'deeds' lies in the 'inherent nature of the subject matter', namely the law of armed conflict, as well as in the special role that *opinio juris sive necessitatis* has in this area due to the existence of the Martens clause, taken as an overarching interpretative and lawmaking-inspiring principle.[39] This attitude stands in sharp contrast to what the ICJ maintained

[36] See G. Arangio-Ruiz, *The United Nations Declaration on Friendly Relations and the System of the Sources of International Law* (Alphen aan den Rijn: Sijthoff and Noordhoff, 1979), 44ff.

[37] *Nicaragua* 1986, para. 176. [38] *Armed Activities*, para. 148.

[39] See *Prosecutor* v. *Tadić*, Decision on the Defence Motion for Interlocutory Appeal on Jurisdiction, Case No. IT-94-1-AR72, A.Ch., 2 October 1995: 'In appraising the formation of customary rules or general principles one should therefore be aware that, on account of the inherent nature of this subject matter, reliance must primarily be placed on such elements as official pronouncements of States, military manuals and judicial decisions' (para. 99). See also para. 527 where as regards the customary rule prohibiting reprisals against civilians, the Appeal Chamber states: 'This is however an area where *opinio juris sive necessitatis* may play a much greater role than *usus* as a result of the aforementioned Martens Clause. In the light of the way States and courts have

in *Nicaragua* as regards the ascertainment of customary rules on the use of force, when it stated that '(t)he mere fact that States declare their recognition of certain rules is not sufficient for the Court to consider them as being part of customary international law.'[40] From this dictum one can reasonably infer that the ICJ intended to privilege what states do rather than what they say, although in the very same *Nicaragua* case the Court gave a lot of weight to General Assembly resolutions and to the official pronouncements of the parties to the case.

The doctrinal debate on which elements to take into account when examining state practice, whether claims submitted in the context of a dispute should count more than acts and/or statements unilaterally made by states and so on, may well carry an old-fashioned flavour with it.[41] Furthermore, it may well be true that '[t]here is no compelling reason for attaching greater importance to one kind of practice than to another'.[42] However, particularly at a time of uncertainty about the state of customary law on the matter, it remains crucial to trace some consensus on whether one should look at 'words' or 'deeds'. Deeds attest to a constant and arguably increasing recourse to force in certain contexts, particularly vis-à-vis terrorist groups and states harbouring terrorists, in the aftermath of 9/11. As regards official pronouncements, the situation is disconcertingly confusing. It suffices to cast a glance at the debates before the Security Council at the occasion of recent uses of force to realize, that despite the adversarial political rhetoric, states consciously characterize in very different legal terms the same factual matrices.[43] Whereas some states qualify certain uses of force as acts of aggression

implemented it, this Clause clearly shows that principles of international humanitarian law may emerge through a customary process under the pressure of the demands of humanity or the dictates of public conscience, even where State practice is scant or inconsistent. The other element, in the form of *opinio necessitatis*, crystallizing as a result of the imperatives of humanity or public conscience, may turn out to be the decisive element heralding the emergence of a general rule of humanitarian law.'

40 *Nicaragua* 1986, para. 184.

41 See, by way of example, A. D'Amato, *The Concept of Custom in International Law* (Ithaca, NY: Cornell University Press, 1971), 88; H. Thirlway, *International Customary Law and Codification: An Examination of the Continuing Role of Custom in the Present Period of Codification of International Law* (Leiden: A.W. Sijthoff, 1972), 58.

42 See M. Akehurst, 'Custom as a Source of International Law' (1974–5) 47 *British Yearbook of International Law* 1, 21.

43 An illustrative example is the debate at the SC, following the Israeli raid into Syria in October 2003 in response to a Palestinian suicide attack in Haifa. Israel justified the raid as an act of self-defence, for Syria allegedly harboured terrorist training camps in its territory. While Syria maintained that the raid was an act of aggression on the part of Israel, other states characterized it as a violation of international law for the

and grave violations of the prohibition of the use of force, others see the very same acts as lawful responses in self-defence or as lawful uses of forces even if they might fall short of the required proportionality.[44] Very little attention is devoted to construing the arguments in a legally plausible sense. One has the impression that the differences in vocabulary hardly hide a more profound division in the legal categories used to evaluate the limits posed by international law to the use of force.

Equally striking is the silence surrounding certain instances in which force is used. The Turkish incursions into Iraqi territory to hit PKK strongholds and militants have not been accompanied by any official justification,[45] nor have they raised particular interest on the part of other states. Similarly, US raids against allegedly terrorist targets in the territories of several states seem to have elicited very few, if any, comments on their legality or lack thereof. If, in some instances such as Yemen, the consent of the territorial state's authorities may have remedied any violation of the territorial state's sovereignty, this is not the case for other instances of use of force against terrorist groups. Indeed, silence towards significant events, potentially affecting the interests of all states, remains enigmatic.[46] All the more so when one realizes that nowadays many are the international fora in which states can express themselves. The relevance of acquiescence and the wider significance of the lack of reaction even by those states that are directly affected by such uses of force ought to be carefully analysed in any serious attempt to discern states' *opinio juris*.[47]

The old debate about the elements of custom, the meaning of general practice and the role of *opinio juris*, perceived by many as outdated, are

disproportionate character of the use of force or for its being an armed reprisal (see Gray, *International Law and the Use of Force*, 236–7).

44 See, for instance, the UNSC debates on 'The situation in the Middle East, including the Palestinian question', UN Doc. S/PV.5493 (2006), at the occasion of the Israeli military intervention against Lebanon.

45 See Gray, *International Law and the Use of Force*, 140ff.

46 It would be but logical to think that states would react to acts affecting their own interests (see *Fisheries* (*United Kingdom* v. *Norway*), Judgment of 18 December 1951 [1951] ICJ Rep. 116, 138–9; *Temple of Preah-Vihear* (*Cambodia* v. *Thailand*), Judgment of 16 June 1962 [1962] ICJ Rep. 6, 31 and *Dubai-Sharjah*, Arbitral Award (1996) 91 *International Law Reports* 623). All the more so, in light of the *erga omnes* character of the prohibition of the use of force.

47 For an attempt to address these issues, see S. Ratner, '*Jus ad Bellum* and *Jus in Bello* after September 11' (2002) 96 *American Journal of International Law* 905, 909–10; A. Bianchi, 'Enforcing International Law Norms against Terrorism: Achievements and Prospects', in A. Bianchi (ed.), *Enforcing International Law Norms against Terrorism* (Oxford: Hart, 2004), 491 and 508.

all the more relevant today at a time in which, particularly in the literature, although not exclusively, customary norms are reconstructed on a fairly flimsy base. A dictum of the ICJ may suffice or a single nineteenth-century diplomatic case of dubious relevance like the *Caroline* case might well do to establish the existence of a custom. Contrary to conventional wisdom, even the ICTY has repeatedly shown a certain lack of rigour in reconstructing customary law rules.[48] An accurate reconstruction of custom and a solid societal agreement on the relevant elements to ascertain its existence seem to be compelling, particularly if such custom modifies rather than complements the UN Charter provisions.

5 The relationship between the law of the Charter and customary law

In assessing the relationship between the law of the Charter and customary law on the use of force one should not depart from what is accepted under general international law. Against the backdrop of what the ICJ said in the *Nicaragua* case about the separate existence of customary rules and the UN Charter provisions, the least problematic case would be the one in which customary law rules integrate and specify the rules laid down in the Charter. The fact that the Charter is silent on the requirements of necessity and proportionality as regards an act of self-defence, or the further condition that the state which is a victim of an armed attack has to expressly call for intervention in collective self-defence make recourse to customary law somewhat easier, as none of these customary-law-based requirements for the exercise of self-defence fundamentally alters the rules of the Charter. Certainly, in so far as these normative standards claim to reflect customary law, their basis on a generality of practice accepted as law must be firmly established.

Along similar lines, the ICJ relied on the wide acceptance by states of certain General Assembly resolutions to complement the law of the Charter as regards other aspects of the use of force. An illustrative example is that concerning the notion of armed attack, which must

[48] See L. Gradoni, 'L'attestation du droit international pénal coutumier dans la jurisprudence du Tribunal pour l'ex Yougoslavie: "Régularités" et "Règles"', in M. Delmas-Marty *et al.* (eds.), *Les sources du droit international pénal: l'expérience des tribunaux pénaux internationaux et le statut de la Cour Pénale Internationale* (Paris: Société de législation comparée, 2004), 25–74.

not necessarily be carried out by the armed forces of a state, but could also emanate from armed bands or irregulars sent by that state or acting on its behalf, as made clear in Article 3(g) of General Assembly Resolution 3314 (XIX) on the definition of aggression, adopted on 14 December 1974.[49]

However, a more difficult instance is that of establishing the existence of a customary rule which markedly departs from the law of the Charter. Although in principle this is a perfectly admissible process, in this case the burden of proof should be more onerous for the proponent. The ICJ admitted the possibility that customary law may develop under the influence of the law of the Charter, but it then qualified this statement by saying that '[t]he essential consideration is that they [i.e., customary rules and Charter provisions] stem from a common fundamental principle outlawing the use of force in international relations.'[50] The Court later restated the idea that the prohibition of the use of force is a 'cornerstone' of the law of the Charter in *Armed Activities in the Territory of the Congo*.[51] The particularly important character of Article 2(4) of the Charter should therefore be taken into account when considering whether to allow uses of force other than those expressly permitted under the Charter, like self-defence under Article 51 and the authorization to use force granted by the Security Council.[52] At the very least a presumption against allowing other uses of force is strong and would make the burden of proving that a derogatory custom has emerged, a particularly exacting one.[53] States are aware of this difficulty and tend to rely on self-defence as a justification, even when their uses of force seem hardly to conform to the notion of self-defence.[54]

An alternative approach consists of submitting that whenever the Security Council is unable to act, the failure of the collective security system would revive the applicability of customary international law, or even customary international law predating the Charter and allow uses of force otherwise prohibited under the Charter. This theory is

[49] The customary character of this proviso was restated by the ICJ in *Armed Activities*, para. 147.

[50] *Nicaragua* 1986, para. 181. [51] *Armed Activities*, para. 148.

[52] Although not expressly contemplated by the Charter, authorization by the SC to use force has come to be accepted by states as consistent with the UN Charter since its first application in Res. 678.

[53] On the particularly onerous burden of proof for establishing a custom that derogates previous law see Akehurst, 'Custom as a Source of International Law', 19.

[54] See section 8 below.

reminiscent of so-called 'fall-back theories' in international law, to which we shall now briefly turn.

6 Fall-back theories and their relevance to the debate

The UN Charter could be characterized or, at least, be eligible for the controversial status of 'self-contained regime'.[55] The widespread diffidence towards the expression has recently caused the ILC to adopt the term 'special regimes' in its stead.[56] Nobody denies that a treaty may derogate from general international law rules on responsibility, so-called 'secondary rules'. What makes certain regimes 'special' is their opting out of the general international law of responsibility by adopting 'a full (exhaustive and definite) set of secondary rules'.[57] The essence of fall-back theories is to maintain that special secondary rules adopted within special regimes should always be given priority over general international law rules, but only in so far as the situation is 'normal'.[58] When secondary rules contained in the special regime are no longer able to induce compliance with the regime's primary rules, the system is deemed to have failed and its parties would be entitled to invoke general international law.[59]

[55] As is well known, the ICJ endorsed the notion of 'self-contained regimes' in the *US Diplomatic and Consular Staff* case, where it was stated that '[t]he rules of diplomatic law . . . constitute a self-contained regime', in that they specify 'the means at the disposal of the receiving State to counter any . . . abuse' of diplomatic privileges and immunities, and '[t]hese means are by their nature, entirely efficacious' (*United States Diplomatic and Consular Staff in Tehran* (*United States* v. *Iran*), Judgment of 24 May 1980 [1980] ICJ Rep. 3, para. 40).

[56] *Fragmentation of International Law: Difficulties Arising from the Diversification and Expansion of International Law*, Report of the Study Group of the International Law Commission (Finalized by M. Koskenniemi), UN Doc. A/CN.4/L.682 (2006), para. 193. As noted by the Study Group, Art. 42 VCLT, which provides, *inter alia*, that the validity of a treaty can only be impeached through the application of the Convention itself 'is the "minimum level" at which the Vienna Convention regulates everything that happens in the world of regime building and regime-administration', so that at least '[t]hrough it . . . every special regime links up with general international law' (*ibid.*, para. 194).

[57] See B. Simma, 'Self-Contained Regimes' (1985) 16 *Netherlands Yearbook of International* Law 111, 117.

[58] A normal situation would be one in which a satisfactory level of compliance exists and there is no perception by the parties that the regime is chronically inefficient and no longer able to accomplish the goals for which it was created.

[59] 'What such failure might consist in has not been explicitly treated by the Commission. However, an analogy could be received from the conditions under which the exhaustion

Regime failure has attracted some interest in specific contexts, such as EU and WTO law, although few are the works that broach the issue in comprehensive terms.[60] Several theories have been advanced to justify fall-back on general international law in case of regime failure. Some rely on a peculiar application of the principle of effective interpretation to assert the existence of a strong, albeit rebuttable, presumption against the continued applicability of special secondary rules in case of regime failure.[61] Others postulate fall-back as a structural feature of the international legal order which should allow states party to a self-contained regime taking extra-systemic countermeasures in case of exceptionally serious violations of the treaty.[62] This power would be inherent in the concept of state sovereignty, of which it is an essential guarantee. More mildly, the ILC seems to take the position that fall-back can be triggered by a material breach of treaty or by a fundamental change of circumstances under Articles 60 and 62 of the Vienna Convention on the Law of Treaties.[63]

The problems with regime failure and fall-back theories in our context are numerous. First, it should be noticed that these theories are little explored and so far they seem to have remained largely confined to the narrow boundaries of academic debates. Their potentially disruptive effects on international cooperation make one hesitant to draw the practical consequences of such intellectual constructs. Second, there is the difficulty of conceiving the UN Charter as a self-contained and autonomous regime, given that the ICJ has repeatedly stated that customary law rules and Charter provisions coexist even within the system of the Charter. In other words, the inside–outside binary category which

of local remedies rule need not be followed. These would be cases where the remedy would be manifestly unavailable or ineffective or where it would be otherwise unreasonable to expect recourse to it' (*Fragmentation of International Law*, para. 152(4)). Note, however, that the same Report *in fine* raises the question as to what may count 'as 'regime failure' in the first place' and recommends that the ILC further examine '[t]he conditions and consequences of regime failure' (*ibid.*, para. 493(2)(e)).

60 An exception is the recent book by L. Gradoni, *Regime failure nel diritto internazionale* (Milan: CEDAM, 2009).

61 B. Simma and D. Pulkowski, 'Of Planets and the Universe: Self-Contained Regimes in International Law' (2006) 17 *European Journal of International Law* 483.

62 G. Arangio-Ruiz, 'Fourth Report on State Responsibility', *Yearbook of the International Law Commission*, 1992, vol. II, pt 1, paras. 112–25.

63 *Fragmentation of International Law*, para. 188. For a critique of these theories see A. Bianchi and L. Gradoni, *Developing Countries, Countermeasures and WTO Law: Reinterpreting the DSU against the Background of International Law* (Geneva: ICTSD, 2008), 17–23.

is the necessary presupposition and fundamental element to trigger the operation of fall-back theories would be blurred by the somewhat peculiar system of the Charter. Lastly, even admitting that failure of the collective security system, which could be categorized as a set of secondary rules to enforce the primary rule on the prohibition of the use of force, might trigger the fall-back on general international law, what could this imply? If the object of fall-back theories is that of securing the effectiveness of the fundamental primary rules of the system, which surely include the prohibition of the use of force, it would be difficult to use such theories to justify an expansion of the exceptions to the general rule of non-use of force. Moreover, it is doubtful that once one falls back on general international law, one would be entitled to revive armed reprisals and other forms and uses of force that in contemporary international law are widely recognized as unlawful. Even the Articles on State Responsibility (ASR), elaborated by the ILC and largely considered to be declaratory of customary international law,[64] exclude the use of force from the range of admissible countermeasures and refer to self-defence in conformity with the Charter as the only admissible circumstance exonerating from responsibility.[65] Furthermore the UN Charter as a whole is considered as *lex specialis* vis-à-vis the Articles.[66]

Finally, the contention that fall-back into customary international law as it existed prior to the entry into force of the Charter should occur is not terribly persuasive. The fall-back theories thus far developed clearly contemplate only fall-back into contemporary general international law. This is perfectly consistent with the logic of a theory founded on a synchronic special–general binary mode, to which diachronic elements are entirely alien. To presume the reviviscence of extinct legal rules allowing the unilateral use of force in international relations would be not only dangerous as a normative choice, but also thoroughly unsubstantiated in theory as well as in practice, as there is no indication that states would like to do away with the prohibition of the use of force as a general rule.

7 The definitional conundrum: use of force and its next of kin

One of the neglected issues that would merit further consideration in relation to the international legal regime on the use of force is whether there is agreement on the interpretation of the content and scope of

[64] UN Doc. A/Res./56/83 (2001). [65] Art. 21. [66] Art. 59.

application of Article 2(4). In particular, what remains rather unclear is the meaning of a 'use of force'. The issue takes up particularly important connotations in light of the widespread conviction that the prohibition of the use of force is a rule of *jus cogens*.[67] Although it may be difficult to provide a clear-cut definition of 'use of force', some distinctions can be drawn with a view to shedding light on such unqualified notion.

A first obvious distinction is that a use of force is not necessarily synonymous with the notion of armed attack under Article 51 of the Charter. If all armed attacks are uses of force, the reverse is not necessarily true. Interestingly enough, however, much of the discussion about use of force has taken place in connection with the notion of armed attack, particularly for the purpose of establishing whether the requirements for a response in self-defence were met. Also the expression 'armed attack' lacks a definition in the Charter. The ICJ may have been accurate in 1986 when it stated that there was then agreement on what acts amounted to an armed attack in international law.[68] Besides 'action by regular armed forces across an international border' the Court considered that customary international law would also consider an armed attack 'the sending by or on behalf of a State of armed bands, groups, irregulars or mercenaries, which carry out acts of armed force as to amount (inter alia) to an actual armed attack conducted by regular armed forces, "or its substantial involvement therein"', directly quoting from Article 3(g) of the General Assembly Resolution 3314 on the Definition of aggression of December 1974.[69] The Court then went on to distinguish in customary international law the case in which the sending by a state of armed bands into the territory of another state to conduct an operation which, 'because of its scale and effects', would have been classified as an armed attack if conducted by regular armed forces, from the case of 'assistance to rebels in the form of the provision of weapons or logistical or other support',[70] which might substantiate a violation of the prohibition of the threat or use of force. The Court restated this distinction later in the judgment by stressing that the supply of arms to armed bands cannot be equated to an armed attack, but may

[67] It is impossible for the limited purposes of this chapter to exhaustively account for the literature on this particular point. See, just as a recent example, the extensive treatment devoted to this very issue by Corten, *Le droit contre la guerre*, esp. 293ff.

[68] *Nicaragua* 1986, para. 195. [69] *Ibid.* [70] *Ibid.*

nonetheless 'constitute a breach of the principle of the non-use of force ... of lesser gravity than an armed attack'.[71] Incidentally, this position was confirmed by the Court in 2005 in the case of *Armed Activities in the Territory of the Congo*, attracting some strong criticism by individual judges who thought that the Court missed an opportunity 'to fine-tune the position it took 20 years ago'.[72]

The use of force seems, therefore, to be a matter of degree. International tribunals have been reluctant to go a further step up the ladder to identify acts of aggression. The ICJ in the *Armed Activities in the Territory of the Congo* case considered that '[t]he unlawful military intervention by Uganda was of such magnitude and duration that the Court considers it to be a grave violation of the prohibition of the use of force.'[73] Not without reason, Judge Simma in his Separate Opinion, criticized the Court for not having called 'a spade a spade' and qualified the military intervention by Uganda as an act of aggression.[74] The same criterion of 'magnitude' was used by the Eritrea–Ethiopia Claims Commission to distinguish such 'relatively minor incidents' as 'localized border encounters between small infantry units, even those involving loss of life' and 'geographically limited clashes between small Eritrean and Ethiopian patrols along a remote, unmarked and disputed border' from armed attacks within Article 51 of the Charter.[75]

A fairly thorny issue is that of determining whether the uses of force prohibited under Article 2(4) are only those directed against the territorial sovereignty or political independence of another state. The issue of which interpretation to give to such an expression has recently emerged, particularly as regards military interventions against groups of terrorists in the territory of another state which are clearly not directed against the territorial integrity or political independence of the state in the territory of which force is used. The theory of lawful 'defensive actions', developed

[71] *Ibid.*, para. 247.

[72] See *Armed Activities* (Judge Kooijmans, Separate Opinion), para. 25. As is well known, Judge Kooijmans's dissent focused on the refusal by the Court to pass judgment on whether a response in self-defence can be lawful even when the armed attack comes from a non-state actor (*ibid.*, paras. 28–9). Judge Kooijmans had already expressed his dissent as regards the finding by the Court in its Advisory Opinion on the Israeli Wall that an armed attack must come from a state for the right to self-defence to apply (*Israeli Wall*, para. 139; and *Armed Activities* (Judge Kooijmans, Separate Opinion), para. 35).

[73] *Armed Activities*, para. 165.

[74] *Ibid.* (Judge Simma, Separate Opinion), para. 2.

[75] Eritrea–Ethiopia Claims Commission, Partial Award on the *Jus ad Bellum* (Ethiopia's Claims 1–8), 19 December 2005, paras. 11–12.

by Judge Simma in his Separate Opinion in the *Armed Activities in the Territory of the Congo* case,[76] as well as the stance taken in the same case by Judge Kooijmans on the legality of uses of force against terrorists in another state,[77] connect with doctrinal contributions[78] to converge at giving a restrictive reading to the prohibition of the use of force. Although this is done indirectly by expanding the notion of self-defence, the ultimate effect is that of narrowing down the scope of the prohibition laid down in Article 2(4) of the Charter.

A further distinction that could be made concerns extraterritorial acts of enforcement that violate the territorial sovereignty of the foreign state but which would not be within the purview of Article 2(4), even if perpetrated by state organs, including regular armed force members of the wrongdoing state. Targeted killings or police operations carried out in a foreign state's territory should be framed under the law of international jurisdiction, which lays down a clear prohibition as regards the carrying out of extraterritorial acts of enforcement in the territory of another state, in the absence of the latter's consent.[79] Further limits to state conduct can obviously be traced to human rights and international humanitarian law, depending on the circumstances.[80] However, a sound argument can be made that such instances should not be framed against the background of the international regulation of the use of force, as their nature and purpose are fundamentally different.

[76] *Armed Activities* (Judge Simma), paras. 11–13.

[77] *Ibid.* (Judge Kooijmans), para. 31.

[78] See for instance the concepts of 'extraterritorial law-enforcement operations' and 'defensive reprisals', elaborated by Y. Dinstein, *War, Aggression and Self-Defence* (Cambridge: Cambridge University Press, 2005), 219ff. See also O. Schachter, 'The Use of Force against Terrorists in Another State' (1989) 12 *Israeli Yearbook of Human Rights* 225, who relies on necessity to justify the use of force against terrorists in another state.

[79] See *SS Lotus case* (*France* v. *Turkey*), PCIJ Rep Ser. A No. 10: 'Now the first and foremost restriction imposed by international law upon a State is that – failing the existence of a permissive rule to the contrary – it may not exercise its power in any form in the territory of another State. In this sense jurisdiction is certainly territorial; it cannot be exercised by a State outside its territory except by virtue of a permissive rule derived from international custom or from a convention' (18–19).

[80] For a comprehensive treatment of the topic of targeted killings, see the recent work by N. Melzer, *Targeted Killing in International Law* (Oxford: Oxford University Press, 2008).

8 Legal qualification and its consequences: the problem of mischaracterization

Legal qualification is an essential tool for lawyers. Legal rules are supposed to be applied to factual matrices that are identified beforehand in general and abstract terms by the lawmaker. In other words, law provides regulation for certain facts or activities that – experience suggests – occur or take place in a certain fashion. Most work by those who are entrusted to apply the law consists of 'characterizing' these facts with a view to determining what the applicable rules are. 'Characterization' or 'qualification' is the interpretative operation whereby the facts are subsumed into legal rules. The outcome of this operation is the identification of the applicable law. Since in international law, the opportunities of having authoritative qualifications by adjudicatory bodies is less frequent than in domestic legal orders, states themselves advance their characterization, which will be accepted or contested by others. This premise is particularly relevant as we set out to explore an additional reason why the international regulation of the use of force is in such a state of confusion and disarray.

A quite distinct trend in recent practice is that states tend as much as possible to use self-defence as a justification for their uses of force. With the notable exception of humanitarian intervention, almost all legal justifications recently provided by states rely on self-defence. Specific characterization of self-defence, such as preventive self-defence and self-defence to rescue citizens abroad (recently invoked by Russia to justify its intervention against Georgia), are but two examples of how the outer limits of the notion of self-defence tend to be stretched. This attitude by states is comprehensible, as self-defence is the only universally accepted exception to the unilateral use of force. The problem is that many instances of uses of force, particularly those related to terrorism, can hardly be amenable within the purview of self-defence, either because the prerequisites for its exercise are absent or because by their nature and purpose they would better fit other qualifications. In particular, states have often resorted to force in response to terrorist attacks in forms that are reminiscent of armed reprisals for their punitive and deterrent character. Such instances as the bombing of Sudan and Afghanistan in 1998, following the terrorist attacks against American embassies in Africa, or the 1993 bombing against Baghdad, to mention just a few cases related to terrorism, are readily identifiable as armed reprisals properly so called, for the punitive character of the action and its intended deterrent effect.[81] The problem is that armed reprisals are almost universally regarded, with few highly controversial exceptions,[82] as having been outlawed in contemporary international law, even by those who carry them out.[83] However, as I wrote elsewhere, 'armed reprisals risk sneakingly making their way back into the reality of international relations if not in its illusive representation'.[84]

The risk of overtly admitting the legality of armed reprisals is self-evident, as this might undermine the general prohibition of the use of force, to which everyone seems committed. On the other hand, to use self-defence as a misnomer to justify uses of force that are clearly punitive and deterrent in character may have the unfortunate consequence of jeopardizing the credibility of the international regulatory system. The blurring of the distinction between distinct legal categories, already highlighted by some commentators,[85] seems to be of even greater significance. If one looks at the debates before the Security Council, emphasis is often placed, in order to determine the lawfulness of uses of force, on their necessity and proportionality regardless of their qualification as acts of self-defence.[86]

Inaccurate and self-serving, purposeful characterizations of uses of force unilaterally advanced by states add up to the confusion and in the absence of authoritative determinations risk obfuscating even more an already murky scenario. Once again, however, it is worth noting that mystifying characterizations and the like are but the symptoms of a

81 See the definition provided by D. Bowett, 'Reprisals Involving Recourse to Armed Force' (1972) 66 *American Journal of International Law* 3.

82 See Dinstein, admitting of the legality of defensive armed reprisals as somewhat amenable within the scope of self-defence (*War, Aggression and Self-Defence*).

83 See the 'categorical position' taken by the United States 'that reprisals involving the use of force are illegal under international law' (M. L. Nash, 'Contemporary Practice of the United States Relating to International Law' (1979) 73 *American Journal of International Law* 476, 491).

84 See Bianchi, 'Enforcing International Law Norms against Terrorism', 506.

85 See P. Klein, 'Vers la reconnaissance progressive d'un droit à des représailles armées?', in K. Bannelier *et al.* (eds.), *Le droit international face au terrorisme: après le 11 septembre 2001* (Paris: Pedone, 2003), 249ff. See also R. W. Tucker, 'Reprisals and Self-Defence: The Customary Law' (1972) 66 *American Journal of International Law* 586, 595, stressing 'the little significance of prohibiting armed reprisals while retaining the customary right of self-defence'.

86 Some statements made by Western states at the occasion of the 2006 Israeli military intervention in Lebanon can be interpreted to this effect (see the minutes of the debate before the SC in UN Doc. S/PV.5493 (2006)).

much more serious disease, namely the lack of consensus on how to use legal categories and interpretative techniques for the purpose of identifying the precise contours of the international regulation of the use of force.

9 Necessity between primary and secondary norms

Necessity is a concept incorporated into many rules of international law. In many ways, it could be characterized as one of those 'interstitial norms',[87] that adjust their content to the normative setting to which they apply. The flexibility and multifunctionality of this and similar concepts (another example could be that of proportionality) make them particularly suitable to shape and to direct the interpretation and application of many primary norms. Necessity is relevant to many normative regimes of international law. It is relevant to the field of human rights, in which it is a prerequisite for the limitation of specific rights in claw-back clauses or, more generally, in derogation clauses. But necessity is also relevant to international humanitarian law by limiting the conduct of hostilities and the use of certain weapons. In the area of the use of force necessity comes into play as a general limitation to any use of force and as a particular prerequisite for the exercise of an action in self-defence.[88] Most of the time associated with the complementary concept of proportionality, necessity is regarded primarily as a component of primary rules on the use of force.

As is well known, however, necessity is also a concept relevant to secondary rules. The plea of 'state of necessity' is one of the circumstances precluding wrongfulness under the law of state responsibility, as codified in the ILC ASR. Well before the completion of the codification process, the ICJ in the *Gabčíkovo–Nagymaros Project* case stated that 'the state of necessity is a ground recognized by customary international law for precluding the wrongfulness of an act not in conformity with an international obligation.' The Court went on to spell out the rigorous conditions for invoking the state-of-necessity defence, relying on the

[87] See V. Lowe, 'The Politics of Law-Making: Are the Method and Character of Norm Creation Changing?', in M. Byers (ed.), *The Role of Law in International Politics: Essays in International Relations and International Law* (Oxford: Oxford University Press, 2000), 207ff.

[88] See, generally, J. Gardam, *Necessity, Proportionality and the Use of Force by States* (Cambridge: Cambridge University Press, 2004).

work of the ILC.[89] Article 25 ASR now codifies necessity as a circumstance precluding wrongfulness under the law of state responsibility.[90] The article as such is widely regarded as declaratory of customary international law. Recently, the plea of state of necessity has been invoked before domestic courts[91] and international arbitral tribunals[92] in connection with the failure by Argentina to repay its creditors in the aftermath of its bankruptcy. Even though tribunals have come up with conflicting views on the applicability of the state of necessity to the economic and financial situation faced by Argentina at the time and to its sovereign debt crisis, the status of the plea under international law and the conditions for its application have not really been called into question. The discrepancies in the various judgments derive mainly from a different interpretation of the applicability of the state-of-necessity plea requirements to the facts of the case.

Most likely, to invoke the plea of necessity in the context of the use of force would be generally regarded as anathema by international lawyers, at least since the time when Roberto Ago, Special Rapporteur of the ILC on state responsibility, decided to disassociate self-defence and necessity, which had been for a long time closely intertwined in international

89 *Gabčíkovo–Nagymaros Project* (*Hungary* v. *Slovakia*), Judgment of 25 September 1997 [1997] ICJ Rep. 7, paras. 51–2. Such rigorous conditions are now codified in Art. 25 (see n. 90 below).

90 Art. 25 (Necessity) reads: '1. Necessity may not be invoked by a State as a ground for precluding wrongfulness of an act not in conformity with an international obligation of that State unless the act: (a) is the only means for the State to safeguard an essential interest against a grave and imminent peril; and (b) does not seriously impair an essential interest of the State or States towards which the obligation exists, or of the international community as a whole. 2. In any case, necessity may not be invoked by a State as a ground for precluding wrongfulness if: (a) the international obligation in question excludes the possibility of invoking necessity; or (b) the State has contributed to the situation of necessity.'

91 See the decision of the *Bundesverfassungsgericht* of 8 May 2007 (for a comment, see S. Schill, 'German Constitutional Court Rules on Necessity in Argentina Bondholder case' (2007) 11 *ASIL Insights*).

92 See the two conflicting ICSID arbitrations: *LG&E Energy Corp., LG&E Capital Corp., and LG&E International Inc.* v. *Argentina*, ICSID Case No. ARB/01/1, Award, 3 October 2006, 46 ILM 36 (2007) and *CMS Gas Transmission Company* v. *Argentina*, ICSID Case No. ARB/01/8, 12 May 2005, 44 ILM 1205 (2005) as well as the Decision of the Ad Hoc Committee on the Application for Annulment of the Argentine Republic in the *CSM* v. *Argentina* case, 46 ILM 1132 (2007). For a comment, see M. Waibel, 'Two Worlds of Necessity in ICSID Arbitration: CMS and LG&G' (2007) 20 *Leiden Journal of International Law* 637.

practice as justifications for forcible measures of self-help.[93] However, at closer scrutiny, to rely on the plea of necessity as a circumstance precluding wrongfulness under the secondary rules of state responsibility in order to justify certain uses of force in exceptional circumstances could have the merit of reversing the presumption of legality. The use of force in cases other than those expressly authorized under the UN Charter and under customary international law would remain prohibited unless it could be proved that a state of necessity, the ascertainment of which would be subject to the strict standards laid down in Article 25 ASR, exists. Such a plea could be successful in case of a clear and imminent danger of an attack with weapons of mass destruction.[94] In such a case, a response by the potential victim could be justified out of a state of necessity, without calling into question the general prohibition of the use of force and the requirement of a prior armed attack under the law of self-defence. Incidentally, this might have been a much more convincing response to the question submitted to the ICJ in the *Legality of the Threat or Use of Nuclear Weapons* case.[95] Rather than answering in a fairly convoluted manner that the 'Court cannot conclude definitively whether the threat or use of nuclear weapons would be lawful or unlawful in an extreme circumstance of self-defence, in which the very survival of a State would be at stake',[96] the Court could have simply said that in such case the threat or use of nuclear weapons in extreme circumstances could be justified, subject to its strict conditions, by a state of necessity. Even the much celebrated passage from the diplomatic correspondence between the US and the UK at the occasion of the *Caroline* case, taken by many as evidence of the existence at the time of a right to preventive self-defence, could be more properly framed under the state

[93] See R. Ago, Addendum to the Eight Report on State Responsibility, UN Doc. A/CN.4/318/ADD.5–7 [1980] II (I) *Yearbook of International Law Commission*, esp. 39–40, 61–3.

[94] While it is true that the invocation of a state of necessity can be abused and that – as the ICJ put it in the *Gabčíkovo–Nagymaros Project* case – the invoking state cannot be the sole judge of its own necessity (para. 51), it is also true that 'a measure of uncertainty about the future does not necessarily disqualify a State from invoking necessity, if the peril is clearly established on the basis of the evidence reasonably available at the time' (Commentaries to Art. 25, para. 16; reproduced in J. Crawford, *The International Law Commission's Articles on State Responsibility. Introduction, Text and Commentaries* (Cambridge: Cambridge University Press, 2002), 184).

[95] *Legality of Threat or Use of Nuclear Weapons*, Advisory Opinion [1996] ICJ Rep. 226.

[96] *Ibid.*

of necessity.[97] When Secretary of State Webster made reference to the 'necessity of self-defence ... instant, overwhelming, and leaving no choice of means and no moment for deliberation',[98] the point that he was attempting to make was that the UK had violated international law and that only evidence of the existence of a state of necessity in the terms just described could have exempted it from responsibility. From a systemic point of view, given the widely shared perception of the centrality of the prohibition of the use of force to international relations, reliance on necessity as a secondary rule exonerating a state from responsibility under strict circumstances seems no more dangerous than widening the range of admissible exceptions to the prohibition of the use of force, the contours of which are still highly controversial as in the case of humanitarian intervention and anticipatory self-defence.[99]

10 The use of different axiological categories: legality vs. legitimacy

As the above remarks have made abundantly clear, the methodological difficulties and hard interpretative choices underlying the legal regulation of the use of force are by themselves quite a skein to unravel, even within the fairly homogeneous traditions of the international legal discourse. Certainly, there was hardly any need to further muddle up the matter by introducing analytical frames that rely on different axiological categories. Reference is here made to the use of the category of 'legitimacy' used in juxtaposition to 'legality' to convey the sense that the use of force by states in certain circumstances can be appraised by a dual (or perhaps double) standard. The issue came dramatically to the fore at the occasion of the military intervention in Kosovo, when even less than a formalistic reading of the Charter would clearly point to the illegality of the intervention. Nor did the arguments that anchored the use of force on an alleged customary law rule on humanitarian intervention sound

[97] In the same sense the ILC's Commentary to Art. 25 (see Crawford, *International Law Commission's Articles on State Responsibility*, 179–80).

[98] See 'Letter from D. Webster, US Secretary of State, to Mr. Fox (24 April 1841)' (1857) 29 *British and Foreign State Papers* 1129, 1138.

[99] On anticipatory self-defence, see Chapter 12 in this volume. As to the objection that Art. 26 ASR would preclude invocation of necessity for acts contrary to peremptory norms, its practical impact would depend on the definition of the content of any such peremptory norm (see section 7 above). If one takes only the prohibition of acts of aggression to be a peremptory norm, there would be room for resorting to the plea of necessity as regards uses of force short of an act of aggression.

terribly convincing. It is a fair speculation to make that the use by some international lawyers of the characterization of the intervention in Kosovo as legitimate, albeit illegal, or not too much illegal, was a desperate attempt to avoid the defeat of having the law (and their own personal authority) discredited by a widespread perception of inefficacy and unfairness.[100]

Legitimacy is a complex category, whose genealogy goes well beyond the limits of these scattered considerations on its impact on the debate on the use of force. Incidentally, some interesting studies on legitimacy have been produced in international law scholarship, particularly the well-known book by Thomas Franck, who developed a theory of legitimacy as an important compliance-inducing factor in international law.[101] However, the appeal and popularity of the dichotomy between legality and legitimacy presumably derives from the well-known essay by Carl Schmitt, which was too historically rooted and context-based to lend itself to the generalizations it later produced.[102] Be that as it may, it is rather along the lines of Schmitt's juxtaposition between the conformity of the law with some pre-legal moral values and the respect for formal rules of the legal order that the debate on the use of force has developed in international legal scholarship.[103] The idea of legitimacy has been fairly simplistically associated with some correspondence of the challenged action with some communal moral and political values, as opposed to compliance with particular legal rules. The tactical as well as the strategic value of the use of the dichotomy are self-evident: in this way, hard cases on the fringe of illegality can be accommodated, their status as legal precedents less easily denied and, like in all good stories, there may be eventually a happy end with legality and legitimacy meeting again and reconciling with each other. For instance, Resolution 1244 passed by the SC in the aftermath of the military intervention in Kosovo was considered by some commentators to have achieved such a noble

[100] See B. Simma, 'NATO, the UN and the Use of Force: Legal Aspects', *European Journal of International Law* 10 (1999), 1; A. Cassese, '*Ex Iniuria Jus Oritur*: Are we Moving towards International Legitimization of Forcible Humanitarian Countermeasures?' (1999) 10 *European Journal of International* Law 23.

[101] T. Franck, *The Power of Legitimacy among Nations* (Oxford: Oxford University Press, 1990).

[102] C. Schmitt, *Legalität und Legitimität* (Berlin: Duncker & Humblot, 1932); translated into English as *Legality and Legitimacy* (Durham, NC: Duke University Press, 2004).

[103] See the interesting considerations advanced by R. Falk, 'Legality and Legitimacy: The Quest for Principled Flexibility and Restraint' (2005) 31 *Review of International Studies* 3.

goal.[104] In any event, the potential for a loose use of the two categories to accommodate specific political interests and produce normative uncertainty cannot be underestimated.[105]

At first sight the use of the concept of legitimacy may be thought to have brought further uncertainties into the legal standards regulating the use of force by states. At closer scrutiny, however, some lessons can be learnt from it. The first and obvious one is that a certain contamination of categories is well under way in international law. The influence of other disciplines, be it economics or international relations, should provide those who still believe in the 'romantic insularity' of international law as an autonomous, and possibly prominent discipline among others, some food for thought. Even more importantly, the legitimacy–legality debate has provided a good opportunity to reflect on the limits of conceiving of the law as detached from the societal body from which it emanates and from its underlying values. Whether this will have an influence in shaping foreign policies and future legal regimes may be 'uncertain at this juncture',[106] but a powerful warning sign may well have positive effects in a long-term perspective.

11 Conclusion: interpretative method and societal consensus

The purpose of the preceding sections was not simply to highlight the thorniest substantive issues in the international regulation of the use of force, but also to show that the main problem lies in the methodology by which the legal discourse is formed. Method, far from being a theoretical preoccupation, lays down the framework in which practice takes place. The credibility and persuasive force of any legal argument depends heavily on the extent to which it fits a generally shared methodology of legal reasoning and interpretation.

The broken societal consensus on many issues related to the use of force has caused interpretative methods to proliferate. The panoply of discourses is a symptom rather than the cause of the current disagreement but risks widening the gap between diverging positions. Any serious attempt to rebuild social consensus on the interpretation of the

[104] See A. Pellet, 'Brief Remarks on the Unilateral Use of Force' (2000) 11 *European Journal of International Law* 385, 389. Pellet conceded, however, that the ex-post legalization of the intervention was not a 'satisfactory picture'.

[105] As an apt illustration, I would quote the article by A.-M. Slaughter, 'Good reasons for going around the UN', *New York Times*, 18 March 2003, A33.

[106] Falk, 'Legality and Legitimacy', 50.

rules governing the use of force must be geared towards seeking a common methodology within the interpretative community that generates the official discourse. It would be illusory to believe that such common method can be traced to the rules of treaty interpretation or to theories of customary lawmaking, as they can be twisted and turned at will, unless there is consensus on how to use them and how to direct the interpretative discourse.

In the constant tension between a formalistic normative mode, which is far removed from social realities, and a cynical acknowledgement of power politics relations, which overlooks the powerful moral and political drive of legal commitments, a point of equilibrium must be found. All the more so in relation to the use of force, in which the legal and political dimensions are indissolubly linked. The politics of the use of force alone cannot accomplish any meaningful goal unless it can rely on a sufficiently generally shared method of legal interpretation to provide it with the necessary level of acceptance by the societal body. At the same time, interpretative methods need to rely on political realities and societal values to have a bearing on normative outcomes.

To bring to the fore and to broach the methodological and interpretative issues raised in this chapter could be a sensible way to try to restore a common starting point. It will not be easy to construe a new societal consensus on the international regulation of the use of force, but the stakes involved are such as to make the effort worthwhile. If method directs the normative outcome, there cannot be any acceptable outcome, unless the method is sufficiently approved and shared by the players of the game.

10

The role of the UN Security Council in relation to the use of force against terrorists

SIR MICHAEL WOOD

> Terrorism is one of the main contemporary threats to international peace and security. Perpetrators of terrorist acts undermine human rights, fundamental freedoms and the rule of law, which are the pillars of international stability and of the action of the United Nations.
>
> The Organization plays a leading role in the fight against terrorism, which calls for a global response.[1]

Given the importance of the UN collective security system and the Security Council's primary responsibility for the maintenance of international peace and security, and given both legal and political doubts concerning the unilateral use of force by states against terrorists,[2] it is important when states feel driven to take forcible measures against terrorist threats that they bear in mind the Security Council's powers to take or authorize the use of force.[3] Collective action is almost always better than individual action, legally, politically and in terms of effectiveness. Collective decisions (or even non-decisions) are often wiser than those taken individually.

The present contribution deals principally with the potential of the Council in this area, less with actual practice, which is sparse.[4] The aim is

I wish to thank Eran Sthoeger for his valuable assistance.

[1] Ban Ki-moon, preface, *International Instruments related to the Prevention and Suppression of International Terrorism* (New York: United Nations, 2008). For a fuller collection, see B. Saul (ed.), *Terrorism* (Oxford: Hart, 2012) ('*Terrorism Documents*').

[2] See Chapters 11–13 in this volume; also L. Moir, *Reappraising the Resort to Force: International Law,* Jus ad Bellum *and the War on Terror* (Oxford: Hart, 2010).

[3] Here the term 'use of force' refers to such use of force internationally as falls to be judged against the international law on the use of force (*jus ad bellum*), not the employment of force in law enforcement activities or by peacekeepers acting in self-defence or in the execution of their mandate.

[4] Practice may be sparse, but the literature is extensive: see, by way of recent contributions, N. Schrijver, 'Responding to International Terrorism: Moving the Frontiers of

to describe the background to the Security Council's potential use of its powers, and to offer some policy suggestions.

As will be seen, the Security Council has by now an extensive practice of determining that acts of terrorism are threats to international peace and security, thus paving the way for action under Chapter VII of the Charter. Its action in this field has so far been confined to the adoption of measures not involving the use of force. But there is no reason why, in appropriate circumstances, the Council should not authorize the use of force against terrorist threats. This could be done both in circumstances where a state which has been attacked may exercise the right of self-defence and where such right is not available, in particular where a terrorist threat, though real, is not imminent and also, possibly, where the attacks are not of such gravity as to give rise to a right to justify self-defence.

It is common to contrast the 'law enforcement' approach to fighting terrorism and the 'armed conflict' approach. The one involves the police, financial regulatory bodies, the courts; the other the armed forces. The Security Council has been concerned with both approaches, within its core function of maintaining international peace and security. So it has been involved in bringing to justice terrorist suspects; equally it has endorsed the taking of military action against terrorist groups such as al-Qaeda in Afghanistan. It is not a matter of *either* law enforcement *or* armed force. The one should be routine; the other exceptional. Both may

International Law for "Enduring Freedom"?' (2001) 48 *Netherlands. International Law Review* 271; N. Rostow, 'Before and After: The Changed UN Response to Terrorism Since September 11th' (2002) 35 *Cornell International Law Journal* 475; J. E. Alvarez, 'The Security Council's War on Terrorism: Problems and Policy Options', in E. De Wet and A. Nollkaemper (eds.), *Review of the Security Council by Member States* (Antwerp: Intersentia, 2003) 119; N. J. Schrijver, 'September 11th and Challenges to International Law', in J. Boulden and T. G. Weiss (eds.), *Terrorism and the UN: Before and After September 11* (Bloomington, IN: Indiana University Press, 2004), 55; B. Fassbender, 'The Security Council and International Terrorism', in A. Bianchi (ed.), *Enforcing International Law Norms against Terrorism* (Oxford: Hart, 2004), 83; G. Guillaume, 'Terrorism and International Law' (2004) 53 *International & Comparative Law Quarterly* 637; S. Szurek, 'La lutte internationale contre le terrorisme sous l'empire du chapître VII: un laboratoire normative' (2005) 109 *Revue générale de droit international public* 5; E. David, 'Les Nations unies et la lutte contre le terrorisme', in J.-P. Cot, A. Pellet and M. Forteau (eds.), *La Charte des Nations Unies: Commentaire article par article* (Paris: Économica, 2005), 163; J. Boulden, 'The Security Council and Terrorism', in V. Lowe *et al.* (eds.), *The United Nations Security Council and War: The Evolution of Thought and Practice since 1945* (Oxford: Oxford University Press, 2008), 608; N. White, 'The United Nations and Counter-Terrorism', in A. Salinas de Frías, K. Samuel, N. White (eds.), *Counter-Terrorism: International Law and Practice* (Oxford: Oxford University Press, 2012), 54–82; Chr. Walter, 'Terrorism', *Max Planck Encyclopedia of Public International Law* (Oxford: Oxford University Press, 2012).

be needed. It is important not to lose sight of the fact that in the 'fight' against terrorism a range of measures is required, among which the use of force should be seen as exceptional, and only a last resort.[5] The work of the United Nations, including the Security Council, in this field has not so far been much concerned with measures involving the use of force in the *jus ad bellum* sense. It has focused on non-forcible measures, including the prevention and punishment of various crimes that may be qualified as 'acts of terrorism' (law enforcement) and the financing of terrorism,[6] as well as the broader matters covered by the General Assembly's Declarations of 1994 and 1996,[7] and the United Nations Global Counter-Terrorism Strategy of 2006.[8] These include promoting a culture of ethnic, national and religious tolerance.

We also need to be aware that the experience of terrorism varies around the globe – though perhaps less so now than in even the recent past. It is important not to view terrorism from the perspective of only one region or state. As the UN General Assembly reaffirmed in its 2006 Counter-Terrorism Strategy, 'terrorism cannot and should not be associated with any religion, nationality, civilization or ethnic group'. The Security Council has emphasized the contribution of international efforts 'to enhance dialogue and broaden the understanding among civilizations, in an effort to prevent the indiscriminate targeting of different religions and cultures'.[9]

[5] This is true of any use of force: Institute of International Law, Resolution on Authorization of the Use of Force by the United Nations, 9 September 2011, Art. 8: 'In all circumstances, the use of force shall only be authorized as a last resort.'

[6] In particular, the conventions and protocols on a series of terrorist crimes, adopted between 1963 and 2010 by the United Nations General Assembly, ICAO, IMO and IAEA (*International Instruments*, 3–156; *Terrorism Documents*, 1–161); and the work of the Counter-Terrorism Committee, established by the Security Council, and the Counter-terrorism Implementation Task Force within the United Nations Secretariat (*Terrorism Documents*, 600–28).

[7] Declaration on Measures to Eliminate International Terrorism, UN Doc. A/Res./49/60 (1994) (*International Instruments*, 349; *Terrorism Documents*, 331); Declaration to Supplement the 1994 Declaration on Measures to Eliminate International Terrorism, UN Doc. A/Res./51/210 (1996) (*International Instruments*, 353; *Terrorism Documents*, 398).

[8] UN Doc. A/Res./60/288 (2006), with annexed Plan of Action (*International Instruments*, 355); UN Doc. A/Res./62/272 (2008); UN Doc. A/Res./64/297 (2010)

[9] Declaration of the Ministers for Foreign Affairs on the Issue of Combating Terrorism, UN Doc. S/Res./1456 (2003), Annex, para. 10 (*International Instruments*, 383; *Terrorism Documents*, 484).

The focus on 'terrorists' or 'terrorist groups' is not legally satisfactory. 'Terrorism' is not a term of art in international law, and there is no generally agreed definition.[10] 'Terrorism' and 'terrorist' have no universally agreed meaning, and are overused. It is all too easy to designate someone or some organization, or even a state, as 'terrorist', with the emotional undercurrents that go with such designation, including the pretext for disregarding human rights. Terrorist groups shade into other non-state actors, including insurgents – the distinction is often in the eye of the beholder. The actions of terrorist groups should be treated mainly as ordinary crimes under domestic law of the various states. Acts such as those of 9/11 in New York, Washington and Pennsylvania, that may qualify as armed attacks for the purposes of the *jus ad bellum* are perhaps the exception. 'Ordinary' terrorist acts, such as those in London in July 2005, should be seen simply as crimes, albeit often crimes of international concern and the subject of international conventions.

1 The Security Council's powers: evolving practice in the field of counter-terrorism

When the Security Council first met, in London on 17 January 1946, no one could have anticipated that the Council would come to play a role in the field of counter-terrorism. It was set up to keep the peace between states, and that is mostly what it tried to do in the early years, though with difficulty given the Cold War. The Council's counter-terrorism work is a good example of how its mandate has developed from what was originally envisaged. It also illustrates some of the principal features

[10] Reference is sometimes made to the 'definition' in the 1999 International Convention for the Suppression of the Financing of Terrorism, 2178 UNTS 197, Art. 2.1(b) (*International Instruments*, 89; *Terrorism Documents*, 115) and to UN Doc. S/Res./1566 (2004), para. 3 (*International Instruments*, 398; *Terrorism Documents*, 499). In a 16 February 2011 Interlocutory Decision, the Appeals Chamber of the Special Tribunal for Lebanon found there was a crime of transnational terrorism under customary international law. This questionable finding has met with fierce criticism: see B. Saul, 'Legislating from a Radical Hague: The United Nations Special Tribunal for Lebanon Invents an International Crime of Transnational Terrorism' (2011) 24 *Leiden Journal of International Law* 677; B. Saul, 'The Emerging Law of International Terrorism', *Terrorism Documents*, lxii, lxx–lxxiii, with further references. In this contribution, the term 'terrorism' does not include 'state terrorism'. However strongly one may feel about the actions of certain states, it is generally misleading, as a matter of law, to describe such actions as terrorist. There are other sets of rules within international law that govern the actions of states, including in particular the law of armed conflict and international human rights law.

of the Security Council that distinguish it from other international bodies: the speed with which it can act, as an organ of limited membership – fifteen members; and its power, when acting under Chapter VII of the Charter of the United Nations, to impose international legal obligations on states, obligations that under Article 103 of the Charter prevail over all other international obligations (except perhaps obligations under *jus cogens* norms). For present purposes, it is particularly important to emphasize that the Council is the only international body which can authorize a use of force which would otherwise be contrary to the *jus ad bellum*. Though acting within other groups may add legitimacy, only the Council can add legality.

The Security Council came to terrorism rather late in the day. While the Council occasionally dealt with particular aspects of the matter, such as the security of civil aviation, or attacks on diplomats, in the 1970s and 1980s, more often than not political divisions within the Council on the nature of attacks by non-state actors, or on the appropriateness of unilateral state actions to address these attacks, led to non-action.[11] It was only from September 2001 that the issue began to play a major role in the Council's work. Before then the emphasis, within the United Nations, had rested with the General Assembly, which continues to play an important role. Entirely appropriately, it was the General Assembly, not the Council, that adopted the United Nations Global Counter-Terrorism Strategy, which is intended to be 'a strategy to promote comprehensive, coordinated and consistent responses, at the national, regional and international levels, to counter terrorism'. In doing so the Assembly reaffirmed 'its role under the Charter, including on questions of international peace and security'. UN specialized agencies also played a role in addressing international terrorism. The International Civil Aviation Organization (ICAO), formed to promote the safe and orderly development of international civil aviation, has been a successful forum for the conclusion of several conventions with counter-terrorism elements, as is also the case with the International Maritime Organization.

On 20 December 2006, the Security Council issued a presidential statement summarizing its basic approach to the fight against terrorism.[12] It reaffirmed that 'terrorism constitutes one of the most serious

[11] For an overview of such instances, see E. C. Luck, 'Tackling Terrorism', in D. Malone (ed.), *The UN Security Council: From the Cold War to the 21st Century* (Boulder, CO: Lynne Reinner, 2004), 88.

[12] UN Doc. S/PRST/2006/56 (2006).

threats to international peace and security'. That has become standard language, both for the Security Council but also – and this is important for the Council's legitimacy – for the plenary organ of the United Nations, in which all states are represented, the General Assembly. The language reflects Article 39 of the UN Charter, the opening provision of Chapter VII, and so affirms the Council's competence, in appropriate cases, to take action against terrorism under that Chapter. In the presidential statement, the Council went on to reiterate 'its determination to combat all forms of terrorism, in accordance with its responsibilities under the Charter of the United Nations'. It was thus asserting its specific role, while not of course claiming exclusivity as against the General Assembly. And the Council further reaffirmed 'the need to combat by all means, in accordance with the Charter of the United Nations [an important qualification], threats to international peace and security caused by terrorist acts'.[13] At the same time, it should be recalled that in the statement the Council reminded states that 'they must ensure that any measures taken to combat terrorism comply with all their obligations under international law, in particular international human rights, refugee and humanitarian law'. This reflects the accepted view that 'effective counter-terrorism measures and the protection of human rights are not conflicting goals, but complementary and mutually reinforcing'.[14] The reference to human rights obligations presumably includes the provisions contained in international treaties for derogation in time of emergency, as well as the Security Council's own powers, under Article 103 of the Charter, to restrict the application of such obligations in certain circumstances.

It is a condition precedent for action under Chapter VII of the Charter that the Security Council determines the existence of a threat to the peace, a breach of the peace or an act of aggression. There is now no doubt that the Security Council may properly determine that particular acts of terrorism, and not only those in which states have some involvement,[15] are threats to international peace and security,[16] and may make recommendations or decide on measures under Chapter VII of the

[13] UN Doc. A/Res./60/288 (2006), annex, section IV, chapeau; see also UN Doc. S/PRST/2006/56 (2006).

[14] UN Doc. A/60/825 (2006), para. 5.

[15] T. Becker, *Terrorism and the State: Rethinking the Rules on State Responsibility* (Oxford: Hart, 2006).

[16] The Council has repeatedly pronounced itself to this effect, e.g., UN Doc. S/PRST/2006/30 (2006); UN Doc. S/PRST/2005/55 (2005); UN Doc. S/PRST/2004/14 (2004).

Charter. This is a relatively recent development. The General Assembly, representing the membership of the United Nations as a whole, has endorsed this approach, for example in its Resolution 62/272 of 5 September 2008, paragraph 1 of which states that

> terrorism in all its forms and manifestations, committed by whomsoever, wherever and for whatever purposes ... constitutes one of the most serious threats to international peace and security.

2 Security Council action in the field of counter-terrorism

So what has the Security Council done in the field of counter-terrorism? It has not succeeded in defining terrorism. Indeed, it has largely avoided that issue. An exception is the general, i.e. non-country or non-situation specific Resolution 1566 which provides a general definition of terrorism, for the purposes of the Council, but by reference to existing international conventions.[17] It may well be argued that it is not the function of the Security Council to operate as a crime-defining agency. At least initially it dealt with terrorist incidents case-by-case; the Council has not been greatly troubled by the ideological debates that have for so long hampered the General Assembly.

The Security Council's role in relation to terrorism has been varied, and has varied over time. Its involvement has taken many forms. Many of its activities, even under Chapter VI (pacific settlement of disputes), assist in resolving, or at least calming, underlying situations which might otherwise spawn terrorist groups. Security Council action specifically directed at terrorism may be viewed in three (overlapping) phases.[18] For a time, the Council confined itself to denouncing terrorist acts and making generalized appeals to states to act appropriately. Then, in the 1990s the Council began to take specific measures in relation to

[17] UN Doc. S/Res./1566 (2004), para. 3, reads: '*Recalls* that criminal acts, including against civilians, committed with the intent to cause death or serious bodily injury, or taking of hostages, with the purpose to provoke a state of terror in the general public or in a group of persons or particular persons, intimidate a population or compel a government or an international organization to do or to abstain from doing any act, which constitute offences within the scope of and as defined in the international conventions and protocols relating to terrorism, are under no circumstances justifiable by considerations of a political, philosophical, ideological, racial, ethnic, religious or other similar nature, and calls upon all States to prevent such acts and, if not prevented, to ensure that such acts are punished by penalties consistent with their grave nature'

[18] M. Wood, 'The Security Council and International Criminal Law' (2007) 5 *Romanian Journal of International Law/Revista Română de Drept Internațional* 160, 169–71.

particular cases, such as requiring the surrender of suspects, or demanding the cessation of support for terrorism (e.g., in response to the bombing of the US embassies in Nairobi and Dar es Salaam). And following 9/11 the Council began to adopt what have been termed 'generic', 'legislative' or 'quasi-legislative' measures, seeking to deal with the phenomenon of terrorism as a whole, not only with particular incidents.

In the first phase, the Security Council developed a practice of *condemning* major acts of international terrorism. Such condemnations became more formal over time, perhaps reflecting greater confidence in the Council's role in this field. Initially the condemnation was contained in a press statement or Presidential statement (e.g. over the *Achille Lauro* incident in 1985, and the bombings at Rome and Vienna airports that same year); now condemnation may also come in the form of a short resolution.[19] The Council has a standing item on its agenda, 'Threats to international peace and security caused by terrorist acts', under which it takes up such attacks.[20] These have become almost pro forma condemnations and expressions of sympathy. But at least they make clear the Council's concern at such acts, and make clear the solidarity of the international community for the affected populations. And in some cases they may serve a political purpose, where for example the terrorist attack may strain relations between states.[21]

In a second period, beginning in the 1990s the Security Council began to call for action in specific cases. In particular, it has demanded or required states to act against the alleged perpetrators of terrorist acts, by arresting them and transferring them to other countries for trial (Libya–Lockerbie/UTA suspects;[22] Sudan – those who attempted to

[19] For example, there were resolutions on Bali (UN Doc. S/Res./1438 (2002)); Moscow (UN Doc. S/Res./1440 (2002)); Mombasa (UN Doc. S/Res./1450 (2002)); Istanbul (UN Doc. S/Res./1516 (2003)): see *Terrorism Documents*, 436–585.

[20] Care is needed in the heat of the moment. There is always pressure to respond instantly, on the day, yet the Council needs to have the facts before it. On one occasion, the Council condemned the attacks that took place in Madrid on 11 March 2003, blaming by name 'the terrorist group ETA', the Basque separatists; it quickly became apparent that they had nothing to do with it (UN Doc. S/Res./1530 (2004)).

[21] An example is the Council's statement strongly condemning the series of bomb attacks that occurred in different parts of India, including Mumbai, on 11 July 2006. The Council underlined the need to bring the perpetrators to justice, and urged all states to cooperate with India in this regard (UN Doc. S/PRST/2006/30 (2006)).

[22] UN Doc. S/Res./731 (1992); UN Doc. S/Res./748 (1992); UN Doc. S/Res./883 (1993); UN Doc. S/Res./1192 (1998).

assassinate President Mubarak;[23] Afghanistan – Osama bin Laden).[24] In each of the cases just mentioned, the Council determined that a particular act of terrorism, or acts of terrorism in general, are threats to the peace.[25] The other major development during this phase was the sanctions regime imposed on al-Qaeda and Taliban (non-state and state actors), accompanied by the procedural innovation of the 1267 Committee.

The third stage, and the most dramatic development in the practice of the Council, began in the immediate aftermath of the attacks in the United States, on the World Trade Center and the Pentagon, on 11 September 2001. The Council imposed a requirement upon all states to criminalize terrorism in their domestic law. This may have revolutionized traditional domestic approaches, which treated terrorism as an ordinary crime. It sidestepped consensual treaty-making processes, and may have made less significant the General Assembly's impasse over a comprehensive terrorism convention. One of the principal measures resorted to by the Security Council in this third phase has been targeted 'sanctions' against terrorist groups and those who support or harbour them. A particular focus of Security Council action has been the financing of terrorism. In Resolution 1373 of 28 September 2001, the Council took upon itself what has been described as a largely legislative role in imposing on states obligations set out in the 1999 Financing of Terrorism Convention, which at the time had not yet entered into force, and which many states had not yet signed or ratified. By the same resolution, the Council set up the Counter-Terrorism Committee, an important and innovative subsidiary organ, whose task is to support and monitor states in their implementation of the obligations laid down by the Security Council. This it does, *inter alia*, through a reporting system. By Resolution 1535 (2004), the Council established the Counter-Terrorism Committee Executive Directorate, thus reinforcing the UN Secretariat's capacity to service the CTC and to assist states in their compliance.

[23] UN Doc. S/Res./1044 (1996); UN Doc. S/Res./1054 (1996); UN Doc. S/Res./1070 (1996); UN Doc. S/Res./1372 (2001).

[24] UN Doc. S/Res./1267 (1999); UN Doc. S/Res./1333 (2000); UN Doc. S/Res./1363 (2001).

[25] The Council may have been too sweeping when it says that *all* acts of terrorism are threats to international peace and security.

3 The Security Council and the use of force

It should first be noted that we are here only concerned with the use of force by or authorized by the Security Council. Notwithstanding the 'Uniting for Peace' resolution, the General Assembly does not have the power to authorize a use of force that would otherwise be contrary to international law and has so far, perhaps prudently, not attempted to recommend the use of force under that resolution.[26]

It is sometimes asked whether the existing rules of international law on the use of force (*jus ad bellum*) are adequate to meet current threats, especially from terrorists and weapons of mass destruction (WMD).[27] Some have from time to time suggested they are or may not be. The General Assembly of the United Nations, meeting at the level of Heads of State and Government, responded in the 2005 World Summit Outcome Document, reaffirming

> that the relevant provisions of the Charter are sufficient to address the full range of threats to international peace and security. We further reaffirm the authority of the Security Council to mandate coercive action to maintain and restore international peace and security. We stress the importance of acting in accordance with the purposes and principles of the Charter.[28]

[26] C. Binder, 'Uniting for Peace Resolution (1950)', *Max Planck Encyclopedia of Public International Law* (Oxford: Oxford University Press, 2012). See the UK government's response to the Foreign Affairs Committee in connection with Kosovo: (2000) 71 *British Yearbook of International Law* 649. As Matheson says in the context of Uniting for Peace, 'the Assembly could only make recommendations to states; it could not authorize a UN force to act without the consent of the state or states involved, to initiate the use of force, or to take enforcement action' (M. Matheson, *Council Unbound: The Growth of UN Decision Making on Conflict and Postconflict Issues after the Cold War* (Washington, DC: United States Institute for Peace Press, 2006), 104); see also Y. Dinstein, *War, Aggression and Self-Defence* (Cambridge: Cambridge University Press, 2011), paras. 901–8; Institute of International Law, resolution on 'Authorization of the Use of Force by the United Nations' of 9 September 2011, Art. 7: 'the General Assembly should exercise its competence under the "Uniting for Peace" resolution to *recommend* such measures as it deems appropriate' (my emphasis). According to the resolution's wording, recommendations to use force may only be made in the event of breaches of the peace or acts of aggression, not threats to the peace.

[27] M. Wood, 'Towards New Circumstances in which the Use of Force May Be Authorized? The Cases of Humanitarian Intervention, Counter-terrorism, and Weapons of Mass Destruction', in N. Blokker and N. Schrijver (eds.), *The Security Council and the Use of Force: Theory and Reality – A Need for Change?* (Leiden: Martinus Nijhoff, 2005), 75–90; M. Wood, lecture no. 3 entitled '*The UN Security Council and International Law*' (2006), available on the website of the Lauterpacht Centre for International Law, University of Cambridge.

[28] UN Doc. A/Res./60/1 (2005), para. 79. In this, they were following similar statements by the United Nations Secretary-General in his report *In Larger Freedom: Towards Development, Security and Human Rights for All* (UN Doc. A/59/2005 (2005)) and the

Of course, in a sense they did not have much choice in the matter. It is unrealistic to think of amending the relevant provisions of the Charter. But they were justified in what they said. Properly interpreted and applied, the rules on the use of force in the Charter and in customary international law are flexible enough to meet the new challenges, given the political will. And they are better than some proposals for new rules that would excessively relax existing constraints and potentially lead to international anarchy.[29]

The rules are to be found in the Charter of the United Nations and in customary international law. The Charter contains, among the Principles of the United Nations, a general prohibition of the threat or use of force (Article 2, paragraph 4). The Charter refers to two (not unrelated) circumstances in which the prohibition does not apply. First, forcible measures taken or authorized by the Security Council, acting under Chapter VII of the Charter. Second, the use of force in self-defence, recognized by Article 51 of the Charter (which may include the rescue of nationals abroad where the territorial state is unable or unwilling to take the necessary action). A possible, but controversial, third exception, not mentioned in the Charter but presumably to be found in customary international law, is the exceptional right to use force to avert an overwhelming humanitarian catastrophe. Other exceptions that have been suggested have received no support from states. The use of force in retaliation (as punishment, revenge or reprisals) is illegal. Nor is there any right to engage in extraterritorial law enforcement, such as the transboundary abduction of suspects.

As one author has explained, '[t]raditionally, there were no terrorism-specific rules in the law on non-intervention and non-use-of-force ... the factual phenomenon of terrorism has assisted in the clarification of the general law, but terrorism is just one manifestation or instantiation of non-State armed force to which the general legal principles apply'.[30]

The Council has authorized the use of force on many occasions.[31] Such authorizations have become so much part of the international

High-level Panel in its report *A More Secure World: Our Shared Responsibility* (UN Doc. A/59/565 (2004)).

29 M. Wood, 'The Law on the Use of Force: Current Challenges' (2007) 11 *Singapore Year Book of International Law* 1.

30 Saul, 'Emerging Law of International Terrorism' *Terrorism Documents*, lxxix–lxxxi.

31 Institute of International Law, Resolution 'Authorization of the Use of Force by the United Nations', 9 September 2011, Art. 1: 'Under Chapters VII and VIII of the Charter of the United Nations, the Security Council, without prejudice to its power to undertake

landscape that we often forget that they are for the most part relatively recent, and how hesitant the Council was in the early days, indeed until the end of the Cold War. One example from the Cold War era is Resolution 221(1966).[32] Since 1990, the Council, acting under Chapter VII or Chapter VIII of the Charter, has authorized the use of force by various 'coalitions of the willing' or regional arrangements or agencies (such as ECOWAS, AU and EU), including those led by the United States (Iraq in 1990/1, Somalia, and Haiti); by France (Operation Turquoise in Rwanda); by Italy (Operation Alba in Albania); by Australia (East Timor); and by the UK (in Afghanistan – ISAF later had other lead countries/organizations). It authorized the first-ever use of force by the North Atlantic Treaty Organization (Bosnia), and then again in Libya in 2011.

Non-forcible Council measures, such as sanctions and arms embargoes against non-state 'terrorist' groups, may help to tip the balance in an internal conflict in favour of the state, and may be an important contribution to resolution of conflict in one direction or other. But we are here concerned with the specific question of the use of force against terrorists taken or authorized under Chapter VII of the UN Charter. It is convenient to begin with self-defence. The Security Council's important functions in connection with the inherent right of individual and collective self-defence, recognized by Article 51 of the Charter, are sometimes overlooked. Under Article 51, the right of self-defence may be exercised only 'until the Security Council has taken measures necessary to maintain international peace and security'. Measures taken in self-defence 'shall be immediately reported to the Security Council'. Moreover, such measures 'shall not in any way affect the authority and responsibility of the Security Council under the present Charter to take such action as it deems necessary in order to maintain or restore international peace and security'. So the priority of action by the Security Council is clear from the Charter, even in situations of

peacekeeping and peace enforcement operations of its own, has the power to authorize Member States or regional arrangements or agencies to take all necessary measures, including the use of force, to maintain or restore international peace and security'; R. Vinuesa, 'Present Problems of the Use of Force in International Law: Authorization to Resort to Force Given by the United Nations' (2007) 73 *Yearbook of the Institute of International Law – Session of Naples* 233.

32 For other authorizations of interception at sea, see UN Doc. S/Res./665 (1990), UN Doc. S/Res./787 (1992) and UN Doc. S/Res./875 (1993). See also UN Doc. S/Res./1540 (2004) and UN Doc. S/Res./1874 (2009).

self-defence.[33] The extent to which the Security Council should have a role in regard to action in self-defence may give rise to controversy.

In its Resolutions 1368 (2001) of 12 September 2001 and 1373 (2001) of 28 September 2001, adopted in the immediate aftermath of 9/11, the Security Council reaffirmed the right of self-defence in the context of terrorist attacks. The third preambular paragraph of Resolution 1368 recognized 'the inherent right of individual or collective self-defence in accordance with the Charter', and the fourth preambular paragraph of Resolution 1373 (2001) reaffirmed 'the inherent right of individual or collective self-defence as recognized by the Charter of the United Nations as reiterated in resolution 1368 (2001)'.

Following the commencement of hostilities, the US and UK wrote to the President of the Security Council stating that the action was taken in accordance with the inherent right of individual and collective self-defence following the terrorist attacks on the United States of 11 September 2001, and they reported orally to the members of the Council on 8 October 2001. Following that meeting, the President of the Council issued a 'press statement on terrorist threats' recording that '[t]he permanent representatives made it clear that the military action that commenced on 7 October was taken in self-defence and directed at terrorists and those harbouring them' and that '[t]he members of the Council were appreciative of the presentation made by the United States and the United Kingdom'.[34]

Notwithstanding some brief and rather opaque, perhaps misunderstood, observations by the International Court of Justice in the *Wall* Advisory Opinion,[35] which were not much clarified in its judgment in the *DRC* v. *Uganda* case,[36] states and authors generally do not consider that the right of self-defence is unavailable in the face of large-scale terrorist attacks. They have found this conclusion confirmed by the reaffirmation of the right of self-defence in the aforementioned resolutions of the Council.[37]

33 According to Art. 51, the inherent right of self-defence exists until the SC takes the necessary measures to maintain or restore peace and security. It is not enough for the Council to consider an issue, or to adopt economic sanctions to terminate the right of self-defence, when military action is warranted.

34 SC press release, UN Doc. AFG/152, SC/7167 (2001).

35 *Legal Consequences of the Construction of a Wall in the Occupied Palestinian Territory*, Advisory Opinion of 9 July 2004 [2004] ICJ Rep. 136, 194.

36 *Armed Activities on the Territory of the Congo* (*Democratic Republic of the Congo* v. *Uganda*), Judgment of 19 December 2005 [2005] ICJ Rep. 168, 223.

37 See Chapter 11 in this volume; E. Wilmshurst, 'Chatham House Principles on Self-Defence' (2006) 55 *International & Comparative Law Quarterly* 936; T. Franck,

The use of force directly by the Security Council itself, using forces at its disposal, as originally envisaged by the Charter, is scarcely realistic today. Instead, the Council has developed the practice of authorizing others, able and willing to do so, to use force in specific circumstances. Such authorizations have taken many forms, ranging from what are essentially law-enforcement operations to authorizations to use force against states. So far such authorizations have not related to cases where the principal objective was to defeat terrorist groups. However, Council action in the field of non-proliferation and piracy demonstrates that the Council is ready to authorize a degree of forceful action against non-state actors in other circumstances, and there is no reason in principle why it should not do so in the counter-terrorism field.

4 The relationship between the Security Council and regional organizations

The relationship between the Security Council and regional organizations in the field of the use of force, including against non-state actors, is a matter of considerable debate. The possible *post factum* Council authorization of the use of force has arisen in particular in connection with regional organizations. The starting point is that states acting collectively within a regional, subregional or other organization have no greater right to use force than they have as individual states. It was not, for example, claimed that NATO, when it attacked the Federal Republic of Yugoslavia in 1999, had any right to use force over and above that of its member states.[38]

This basic legal position is reflected in Article 53 of the Charter, which provides that the Council may utilize regional organizations for enforcement action under its authority, but which goes on to provide that 'no enforcement action shall be taken under regional arrangements or by

'Terrorism and the Right of Self-Defence' (2001) 95 *American Journal of International Law* 839, 840. See also the Israeli Supreme Court judgment following the ICJ's *Wall* Advisory Opinion, in HCJ 7957/04 *Mar'abe* v. *Prime Minister of Israel*, Judgment of 15 September 2005, para. 23, at http://elyon1.court.gov.il/files_eng/04/570/079/a14/04079570.a14.pdf. I do not here discuss the question of imminent attacks and 'pre-emptive' action: see Chapter 12 in this volume.

[38] A possible, though controversial, exception to this is where the constituent instrument of the regional organization itself provides for armed intervention in the territory of a member state, as may now be the case with the African Union. This could be seen as consent to armed intervention, given in advance, and compared with (relatively uncontroversial) cases where the armed forces of one state enter the territory of another with its consent, for example to help maintain order or fight an insurrection.

regional agencies without the authorization of the Security Council'.[39] There have been a few cases where a regional or subregional organization has taken enforcement action without the prior authorization of the Council, and the Council has subsequently indicated its support.[40] This practice has led some to suggest that is sufficient, to comply with Article 53 of the Charter, if the Council's authorization for enforcement action by a regional organization is given after the event or at least after the use of force has commenced. Thus the Secretary-General's High-level Panel correctly stated that '[a]uthorization from the Security Council should in all cases be sought'. But it then went on to recognize 'that in some urgent cases that authorization may be sought after such operations have commenced'.[41] It is, perhaps, significant that this point was not taken up by the Secretary-General in his report *In Larger Freedom* or in the 2005 Summit Outcome Document. Council authorization may be sought, and if obtained it would presumably avoid the state concerned incurring responsibility for their unlawful act, but that is not the same as saying it becomes lawful.[42]

39 'Enforcement action' is not defined, though a similar expression – 'enforcement measures' – occurs in Art. 2, para. 7.

40 A case often referred to is the armed intervention by the Economic Community of West African States (ECOWAS), led by Nigeria, in Liberia in 1990. In a note by the President of the Security Council, issued on 22 January 1991, the Council commended 'the efforts made by the ECOWAS Heads of State and Government to promote peace and normalcy in Liberia' and called on all warring sides to cooperate with ECOWAS and the ceasefire signed under its auspices (UN Doc. S/22133 (1991)). These sentiments were later repeated in an additional note by the President of the Council (S/23886 of 1992) and Res. 788 of 19 November 1992.

41 Para. 272(a). The reference to *ex post facto* authorization was not repeated in the recommendations: see Annex I, recommendation 86(a). See also M. Matheson, *Council Unbound: The Growth of UN Decision Making on Conflict and Postconflict Issues after the Cold War* (Washington, DC: United States Institute for Peace Press, 2006), who suggests that '[e]xpress advance authorization is always preferable, but if the Council were to indicate clearly its acceptance of such regional intervention without formally authorizing it, the failure to obtain prior formal authorization would not seriously challenge to the Charter structure' (26). I doubt this is so even as a matter of policy; in any event, Matheson does not appear to be saying that such intervention would therefore be lawful. The notion of 'formal' authorization is, in fact, no clearer than that of 'express' authorization.

42 Compare the position under the law of state responsibility where a state consents after the event to an unlawful act, leading to the loss of the right to invoke responsibility but not to the lawfulness of the act: articles on state responsibility, commentary (3) to Art. 20. The taking of forcible measures with the ad hoc consent of the territorial state, or possibly with its consent given in advance pursuant to a treaty, as may be the case with

5 Recommendations

The Security Council has primary responsibility under the UN Charter for the maintenance of international peace and security. It has long described acts of terrorism as threats to international peace and security. It has adopted important and effective non-forcible measures, in particular financial and other sanctions, under Article 41 of the Charter. It also has an important potential role in combating terrorism by forcible means. Given the limits and uncertainties surrounding the right of self-defence, particularly against non-state actors, and given the political advantages for states, domestic and international, of acting with Security Council authority, states should be more ready than in the past to have recourse to the Security Council for authorization or endorsement of the use of force in the fight against terrorism.

The following recommendations are essentially on matters of policy, though to some degree that policy is 'legal policy'.

- Consideration should be given to enhancing the Security Council's role in respect of the use of force against terrorists, so as to develop multilateral approaches to the matter wherever possible. This is best done case-by-case, not by way of a general declaration (such as a Council presidential statement). There may of course be 'legitimacy' problems, given the difficulty of determining who is a terrorist, and the fact that the Council will inevitably act against some 'terrorists' but not others. But, given that it is a highly political body, selectivity is inevitable in the Council's actions and should not be seen as a reason for inaction.
- It should be recognized that Security Council authorization under Chapter VII is sometimes legally necessary (not in cases of self-defence, though even in the case of self-defence the Council has a role under the Charter).
- Security Council endorsement should be seen as politically desirable, even in cases of self-defence (and need not affect the right of self-defence). Measures taken with Security Council endorsement will usually have stronger domestic and international support, and for that reason should be more effective than if they are taken without such endorsement. A state contemplating the use of force against

the African Union, is not a true exception to the general prohibition, but may be of considerable practical importance. There is, however, a difficult question with, say, the African Union treaty, as to whether the Charter prohibition on the use of force may not prevail by virtue of Art. 103.

terrorists abroad should therefore normally first go to the Security Council, except when there is no time, or where the Security Council is manifestly unable to act. This would be desirable as a matter of policy, even if a state is considered to be legally acting in self-defence against non-state actors.

- Care is needed to ensure that regional organizations, such as the African Union, play an appropriate role in respect of any use of force against terrorist groups, one that does not undermine the Security Council's role under the Charter.

This chapter has sought to describe the important role that the Security Council has played in the fight against terrorism – both as regards law enforcement, where its involvement has become central, and as regards the use of armed force, which remains exceptional. Under the UN Charter, the Security Council has unique and important powers, granted to it by all the members of the United Nations, which have been – and surely will continue to be – used in the fight against terrorism. It is the only international body with the power to impose legal obligations on states that override their other international obligations. This happens routinely when the Council imposes sanctions. And it is the only body that can authorize states to use force which would otherwise be in violation of the prohibition on the use of force in international law. The Security Council is not perfect. It is criticized – and often rightly so – for failing to act, and less often for acting. But it is the central organ of the collective security system established by the UN Charter. It is a key instrument for multilateralism in a world where unilateralist pressures are all too great.

11

Self-defence against terrorists: the meaning of armed attack

STEVEN R. RATNER

1 Introduction

In light of the sporadic authorization of force by the Security Council for the maintenance of international peace and security, Article 51 becomes central to any consideration of the lawful use of military coercion against non-state actors deploying terrorist tactics. This chapter focuses principally on the threshold question of determining whether and which acts by terrorists constitute an armed attack that triggers the right of individual or collective self-defence under Article 51. Because the definition of an armed attack is linked to the question of which entity is responsible for the attack, the chapter also considers, though not exhaustively, the related question of the permissible target of self-defence measures. It will examine the current legal position, address the practical and legal challenges, and offer recommendations for the future. It is not meant to be an exhaustive treatment of the subject, which is now offered by a number of scholars cited in this chapter. This chapter will assume that the scope of permissible self-defence under contemporary international law is wholly determined by Article 51 and avoid debates, well addressed in Chapter 10, over the possibility of some broader right of self-defence independent of the Charter.

2 The current legal position

The first sentence of Article 51 reads, in English and French:

> Nothing in the present Charter shall impair the inherent right of individual or collective self-defence if an armed attack occurs against a Member of the United Nations, until the Security Council has taken measures necessary to maintain international peace and security.

> Aucune disposition de la présente Charte ne porte atteinte au droit naturel de légitime défense, individuelle ou collective, dans le cas où un Membre des Nations Unies est l'objet d'une agression armée, jusqu'à ce que le Conseil de sécurité ait pris les mesures nécessaires pour maintenir la paix et la sécurité internationales.

States have invoked the iconic language of Article 51 hundreds, if not thousands, of times to justify military action against other states and against non-state actors. Yet significant disagreements remain over the meaning of an armed attack, a term that has never been defined as such by any organ of the United Nations.[1] For purposes of determining the relevance of this term to acts by terrorist groups, five issues will be considered: (1) the source of the attack; (2) the target of the attack; (3) the scale of the attack; (4) the military nature of the attack; and (5) the attribution to states of the attack in so far as it affects the response of the attacked state.

2.1 *The source of the attack*

2.1.1 States vs. non-state actors

As repeatedly noted by states and scholars, the text of Article 51 does not limit armed attacks to actions carried out by states. States always understood that Article 51 applied to attacks by states, although they also knew that states could carry out armed attacks through the vehicle of non-state actors. Thus, the Definition of Aggression, which does not define armed attack per se but seems helpful in understanding its contours, refers to the 'sending by or on behalf of a state of armed bands, groups, irregulars or mercenaries' as acts that can amount to aggression (subject to a qualitative threshold discussed later).[2] In this sense, Article 51 has always included attacks by terrorist groups, but the assumption was that those acts were imputable to states.

Only recently have many states begun to grapple with the claim that attacks by non-state actors can constitute armed attacks *regardless of the role of a state*. The most authoritative pronouncement that states do consider terrorist acts as within the scope of Article 51 is the preambular

[1] As discussed further below, even the *Nicaragua* judgment itself does not offer a definition but rather an illustrative set of acts. See *Military and Paramilitary Activities in and against Nicaragua* (*Nicaragua* v. *United States of America*), Judgment of 27 June 1986 [1986] ICJ Rep. 14.

[2] UN Doc. A/Res./3314 (XXIX) (1974) [hereafter Definition of Aggression].

paragraphs of the unanimously passed Security Council Resolutions 1368 (12 September 2001) and 1373 (28 September 2001) ('Recognizing the inherent right of individual or collective self-defence in accordance with the Charter'). Both resolutions were specifically aimed at responding to a major terrorist incident carried out by a non-state actor, at a time when no state was asserting that the acts were carried out by any state (although the United States was already asserting that it would make no distinction between terrorists and the states that harbour them).[3] The references by states to 'attacks' by al-Qaeda – even if most of those attacks have not led to a use of military force – strongly suggests that it is now a settled interpretation of Article 51 that the term armed attack includes actions by non-state actors without a need to demonstrate attribution to a state.[4] International reactions to claims of self-defence against non-state actors in other situations since 2001, including by Turkey against PKK guerrillas operating from Iraq, by Russia against Chechen guerrillas operating from Georgia, and by Israel against Hezbollah guerrillas operating from Lebanon, point to, at a minimum, widespread acquiescence, and more likely acceptance, of the general claim that self-defence may be invoked in principle against such actors regardless of their ties to other states.[5] At the same time, some scholars resist this view, some more carefully than others.[6]

[3] George W. Bush, President, Address to the Nation on the Terrorist Attacks (11 September 2001), in 2001–1 *Pub. Papers of the Presidents* 1099, 1100 (2001).

[4] See, e.g., Organization of American States, *Convocation of the Twenty-Third Meeting of Consultation of Ministers of Foreign Affairs*, OAS Doc. OEA/Ser.G/CP/RES 796 (1293/01) (2001), at www.oas.org/consejo/resolutions/res796.asp; Lord Robertson, Statement Regarding NATO's Response to the September 11th Attacks (2001), at www.nato.int/docu/speech/2001/s011002a.htm.

[5] For reviews of state practice supporting this view, see C. J. Tams, 'The Use of Force Against Terrorists' (2010) 20 *European Journal of International Law* 359, 378–81; G. Wettberg, *The International Legality of Self-Defense against Non-State Actors: State Practice from the UN Charter to the Present* (Frankfurt am Main: Peter Land, 2007); T. Reinold, 'State Weakness, Irregular Warfare, and the Right of Self-Defense Post-9/11' (2011) 105 *American Journal of International Law* 244; R. van Steenberghe, 'Self-Defence in Response to Attacks by Non-state Actors in the Light of Recent State Practice: A Step Forward?' (2010) 23 *Leiden Journal of International Law* 183, 197–9. For other endorsements, see J. Lee, 'Terrorism Prevention and the Right of Preemptive Self-Defense' (2008) 1 *Journal of East Asia and International Law* 291, 300–1; N. Shah, *Self-Defense in Islamic and International Law: Assessing Al-Qaeda and the Invasion of Iraq* (Basingstoke: Palgrave Macmillan, 2008), 95–8.

[6] For the best argued (though, in my view, ultimately unconvincing) position, see T. Ruys, *'Armed Attack' and Article 51 of the UN Charter: Evolutions in Customary Law and*

The International Court of Justice (ICJ), for its part, has adopted a confusing approach to this question. In *Nicaragua* v. *United States* (1986),[7] it never considered the possibility that military activity by either the Frente Farabundo Martí para la Liberación Nacional (FMLN) (the Salvadoran guerrillas) or the contras was itself an armed attack, instead addressing whether those actions could either be imputed to, or were otherwise actions of, Nicaragua or the United States. In the *Wall Opinion* (2004),[8] the Court stated, with no argument, that 'Article 51 of the Charter thus recognizes the existence of an inherent right of self-defence in the case of armed attack by one State against another State', and found self-defence inapplicable in part because Israel did not allege that the acts were imputable to a foreign state.[9] And in *Armed Activities on the Territory of the Congo* (2005),[10] as pointed out by Judge Kooijmans, it offered two different positions on the question in two adjacent paragraphs – one stating, *per Nicaragua*, that attacks by armed groups could not trigger Article 51 because they were 'non-attributable to the DRC', and another stating instead that the Court would not address whether self-defence applies against 'large-scale attacks by irregular forces'.[11] It seems safe to say that the ICJ has at best shied away from this important question of contemporary international law and at worst clung to an antiquated understanding of an armed attack. The ICJ's view was notably rejected in 2011 by the Secretary-General's Panel of Inquiry on the Israeli attack on the Turkish flotilla near Gaza.[12]

Practice (Cambridge: Cambridge University Press, 2010), 486–9. For other critiques, see V. Kattan, 'The Use and Abuse of Self-Defence in International Law: The Israel–Hezbollah Conflict as a Case Study' (2005–6) 12 *Yearbook of Islamic and Middle Eastern Law* 31, 41–3; C. Antonopoulos, 'Force by Armed Groups as Armed Attack and the Broadening of Self-Defence' (2008) 50 *Netherlands International Law Review* 159, 169–71; S. Mahmoudi, 'Self-Defence and International Terrorism', in P. Walgren (ed.), *Perspectives on Jurisprudence: Essays in Honor of Jes Bjarup* (Stockholm: Stockholm Institute for International Law, 2005), 203.

[7] *Nicaragua*.

[8] *Legal Consequences of the Construction of a Wall in the Occupied Palestinian Territory*, Advisory Opinion [2004] ICJ Rep. 136.

[9] *Ibid.*, para. 139. For a forceful critique, see Sean D. Murphy, 'Self-Defense and the *Israeli Wall* Advisory Opinion: An *ipse dixit* from the ICJ?' (2005) 99 *American Journal of International Law* 62.

[10] *Armed Activities on the Territory of the Congo* (*Democratic Republic of the Congo* v. *Uganda*), Judgment of 19 December 2005, ICJ Rep. 168.

[11] *Ibid.*, paras. 146–7.

[12] Report of the Secretary-General's Panel of Inquiry on the 31 May 2010 Flotilla Incident, July 2011, Annex I, para. 41, 93, at http://graphics8.nytimes.com/packages/pdf/world/Palmer-Committee-Final-report.pdf.

2.1.2 Geographical source

Just as Article 51 does not require that an armed attack emanates from another state, it does not include a requirement regarding the geographic origin of the attack. Indeed, the Definition of Aggression includes as aggression actions by foreign forces stationed within a state without the consent of the latter state.[13] The reference to armed attack in the two post-11 September resolutions supports this presumption in light of various domestic aspects of those events, including the location of the airplanes, the residency of the terrorists, and the source of some of their training. As Sean Murphy has pointed out, this makes the ICJ's statement on this point in the *Israeli Wall Opinion* – that because 'the threat [cited by Israel to justify the barrier]. . . originates within, and not outside [Israeli] territory', Article 51 cannot apply – somewhat bizarre.[14]

At the same time, there does seem to be some sense in which states agree that an armed attack for purposes of Article 51 necessarily has some transnational element to it because of the very purpose of Article 51, which is to preserve or provide an authorization for a state to use military force against another state notwithstanding Article 2(4). Thus, it would be strange for states to invoke Article 51 in situations in which they have no intention to use force abroad. If, for instance, an organized crime syndicate planted a large bomb in a city of one state, with no proof whatsoever of foreign involvement, it would seem silly for the affected state to invoke Article 51. The 2006 Chatham House principles offer a possible compromise in requiring that an armed attack be 'directed from outside territory controlled by the State'.[15]

2.2 The target of the attack

The scope of the term 'against a Member of the United Nations' has led to significant debate over the years. One aspect, the limitation to UN members, is effectively moot, as all states are now UN members (although it does invite consideration of whether attacks on Taiwan or Palestine would be covered). The more important question remains

[13] Definition of Aggression, Art. 3(e).

[14] *Israeli Wall Opinion*, para. 139; Murphy, 'Self-Defense and the *Israeli Wall* Advisory Opinion', 68.

[15] E. Wilmshurst, 'The Chatham House Principles of International Law on the Use of Force in Self-Defence' (2006) 55 *International and Comparative Law Quarterly* 963, 965 [hereafter Chatham House principles].

whether Article 51 is limited to attacks on a state's territory. Here the accepted view is that Article 51 contains no such territorial limitation, although there remains disagreement on the non-territorial aspect of Article 51. The most significant evidence of at least some extraterritorial scope remains the Definition of Aggression, which lists 'an attack by the armed forces of a State on the land, sea or air forces, or marine and air fleets of another State'.[16] In the *Oil Platforms* case, for instance, the ICJ seems to have assumed that an armed attack on a US warship and a US-reflagged ship would both constitute an armed attack on the United States.[17]

Two interpretative questions remain critical. First, does Article 51's coverage of attacks on certain objects of the state beyond its territory extend to attacks on those objects by non-state actors? The Definition of Aggression addresses only attacks by another state's armed forces. Here, state practice is not extensive, as attacks on a state's assets outside its territory are infrequent. The United States apparently considered the attack on the *USS Cole* in Yemen in 2000 as a basis for its attacks on Afghanistan in October 2001. As a logical matter, the source (state against non-state) of the attack should not affect whether Article 51 addresses extraterritorial attacks (assuming, as discussed below, the extraterritorial attack is indeed directed against the state).

Second, what sorts of targets not on a state's territory are covered by the term armed attack in Article 51? There seems to be a consensus, seen in the Definition of Aggression excerpt above, that it includes a state's foreign military bases and fleets.[18] Moreover, it also seems clear that it does not include private property owned by nationals of the state, for Article 2(4) is meant to preclude the use of force for the protection of economic interests.[19] Far more contentious are the following categories: (1) diplomatic and consular missions; (2) ships and aircraft of the flag of the state; (3) individual nationals. State practice on these matters is unclear, and each is subject to significant academic disagreement.[20]

[16] Definition of Aggression, Art. 3(d).

[17] *Oil Platforms* (*Islamic Republic of Iran* v. *United States of America*), Judgment of 6 November 2003 [2003] ICJ Rep. 161, paras. 57, 72. For a useful critique, see D. Raab, '"Armed Attack" after the Oil Platforms Case' (2004) 17 *Leiden Journal of International Law* 719.

[18] See above n. 2; see also A. Randelzhofer, 'Article 51', in Bruno Simma (ed.), *The Charter of the United Nations: A Commentary* (Oxford: Oxford University Press, 2nd edn, 2002), 788, 797.

[19] *Oil Platforms*, para. 64 (attack on US-owned vessel is not an attack on the US).

[20] For a review of the positions, see Ruys, *'Armed Attack' and Article 51 of the UN Charter*, 199–249; Randelzhofer, 'Article 51', 798–9.

The United States specifically cited Article 51 in taking military action against Libya and Iraq after accusing them of trying to kill US nationals, although the targets had some official status (service members in one case, a former president in the other).[21] Given the likelihood that terrorists will not confine their attacks to the territory of a target state, clarification of these matters would be very helpful.[22]

2.3 *The scale of the attack*

Disagreements about the threshold of attack needed to trigger Article 51 are as old as the Charter itself, which mentions and ultimately proscribes three different categories of coercion – the use of force (Article 2(4)), aggression (Chapter VII) and armed attack (Article 51). On the initial question of whether an armed attack is limited to a particularly large use of force – creating a gap in the Charter that would prohibit self-defence against admittedly illegal uses of force – it is difficult to find contemporary state views on this question. Certainly the *Nicaragua* and *Oil Platforms* judgments endorse such a gap, as likely do the views of the majority of scholars until recently.[23] The United States has in the past rejected such a gap, arguing that any illegal use of force is an armed attack that triggers the right of self-defence.[24] The 2006 Chatham House principles also rejected the idea of any threshold of intensity.[25] It is safe to say that there is no consensus over this important question. (The related question of the timing of the attack and the response is addressed in Chapter 12 in this volume.)

21 M. Nash and M. Nash Leich (eds.), *Cumulative Digest of United States Practice in International Law 1981–1988* (Washington, DC: United States Government Printing, 1994), 3405; 'Raid on Baghdad: excerpts from UN Speech: the case for Clinton's strike', *New York Times*, 28 June 1993, at www.nytimes.com/1993/06/28/world/raid-on-baghdad-excerpts-from-un-speech-the-case-for-clinton-s-strike.html; see also A. D. Sofaer, 'Terrorism, the Law, and the National Defense' (1989) 126 *Military Law Review* 89.

22 For an interesting religious perspective, see A. Ghafar Hamid and K. Maung Sein, 'Islamic International Law and the Right of Self-Defense of States' (2009) 2 *Journal of East Asia and International Law* 67, 97–8.

23 *Nicaragua*, paras. 191, 210–11, 247–9; *Oil Platforms*, paras. 51, 64. For a rundown on scholarly views, see Randelzhofer, 'Article 51', 79–91. For an endorsement of greater flexibility based on state practice, see Tams, 'Use of Force Against Terrorists', 197–89. For a view that this goes so far as to include imminent threats, see K. Chainoglu, 'Reconceptualising Self-Defence in International Law' (2007) 18 *King's Law Journal* 61, 70–1.

24 See Sofaer, 'Terrorism, the Law'.

25 Chatham House principles, 966 (dismissing ICJ views as 'not generally accepted').

Compounding this difficulty is whether a different set of considerations should apply when the attack is carried out by non-state actors. Does the involvement by non-state actors increase the threshold at which an attack becomes an armed attack? Views can differ on this issue; the same Chatham House principles that reject a threshold of intensity for an armed attack note that the right of self-defence against terrorist attacks applies only when the attack is 'large-scale', defending this position with recourse to *Nicaragua*'s view that acts by an armed group on behalf of a state must be of such a gravity as to amount to an armed attack by regular forces.[26] But the ICJ took that test from the Definition of Aggression, which, when it discusses acts by armed bands, states that such acts are aggression 'of such gravity as to amount to the acts listed above',[27] meaning that such acts by terrorists need only have the *same* gravity as those by states, not a greater gravity, in order to be armed attacks. Thus, the absence of a requirement in Article 51 that an armed attack emanate from a state does not introduce a new scale requirement into the definition of armed attack (assuming one even exists at all) for attacks by non-state actors. Rather, whatever scale requirement might prevail should apply equally to attacks by states and non-state actors.

Assuming a scale requirement applies to Article 51, there is very little guidance from states as to its contours. *Nicaragua*'s test is to examine whether the attack, 'because of its scale and effects, would have been classified as an armed attack rather than as a mere frontier incident had it been carried out by regular armed forces'.[28] But this muddies the waters because some frontier incidents can be quite severe and would be the basis for claims of self-defence (e.g., between Eritrea and Ethiopia).[29] Even distinguishing based on whether people are killed is not sufficient, as this would exclude significant property damage in a cross-border raid. The precise threshold, should it exist, remains uncertain.

At the same time, some understanding has emerged in recent years on the important question of whether a series of relatively small cross-border

[26] *Ibid.*, 971. [27] Definition of Aggression, para. 3(g). [28] *Nicaragua*, para. 195.

[29] See, e.g., *Jus Ad Bellum* Claims Ethiopia's Claims 1–8 (*Ethiopia* v. *Eritrea*), Partial Award of 19 December 2005, paras. 16, 20, at www.pca-cpa.org/upload/files/FINAL%20ET%20JAB.pdf (classifying Eritrean actions as violations of 2(4) and armed attacks). For commentary, see C. Ponti, 'The Eritrea–Ethiopia Claims Commission on the Threat or the Use of Force and on Self-defence', in A. de Guttry *et al.* (eds.), *The 1998–2000 War Between Eritrea and Ethiopia: An International Legal Perspective* (The Hague: TMC Asser Institute, 2009), 267.

attacks over time can amount to an armed attack, known in the literature as the accumulation doctrine. Notably, the acquiescence of states to the claims of Israel, Turkey and Colombia to respond in self-defence after a relatively small single event, following a series of others, suggests significantly greater acceptance of that doctrine.[30] Even the ICJ stated, albeit backhandedly, in the *Oil Platforms* case that a series of attacks, none of which individually could amount to an armed attack, might together constitute an armed attack.[31]

2.4 *The military nature of the attack*

State expectations of Article 51 have always recognized that an armed attack involves the use of military force and not economic power, however devastating the effects of the latter on a target state. Thus, the Definition of Aggression – which arguably covers a broader set of acts than included in the notion of armed attack – refers only to 'armed force' and does not include the notion of so-called economic aggression.

Given the nature of most terrorist attacks today, this limitation has little practical impact. The one exception to this general statement would be in the area of cyber-terrorism, where terrorists using hacking and malicious software could wreak immediate and significant destruction on a victim state akin to that arising from an armed attack. These could include harm to a nation's air traffic control systems, nuclear safety systems, and electrical grid. Although states, international organizations, NGOs and scholars have addressed this issue for only about a decade, there is emerging support for the idea that some computer attacks are uses of force and indeed can also amount to armed attacks. This position has, for instance, received support from within the US Department of Defense.[32] The current treatment in governmental and scholarly circles

[30] See Tams, 'Use of Force Against Terrorists', 387–9; Reinold, 'State Weakness, Irregular Warfare', 271, 281, 284; van Steenberghe, 'Self-defence in Response to Attacks by Non-state Actors in the Light of Recent State Practice', 202; Shah, *Self-Defense in Islamic and International Law*, 98.

[31] *Oil Platforms*, para. 65.

[32] See M. Anderson and E. Zukauskas (eds.), *Operational Law Handbook* (Charlottesville, VA: United States Army, 2008), 146–7; see generally Office of General Counsel, US Department of Defense, *An Assessment of Legal Issues in Information Operations* (Washington, DC: Department of Defense, 1999).

focuses largely on the impact of the computer attack.[33] At the same time, writers recognize the special difficulties associated with attribution of such attacks and thus the consequences for invoking self-defence. The full range of state attitudes on this question remains unknown.

2.5 *Attribution of armed attacks and the targets of self-defence*

Beyond the definition of armed attack strictly, Article 51 leaves unanswered important questions regarding the lawful targets of self-defensive action. The assumption underlying Article 51 was always that the state(s) engaging in the armed attack – whether on their own or through non-state agents – would be the permissible target of self-defence. Recent self-defensive attacks in which terrorists are not agents of states clearly question this presumption. State practice is limited, principally to Israel (in Lebanon), the United States (in Afghanistan and elsewhere), Turkey (in Iraq), Russia (in Georgia) and Colombia (in Ecuador). These states appear to be making essentially one of *two distinct claims*: (1) a right to respond militarily against a state that has in some sense *harboured* – in the general sense of offering some positive support to or being complicit with – transnational terrorists; and (2) a right to attack terrorists and terrorist bases in other states *where the state has not harboured* terrorists. (I leave aside for now whether that self-defensive response can target only terrorist-related sites or may also target governmental facilities.)

2.5.1 Military responses against so-called harbouring states

The United States asserted this claim to justify its air strikes on Afghanistan and Sudan in August 1998 after the bombing of US embassies in Africa as well as its invasion of Afghanistan beginning in October 2001.[34] The US engaged in attacks not only against suspected al-Qaeda training areas, but against the state and government of Afghanistan

[33] See, e.g., M. N. Schmitt, 'Computer Network Attack and Use of Force in International Law: Thoughts on a Normative Framework' (1999) 37 *Columbia Journal of Transnational Law* 885; T. C. Wingfield, *The Law of Information Conflict: National Security Law in Cyberspace* (Falls Church, VA: Aegis Research Corp., 2000).

[34] See W. J. Clinton, Address to the Nation on Military Action Against Terrorist Sites in Afghanistan and Sudan (20 August 1998), in 1998 *Pub. Papers of the Presidents* 1460, 1461 ('[C]ountries that persistently host terrorists have no right to be safe havens'); US letter to the Security Council, 7 October 2001, UN Doc. S/2001/946 ('[T]he ongoing threat to the United States ... has been made possible by the decision of the Taliban regime to allow the parts of Afghanistan that it controls to be used by [al-Qaeda] as a base of operation').

itself, leading eventually to the government's fall. The claim appears to have been picked up by Israel in its invasion of Lebanon in 2006 and Colombia in its intervention in Ecuador in 2008. This claim could itself be interpreted in two ways:

- Under one view, it was a major departure from traditional views of state responsibility – the secondary rules of international law that address all violations of primary rules. The secondary rule had held that a state could only be responsible for the acts of non-state actors in very limited circumstances, e.g., if they were organs or agents of the state, whereas the United States was suggesting that a state was now responsible for illegal conduct if it facilitated, encouraged, or even simply tolerated the conduct.[35]
- Under a second view, the United States was advocating a new primary rule with respect to the law on the use of force. Rather than seeing the acts of the groups as imputed to the state, this view, which might itself be said to have two versions, either: (1) regards a state as having committed the armed attack by virtue of harbouring the terrorists, permitting a victim state to engage in self-defence against the state; or potentially (2) permits a state to engage in self-defence against a state even without regard to whether the state committed an armed attack.[36] Version (1) is at odds with *Nicaragua*, which had limited the use of force that triggers self-defence to the sending by a state of armed bands or a substantial involvement therein, and would extend the notion of armed attack to a state's offering terrorists safe haven. Version (2) is an even bolder claim, for although a state's harbouring of terrorists is clearly a violation of international law,[37] the Charter bans states from responding with force to most international law violations by another state, limiting the use of force to respond only to another state's armed attack against it.[38]

[35] International Law Commission, *Draft Articles on Responsibility of States for Internationally Wrongful Acts* (UN Doc. A/Res./56/83 (2001), Arts. 8–9, 11); see also S. R. Ratner, '*Jus ad bellum* and *jus in bello* after the Cold War' (2002) 96 *American Journal of International Law* 905.

[36] For endorsement of this view, see D. Jinks, 'State Responsibility for Sponsorship of Terrorist and Insurgent Groups: State Responsibility for the Acts of Private Armed Groups' (2003) 4 *Chicago Journal of International Law* 83; Randelzhofer, 'Article 51', 801.

[37] See, e.g., UN Doc. S/Res./1373 (2001); Declaration on Principles of International Law Concerning Friendly Relations and Co-operation Among States in Accordance with the Charter of the United Nations (UN Doc. A/Res./25/2625 (XXV) (1970), princ. 1, para. 9).

[38] On the question of primary vs. secondary rules, see Ruys, *'Armed Attack' and Article 51 of the UN Charter*, 489–93.

Global reactions to the US incursion in Afghanistan were generally positive or muted. This could suggest a significant degree of international endorsement of the US view about either a new primary rule or a new secondary rule.[39] However, ambiguities remain in determining international expectations, as states may not share a common meaning of the concept of harbouring. For some states, harbouring might well be tantamount to active support for the terrorists, whereas for others, it might be more akin to passive toleration of their activities. Christian Tams has suggested that current state attitudes suggest that attribution ought to apply when the state is complicit in terms of support or provision of haven, akin to the idea of aiding and abetting.[40]

2.5.2 Military responses against terrorist groups irrespective of host state so-called harbouring

The second claim, which extends beyond the Afghanistan context, has been made to justify the deployment of US military and CIA forces against suspected terrorists globally, as well as responses by other states against terrorist bases but not the apparatus of the state on which the terrorists operate, e.g., Turkey's attacks on Kurds in northern Iraq and Russia's raids into Georgia in 2002–3.[41] In the case of the United States, these uses of force have included targeted killings against suspected terrorists in Yemen, Pakistan and Syria since 2001.[42] The scope of the US claim to attack terrorists globally is somewhat unclear. The Legal Adviser to the State Department under the Bush Administration stated: '[A] state must prevent terrorists from using its territory as a base for launching attacks. As a legal matter, where a state is *unwilling or unable* to do so, it may be lawful for the targeted state to use military force in

39 See Ratner, '*Jus ad bellum* and *jus in bello*; Reinold, 'State Weakness, Irregular Warfare', 284–5. For a less definitive view, see Chatham House principles, 970 (right of victim state to take action against harbouring state is still 'questioned').

40 Tams, 'Use of Force Against Terrorists', 385–7 (addressing the targets of the self-defensive attack through the notions of necessity and proportionality).

41 See Reinold, 'State Weakness, Irregular Warfare', 252–7, 268–72. As discussed further in Wettberg, *International Legality of Self-Defense*, 141–9, Turkish strikes against Kurds in Iraq before 2003 were undertaken either with the consent of Saddam Hussein or, after 1991, when northern Iraq was beyond the control of Iraq's government due to the no-fly zone.

42 For a detailed elaboration of the Bush administration's legal view, see posting of J. Bellinger, Armed Conflict with Al Qaida?, Opinio Juris Blog, www.opiniojuris.org/2007/01/15/armed-conflict-with-al-qaida.

self-defence to address that threat.'[43] His successor under the Obama administration stated in 2010:

> Al Qaeda has not abandoned its intent to attack the United States, and indeed continues to attack us. Thus, in this ongoing armed conflict, the United States has the authority under international law . . . to use force, including lethal force, to defend itself, including by targeting persons such as high-level al Qaeda leaders who are planning attacks... [W]hether a particular individual will be targeted in a particular location will depend upon considerations specific to each case, including those related to the imminence of the threat, the sovereignty of the other states involved, and the *willingness and ability* of those states to suppress the threat the target poses.[44]

These legal arguments are distinct from the claim for attacking a state that has harboured terrorists, although from the perspective of the target state, it may be forgiven for not appreciating that an attack against terrorist bases on its territory is not actually an attack against the state.[45] The 'unwilling or unable' standard appears in doctrines as varied as espousal of international claims by states of nationality and complementarity of the International Criminal Court.[46] It is clearly a lower threshold of state involvement than that entailed in harbouring.

The extent of international endorsement of the 'unwilling or unable' theory is difficult to determine. Judges Kooijmans and Simma seemed to endorse at least part of this concept in their separate opinions in the *Armed Activities* case. They assert that if terrorist acts meeting the definition of armed attacks (by which they mean large-scale uses of force, endorsing the ICJ's position on scale) originate from parts of a state in which there is no governmental authority, then the victim of such attacks may respond in self-defence in that state.[47] The Chatham House principles endorse the 'unable or unwilling standard' as a basis for acting against terrorists in the territory of another state.[48] While this standard

[43] *Ibid.* (my emphasis).

[44] H. H. Koh, 'The Obama administration and international law', speech to the Annual Meeting of the American Society of International Law, 24 March 2010, at www.state.gov/s/l/releases/remarks/139119.htm (my emphasis).

[45] See generally S. R. Ratner, 'Predator and Prey: Seizing and Killing Suspected Terrorists Abroad' (2007) 15 *Journal of Political Philosophy* 251.

[46] 1998 Rome Statute for the International Criminal Court, 2187 UNTS 3, Art. 17.

[47] *Armed Activities*, para. 30 (Judge Kooijmans, Separate Opinion); *ibid.*, para. 12 (Judge Simma, Separate Opinion).

[48] Chatham House principles, 969. The phrase is 'unwilling or unable to deal with the non-state actors itself', without an explanation of what 'deal with' means. See also Ruys,

has great intuitive appeal, the result in practice has been, as Teresa Reinold has noted, 'that states are making indiscriminate use of the unwillingness and inability scenarios',[49] often claiming that target states are unwilling to prevent terrorism when they are actually unable to do so.

Whatever the scope of international endorsement, the parameters of each prong raise numerous interpretive questions. At what point is a state truly unable to stop terrorists from using it as a base for operations? This may seem like an easy question for so-called failed states, or states that fit in the model described by Judge Kooijmans above. But many states with fully functioning governments have not succeeded in preventing their territories from being used by terrorists despite bona fide criminal law enforcement and prevention efforts. Certainly Germany and Malaysia were unable to stop the 9/11 hijackers from carrying out key planning activities there. Nobody has seriously suggested that such states meet the 'unable' test, yet if one chooses to adopt such a test it becomes incumbent to identify the criteria for the inability of a state to prevent terrorists from using its soil for attacks. If states chose to act on this theory in situations where governments are merely weak or poor, it would clearly exacerbate interstate tensions.

Similarly, the standard of a state unwilling to act is also prone to interpretive disputes and ultimately abuse. States have numerous domestic priorities and financial limitations, so at what point can another state reasonably conclude that the state is unwilling to prevent terrorists from using it? Presumably this standard is lower than the harbouring standard for using self-defensive force against the state, but the same difficulties in determining harbouring arise with respect to determining unwillingness.

In the end, states will probably see it in their interest to limit the scope of the concepts of harbouring, inability and unwillingness. The notions of necessity and proportionality, a key part of *jus ad bellum* and the subject of Chapter 13, might provide guidance to them. The United States, which has served as the chief claimant of these ideas, has limited the argument to a very small number of states; and indeed in the case of Pakistan, it seems likely that the use of Predators for targeted killings has the acquiescence of the Pakistani government.[50]

'Armed Attack' and Article 51 of the UN Charter, 502–6 (proposing a standard of 'manifest and persistent unwillingness or inability to prevent non-state attacks').

49 Reinold, 'State Weakness, Irregular Warfare', 285.

50 See J. Mayer, 'The predator war', *New Yorker*, 26 October 2009.

3 Practical challenges and outstanding legal issues

The above review of current international expectations regarding the nature of an armed attack that triggers the right of self-defence and the consequences of that determination suggests important areas of agreement – most significantly on the non-limitation of armed attacks to attacks by states – as well as some significant interpretive differences.

3.1 Outstanding legal issues

The principal outstanding legal questions appear to be:

(1) Beyond attacks on the territory of a state and its military assets abroad (e.g., ships, aircraft and bases), what other kinds of attacks in terms of targets may be considered attacks against the state? Is the list of targets any different if the attack emanates from terrorists as opposed to other states?
(2) Must a terrorist attack achieve a certain scale in order to constitute an armed attack under Article 51? If so, what are the indicia of scale and are they any different from those for an attack by a state? How far should the accumulation doctrine extend?
(3) Under what circumstances might a computer-based attack on a state by terrorist groups amount to an armed attack under Article 51?
(4) What relationship between a terrorist group and a state on whose territory it conducts preparatory operations, in situations short of attribution of the state for the group's conduct, triggers the right of the victim of an armed attack by the group to respond in lawful self-defence against the *terrorist group alone*?
(5) What relationship between a terrorist group and a state on whose territory the group conducts preparatory operations, in situations short of attribution of the state for the group's conduct, triggers the right of the victim of an armed attack by the group to respond in lawful self-defence against the *government of the state*?

3.2 Practical challenges to determining an armed attack

If a state seeks to rely upon Article 51 to respond against an armed attack by terrorist groups, it will face a number of special practical impediments distinct from those that arise in the interstate context.

3.2.1 Locating the source of the attack

An act of transnational terrorism may take place in a few states or a large number. A simple scenario involves a group preparing in State A conducting attacks in State B. Even in that scenario, however, funds, equipment, and weapons will typically come from abroad – although the involvement of outside states as sources of funds or equipment does not seem to be regarded currently as triggering a right of self-defence against those states. Under a more complex scenario that has characterized some al-Qaeda operations, terrorists prepare in several states before launching the operation in the victim state. Tracing that preparation back to specific states will require sophisticated intelligence. Such knowledge may be relatively simple for rich states (or those sharing intelligence with them) to obtain. But it is likely to be far more difficult for a developing state to determine the source of a foreign terrorist attack. The 2008 Mumbai attacks and the rumours and confusion regarding the role of Pakistan highlight these challenges. And the problem of cyber-warfare multiplies these difficulties significantly.

3.2.2 The threshold question

In many situations of terrorism, a state may not need to consider whether a terrorist act or series of acts amounts to an armed attack because it has no intention or capacity to engage in any kind of self-defensive response. Other states, which wish to leave individual or collective self-defence on the table as a possible response, will need to make critical judgements as to whether the act(s) cross(es) the threshold to an armed attack. Indeed, because some states will not be considering military options, we are likely to witness situations where attacks of similar intensity are characterized differently by states, leading to even more practical uncertainty as to the attacks that trigger the right to self-defence under Article 51. And even if some criteria could be developed to answer question 2 above, such determinations will inevitably be greatly influenced by domestic politics.

3.2.3 Managing the attribution question

In each case of a transnational terrorist attack in which the victim state contemplates invoking Article 51, it will need to consider very carefully the role of foreign states in the particular attack. The exact relationship between the foreign government(s) and the terrorists will need to be parsed, as it may range from the former's powerlessness due to lack of control over territory, to inadequate financial resources to prevent the terrorists' operations, to a fear of antagonizing the group or its internal supporters, to various modes of active encouragement of the group, all the way up to sponsorship of the group. Once questions 4 and 5 above are answered, then the facts will determine the permissible legal options for the victim state.

In implementing these options, the victim state must guard against two contingencies, one before responding and one after. First, it will need to characterize carefully the relationship between the state and the terrorist group. The US administration offered NATO officials classified briefings on this matter in the fall of 2001, but it did not, at the time of the Afghanistan operation, offer a public brief on the exact relationship between al-Qaeda and the Taliban government of Afghanistan. Other states have fallen short in this regard as well. Gaining public support (more abroad than at home, where military action will typically prove popular) as well as convincing other states to join in the Article 51 action[51] will turn on the care of the presentation in its casting of blame beyond the terrorist group itself. Many of the condemnations of Israel's actions in Lebanon in 2006 accepted Israel's right of self-defence in principle to respond to the attacks by Hezbollah, but rejected the extension of the response to infrastructure of the Lebanese government in the absence of closer links between the government and Hezbollah.[52]

Second, if the victim state engages in military action against the terrorist bases or personnel alone, it will face the almost impossible task of convincing the government and population of the state where those bases or personnel are located that the military action is directed against the terrorist group and not the state. This predicament currently faces the United Sates with respect to drone flights over Pakistan and its raid that killed Osama bin Laden. The responding state will need to discriminate carefully between terrorist targets and other targets (which is not the same as the distinction in IHL as between military and civilian objects). The overriding principles of necessity and proportionality (as discussed in Chapter 13) will play a role here, but the political difficulties of convincing a state that it is not in fact the target of an attack will remain.

[51] I do not discuss here the ICJ's unsubstantiated view in *Nicaragua* and *Armed Activities*, that a state may not invoke collective self-defence unless it has publicly declared itself the victim of an armed attack.

[52] Reinold, 'State Weakness, Irregular Warfare', 264–8.

4 Recommendations

I now offer some brief suggestions with respect to the five sets of legal questions identified above. It is not an attempt to arrive at some kind of authoritative restatement of the law of the Charter regarding the notion of armed attacks by terrorists for two reasons. First, despite the significant global concern with transnational terrorism, most states, because they have not taken self-defensive actions against terrorists, do not have clear views about the questions identified earlier. If they have taken any actions against terrorists abroad, they may still lack a clear legal position. Even the United States, which has addressed the issue most directly, has still left many issues undecided. Thus it is impossible to offer a restatement of the law. Second, with a view to fostering dialogue and derive useful recommendations for governments, a descriptive exercise is far less useful than an overtly prescriptive one. Indeed, if we were to assume against the facts that there were some consensus on the numerous issues identified above, that consensus might well be antiquated and not prepared to respond to modern terrorist threats.

4.1 *Question 1: Targets of attacks*

Beyond the clear cases of attacks on a state's territory and armed forces, terrorist attacks against a state's diplomatic and consular properties and personnel should be considered an armed attack on a state. Terrorist attacks on vessels or persons with a state's nationality alone should generally not be considered armed attacks on the state, although it is worth discussing whether to classify such acts as armed attacks if they were based solely on the vessel's or person's nationality. The problem with this test is that international responsibility does not typically turn on the mental state of the perpetrator (genocide is one exception), and it seems odd to introduce a mental state for attacks on some targets but not others.[53]

4.2 *Question 2: Scale and their indicia*

For terrorist action attributable to states under generally accepted notions of state responsibility, the current position, which lacks a

[53] The Chatham House principles talk of an 'intention and capability to attack', for all attacks, 965, but this does not address whether the attack is based on the nationality of the target.

threshold requirement, should be maintained. The issue is more difficult with respect to action that lacks such attribution. On the one hand, a strong argument remains that Article 51 should be interpreted to lack a requirement of scale for an armed attack by any terrorists, regardless of state involvement. Such a requirement is impossible to devise, and it is unreasonable to expect state compliance with it. The term large scale is very vague and subject to manipulation. Is a suicide bomb in London that kills ten people large scale? What if it kills one person? What if it only destroys a building? The same inadequacies of the concept in the case of state-sponsored terrorism apply here. As for the argument that the absence of a scale requirement will trigger abuse and hasty recourses to armed force abroad, these possibilities for abuse can be addressed through self-interested restraint (states will not use military resources against de minimus attacks) and the concepts of necessity and proportionality.

At the same time, I recognize, and ultimately endorse, the position taken in the *Leiden Policy Recommendations* that Article 51 'should be read to require that the attack be large-scale' in the case of terrorism not attributable to states. The position adopted is acceptable for two reasons. First, as a matter of form, it is modest in its choice of words, not purporting to describe a clearly accepted *lex lata* but rather the best position from a policy-oriented perspective on an issue on which there is still disagreement. Second, in terms of the substantive policy choice made in including the requirement, I agree that the absence of attribution means that the public order consequences of a self-defensive response – and the harm that ultimately results to the target state – counsel against permitting armed responses unless the attack meets a high threshold. Moreover, the recognition in the same paragraph that multiple small-scale activities can together constitute a large-scale activity means that, at a certain point, the target state can react to the failure of the host state to prevent small-scale actions.

Nevertheless, the position has shortcomings (in addition to those arguments above used to endorse the absence of a requirement). In situations short of attribution to the state, the state may be unable to stop terrorists; it may choose not to try to stop them; or it may even be somewhat complicit in their actions. Yet the position of the *Leiden Recommendations* prohibits self-defence after small- or medium-scale attacks by terrorists with active or passive assistance from the state. This, I suppose, is the price to pay for avoiding self-defensive action that will likely harm the host state and not merely the terrorists operating on its soil.

4.3 Question 3: Computer-based attacks

Any computer attack that causes damage akin to that caused by a military attack should be regarded as an armed attack. Immediate destruction of life is not a prerequisite.

4.4 Questions 4 and 5: Criteria for self-defence against the terrorist groups and against the state on whose territory terrorists operate where those acts are not attributable to the state

In situations where the activities of the terrorist group cannot be attributed to the state, the *Leiden Recommendations* end up relying upon the notions of necessity and proportionality inherent in Article 51 to determine the scope of the self-defensive response.[54] Utilization of these principles to identify the acceptable targets of the self-defence action fits well into accepted doctrine. However, because these principles are somewhat vague in theory and hard to enforce in practice, it is still useful to consider how the notions of necessity and proportionality should play out with respect to the two key targets identified earlier, i.e., the group itself and the state on which it operates.

- If the terrorist group undertook active training in a state, then the victim state may use force against terrorist groups in that state. In these cases, the victim state may not respond against other targets in the state (Scenario 1). The victim state may not use force against the terrorist group in that state if the group was engaged in actions short of training, such as fundraising or arms purchases, in that state.
- If the state from which the terrorist group operates actively enables the group to work on its territory such that, absent that affirmative action by the state, the group could not operate, then the victim state may respond in self-defence against that state, and not merely against the terrorist groups. Such action by the target state includes provision to the group of bases and other real property, logistical and infrastructural support, travel documentation, licences to receive and operate weapons, etc. The state's involvement does not have to cross the line to the organization and sponsorship of the terrorist group in order for the state to be the target of the self-defensive measure. The *Leiden*

[54] See generally Tams, 'Use of Force Against Terrorists'; Reinold, 'State Weakness, Irregular Warfare', 5.

Recommendations endorse a similar position in paragraph 43 (Scenario 2).

- In both scenarios, the victim state of a terrorist attack must exhaust all reasonable possibilities to persuade and assist the state to terminate the terrorists' activities itself before engaging in self-defence. However, reasonableness regarding exhaustion will differ between the two scenarios above – if the victim state can demonstrate the close relationship in the second scenario, it would not need to wait as long as in the first scenario before using force. In addition, reasonableness will depend upon the urgency of the situation, e.g., if the victim state knows that future attacks are imminent, it will not need to wait long to act in self-defence if the state does not terminate the terrorists' activities.
- In carrying out self-defensive actions, in scenario 1, the victim state must scrupulously limit its deployment of force to the terrorist targets; in case of doubt as to the status of the target, it should be presumed to belong to the state and not the terrorist group. To avoid casualties to civilians in the state (which is, after all, not the target of the attack in Scenario 1), a very high standard should obtain with respect to collateral damage, one stricter than the proportionality test in Article 51(5)(b) of Additional Protocol I.

5 Future steps

With the publication and dissemination of the *Leiden Recommendations*, further work on the scope of an armed attack could take place on several fronts. One prong could be *inductive*, describing scenarios in which an attack by terrorist groups should or should not give rise to self-defence under Article 51. Such a list of scenarios could include both actual scenarios, in which the claim to self-defence was generally accepted or generally rejected by international actors; as well as a series of hypothetical scenarios. In each case, a legal argument for accepting or rejecting the claim should be offered in as much detail as possible (especially if, in the case of actual scenarios, international actors did not themselves offer detailed legal justifications). This process would give a sense of the best – and suboptimal – practices to invoking Article 51.

A complementary strategy is that begun with the *Leiden Recommendations*, which would entail a set of *legal principles* fleshing out in some detail the issues raised in this chapter. These principles could be expanded or operationalized through the preparation of a *checklist of questions* that will require satisfactory answers before a state engages in self-defence. These questions could even be directed to different agencies of a government, e.g., defence, intelligence, foreign affairs. This would provide a template for policy considerations. Over time, the *Leiden Recommendations*, along with the template, could form the basis for more formal prescription of law and policy within governments, regional organizations, and the United Nations. A Security Council resolution could incorporate some of its insights; so could an opinion of the International Court of Justice should it be willing to assume its responsibilities in this area.

12

Anticipatory self-defence against terrorists

ELIZABETH S. WILMSHURST

1 Introduction

In the years since 9/11 existing interpretations of international law have been challenged as a result of military measures taken in response to terrorism. The law on the right to use force in self-defence is at the heart of the international legal regulation of military force but its interpretation and application have come into question in the light of counter-terrorism measures taken by states.

The question whether the right of self-defence may lawfully be exercised in anticipation of an armed attack is a controversial issue even outside the terrorism context, although there the controversy may be more in the theory than in the practice. But the doctrine of anticipatory self-defence is particularly difficult to apply in relation to military measures taken against terrorist attacks. This chapter considers whether the law in this area is undergoing a process of change, as some writers assert.[1]

The chapter first summarizes the arguments as to whether international law allows to states a right of anticipatory self-defence against attacks and threats from other states, and then examines the exercise of the right in response to threats by non-state actors operating from outside the victim state.

[1] See, e.g., T. Reinold 'State Weakness, Irregular Warfare, and the Right to Self-Defense post-9/11' (2011) 105 *American Journal of International Law* 244, 245: the writer states that a process of transformation of the law is clearly indicated by state practice, visible 'in States' changed interpretations of the principles of immediacy and necessity, which are nowadays understood in more contextualized and permissive terms'. And in the view of C. J. Tams, 'in the course of two decades the legal rules governing the use of force have been re-adjusted so as to permit forcible responses against terrorism under more lenient conditions' ('The Use of Force against Terrorists' (2009) 20 *European Journal of International Law* 359, 361).

2 Anticipatory self-defence

There is a long-standing controversy over whether the use of force by one state against an anticipated, as opposed to an ongoing, attack by another state is permissible under international law. Arguments that force may be used where an attack is imminent but has not yet begun rely on pre-existing customary law or refer to state practice in interpreting Article 51. They also point out the impracticability of having to await an attack before defence is permitted, and the implausibility of states having accepted that the Charter could have imposed such a limitation on their actions. Other commentators rely on the wording of Article 51, which preserves the right of self-defence 'if an armed attack occurs', to maintain that the use of force is not lawful, without Security Council authorization, to prevent an attack before it has begun. They deny the continued relevance of pre-existing customary law, and stress the need to accept the 1945 revolution in favour of *collective* action for the maintenance of international peace and security; they point to the prospects for abuse of anticipatory self-defence since there is no possibility of testing the reality of its need when no attack has taken place.[2]

The debate is sometimes clouded by different usages of the terms 'anticipatory', 'preventive' or 'pre-emptive' defence.[3] In the sense employed here, 'anticipatory self-defence' refers to the use of defensive force necessary to avert an attack which is imminent but has not yet begun. Assertion of a right to use 'pre-emptive' force, on the other hand, does not acknowledge the need for an imminent threat of attack and assumes the right to act before a threat has crystallized. In his 2003 State of the Union address, for example, President Bush stated '[s]ome have said we must not act until the threat is imminent. Since when have terrorists and tyrants announced their intentions, politely putting us on notice before they strike? If this threat is permitted to fully and

[2] For classic expressions of views opposing a right of anticipatory defence, see I. Brownlie, *International Law and the Use of Force by States* (Oxford: Oxford University Press, 1963), 275–8; B. Simma *et al.* (eds.) *The Charter of the United Nations: A Commentary* (Oxford: Oxford University Press, 2002), vol. I, 803. For the contrary view, see e.g. H. Waldock 'The Regulation of the Use of Force by Individual States in International Law' (1952) 81 *Recueil des cours L'Académie de Droit International de la Haye*, vol. II, 455, 495–505; C. Greenwood, 'International Law and the United States' Air Operation against Libya' (1987) 89 *West Virginia Law Review* 933, 942.

[3] The terms 'pre-emptive' and 'anticipatory' are used interchangeably by some commentators, for example in A. Sofaer, 'On the Necessity of Pre-emption' (2003) 14 *European Journal of International Law* 209, 214.

suddenly emerge, all actions, all words, and all recriminations would come too late.'[4] Outside the US the Bush doctrine has had little or no support from states or commentators, and is widely rejected as impermissible under international law.[5]

Governments have expressed differing views on anticipatory self-defence. One discussion of the use of force in an intergovernmental forum illustrates the controversy. The UN High-level Panel's report *A More Secure World: Our Shared Responsibility* (A/59/565) and the Secretary-General's Report *In Larger Freedom: Towards Development, Security and Human Rights for All* both affirmed that the right of self-defence extends to the case of an imminent attack.[6] But when the General Assembly came to debate *In Larger Freedom* in April 2005, a large number of government statements denied a right of anticipatory self-defence.[7] General Assembly Resolution 60/1 (the 2005 World Summit Outcome) did not mention the issue. As an expression (or non-expression) of government views this is interesting, but what is said in such a forum is not always reflected in practice or in responses to other states' practice. There is some indication of development in state practice towards an acceptance of anticipatory defence, expressed in publicly stated views.[8]

The International Court of Justice has not clarified the issue. The Court expressly left open the issue of the lawfulness of a response to

[4] Keesing's Record of World Events, vol. XLIX, January, 2003 International, 45178, 45181. The 2002 National Security Strategy of the United States of America (White House, September 2002) is also often quoted in this connection, though it did not make the point so starkly.

[5] See e.g. the statement by the UK's Foreign Secretary, Foreign Affairs Committee, Foreign Policy Aspects of the War against Terrorism, Session 2002–3 Cm 5793, 8; *In Larger Freedom*, UN Doc. A/59/2005 (2005) paras. 188–92; C. Gray 'The US National Security Strategy and the New "Bush Doctrine" on Pre-emptive Self-Defence' (2002) 1 *Chinese Journal of International Law* 437; C. Greenwood 'International Law and the Pre-emptive Use of Force: Afghanistan, al-Qaeda and Iraq' (2003) 4 *San Diego International Law Journal* 7. For support within the US, see, e.g., R. Wedgwood, 'The Fall of Saddam Hussein: Security Council Mandates and Preemptive Self-Defense' (2003) 97 *American Journal of International Law* 576, 582–5.

[6] *Ibid.*, *In Larger Freedom*, paras. 188 and 124, respectively.

[7] See C. Gray, 'A Crisis of Legitimacy for the UN Collective Security System?' (2007) 56 *International and Comparative Law Quarterly* 157, 163–4.

[8] See, for example, statements of Germany, the Netherlands and Russia, quoted in M. Wood 'Towards New Circumstances in Which the Use of Force May Be Authorized? The Cases of Humanitarian Intervention, Counter-Terrorism and Weapons of Mass Destruction', in N. Blokker and N. Schrijver (eds.), *The Security Council and the Use of Force* (Leiden: Martinus Nijhoff, 2005), 75, 81.

the threat of an imminent armed attack in the *Nicaragua* case[9] and in the *Armed Activities* case.[10]

In any event, the opposing views do not produce practical outcomes which differ as much as might be expected. Some who deny a right of anticipatory self-defence give an expansive interpretation to the phrase 'armed attack' in Article 51, thus accepting as permissible the use of force to prevent an attack which has not actually begun but which has been planned and prepared for, and where there is an intention to launch it imminently.[11] Other commentators characterize as 'classic' self-defence the use of force to prevent *further* attacks once there has been an attack from a particular source. This was indeed the situation in the *Caroline* incident in 1837. But others consider *Caroline* to be an example of anticipatory self-defence since it concerned an attack which was still threatened.

The debate has been continuing for so long that there is little more to add to it on either side. For this writer, state practice and a contextual approach both lead to an interpretation of Article 51 wide enough to read 'armed attack' as encompassing an imminent attack. The robust words of Professor Bowett writing in 1972 are just as valid today: 'the rejection of an anticipatory right is, in this day and age, totally unrealistic and inconsistent with general State practice.'[12] The reasoning given by Dame Higgins, formerly President of the International Court of Justice, holds good:

> In a nuclear age, common sense cannot require one to interpret an ambiguous provision in a text in a way that requires a state passively to accept its fate before it can defend itself. And, even in the face of conventional warfare, this would also seem the only realistic interpretation of the contemporary right of self-defence. It is the potentially devastating consequences of prohibiting self-defence unless an armed attack has already

[9] *Military and Paramilitary Activities in and against Nicaragua* (*Nicaragua* v. *United States of America*), Judgment of 27 June 1986 [1986] ICJ Rep. 14, para. 194 ('the issue of the lawfulness of a response to the imminent threat of armed attack has not been raised. Accordingly, the Court expresses no view on that issue').

[10] *Armed Activities on the Territory of the Congo* (*Democratic Republic of the Congo* v. *Uganda*), Judgment of 19 December 2005 [2005] ICJ Rep. 168, para. 143.

[11] See, for example, the 'interceptive self-defence' discussed by Y. Dinstein, *War, Aggression and Self-Defence* (Cambridge: Cambridge University Press, 2005): an armed attack has begun when the 'other side has committed itself to an armed attack in an ostensibly irrevocable way' (191).

[12] D. Bowett, 'Reprisals Involving Recourse to Armed Force' (1972) 66 *American Journal of International Law* 1, 4.

> occurred that leads one to prefer this interpretation – although it has to be said that, as a matter of simple construction of the words alone, another conclusion might be reached.[13]

Anticipatory self-defence is permissible however only if confined by the requirements of necessity, imminence, and proportionality. The formulation of the conditions following the *Caroline* incident, although dating from an earlier era, is still valid. The conditions are taken from the letter of US Secretary of State Webster, who specified that a government using force had to 'show a necessity of self-defence, instant, overwhelming, leaving no choice of means, and no moment of deliberation' and the military action must not be 'unreasonable or excessive, since the act, justified by the necessity of self-defence, must be limited by that necessity, and kept clearly within it'.

The requirements of necessity and proportionality are discussed elsewhere in this volume.[14] As summarized in the Chatham House principles, the criterion of necessity requires that

> [f]orce may be used in self-defence only when this is necessary to bring an attack to an end, or to avert an imminent attack. There must be no practical alternative to the proposed use of force that is likely to be effective in ending or averting the attack. . .Thus, all peaceful means of ending or averting the attack must have been exhausted or be unavailable.

The criterion of proportionality requires that the force used must not be excessive in relation to the need to avert the attack but since 'the right of self-defence does not allow the use of force to punish an aggressor, proportionality should not be thought to refer to parity between a response and the harm already suffered from an attack, as this could either turn the concept of self-defence into a justification for retributive force, or limit the use of force to less than what is necessary to repel the attack.'[15]

[13] R. Higgins, *Problems and Process: International Law and How We Use It* (Oxford: Oxford University Press, 1994), 242.

[14] See Chapter 13 in this volume.

[15] 'The Chatham House Principles of International Law on the Use of Force in Self-Defence' (2006) 55 *International and Comparative Law Quarterly* 963, 966 and 968. The principles were drawn up as a result of a study undertaken by Chatham House in 2004/5 with participation by a group of international law academics and practitioners and international relations scholars in the UK.

2.1 Imminence

It is a crucial condition for the lawful exercise of anticipatory self-defence that a state may use force against a threatened attack only if that attack is 'imminent'. The criterion of imminence requires that any delay in countering the intended attack will result in the inability of the defending state effectively to defend against or avert the attack. It must be necessary to act before it is too late.

Because of this close relationship between necessity and imminence it has been argued by Professor Tams (Chapter 13 in this volume) that an immediacy criterion does not act as a restraint additional to necessity and can be dispensed with.[16] The criterion can indeed be seen as an aspect of necessity, inasmuch as it requires that there be no time to pursue non-forcible measures with a reasonable chance of averting or stopping the attack; hence the necessity of armed measures. Used in an expansive manner, the criterion of necessity can be seen to address all the questions about the legality of use of force in self-defence, including questions of proportionality and imminence: it responds to the question whether a particular military action, at this time, in this place and with exactly this scope and extent is necessary to avert or put an end to this particular attack.[17] It is, however, useful to consider the temporal element separately from necessity; it is a defining part of anticipatory self-defence and it emphasizes that the use of force before an attack has begun is exceptional and requires a high level of justification. The criterion of imminence may also serve to distinguish self-defence from (illegal) reprisal for an attack that has gone before. It is thus that it has traditionally been regarded and it is one of the criteria used by those governments which accept the right of anticipatory self-defence.[18]

The application of the criterion is not easy. The *Caroline* formulation appears a little exaggerated. And it is to be hoped that there will indeed be a 'moment of deliberation' before military measures are undertaken. To quote again from the Chatham House principles,

> the criterion of imminence must be interpreted so as to take into account current kinds of threat and it must be applied having regard to the particular circumstances of each case...

[16] See Chapter 13 in this volume (section 2.2.3).

[17] Though Tams argues that the criterion of necessity is narrower, and does not overlap with proportionality (see Chapter 13, section 2.1 of this volume).

[18] For the UK, see, e.g., statement of the Attorney General below n. 37.

- Force may be used only when any further delay would result in an inability by the threatened State effectively to defend against or avert the attack against it.
- In assessing the imminence of the attack, reference may be made to the gravity of the attack, the capability of the attacker, and the nature of the threat, for example if the attack is likely to come without warning.
- Force may be used only on a proper factual basis and after a good faith assessment of the facts.

There must exist a circumstance of irreversible emergency. Whether the attack is 'imminent' depends upon the nature of the threat and the possibility of dealing effectively with it at any given stage.[19]

There have been attempts to stretch the criterion. For example, it has been argued 'that there may be some advantage to the development of a new concept of "catastrophic threat", or more properly, the "threat of catastrophic attack". Faced with a threat of attack of this kind, it would . . . be appropriate to begin to think beyond imminence to reasonable foreseeability, *i.e.*, away from temporal notions of threat and towards action required to neutralize the risk of catastrophic harm.'[20] But such approaches fail to recognize the extent to which the doctrine of anticipatory self-defence is itself considered controversial. Military action in these circumstances is at the limit of an already exceptional legal category, and the criterion of imminence requires a correspondingly high level of justification. As Professor Franck said, 'The problem with recourse to anticipatory self-defence is its ambiguity. In the right circumstances, it can be a prescient measure that, at low cost, extinguishes the fuse of a powder keg. In the wrong circumstances, it can cause the very calamity it anticipates.'[21]

3 Anticipatory self-defence against non-state actors in the territory of another state: military measures in response to terrorist attacks

3.1 Threats from non-state actors

Before considering the right to use *anticipatory* measures to avert terrorist attacks, the question must be addressed of the circumstances in

[19] 'Chatham House Principles', 967–8.

[20] D. Bethlehem (before becoming FCO Legal Adviser) in evidence before the UK House of Commons Foreign Affairs Select Committee.

[21] T. Franck, *Recourse to Force: State Action against Threats and Armed Attacks* (Cambridge: Cambridge University Press, 2002), 107.

which *any* measures against non-state actors in other states are legally justifiable. While there is wide agreement that large-scale acts of terrorism by private groups which are attributable to the state from which they operate – the territorial state – can give rise to the right of self-defence by another state,[22] opinions are divided on whether there has to be attribution to the territorial state before the right can be exercised against the groups in that state.[23]

Thus, in relation to the operations of al-Qaeda in 2001, the issue for many governments and commentators at the time was whether the acts were attributable to the Taliban regime, such that the latter became responsible for those acts.[24] For those who questioned whether the evidence showed that the Taliban regime was indeed responsible, Operation Enduring Freedom was unlawful either in whole or in part.[25]

To take an example from another region, Israel's claims to legal justification for its armed responses to attacks by groups in neighbouring countries have been generally based on some form of responsibility by

[22] See, e.g., A. Randelzhofer 'On Article 51', 802, paras. 34–6.

[23] For some of the extensive literature, see C. Greenwood, 'International Law and the "War on Terrorism"' (2002) 78 *International Affairs* 301; S. Murphy, 'Self-Defence and the *Israeli Wall* Advisory Opinion: An *ipse dixit*' (2005) 99 *American Journal of International Law* 62; Dinstein *War, Aggression and Self-Defence*; T. Franck, 'Editorial Comments: Terrorism and the Right of Self-Defence' (2001) 94 *American Journal of International Law* 839; D. Brown, 'Use of Force against Terrorism after September 11th: State Responsibility, Self-Defence and Other Responses' (2003) 11 *Cardozo Journal of International and Comparative Law* 1; C. Stahn, 'Terrorist Acts as "Armed Attack": The Right to Self-Defense, Article 51 (1/2) of the UN Charter, and International Terrorism' (2003) 27 *Fletcher Forum World Affairs* 35. For arguments against a right against non-state actors, see A. Cassese, 'Terrorism Is Also Disrupting Some Crucial Legal Categories in International Law' (2001) 12 *European Journal of International Law* 993.

[24] See, e.g., letter of 7 October 2001 from the United Kingdom to the President of the Security Council, UN Doc. S/2001/947 (2001): 'This military action ... is directed against Usama Bin Laden's Al-Qaeda terrorist organization and the Taliban regime that is supporting it.' See also H. Duffy, *The War on Terror and the Framework of International Law* (Cambridge: Cambridge University Press, 2005), 48. The position requiring attribution is put clearly in G. Travalio and J. Altenburg, 'State Responsibility for Sponsorship of Terrorist and Insurgent Groups: Terrorism, State Responsibility, and the Use of Military Force' (2003) 4 *Chicago Journal of International Law* 97: 'Because an attack against the terrorists violates the territorial integrity of the host state, the "armed attack" of the terrorists must be attributable to that state. Only then can force be used against the terrorists in that state or against the forces of that state itself' (102).

[25] See, e.g., discussion by J. Paust in 'Use of Armed Force against Terrorists in Afghanistan, Iraq, and Beyond' (2002) 35 *Cornell International Law Journal* 533.

those countries. Thus Israel defended its launch of guided missiles in Syria in October 2003 on the basis that Syria had encouraged, harboured and offered support to terrorist organizations, and that the missiles represented an act of self-defence against terrorist training facilities in Syria to 'prevent further armed offences against Israeli civilians in which Syria is complicit'.[26] The 'Second Lebanon War' in 2006 was another instance where Israel, in at least some of its official statements, held the territorial state, Lebanon, responsible for not stopping the attacks by Hezbollah.[27]

The debate about the extent of responsibility by the territorial state often revolves around discussion of what the rules of attribution are or should be.[28] But state practice – or at least the practice of some states – appears to be developing towards a view that it is neither necessary nor relevant to prove attribution, in whatever form, of the conduct of the non-state actor to the territorial state. While foreign affairs legal advisers have not generally given detailed analyses of the legal positions taken by their respective governments, there is some support for the proposition that action against non-state actors in other states' territory is lawful when the territorial state is 'unwilling or unable' to prevent the attack.[29] While this formulation does refer to a link with the territorial state, it does not provide a justification in terms of state responsibility for the violation of the state's sovereignty or territorial integrity. It relies instead on the notion that if it is necessary to use force in self-defence, Article 51 provides an exception to the prohibition in Article 2(4) vis-à-vis *any* state which may be involved or affected. The same notion supports the

[26] UN Doc. S/PV.4836 (2003). Many of the speakers in the SC debate which followed condemned Israel's action as a breach of international law.

[27] See, e.g., identical letters dated 12 July 2006 from the Permanent Representative of Israel to the United Nations addressed to the Secretary-General and the President of the Security Council (UN Docs. A/60/937-S/2006/515 (2006)).

[28] C. Stahn discusses the different models of attribution and responsibility in 'Self-defence under Art. 51 UN Charter and International Terrorism', in C. Walter *et al.* (eds.), *Terrorism as a Challenge for National and International Law: Security versus Liberty?* (Berlin: Springer, 2004), 827. See also J. Brunee and S. Toope, 'The Use of Force: International Law after Iraq' (2004) 53 *International and Comparative Law Quarterly* 805; and Greenwood, 'International Law', 313.

[29] See, e.g., M. Wood 'The Law on the Use of Force: Current Challenges' (2007) 11 *Singapore Yearbook of International Law* 1, 7; he also quotes the then US State Department Legal Adviser as stating 'As a legal matter, where a state is unwilling or unable to do so, it may be lawful for the targeted state to use military force in self-defence to address [the] threat.' See also Reinold, 'State Weakness, Irregular Warfare'; and Chatham House principles, 969, 970.

use of force to rescue nationals, which is regarded by many as an example of self-defence, even where the territorial state is not involved in any way.[30] The matter is the subject of another chapter in this volume.[31]

For the purposes of this chapter it is recognized, first, that the right of self-defence is a right to use proportionate force where necessary to avert an attack, and that the source of the attack, whether a state or a non-state actor, is not determinative of the existence of the right. Second, while defensive measures against a non-state group within a state will inevitably constitute the use of force *on* the territorial state and will therefore have an impact on its territorial integrity, such action can be legally justified not only if there is some form of international responsibility on the part of the territorial state but also, in the absence of such responsibility, if there are no other means of averting attacks from the group.

3.2 *Anticipatory force against imminent attacks*

The principles applicable to anticipatory self-defence against states are the same with regard to threats from non-state actors. Thus the military operation launched in Afghanistan in October 2001 was described as self-defence against further terrorist attacks from al-Qaeda, supported by the Taliban: the US described its actions as 'designed to prevent and deter further attacks on the United States'; the UK notified to the Security Council its participation in the operation 'to avert the continuing threat of attacks'.[32] These actions are properly classed as an exercise of anticipatory self-defence, with the necessity of armed response made clear by the past attacks and the continuing threats, and the proportionality of the response being judged by reference to both. If the October operation is viewed simply as a response to the attack on the Twin Towers it would have been unlawful, as being merely retaliatory.

But the phenomenon of terrorism often presents a problem for the application of the criterion of imminence in relation to the right of anticipatory self-defence. One of the particular characteristics of terrorism is the intention to cause a maximum of damage at unpredictable times and by unpredictable means. The uncertainty about time and

[30] See e.g. Dinstein, *War, Aggression and Self-Defence*, 231.

[31] See Chapter 11 in this volume.

[32] Letter of 7 October 2001 from the United States to the President of the Security Council, UN Doc. S/2001/946; letter of 7 October 2001 from the United Kingdom, UN Doc. S/2001/947.

means helps to create the very climate of fear which is the objective of the terrorist organization.[33] The operating methods of modern terrorist groups can make a strict temporal assessment of the threat of the next terrorist attack difficult or impossible.

It has been suggested therefore that against terrorist groups the right of self-defence does not apply only where the threat is imminent but also where the danger is real but more remote.[34] A wide interpretation of the temporal requirement 'corresponds to the specific nature of terrorism, which does not manifest itself in sustained operations, but rather in intermittent acts of violence the times and places of which are difficult, if not impossible to predict'.[35] Indeed some commentators go so far as to say that a state may act on the assumption that an attack from some international terrorist organizations is always 'imminent', given their nature and methods of operation.

> If a terrorist organization has committed prior attacks, or has explicitly or implicitly announced its intention to do so, then any future attack can be considered imminent for purposes of the Webster standard [i.e., the standard laid down in the *Caroline* incident]. Reasonably interpreted in this way – adapted to the political and operational realities of transnational terrorism – Webster's definition of anticipatory self-defense is as relevant and workable today as it was in the 19th and 20th centuries.[36]

There is however a need to distinguish between lawful self-defence on the one hand and unlawful reprisals or retaliation on the other. The law on self-defence is intended for defensive, preventive purposes not for retribution. The distinction is lost if the victim state may use military action in response to a terrorist attack without the need to avert future attacks of which there is real evidence. Further, because it is in the first place for the territorial state itself to deal with a threat from terrorist

[33] See discussion in G. Travalio, 'Terrorism, International Law, and the Use of Military Force' (2000) 18 *Wisconsin International Law Journal* 145, 165.

[34] See e.g. J. Yoo 'International Law and the War in Iraq' (2003) 97 *American Journal of International Law* 563: the indicators for the imminence criterion 'should now include the probability of an attack; the likelihood that this probability will increase, and therefore the need to take advantage of a limited window of opportunity; whether diplomatic alternatives are practical; and the magnitude of the harm that could result from the threat' (574).

[35] R. Grote, 'Between Crime Prevention and the Laws of War: Are the Traditional Categories of International Law Adequate for Assessing the Use of Force against International Terrorism?', in C. Walter *et al.* (eds.), *Terrorism as a Challenge for National and International Law: Security versus Liberty?* (Berlin: Springer, 2004), 979.

[36] Travalio and Altenburg, 'State Responsibility', 116.

groups on its soil, anticipatory self-defence by another state can lawfully be exercised only in the most compelling emergencies. As with the assessment of whether an attack from a *state* is 'imminent', a calculation of the intentions, capabilities, planning and ongoing preparations by the non-state actor must be made, as well as an assessment of the possibility of averting the threats by non-forcible means. The statement made in 2004 by the then UK Attorney General sets out what is perhaps at the very limit of legality:

> The concept of what constitutes an 'imminent' attack will develop to meet new circumstances and new threats. For example, the resolutions, passed by the Security Council in the wake of 11 September 2001 recognised both that large-scale terrorist action could constitute an armed attack that will give rise to the right of self-defence and that force might, in certain circumstances, be used in self-defence against those who plan and perpetrate such acts and against those harbouring them, if that is necessary to avert further such terrorist acts ... It must be right that states are able to act in self-defence in circumstances where there is evidence of further imminent attacks by terrorist groups, even if there is no specific evidence of where such an attack will take place or of the precise nature of the attack.[37]

The concept of anticipatory self-defence is relevant only where an imminent attack is threatened; where an attack is *ongoing*, there is a right of 'classic' self-defence. In the context of defence against terrorist attacks, discussion of the meaning of 'imminence' sometimes gives way to the question whether separate attacks are linked together so as to be properly treated as a continuing attack. Where attacks come in a more or less continuous series, the use of force in self-defence may be regarded as countering a continuing attack rather than defending against an imminent attack in the future.

Does this show a movement towards the acceptance of the so-called 'accumulation of events' doctrine? According to this doctrine, a pattern of minor terrorist attacks may be considered as a continuing attack, even though no one attack on its own would justify a response. The doctrine was discussed as early as 1972 by Professor Bowett with reference in particular to Israeli operations dating from 1953 onwards and a British attack on Yemen in 1964, following a series of Yemeni attacks on the

[37] Statement in the House of Lords (21 April 2004); HL Debates vol. 660 cols. 370–1. But this has been criticized by Gray as depriving 'the requirement of "imminence" of any content' (*International Law and the Use of Force*, 215).

territory of the then South Arabian Federation.[38] The Security Council appears to have opposed the doctrine on the occasions mentioned. Writing in 1987 Professor Greenwood stated:

> Since States appear to rely upon this approach to self-defence and since it is suggested that it accords more with the reality of international relations in an age in which armed attacks are as likely to take the form of terrorist 'pinprick' attacks as conventional invasions or bombardment, one must question whether the Security Council's rejection of the accumulation of events approach still represents international law, or whether it ought to do so . . . [I]t is better that international law should adapt to take account of State practice than continue to set a standard which is ignored in practice.[39]

He points out that to adopt this somewhat wider approach to the right of self-defence is more desirable than to claim a right to take reprisals.

The doctrine presents more risks of abuse than does anticipatory self-defence and could become an open-ended licence to use force. Nevertheless, some governments prefer to argue for this extended interpretation of armed attack rather than accept the doctrine of anticipatory defence.[40] The risks are clear. If a series of small attacks, none of which causes much damage, can be accumulated to comprise one continuing attack against which a state is entitled to defend itself by force, there is the possibility of ratcheting up the scale of a conflict, responding always to what has gone before rather than relying on evidence of what is to be averted in the future, and maintaining a conflict that may continue indefinitely.

The approach raises questions in relation to the requirement for a threshold of gravity in assessing what is an 'armed attack' under Article 51; the matter is considered elsewhere in this volume.[41] Whether or not the approach is a useful or acceptable one in making this assessment, using the 'accumulation of events' doctrine in relation to the 'imminence' requirement could render it unnecessary to assess when the next attack will take place since it assumes the existence of a continuing attack. It could thus remove the temporal element altogether. Professor Schmitt has said:

[38] Bowett, 'Reprisals', 1. [39] Greenwood, 'International Law', 955–6.

[40] See Gray, *International Law and the Use of Force*, 165. There have also been a couple of inconclusive nods by the ICJ towards the doctrine in *Nicaragua*; and in *Oil Platforms* (*Islamic Republic of Iran* v. *United States of America*), Judgment of 6 November 2003 [2003] ICJ Rep. 161.

[41] See Chapter 11 in this volume.

> Treating a series of actions as a unitary whole makes particular sense in the context of terrorism ... [I]t is reasonable to interpret self-defense as permitting the use of force against terrorists who intend, and have the capability, to conduct further attacks against the victim. By this interpretation, it is not the imminency of an isolated action that is relevant, but rather the relationship between a series of attacks. Once the first of the related attacks has been launched, the question becomes whether the victim State has sufficient reliable evidence to conclude that further attacks are likely, not whether those further attacks are themselves imminent.[42]

He concludes:

> The acceptability of viewing separate acts of terrorism conducted by the same organization (or closely related organizations acting in concert) as a single ongoing attack appears clear in the aftermath of the response to 9/11 ... [T]he understanding of armed attack has evolved from one looking at particular operations in isolation, and asking whether each is imminent or ongoing in and of itself, to one where terrorists are viewed as conducting campaigns. Once it is established that an ongoing campaign is underway, acts of self-defense are acceptable throughout its course.[43]

There are other scholars who agree that state practice supports this approach, although the state practice used for such assertions is difficult to interpret.[44] As regards the 'war against al-Qaeda', there must at least be doubt as to whether the separate incidents following 9/11 (in London, Madrid, Bali, Pakistan, Syria, Somalia and Yemen) can in reality be treated as part of one continuing attack. And can al-Qaeda be described

42 M. Schmitt, 'Counter-Terrorism and the Use of Force in International Law' (2002) 5 *Marshall Center Papers* 24–5.

43 *Ibid.*, 65.

44 For example Reinold, 'State Weakness, Irregular Warfare', 266–75, regards Israel's intervention in Lebanon against Hezbollah in 2006, Turkey's operation in Iraq against the PKK in 2008 and Colombia's intervention in Ecuador against the FARC in 2008 as illustrating the international community's tacit acceptance of the accumulation of events doctrine at the expense of the immediacy criterion in anticipatory self-defence. But the practice is inconsistent and ambiguous; the acceptance by states of Israel's right of self-defence in 2006 related to the specific attacks by Hezbollah two days before the IDF response and the criticism that the IDF response was disproportionate was measured against the Hezbollah attacks in July not a continuing series of attacks (see statements made in SC meetings of 13 July 2006 (UN Doc. S/PV.5488) and 14 July 2006 (UN Doc. S/PV.5489) and of 21 July 2006 (UN Doc. S/PV.5493 (Resumption 1)). It is difficult to draw firm inferences from the scarcity of international comment on Turkey's intervention in Iraq against the PKK. As for the intervention by Colombia into Ecuador in 2008, this was regarded as a violation of 'principles of international law' by the OAS, the regional organization (resolution of the Permanent Council CP/RES. 930 (1632/08)).

as a distinct and organized armed group, as opposed to a network of loosely affiliated groups with similar ideologies?[45] If they are undertaken by separate groups from separate countries, without the same command and control, it is problematic to regard the attacks as a unitary and continuing whole.

The difficulty of reaching firm conclusions about state practice from states' reactions to military measures taken under a claim of self-defence is illustrated by the reactions to 'Operation Cast Lead', launched by Israel in Gaza in 2008/9. Israel claimed that it was 'compelled to resort to a military operation after many weeks – indeed, months and years – during which its civilians were subjected to deliberate terrorist attacks carried out by Hamas and other Palestinian terrorist organizations operating from the Gaza Strip'.[46] Leaving aside the question whether the principles of self-defence as such are applicable in a situation which many classed as one of occupation, the constant rocket attacks from Gaza into Israel would indeed seem to raise the issue of whether this was a continuing attack justifying military measures, if the latter were necessary and proportionate. According to the Israel Security Agency (Shin Bet), there were 1, 276 rocket launchings from Gaza in 2007 and 1,785 in 2008 before the start of Operation Cast Lead.[47] Reactions in the Security Council were however divided. Of course statements in that forum have political motivations, but there were divisions even among those who are not always critical or always supportive of Israel. On the one hand, there was the remark that 'legitimate self-defence does not sanction reprisals such as those carried out by Israel in its attacks of recent days' (Costa Rica), and on the other, recognition that Israel was exercising the right to self-defence (Italy, Vietnam) but was to be criticized for using military measures which were disproportionate and excessive (South Africa, Vietnam, Indonesia, France).[48]

In conclusion, there is insufficient state practice to justify dropping the immediacy criterion from the assessment of the legality of military measures to avert future attacks. An assessment of what is a 'continuing' attack, such as to justify a response without considering whether

[45] See discussion by N. Lubell in 'The War (?) against al-Qaeda', in E. Wilmshurst (ed.), *International Law and the Classification of Conflicts* (Oxford: Oxford University Press, 2012), 421–54.

[46] Statement by Israel (UN Doc. S/PV 6060 (2008)).

[47] Statistics interpreted by the Foreign Affairs Committee, *Fifth Report of Session 2008–2009*, para. 9 (UK).

[48] Statements (UN Doc. S/PV 6060 (2008)).

'anticipatory' action is permissible, must crucially rely on evidence as to whether one or more terrorist attacks from the same source have come to an end or are a part of an ongoing series. The pattern of past attacks can form a part of an assessment as to whether they will continue. Where a group is undertaking a series of terrorist attacks from one state of a sufficiently high threshold to engage defensive military operations by another state, a decision whether to launch such defensive action must include an assessment as to whether the attacks are from one source, form a coherent pattern and are not sporadic incidents separated by long periods of time; there must be clear evidence of the likelihood of the attacks continuing from that source and they must be closely linked in time. There is not a continuing 'global war on terror', which justifies the targeted killing of any alleged terrorist anywhere in the world.

4 Conclusions

No discussion on the use of military force against terrorist attacks should begin or end without emphasizing the place of the criminal law on the one hand and, on the other, the role of the Security Council. Terrorists are criminals and should be dealt with as far as that is possible by criminal law, rather than by military force. If they are located in another state, the possibilities of asking for extradition or offering support for local investigations and prosecutions should be thoroughly explored. A victim state should generally request the territorial state to deal with the offending groups itself unless there is clear intelligence that there is insufficient time or inclination for this on the part of the territorial state. As for the role of the Security Council, states should consider whether resort to the Council is possible before taking their own action in self-defence. The UN Charter instituted a system of collective defence to which self-defence is an exception and the Council has the right and responsibility itself to authorize collective military action to deal with threatened attacks.

There is a plethora of writings and commentaries on the question of using military force against attacks by terrorists; on a matter so central to international law it is desirable to attempt to narrow differences of view, in both governmental and non-governmental debate. The 2005 experience in the General Assembly[49] shows that it may not be wise to use that forum with its large numbers and particular atmosphere for the purpose

[49] Debate on the report *In Larger Freedom*.

of attempting a closer consensus. Nor would the Security Council be amenable to having its own powers circumscribed by principles in this area, even were it possible for it to agree on any. One exercise in a non-governmental forum to attempt agreement on the law on self-defence generally was made in the Chatham House principles on the use of force in self-defence, elsewhere referred to in this chapter.[50] The *Leiden Policy Recommendations on Counter-Terrorism and International Law*, for which this volume is written, is an example of a wide consultation exercise involving academics, practitioners and governmental experts. Another exercise, the transatlantic legal advisers' dialogue in an intergovernmental context, relates to self-defence against attacks of non-state actors, and appears to have reached some level of agreement on certain propositions.[51]

The question whether particular instances of military action are justified on the basis of self-defence must be subjected to the debate and commentary of different communities of international law, including states – individually and in the UN Security Council and General Assembly – academics, non-governmental organizations and the International Court of Justice. It is in the first place for an individual state to determine for itself the need for military measures. But a state which uses force in anticipatory self-defence must be prepared to justify itself after the event as to the law and the facts, by disclosing as much information in support of the necessity of military operations as is practically possible for it to do, including as much of the intelligence as may reasonably be produced. In spite of the difficulty in achieving consensus on what international law requires in this area, it remains important to test governments' actions by reference to the law, and to continue to enjoin on governments compliance with the law.

[50] Paust in 'Use of Armed Force', 963.

[51] Daniel Bethlehem, 'Self-Defense against an Imminent or Actual Armed Attack by Nonstate Actors' (2012) 106 *American Journal of International Law 769.*

13

The necessity and proportionality of anti-terrorist self-defence

CHRISTIAN J. TAMS

1 Introduction

Necessity and proportionality are broad principles that apply to a variety of different settings under international law, including the law of self-defence. This seems undisputed today, even though Article 51 of the Charter of the United Nations (UN Charter) does not mention 'proportionality/proportionate' at all, and 'necessity/necessary' only in relation to the Security Council.[1] Yet Article 51 UN Charter does not regulate the right to self-defence comprehensively; in order for it to be applicable, 'external factors' need to be taken into account. That necessity and proportionality are two such factors is generally agreed. Pursuant to the jurisprudence of the ICJ '[t]he submission of the exercise of the right of self-defence to the conditions of necessity and proportionality is a rule of customary international law'.[2] In this respect, the Court was surely correct to note that '[t]he conditions for the exercise of the right of self-defence are well settled'.[3]

'Ritual incantations'[4] of necessity and proportionality, however, do not solve problems of application. These appear at two levels. Predictably, when

[1] Cf. Art. 51, clause 1 (in fine): 'until the Security Council has taken measures necessary to maintain inter national peace and security'.

[2] *Legality or Threat or Use of Nuclear Weapons*, Advisory Opinion of 8 July 1996 [1996] ICJ Rep. 226, para. 41 (citing para. 176 of the *Military and Paramilitary Activities in and against Nicaragua* (*Nicaragua* v. *United States of America*), Judgment of 27 June 1986 [1986] ICJ Rep. 14.). See further *Oil Platforms* (*Islamic Republic of Iran* v. *United States of America*), Judgment of 6 November 2003 [2003] ICJ Rep. 161, para. 76.

[3] *Oil Platforms*. See further C. Gray, *International Law and the Use of Force* (Oxford: Oxford University Press, 2008), 147; J. C. Gardam, *Necessity, Proportionality and the Use of Force by States* (Cambridge: Cambridge University Press, 2004), 138ff; E. Roucounas, *Preliminary Report on Self-Defence, Annuaire de l'Institut de droit international* (2007), 72, 99.

[4] See Gray, *International Law*, 118.

measuring specific acts of self-defence against the yardsticks of necessity and proportionality, lawyers are likely to reach different results. In so far as this reflects different assessments of the facts, this may be in the nature of things. There is however a second problem: necessity and proportionality are 'consistently referred to ... but rarely, if ever, analysed in relation to the Charter scheme on self-defence'.[5] As a consequence, there is much uncertainty about the precise content of the 'necessity test' and the 'proportionality equation', and about their interrelation. As these difficulties affect the application of self-defence generally, section 2 of this contribution seeks to clarify the meaning of the two requirements. On that basis, the application of necessity and proportionality to measures of anti-terrorist self-defence will be assessed (section 3). Before proceeding with the analysis, two important caveats need to be added.

The *first* concerns the role of necessity and proportionality within the law of self-defence. As noted above, both govern 'the *exercise* of the right of self-defence'.[6] As restraints (or limitations) on the *exercise* of a right, necessity and proportionality need to be distinguished from conditions governing the *availability of a right.* Restraints or limitations governing the exercise of a right only need to be addressed if it is established that that right could be invoked at all. In the present context, the necessity and proportionality of self-defence against attacks by terrorists need only be addressed if it is accepted that attacks by terrorists can give rise to a right of self-defence. The subsequent considerations therefore are based on three assumptions:

(1) International law, under certain conditions, recognizes the right of states to use force unilaterally against terrorists operating in a different country.[7]

[5] Gardam, *Necessity*, 149 (citing I. Brownlie, *International Law and the Use of Force by States* (Oxford: Oxford University Press, 1963), 429). While this observation refers to necessity, Gardam and Brownlie make very similar statements on the lack of detailed analysis of the proportionality requirement (see Gardam, *Necessity*, 155; Brownlie, *International Law*, 261).

[6] *Nuclear Weapons*, para. 41.

[7] The subsequent considerations focus on the use of force on the territory of another state. Forcible measures against terrorists operating within the responding state's territory (or other areas of its jurisdiction) are not covered, as they usually do not involve question of the *jus ad bellum*. For reasons of convenience, forcible responses against terrorists operating in areas outside any state's jurisdiction (notably the High Seas) are not covered either.

(2) The right to use extraterritorial force against terrorists is part of the inherent right of self-defence, and subject to the legal regime of self-defence; it is not part of an allegedly 'reviving' right to resort to armed reprisals, or an emerging regime of forcible law enforcement in the general interest.
(3) Self-defence is only available against armed attacks. In order to qualify as an armed attack, international jurisprudence suggest that an attack must involve large-scale violence;[8] the notion of 'armed attack' thus comprises – in the words of the ICJ – only 'the most grave forms of the use of force'.[9]

As is clear, these assumptions by no means command universal support. Since they are explored in other contributions to this volume, they will not be addressed here.[10]

The *second* caveat concerns the relationship between different branches of international law that impose limitations based on necessity and proportionality. The subsequent considerations focus on necessity and proportionality under the *jus ad bellum*; by contrast, they do not address necessity and proportionality as imposed by rules governing the conduct of hostilities. Proceedings such as the *Nuclear Weapons* opinion[11] suggest that the two different sets of limitations are not always clearly separated.[12] However, the two tests follow different rationales – the *jus ad bellum* regulates the

[8] This approach has remained controversial, but would seem to follow from the Court's jurisprudence in *Nicaragua*, para. 191; *Oil Platforms*, paras. 51 and 62; and *Armed Activities on the Territory of the Congo* (*Democratic Republic of the Congo* v. *Uganda*), Judgment of 19 December 2005 [2005] ICJ Rep. 168, para. 147). See also the Eritrea–Ethiopia Boundary Commission Award on Ethiopia's *jus ad bellum* claims 1–8, *Eritrea Ethiopia Claims Commission*, 19 December 2005 (2006) 45 *International Law Materials* 430.

[9] *Nicaragua*, para. 191.

[10] See notably Ratner, Chapter 11 in this volume, and further C. J. Tams, 'The Use of Force against Terrorists' (2009) 20 *European Journal of International Law* 359; and C. J. Tams, 'Light Treatment of a Complex Problem' (2005) 16 *European Journal of International Law* 963; T. Bruha and C. J. Tams, 'Self-Defence against Terrorist Attacks: Considerations in the Light of the ICJ's *Israeli Wall* Opinion', in C. Dicke *et al.* (eds.), *Weltinnenrecht: Liber Amicorum Jost Delbrück* (Berlin: Duncker & Humblot, 2005), 85; C. J. Tams and J. Devaney, 'Applying Necessity and Proportionality to Anti-Terrorist Self-Defence' (2012) 45 *Israel Law Review* 91.

[11] *Nuclear Weapons*, 226.

[12] For debate on their interrelation, see E. Cannizaro, 'Contextualizing Proportionality: *Jus ad bellum* and *jus in bello* in the Lebanese War' (2006) 88 *International Review of the Red Cross* 779; and the contributions of J. C. Gardam and C. Greenwood to L. Boisson de Chazournes and P. Sands (eds.), *International Law, the International Court of Justice and Nuclear Weapons* (Cambridge: Cambridge University Press, 1999), 247 and 275, respectively.

entitlement and scope to use force, whereas necessity and proportionality under the *jus in bello* mainly govern the employment of force in concrete military encounters. These latter considerations will be taken up only to the extent that they influence the necessity and proportionality tests under the *jus ad bellum.*

2 Clarifying the 'necessity test' and the 'proportionality equation'

Notwithstanding the caveats, necessity and proportionality do of course play an important role within the legal rules restraining the use of force. The subsequent section seeks to clarify the meaning of the 'necessity test' and the 'proportionality equation', so to set the stage for the subsequent discussion of anti-terrorist self-defence. Before that, it is necessary to assess the interrelation between necessity and proportionality.

2.1 Necessity and proportionality

As a preliminary issue, the relationship between the two concepts needs to be assessed. This is by no means a straightforward matter. Closer scrutiny reveals at least four different approaches to this question:

- some commentators openly question whether they can operate separately;[13]
- most writers state that they are closely interlinked[14] (without however necessarily exploring the link);
- some view necessity as part of an overall test of proportionality;[15] and
- others keep necessity and proportionality separate but describe proportionality as variation on the theme of necessity.[16]

[13] See Gray, *International Law*, 150.

[14] T. Gazzini, *The Changing Rules on the Use of Force in International Law* (Manchester: Manchester University Press, 2006), 147; Roucounas, *Preliminary Report on Self-Defence*, 98; C. Wicker, *The Concepts of Proportionality and State Crimes in International Law* (Frankfurt am Main: Peter Lang, 2005), 39.

[15] J. Delbrück, 'Proportionality', in R. Bernhardt *et al.* (eds.), *Encyclopedia of Public International Law* (Oxford: Oxford University Press, 1997), vol. III, 1140; M. Krugmann, *Der Grundsatz der Verhältnismäßigkeit im Völkerrecht* (Berlin: Duncker & Humblot, 2004).

[16] See, e.g., principle 3 of the Chatham House principles, pursuant to which proportionality 'requires that the level of force used is not greater than that necessary to end the attack or remove the threat' (E. Wilmshurst, 'The Chatham House Principles of

This chapter is not the place to address these issues in a detailed manner; however four points seem in order:

(1) Failure to distinguish between necessity and proportionality would seem to be one of the key factors contributing to the uncertainty surrounding both concepts. To merge two broad concepts into an overall test of 'necessity and proportionality' further complicates their application. In order to apply necessity and proportionality meaningfully, they ought to be distinguished.
(2) Contrary to what is at times alleged, necessity and proportionality *can* be distinguished. The distinction can be drawn differently, and is drawn differently in different legal systems employing both concepts.[17] What is more, the references given above suggest that even within the law of self-defence, it is not always drawn consistently. The most meaningful distinction, it is submitted, proceeds from the literal meaning of both terms:
(3) Dictionaries define 'necessity' as a situation which compels a certain course of conduct, and leaves no choice of alternatives.[18] Proportionality derives from 'proportion', which denotes the 'due relation of one part to another'.[19] While clearly in need of substantiation, these definitions offer the correct starting point for a reasonably clear distinction between necessity and proportionality. The 'necessity test' requires a comparison between the conduct under scrutiny (forcible self-defence) and potential alternatives; necessity thus concerns the *choice between alternative modes of response*. In contrast, the 'proportionality equation' amounts to a balancing exercise juxtaposing the interests harmed by the conduct under scrutiny (in the present case: an act of self-defence) on the one hand and the factors justifying it on the other; it is not about alternatives but questions whether necessary forms of responses are unlawful because they entail disproportionate consequences.
(4) International practice and jurisprudence moreover suggest that necessity and proportionality come into play at different levels of a

International Law on the Use of Force in Self-Defence' (2006) 55 *International and Comparative Law Quarterly* 963).

17 Delbrück, 'Proportionality', 1140–1. For a comparative assessment, see Krugmann, *Der Grundsatz der Verhältnismäßigkeit im Völkerrecht*, 41–66.

18 See, e.g., B. A. Garner and H. C. Black, *Black's Law Dictionary* (St Paul, MN: West Group, 1991) ('necessity').

19 C. Soanes and A. Stevenson (eds.), *Concise Oxford English Dictionary* (Oxford: Oxford University Press, 2008) ('proportion').

self-defence operation. The 'necessity test' is applied to determine whether a use of force is at all required to respond against an armed attack.[20] Proportionality may also affect that question, but it mainly functions as a limit on the scope or intensity of responses; it thus may be said mainly to concern the 'implementation' of self-defence.[21]

2.2 *Necessity*

The general position that force should only be used if necessary is not disputed. It is informed by the comprehensive character of the ban on use of force enshrined in Article 2(4) UN Charter which suggests a narrow construction of exceptions. For a variety of reasons most states refrain from resorting to force lightly; in that respect, necessity can indeed be said to 'constitute a real restraint on the resort to force by States'.[22] Whether states indeed feel restrained by legal factors is another matter. In this respect, one cannot fail to observe that practice, courts and commentators have formulated different 'necessity tests'. The following considerations suggest which aspects of the test are genuinely relevant, and provide the basis for the subsequent discussion of necessity in the context of anti-terrorist attacks.

2.2.1 Necessity and the functions of self-defence

Necessity cannot be determined in the abstract, but only in relation to a specific purpose. Necessity is influenced by the goals to be achieved ('necessary to achieve *what result*?'). Within the law of self-defence, this 'functional argument',[23] at least in theory, imposes an important restriction.[24] As the term 'self-defence' itself indicates, measures of self-defence are defensive in nature; they are directed against an armed attack and only permitted if 'necessary to respond to it'[25] (or potentially to avert it). This functional approach makes necessity dependent on external factors: assessments of necessity are notably influenced by what is

20 K. N. Trapp, 'Back to Basics: Necessity, Proportionality, and the Right of Self-Defence against Non-State Terrorist Actors' (2007) 56 *International and Comparative Law Quarterly* 141, 146.

21 *Ibid.* 22 Gardam, *Necessity*, 186.

23 Cannizaro, 'Contextualizing Proportionality', 82.

24 *Ibid.*; Bowett, 'Reprisals Involving Recourse to Armed Force' (1972) 66 *American Journal of International Law* 3; Gazzini, *Changing Rules*, 129.

25 *Nicaragua*, para. 176; see also *Nuclear Weapons*, para. 41.

meant by an armed attack, and the range of state interests that are considered worthy of protection by means of self-defence (a state's territory, its population, its ships, its security in a more comprehensive sense, etc.). Clearly however, the functional understanding narrows the scope of self-defence by excluding measures taken for non-defensive purposes such as revenge, retaliation or law enforcement.[26]

In practice, this aspect of the rules of necessity has been applied pragmatically. While stressing the defensive character of self-defence, international practice has admitted responses that were taken after the completion of an armed attack, as long as the attack continued to produce effects and the situation remained volatile.[27] It has also been prepared to admit that at least in cases involving a risk of repetition, the state responding itself may do more than to merely repel an attack, but also take measures aimed at forestalling future attacks; the limits of this broader approach to self-defence have however remained controversial.[28] This latter aspect in particular has blurred the distinction between the defensive functions of self-defence and other motives. More generally, during long-standing conflicts involving frequent clashes, states have claimed their reaction was necessary to prevent future attacks.

These claims raise difficult issues going to the legitimate functions to be pursued by self-defence and may also be affected by difficult discussion about the 'accumulation of events doctrine' (suggesting that different attacks could be added together, but presumably also prolonging the period during which defensive measures could be taken). For present purposes, it is important to note that they affect the application of the necessity test and that the functional understanding of self-defence is not applied inflexibly. In fact, it may be precisely because of this flexible interpretation that states seem to have accepted the defensive character of self-defence as a means of repelling or averting an armed attack.

[26] See Gazzini, *Changing Rules*, 129, according to whom self-defence has 'a defensive character since it is directed at preventing the armed attack from proceeding, succeeding and achieving its purpose'.

[27] The second Gulf War (if considered relevant for the purposes of self-defence) may be a case in point – it suggests that when States protest against the use of armed force, they are not prevented from resorting to self-defence at a time when the attack had long been completed and its goals accomplished

[28] Contrast Gazzini, *Changing Rules*, 148–9, and Y. Dinstein, *War, Aggression and Self-Defence* (Cambridge: Cambridge University Press, 2005), 237–8.

2.2.2 Necessity as 'absence of reasonable alternatives'

To assess the functions of self-defence is only the first step in operationalizing the necessity test. The second step concerns the content of necessity proper, i.e. the relationship between forcible measures of self-defence by the victim state on the one hand and potential alternatives on the other. As noted above, necessity can be defined as a situation which compelled a certain course of conduct. This implies that in order to meet the necessity test, the victim state must consider potential alternatives to the unilateral use of force. Given the comprehensive character of the ban on unilateral force, it is clear that the necessity test is formulated rather strictly: in order to be necessary, measures of self-defence have to be the *only* reasonable option of addressing the armed attack.[29] Other responses have to be unavailable; the responding state must have – to use the language of the *Caroline* formula – 'no choice of means',[30] or at least, to put things more realistically, no choice of other effective ways of responding to the attack or averting it.[31] This aspect of necessity is mainly understood to concern the relationship between forcible and non-forcible unilateral responses, but can also be applied in relation to institutional responses.

Non-forcible responses Forcible measures of self-defence may fail the 'necessity test' if the victim state can address the armed attack by non-forcible means. This is often seen as the essence of necessity, which brings out very clearly the 'ultimate' character of forcible responses.[32] Potential alternatives would notably include economic or political pressure, threats of force, or resort to forms of peaceful dispute resolution.

Of course, nearly all victim states will be in a position to resort to one or more of these non-forcible options; almost inevitably, victim states

[29] Gardam, *Necessity*, 148–50; Gray, *International Law*, 150; Gazzini, *Changing Rules*, 146.

[30] *British and Foreign State Papers*, vol. 29, 1129, 1138 (1840–1) (Mr Webster's statement).

[31] This latter qualification is frequently overlooked. See however the very clear formulation in principle 3 of the Chatham House principles.

[32] See, e.g., R. Ago, *Eighth report on State responsibility (Addendum)*, Yearbook of the International Law Commission vol. II/1 (1980), 60: 'The reason for stressing that action taken in self-defence must be necessary is that the State attacked (or threatened with imminent attack, if one admits preventive self-defence) must not, in the particular circumstances, have had any means of halting the attack other than recourse to armed force. . .*The point is self-evident and is generally recognized; hence it requires no further discussion*' (para. 120, my emphasis).

therefore do have 'a choice of means' – they can break off diplomatic relations, they can suspend treaties, etc. Focusing on *effective* alternatives, it seems preferable to require that a victim state thus must assess, in good faith and on the basis of the available evidence, whether it could repel or avert the attack without resorting to force.[33] This assessment depends on a broad range of factors that would typically include: the scale and effects of the armed attack; the relative strength of the attacker and victim state; or the history of the conflict of which the armed attack forms part.[34] It seems fair to say that given these qualifications, the real impact of this aspect of the necessity test, at least in traditional interstate disputes involving 'the most grave forms of the use of force',[35] is usually limited.[36] This is mainly due to two factors.

First, the Court's consistent interpretation of the armed attack requirement has restricted self-defence to qualified breaches of the ban on force.[37] In response to breaches of a lesser character (i.e. not reaching the threshold of an armed attack), self-defence is not available in the first place.[38] Arguably, these lesser breaches would be more likely to be settled without resort to force. *Second*, unlike in national legal systems, recourse to courts and tribunals will hardly ever be a practical alternative excluding self-defence (even though it may be one aspect of the victim state's defensive strategy).[39] Recourse to courts presupposes the consent of both parties; what is more, intrusive forms of dispute settlement often follow cumbersome procedures not designed to address ongoing conflicts. As a consequence, a state instituting legal proceedings can usually not be said to renounce other forms of responses. More generally, the narrow construction of self-defence means that effective alternatives are often unavailable.

Victim state responses versus measures by other actors Measures of self-defence are equally unnecessary if the armed attack can be averted or repelled by other actors whose reaction is judged preferable to that of the victim state; if this is the case, there is no reason to permit the victim

[33] See commentary to principle 3 of the Chatham House principles. [34] *Ibid.*

[35] *Nicaragua*, para. 191.

[36] Dinstein, *War, Aggression and Self-Defence*, 237; O. Schachter, *International Law in Theory and Practice* (Dordrecht: Martinus Nijhoff, 1991), 152.

[37] See above, references in section 1.

[38] Dinstein, *War, Aggression and Self-Defence*, 209–10.

[39] As witnessed by the increasing number of international proceedings initiated by States claiming to have suffered from an armed attack.

state to resort to force. Of course, usually, the victim state as the actor 'specially affected'[40] by an armed attack should be the one to respond. The UN Charter addresses the main[41] exception by clarifying the relationship between unilateral measures of self-defence and institutional responses. According to Article 51 UN Charter, measures of self-defence can be taken only 'until the Security Council has taken measures necessary to maintain international peace and security'. This is formulated as a temporal limitation, but implies a general statement on the relationship between self-defence and collective security measures, expressing the Charter's preference for 'institutional' action over 'private' reactions.[42]

The crucial question is what types of Security Council measures would qualify as 'necessary measures'.[43] As a general rule, since Security Council measures are to exclude a fundamental right of states, they must be designed to remove the threat posed by the armed attack, and must be authoritative. It would therefore not be sufficient for the Security Council to be seized of a matter, or to issue non-binding calls for the cessation of hostilities. Rather, for collective measures to be considered 'necessary to maintain international peace and security', one would normally expect a binding resolution, by the Council, requiring a stay of violence (e.g. the imposition of a ceasefire) or another effective sanction directed specifically against the armed attack.[44] In that latter scenario, the required degree of Security Council action would notably seem to depend on the scale and effects of the armed attack, the amenability of the attacker to UN pressure, and the importance of a swift

[40] To borrow the term used in Art. 42(b) of the ILC's Articles on State Responsibility (reproduced in J. Crawford, *The International Law Commission's Articles on State Responsibility: Introduction, Text and Commentaries* (Cambridge: Cambridge University Press, 2002)) and Art. 60(2)(b) VCLT.

[41] A further exception would seem to apply in the case of collective self-defence: As the Court's jurisprudence clarifies, States other than the direct victim of an armed attack can exercise collective self-defence only if so requested by the direct victim. See C. J. Tams, *Enforcing Obligations Erga Omnes in International Law* (Cambridge: Cambridge University Press, 2005), 300–2.

[42] See S. A. Alexandrov, *Self-Defense against the Use of Force in International Law* (The Hague: Kluwer Law International, 1996), 104–5, 130ff., for details and references.

[43] The point is much neglected. For comment see Dinstein, *War, Aggression and Self-Defence*, 215–16; Gray, *International Law*, 126–8.

[44] Dinstein, *War, Aggression and Self-Defence*, 216. Hence the SC's determination, in SC Res. 502 (UN Doc. S/Res./502 (1982)), that Argentina's invasion of the Falklands/Malvinas amounted to a breach of the peace, was as such not sufficient to display the United Kingdom's right of self-defence. See further, Gray, *International Law*, 125.

response.[45] Finally, it is clear that if the Security Council authorizes the use of force against the state responsible for the armed attack, and if it decides that institutional action is to replace individual action,[46] self-defence measures may be transformed into measures of UN law enforcement.[47] Absent such – relatively far-reaching – Security Council involvement, measures of self-defence as a general rule remain necessary.

2.2.3 The alleged temporal dimension of necessity ('imminence'/'immediacy')

Finally, there have been attempts to concretize the necessity test by introducing a temporal link between attack and response, at times also referred to as an issue of 'imminence' or 'immediacy'.[48] The purpose of that requirement is clear: as a reaction against an armed attack, self-defence would normally be expected to begin quickly after the initial attack has been launched, and one way of providing for this is by establishing a temporal link. If an attack is ongoing, this temporal requirement is met. This in turn makes necessity dependent upon the interpretation of the armed attack requirement; this dependence is an important factor in recent debates about the 'accumulation of events doctrine' potentially extending the period of armed attacks.

Matters are different when it comes to anticipatory '(re)actions' and belated responses. There is much authority in the literature suggesting these might be 'unnecessary' for lack of immediacy. On substance, it is not disputed that in order to be lawful, measures of self-defence must already, and must still, have been necessary to repel an armed attack.[49] It is another matter whether this should be put as a problem of immediacy. Two observations suggest that it should not:

45 On that basis, it would generally seem doubtful whether SC action outside the framework of Chapter VII, or non-military sanctions adopted under UN Charter, Art. 41 could exclude the right of self-defence.

46 This should not be lightly assumed: see UN Doc. S/Res./561 (1991) (preserving Kuwait's right of self-defence).

47 This in fact was already envisaged by H. Kelsen, *The Law of the United Nations: A Critical Analysis of Its Fundamental Problems* (New York: Praeger, 1951), 800–2.

48 See, e.g., Gardam, *Necessity*, 149–53; Roucounas, *Preliminary Report*, 99. Others treat imminence as a self-standing criterion independent of necessity: see notably Dinstein, *War, Aggression and Self-Defence*, 209, 242ff.; Y. Dinstein, 'Comment', *Proceedings of the 86th Annual Meeting of the American Society of International Law* (1992), 57; Gazzini, *Changing Rules*, 143–146.

49 Dinstein, *War, Aggression and Self-Defence*, 57; Gardam, *Necessity*, 149–53.

(1) While references to 'immediacy' are frequent, 'what the requirement of immediacy [addressed within the framework of necessity] consists of under the Charter is by no means clear'.[50] The reasons for that are evident: depending on the scale and type of an armed attack, states may need to prepare for their measure of self-defence rather than responding prematurely. Where the attack is directed against far-off locations, the victim state may need time to deploy troops (as with respect to the United Kingdom's response against the Argentine invasion of the Falklands/Malvinas).[51] Perhaps most importantly, a victim state that takes seriously its obligation to exhaust non-forcible means may even be under a duty to wait before resorting to force; as a consequence, respect for necessity (in the sense of 'absence of alternatives') may require victim states to postpone responses.[52] Rather than prescribing an absolute limit, immediacy, then, seems to require little more than *some* temporal connection between the armed attack and the response.

(2) If this understanding is accepted, then issues of 'immediacy' largely duplicate other limitations of the right of self-defence. *Belated responses* are said to fail the immediacy test if they are no longer required to repel an attack. If this is so, however, self-defence is no longer necessary in the first place. For example, the attack may have already been repelled[53] – in which case it is no longer 'necessary to respond to it',[54] i.e. no measure of self-defence is required any more.[55] Alternatively, self-defence may come too late because 'the Security Council has taken measures necessary to maintain international peace and security' – in which case self-defence has become unnecessary because other means are available.[56] The immediacy criterion therefore seems unnecessary to exclude belated responses. Conversely, to the extent that belated responses, following the flexible handling of the functional approach to self-defence,[57] are accepted, immediacy does not act as an additional restraint.

[50] Gardam, *Necessity*, 150.

[51] Cf. A. Constantinou, *The Right of Self-Defence under Customary International Law and Article 51 of the United Nations Charter* (Brussels: Bruylant, 2000), 160.

[52] Dinstein, *War, Aggression and Self-Defence*, 210; Dinstein, 'Comment', 57.

[53] As with respect to measures taken by the United States against Nicaragua in December 1981, at a time when 'the major offensive of the armed opposition against the government of El Salvador had been completely repulsed' (*Nicaragua*, 122).

[54] *Ibid.*, para. 176; see also *Nuclear Weapons*, para. 41.

[55] See section 2.2.1 above.

[56] See section 2.2.2 above.

[57] See section 2.2.1 above.

By the same token, a temporal reading is of little help in determining the legality of *anticipatory* '*(re)actions*'. In this case, the real question is not one of necessity or immediacy, but goes to the existence of a right of self-defence as such.[58] All depends on whether a state is entitled to resort to self-defence in the first place. If it is accepted that states can invoke self-defence against imminent attacks, then such anticipatory reactions would also fulfil the necessity test; again, immediacy does not act as an additional restraint.

2.2.4 Interim conclusions

To sum up, necessity is accepted as a restraint on the use of force in self-defence, and is applied in a range of different ways. The main aspects of the necessity test can be formulated in three questions:

(1) Was self-defence *required to repel or avert an armed attack* (or exceptionally, to preclude future attacks)?
(2) Was a *response by the victim state* required, or could the armed attack be repelled or averted by other actors, notably the Security Council?
(3) Was the use of *military force* required to repel or avert the armed attack, or could that goal be met by non-forcible measures?

The subsequent section applies these questions (with modifications where required), to the specific setting of self-defence against terrorist attacks. Before that, some remarks on the role and function of proportionality are called for.

2.3 Proportionality

Proportionality is considered to be the more complex limitation restricting the exercise of self-defence.[59] Requirements of proportionality apply in many areas of law, from human rights law to international humanitarian law, but also the rules governing countermeasures or self-defence.[60] While always concerning a balancing of interests, it is crucial to note that the application of proportionality in these different fields

[58] For detail, see Chapter 12 in this volume. [59] Roucounas, *Preliminary Report*, 99.

[60] Jost Delbrück's entry in the Encyclopedia of Public International Law ('Proportionality') provides a good overview. See also the detailed treatment by T. Franck, 'On Proportionality of Countermeasures in International Law' (2008) 102 *American Journal of International Law* 715.

serves different functions, which in turn influences the formulation of the respective proportionality equations.[61] Within the law of self-defence, proportionality serves two distinct functions which are not always kept separate. *First*, it is an additional factor determining whether states are at all entitled to resort to self-defence. Even if the requirement of necessity is met, a state may be precluded from responding by means of force if this use of force would entail harm that is completely out of proportion to the harm expected from the initial attack. This however is a highly unlikely scenario, as it implies that a state suffering from an armed attack (i.e. a grave breach of Article 2(4) UN Charter) would have to refrain from defending itself by military means; one would be hard pressed to find realistic examples where international law would force states to turn the other cheek when attacked by military force. Conversely, in most situations where the use of force would be out of proportion (e.g. with respect to relatively minor incidents just meeting the threshold of an armed attack), forcible self-defence would probably not be necessary in the first place.

In contrast, the *second* function of proportionality is of much greater practical relevance, and the subsequent discussion will focus on it. State practice and jurisprudence view proportionality as a factor restricting the scope or intensity of lawful self-defence. The guiding principle is that self-defence, even if it could be resorted to, must not involve the use of excessive force.[62] Notwithstanding broad agreement on the principle, proportionality often remains a mere 'rhetorical tool'[63] in debates about self-defence, and it is by no means clear how it can be applied meaningfully. In fact, there is much discussion about the parameters of the proportionality equation as well as the factors influencing its application. Both aspects are addressed in the following.

2.3.1 The proportionality equation

Just as necessity, proportionality cannot be determined in the abstract. As it involves a balancing of interests, the conduct under scrutiny must be related to something else; the 'due relation' of an act of self-defence

[61] A point rightly stressed by N. Lubell, 'Use of force against individuals and groups abroad' (Ph.D. thesis, Galway, ms on file with the author), 69–70.

[62] See principle 5 of the Chatham House principles, which prescribes: 'The force used, taken as a whole, must not be excessive in relation to the need to avert or bring the attack to an end. The physical and economic consequences of the force used must not be excessive in relation to the harm expected from the attack.'

[63] Gardam, *Necessity*, 187.

can only be evaluated if it is clear to what it should be compared.[64] Curiously, courts and commentators have so far adopted diverging approaches to this problem.

In its (admittedly cursory) treatment of proportionality, the ICJ seems to have followed a rather straightforward test.[65] In *Nicaragua*[66] and *Oil Platforms*[67] it assessed whether the victim state's response was proportionate *to the armed attack*. This seemed to imply a comparison between the injurious effects of the armed attack and those of the response in self-defence.[68] Hence, to give just one example, the United States' destruction of two Iranian oil platforms, carried out as part of a more extensive operation, was held out of proportion to Iran's previous conduct, namely 'the mining, by an unidentified agency, of a single United States warship, which was severely damaged but not sunk, and without loss of life'.[69] This seems to suggest almost a quantitative evaluation of harm; what is more, the proportionality of self-defence was assessed retrospectively, against harm already inflicted.[70]

Most commentators addressing the issue adopt a different approach.[71] They note that self-defence, even when directed against an ongoing attack, aims at avoiding future consequences, and thus is a response against a threat as much as against an attack already inflicted. What is

[64] R. Higgins, *Problems and Process: International Law and How We Use It* (Oxford: Oxford University Press, 1994), 231; Wicker, *Concepts of Proportionality*, 40.

[65] Curiously, even commentators otherwise placing great emphasis on the value of ICJ judgments seem to ignore the Court's statements on the assessment of proportionality. But contrast the very detailed treatment by T. Christodoulidou and K. Chainoglou, 'The Principle of Proportionality in Self-Defence and Humanitarian Intervention' (2007) 20 *Humanitäres Völkerrecht* 79, 80–3.

[66] See *Nicaragua*, para. 237: 'Whatever uncertainty may exist as to the exact scale of the aid received by the Salvadorian opposition from Nicaragua, it is clear that these . . . United States activities . . . could not have been proportionate to that aid'.

[67] See *Oil Platforms*, para. 77 (cited in the text).

[68] Christodoulidou and Chainoglou, 'Principle of Proportionality', 83; F. L. Kirgis, 'Some Proportionality Issues Raised by Israel's Use of Armed Force in Lebanon' (2006) 10/20 *ASIL Insight* (at www.asil.org/insights060817.cfm#_ednref3).

[69] *Oil Platforms*, para. 77.

[70] For a similar approach see J. L. Hargrove, 'The Nicaragua Judgment and the Future of the Law of Force and Self-Defence' (1987) 81 *American Journal of International Law* 136; and see Wicker, Concepts of Proportionality, 40–1.

[71] See, e.g., Ago, *Eighth report*, 60 (para. 121); Alexandrov, *Self-Defense*,185; Constantinou, *Right of Self-Defence*, 162; Gardam, *Necessity*, 403–6; C. Greenwood, 'Self-Defence and the Conduct of International Armed Conflict', in Y. Dinstein (ed.), *International Law at a Time of Perplexity: Essays in Honour of Shabtai Rosenne* (Dordrecht: Martinus Nijhoff, 1989), 273.

more, it is a response that is legitimate to repel or avert a threat posed by a grave breach of international law.[72] Taking into account both factors, commentators have argued for a qualitative–prospective approach, which assesses proportionality against the threat posed by the armed attack, and which also takes into account the victim state's 'superior right'[73] to defend itself. The greater that threat, the more intensive measures of self-defence the victim state can take. What is more, since no state has to endure an armed attack, its repulsion is a legitimate goal. This in turn means that self-defence can involve the use of more severe measures than those employed during the armed attack, and does not require the victim state to settle on 'an eye for an eye', or to stop when its response has resulted in a number of casualties equivalent to those suffered as a result of the attack.[74] Instead, the 'due relation' must be maintained between the means employed and the legitimate aims of self-defence.

While this renders proportionality much more difficult to apply in practice, this prospective–qualitative approach is indeed based on a convincing understanding, which takes due account of the future-looking character of self-defence measures and of the characterization, in Article 51, of self-defence as an 'inherent right'. What is more, international practice, without much debate, seems to have followed a prospective–qualitative approach rather than adopting the quantitative evaluation favoured by the ICJ. During the Falklands campaign or (to the extent this instance is considered relevant for the law of self-defence) the second Gulf War, the international community for example was prepared to countenance counter-force of greater scale and effects than the initial attacks.[75] Given these considerations, the ICJ's focus on harm

[72] Hence Cannizzaro speaks of the victim state's 'superior right' to defend the attack, E. Cannizzaro, 'Contextualizing Proportionality: *Jus ad bellum* and *jus in bello* in the Lebanese War' (2006) 88/864 *International Review of the Red Cross* 785.

[73] *Ibid.*

[74] Gardam, *Necessity*, 160–1; Ago, *Eighth report*, 69; M. S. McDougal and F. P. Feliciano, *Law and Minimum World Public Order: the Legal Regulation of International Coercion* (New Haven, CT: Yale University Press, 1961), 244.

[75] In response to the invasion, the United Kingdom amassed a considerable amount of firepower to dislodge Argentinean forces from the Falkland islands, while during the second Gulf War of 1991, coalition forces used force on a massive scale in order to secure Iraq's withdrawal from Kuwait. In both instances, measures of self-defence clearly entailed more harm than the initial attacks against which they were directed, yet this in itself (as opposed to specific aspects of the Falklands or Gulf campaigns) was not considered to render them disproportionate. The international community seemed to agree that since the response was lawful, it could very well be more injurious than the

already sustained is probably best explained by reference to the specific facts of the cases before it. These involved doubtful invocations of self-defence in cases in which the risk of future harm was not clearly established. In fact, in *Oil Platforms*, a number of judges described the United States attacks as punitive measures.[76]

To sum up, the proportionality of self-defence should be understood to require a due relation between the forcible response and the threat against which it was directed. To the extent that responses against completed attacks without a relevant prospective element are exceptionally qualified as self-defence, the threat may be of limited relevance; instead, it may be possible to rely on a quantitative approach to proportionality.[77] Still, as a general rule, proportionality is best formulated as a prohibition against measures that are excessive *in relation to the injury expected from the attack.*[78]

2.3.2 Factors relevant to the assessment of proportionality

If the formulation of the proportionality equation remains strangely controversial, its application to specific fact-patterns escapes a clear-cut legal formulation. This is primarily due to the asymmetric and open-ended character of the test: in order or decide whether self-defence is proportionate, it is necessary to evaluate the magnitude of the threat posed by an armed attack, and to compare it to the effects and 'scale of the whole [self-defence] operation'.[79] This requires a comparison between what has been termed 'disparate integers',[80] or 'apples and oranges',[81] namely the injury to a right and the harm entailed by self-defence. Whether a response is excessive or not largely depends on the circumstances and their evaluation. The evaluation in turn is often largely prognostic and has to take account of factual uncertainties.

initial armed attack – in fact, the retaking of the Falklands cost 907 lives, as compared to 0 casualties caused by their taking.

76 *Oil Platforms* (Judge Simma, Separate Opinion) and (Judge Elaraby, Dissenting Opinion).

77 This in turn suggests that the proportionality equation may depend on the functions of self-defence, a point made e.g. by Higgins, *Problems and Process*, 231–2, and developed by Dinstein, *War, Aggression and Self-Defence*, 57–8.

78 See for a similar formulation, principle 5 of the Chatham House principles.

79 *Oil Platforms*, para. 77. See also McDougal and Feliciano, *Law and Minimum World Public Order*, 243; and Gardam, *Necessity*, 159.

80 Franck, 'On Proportionality', 729.

81 M. N. Schmitt, 'Fault Lines in the Law of Attack', in S. C. Breau and A. Jachec-Neale Breau *et al.* (eds.), *Testing the Boundaries of International Law* (London: British Institute of International and Comparative Law, 2006), 293.

These general problems of proportionality are exacerbated by the relative lack of international practice – unlike in other areas of proportionality (e.g. in the law of human rights), there is no regular procedure for evaluating the lawfulness of states' responses in self-defence in any detail: courts hardly ever are competent to address the matter (and if so, have provided little guidance), and states criticizing acts of self-defence as disproportionate usually do so in general terms only.[82]

These considerations suggest that attempts to concretize the proportionality test are unlikely to produce a definite set of rules that could simply be applied to a given case. Yet international practice and jurisprudence do help to identify a number of factors that have generally been considered relevant to an assessment of proportionality.

Evaluating the injury expected from the attack Very little is usually said about the armed attack. Yet, of course, the permissible scope of self-defence crucially depends on how the armed attack is perceived. Two factors would seem relevant.

The gravity of the armed attack: the crucial factor is to assess the gravity of the armed attack. This cannot be done mathematically, but it should take account of tangible evidence. It notably depends on the scale and effects of the attack, i.e. the number of forces or the destructive scope of weapons employed, as well as harm already inflicted on nationals and property within the victim state. The aims pursued by the attack are of equal importance; they e.g. permit a distinction between 'total wars' aimed at the destruction of the enemy and more limited campaigns. Finally, the gravity of the attack may depend on normative considerations: the conduct of the parties in the run-up to the conflict; the character of the attack; the way it is being conducted.

The likelihood of its success: the injury expected from the attack furthermore depends on the likelihood of its success. Serious threats need to be distinguished from far-reaching war aims that stand no chance of realization. The distinction notably depends on the relative military strengths of the parties to the conflict. In ongoing conflicts, it crucially depends on whether the armed attack has already been successful. In long-standing conflicts it will also be influenced by past experience. Finally, it may depend on the attitude of third states potentially supporting a party to the conflict.

[82] Cf. Franck, 'On Proportionality', 729. The point is taken up below.

Evaluating the effects of self-defence In order to assess the proportionality of self-defence, the injury expected from the attack must be compared to the injurious consequences produced by the self-defence operation as a whole.[83] It can only be repeated that this involves an evaluation based on a set of very diverse factors; it is therefore not a mechanical operation and will often not lead to obvious results. What seems agreed, at least, is the overarching requirement: measures of self-defence must not entail physical and economic consequences that are excessive in relation to the injury expected from the armed attack.[84] The range of factors that need to be taken into account is in principle unlimited. However, a number of aspects seem particularly important.

The scale of the response: in evaluating the victim state's response, the scale of self-defence operations provides the natural starting point.[85] In order to assess the scale, the destructive force of the response is of crucial importance. This involves factors such as casualties among the attackers, but also the choice of weapons. Since these aspects are addressed in specific rules of international humanitarian law and human rights law, it is important to note that the proportionality test imposed by the *jus ad bellum* is an autonomous requirement.[86] The test is not whether the use of a specific weapon is unlawful as a matter of international humanitarian law, or whether a specific target is a legitimate military target. Instead, the victim state's means and methods of warfare must have been necessary to repel the attack – sometimes described as an issue of 'strategic' rather than 'tactical' proportionality:[87] unlike the specific rules of IHL, this more general test produces few clear-cut rules. However, the scale of responses operates as a relative factor: if its response entails immense physical and economic harm, the victim state will be required to provide convincing evidence why the degree of force employed was required to meet the threat of the attack.

Geographical scope: the geographical scope of self-defence operations provides another indication. There is support for the view that the forcible response must remain confined to 'the area of the threat which it is designed to meet'.[88] In the *Congo–Uganda* case, the ICJ took account

[83] *Oil Platforms*, para. 77. [84] See principle 5 of the Chatham House principles.

[85] Cf. Gardam, *Necessity*, 162ff.

[86] *Ibid.*, 169; Greenwood, 'Self-Defence', 279; Cannizzaro, 'Contextualizing Proportionality', 785ff.; UK Ministry of Defence, *The Joint Service Manual of the Law of Armed Conflict* (2004), para. 2.8.1.

[87] Greenwood, 'Self-Defence'.

[88] *Ibid.*, 277. See further Constantinou, *Right of Self-Defence*, 171; Higgins, *Problems and Process*, 232; Gardam, *Necessity*, 163–5.

of this fact when observing that Uganda's use of force was out of proportion (as well as unnecessary) since it affected 'airports and towns many hundreds of kilometres from Uganda's border' (supposedly violated by armed attacks).[89] Just as the scale of the response, this criterion does not impose strict limitations. It is relative in that it depends on the geographical scope of the attack. The victim state is of course not prevented from directing its response against targets located elsewhere if there is a risk that conflicts might 'spill over'. However, it would have to provide convincing arguments explaining why the conflict had to be carried into other areas.

Temporal scope: the scope of permissible self-defence may moreover depend on developments over time.[90] What may have been a proportionate response at one point over time may lose that character once the threat of further harm decreases. In the *Nicaragua* case, the ICJ e.g. considered disproportionate measures that were 'continued long after the period in which any presumed armed attack by Nicaragua could reasonably be contemplated'.[91] Again, there can be no fixed time-frame. However, the duration of a response plays an indicative role – the longer a state invokes its right of self-defence, the more credible must be its claim that further action against attacks or threats is indeed required.

Collateral damage: finally, the proportionality of self-defence depends on what may be subsumed under the broad notion of 'collateral damage'.[92] That term would seem to comprise injurious consequences of self-defence affecting legal positions or values of actors not involved in the conflict, such as third states, but also civilians not participating in the conflict. Traditionally, the rights and duties of third states affected by belligerent conduct were governed by the rules of neutrality; to what extent these continue to apply is a matter of dispute.[93] What is beyond dispute is that the effects of self-defence on 'others' may affect the evaluation of proportionality. In *Nicaragua*, one of the reasons leading the Court to declare United States' mining of, and armed attacks on, Nicaraguan ports to be disproportionate was that these mainly affected

[89] *Armed Activities*, para. 147.

[90] Greenwood, 'Self-Defence', 275–6; Gardam, *Necessity*, 167–8; Christodoulidou and Chainoglou, 'Principle of Proportionality', 87–8. Others would probably approach this issue as a problem of necessity: see e.g. Gazzini, *Changing Rules*, 46–147.

[91] *Nicaragua*, para. 237.

[92] Cf. Gardam, *Necessity*, 173–9; Greenwood, 'Self-Defence', 281–5.

[93] See para. 6 of the ILC's commentary on Art. 21 of the Articles on State Responsibility.

civilians and third states.[94] In the *Nuclear Weapons* opinion, the Court went further and noted that 'respect for the environment is one of the issues that go to assessing whether an action [of self-defence] is in conformity with the principl[e] of proportionality'.[95] While self-defence operations must be justified by a military motive (and not involve the wanton violation of rights of others),[96] rights of neutrals, of civilians and global public goods of course may be affected to the extent that it is indispensable to the pursuit of self-defence. However, the greater the losses, the more detailed the victim state's justification for violating them will have to be.

2.3.3 Interim conclusions

To sum up, it is not disputed that responses in self-defence must not be *excessive in relation to the injury expected from the attack*. This means that the usual test is one of prospective–qualitative proportionality, and only in exceptional instances of responses to past attacks can proportionality be assessed by comparing levels of harm inflicted.

Unlike issues of necessity, proportionality cannot be broken down into different sets of questions. It involves an overall balancing of interests that depends 'on the contingencies of an operation'.[97] Given its elasticity, proportionality is unlikely to produce predictable results unless supplemented by guidelines, established 'under the aegis of a credible decision-making process';[98] on how to evaluate the different variables of the equation. The preceding considerations suggest that within the international law of self-defence, such general 'supplementary rules' have yet to emerge: jurisprudence and state practice have identified relevant factors but, in the absence of regular procedures allowing for a detailed scrutiny of self-defence operation, have provided relatively little guidance on their evaluation. Despite general acceptance as a principle, proportionality therefore has so far remained difficult to operationalize.[99]

94 *Nicaragua*, para. 237. See further Constantinou, *Right of Self-Defence*, 170.

95 *Nuclear Weapons*, para. 30. Curiously, the Court also referred to the principle of necessity.

96 See, *ibid.* (Judge Higgins, Separate Opinion), para. 22.

97 See D. P. O'Connell, *The Influence of Law on Sea Power* (Manchester: Manchester University Press, 1975), 64.

98 Franck, 'On Proportionality', 718.

99 Gardam, *Necessity*, 186.

3 The necessity and proportionality of self-defence against terrorists

If self-defence is available against armed attacks by terrorists, it is subject to the limitations of necessity and proportionality. This much seems beyond dispute. What is more, the application of these limitations to anti-terrorist measures does not raise conceptual problems. Contrary to what is sometimes alleged, necessity and proportionality can be applied to measures of self-defence directed against non-state actors. In fact, it may be worth reminding that the law of self-defence – including the requirements of necessity and proportionality – has been shaped by judgments that concerned claims of self-defence against 'indirect attacks' by irregular forces, such as *Congo–Uganda* or *Nicaragua*.

In order to be applicable to anti-terrorist measures, various aspects of necessity and proportionality as discussed in the preceding section however need to be adapted. This is primarily due to two factors:

- It results from the specific character of armed attacks by terrorists. These are often 'one-off', 'instant' or 'pin prick' attacks of limited duration, and typically involve an element of surprise. This in turn means that victim states often do not have the chance to react while the attack is still ongoing.[100] Instead, their response is likely to take place either before a specific attack has begun or after it has ended.
- It follows from the fact that if self-defence against terrorist attacks is admitted, it requires the modification, or bypassing, of traditional rules on attribution, thus allowing responses against 'host states' supporting or harbouring terrorist organizations, or even against states unable to stop terrorists from operating on their territory.

The following section seeks to explore whether and how these factors affect the application of necessity and proportionality to measures of anti-terrorist self-defence. In order to illustrate the practical working of both principles, the analysis is preceded by three case studies, on which the subsequent discussion will draw.

[100] The situation would be different if the 'accumulation of events' doctrine were admitted. Whether it should is mainly a matter of construing the requirement of 'armed attack' and therefore outside the scope of the present contribution. Recognition of the doctrine would help avoid the sometimes artificial separation of multiple attacks into separate incidents; on the other hand, it would risk turning self-defence into an open-ended licence to use counterforce. This suggests that much further debate on the conditions permitting the accumulation of separate events is required.

3.1 *Case studies*

Instances in which states have invoked self-defence to justify their anti-terrorist operations have been frequent. They involve conduct of states as diverse as the United States, Israel, Iran, Colombia, Russia, Turkey, Ethiopia, as well as the collective efforts of states participating in Operation Enduring Freedom.[101] The following three case studies present a reasonably representative sample of responses.

3.1.1 Turkey – Kurds – Iraq (2007–8)

Since the 1990s, Turkey has repeatedly invoked a right to use force against Kurdish PKK bases in northern Iraq.[102] The 1999 Washington Accord between the competing Kurdish political factions of Iraq required the elimination of all terrorist bases. Nevertheless Kurdish attacks, from 2004, intensified, and in October 2007, led to an unprecedented escalation, as a result of which dozens of Turkish guards and soldiers were killed. In response, Turkey amassed tens of thousands of troops in the border region. In response to further ambushes, Turkish forces conducted air raids targeting PKK bases within approximately 100 kilometres from the Turkish–Iraqi border between late October 2007 and January 2008; these were accompanied by cross-border artillery bombardments. On 21 February 2008, several thousand Turkish ground forces moved deep into Iraqi territory, where they stayed until 29 February. After the end of this operation (Operation Sun), occasional air raids continued. The Turkish military claimed that approximately 540 PKK members were killed during the offensive, which also led to the destruction of 800 shelters, weapon stores and other PKK positions.[103] In a *note verbale* to the UN Human Rights Council, Turkey claimed its operation had been 'limited in scope, geography and duration. It targeted solely the PKK/KONGRA–GEL terrorist presence in the

[101] State practice (including pre-9/11 practice) is conveniently summarized by G. Wettberg, *The International Legality of Self-Defense against Non-State Actors: State Practice from the UN Charter to the Present* (Frankfurt am Main: Peter Lang, 2007), and, more cautiously, by Gray, *International Law*, 193ff. For a brief summary, see Tams, 'Self-Defence', 375–8.

[102] The following draws on the detailed account by T. Ruys, '*Quo vadit jus ad bellum*? A Legal Analysis of Turkey's Military Operations against the PKK in Northern Iraq' (2008) 12 *Melbourne Journal of International Law* 334. See also Wettberg, *International Legality*, 144–51, for details.

[103] See Turkish General Staff, *Final Report Regarding Operation Sun*, at www.tsk.tr/10_ARSIV/10_1_Basin_Yayin_Faaliyetleri/10_1_Basin_Aciklamalari/2008/BA_25.html.

region. Turkish military authorities took all possible measures to ensure the security of civilians and to avoid collateral damage'.[104]

The international community's reaction was characterized by a 'mixture of sympathy and concern'[105] for Turkey's conduct. Despite its magnitude, Operation Sun was never discussed in the Security Council. In their reactions, few states disputed that Turkey could use force against PKK fighters operating from northern Iraq. The PKK's attacks of October 2007 were widely condemned;[106] many states accepted that Turkey had a right to defend its population against terrorist attacks (including, it seems, by means of extraterritorial force). On the other hand, there was widespread concern about the scope of Turkey's use of force. EU statements frequently warned Turkey not to take disproportionate action, and not to destabilize the region. Most statements stressed that civilian lives had to be protected. US Secretary of Defence Gates for example declared the Turkish invasion should be 'as short and precisely targeted as possible'.[107] When Turkish troops left Iraqi territory, these concerns quickly ebbed away. States and international organizations expressed satisfaction that Turkey had refrained from excessive violence.[108] After a detailed study, one commentator observed that 'the Turkish intervention poses few problems in terms of proportionality'.[109]

3.1.2 Israel – Hezbollah – Lebanon (2006)

On 12 July 2006, Hezbollah mounted a cross-border operation into northern Israel, killed eight Israeli soldiers and abducted two. Israel responded with increasingly extensive attacks on Lebanon, culminating

[104] *Note verbale* from Turkey to the secretariat of the HRC (UN Doc. A/HRC/7/G/15 (2008)).

[105] Ruys, '*Quo vadis*', 344.

[106] See e.g. 'EU Presidency Statement on the Terrorist Attacks of the PKK in Turkey over the Weekend' (press release, 22 October 2007), at www.eu2007.pt/UE/vEN/Noticias_Documentos/Declaracoes_PESC/20071022PESCPKK.htm.

[107] 'Turkey must end Iraq raid – Bush', BBC News, 28 February 2008, at www.news.bbc.co.uk/2/hi/europe/7268345.stm.

[108] For example, the Belgian Foreign Minister noted that the Turkish attack 'was precisely targeted and aimed only at PKK targets, without harming the population of northern Iraq or local factions' (Questions et réponses écrites, Chambre des représentants de Belgique, 21 February 2008, QRVA 52 010, 1357, www.dekamer.be/QRVA/pdf/52/52K0010.pdf). His Dutch colleague observed that 'the Turkish actions appear to be restricted to specific actions against PKK targets in the border area of northern Iraq' (Maxime Verhagen, 'Beantwoording vragen van het lid Van Bommel over een Turkse invasie in Noord-Irak' (ministerial statement, 3 March 2008), at www.minbuza.nl/nl/actueel/brievenparlement,2008/03/Beantwoording-vragen-van-het-lid-Van-Bommel-over-e.html).

[109] Ruys, '*Quo vadis*', 363.

in a ground invasion.[110] Lebanon denied responsibility for the attacks of 12 July of which it claimed not to have been aware. Israel alleged Lebanon, Syria and Iran to be responsible for Hezbollah's conduct,[111] but said it was acting against Hezbollah targets only.[112] Subsequent UN investigations confirmed that Israel's attacks had claimed the lives of approximately 1,100 Lebanese civilians, injured some 4,400 and displaced about 900,000 residents; in addition, it destroyed airports, roads, ports and power stations within Lebanon.[113] Hezbollah, for its part, fired large numbers of rockets into Israel, which claimed the lives of approximately 50 civilians and 114 military deaths.

The international community's reaction was overshadowed by long-standing controversies about the Israeli–Palestine conflict. As regards the legal assessment, there seems to have been a considerable shift over time. Initially, a large number of states accepted that Israel could invoke self-defence against Hezbollah's attacks.[114] From the beginning, states however stressed that Israel would have to 'exercise utmost restraint' and should 'avoid casualties among innocent civilians and damage to civilian infrastructure and to refrain from acts that would destabilize the Lebanese government'.[115] As the Israeli use of force intensified, the strong majority of states criticized Israel's use of force as excessive.[116]

110 See the Secretary-General's Report on UNIFIL (UN Doc. S/2006/560 (2006)); and Gray, *International Law*, 237–44. For a detailed legal analysis, see A. Zimmermann, 'The Second Lebanon War: *jus ad bellum, jus in bello* and the Issue of Proportionality' (2007) 11 *Max Planck Yearbook of United Nations Law* 99; and Cannizzaro, 'Contextualizing Proportionality', 779.

111 Identical letters from Israel addressed to the Secretary-General and the President of the Security Council (UN Doc. S/2006/515 (2006)).

112 See Cabinet communiqué of 16 July 2006, at www.mfa.gov.il/MFA/Government/Communiques/2006/Cabinet%20Communique %2016-Jul-2006.

113 See Report of the Commission of Inquiry on Lebanon pursuant to Human Rights Council resolution S-2/1 (UN Doc. A/HRC/3/2 (2006), paras. 11 and 20).

114 During the SC meeting of 14 July, only China and Qatar expressly rejected Israel's reliance on self-defence (UN Doc. S/PV.5489 (2006), at www.un.org/depts/dhl/resguide/scact2006.htm). In contrast, Israel's right was recognized by Argentina (9); Japan (12); the United Kingdom (12); Peru (14); Denmark (15); Slovakia (16); Greece (17); France (17) and the United States of America (17) (*ibid.*). The UN Secretary-General also acknowledged Israel's right to defend itself against Hezbollah attacks under Art. 51 UN Charter (UN Doc. S/PV.5492 (2006) 3; UN Doc. S/PV.5498 (2006) 3).

115 Cited from the statement of the G8 leaders meeting of 16 July 2006, at www.mfa.gov.il/MFA/MFAArchive/2000_2009/2006/Statement%20by%20Group%20of%20Eight%20Leaders%20-%20G8%20Summit%202006%2016-Jul-2006.

116 In its Report, the Commission of Inquiry on Lebanon noted that 'while Hezbollah's illegal action under international law of 12 July 2006 provoked an immediate violent

Predictably, this approach was followed by the Non-Aligned-Movement. However, it was also shared by states that had initially supported Israel's position such as France and Argentina, as well as, e.g. Brazil, Chile, Djibouti, Switzerland and New Zealand.[117] The Security Council for a long while did not take any decisive action, but in SC Res 1701 (2006) ordered a qualified ceasefire, which required Hezbollah to cease all attacks and Israel to refrain from 'all *offensive* military operations'.

3.1.3 United States – Afghanistan – Sudan (1998)

In early August 1998, terrorists attacked the US embassies in Nairobi and Dar es Salam, killing more than 200 individuals and wounding approximately 4,000.[118] Evidence suggested that Osama bin Laden's terror network was responsible for the attacks, which were widely condemned, including by the Security Council.[119] On 20 August 1998, the United States responded by missile attacks on two targets: a terrorist training camp in Afghanistan and the El-Shifa pharmaceutical plant in Khartoum, allegedly used to produce chemical weapons for Osama bin Laden. In its report to the Security Council,[120] the United States claimed a right to respond against the embassy bombings and in order to prevent their repetition. The United States also claimed that neither Sudan nor Afghanistan had been willing to comply with requests to suppress bin Laden's activities on their respective territories, and that the attacks had been 'carefully designed to minimize risks of collateral damage to civilians and to comply with international law, including the rules of necessity and proportionality'.[121] Soon after the attacks, it was revealed that while the target in Afghanistan had in fact been used as a training camp, the El-Shifa factory in Sudan had long severed its ties with bin Laden and that it could hardly be used to produce chemical weapons (or precursors). Although the Sudan strikes thus in all likelihood had been based on 'faulty factual premises',[122] the United States (unlike for example in the aftermath of its 1986 raid on Libyan targets) refused to disclose evidence and blocked an international investigation. The international reaction to

reaction by Israel, it is clear that, albeit the legal justification for the use of armed force (self-defence), Israel's military actions very quickly escalated from a riposte to a border incident into a general attack against the entire Lebanese territory' (UN Doc. A/HRC/3/2 (2006), para. 61).

117 Gray, *International Law*, 241.

118 For a clear account see J. Lobel, 'The Use of Force to Respond to Terrorist Attacks: The Bombing of Sudan and Afghanistan' (1999) 24 *Yale Journal of International Law* 537.

119 UN Doc. S/Res./1189 (1998). 120 UN Doc. S/Res./780 (1998). 121 *Ibid.*

122 Lobel, 'Use of Force', 544.

the US action was surprisingly muted.[123] Most of its allies supported the United States' position.[124] China, Russia, Arab countries and the Non-Aligned Movement condemned it, as did (at least implicitly) UN Secretary-General Kofi Annan.[125] While few states openly challenged the United States' factual assertions, the evaluation of evidence seems to have influenced the international reaction: hence the attacks on Sudan, despite the disdain for Sudan's government, arguably was condemned in stronger terms than the attacks on targets in Afghanistan.[126]

3.2 *The necessity of anti-terrorist self-defence*

The case studies do not provide detailed rules about the application of necessity to measures of anti-terrorist self-defence. Politically as well as legally, the various instances have remained controversial, and this has clearly clouded states' views on the necessity (or otherwise) of self-defence. Practice however suggests that states invoking self-defence in order to justify forcible responses against terrorists abroad do consider necessity to be relevant. In fact, as will be shown, it arguably plays a more important role than in traditional instances of interstate self-defence. While necessity is not always clearly separated from proportionality, it is possible to filter out some guidelines governing the application of the necessity test to measures of anti-terrorist self-defence. Taking account of the different questions singled out in the preceding sections, four observations can be made:

3.2.1 The functions of self-defence

The first concerns the functions of self-defence. As noted above, measures taken in self-defence are to be *defensive* in character: they must serve to repel an armed attack or avert imminent armed attacks. This criterion – always flexibly applied – has come under considerable strain. States have invoked a right of self-defence against terrorists even where their primary motive was not the repulsion of ongoing, or the prevention

123 *Ibid.*, 556–7, for much more on this point; Wettberg, *International Legality*, 157–9, for a summary of responses.

124 See the references in W. Drozdiak, 'European allies back US strikes; Japan says it "understands"', *Washington Post*, 21 August 1998, A 20.

125 Cf. H. Schneider and N. Boustany, 'A barrage of criticism in Mideast; US accused of "state terrorism"', *Washington Post*, 21 August 1998, A 20.

126 T.M. Franck, *Recourse to Force: State Action against Threats and Armed Attacks* (Cambridge: Cambridge University Press, 2002), 95–6.

of imminent, attacks. Rather, the campaigns pursued by Israel or Turkey, just as the United States' air strikes against Afghanistan and Sudan, seemed to serve a variety of different goals. The United States for example certainly claimed that its strikes would prevent future attacks, but did not suggest these had been imminent.[127] Israel and Turkey, for their part, made clear that in addition to repelling or averting specific attacks, they would weaken Hezbollah and PKK decisively.[128] Finally, it does not seem far-fetched to suggest that the real motive may have been to punish terrorists for their previous conduct or to retaliate.[129] In short, recent anti-terrorist practice seems to serve a variety of functions.

To some extent, this may be in the nature of things. As noted above, terrorist attacks frequently do not take the form of military campaigns with a clear beginning and ending. Rather, even if they are part of general policies of terror directed against a particular state (such as Israel), the specific attacks tend to be irregular, unpredictable, and usually of limited duration. This means that by the time a state is in a position to act, a particular terrorist attack may already have been completed – or alternatively the next attack may not yet be imminent. A strict application of the traditional test (that measures of self-defence be necessary to repel or avert an attack) therefore would exclude reliance on self-defence in many instances.

Recent practice suggests modifications to this traditional approach. How the new practice can be accommodated is not yet clear. Acceptance of the 'accumulation of events doctrine' might be one way of overcoming the problem.[130] Perhaps more pragmatically, recent practice can be explained as a move towards an even more flexible understanding of the functions of self-defence. The response to Turkey's invasion

[127] This especially applies to the attack on Sudan, as rightly noted by Lobel: 'The United States has not claimed that bin Laden used chemical weapons, or that he was going to use them imminently' ('Use of Force', 543).

[128] As regards Israel, see statements made during the SC's 5493rd meeting (UN Doc. S/PV.5493 (2006)), 4–5. With respect to Turkey cf. Ruys, *'Armed Attack'*, 338–9.

[129] See Gray's comment on pre-9/11 practice (including the United States strikes on Afghanistan and Sudan): 'on the basis of explanations given by [Israel and] the USA themselves the actions look more like reprisals, because they were punitive rather than defensive ... it is difficult to see how the use of force was necessary, given that the attacks on the nationals had already taken place' (*International Law*, 197–8). See Alexandrov, *Self-Defense*, 183–4, for a similar observation.

[130] As noted above, the accumulation doctrine will not be discussed here, as it primarily relates to the character of an armed attack, which is addressed in a Chapter 11 in this volume.

e.g. suggests that where the fear of future attacks seems genuine, victim states are allowed to use self-defence to avert attacks that are not yet imminent. The same seems implicit in the initial response to Israel's reaction against Hezbollah (even though the matter was more controversial). Perhaps more critically, the response to the United States' 1998 bombings seems to suggest that as long as victim states claimed to act defensively, other states are likely to accept their explanation, even if the real motive might have been to retaliate or punish.[131] As a result, while self-defence against terrorists ostensibly must serve defensive purposes, recent practice indicates that this aspect is not seriously scrutinized.

3.2.2 Security Council action

The case studies provide relatively little evidence about the relationship between self-defence and Security Council action. With respect to the operations by Turkey and the United States, the issue hardly arose, as the Security Council did not adopt sanctions against the PKK attacks of October 2007 and the 1998 embassy bombings (even though it condemned the latter).[132] To the extent that measures of self-defence were considered necessary to repel the attack or prevent their repetition, unilateral conduct was not blocked by institutional action. In the Turkish case, one might add that this view of the relationship between self-defence and Security Council action implies that the broad range of anti-terrorism measures enacted by the Council since the late 1990s are in and of themselves not sufficient to exclude measures of self-defence. This in fact is not surprising, as the Council has mostly addressed terrorism at a more general level – by prescribing rules governing the conduct of states vis-à-vis terrorist organizations, by seeking to prevent terrorists from acquiring or using funds, etc. In so far as the Security Council has addressed armed attacks by terrorists, it has mostly done so through non-military sanctions in the sense of Article 41 UN Charter, but has so far not authorized the use of military measures against terrorists.[133]

The Israeli measures against Lebanon raise much more complex issues.[134] As noted above, the Security Council ordered a ceasefire on 11 August 2006. In line with what has been stated above, this could have

[131] According to Gray, *International Law*, it seems nowadays sufficient that States often merely 'pay lip-service to the need to act in self-defence' (166).

[132] UN Doc. S/RES/1189 (1998).

[133] See Tams, 'Use of Force', 375–8.

[134] For a clear summary see Gray, *International Law*, 243–4.

had the effect of disapplying Israel's right to use self-defence (if it existed in the first place); however, the terms of SC Res. 1701 (2006) only required Israel to cease all 'offensive' military operations. The matter came to the fore when Israel continued to use force after 11 August 2006.[135] Predictably, Israel argued that its use of force was defensive in character. The express language of the resolution favoured this approach; even though many states and the UN Secretary-General expressed criticism.[136] For present purposes, the episode is relevant in that it underlines the high threshold of Security Council involvement that is required to disapply the right of self-defence. SC Res. 1701 (2006) suggests that in the anti-terrorism context, the Security Council, even when it does address a conflict, may be unable or unwilling to preclude self-defence even where its exercise has been extremely controversial. It is thus further evidence of the blurring of lines between unilateral and institutional conduct, and suggests that Security Council action only in exceptional circumstances excludes self-defence against terrorist attacks.

3.2.3 Responses by the host state

Whereas the previous paragraphs address smaller modifications to the traditional understanding of necessity, the case studies, in at least one respect, show that when applied to anti-terrorist self-defence, the necessity test assumes a new dimension. This new dimension concerns the relationship between the victim state and the host state on whose territory the terrorists operate. If it is accepted that self-defence can be used against host states that do not direct or control terrorist activities,[137] then 'there is an additional rung in the ladder of available options, namely the possibility of seeking a solution via the territorial [host] state'.[138] This 'additional rung in the ladder' is crucial because repressive measures by the host state against terrorists are clearly an alternative option, a 'choice

[135] See Report of the Secretary-General on the Implementation of SC Res. 1701 (2006) (UN Doc. S/2007/147 (3–8)) for details.

[136] Contrast UN press release SG/SM/10602 ('UN Secretary-General deeply concerned about Israeli violation of ceasefire on 19 August') on the one hand, and the statement by the Israeli Ministry of Foreign Affairs on the other (IDF Bekaa operation in response to violation of ceasefire, www.mfa.gov.il/MFA/About+the+Ministry/MFA+Spokesman/2006/MFA+IDF+Bekaa+operation+in+response+to+violation+of+cease-fire+20-Aug-2006.htm).

[137] As noted in section 1, this is by no means accepted. The understanding of 'necessity' is inevitably influenced by the debate about required degree of host state involvement in the armed attacks of terrorists.

[138] Lubell, 'Use of force', 47.

of means'[139] much preferable to the extraterritorial use of armed force by the victim state. As a general rule, it would seem to follow that for self-defence to be considered necessary, the victim state has to make an attempt to have the host state suppress the terrorist threat, or alternatively to seek the host state's consent to extraterritorial anti-terrorist measures.[140] This in fact is brought out, at least implicitly, by the different instances examined above. In order to justify their conduct, Turkey and the United States for example asserted that the respective host states affected by their operations had been unwilling or unable to prevent the terrorist threat/attack. Israel went further in that it alleged (controversially) that Lebanon had supported Hezbollah's activities and therefore bore responsibility. Whether or not these allegations were true on the facts, they clearly show that victim states accept the primacy of host state enforcement as a matter of principle.

The question remains under what circumstances victim states can legitimately claim that notwithstanding the possibility of host state enforcement, they are entitled to use force against terrorists. Practice examined above suggests that this notably depends on the relationship between the host state and the terrorist organization in question and the type of anti-terrorist action taken. In both respects, international practice has yet to produce clear-cut rules. A number of points however can be made.[141]

Whether or not self-defence is necessary largely depends on the host state's attitude towards the terrorist organization responsible for the attack: states that openly or covertly support terrorists cannot be expected to take effective enforcement action against them. In this case, reactions by the victim state have been considered necessary as host state enforcement was not a realistic option. While the role of Lebanon has remained controversial (as many states did not accept Israel's claim) this is brought out, e.g., by the international response

[139] See *British and Foreign State Papers* (1840–1), 1138.

[140] See Chatham House principles: 'If the right of self-defence . . . is to be exercised in the territory of another state, it must be evident that that state is unable or unwilling to deal with the non-state actors itself, and that it is necessary to use force from outside to deal with the threat in circumstances where the consent of the territorial state cannot be obtained' (principle 6).

[141] The subsequent discussion focuses on the relationship between host states and terrorists in so far as it is relevant to the question of necessity. If self-defence is construed as a self-standing right against terrorists (irrespective of attribution), similar considerations would apply to the question whether the exercise of self-defence could violate right of the host state.

against al-Qaeda operating from Afghanistan. In that case, at least from the late 1990s, the international community seemed to accept that the Taliban regime did support the terrorists; as a consequence, the necessity of some action against al-Qaeda targets in Afghanistan was not disputed.[142] The matter in fact is largely one of establishing the host state's support for terrorists.

Where there is no evidence that the host states supports terrorists, the matter is more complex. Practice suggests that acts of self-defence may be considered necessary if the host state tolerates terrorist activities on its territory or harbours terrorists. This is evidenced e.g. by the international response to Turkey's invasion of northern Iraq (accepted largely because of the passive attitude adopted by the Northern Iraqi authorities). Outside the examples mentioned above, states such as Russia or Iran have claimed a right to use force where host states had tolerated (as opposed to supported) terrorists operating on their soil.[143] Possibly, this approach might be explained by reference to the duty of states to suppress terrorist activities.[144] Such a duty is enshrined in modern Security Council resolutions and anti-terrorism conventions, and it may also be derived from the general duty of states not to knowingly allow their territory to be used for violations of rights of other states.[145] It seems also implicit in modern international conventions such as 2005 the *African Union Non-Aggression and Common Defence Pact* which expressly qualifies the harbouring of terrorists, as well as any provision of support for them, as an act of aggression.[146]

By the same token, recent practice indicates that acts of self-defence can even be considered necessary where the host state is merely *unable* to

[142] But see below for comment on whether actions against the Taliban themselves were justified.

[143] See e.g. Letter from the Russian Federation addressed to the Secretary-General (UN Doc. S/2002/1012 (2002)) (claiming that '[t]he continued existence in separate parts of the world of territorial enclaves outside the control of national governments, which, owing to the most diverse circumstances, are unable or unwilling to counteract the terrorist threat is one of the reasons that complicate efforts to combat terrorism effectively').

[144] See explanation to principle 6 of the Chatham House principles.

[145] *Corfu Channel* (*United Kingdom of Great Britain and Northern Ireland* v. *Albania*), Judgment of 9 April 1949 [1949] ICJ Rep. 4.

[146] See Art. 1(c)(xi): 'The following shall constitute acts of aggression ... the encouragement, support, harbouring or provision of any assistance for the commission of terrorist acts and other violent trans-national organized crimes against a Member State' (at www.africa-union.org/root/AU/Documents/Treaties/text/Non%20Aggression%20Common%20Defence%20Pact.pdf).

suppress terrorist activities on its territory. The Israeli invasion of Lebanon for example seemed initially acceptable to many states even though Lebanon arguably was not in a position to suppress Hezbollah's activities. Other states invoking self-defence have equally asserted a right to act if the host state seemed incapable (rather than unwilling) to suppress terrorist threats.[147] Two considerations may be offered to support that position. For once, the line between situations of 'unwillingness' and 'inability' may be extremely thin, and not suited to distinguish illegal acts of force from instances of necessary self-defence. Perhaps more importantly, states that are unable to suppress terrorist activities on their territory would still be under a duty to do so – an inability to comply does not relieve states of their obligations.[148] But it is clear that this approach stretches the limits of self-defence to a remarkable extent.

Notwithstanding these attempts to filter out some legal standards, the relationship between host state and victim state responses against terrorists remains one of the main areas of uncertainty. The limited amount of practice so far has not produced clear guidance. In particular, third states have so far shown a curious reluctance to express their views on whether particular acts of self-defence were in fact necessary. Actual uses of self-defence have not been seriously scrutinized – in fact, states relying on self-defence (such as the United States with respect to the 1998 bombings) have often not been asked to 'make their case' before international fora, for example, in the Security Council,[149] even where the host state did require a public debate.

Pragmatically, one might suggest that in order to establish the necessity of its conduct, the victim state would be required to call on the host state to suppress terrorist activities on its territory, and even to reinforce its demands through economic or political pressure (whether through the UN or on a bilateral level). If the host state is willing, but unable to take effective anti-terrorist action, the victim state might even have to sound the possibility of a joint operation or share information enabling the host state to act more effectively. It also bears underlining that the application of the necessity test has to take account of the character of the

[147] See e.g. UN Doc. S/2002/1012 (for Russia's claim mentioned above); and see Tams, 'Self-Defence', 379–81 for a summary of similar claims.

[148] A point rightly stressed in the comment to Principle 6 of the Chatham House principles.

[149] A point emphasized by Lobel, 'Use of Force', 552–3.

particular anti-terrorist operation in question. By way of illustration, it may well be that a state unwilling or unable to mount a massive operation against terrorists would be willing and able to arrest individual leaders, or to prevent terrorists from acquiring specific weapons. Finally, the required degree of host state involvement may also depend on the urgency of the situation.

These considerations suggest that, as with necessity generally, the relationship between host state and victim state responses is heavily fact dependent. When assessing the facts, one should not lose sight of the exceptional nature of the self-defence against terrorists operating abroad. Victim states asserting a right of self-defence against terrorists abroad in effect require a licence to violate another state's territorial integrity even if that other state cannot be held responsible for the armed attack in question. The application of the necessity test ought to reflect the exceptional nature of this licence.

3.2.4 Non-forcible measures

Finally, the instances of anti-terrorist self-defence referred to above suggest that the principle of necessity is being adapted in yet another respect. Just as in the traditional, interstate setting, self-defence against terrorists is necessary only if the armed attack cannot be repelled or averted by non-forcible means. That much is admitted for example in the United States letter to the Security Council suggesting that, when striking targets in Afghanistan and Sudan, it 'had no choice but to use armed force to prevent these [terrorist] attacks from continuing'.[150] The application of this aspect of necessity however involves considerations quite different from those obtaining in traditional interstate disputes. This is largely due to three factors.

(1) The usual non-forcible means of averting or repelling armed attacks are unlikely to be effective when employed against terrorist organizations. Given the general condemnation of terrorism, it would for example be unrealistic to assume that 'diplomatic' pressure could be of much use against terrorist organizations; equally, economic blockades or treaty suspension will often not be a viable option.
(2) In contrast, states can exercise jurisdiction over terrorist offenders. They can thus pursue a 'law enforcement' strategy against terrorists

[150] Letter from the United States of America addressed to the President of the Security Council (UN Doc. S/1998/780 (1998)).

which usually is ineffective (or impossible, given rules on immunity) as a means of responding to interstate armed force. Moreover, since terrorist attacks often are of limited duration, the window of opportunity for non-forcible responses is arguably open for longer periods of time.

(3) The success of a law enforcement strategy crucially depends on the cooperation between the victim state and the host state in whose territory terrorists are based. Non-forcible responses will typically require the consent of the host state. As a consequence, the necessity of forcible responses depends on the relationship between host state and victim state.

These considerations suggest that potential non-forcible responses to be pursued against terrorists are likely to be different from those that a victim state might adopt against other states. They would notably seem to include measures designed to arrest and prosecute terrorist offenders; prevent them from acquiring weapons or supplies; or freeze bank accounts or other funds used by terrorist organizations. Whether these reactions are likely to repel or avert an armed attack may depend on a variety of factors, including the degree of information available about the aims and activities of terrorists, and the structure of their organization; the terrorists' dependence on logistic and other support to carry out attacks. Most importantly however, they depend on the attitude of the host state vis-à-vis terrorists operating on its territory. Without host state cooperation, non-forcible responses are unlikely to be successful. This in turn means that potentially effective non-forcible means crucially depend on the relationship between host state and victim state, and are affected by the lack of clear rules mentioned in the previous section.

3.2.5 Interim conclusions

These considerations suggest that while self-defence against terrorist attacks is subject to the necessity test, that test is adapted to the special circumstances of anti-terrorist force, and arguably can be applied more meaningfully than in the traditional interstate setting. While the relationship between unilateral conduct and Security Council action follows the general rules, the necessity test acquires a new meaning because it has to take into account the possibility of host state enforcement. As shown in the preceding section, the necessity of victim state action crucially depends on the attitude of the host state. Details of the relationship between host and victim state have yet to be clarified. Yet the preceding considerations bring out four general points:

- The primacy of host state action is undisputed as a matter of principle.
- Victim states must establish that host state action cannot be expected to repel or avert armed attacks by terrorists.
- Recent practice seems to suggest that this can be done in a range of different scenarios: clearly in cases of support, but also – more controversially – where host states are genuinely unwilling or unable to combat terrorist activities on their territory.
- In order to establish the necessity of their self-defence operations, victim states should typically be required to seek the host state's cooperation to combat terrorists by means of law enforcement unless the circumstances suggest the futility of any such attempt. In practice, this requirement has not been seriously tested.

3.3 The proportionality of anti-terrorist self-defence

Just as with respect to necessity, recent practice provides no detailed rules governing the proportionality of anti-terrorist self-defence. They do however clearly underline the crucial function of proportionality: whatever their views of a particular conflict, third states inevitably seem to voice concern that force remain proportionate (just as states invoking self-defence inevitably claim that it does). In times of protracted debates about the availability of self-defence or the required degree of cooperation between terrorists and host states, the international community has come to see proportionality as a convenient yardstick against which the states' responses can be measured, even if issues of legal principle remain disputed.[151] What is more, when assessing the proportionality of responses, the international community seems to have mainly taken account of the different, broadly defined, factors identified above – i.e. the scale of attacks, the geographical and temporal scope of responses, and issues of collateral damage. As regards the application of these factors, even a cursory assessment of practice suggests that within an anti-terrorist context – just as in with respect to traditional instances of interstate self-defence, proportionality does act as a restraint on extreme forms of abuse of self-defence – the response to Israel's invasion suggests that there *can* be near-unanimous agreement on the application of the proportionality principle.

Beyond that, the different case studies suggest while broadly following the same lines, the assessment of proportionality of anti-terrorist

[151] See Gray, *International Law*, 154.

self-defence displays a number of specific features. Six observations can be made.

3.3.1 A prospective–qualitative approach

The first point concerns the formulation of the proportionality equation. Practice confirms that self-defence requires the victim state to observe proportionality in a qualitative or prospective sense. In fact, the case studies clearly show that even where responses were directed against completed attacks, the effects of the armed attack were measured to the threat of terrorist attacks. Predictably, states responding against terrorist attacks have adopted that view. More importantly, third states accepted that measures of self-defence against terrorists could involve a more intensive use of force than the initial attack. As regards the instances referred to above, this is brought out clearly by the evaluation of the Turkish and Israeli invasions. It was beyond doubt that the full-scale invasions of Lebanon and northern Iraq would involve counter-force clearly exceeding that of the initial attacks prompting them. In its official statements, Israel expressly noted that it would take action proportionate to the threat Hezbollah's attacks posed to the border as well as stability in the region.[152] Turkey, by implication, took the same approach, as it strongly asserted the proportionality of Operation Sun, even though, on its own admission, it had clearly caused more damage than the initial attacks against which it had been directed,[153] and third states evaluating this claim did not seem to view this as a problem. Hence the EU Presidency, at the height of the ground offensive, called upon Turkey 'to limit its military activities to those which are absolutely necessary *for achieving its main purpose* – the protection of the Turkish population from terrorism',[154] thus deliberately avoiding a quantitative comparison of levels of harm inflicted. In short, recent practice indicates that when resorting to self-defence against terrorist attacks, states have to observe proportionality in a qualitative/prospective sense.

[152] Israel expressly referred to the grave threat, see UN Doc. S/2006/515 (2006). For the United States' arguments see UN Doc. S/1998/780 (1998).

[153] For the figures, see section 3.1.1 above.

[154] 'EU presidency statement on the military action undertaken by Turkey in Iraqi territory' (press release, 25 February 2008) www.eu2008.si/en/News_and_Documents/CFSP_Statements/February/0225MZZturkey.html.

3.3.2 Self-defence as a right to use force against terrorists

The case studies provide clarity also in another respect. They indicate that when assessing proportionality, the threat of the attack is to be compared to the injury suffered by the attackers, i.e. *the terrorists themselves*. At least in the three instances referred to, victim states have not claimed a right to take action against the host state. Of course, they have implicitly asserted a right to violate the host state's rights in so far as this seemed required by the exigencies of anti-terrorist force. Yet states have not claimed a right to respond against the host state irrespective of any such 'terrorist link'. The point was made expressly by Turkey and Israel,[155] and it is implicit in the United States' claim that its strikes had been carefully targeted to exclude collateral damage.[156] These claims are in line with the practice of other states invoking self-defence against terrorists, such as Russia, Iran or Colombia. As observed by one commentator, 'all invocations of the right to use force in self-defence against terrorist attacks since the 2001 US-led campaign in Afghanistan purport to be based on a right to use defensive force against non-State terrorist actors, not against the State acquiescing in their activities.'[157] Conversely, the failure of victim states to comply with this restriction on force was a crucial factor leading the international community to qualify self-defence operations as disproportionate.[158]

As is well known, the restriction of self-defence as a right to use force *against terrorists* (even if accepted) admits of a famous exception – the OEF campaign against Afghanistan begun in 2001 was, from its beginning, directed against terrorists *as well as* the Taliban regime.[159] This may be explained with reference to the special circumstances of the self-defence operation, which responded against a terrorist attack of a

[155] See Israeli Cabinet communiqué of 16 July 2006 and Turkish Note Verbale to the Human Rights Council (referred to in sections 3.1.1 and 3.1.2 above).

[156] UN Doc. S/1998/780 (1998). [157] Trapp, 'Back to Basics', 155.

[158] See further section 3.3.5 below.

[159] See the United States' letter to the Security Council (UN Doc. S/2001/946): 'In response to these attacks [of 9/11], and in accordance with the inherent right of individual and collective self-defence, United States armed forces have initiated actions designed to prevent and deter further attacks on the United States. These actions include measures against Al-Qaeda terrorist training camps and military installations of the Taliban regime in Afghanistan.' Whether the use of force against the Taliban was covered by Art. 51 (even admitting that it included a right to use force against terrorists) was of course much discussed: for criticism see e.g. J. J. Paust, 'Use of Force against Terrorists in Afghanistan, Iraq and Beyond' (2002) 35 *Cornell International Law Journal* 533, 540–3.

particular brutality. Perhaps more importantly, it might indicate that self-defence measures could be directed against states as well if (but only if) that state's support for terrorists was well established; this in turn would mean that proportionality (and not just necessity) depended on the relationship between the host state and the terrorists. Yet for present purposes, it is crucial to note that the broad focus of OEF is an exception, and that anti-terrorist self-defence has otherwise been understood as a justification to use force against terrorists, *not* against host states.[160]

3.3.3 The assessment of the terrorist threat

A third observation concerns the assessment of the terrorist threat. As noted above, in so far as self-defence must not be excessive in relation to the injury expected from the attack, this assessment crucially influences the scope and intensity of permissible self-defence.[161] Of course, very little express evidence is available on this – states do not 'rate' terrorist threats on a scale, or situate their relevance on a spectre. The matter therefore involves a degree of second-guessing or speculation. Yet with due caution, it seems fair to say that in recent years, terrorist threats have been considered to be of considerable gravity. As noted above, the gravity of an attack primarily depends on its scale and the likelihood of its success, but may also be influenced by normative considerations. As regards the former criteria, since the 1990s, a number of states have had to experience the very real consequences of terrorism, and the threat posed by it has become much more palpable. Perhaps as importantly, this has forged a 'strong international policy against terrorism':[162] the international community has progressively come to regard terrorist attacks, irrespective of their causes, as horrendous. The growing consensus against terrorism is evidenced by the massive proliferation of anti-terrorist rules and by the principled condemnation of terrorism in international declarations, resolutions of UN organs or international conventions.[163] These imply that, irrespective of the 'objective' dangers of terrorism, states consider it legitimate to eliminate the terrorist threat, and to take decisive action against it.

160 For many references on this point see Trapp, 'Back to Basics', 152–5.

161 See section 2.2.1 above.

162 See O. Schachter, 'The Lawful Use of Force by a State against Terrorists in another Country' (1989) 19 *Israel Yearbook on Human Rights* 209, 218.

163 For the best survey see P. Klein, 'Le droit international à l'épreuve du terrorisme' (2006) 321 *Recueil des cours, L'Académie de Droit International de la Haye* 203.

The new consensus against terrorism of course has been felt in many areas of international law. It is manifest e.g. in the willingness of states to derogate from human rights or in the surprisingly quick recognition of a right to use self-defence against terrorist attacks that are not imputable to another state. For present purposes, it is important to note that the normative 'reorientation', even where this is not made express, almost inevitably affects the application of the proportionality principle. Where an evaluation of an attack is influenced by normative considerations, the 'strong international policy against terrorism'[164] is likely to be an aggravating factor. This means that terrorist threats have been considered grave even where the likelihood that they could be realized, or that their realization would put the survival of the victim state at risk, realistically is not great.

3.3.4 The scale of the permissible force against terrorists

The assessment of the terrorist threat affects the scope of lawful responses. In particular, it may be a crucial factor explaining why responses by states have not been considered excessive even where they involved the large-scale use of force against terrorists. Turkey's invasion of Northern Iraq may serve to illustrate the point: As noted above, it was prepared by massive air raids and artillery fire and involved the deployment of large numbers of fully armed ground troops, which occupied a relevant sector of foreign territory. What is more, on Turkey's own admission, casualties among the PKK were twenty times higher than the number of Turkish nationals killed in attacks preceding the invasion.[165] Nevertheless, the invasion generally was not considered excessive; in fact, many states lauded the precision of Turkey's use of force, without discussing the number of losses among the PKK.[166] This in turn suggests that where responses are directed against terrorists as such, while avoiding collateral damage and sparing the civilian population,[167] counter-force used against terrorists may be massively more intensive than the initial armed attacks.

Perhaps as importantly, practice suggests that when invoking self-defence against terrorists, states are not prevented from pursuing

[164] Schachter, 'Lawful Use of Force', 218.
[165] See the figures given in section 3.1.1 above.
[166] See statements by the Dutch and Belgian foreign ministers cited above, section 3.1.1.
[167] A point to be addressed below (section 3.3.5).

far-reaching aims going beyond the repulsion of ongoing, or prevention of imminent, attacks.[168] Where there is a well-founded fear of repetition (e.g. because of the long history of separatist or terrorist violence, as in the case of Turkey and Israel), the international community seems to have accepted that states are entitled to use self-defence as a means of severely weakening the terrorist organization. The point has been made already with respect to the legitimate functions of necessity but also affects the application of proportionality. During the 2006 conflict, Israel's proclaimed aim of destroying Hezbollah's operational base in Lebanon[169] as such was condemned only by a few states. More clearly, the international community seemed to accept that Turkey's invasion was primarily aimed at destroying PKK bases in northern Iraq. With respect to the more limited 1998 strikes on Afghanistan and Sudan, the United States aimed at preventing future attacks that were not yet imminent.[170] For present purposes, it is crucial to note that the recognition of broadly defined aims of self-defence renders the proportionality analysis even more elusive than it usually is. If states invoking self-defence can legitimately seek to prevent future threats irrespective of their 'imminence', then the duty not to inflict injury that is *excessive in relation to the aims pursued* can hardly act as a restraining factor any more (at least as far as attacks on terrorists themselves are concerned). In this respect, the case studies evidence the further erosion of the proportionality test.[171]

3.3.5 Limitation of collateral damage as the key concern

While proportionality seems to place only few real constraints on responses against terrorists, the case studies suggest that the prevention or limitation of collateral damage has emerged as the key concern. When assessing measures of self-defence, the international community has placed crucial relevance on the protection of civilian losses and to damage sustained by the state (as opposed to terrorists operating on its territory). States invoking self-defence claimed their conduct had been 'carefully designed to minimize risks of collateral damage to civilians'.[172]

[168] See section 3.2.1, commenting on the broader functions of self-defence in the anti-terrorism context.

[169] See reference in section 3.1.2 above. [170] See Lobel, 'Use of Force', 543.

[171] See Gardam, *Necessity*, 183, who observes that 'discussions of proportionality take on a somewhat unreal air'.

[172] See UN Doc. S/1998/780 (justifying the US strikes on Sudan and Afghanistan). Similar arguments were advanced by Turkey (see note verbale to the HRC (UN Doc. A/HRC/7/G/15)) and Israel (UN S/2006/515).

In their responses, states and international organizations have almost inevitably called for 'utmost restraint' and in particular stressed the need to protect civilian life.[173] This is not to suggest that self-defence operations could involve no civilian losses at all: especially where terrorists form an integral part of the host state's population, a system permitting anti-terrorist responses cannot completely exclude civilian losses. Yet the various pronouncements mentioned above suggest that in the assessment of proportionality (under the *jus ad bellum* as well as the *jus in bello*), prevention or minimization of collateral damage – including damage sustained by the state as such[174] – has been of crucial relevance. In the Israeli case, this seemed the decisive factor leading states to criticize Israel's use of force as excessive – hence criticism intensified once large numbers of civilian casualties were reported, once Israel had destroyed targets without an obvious Hezbollah link (such as the Beirut airport), and more generally, once the Israeli operation came to be seen as a 'collective punishment' of the Lebanese people.[175] Conversely, as noted above, Turkey's invasion of northern Iraq was accepted precisely because it (while entailing heavy losses among PKK fighters) was felt to have only entailed relatively limited infringements of civilian rights.[176] While the matter remains more speculative, the same reasoning might at least partly explain why the international condemnation of the United States' 1998 strikes on Afghanistan remained muted.

Again, the three case studies are a far cry from establishing a new clear-cut proportionality test. What they seem to indicate, however, is that in the assessment of forcible responses, the international community has placed crucial emphasis on the scale of collateral damage, especially injuries sustained by the host state's population.

[173] See e.g. the various statements by UN Secretary-General Ban Ki-Moon on the Turkish operations in northern Iraq: See, e.g., 'Secretary-General concerned at Turkish move on attacking Kurdish Targets in Iraq' (UN News Service, 19 October 2007, at www.un.org/apps/news/story.asp?NewsID=24355&Cr=iraq&Cr1=turkey); 'Ban Ki-moon voices concern over Turkish air attacks against Iraq' (UN News Service, 17 December 2007, at www.un.org/apps/news/story.asp?NewsID=25098&Cr=iraq&Cr1=turkey); 'Ban Ki-moon calls for "utmost restraint" in Turkey–Iraq border actions' (UN News Service, 22 February 2008, at www.un.org/apps/news/storyAr.asp?NewsID=25722&Cr=iraq&Cr1=turkey).

[174] See section 3.2.2 above.

[175] For statements to this effect see e.g. UN Doc. S/PV.5492 (2006) 3 (Secretary-General) or UN Doc. S/PV.5489 (2006) 9 (Argentina).

[176] See the statements cited in section 3.1.1.

3.3.6 The limited relevance of geographical limitations

In contrast, the geographical scope of responses seems to have been of limited relevance in assessing the proportionality of responses. This is not to say that it played no role at all: Turkey for example underlined that Operation Sun had been 'limited in scope, *geography* and duration'.[177] However, recent practice seems to suggest that the geographical criterion is applied with more flexibility than in traditional interstate settings. This, in fact, would seem to be but a reflection of the new, 'global' dimension of terrorist activities. The 'global' dimension of permissible responses is brought out rather clearly by the United States' strikes against al-Qaeda cells in countries as diverse as Sudan or Afghanistan. While these strikes were by no means generally accepted, the fact that they carried the fight against terrorism into far-away countries seemed to be a factor of limited relevance.

More generally, it seems fair to say that the ubiquitous character of at least some modern terrorist organizations reduces the importance of geographical limitations on self-defence. In so far as armed attacks by terrorists are directed from remote bases, or even multiple bases in different countries, proportionality as applied in recent practice does not require the victim state to restrict its response to the geographically limited area of the attack itself. In fact, if terrorists are organized as networks operating from cells in different countries, it will often be impossible to identify a primary area of conflict. If the use of force against multiple cells is considered necessary (i.e. if the different host states are unwilling or incapable of suppressing terrorists operating on their territory),[178] it would e.g. be difficult to see why it should fail the proportionality test because of geographical considerations.[179]

3.3.7 Interim conclusions

Recent practice suggests that proportionality, just as in the traditional setting of self-defence, is a powerful rhetorical tool. The preceding considerations show that it can be applied and that the factors relevant to proportionality generally 'resurface' in debates about anti-terrorist self-defence. Nevertheless, the evaluation reveals certain specific features:

177 *Note verbale* to the HRC (UN Doc. A/HRC/7/G/15).

178 See section 3.2.3 above, on the relationship between host state and victim state responses.

179 For further discussion see Lubell, 'Use of force', 73–4.

(1) With the notable exception of Operation Enduring Freedom, self-defence has been construed as a right to use force against terrorists, not against the host state (which of course is affected by forcible measures, but not their principle target).
(2) Influenced by the growing consensus against terrorism, the international community's approach to proportionality has on balance been surprisingly lenient. In particular, drastic measures taken against terrorists have not been considered excessive even where they involved the use of force on a massively larger scale than the initial attacks. What is more, states have been permitted to weaken terrorist organizations rather than merely repelling or averting imminent attacks. This affects the scale of permissible responses.
(3) In contrast, international responses suggest that the international community does not seem prepared to condone large numbers of civilian losses, or collateral damage more generally; where this has occurred, the victim state's response has been criticized as disproportionate.

The special features to some extent concretize the application of the proportionality test: they suggest which factors are relatively relevant (collateral damage), and which are of relatively limited concern (casualties among the terrorists; as well as the geographical focus of responses). On the other hand, it may be exaggerated to hope for a real increase in predictability. State practice is too limited, and the various features remain tentative. Perhaps more importantly, the potential increase in predictability has to be weighed against new uncertainty about the legitimate aims of self-defence. This of course is a general problem complicating the assessment of proportionality of self-defence. Recent practice suggests that it is however particularly acute with respect to anti-terrorist self-defence.

4 Conclusions and recommendations

The preceding considerations suggest that necessity and proportionality limit the right of states to resort to self-defence against armed attacks by terrorists, but that their restraining impact is not always clear. Their application to anti-terrorist measures raises no conceptual difficulties but poses a number of special problems. It should be underlined that these problems are not caused by a lack of legal clarity – but for one (albeit important) aspect, the legal rules are clear: force must not be used unless necessary, and it must not be disproportionate. However, these rules are indeterminate: they can be applied to individual instances of self-defence, but the application is likely to remain case specific and therefore unpredictable, unless the indeterminate rules are supplemented by standards or guidelines on how they should be applied to future cases.

(1) With respect to necessity, at least in the traditional interstate setting of self-defence, such standards or guidelines seem to have emerged. Article 51 UN Charter clarifies that Security Council 'trumps' self-defence, and international practice clearly underlines that forcible self-defence can only be resorted to if the armed attack cannot be repelled/averted by non-forcible means. These standards are clear, but they rarely preclude a state that has suffered an armed attack from responding by forcible means. This in turn is not due to the rigidity of the necessity test, but because most armed attacks cannot be repelled or averted by other means: the Security Council has rarely acted; what is more, international jurisprudence has adopted a narrow understanding of the concept of 'armed attack', which means that if the use of force in international relations reaches the threshold level, it will usually be necessary to respond 'in kind'.

In contrast, with respect to special problems of anti-terrorist self-defence, practice so far does not provide clear guidance on the application of necessity. The key, novel, aspect concerns the relationship between the victim state targeted by an attack and the host state on whose territory terrorists are based. This adds 'an additional rung in the ladder of available options, namely the possibility of seeking a solution via the territorial [host] state'.[180] The primacy of host state action is universally accepted in principle, but there is no agreement on the scope of exceptions to the principle. The preceding discussion suggests that the host state's attitude vis-à-vis the terrorists is the key factor in applying the necessity test, and that the victim state has to establish that host state action would not be effective in repelling or averting the terrorist attack. Practice also indicates that the matter cannot be settled by identifying categories of host state conduct such as 'toleration', 'aiding'/'abetting' or 'inability to combat terrorists'. Beyond that, a proper balance

[180] *Ibid.*, 47.

between host state and victim state interests that takes due account of the exceptional nature of any forcible conduct on foreign territory has yet to be struck. Leaving aside the difficulty of agreeing on acceptable guidelines, this seems due to the fact that third states have so far rarely expressed views on whether a specific measure of anti-terrorist self-defence was necessary; unlike with respect to proportionality, public discussion about the necessity of anti-terrorist force has remained curiously muted.

(2) As regards proportionality, matters are more complex. Unlike necessity, the proportionality test cannot be broken down into a set of questions; it involves a comprehensive balancing of interests rather than a set of distinct questions. The balancing exercise has to take account of the prospective nature of self-defence and of the 'superior right' of the victim state to repel or avert attacks. This complicates the proportionality equation, as it means that attempts to measure proportionality in a quantitative way are inappropriate, and there is no objective way of measuring levels of injury. Proportionality judgments are difficult to predict, and depend on the assessment of the gravity of threats just as on the value judgments of what level of response is permissible. Unlike with respect to necessity, states have not shied away from pronouncing on these matters. However, they have usually been content to assert proportionality or lack of proportionality in very general terms. The point is well put by Franck: 'Although . . . commentators [including states] frequently endorse the principle of proportionality, they have been less than fastidious in explaining the exchange rate they have used to equate disparate integers'.[181] Since international jurisprudence has hardly been more specific, the requirement of proportionality, while much discussed, has yet to be fully operationalized.

That said, international responses to measures of anti-terrorist self-defence provide at least some guidance on what level of response is still regarded as proportionate. Taking account of the general condemnation of terrorist activities, the international community has been prepared to accept that states can take rather drastic measures against terrorists themselves. In contrast, it has been much less willing to condone collateral damage, especially civilian losses. These however are rather general guidelines.

[181] Franck, 'On Proportionality', 729.

(3) Finally, in one respect, necessity and proportionality lack the required degree of legal clarity: there is increasing uncertainty about the legitimate aims of self-defence. The defensive function of self-defence is typically asserted but applied very flexibly. Recent experience suggests that by defining their defensive aims broadly, states are able to subsume far-reaching military goals under a broadly-defined concept of self-defence. This 'normative drift' of self-defence indirectly affects the application of necessity and proportionality, as both can only be assessed in relation to the legitimate aims pursued by self-defence operations. Unlike with respect to the threshold requirement of 'armed attack', in respect of which the majority of states seems to have resisted attempts to 'open the floodgates', the international community seems surprisingly unconcerned about the scope of permissible self-defence. This approach limits the restraining potential of both necessity and proportionality.

The full potential of necessity and proportionality as limitations on the use of force has yet to be realized. The preceding considerations suggest that this problem is unlikely to be tackled by legal reform, and given the controversial nature of recent developments within the law of self-defence, it seems unrealistic to hope for authoritative restatements that command general support. Realistically, it may be hoped that the content of necessity and proportionality could be clarified and concretized through further debate between states amounting to a decentralized, but 'credible decision-making process', which in turn would produce a 'general system of subsidiary rules ... that demonstrably affects outcomes'.[182] This would primarily involve the scrutiny of (the necessity and proportionality of) specific invocations of self-defence. In addition, the relationship between host states and victim states might beneficially be addressed in a more abstract way.

Pragmatically, the following three measures might be recommended.

(1) Clarification of the legitimate aims of self-defence:
- At the 'legal' level, further debate on the legitimate aims of self-defence is of crucial relevance. This debate might take the form of, or be initiated by:
  - international studies;
  - express reactions by states to broadly-defined measures of self-defence (whether endorsement or protest); and

[182] *Ibid.*, 718.

- demands on states to define the aims pursued by self-defence operations (e.g. in Security Council discussions on states' reports under Article 51 clause 2 UN Charter).

While debates are unlikely to produce consensus, they might be hoped to raise awareness for the problem, and indirectly increase pressure on states to be more transparent about the aims of self-defence.

(2) A more active debate of necessity:
- With respect to necessity, international practice would notably have to clarify the relationship between victim state and host state action, and establish under which conditions victim states can reasonably claim that, notwithstanding the potential for host state enforcement, *they* had to use force to repel/avert an attack. In order to facilitate debate on this aspect, the following measures might be helpful:
  - Victim states resorting to self-defence should be asked to make public the reasons for their conduct, and especially to release information about why host state enforcement was no effective alternative.
  - Requests by host states for a debate about the specific self-defence operation (whether in the Security Council or in another forum) should, as a rule, be endorsed.
  - States should be more forthcoming in expressing views on the necessity of self-defence operations; in this respect, they would also have to separate issues of necessity and proportionality more clearly.

(3) More detailed comments on proportionality:
- As noted above, states do use proportionality as an argument in debates about (the scope) of self-defence, especially in recent instances of anti-terrorist self-defence. In order to identify the content of proportionality, it is however crucial to move from the level of general assertion to a more detailed assessment of proportionality. This would imply statements about proportionality that are more transparent and more specific than the standard pledges common at present. While outside observers often lack detailed information, it does not seem overly optimistic to expect statements that:
  - identify, in a concrete way, *the specific self-defence operations* whose proportionality seems questionable (e.g. the destruction of the Beirut airport during the 2006 July war); and
  - reveal the considerations on which the assessment is based (e.g. no military target; no obvious relation to terrorists, etc.).

Of course, outside observers will often not have the full facts of a situation. However, by moving towards a more detailed assessment of proportionality, outside observers might exercise pressure on victim states to release further details, and thereby contribute to a more transparent assessment.

Admittedly, these recommendations are unlikely to bring about quick clarification. What is more, they would require states to be more outspoken in some respects, which may be unpopular. However, it is believed that a more transparent discourse among states is the most effective way of operationalizing the concepts of necessity and proportionality.

PART III

Intersection between international human rights law and international humanitarian law in the fight against terrorism

14

Armed conflict and terrorist organizations

CHARLES GARRAWAY

1 Introduction

> Our war on terror begins with Al Qaeda, but it does not end there. It will not end until every terrorist group of global reach has been found, stopped and defeated.[1]

With these words to Congress, said in the presence of British Prime Minister, Tony Blair, President George W. Bush inaugurated a debate that was to outlive his presidency. What is a 'war on terror'? Is it a political phrase or a legal construct? Can you have a war against a tactic? How does it differ from phrases like the 'war on drugs' or the 'war on poverty'? Even as people began to back away from the phrase itself, it was clear that the United States was not backing away from insisting that it was at 'war' with al-Qaeda. In his memorandum of 7 February 2007, President Bush stated:

> (1) Our recent extensive discussions regarding the status of al Qaeda and Taliban detainees confirm that the application of Geneva Convention Relative to the Treatment of Prisoners of War of August 12, 1949, (Geneva) to the conflict with al Qaeda and the Taliban involves complex legal questions. By its terms, Geneva applies to conflicts involving 'High Contracting Parties', which can only be states. Moreover, it assumes the existence of 'regular' armed forces fighting on behalf of states. However, the war against terrorism ushers in a new paradigm, one in which groups with broad, international reach commit horrific acts against innocent civilians, sometimes with the direct support of states. Our nation recognizes that this new paradigm – ushered in not by us, but by terrorists – requires

[1] Speech by President George W. Bush to a Joint Session of Congress on 20 September 2001, at www.washingtonpost.com/wp-srv/nation/specials/attacked/transcripts/bushaddress_092001.html.

new thinking in the law of war, but thinking that should nevertheless be consistent with the principles of Geneva.

(2) Pursuant to my authority as commander in chief and chief executive of the United States, and relying on the opinion of the Department of Justice dated January 22, 2002, and on the legal opinion rendered by the attorney general in his letter of February 1, 2002, I hereby determine as follows:

   (a) I accept the legal conclusion of the Department of Justice and determine that none of the provisions of Geneva apply to our conflict with al Qaeda in Afghanistan or elsewhere throughout the world because, among other reasons, al Qaeda is not a High Contracting Party to Geneva.

   (b) I accept the legal conclusion of the attorney general and the Department of Justice that I have the authority under the Constitution to suspend Geneva as between the United States and Afghanistan, but I decline to exercise that authority at this time. Accordingly, I determine that the provisions of Geneva will apply to our present conflict with the Taliban. I reserve the right to exercise the authority in this or future conflicts.

   (c) I also accept the legal conclusion of the Department of Justice and determine that common Article 3 of Geneva does not apply to either al Qaeda or Taliban detainees, because, among other reasons, the relevant conflicts are international in scope and common Article 3 applies only to 'armed conflict not of an international character'.

   (d) Based on the facts supplied by the Department of Defense and the recommendation of the Department of Justice, I determine that the Taliban detainees are unlawful combatants and, therefore, do not qualify as prisoners of war under Article 4 of Geneva. I note that, because Geneva does not apply to our conflict with al Qaeda, al Qaeda detainees also do not qualify as prisoners of war.

(3) Of course, our values as a nation, values that we share with many nations in the world, call for us to treat detainees humanely, including those who are not legally entitled to such treatment. Our nation has been and will continue to be a strong supporter of Geneva and its principles. As a matter of policy, the United States Armed Forces shall continue to treat detainees humanely and, to the extent appropriate and consistent with military necessity, in a manner consistent with the principles of Geneva.

(4) The United States will hold states, organizations, and individuals who gain control of United States personnel responsible for treating such personnel humanely and consistent with applicable law.

(5) I hereby reaffirm the order previously issued by the secretary of defense to the United States Armed Forces requiring that the detainees be treated humanely and, to the extent appropriate and consistent with military necessity, in a manner consistent with the principles of Geneva.

(6) I hereby direct the secretary of state to communicate my determinations in an appropriate manner to our allies, and other countries and international organizations cooperating in the war against terrorism of global reach.[2]

In this memorandum, the President clearly spoke of 'our conflict with al Qaeda in Afghanistan or elsewhere throughout the world' and drew a distinction between that conflict which was outwith the constructs of the Geneva Convention and the separate conflict with the Taliban, acting as the de facto government of Afghanistan, which he acknowledged was defined by the terms of the Geneva Conventions, even though he held that Taliban fighters did not qualify as prisoners of war under Article 4 of the Third Geneva Convention.[3]

But how does this bifurcation of conflict fit into the traditional legal construct? Can one have an armed conflict against a transnational terrorist group and if so, what are the applicable rules?

2 Definitions

Since the Treaty of Westphalia, war has been traditionally considered the prerogative of states. The construct of the modern laws of war[4] has grown up around that concept. Thus in the earliest treaties on the laws of war, the subject matter was limited to wars between states. The St Petersburg Declaration of 1868 stated that: '*The Contracting Parties* engage mutually to renounce, *in case of war among themselves*, the employment by their military or naval troops of any projectile of a weight below 400 grammes, which is either explosive or charged with fulminating or inflammable substances' (my emphasis).[5]

Only states were subjects of international law and therefore only states could be bound by international law. Although this general premise changed during the twentieth century, the principle that the laws of war applied only to conflicts between states did not. After the Second

2 White House memo, 'Humane treatment of Al Qaeda and Taliban detainees', 7 February 2002 (printed in K. Greenberg and J. Dratel (eds.), *The Torture Papers: The Road to Abu Ghraib* (Cambridge: Cambridge University Press, 2005), 134).

3 1949 Geneva Convention Relative to the Treatment of Prisoners of War of 12 August 1949, 75 UNTS 135 (reprinted in A. Roberts and R. Guelff (eds.), *Documents on the Laws of War* (Oxford: Oxford University Press, 2000), 244).

4 The terms 'laws of war', 'law of armed conflict' and 'international humanitarian law' in this chapter carry the same meaning and are used interchangeably according to context.

5 1868 St Petersburg Declaration (reprinted in Roberts and Guelff, *Documents on the Laws of War*, 55).

World War, the ICRC hoped to extend the ambit of the new Geneva Conventions being considered by the Diplomatic Conference in 1949 so that they covered both international and non-international armed conflict.

However, they did not succeed. Common Article 2 to the four Conventions was worded as follows:

> In addition to the provisions which shall be implemented in peacetime, the present Convention shall apply to all cases of declared war or of any other armed conflict which may arise between two or more of the High Contracting Parties, even if the state of war is not recognized by one of them.
>
> The Convention shall also apply to all cases of partial or total occupation of the territory of a High Contracting Party, even if the said occupation meets with no armed resistance. Although one of the Powers in conflict may not be a party to the present Convention, the Powers who are parties thereto shall remain bound by it in their mutual relations. They shall furthermore be bound by the Convention in relation to the said Power, if the latter accepts and applies the provisions thereof.[6]

The Commentary made the meaning of this article clear when it said: 'Any difference arising between two States and leading to the intervention of armed forces is an armed conflict within the meaning of Article 2, even if one of the Parties denies the existence of a state of war. It makes no difference how long the conflict lasts, or how much slaughter takes place.'[7]

However, that was not the end of the matter. Common Article 3 to the Conventions specifically applied to 'armed conflict not of an international character occurring in the territory of one of the High Contracting Parties'.[8] The Commentary makes it clear that this was designed to apply to 'civil wars'. However, the International Committee of the Red Cross did not wish to be quite as restrictive. The Commentary asks 'What is meant by 'armed conflict not of an international character'?' and goes on to say:

> That was the burning question which arose again and again at the Diplomatic Conference. The expression was so general, so vague, that many of the delegations feared that it might be taken to cover any act committed by

[6] Common Article 2 to the four Geneva Conventions of 12 August 1949 (reprinted in Roberts and Guelff, *Documents on the Laws of War*, 198, 222, 244 and 301, respectively).

[7] J. Pictet (ed.), *Commentary to the First Geneva Convention for the Amelioration of the Condition of the Wounded and Sick in the Armed Forces in the Field* (Geneva: ICRC, 1952) [hereafter Pictet I], 31.

[8] Common Article 3 to the four Geneva Conventions of 12 August 1949 (reprinted in Roberts and Guelff, *Documents on the Laws of War*, 198, 223, 245 and 302, respectively).

> force of arms – any form of anarchy, rebellion, or even plain banditry. For example, if a handful of individuals were to rise in rebellion against the State and attack a police station, would that suffice to bring into being an armed conflict within the meaning of the Article? In order to reply to questions of this sort, it was suggested that the term 'conflict' should be defined or, which would come to the same thing, that a certain number of conditions for the application of the Convention should be enumerated. The idea was finally abandoned – wisely, we think.[9]

Later, the Commentary says:

> We think ... that the Article should be applied as widely as possible. There can be no reason against this. For, contrary to what may have been thought, the Article in its reduced form does not in any way limit the right of a State to put down rebellion. Nor does it increase in the slightest the authority of the rebel party. It merely demands respect for certain rules, which were already recognized as essential in all civilized countries, and enacted in the municipal law of the States in question, long before the Convention was signed. What Government would dare to claim before the world, in a case of civil disturbances which could justly be described as mere acts of banditry, that, Article 3 not being applicable, it was entitled to leave the wounded uncared for, to inflict torture and mutilations and to take hostages?[10]

This Article was the first foray of international humanitarian law outside international armed conflict and into the murky waters of activities by non-state actors. It left two crucial areas in a state of ambiguity. First the text limited the applicability of Common Article 3 to 'armed conflict not of an international character *occurring in the territory of one of the High Contracting Parties*' (my emphasis). Of course, in 1949, the anticipation was for civil wars and colonial wars – not what are sometimes now referred to as 'transnational conflicts' – conflicts between a state and a non-state actor that cross international boundaries. The phrase, 'occurring in the territory of one of the High Contracting Parties', was included in early drafts of the text at the Diplomatic Conference[11] and does not appear to have attracted much debate. Indeed, there is comparatively little debate in the Commentaries, though the Commentary to the Third Geneva Convention makes clear the intent in saying: 'Speaking generally, it must be recognized that the conflicts referred to in Article 3 are armed conflicts, with "armed forces" on either side engaged

[9] Pictet I, 49. [10] *Ibid.*, 50. [11] *Ibid.*, 45.

in "hostilities" – conflicts, in short, which are in many respects similar to an international war, but take place within the confines of a single country.'[12]

The second area of ambiguity was more deliberate. As has already been noted, there is no definition of armed conflict. That this was indeed deliberate is made clear in the Commentary to the Third Geneva Convention.[13] This of course fitted with the ICRC view that the provisions of the Article should be applicable as widely as possible without too much concern on the technical definition of terms such as 'armed conflict'.

In 1977, when the two Additional Protocols to the 1949 Geneva Conventions were adopted, the same two points arose again. Additional Protocol I, which dealt with international armed conflicts, adopted the scope of application contained in Common Article 2.[14] However, in a controversial provision, it extended the scope to include: '[A]rmed conflicts in which peoples are fighting against colonial domination and alien occupation and against racist régimes in the exercise of their right of self-determination, as enshrined in the Charter of the United Nations and the Declaration on Principles of International Law concerning Friendly Relations and Co-operation among States in accordance with the Charter of the United Nations.'[15]

It should be noted that this has no territorial restriction. Most of the colonial conflicts of that time involved cross-border activity.

On the other hand, Additional Protocol II, dealing with non-international armed conflict and seeking to expand the provisions of Common Article 3, was adopted with a much more restricted field of application. It applied only to:

> [A]ll armed conflicts which are not covered by [Additional Protocol I] and which take place in the territory of a High Contracting Party between its armed forces and dissident armed forces or other organized armed groups which, under responsible command, exercise such control over a part of its territory as to enable them to carry out sustained and concerted military operations and to implement this Protocol.[16]

[12] J. Pictet (ed.) *Commentary to the Third Geneva Convention Relative to the Treatment of Prisoners of War* (Geneva: ICRC, 1958) [hereafter Pictet III], 37.

[13] Pictet I, 49.

[14] 1977 Protocol Additional to the Geneva Conventions of 12 August 1949, and Relating to the Protection of Victims of International Armed Conflicts (Additional Protocol I), art. 1(3) (reprinted in Roberts and Guelff, *Documents on the Laws of War*, 423).

[15] *Ibid.*, Art. 1(4).

[16] 1977 Protocol Additional to the Geneva Conventions of 12 August 1949, and Relating to the Protection of Victims of Non-International Armed Conflicts (Additional Protocol II), Art. 1 (reprinted in Roberts and Guelff, *Documents on the Laws of War*, 484).

Here again is the geographic limitation, 'in the territory of a High Contracting Party'. Perhaps surprisingly, this is not specifically referred to in the Commentary which concentrates on the other restrictions which distinguish the application of Additional Protocol II from Common Article 3, namely that the conflict must be 'between its armed forces and dissident armed forces or other organized armed groups which, under responsible command, exercise such control over a part of its territory as to enable them to carry out sustained and concerted military operations and to implement this Protocol'.[17]

Also, the arguments over the definition of 'armed conflict' reappeared. Neither Protocol sought to solve that conundrum but Additional Protocol II did seek to define what did not amount to an armed conflict. Article 1(2) states: 'This Protocol shall not apply to situations of internal disturbances and tensions, such as riots, isolated and sporadic acts of violence and other acts of a similar nature, as not being armed conflicts.'[18]

The Commentary explained this as follows:

> 4446 . . . As the heading indicates, Article 1 defines the material field of application of the Protocol, i.e., it determines the circumstances in which it applies. This provision constitutes the keystone of the instrument. It is the result of a delicate compromise, the product of lengthy negotiations, and the fate of the Protocol as a whole depended on it until it was finally adopted in the plenary meetings of the Conference.[19]

Specifically in relation to Article 1(2), the Commentary stated:

> 4473 This paragraph was taken from the ICRC draft and made sense in the context of the original draft article. Its purpose was to define the lower threshold of the concept of armed conflict, assuming that the field of application of common Article 3 and the Protocol would be identical. The paragraph was not questioned and was retained and adopted without lengthy debates.
>
> 4474 No real definitions are given. The concept of internal disturbances and tensions may be illustrated by giving a list of examples of such situations without any attempt to be exhaustive: riots, such as demonstrations without a concerted plan from the outset; isolated and sporadic

[17] Y. Sandoz *et al.* (eds.), *Commentary on the Additional Protocols of 8 June 1977 to the Geneva Conventions of 12 August 1949* (Geneva: ICRC, 1987) [hereafter Sandoz, *Commentary*], 1347ff.

[18] APII, Art. 1(2) (reprinted in Roberts and Guelff, *Documents on the Laws of War*, 484).

[19] Sandoz, *Commentary*, 1348.

> acts of violence, as opposed to military operations carried out by armed forces or armed groups; other acts of a similar nature, including, in particular, large scale arrests of people for their activities or opinions.
>
> 4476 As regards 'internal tensions', these could be said to include in particular situations of serious tension (political, religious, racial, social, economic, etc.), but also the sequels of armed conflict or of internal disturbances. Such situations have one or more of the following characteristics, if not all at the same time:
>
> - large scale arrests;
> - a large number of 'political' prisoners;
> - the probable existence of ill-treatment or inhumane conditions of detention;
> - the suspension of fundamental judicial guarantees, either as part of the promulgation of a state of emergency or simply as a matter of fact;
> - allegations of disappearances.
>
> 4477 In short, as stated above, there are internal disturbances, without being an armed conflict, when the State uses armed force to maintain order; there are internal tensions, without being internal disturbances, when force is used as a preventive measure to maintain respect for law and order.[20]

It will be noted that the ICRC recognized that not every deployment of armed force necessarily amounts to a non-international armed conflict. There is a growing scale of internal violence running from internal tensions through internal disturbances to non-international armed conflict. Article 1(2) was designed to provide a bottom threshold for both Additional Protocol II and Common Article 3; hence the final words, 'as not being armed conflicts'.

Thus, with the adoption of the Additional Protocols, there was a graduated list of legal regimes. First, there were 'situations of internal disturbances and tensions, such as riots, isolated and sporadic acts of violence and other acts of a similar nature'. These were excluded from the definition of 'armed conflict' and hence international humanitarian law did not apply at all. Second, there were armed conflicts 'not of an international character occurring in the territory of one of the High Contracting Parties', governed by Common Article 3. Third, there were the more restricted and high-intensity non-international armed conflicts, governed by Additional Protocol II. Fourth came 'armed conflicts in which peoples are fighting against colonial domination and alien occupation and against racist régimes in the exercise of their

[20] *Ibid.*,1354.

right of self-determination, as enshrined in the Charter of the United Nations and the Declaration on Principles of International Law concerning Friendly Relations and Co-operation among States in accordance with the Charter of the United Nations', which, by virtue of Article 1(4) of Additional Protocol I, were equated to full international armed conflicts. Finally came 'all cases of declared war or of any other armed conflict which may arise between two or more of the High Contracting Parties', governed by Common Article 2 and amounting to full international armed conflict.

Although attempts have been made through judicial decisions, particularly by the International Criminal Tribunal for the Former Yugoslavia, and also by the International Committee of the Red Cross in its study *Customary International Humanitarian Law*,[21] to bring some coherence to this jungle by introducing more of the provisions applicable in international armed conflict into other forms of conflict, the basic legal framework has remained the same since the mid-1970s. The ICTY did try to resolve the definition of armed conflict in the *Tadić* case and arrived at the following summation:

> an armed conflict exists whenever there is a resort to armed force between States or protracted armed violence between governmental authorities and organized armed groups or between such groups within a State. International humanitarian law applies from the initiation of such armed conflicts and extends beyond the cessation of hostilities until a general conclusion of peace is reached; or, in the case of internal conflicts, a peaceful settlement is achieved. Until that moment, international humanitarian law continues to apply in the whole territory of the warring States or, in the case of internal conflicts, the whole territory under the control of a party, whether or not actual combat takes place there.[22]

3 Terrorism and armed conflict

However, where in all this does terrorism fit in? Of course the answer to that depends to a certain extent on one's definition of 'terrorism' and there perhaps lies the rub.

[21] J. M. Henckaerts and L. Doswald-Beck (eds.), *Customary International Humanitarian Law* (Cambridge: Cambridge University Press, 2005) (ICRC Study).

[22] *Prosecutor* v. *Tadić*, Decision on the Defence Motion for Interlocutory Appeal on Jurisdiction, Case No. IT-94-1-AR72, A.Ch., 2 October 1995, para. 70.

Terrorist acts have been committed for centuries by different groupings. Some were anarchists, some revolutionaries and during the latter half of the twentieth century, many were involved in what were seen as 'liberation struggles' – freeing their countries from the yoke of colonialism, apartheid or occupation. Some sought to justify such acts according to the motive which caused them to be committed. Most terrorist acts were committed in a national environment and the response, in keeping with the view that civil disturbances were a matter primarily for national law, treated them as criminal matters under local jurisdiction. International criminal justice as we know it today with the various international criminal tribunals and the International Criminal Court was still a dream.

As early as 1937, there had been an attempt to produce a Convention for the Prevention and Punishment of Terrorism which defined terrorism as '[a]ll criminal acts directed against a State and intended or calculated to create a state of terror in the minds of particular persons or a group of persons or the general public'.[23] This Convention never came into force but illustrates that terrorism was seen as principally a matter of criminal law. When acts of terror became more international, particularly with the spate of aircraft hijackings in the 1970s, the response was to seek greater international cooperation in law enforcement. There was already a Convention on Offences and Certain Other Acts Committed on Board Aircraft dating from 1963[24] and this was followed by a succession of other Conventions dealing with specific acts of terrorism from the 1970 Convention for the Suppression of Unlawful Seizure of Aircraft[25] to the 1999 International Convention for the Suppression of the Financing of Terrorism.[26] What is notable about all of these is that they continued to look upon acts of terror as a matter principally for criminal jurisdiction.

Of course this did not exclude the commission of acts of terror in armed conflict. The Fourth Geneva Convention specifically prohibited

[23] 1937 Convention for the Prevention and Punishment of Terrorism, 19 League of Nations OJ 23, League of Nations Doc.C.546(I)M.383(I) 1937 V (1938), Art. 2(1).

[24] 1963 Convention on Offences and Certain Other Acts Committed on Board Aircraft, 1248 UNTS 451.

[25] 1970 Convention for the Suppression of Unlawful Seizure of Aircraft, 860 UNTS 105.

[26] 1999 International Convention for the Suppression of the Financing of Terrorism, 2178 UNTS 197.

'all measures of intimidation or of terrorism'.[27] Additional Protocol I extended this to prohibit '[a]cts or threats of violence, the primary purpose of which is to spread terror among the civilian population'[28] and, in non-international armed conflict, 'acts of terrorism' were prohibited 'at any time and in any place whatsoever' under Additional Protocol II.[29]

But international humanitarian law did not equate acts of terror to armed conflict. Indeed the United Kingdom statement on ratification of Additional Protocol I made this quite clear when, in relation to Article 1(4) and Article 96(3), it stated: 'It is the understanding of the United Kingdom that the term 'armed conflict' of itself and in its context denotes a situation of a kind which is not constituted by the commission of ordinary crimes including acts of terrorism whether concerted or in isolation.'[30]

It should be recalled that this statement was made by a country that had just come out of some thirty years of terrorism conducted in relation to the 'Troubles' in Northern Ireland. It was a clear acknowledgement that 'terrorism', in itself, did not amount to an armed conflict sufficient to bring the laws of armed conflict into play.

4 The effect of 9/11

The events of 9/11 cast this carefully constructed edifice into doubt. The attacks on New York and Washington, DC were undoubtedly criminal acts under domestic law. Indeed, most would argue that the attacks on the World Trade Centre also were international crimes – i.e., crimes against humanity under the definition contained in the Rome Statute of the International Criminal Court.[31] However, did they constitute 'acts of war' sufficient to amount to an 'armed conflict'? Certainly, so far as President Bush was concerned, there was no doubt. In his Military Order of 13 November 2001, he stated:

[27] Geneva Convention Relative to the Protection of Civilian Persons in Time of War of 12 August 1949 (Geneva Convention IV), Art. 33(1) (reprinted in Roberts and Guelff, *Documents on the Laws of War*, 312).

[28] API, Art. 51(2) (reprinted *ibid.*, 448). [29] APII, Art. 4(2)(d) (reprinted *ibid.*, 485).

[30] United Kingdom statement (d) on ratification of API (reprinted *ibid.*, 510).

[31] 1998 Rome Statute of the International Criminal Court, 2187 UNTS 3, Art. 7 (reprinted *ibid.*, 674). Different considerations would apply to the Pentagon as it was not an 'attack directed against any civilian population'.

> International terrorists, including members of al Qaida, have carried out attacks on United States diplomatic and military personnel and facilities abroad and on citizens and property within the United States on a scale that has created a state of armed conflict that requires the use of the United States Armed Forces.[32]

But if there was an armed conflict, what sort was it and what rules applied?

The initial response of the United States to the attacks of 9/11 was to launch attacks against Taliban and al-Qaeda targets in Afghanistan. To most observers, these attacks fell within the traditional framework of law. The Taliban was the de facto government of Afghanistan and, although there was undoubtedly an existing non-international armed conflict taking place in Afghanistan between the Taliban and the Northern Alliance, the intervention of the United States and its allies was separate from that. The United States was invoking 'its inherent right of individual and collective self-defense following armed attacks that were carried out against the United States on September 11, 2001'.[33] There was thus a new international armed conflict between the United States with its allies, and Afghanistan. However, the United States letter to the President of the Security Council was more ambivalent. It stated:

> The attacks on September 11, 2001, and the ongoing threat to the United States and its nationals posed by the Al-Qaeda organization have been made possible by the decision of the Taliban regime to allow parts of Afghanistan that it controls to be used by this organization as a base of operation. Despite every effort by the United States and the international community, the Taliban regime has refused to change its policy. From the territory of Afghanistan, the Al-Qaeda organization continues to train and support agents of terror who attack innocent people throughout the world and target United States nationals and interests in the United States and abroad.[34]

While this clearly sought to link al-Qaeda with the Taliban, the letter also contained a more ominous phrase: 'We may find that our self-defense

[32] Military Order on the Detention, Treatment, and Trial of Certain Non-Citizens in the War against Terrorism, of 13 November 2001, Federal Register, 16 November 2001, 66 (*Presidential Documents*, 57831–6).

[33] Letter of John Negroponte to the President of the Security Council, 7 October 2001, at www.yale.edu/lawweb/avalon/sept_11/un_006.htm.

[34] *Ibid.*

requires further actions with respect to other organizations and other States.'[35]

There seem to have been two schools of thought within the Administration at the time. These were roughly reflected in a split between the Department of Justice, supported to a large extent by the civilian lawyers of the Pentagon, and the Department of State, supported by the military lawyers. Much of this debate was behind closed doors and is still not fully in the public domain but some has been revealed in what have become known as 'the torture papers'[36] and in other documents now placed in the public domain. The end result was the decision by President Bush in his memorandum of 7 February 2002[37] and the split of the Afghan conflict into two parts, an international armed conflict against Afghanistan, as represented by the Taliban, and a separate conflict against al-Qaeda with no geographic boundaries. As a result of this decision, all activities against al-Qaeda, across the world, could be governed by the laws of war rather than by law enforcement rules (though the option of using law enforcement rules remained). Until papers currently still classified are released, it will not be possible to ascertain the exact legal basis on which that decision was reached, if there was a legal basis at all. An attempt to reconstruct the reasoning from currently available sources indicates that this may almost have been a legal accident rather than a deliberate decision.[38] The argument seems to have centred on the applicability of all of the Geneva Conventions with Department of Justice officials keen to argue that they were not applicable for various reasons, including that Afghanistan was a 'failed state'.[39] As late as 2 February, William Taft, Legal Adviser to the State Department, was arguing that the issue was 'whether the Geneva Conventions apply to the conflict in Afghanistan in which U.S. armed forces are engaged'.[40] The singular use of the word 'conflict' should be noted. He went on to urge: 'It is not inconsistent with the DOJ opinion

[35] *Ibid.* [36] See *Torture Papers.* [37] *Ibid*, 134.

[38] See C. Garraway, 'Afghanistan and the Nature of Conflict' (2009) 39 *Israel Yearbook on Human Rights* 1.

[39] J. Yoo and R. Delahunty, *Memorandum for William J Haynes II, General Counsel*, Department of Defense, 'Re. Application of Treaties and Laws to al Qaeda and Taliban Detainees', 9 January 2002 (*Torture Papers*, 30).

[40] Memorandum from William H. Taft IV, Legal Adviser, Department of State to Counsel to the President, Comments on Your Paper on the Geneva Conventions, 2 February 2002 (*Torture Papers*, 129).

that the Conventions generally do not apply to our world-wide effort to combat terrorism and to bring al Qaeda members to justice'.[41]

He concluded by challenging the Department of Justice paper on which he was commenting in the following terms:

> The structure of the paper suggesting a distinction between our conflict with al Qaeda and our conflict with the Taliban does not conform to the structure of the Conventions. The Conventions call for a decision whether they apply to the conflict in Afghanistan. If they do, their provisions are applicable to all persons involved in that conflict – al Qaeda, Taliban, Northern Alliance, U.S. troops, civilians etc. If the Conventions do not apply to the conflict, no one involved in it will enjoy the benefit of their protections as a matter of law.[42]

However, this was to no avail. While the President was not prepared to go along with the Department of Justice view that the Geneva Conventions did not apply at all, he did bifurcate the conflict to exclude their direct application to al-Qaeda. The 'war on terror' was now official.

5 The ongoing legal debate

The argument in relation to Afghanistan was, to an extent, academic as the dispute was principally over the nature of the conflict rather than whether there was a conflict at all. However, the issue was thrown into sharper contrast in November 2002 in relation to the attack by an unmanned United States Predator drone, operated allegedly by the CIA, which launched a Hellfire missile killing a number of suspected al-Qaeda operatives in the Marib area of Yemen. The United States made their legal position seemingly clear in a Department of State response to an enquiry from a United Nations Special Rapporteur.

The United States asserted: 'The Government of the United States respectfully submits that inquiries related to allegations stemming from any military operations conducted during the course of an armed conflict with Al Qaida do not fall within the mandate of the Special Rapporteur . . . Al Qaida and related terrorist networks are at war against the United States.'[43]

[41] *Ibid.* [42] *Ibid.*

[43] See Response of the Government of the United States of America to the letter from the Special Rapporteur on Extrajudicial, Summary or Arbitrary Executions Asma Jahangir's letter to the Secretary of State, 15 November 2002 and to the findings of the Special

This should be set in contrast with the more conservative views expressed on the website of the International Committee of the Red Cross, and shared by many, both states and non-governmental organizations:

> Specific aspects of the so-called 'war on terrorism' launched after the attacks against the United States on 11 September 2001 amount to an armed conflict as defined under IHL. The war waged by the US-led coalition in Afghanistan that started in October 2001 is an example. The 1949 Geneva Conventions and the rules of customary international law were fully applicable to that international armed conflict, which involved the US-led coalition, on the one side, and Afghanistan, on the other side. However, much of the ongoing violence taking place in other parts of the world that is usually described as 'terrorist' is perpetrated by loosely organized groups (networks), or individuals that, at best, share a common ideology. On the basis of currently available factual evidence it is doubtful whether these groups and networks can be characterised as a 'party' to a conflict within the meaning of IHL.[44]

The ICRC added: 'Even if IHL does not apply to such acts they are still subject to law. Irrespective of the motives of their perpetrators, terrorist acts committed outside of armed conflict should be addressed by means of domestic or international law enforcement, but not by application of the laws of war.'[45]

On the other hand, those who sought to uphold the position of the United States administration argued with vehemence that the old concepts where states alone had a monopoly on the use of force were now outdated. A non-state actor could command as much capability to use force as many states and to say that such use of force was not an 'armed conflict', either because one side was not a state (international) or because it crossed state borders (non-international) was to allow such conflicts to become unregulated. Law enforcement, governed by its peacetime restrictions, was not a suitable vehicle for handling such cases.

There were probably some who were content for such conflicts to fall outside traditional boundaries as this permitted a 'pick and mix' approach to law. As this was a hybrid conflict to which neither Common Article 2 nor Common Article 3 applied, it was open to a

Rapporteur contained in her report to the Commission on Human Rights (UN Doc. E/CN.4/2003/3 (2003), Annex to UN Doc. E.CN.4/2003/G/80 (2003)).

[44] ICRC, *International Humanitarian Law and Terrorism: Questions and Answers*, at www.icrc.org/web/eng/siteeng0.nsf/htmlall/terrorism-faq-050504?opendocument#a3.

[45] *Ibid.*

state involved in such a conflict to apply by analogy those parts of the law which seemed most appropriate. This would inevitably mean those parts that were most advantageous. The term 'transnational armed conflict' was coined to cover such conflicts.

6 Transnational armed conflicts

Some of those who have argued for this new category of conflict saw the danger of the 'pick and mix' approach and indeed see this categorization as the only way to avoid it. Professor Geoff Corn, a former Special Assistant for Law of War Matters to the United States Army Judge Advocate General has written:

> It is essential that the applicability of the principles of the laws of war – principles that operate to limit the brutality of war and mitigate the suffering of victims of war – not be restricted by an overly technical legal triggering paradigm. Accordingly, the ongoing evolution in the nature of warfare requires acknowledgment that *any* armed conflict triggers the foundational principles of the laws of war. Many have argued that this outcome can be achieved by characterizing such military operations as 'common Article 3' conflicts. This concept of an 'internationalized' Common Article 3 conflict is certainly more logical than assertions that Al Qaeda and other non-state transnational groups should be treated as *de facto* states for purposes of satisfying Common Article 2. However, even this 'internationalized' application of Common Article 3 is limited in its effect, for it triggers only the humane treatment obligation of that treaty provision. What is necessary is to acknowledge that these 'transnational' armed conflicts trigger not only the humane treatment mandate, *but also* additional customary LOAC principles such as necessity, distinction, proportionality, and the prohibition against inflicting unnecessary suffering. Only such an expanded conception of LOAC application will ensure the regulatory purpose of the law is achieved. This is the basis for adopting the more pragmatic characterization of *transnational* armed conflict.[46]

But is this necessary? The United States Supreme Court, when faced with a variant of this question in the Hamdan case, adopted a slightly more cautious approach. Rather than adopt the 'transnational armed conflict' concept, the Court preferred a nuanced version of the traditional distinction between Common Article 2 and Common Article 3. Justice Stevens commented as follows:

[46] G. Corn, 'Making the Case for Conflict Bifurcation in Afghanistan: Transnational Armed Conflict, Al Qaeda, and the Limits of the Associated Militia Concept' (2009) 39 *Israel Yearbook on Human Rights* 31–2.

> The Court of Appeals thought, and the Government asserts, that common Article 3 does not apply to Hamdan because the conflict with al Qaeda, being 'international in scope', does not qualify as a 'conflict not of an international character'. That reasoning is erroneous. The term 'conflict not of an international character' is used here in contradistinction to a conflict between nations. So much is demonstrated by the 'fundamental logic [of] the Convention's provisions on its application', common Article 2 provides that 'the present Convention shall apply to all cases of declared war or of any other armed conflict which may arise between two or more of the High Contracting Parties'. High Contracting Parties (signatories) also must abide by all terms of the Conventions *vis-à-vis* one another even if one party to the conflict is a nonsignatory 'Power', and must so abide *vis-à-vis* the nonsignatory if 'the latter accepts and applies' those terms. Common Article 3, by contrast, affords some minimal protection, falling short of full protection under the Conventions, to individuals associated with neither a signatory nor even a nonsignatory 'Power' who are involved in a conflict 'in the territory of' a signatory. The latter kind of conflict is distinguishable from the conflict described in common Article 2 chiefly because it does not involve a clash between nations (whether signatories or not). In context, then, the phrase 'not of an international character' bears its literal meaning.[47]

However, this reinterpretation of Common Article 3 would still not satisfy the Corn test as it would seem to trigger 'only the humane treatment obligation of that treaty provision'. But that may of itself be incorrect. Certainly it is now accepted that, as a matter of customary law, large parts of what might be described as the law governing the conduct of hostilities (once known as 'Hague law' to distinguish it from 'Geneva law' providing protection to victims of armed conflict) have been transposed across into non-international armed conflict as a matter of customary law. This trend perhaps started in the seminal decision in the *Tadić* case at the International Criminal Tribunal for the former Yugoslavia where the Appeals Chamber stated:

> Notwithstanding these limitations, it cannot be denied that customary rules have developed to govern internal strife. These rules... cover such areas as protection of civilians from hostilities, in particular from indiscriminate attacks, protection of civilian objects, in particular cultural property, protection of all those who do not (or no longer) take active part in hostilities, as well as prohibition of means of warfare proscribed in international armed conflicts and ban of certain methods of conducting hostilities.[48]

[47] *Hamdan* v. *Rumsfeld*, 126 S. Ct 2669, 2795–6 (citations omitted) (2006).

[48] *Tadić*, para. 127.

This was followed by the Statute of the International Criminal Court which went beyond the victim protection provisions of Common Article 3 and included, in relation to non-international armed conflicts, some limited provisions on the conduct of hostilities.[49] The ICTY continued to advance the arguments put forward in *Tadić* in subsequent cases but these tentative steps were dwarfed by the impact of the study *Customary International Humanitarian Law* published by the ICRC in 2005.[50] This study found 161 'rules' of customary international law relating to armed conflict, 159 applied to international armed conflict and 2 were only applicable to non-international armed conflict. However, of the 159, 146 of these rules were applicable across the board to international and non-international armed conflict alike. Essentially, in so far as the conduct of hostilities was concerned, the rules were the same. A similar line was taken by the San Remo *Manual Law of Non-International Armed Conflict*.[51]

If it is to be argued that 'transnational armed conflicts' are in fact covered by Common Article 3, then it is a short step to adopting the conduct of hostilities provisions as well so that there is a mass of regulation for these types of conflict and no need for a new category to be created.

There is a degree of simplicity to this that is attractive and it is indeed that very simplicity that is the greatest weakness. As Corn puts it: 'the time is ripe to consider whether the pragmatic logic that has animated military policy on this subject for decades should not be regarded as something more, to wit a reflection of a general principle of law requiring that all military operations involving the employment of combat power fall under the regulatory framework of the LOAC.'[52]

In support of this, Corn cites 'a clear and simple mandate codified in the Department of Defense Law of War Program: comply with the principles of the law of war during all military operations'.[53] But it

49 See Rome Statute, Art. 8(2)(e) (reprinted in Roberts and Guelff, *Documents on the Laws of War*, 679).

50 ICRC Study.

51 M. Schmitt *et. al* (eds.) *Manual on the Law of Non-International Armed Conflict*, special supplement to the (2006) 36 *Israel Yearbook on Human Rights*.

52 Corn, 'Making the Case', 48.

53 *Ibid.*, 50, citing United States Department of Defense, Directive 5100.77, DoD Law of War Program (9 December 1998). The exact policy mandate required that each component of the armed forces ensure that the members of their DoD components comply with the law of war during all armed conflicts, however such conflicts are characterized, and with the principles and spirit of the law of war during all other operations.

must be questioned whether the reason why such a mandate was inserted was to widen the rights of service personnel or to provide guidance on the restrictions that should be imposed on operations. Not every deployment of armed forces amounts to an 'armed conflict'. However, Corn seeks to argue that wherever a state employs what he describes as 'combat power', the law of armed conflict should apply. In effect, he introduces the exercise of combat power as a definition of 'armed conflict'. Again, there is logic in this. In international armed conflict, it is possible to find support in the ICRC Commentaries to the 1949 Geneva Conventions. In seeking to define 'armed conflict', Jean Pictet stated that: 'Any difference arising between two States and leading to the intervention of members of the armed forces is an armed conflict within the meaning of Article 2, even if one of the Parties denies the existence of a state of war.'[54]

It is correct that Pictet wanted the threshold for international armed conflict (as described above) to be as low as possible but that was to enable the protections provided within the four Conventions to be effective in as wide circumstances as possible. Corn's wish is in fact precisely the opposite. He fully recognizes that 'the most fundamental distinction between law enforcement and armed conflict is manifested in the scope of use of deadly force authority. Law enforcement activities, governed by international human rights standards, reserve the use of deadly force as a measure of last resort. In contrast, use of deadly force against a military objective is a legitimate measure of first resort during armed conflict'.[55] As Corn later argues: 'While characterizing counter terror operations under the LOAC framework will undoubtedly trigger more expansive authorities than law enforcement operations, requiring compliance with LOAC principles of constraint will limit the scope of that authority.'[56] His purpose therefore is not so much to increase protection but to widen the authority for armed forces to use lethal force.

The United States historically does not use its regular forces in law enforcement. Indeed the Posse Comitatus Act[57] substantially restricts the power of the federal government in that regard. Other countries have a different tradition. In the United Kingdom, for example, the government used the armed forces in a law enforcement mode operating under domestic law for many years in Northern Ireland. The British Army is used therefore to operating on restricted rules of engagement based on

[54] Pictet III, 23. [55] Corn, 'Making the Case', 56 (citations removed). [56] *Ibid.*, 65–6.
[57] 18 USC sec. 1385.

law enforcement principles. Is it therefore that there is a cultural difference which pushes the United States towards the 'war' paradigm when their armed forces are deployed?

7 Lebanon

Of course, Afghanistan and the United States conflict with al-Qaeda are not the only situations in which the issues arising from the participation by non-state actors in conflict has arisen. Similar arguments arose in 2006 when Israel responded to Hezbollah actions by a concerted military operation aimed at Hezbollah positions in Lebanon. There was much debate over the characterization of the conflict. The conflict took part largely in Lebanese territory and few would argue that the level of violence did not amount to an armed conflict. But what was the nature of that conflict? At the start of the conflict, there was clear confusion in the public statements. In a special Cabinet communiqué on 12 July 2006, Israel pronounced: 'Israel views the sovereign Lebanese Government as responsible for the action that originated on its soil and for the return of the abducted soldiers to Israel. Israel demands that the Lebanese Government implement UN Security Council Resolution 1559.'[58]

Prime Minister Olmert is reported to have claimed that the Hezbollah actions were an 'act of war' by Lebanon.[59] Yet only four days later, Prime Minister Olmert was quoted as saying that: 'Israel is not fighting Lebanon but the terrorist element there, led by Nasrallah and his cohorts, who have made Lebanon a hostage and created Syrian- and Iranian-sponsored terrorist enclaves of murder.'[60]

The Lebanese government, which included Hezbollah members, issued similarly conflicting statements. The Lebanese Prime Minister, Fuad Siniora, was reported as saying: 'The government was not aware of and does not take responsibility for, nor endorses what happened on the international border.'[61]

[58] Special Cabinet communiqué – Hezbollah attack, 12 July 2006, accessed at www.mfa.gov.il/MFA/Government/Communiques/2006/Special+Cabinet+Communique+-+Hizbullah+attack+12-Jul-2006.htm.

[59] 'Hezbollah seizes Israel soldiers', BBC News, 12 July 2006, at http://news.bbc.co.uk/1/hi/world/middle_east/5171616.stm.

[60] Cabinet communiqué, 16 July 2006, at www.mfa.gov.il/MFA/Government/Communiques/2006/Cabinet+Communique+16-Jul-2006.htm.

[61] 'Hezbollah warns Israel over raids', BBC News, 12 July 2006, at http://news.bbc.co.uk/1/hi/world/middle_east/5173078.stm.

Yet, on coming to power, the same Prime Minister had told Parliament: 'The government considers the resistance [Hezbollah] a natural and honest expression of the Lebanese people's national rights to liberate their land and defend their honor against Israeli aggression and threats.'[62]

The relationship between the Lebanese government and Hezbollah is tangled, to say the least and tests of 'effective control' such as was laid down by the International Court of Justice in the *Nicaragua* case[63] are not particularly helpful. Hezbollah appears to be a separate entity with its own command and control system operating with, rather than under the control of, the Lebanese government. During the conflict, while Israel maintained that it only attacked targets linked to Hezbollah and not directly Lebanese military targets, it is hard to see how attacks on the main airport of a country and a blockade of its sea ports can be anything other than an armed conflict against that state. It follows that the question is again one of bifurcation. Even if there was a conflict against Lebanon, was there a separate conflict against Hezbollah or was this part and parcel of a single conflict?

Both the conflicts in Lebanon and Afghanistan were comparatively limited in geographic scope. Those who argue for a separate conflict against non-state actors, be they al-Qaeda or Hezbollah, seek the authority to extend the application of the laws of armed conflict to operations beyond the geographic boundaries of the specific conflicts.

Certainly in international armed conflict, there is authority for that. Subject to the laws of neutrality, in law a combatant may be targeted wherever he or she may be found. But is this applicable to actions against terrorists?

8 Armed conflict vs. law enforcement

Professor Yoram Dinstein agrees that action may be taken but he does not see this as an extension of armed conflict but rather an extension of law enforcement. He has long argued that a state may take forcible counter-measures against non-state actors operating from outside its

[62] 'New Lebanon govt defends Hezbollah role', Arab News, 29 July 2005, at www.arabnews.com/?page=4&section=0&article=67672&d=29&m=7&y=2005&pix=world.jpg&category=World.

[63] *Military and Paramilitary Activities in and against Nicaragua* (*Nicaragua* v. *United States of America*), Judgment of 27 June 1986 [1986] ICJ Rep. 14, para. 115.

territory as a form of 'extra-territorial law enforcement'.[64] Dinstein does not exclude the application of the laws of armed conflict in appropriate cases but prefers to use the law enforcement paradigm for transnational operations of the type seen in Yemen.[65]

In some ways, the current debate was inevitable. In the early part of the twentieth century, the division between war and peace was comparatively clear-cut. However times have changed. International law, which until the mid-twentieth century had no direct interest in matters other than relations between states, has now moved into areas which previously were the sole prerogative of domestic law. Human rights law expanded after the Second World War to provide a comprehensive framework for the relations between a state and those who fell within the jurisdiction of that state. Originally seen as a system to govern relationships within the territorial borders of a state in peacetime, it has evolved into a system that has extended the concept of 'jurisdiction' to cover many extraterritorial activities carried on by states, both in peace and war. At the same time, the laws of war have changed into the laws of armed conflict and now the more modern term, international humanitarian law. No longer do they limit themselves to war between states but have extended their jurisdiction into non-international armed conflicts. Here they have come into direct juxtaposition with law enforcement and human rights principles. The need to reconcile these two opposing philosophies was recognized by the International Court of Justice which acknowledged the application of human rights law in general to situations of armed conflict.[66] However, to acknowledge its application is one thing; to deal with its relationship with international humanitarian law is quite another. In the 'Barrier case', the Court sought to explain this relationship in the following manner:

> As regards the relationship between international humanitarian law and human rights law, there are thus three possible situations: some rights may be exclusively matters of international humanitarian law; others may be exclusively matters of human rights law; yet others may be matters of both these branches of international law. In order to answer the question put to it, the Court will have to take into consideration both

64 See Y. Dinstein, *War, Aggression and Self-Defence* (Cambridge: Cambridge University Press, 2005).

65 See n. 43 above.

66 See, for example, *Legality of the Threat or Use of Nuclear Weapons*, Advisory Opinion of 8 July 1996 [1996] ICJ Rep. 226, para. 25.

> these branches of international law, namely human rights law and, as *lex specialis*, international humanitarian law.[67]

Unfortunately, the Court did not go on to explain what those situations are or even what it meant by '*lex specialis*'. There has thus developed a vigorous academic debate ranging from those who argue that, in time of war, international humanitarian law 'trumps' human rights law to those who argue that human rights law governs at all times and international humanitarian law can only be applied where it is consistent with human rights law. In between are a range of other views and opinions. The disagreements on terrorism are just part of this debate.

Professor Corn astutely identifies one of the major areas of conflict here, the use of force. Whereas the use of lethal force in international armed conflict is based primarily on a status ruling – combatant or non-combatant, the use of force under law enforcement and human rights law is primarily threat based.

Terrorism was traditionally seen as on the law enforcement side of the dividing line. However, with the increased power wielded by non-state actors, that dividing line has become obscured so that some want it removed altogether so far as terrorists are concerned. A terrorist is seen as a modern day outlaw – outwith the protection of the law and able to be killed at will. But is this a realistic step forward or in fact a return to the dark ages? If there is a 'spectrum of violence' where, in that spectrum, does terrorism fit? And where does the application of the law of armed conflict start and finish? To put it another way, what is an 'armed conflict'.

9 Conclusions

The first task is to define terrorism. The failure to do so has meant that there are numerous and different definitions. They could include, for example, acts committed by criminal groupings such as animal rights activists targeting the fur trade or acts committed by state armed forces during international armed conflict. To equate terrorism to armed conflict and thus terrorists to participants in an armed conflict seems to go too far. Terrorism and terrorists come in all shapes and sizes. The response to them needs to be similarly multifaceted. At the lower spectrum, law enforcement is the appropriate model. Similarly, where an

[67] *Legal Consequences of the Construction of a Wall in the Occupied Palestinian Territory*, Advisory Opinion of 9 July 2004 [2004] ICJ Reports 136.

armed conflict is taking place, the response should be governed by the law of armed conflict. Terrorist acts, where in breach of the laws of armed conflict, are war crimes and similarly subject to law enforcement procedures whether national or international.

Looked at in this way, terrorist acts are to be found throughout the spectrum of violence. They do not form a specific category of themselves. It is perhaps ironic that one of the best known examples of transnational terrorism actually found the United States on the 'wrong side'. In the famous *Caroline* case, it was British forces responding to transborder incursions by rebels from the United States, who crossed into United States territory and set the *Caroline* adrift across the Niagara Falls.[68] From that case came the long-standing *Caroline* principles on the use of force in self-defence. When Alexander McCleod was unwise enough to boast of his part in the proceedings within United States jurisdiction, he was arrested and brought before a United States court. This was seen by both sides as a matter for domestic jurisdiction.

The United States administration seems now to be slowly drawing back from some of the wilder assertions made during the early days of operations against al-Qaeda and there seems to be a growing appreciation that the 'law of war' paradigm may not be the panacea that it was once thought to be. The answer may be to look again at the balance between law enforcement and armed conflict, particularly in relation to the use of force. In international armed conflict, as traditionally defined,[69] the law of armed conflict should be the preeminent legal framework. However, that does not mean that there is no place for law enforcement. Acts of terrorism should be defined in such a way as to ensure that actions that are legitimate under the law of international armed conflict cannot be included in such a definition.

This raises the first requirement – a clear definition for the meaning of terrorism and terrorist acts.

At the other end of the spectrum, are acts that fall clearly within the domestic sphere, such as bombings and the like carried out in the course of criminal activities. Here, the law enforcement paradigm is the appropriate response.

It is more difficult when considering acts of terrorism carried out for a political motive within the domestic sphere. In principle, these remain

[68] See *British–American Diplomacy: The Caroline Case*, Avalon Project, at http://avalon.law.yale.edu/19th_century/br-1842d.asp.

[69] Common Article 2 to the four Geneva Conventions of 12 August 1949.

governed by the law enforcement paradigm as domestic law continues to apply. However, where the level of violence reaches the level of armed conflict, the law of armed conflict begins to impinge. A difficulty is caused here by the expansion of the law relating to the conduct of hostilities into non-international armed conflict. The original intention of Common Article 3 was to extend protection. This extension creates an inevitable dichotomy. Attacks on legitimate targets are excused from international criminal liability even though they remain illegal under domestic law – and there is no combatant immunity. It is therefore necessary to ensure that any definition of terrorism and terrorist acts does not undermine the law of armed conflict by criminalizing on the international stage acts which are not illegal under international humanitarian law such as attacks on legitimate military objectives.

A further issue arises here in the need to define the point at which the law relating to the conduct of hostilities begins to bite. At present, there is little differentiation between low intensity armed conflicts governed by Common Article 3 and higher intensity conflicts governed by Additional Protocol II. However, it is precisely here that the two tectonic plates of human rights law and international humanitarian law collide. The point of the latter is that it applies equally to all parties but that must mean that if it is legitimate under international law for a dissident to shoot to kill a member of the government fighting forces on the basis of status, then it must be equally legitimate for a member of the government fighting forces to shoot to kill a member of the dissident fighting forces on the basis of status. Yet, this would seem to fly in the face of human rights law and encourage states to declare a situation one of non-international armed conflict, thus legitimizing a 'shoot to kill' policy. On the other hand, in conflicts which bear all the hallmarks of an international armed conflict other than that one of the parties is not a state, to introduce a law enforcement paradigm flies in the face of reality. The fighting in 2009 in Helmand Province in Afghanistan comes to mind. In such cases, it would seem most appropriate for the law of armed conflict paradigm to govern though acts of terrorism, properly defined, would still be criminal under both domestic and international law.

It was partly in response to this that, in 2003, the ICRC in conjunction with the TMC Asser Institute in the Netherlands, began an 'expert process' to look at the meaning of 'taking a direct part in hostilities'.[70]

[70] See N. Melzer, *Interpretative Guidance on the Notion of Direct Participation in Hostilities under International Humanitarian Law* (Geneva: ICRC, 2009).

In the light of the current disputes, it is perhaps not surprising that the experts were unable to agree. Nevertheless, the ICRC, encouraged by the amount of agreement that there was, decided to publish its own 'Interpretive Guidance' based on the process.[71]

As the Introduction states, the Guidance 'is widely informed by the discussions held during these expert meetings but does not necessarily reflect a unanimous view or majority opinion of the experts'.[72] The ICRC have therefore expressed their own views 'informed by' but not necessarily reflective of the views of the experts. This is an important factor to bear in mind when considering the Guidance.

The ICRC appreciated the difficulties of merging status-based and threat-based rules and realized that perhaps the key issue in non-international armed conflict is the question of who is a civilian. It is here that the ICRC has broken new ground in recognizing a degree of reality. Their second principle states:

> For the purposes of the principle of distinction in non-international armed conflict, all persons who are not members of state armed forces or organized armed groups of a party to the conflict are civilians and, therefore, entitled to protection against direct attack unless and for such time as they take a direct part in hostilities. In non-international armed conflict, organized armed groups constitute the armed forces of a non-state party to the conflict and consist only of individuals whose continuous function it is to take a direct part in hostilities ('continuous combat function').[73]

A form of combatant status is thus introduced into non-international armed conflict. Non-state armed forces cannot be given the privileges of a combatant under domestic law, namely the right to use force in accordance with international humanitarian law, but they are recognized as constituting a separate class, distinct from civilians. Thus, targeting rules in relation to such actors will be similar to those relating to regular armed forces in international armed conflict, namely status based rather than conduct based. On the other hand, for those who qualify as civilians, the test remains one of conduct; are they or are they not 'taking a direct part in hostilities'? The Guidance provides some useful indicators as to what this phrase means and when it should apply.

[71] 'Interpretive Guidance on the Notion of Direct Participation in Hostilities under International Humanitarian Law' (2008) 90 *International Review of the Red Cross* 991.
[72] *Ibid.*, 992. [73] *Ibid.*, 995.

But was the creation of this new category necessary? Could the same result have been achieved by holding that such actors, while remaining 'civilians', lost their protection on a continuous basis for as long as they remained within the definition of non-state armed forces?

To balance this concession on status, the ICRC included a very controversial recommendation entitled 'Restraints on the Use of Force'. This reads:

> In addition to the restraints imposed by international humanitarian law on specific means and methods of warfare, and without prejudice to further restrictions that may arise under other applicable branches of international law, the kind and degree of force which is permissible against persons not entitled to protection against direct attack must not exceed what is actually necessary to accomplish a legitimate military purpose in the prevailing circumstances.[74]

The question is what exactly does this mean. Does it mean that there has to be a graduated approach to the use of force even against those who are not entitled to protection as civilians? If so, then does this apply across the board, even to combatants in international armed conflict? This would seem to introduce more of a human rights standard. The commentary text is not helpful here. It states:

> Clearly, the fact that a particular category of persons is not protected against offensive or defensive acts of violence is not equivalent to a legal entitlement to kill such persons without further considerations. At the same time, the absence of an unfettered 'right' to kill does not necessarily imply a legal obligation to capture rather than kill regardless of the circumstances.[75]

Later on the text says:

> In sum, while operating forces can hardly be required to take additional risks for themselves or the civilian population in order to capture an armed adversary alive, it would defy basic notions of humanity to kill an adversary or to refrain from giving him or her an opportunity to surrender where there manifestly is no necessity for the use of lethal force. In such situations, the principles of military necessity and of humanity play an important role in determining the kind and degree of permissible force against legitimate military targets. Lastly, although this Interpretive Guidance concerns the analysis and interpretation of IHL only, its conclusions remain without prejudice to additional restrictions on the use of force, which may arise under other applicable frameworks of international law such as, most notably, international human rights law or the law governing the use of interstate force (*jus ad bellum*).[76]

[74] *Ibid.*, 996. [75] *Ibid.*, 1041. [76] *Ibid.*, 1043.

A possible such solution to the dilemma might lie in the much-maligned threshold introduced by Additional Protocol II.[77] In international armed conflict, international humanitarian law has the lead and human rights law applies to the extent that it is not incompatible. Where there is no armed conflict, human rights law obviously prevails as international humanitarian law has no place. In low-intensity conflicts governed by Common Article 3,[78] the use of force would be governed by human rights principles. However, in high-intensity conflicts where territory was controlled by both sides in accordance with the threshold under Additional Protocol II,[79] the use of force would be governed primarily by international humanitarian law.

This difficulty does not arise in relation to the protection provisions of international humanitarian law, that part which used to be known as 'Geneva law' and which is in the main compatible with human rights law. These would continue to apply across the spectrum of armed conflict.

This leaves still the issue of cross-border terrorism. There can be no simple answer and it may be that each case would need to be handled on an individual basis. Much of the terrorism conducted in Northern Ireland during the 'Troubles' was cross border with the Irish Republican Army operating from training camps and 'safe houses' south of the border with the Irish Republic. But on both sides of the border, this was treated with a law enforcement paradigm despite the deployment of military forces. Those forces themselves were subject to domestic law and excessive use of force under law enforcement rules could, and did, lead to murder charges.

On the other hand, Afghanistan in 2001 and Lebanon in 2006 were clearly armed conflicts governed most appropriately by the law of armed conflict. But is there any need to change traditional paradigms for this to apply? In 2001, the United States chose to attack both al-Qaeda and Taliban targets. By including Taliban targets, an armed conflict existed between Afghanistan and the United States. Al-Qaeda fighters formed part of that armed conflict and were subject to the relevant international law. There was no need to bifurcate the conflict, as was succinctly pointed out by the Legal Adviser to the State Department.[80] The same applies to the Lebanon conflict. On the other hand, most attempts to deal

77 AP II, Art. 1(1) (reprinted in Roberts and Guelff, *Documents on the Laws of War*, 484).

78 Common Article 3 to the four Geneva Conventions of 12 August 1949.

79 AP II, Art. 1(1) (reprinted in Roberts and Guelff, *Documents on the Laws of War*, 484).

80 Memorandum from William H. Taft IV, 2 February 2002 (*Torture Papers*, 129).

with al-Qaeda outside Afghanistan use the law enforcement mode as with the aftermath of the Bali, London and Madrid bombings. There is a place for 'extraterritorial law enforcement', perhaps best illustrated by the deployment of forces overseas to conduct hostage rescue operations. Where these are conducted with the consent of the host country, it will be the domestic law of that country that applies. But there are occasions when a state is unwilling or unable to act – or to give consent. In those circumstances, where it is necessary for a state to act in self-defence of itself or its citizens, and it limits itself to taking action against the offenders themselves and not the state where they are located, then the situation is less clear-cut. In the Entebbe raid in 1976, after an Air France flight to Tel Aviv had been hijacked and diverted to Entebbe, the Israelis had sought the cooperation of the Ugandan authorities without success. Indeed, there were suspicions that Idi Amin, the Ugandan leader, was complicit with the hijackers. However, the intention was to attack the plane and the hijackers though contingency plans were made in case of an intervention by Ugandan forces. The rescue mission was successful. It would perhaps be best to see that as an example of 'extraterritorial law enforcement' but if the Israeli forces had found themselves in conflict with Ugandan forces, then the law of armed conflict would have applied.

In short, there are no straightforward answers. I have sought to look at the matter from a general overview. Specific areas are covered in other chapters of this book with perhaps differing viewpoints. I would suggest that the increased pressure from human rights organizations to limit the use of force by military forces even in armed conflict has led to a 'push back' in some quarters to extend the more relaxed rules on the use of force to be found in international armed conflict to areas for which they were not designed. This should be resisted. But at the same time, attempts to restrict the use of force by states to the extent that they put their own peoples and their own forces at unacceptable risk must also be resisted. Joining the military is not a suicide pact! The answer as always lies in a balance, with compromises needed by all sides. Human rights activists and international humanitarian law experts need to sit down together and work out a *modus vivendi*. Otherwise, everyone will be a loser.

15

Extraterritorial application of the rights to life and personal liberty, including habeas corpus, during situations of armed conflict

ROBERT K. GOLDMAN

1 Introduction

In the aftermath of the September 11, 2001 attacks, the United States and its coalition partners – all parties to various human rights instruments – initiated the so-called 'war on terror' by invading Afghanistan where their armed forces killed or captured hundreds of 'terrorist suspects'. Some of those detained were taken to the US military facility at Guantánamo Bay, Cuba, while others have languished in US custody in Afghanistan. These actions raise the question whether a state is bound by its human rights obligations when its agents operate outside of national territory. And, if so, how do those obligations interrelate with the state's other obligations under international humanitarian law when its counter-terrorism operations coincide with situations of armed conflict.

This chapter addresses these questions. In particular, it examines the extraterritorial reach of two fundamental human rights during two situations recognized in international law. These rights are the right to life and the right to liberty and the related procedural safeguard of habeas corpus. The two situations examined are (1) international armed conflicts, including occupation and (2) non-international armed conflicts. The paper surveys the jurisprudence on the extraterritorial application of the International Covenant on Civil and Political Rights (ICCPR), the American Convention on Human Rights (American Convention) and American Declaration of the Rights and Duties of Man (American Declaration) and the European Convention on Human Rights (European Convention) and the extent to which rights in these instruments can be derogated from. It also examines how the treaty bodies supervising these instruments view the relationship between international human rights (HRL) and international humanitarian law (IHL) in situations of armed conflict. Relevant decisions of the International Court of Justice are also referenced in this connection. The paper also identifies certain gaps in legal protection.

2 Derogation from human rights treaties

As a preliminary matter, it is worth recalling that the UN Security Council in 2001 made clear that any measure taken by states to combat terrorism must comply with all their obligations under international law, including HRL and IHL.[1] This injunction unambiguously requires that states respect both bodies of law while countering terrorism, *whether at home or abroad*, and implicitly recognizes that upholding human rights and protecting the public from terrorist acts are not antithetical, but complimentary responsibilities of states.[2]

When drafting the International Covenant on Civil and Political Rights (ICCPR) and various regional human rights instruments, states were aware of the need to strike a realistic balance between the requirements of national security and the protection of human rights. Accordingly, states included in these instruments provisions that permit them when confronting an emergency situation – which may include actual or imminent terrorist violence, or armed conflict – to derogate from (suspend) certain rights in these instruments.

The ability of states to derogate from rights under these instruments, however, is *not* automatic in the face of such imminent terrorist violence or outbreak of armed conflict. Rather, it is governed by several conditions which are in turn regulated by the generally recognized principles of proportionality, necessity and non-discrimination. For example, Article 4 ICCPR sets forth the following procedural and substantive safeguards regarding the declaration and implementation of a state of emergency: the nature of the emergency must threaten the life of the nation; the existence of the emergency must be officially proclaimed; the measures adopted are strictly required by the exigencies of the situation; derogations cannot be incompatible with the derogating state's other obligations under international law; the derogation must not be

[1] UN Doc. S/Res./1373 (2001).

[2] But see Chapter 14 in this volume, which concludes that the failure to define terrorism precludes states from reconciling their obligations under IHL and HRL with their current efforts to combat terrorism.

discriminatory; and the derogating state must notify other state parties through the UN Secretary-General of the provisions it has derogated from and the reasons for such derogation, as well as of the date the derogation has ceased to apply. Thus, a state that has not declared an emergency may not derogate from its human rights obligations which remain fully in effect save for permissible limitations imposed on certain rights.

The key ground for derogation that the emergency threatens the life of the nation is especially relevant to some issues explored later in this paper. That ground might well be satisfied by the existence of a large-scale internal armed conflict within or invasion of national territory by foreign armed forces since these situations could entail a real threat to the political independence, territorial integrity and/or population of the country. It is questionable, however, whether this ground could be invoked by a state that is engaged in military operations, whatever their nature or origin, that occur exclusively in the territory of another state, particularly if that state's military cannot respond in kind.

While conceding states ample discretion in adopting anti-terrorism measures, the ICCPR and other instruments also specify certain rights that may not be derogated from even during emergency situations. The list of non-derogable rights in the ICCPR is contained in Article 4(2). These are, namely, right to life (Article 6); prohibition of torture or cruel, inhuman or degrading treatment or punishment (Article 7); prohibition of slavery, slave trade and servitude (Article 8(1–2)); prohibition of retroactive criminal laws (Article 15); the recognition of everyone as a person before the law (Article 16); and freedom of thought, conscience and religion (Article 18). Moreover, in 2001 the Human Rights Committee (HRC) in its General Comment No. 29[3] indicated that the following provisions in the Covenant were not lawfully derogable during emergencies: the prohibition of hostage taking, abductions or unacknowledged detentions; and the prohibition of unlawful deportation or transfer of populations.

The jurisprudence of the HRC and regional supervisory bodies indicates that derogations are always exceptional and temporary measures. Accordingly, such measures should be lifted as soon as the emergency which justified their imposition no longer exists or can be managed by less intrusive means under the relevant instrument.

[3] General Comment No. 29, States of Emergency (Article 4), UN Doc. CCPR/C/21/Rev.1/Add. 11, 31 August 2000.

3 Extraterritorial application of human rights law

The HRC, the European Court of Human Rights (ECtHR) and the former European Commission on Human Rights (ECHR), as well as the Inter-American Commission on Human Rights (IACHR), have all found their respective instruments to apply extraterritorially, even in situations governed by IHL. These treaty bodies seem to agree that extraterritorial jurisdiction attaches in principle when a state exercises effective control over territory and/or persons.

3.1 International Covenant on Civil and Political Rights

The Committee's case law has long given extraterritorial effect to the ICCPR. In 1981, it found that Uruguay had violated the Covenant when its agents abducted in Argentina and Brazil several Uruguayan citizens who opposed that country's military regime.[4] The Committee reasoned that 'it would be unconscionable to so interpret the [state's] responsibility under Article 2 of the Covenant as to permit a state party to perpetrate violations of the Covenant on the territory of another state, which violations it could not perpetrate in its own territory.'[5]

The HRC's most comprehensive statement on the extraterritorial reach of the Covenant is found in its General Comment 31.[6] It observed therein that a state party's duty to respect and ensure rights to all persons within their territory and subject to their jurisdiction includes 'anyone within the power or effect control of the State Party, even if not situated in the territory of the State Party . . . This Principle also applies to those within the power or effective control of the forces of the State Party acting outside its territory, regardless of the circumstances in which such power or effective control was obtained, such as forces constituting a national contingent of a State Party assigned to an international peacekeeping or peace-enforcement operation.'[7] Additionally, the HRC has specifically affirmed the ICCPR's extraterritorial application to military and peacekeeping operations outside of the territory of the state concerned.[8]

4 *Lopez Burgos* v. *Uruguay*, Views of 29 July 1981, UN Doc. CCPR/C/13/D/52/1979; *Celiberti* v. *Uruguay*, Views of 29 July 1981, UN Doc. CCPR/C/13/D/56/1979.

5 *Lopez Burgos*, para. 12.3.

6 General Comment No. 31, Nature of the General Legal Obligation Imposed on States Parties to the Covenant, UN Doc. CCPR/C/21/Rev 1/Add.13 (2004).

7 *Ibid.*, para. 10.

8 See Concluding Observations on the second periodic report of Israel, UN Doc. CCPR/CO/78/ISR (2003), para. 178.

Several states, most particularly Israel and the United States, have disputed the Committee's position on the Covenant's extraterritorial reach. However, the International Court of Justice in its 2004 Advisory Opinion *The Legal Consequences of the Construction of a Wall in Occupied Palestinian Territory*,[9] confirmed the Committee's views. After examining the Covenant's *travaux préparatoires* and the Committee's practice, the Court rejected the argument that the Covenant was not applicable outside of a state's territorial borders and, more particularly, in occupied territory. While recognizing that a state's jurisdiction is primarily territorial, the Court concluded that the Covenant's reach extends to 'acts done by a State in the exercise of its jurisdiction outside its own territory'.[10]

Accordingly, it would appear well settled that the ICCPR has a truly global reach, extending to any territory or person within the power or effective control of a party to that treaty.

3.2 *The European Convention on Human Rights*

The Strasbourg organs also have considerable case law affirming the extraterritorial scope of the European Convention. In 1975, the former ECHR addressed this issue in *Cyprus* v. *Turkey*[11] in which Cyprus charged Turkey with violations of the Convention in that part of Cypriot territory invaded by Turkish armed forces. Turkey claimed that the Commission's competence was limited to the examination of acts committed by a contracting party in its own national territory and that it had not extended its jurisdiction to any part of Cyprus. The Commission rejected this argument stating:

> In Article 1 of the Convention, the High Contracting Parties undertake to Secure the rights and freedoms defined in Section 1 to everyone 'within their jurisdiction' ... The Commission finds that this term is not ... equivalent to or limited to the national territory of the High Contracting Party concerned. It is clear from the language ... and the object of this article, and from the purpose of the Convention as a whole that *the High contracting parties are bound to secure the said rights and freedoms*

[9] *Legal Consequences of the Construction of a Wall in the Occupied Palestinian Territory*, Advisory Opinion of 9 July 2004 [2004] ICJ Rep 136.

[10] *Ibid.*, para. 111.

[11] *Cyprus* v. *Turkey*, Appl. No. 6780/74 and 6950/75, Report of the ECHR adopted on 10 July 1976.

> *to all persons under their actual authority and responsibility, whether that authority is exercised within their own territory or abroad.* [my emphasis][12]

This understanding of jurisdiction as a notion linked to authority and effective control, and not merely to territorial boundaries, has been confirmed in other cases decided by the former Commission and the ECtHR. In *Loizidou* v. *Turkey*,[13] the Court reaffirmed that the term jurisdiction in Article 1 was not limited to national territory, noting that 'responsibility of Contracting Parties can be involved because of acts of their authorities, whether performed within or outside national boundaries, which produce effects outside their own territory.'[14] The Court added that based on the Convention's object and purpose '*the responsibility of a Contracting Party may also arise when as a consequence of military action – whether lawful or unlawful – it exercises effective control of an area outside its national territory. The obligation to secure, in such an area, the rights and freedoms set out in the Convention derives from the fact of such control whether it be exercised directly, through its armed forces or through a subordinate local administration*' [emphasis supplied].[15] The Court has explained that any other finding 'would result in regrettable vacuum in the system of human-rights protection in the territory in question by removing from individuals there the benefit of the Convention's fundamental safeguards and their right to call a High Contracting Party to account for violations of their rights in proceedings before the Court'.[16]

In the *Banković*[17] case, the European Court appeared to depart from its previous case law. This case was brought against seventeen European members of NATO for an air strike in 1999 which hit a communications facility in Belgrade, resulting in the deaths of applicants' relatives. In contrast to a situation of occupation, where a state can be regarded as exercising jurisdiction extraterritorially by virtue of its effective control over territory, the Court found no such jurisdictional link between the victims of the extraterritorial bombardment in question and the respondent states in this case. The Court noted that jurisdiction under Article 1 is primarily territorial and that it had recognized only

12 *Ibid.*

13 *Loizidou* v. *Turkey*, Preliminary Objections, Judgment of 23 March 1995 [1995] ECHR Series A No. 310.

14 *Ibid.*, para. 62. 15 *Ibid.* 16 *Cyprus* v. *Turkey*, para. 78.

17 *Banković and others* v. *Belgium and others*, App. No. 52207/99, Admissibility Decision [GC], 12 December 2001.

exceptionally extraterritorial acts as constituting an exercise of jurisdiction.[18] Regarding whether its finding would defeat the '*ordre public* mission of the Convention and leave a regrettable vacuum in the Convention system of human rights protection', the Court indicated that the Convention was meant to operate in an essentially regional context, ie within the Council of Europe (CoE), and not throughout the world, 'even in respect of the conduct of contracting states'.[19]

If the Court in *Banković* meant to limit jurisdiction under the Convention to the geographical confines of the CoE, its subsequent judgments in the *Ocalan* and *Issa* cases appear to retreat from this view. In *Ocalan*,[20] the applicant was arrested by Turkish agents while he was aboard an aircraft in Kenya. The Court found that once the Kenyan authorities delivered Ocalan to Turkish officials he 'was under effective Turkish authority and therefore was brought within the 'jurisdiction' of that state for the purpose of Article 1 of the Convention, even though Turkey exercised its authority outside its territory'.[21] The Court distinguished the circumstances in this case from those in *Banković* noting that Ocalan 'was physically forced to return to Turkey by Turkish officials and was subject to their authority and control following his arrest and return to Turkey'.[22]

The Court in *Issa*[23] again dealt with events taking place outside of the 'legal space' of the CoE. The case was lodged by Iraqi nationals who charged that Turkish forces murdered their relatives during military operations in northern Iraq. While referring to *Banković*, the Court made clear that contracting states 'may also be held accountable for violations of the Convention rights and freedoms of persons who are in the territory of another state but who are found to be under the former state's authority and control through its agents operating – whether lawfully of unlawfully – in the latter state'.[24] Then, citing decisions of the HRC and the IACHR, the Court added: 'Accountability in such situations stems from the fact that Article 1 of the Convention cannot be interpreted so as to allow a State party to perpetrate violations of the Convention on the territory of another State, which it could not perpetrate in its own territory.'[25] The Court then seemed to posit a new test at odds with *Banković* by stating that it did not exclude 'the possibility that,

[18] *Ibid.*, paras. 61, 67. [19] *Ibid.*, para. 80.
[20] *Ocalan* v. *Turkey*, Judgment of 12 March 2003. [21] *Ibid.*, para. 93. [22] *Ibid.*
[23] *Issa and others* v. *Turkey*, Judgment of 16 November 2004. [24] *Ibid.*, para. 71.
[25] *Ibid.*

as a consequence of this military action, the respondent State could be considered to have exercised, temporarily, effective overall control of a particular portion of the territory of northern Iraq'.[26] However, because the applicants failed to establish that Turkish troops were in the area where the victims were killed, the Court found that the victims were not within the 'jurisdiction' of Turkey.

More recently, the Court in the *Al-Skeini*[27] case further clarified its views on the extraterritorial reach of the European Convention. *Al-Skeini* involved the killing of five Iraqis by British troops in Basrah in southern Iraq. The Law Lords, while acknowledging that the United Kingdom was an occupying power in southern Iraq, nonetheless, found that the Iraqi victims were not within the jurisdiction of the UK for purposes of the European Convention because British troops did not effectively control the area where the killings occurred. The European Court disagreed, holding that the UK had exercised jurisdiction over the victims at the time of their deaths. Referring to the general principle in its case law that a state's jurisdiction under Article 1 is primarily territorial, the Court reiterated in *Al-Skeini* that whenever a state's agents, including its military, exercise physical control and authority over an individual outside its territory, it is obliged under Article 1 to secure to that individual 'the rights and freedoms under Section 1 of the Convention that are relevant to the situation of that individual'.[28] The Court also reaffirmed that another exception to the territorial principle occurs when a state, whether by lawful or unlawful military action, exercises effective control over an area outside of its national territory.[29] Importantly, the Court, citing *Issa*, *Ocalan* and *Al-Saadoon and Mufdhi* v. *the United Kingdom*,[30] made clear that jurisdiction under Article 1 of the

26 *Ibid.*, para. 74.

27 *Al-Skeini and others* v. *United Kingdom*, App. No. 55721/07, Council of Europe: ECtHR, 7 July 2011, at www.unhcr.org/refworld/docid/4e2545502.html.

28 The Court also noted that '[i]n this sense, therefore, the Convention rights can be "divided and tailored"'. Compare with *Banković and others* v. *Belgium and others*, App. No. 52207/99, Admissibility Decision [GC], 12 December 2001.

29 Citing *Cyprus* v. *Turkey*, the Court indicated that the controlling state has the responsibility 'under Article 1 to secure, within the area under its control, the entire range of substantive rights set out in the Convention and those additional Protocols which it has ratified' (*Cyprus* v. *Turkey* [GC], App. No. 25781/94, paras. 76–7, ECHR 2001-IV).

30 *Al-Saadoon and Mufdhi* v. *the United Kingdom* (December), App. No. 61498/08, 30 June 2009.

Convention could exist outside the territory covered by CoE member states. Applying these principles, the Court pointedly noted that when the Iraqi victims were killed, the UK was an occupying power within the meaning of the Hague Regulations and had thereby 'assumed authority and responsibility for the maintenance of security in South East Iraq'. Accordingly, the Court found that in these 'exceptional circumstances', the UK had, through its soldiers' engagement in security operations in Basrah during the relevant period, 'exercised authority and control over the individuals killed in the course of such security operations, so as to establish a jurisdictional link between the deceased and the United Kingdom for purposes of Article 1 of the Convention'.[31]

Although the Court's jurisprudence on the extraterritorial reach of the European Convention is somewhat confusing, if not contradictory, it would appear, nonetheless, that a contracting party would be exercising jurisdiction when its agents (1) detain or exercise physical power and control over a person anywhere in the world or (2) occupy or otherwise effectively control the territory of another CoE member state or perhaps, as indicated in *Issa* and *Al-Skeini*, that of a non-member state.

A contracting party, however, would apparently incur no responsibility if its agents targeted and killed a person in another state whose territory, at the time, was neither occupied nor otherwise subject to its effective control. Unlike a detainee who is killed in custody, the person so attacked would be remediless under the Convention. This result creates a glaring and unseemly gap in legal protection. One remedy, proposed by Françoise Hampson, would be for the ECtHR not to look to control of territory as the test for determining whether the victim comes within the jurisdiction of the state launching the attack, but rather to 'control over the effects said to constitute a violation, subject to a foreseeable victim being foreseeably affected by the act'.[32] As she notes, such an approach would only go to the admissibility, not the merits of the complaint. Another solution would be to posit that the right to life's negative dimension, i.e., the duty of states to refrain from violating that right, has acquired the status of customary international law and, as such, is

[31] *Al-Skeini*, para. 149.

[32] F. Hampson, 'The Relationship between International Humanitarian Law and Human Rights Law from the Perspective of a Human Rights Treaty Body' (2008) 90 *International Review of the Red Cross* 570.

binding on all states and their agents in all circumstances. Thus, overseas killings by state agents that are unlawful under IHL would violate customary HRL. Both approaches are plausible and merit further study.

3.3 *The Inter-American human rights instruments*

The Inter-American Commission on Human Rights has also found that persons falling within a state's authority and control outside of national territory are effectively within that state's jurisdiction and holders of enforceable rights under applicable instruments. Interestingly, virtually all of the case law to date on the subject has been made by the Commission and not by the Inter-American Court. This is because most cases have involved the United States, which has not ratified the American Convention and thus is bound by the American Declaration by virtue of its membership in the Organization of American States (OAS). Furthermore, most of these cases have involved claims arising from US military operations within the region.

The Commission's most complete statement concerning the American Declaration's extraterritorial reach is found in *Coard et al.* v. *United States*,[33] which involved the detention of seventeen persons by US forces immediately following the US invasion of Grenada in October 1983. The Commission stated that 'under certain circumstances, the exercise of jurisdiction over acts with an extraterritorial locus will not only be consistent with but required by the norms which pertain … Given that individual rights inhere simply by virtue of a person's humanity, each American State is obliged to uphold the protected rights of any person subject to its jurisdiction.'[34] It added:

> While this most commonly refers to persons within a state's territory, it may, under given circumstances, refer to conduct with an extraterritorial locus where the person concerned is present in the territory of one state, but subject to the control of another state – usually through acts of the latter's agents abroad. In principle, the inquiry turns not on the presumed victim's nationality or presence within a particular geographic area, but on whether, under the specific circumstances, the State observed the rights of the person subject to its authority and control.[35]

[33] *Coard et al.* v. *United States*, Case 10.951, Report No. 109/99, Annual Report 1999, OEA/ ser. l/V/II. 106.doc.3rev. 1999.

[34] *Ibid.*, para. 37. [35] *Ibid.*

The Commission similarly gave extraterritorial application to the American Convention in its recent admissibility decision[36] in the inter-state complaint filed by Ecuador against Colombia for the killing of one of its citizens during a military operation by Colombian security forces against FARC rebels on Ecuadorian soil. Citing its own case law and the jurisprudence of other treaty bodies, the Commission concluded that Colombia had exercised jurisdiction over the area attacked and the victim in question. It specifically found the following factors essential for establishing jurisdiction:

> the exercise of authority over persons by agents of a State even if not acting within their territory, without necessarily requiring the existence of a formal, structured and prolonged legal relation in terms of time to raise the responsibility of a State for acts committed by its agents abroad. At the time of examining the scope of American Convention's jurisdiction, it is necessary to determine whether there is a causal nexus between the extraterritorial conduct of the State and the alleged violation of the rights and freedoms of an individual.[37]

The Commission also noted that during such time as its agents exercise such authority over persons abroad, the state is obliged to respect those persons' rights, particularly, the right to life and humane treatment.[38]

The Commission has also found a state extending its jurisdiction extraterritorially in circumstances not entailing its physical control of territory or custody of persons. Specifically, in *Alejandre et al.*[39] it held that Cuba had violated the right to life of four persons resulting from its agent's shooting down of two unarmed civilian aircraft in international airspace. The Commission found that, unlike the victims in *Banković*, the pilots of the doomed planes were under Cuba's 'authority' when its air force attacked them.[40] The Commission also relied on this notion of authority and control when in 2003 it adopted precautionary measures[41] requesting that the United States have a competent tribunal determine the legal status of the detainees at Guantánamo Bay, Cuba. The

36 *Franklin Guillermo Aisalla Molina, Ecuador* v. *Colombia*, Admissibility, Case IP-02, Report No. 112/10, OEA/Ser.L/V/II. 140 Doc. 10 (2010)

37 *Ibid.*, para. 99. 38 *Ibid.*, para. 100.

39 *Alejandre et al.* v. *Cuba*, Case 11.589, Report No. 86/99, Annual Report 1999, OEA/Ser. L/V/11.06 Doc. 3 rev. 1999.

40 *Ibid.*, para. 25.

41 *Request for Precautionary measures Concerning the Detainees at Guantánamo Bay, Cuba*, Decision of 12 March 2002 (2002) 41 International Legal Materials 532.

Commission in 1993 also declared admissible a case[42] arising out of the US invasion of Panama in 1989. In so doing, it simply stated: 'where it is asserted that a use of military force has resulted in non-combatant deaths, personal injury and property loss, the human rights of non-combatants are implicated . . . The case sets forth allegations cognizable within the framework of the [American] Declaration. Thus, the Commission is authorized to consider the subject matter of the case.'[43] A merits decision in the matter is still pending.

Its case law to date suggests that the Commission views the region's human rights system as applying solely within the geographic boundaries of the Western hemisphere. This may explain why it has never opened a case or issued precautionary measures based on the petitions it has received since 2002 concerning the detention of persons in Iraq and Afghanistan who are under the control of US agents. As previously discussed, such detentions abroad by a party to the European Convention would constitute an exercise of jurisdiction, entitling the detainee(s) to the Convention's protections. However, in the *Saldaño* case,[44] in which it interpreted the scope of Article 1(1) of the American Convention, that treaty's jurisdictional clause, the Commission recognized that 'nationals of a state party to the American Convention are subject to that state's jurisdiction in certain respects when domiciled abroad or otherwise temporarily outside of their country or state and that state party must accord them when abroad the exercise of certain convention based rights'.[45] Thus, an OAS member state whose agents kill or abduct one of its nationals outside of the hemisphere would be exercising jurisdiction over that person and incur responsibility under the American Convention for those illicit acts. The Commission's reasoning would apply equally to those OAS member states bound only by the American Declaration. If the victim, however, were a non-national, the Commission could not entertain a claim based upon these same acts – which bespeaks of a clear gap in legal protection.

42 *Salas* v. *United States*, Case No. 10.573, Report No. 31/93, Annual Report 1993, OEA/Ser.L/V85, doc. 9 rev. 1993.

43 *Ibid.*, para. 6.

44 *Victor Saldaño* v. *Argentina*, Report No. 38/99, Annual Report 1998, OEA/Ser.L/II.95, Doc. 7 rev. 1998.

45 *Ibid.*, para. 20.

4 The relationship between international human rights and international humanitarian law

Before examining how the various treaty bodies view the relationship between HRL and IHL, it is instructive to consider the views of the International Court of Justice (ICJ) on this subject. The ICJ has made clear that HRL does not cease to apply during armed conflict. In its advisory opinion *The Legality or the Threat of Use of Nuclear Weapons*[46] the Court stated the following regarding the right to life in the ICCPR: 'In principle, the right to not arbitrarily be deprived of one's life also applies in hostilities. The test of what is an arbitrary deprivation of life, however, then falls to be determined by the applicable *lex specialis*, namely, the law applicable in armed conflict which is designed to regulate the conduct of hostilities.'[47] The Court in its 2004 advisory opinion *The Legal Consequences of the Construction of a Wall in the Occupied Palestinian Territory*[48] confirmed this view stating that it: 'considers that the protections offered by human rights conventions does not cease in case of armed conflict, save through the effect of provisions for derogation of the kind to be found in Article 4 of the [ICCPR]'.[49] Concerning the relationship between human rights and humanitarian law, it added: 'there are thus three possible situations: some rights may be exclusively matters of international humanitarian law; others may be exclusively matters of human rights law; yet others may be matters of both these branches of international law.'[50] The Court, however, provided no guidance on how this *lex specialis* doctrine should apply in practice.[51]

Human rights treaty bodies have no common approach on how HRL and IHL interrelate when state parties are engaged in situations of armed conflict within their *own* territory, much less in hostilities *abroad*. For its

[46] *Legality or Threat or Use of Nuclear Weapons*, Advisory Opinion of 8 July 1996 [1996] ICJ Rep. 226.

[47] *Ibid.*, para. 25. [48] *Wall Opinion*. [49] *Ibid.*, para. 106.

[50] *Ibid.* The Court confirmed this approach in *Armed Activities on the Territory of the Congo* (*Democratic Republic of the Congo* v. *Uganda*), Judgment, ICJ Reports 2005, 168, paras. 216–20. See also Chapter 16 in this volume, which recognizes that the ambiguity of where the *lex specialis* doctrine applies may raise questions as to the requirements of legality and certainty.

[51] See also Chapter 16 in this volume, which recognizes that some commentators also argue that the relationship between IHL and HRL may be defined through either a complementarity approach that emphasizes harmonious interpretation, or as an interpretative tool pursuant to Art. 31 VCLT.

part, the HRC has yet to fashion a comprehensive theory on the subject. However, in its General Comment No. 31, the Committee stated: 'As implied in general comment 29, the Covenant applies to situations of armed conflict to which the rules of international humanitarian law are applicable. While, in respect of certain Covenant rights, more specific rules of international humanitarian law may be specially relevant for purposes of the interpretation of Covenant rights, both spheres of law are complementary, not mutually exclusive.'[52] This would suggest that where a rule of IHL is *lex specialis*, it does not as such derogate from the Covenant right, but rather must be consulted to determine whether that right has been violated.

The Inter-American Commission's case law most closely tracks the views of the ICJ. The Commission[53] has stated that human rights law is not displaced by IHL during armed conflicts and remains fully applicable save for permissible derogations. It has recognized, however, that the test for evaluating the observance of a particular human right during armed conflict may be distinct from that applicable in peacetime. The Commission, therefore, has looked to IHL rules as sources of authoritative guidance or as the *lex specialis* in interpreting the American Convention and Declaration to resolve claimed violations of those instruments in combat situations.

In contrast, the European Court of Human Rights has to date not expressed an opinion on the relationship between these two bodies of law. Moreover, its consistent jurisprudence applying essentially law enforcement rules to killings during armed conflicts suggests that it does not regard IHL as *lex specialis* in such situations.

5 The right to life

The right to life is the most fundamental right guaranteed in human rights law. Articles 6 and 4 of the ICCPR and the American Convention, respectively, prohibit the 'arbitrary' deprivation of life. This right, moreover, is not subject to derogation or limitations under either instrument. In contrast, Article 2 of the European Convention guarantees this right by prohibiting 'intentional' deprivations of life and stipulates the only circumstances when lethal force can lawfully be employed by state

52 General Comment No. 31, para. 11.

53 See Inter-American Commission on Human Rights, *Report on Terrorism and Human Rights* (22 October 2002), OEA/Ser.L/V/II.116, Doc. 5 rev. 1 corr., paras. 57–62.

agents. Article 15 of the treaty provides an additional ground for use of deadly force in situations of armed conflict by permitting derogation from Article 2 for deaths resulting from 'lawful acts of war'.

This section examines the protection of this right in the following situations: (1) an extraterritorial situation of international armed conflict, including occupation, such as when the United States and its coalition partners invaded and subsequently occupied Iraq; and (2) an extraterritorial situation of non-international armed conflict, such as the current involvement of various NATO member states in the ongoing internal hostilities in Afghanistan at the invitation of the Afghan government.

5.1 *Situations of international armed conflict*

Human rights treaty bodies have developed an extensive and basically similar jurisprudence on the duty of states to uphold the right to life by essentially employing a law enforcement paradigm that places limits on the use of lethal force by state agents. In principle, state agents may use lethal force only in certain situations where strictly unavoidable to protect themselves or others from imminent threat of death or serious injury, or to maintain law and order where strictly necessary and proportionate. In addition, the case law indicates that state agents should attempt to arrest rather than kill persons posing a threat and should plan their operations accordingly.

In contrast, IHL, while placing restraints on the conduct of hostilities, permits deadly force to be used directly against combatants at all times until they have been captured or rendered *hors de combat*. Similarly, civilians lose their immunity from direct attack for such time as they directly participate in hostilities.[54] And, unlike HRL, IHL also does *not* require that an attempt be made to arrest or capture these persons before they are attacked.

If enemy combatants and civilians directly participating in hostilities may be lawfully attacked under IHL during international conflicts, how should their deaths be treated under human rights law? The answer

[54] See N. Melzer, *Interpretive Guidance on the Notion of Direct Participation in Hostilities under International Humanitarian Law* (Geneva: ICRC, 2009), at www.icrc.org/web/eng/htmlall/direct-participation-ihl-feature-020609?opendocument. See Chapter 14 in this volume, which notes the current debate about whether state action to confront terrorists ought to be governed by HRL or, alternatively, by IHL.

might well turn on the particular treaty body's views on the interrelationship of HRL and IHL. Before addressing this issue, the treaty body would have to determine whether the invading state's human rights obligations apply in the country where the hostilities are underway. As previously noted, if the invaded country is outside of the geographic boundaries of the OAS or the CoE, these regional bodies' respective instruments would not apply, and any complaint based on these deaths would be inadmissible. If, however, the invaded country were within one of these regions, the question then becomes whether the victims at the time they were killed were within the jurisdiction of the invading state.

The Inter-American Commission's case law would suggest that persons targeted and killed by the invading states' forces were subject to that state's authority.[55] On the merits, the Commission, which regards IHL as the *lex specialis*, should find that killings sanctioned by IHL would not constitute arbitrary deprivations of life under the American Declaration or Convention.[56]

Given the ICCPR's global reach, the location of the event is not critical; but, the Committee would have to decide whether the victims when attacked were within 'the power or effective control' of the invading state's forces. If it so determined, the thrust of General Comment 31 would suggest that the Committee would reach the same conclusion as the IACHR, finding no violation of the right to life.

Resolution of these issues is more complicated under the European Convention for a variety of reasons. For example, assuming that the invaded country were a CoE member, it is doubtful under the ECtHR's jurisprudence that the victims would be found subject to the jurisdiction of the invading state if that state's forces did not exercise effective control over the territory or the victims at the time of their deaths. And, even assuming that jurisdiction did attach, none of the grounds specified in Article 2 of the European Convention authorizing the use of deadly force, which are based on a law enforcement paradigm, could plausibly be invoked by the invading state. These deaths, for instance, could hardly be justified for the purpose of quelling a riot or insurrection. Because these deaths do not come within any of Article 2's exceptions, the invading state could derogate from Article 2 in respect of 'deaths resulting from lawful acts of war'. But, no European state has ever filed such a

[55] See *Salas*.

[56] See *Juan Carlos Abella* v. *Argentina*, Case No. 11.137, Report No. 355/97, Annual Report 1997, OEA/Ser.L/II.98, doc.6 rev. 1998.

derogation under Article 15 based on its involvement in an extraterritorial international armed conflict. Moreover, as noted previously, it is questionable whether a state could claim that its engagement in a wholly extraterritorial armed conflict would constitute the kind of emergency that would justify its derogating from the European Convention. Furthermore, if such a derogation were invalid, then the only remaining option for the ECtHR would be to use IHL to interpret Article 2 so as to find that deaths resulting from lawful acts of war do not violate the right to life – something that the Court has shown little inclination to do.

5.2 Occupation

The jurisprudence of the treaty bodies surveyed indicates that human rights law applies during a situation of occupation, which is also governed by IHL rules. As the state party to the treaty is obliged to respect the right to life in occupied territory, it is crucial to know when territory is occupied and what body of law – IHL or HRL – controls that determination. Professor Hampson notes that human rights treaty bodies have not had to 'define occupation or to determine whether the definition under human rights law is the same as that under IHL'.[57] She correctly states that 'If IHL is the *lex specialis* but human rights law remains applicable, a human rights body should presumably apply IHL to determine whether the situation is one of occupation'.[58]

In this regard, territory is considered occupied under IHL when it is actually placed under the authority of the hostile army, i.e., organized resistance must have been overcome and the invading power has substituted its own authority for that of the legitimate government. Additionally, the occupation extends only to territory where such authority has been established and can be exercised. As indicated, extraterritorial application of human rights treaties requires the state to exercise effective control over territory, which may well be coextensive with belligerent occupation. However, as one commentator[59] observes, the effective control test under human rights law may be broader and at times have a lower threshold than that for occupation under IHL. One

[57] Hampson, 'Relationship between International Humanitarian Law and Human Rights Law', 567.

[58] *Ibid.*

[59] C. Droege, 'The Interplay Between International Humanitarian Law and International Human Rights Law in Situations of Armed Conflict' (2007) 40 *Israel Law Review* 310, 325.

example would be the *Illascu* v. *Moldova* case[60] where the ECtHR found Russia responsible for human rights violations in territory it controlled, but could not be said to occupy under IHL. Similarly, the IACHR in *Coard*[61] found violations of the American Declaration and actually invoked occupation law when the United States legally was not occupying Grenada.

Another important question is whether IHL or HRL rules govern the use of lethal force by the occupying power in occupied territory. The answer should depend on the nature of the occupation. In a relatively 'calm' occupation, the occupying power, consistent with its duty under IHL to ensure public order and safety, should operate under a law enforcement paradigm. Thus, its armed forces would have to attempt to arrest or capture criminal suspects before using deadly force against them, which would preclude, in principle, 'targeted killings' of suspected terrorists.[62]

If, however, there is an outbreak or resumption of hostilities in the occupied territory entailing military operations by the occupying power's forces against an organized resistance movement and/or the armed forces of the ousted government, then IHL rules should fully apply to the conduct of hostilities with opposing combatants being directly targetable on sight. The killing of civilians in the process of committing terrorist or other hostile acts, amounting to direct participation in hostilities, should also be deemed lawful under both IHL and HRL. Law enforcement rules, however, should continue to apply in connection with ordinary criminal activity not linked to the hostilities.

5.3 *Situations of non-international armed conflict*

It is important to note that under this scenario State X's armed forces are *not* engaged in a non-international armed conflict (NIAC) within State X, but rather are assisting State Y's military to suppress an insurrection within State Y. While there is considerable case law on the application of human rights law in the former situation, there is virtually no

[60] *Illascu and others* v. *Russia, Moldova*, 48787/99, Judgment of 8 July 2004.

[61] *Coard*.

[62] See Concluding Observations on Israel, para. 15, in which the HRC expressed concern about Israel's targeted killings of suspected terrorists in the Occupied Territories. See also *The Public Committee against Torture in Israel et al.* v. *the Prime Minister of Israel et al.*, the Supreme Court of Israel sitting as High Court of Justice, Judgment of 14 December 2006.

jurisprudence at least from human rights treaty bodies on the extraterritorial application of human rights law in the latter situation. Moreover, many of the same threshold issues discussed in the international hostilities section would similarly be posed by State X's extraterritorial involvement in State Y's NIAC.

For example, neither the European Convention, nor the Inter-American instruments would be applicable if the state party were involved in an NIAC outside of the respective region's geographical boundaries. Thus, unlawful killings by State X's forces would not engage its responsibility under these instruments. And, even if State X's forces were fighting within another state party's territory, the treaty body would still have to determine whether the victims, when killed, were within State X's jurisdiction. In addition, extraterritorial killings in an NIAC would not easily satisfy any of the grounds in Article 2 of the European Convention authorizing the use of deadly force. The permissible ground to quell an insurrection most certainly refers to actions taken by the state party within its *own* territory, not within that of another state involved in an NIAC. Furthermore, State X's involvement in State Y's NIAC arguably would provide no more justification for derogating from the European Convention than would its engagement in an overseas international armed conflict.

Assuming that the treaty body were seized with the matter, how should it treat killings that are lawful under IHL rules applicable in NIACs? More particularly, which law – IHL or HRL – should determine whether the use of deadly force was permissible? If the treaty bodies apply the same standards to determine the lawfulness of these extraterritorial killings as they would to killings by state agents in an NIAC at home, then they probably would reach different results.

The Inter-American Commission, based on its practice, would likely treat members of government armed forces and of organized armed groups as combatants and, as such, directly targetable, whether they are *on or away* from the battlefield. Moreover, it would apply IHL as *lex specialis* to determine the lawfulness of the killings under the American Declaration or Convention. In contrast, the HRC[63] and the especially the European Court[64] have applied law enforcement and not

[63] See *Guerrero* v. *Colombia*, Communication No. R.11/45, UN Doc. Supp. No. 40(A/37/40). 31 March 1992.

[64] See, e.g., *Gul* v. *Turkey*, Judgment of 14 December 2000; *Ogur* v. *Turkey*, Judgment of 20 May 1999; *Gulec* v. *Turkey*, Judgment of 27 July 1998: *McCann and others* v. *the United Kingdom*, Ser. A, No.324, App. No. 18984/91 (1995).

IHL rules to find violations of the right to life where state agents have directly targeted members of armed opposition groups *off* the battlefield. However, the Committee would probably find combat-related deaths that are lawful under IHL to not violate the ICCPR.[65]

Whether the European Court would reach this same conclusion is unclear. The Court has taken into account various IHL principles in some recent Turkish[66] and Russian[67] cases involving clashes between governmental and armed opposition forces. However, it has never relied on IHL as *lex specialis* in assessing the legality of deaths arising out of such clashes, but instead has effectively applied HRL to make such determinations. By so doing, the Court risks finding killings that are lawful under IHL as violating the European Convention – a result which, it is submitted, could significantly undermine confidence in both IHL and HRL.

6 The right to liberty and habeas corpus

Articles 9 and 7 of the ICCPR and the American Convention, respectively, address the protection of personal liberty by prohibiting arbitrary arrest or detention. Article 5 of the European Convention takes a different approach by exhaustively listing the grounds for lawful arrest or detention. This section examines the protection of this basic right in (a) extraterritorial situations of international armed conflict, including occupation, and in (b) extraterritorial situations of non-international armed conflict.

6.1 Situations of international armed conflict

Human rights jurisprudence requires, *inter alia*, that any deprivation of liberty be based upon grounds and procedures established by law, that detainees be informed of the reasons for the detention and promptly notified of the charges against them in case of criminal detention, and that they be provided access to legal counsel. Prompt and effective

[65] But see Chapter 16 in this volume, in which it is posited that the line between IHL and HRL may not always be clear, as 'there is still an on-going dynamic interrelationship such that the binding norm can be applied by reference to the principles and provisions of the other area of law.'

[66] See *Ahmet Ozkan and others* v. *Turkey*, Judgment of 6 April 2004; *Ergi* v. *Turkey*, Judgment of 28 July 1998.

[67] See *Isayeva, Yusupova and Bazayeva* v. *Russia*, Judgment of 24 February 2004.

oversight of detention by a judge or other officer authorized by law to exercise judicial power must be ensured to verify the legality of detention and to protect other fundamental rights of the detainee.

The right to personal liberty applies during armed conflicts, except to the extent that it may be subject to lawful derogation. In this regard, the right to liberty is not included among the non-derogable rights in the ICCPR or the European or American Conventions. However, a state's ability to suspend this right has been strictly and narrowly defined by the treaty bodies. The Human Rights Committee, for instance, has indicated that in order to protect non-derogable rights, the right to habeas corpus must not be diminished by a state's decision to derogate from the Covenant.[68] The Inter-American Court has similarly found that habeas corpus and *amparo* cannot be derogated from during emergencies.[69] While never finding habeas corpus to be non-derogable, the ECtHR has ruled that deprivations of liberty without habeas corpus proceedings to review the decision to detain an individual violates Article 5(4) of the European Convention.[70]

IHL permits the capture and detention of adversaries as a lawful incidence of war. During international armed conflicts, the Third and Fourth Geneva Conventions of 1949 contain provisions addressing the circumstances under which prisoners of war (POWs) and civilians, respectively, may be interned or detained and the manner in which their internment/detention must be monitored, including access by the International Committee of the Red Cross (ICRC). The Third Convention (GC III) permits the internment of combatants as PoWs until their repatriation at the cessation of active hostilities or the completion of any criminal proceedings or punishment for an indictable offence pending against a POW. The Fourth Convention (GC IV) permits the internment of civilians either in a party's own territory,[71] as well as in occupied territory (see below) provided certain conditions are met. Among them is that the person represents a serious security threat, that he or she has the right to request review of the internment decision, that such review is to be carried out by a court or administrative board and that it must be periodic (every six months).

68 General Comment No. 29, para. 16.

69 Advisory Opinion OC-9/87, Judicial Guarantees in States of Emergency (Articles 27(2), 25 and 8 of the American Convention on Human Rights, 6 October 1987).

70 *Chahal* v. *United Kingdom*, Judgment of 15 November 1996.

71 See Fourth Geneva Convention, Arts. 41–3.

In addition, persons detained/interned by a party to an international armed conflict and who do not benefit from more favourable treatment under the Geneva Conventions or Additional Protocol I (AP I) are entitled to certain *minimum* protections under Article 75, AP I, which reflects customary international law. Such persons would include civilians who directly participate in the hostilities, but who do not qualify as PoWs under GC III or for protection under GC IV because of the nationality criteria stipulated therein.

Article 75 contains no provisions on permissible grounds for, or review of the lawfulness of detention. However, it stipulates that affected persons must be promptly informed of the reasons for their detention/internment and requires that they 'shall be released with the minimum delay possible and in any event as soon as the circumstances justifying the arrest, detention or internment have ceased to exist'. Article 75's text thus suggests that detention/internment is an exceptional measure which should never be prolonged or indefinite. Moreover, Article 72, AP I makes clear that Article 75's minimum guarantees are supplemented by HRL.

Since IHL authorizes the detention of combatants during international armed conflicts, how should such detentions be treated under HRL? Must a state derogate from the right to personal liberty in order to lawfully detain persons in such conflicts? And, do wartime detainees have a right to habeas corpus? There is little or no human rights jurisprudence on most of these questions. The Inter-American Commission more than any other treaty body has addressed or dealt with some of these issues.

The Commission has said that during international hostilities consideration must be given to IHL rules as the applicable *lex specialis* in interpreting and applying the right to personal liberty, 'with due regard to the overarching principles of necessity, proportionality, humanity and non-discrimination'.[72] Thus, the Commission would look to IHL to determine which grounds of deprivation of liberty are lawful during international hostilities. Since IHL permits the detention of enemy combatants in such hostilities, the Commission would find that such detentions do not constitute 'arbitrary' deprivations of liberty under the American Convention (or Declaration). Accordingly, there would be no need to derogate from Article 7 of the American Convention. Indeed, no OAS member state has ever derogated from the Convention based on its

[72] IACHR, *Report on Terrorism*, para. 141.

involvement, whether at home or abroad, in an international armed conflict. Further, as noted in the previous section, any such derogation would be problematic in terms of satisfying the condition that there be an emergency threatening the life of the nation. And, due to the limited geographical reach of the American Convention and Declaration, detention of persons, other than of nationals, by a member state outside of the Western hemisphere would not generate any state responsibility under either instrument.

As PoWs are interned for reasons of military necessity, i.e., to prevent them from returning to the battlefield, and not as criminal suspects, GC III does not afford them the procedural protections, including judicial review, that HRL provides to criminal suspects in peacetime. Thus, the IACHR has recognized that POWs are not entitled 'to be informed of the reasons for their detention, to challenge the legality of their detention, or, in the absence of disciplinary or criminal proceedings, to be provided with access to legal counsel'.[73] While carving out this exception to regional doctrine on habeas corpus, the Commission has indicated that in uncertain or protracted situations of armed conflict and occupation IHL rules and procedures governing detention/internment might prove 'inadequate' to safeguard the minimum human rights of detainees, including the right to personal liberty.[74] In which case, the Commission has indicated that the supervisory mechanisms and judicial guarantees under HRL and domestic law, including habeas corpus, 'may necessarily supersede international humanitarian law'.[75] This was precisely the rationale underlying the Commission's issuance of precautionary measures on behalf of the Guantánamo Bay detainees – all of whom were captured in the 2002 Afghan hostilities and disqualified, without individual status determinations, by the United States from protection under the Geneva Conventions.

In 2004, the US Supreme Court ruled in *Rasul* v. *Bush*[76] and again in 2008 in *Boumediene* v. *Bush*[77] that Guantánamo detainees only had the right to challenge the lawfulness of their detention in federal court through a habeas corpus petition based on the fact that the naval base is under legal and effective US control. Although the court never expressly referenced human rights law in either case, its rulings are broadly consistent with human rights jurisprudence concerning the non-suspendability of habeas relief during emergencies.

[73] *Ibid.*, para. 142. [74] *Ibid.*, para. 146. [75] *Ibid.*
[76] *Rasul* v. *Bush*, 542 US 466 (2004). [77] *Boumediene* v. *Bush*, 553 US (2008).

The HRC has found that extraterritorial detentions constitute an exercise of jurisdiction under the ICCPR. However, it has never decided a case based on the applicability of IHL to wartime detentions under the Covenant. Walter Kalin, a former Committee member, does provide some insight into how the Committee might deal with this issue. He states that during armed conflicts 'IHL determines what is 'arbitrary' in terms of Covenant rights protecting against arbitrary deprivations of a specific right' and concludes that a detention would not be arbitrary under Article 9 'if it is permitted by IHL which, as *lex specialis*, determines which ground for deprivation of liberty are lawful in times of armed conflict'.[78] Accordingly, the Committee would likely reach this decision without regard to the question of derogation under the Covenant. Moreover, a derogation from Article 9 based on the state's involvement in a wholly extraterritorial armed conflict may not pass muster for reasons previously explained.

Presumably, the Committee, like the IACHR, would also find that PoWs are not entitled to habeas relief, at least when IHL supervisory mechanisms are adequately functioning. Professor Kalin does, however, suggest that a right to periodic review of detention 'would seem possible and required to interpret a provision of Article 75, paragraph 3 [of] Additional Protocol I on the guarantees for persons detained for acts in relation to the armed conflict in light of Article 9 of the Covenant and to apply both provisions cumulatively'.[79] It is also arguable that such security detainees, by analogy to civilian internees under GC IV, should have a right to periodic review of the lawfulness of continued detention as a matter of customary international law.

The ECtHR in *Ocalan* and more recently in *Al-Saadoon and Mufdhi*, also made clear that extraterritorial detentions entail the exercise of authority and control by the state over the detainee. Such detentions during *overseas* international armed conflicts pose many of the same problems as discussed previously. Again, none of the grounds listed in Article 5 of the European Convention could justify detaining combatants or civilians in such situations. Yet, the former European Commission found in *Cyprus* v. *Turkey* that since Turkey had not derogated from

[78] W. Kalin, 'The Covenant on Civil and Political Rights and Its Relationship with International Humanitarian Law', in University Center for International Humanitarian Law, *Expert Meeting on the Supervision of the Lawfulness of Detention During Armed Conflict*, at www.cidh-geneva.ch/experts/meetings/year. php?year =2004, 32.

[79] *Ibid.*

Article 5, its detention of Cypriot troops as POWs violated the Convention.[80] Professor Hampson terms this result 'absurd'.[81] She suggests that such a result could be avoided by the state's derogating to introduce additional grounds for detention permitted by IHL or by the Court's use of IHL as a matter of law.[82] Whether the state should or could derogate in these circumstances requires further study and analysis.

6.2 Occupation

Article 78, GC IV permits, as an exceptional measure, an occupying power 'for imperative reasons of security' to intern or place civilians in assigned residences. Such decisions must be made according to a 'regular procedure' which includes the right of detainees to have the decision appealed with the least possible delay and, if upheld, subject to review 'if possible' every six months 'by a competent body' established by the occupying power. Jelena Pejic suggests that this appeal is essentially akin to a habeas action since its purpose 'is to enable the competent body to determine whether the person was deprived of liberty for valid reasons and to order his or her release if that was not the case'.[83] She also mentions that 'the authority that initially deprived the person of liberty and the body authorized to conduct the review on appeal must not be the same if the right to petition is to be effective.'[84] Further, citing the Commentary to GC IV's requirement that the reviewing authority be independent and impartial, she argues that such a body must have authority to render final decisions on internment or release.[85] On a related issue, the International Tribunal for the former Yugoslavia has determined that an initially lawful internment becomes unlawful if the detaining power does not respect a detainee's basic procedural rights and does not establish an appropriate review mechanism as required by Article 43 of GC IV.[86] The Tribunal's reasoning should similarly apply to detainees in occupied territory under Article 78.

[80] *Cyprus* v. *Turkey*.

[81] Hampson, 'Relationship between International Humanitarian Law and Human Rights Law', 565.

[82] *Ibid.*, 566.

[83] J. Pejic, 'Procedural Principles and Safeguards for Internment/Administrative Detention in Armed Conflict and Other Situations of Violence' (2005) 87 *International Review of the Red Cross* 375, 386.

[84] *Ibid.* [85] *Ibid.*, 387.

[86] *Prosecutor* v. *Zejnil Delalic and others*, Appeal Judgment, Case No. IT-96-21-A, A.Ch., 20 February 2001, para. 22.

The Inter-American Commission's decision in the *Coard* case essentially echoes these views. Although the United States did not legally occupy Grenada after it invaded the island in 2003, the IACHR, nonetheless, invoked parts of occupation law in its analysis of the case. Specifically, it found Article 78, GC IV applicable and noted that it was generally consistent with the supervisory control required by the American Declaration's prohibition of arbitrary arrest.[87] While affirming that valid security reasons initially justified the United States' detention of petitioners, the Commission indicated that the same IHL rules which authorized this 'as an exceptional security measure' also required a regular procedure which permitted the detainees to be heard and to promptly appeal the decision. Such a procedure, which it suggested could be undertaken by a judicial or quasi-judicial body, 'ensures that the decision to maintain a person in detention does not rest with the agents who effectuated the deprivation of liberty, and ensures a minimal level of oversight by an entity with the authority to order release if warranted.'[88] It noted, moreover, that such supervisory control over detention is an 'essential rationale of the right of habeas corpus, a protection which is not susceptible to abrogation.'[89] Because petitioners were held for six to nine days after the end of hostilities without any such review, it found their detention violated the Declaration 'as understood with reference to Article 78 of the Fourth Geneva Convention.'[90]

The HRC has dealt with detentions during a situation of occupation. For example, it has addressed Israel's detention of Palestinians from the Occupied Territories in connection with its derogation from Article 9 of the ICPR. In its Concluding Observations on Israel's second periodic report, the Committee recognized Israel's 'serious security concerns in the context of the present conflict', including suicide bombings associated with the second intifada, which led it to declare a state of emergency and derogate from Article 9 of the ICCPR.[91] Nonetheless, it expressed concern about Israel's use of various forms of administrative detention, restricting access to counsel and disclosure of full reasons for detentions. The Committee stated 'these features limit the effectiveness of judicial review, thus endangering the protection against torture and other inhuman treatment prohibited under article 7 and derogating from article 9 more extensively than what in the Committee's view is permissible pursuant to article 4.'[92] Presumably, the European Court would also

[87] *Coard*, para. 55. [88] *Ibid.*, para. 58. [89] *Ibid.*, para. 55. [90] *Ibid.*, para. 57.
[91] Concluding Observations on Israel, para. 3. [92] *Ibid.*, para. 12.

find persons detained during an occupation entitled to a habeas or equivalent proceeding.

6.3 *Situations of non-international armed conflict*

Although IHL applicable to NIACs envisions the detention of fighters and civilians for reasons related to the conflict, it contains no rules authorizing or regulating such detentions.[93] These are matters governed exclusively by domestic law and HRL.[94] Thus, a state engaged in an NIAC can detain, try and punish insurgents consistent with its human rights obligations. If it instead wants to administratively detain or intern them, then it would have to derogate from the right to personal liberty, which would entail declaring an emergency. However, human rights jurisprudence, as indicated, would preclude it from suspending habeas corpus in such situations.

If that state requests other states to help it quell the insurrection within its territory, those states' legal authority to detain insurgents and other persons, unless stipulated otherwise in a legal arrangement, would not be based on their *domestic* laws, but that of the host state. Moreover, any such extraterritorial detentions would also constitute an exercise of jurisdiction under the ICCPR, the European Convention, and the American Convention or Declaration (if carried out in an OAS member state). No human rights treaty body has yet ruled on the lawfulness of extraterritorial detentions in these particular circumstances. The Human Rights Committee and the IACHR arguably would not find such detentions to be 'arbitrary' if they were lawful under the law of and duly authorized by the host state. However, such detentions do not facially satisfy any of the grounds for deprivation of liberty in Article 5 of the European Convention. And, any attempt by a CoE state to derogate from that article based on its involvement in a purely extraterritorial NIAC would be questionable for reasons previously explained. Finally, any person detained, administratively or otherwise, by agents of the invited states should be entitled to file habeas or equivalent actions before the

[93] But see Chapter 17 in this volume, which indicates that 'both customary and treaty IHL contain an inherent power to intern and may thus be said to provide a legal basis for internment in NIAC.'

[94] See Chapter 16 in this volume, which notes that at least one commentator has suggested that applying HRL by reference to IHL 'may "relax" the human rights requirements in some situations'.

courts of the *host* state. US case law also suggests that the courts of the *detaining* country might also entertain such petitions.

7 Conclusion

In examining the extraterritorial application of two 'preferred' human rights, this chapter has identified serious gaps in legal protection of the right to life under the European and Inter-American human rights systems, which should be remedied. It also has noted potentially significant problems with derogations from these rights based on a state's involvement in purely overseas armed conflicts. Its exploration of how treaty bodies deal with the relationship between IHL and HRL during armed conflicts has revealed major differences in approach, particularly the European Court's failure to use IHL to assess the legality of combat-related killings during armed conflicts. The chapter also points out the need to clarify whether human rights bodies should apply IHL or HRL to determine when territory is occupied, and which body of law should govern the use of deadly force in such situations. Finally, it notes that, with the exception of PoWs and civilian internees under GC IV, all other persons deprived of liberty during emergency situations, including armed conflicts, should have, in principle, a right to challenge the lawfulness of his/her detention.

16

Harmony or conflict? The interplay between human rights and humanitarian law in the fight against terrorism

HELEN DUFFY

A selective and at times confused approach to international law, and human rights and humanitarian law in particular, has blighted discourse surrounding appropriate responses to terrorism in recent years. In many cases problems relate more to an unwillingness to be constrained by law, or to apply consistently international law, than genuine lack of clarity as to its scope.[1] But manipulation of the legal framework should not obscure areas of genuine uncertainty and complexity. One such area may be the interplay between IHL and IHRL in the context of the fight against terrorism. While in most areas IHL and IHRL will overlap and drive in the same direction, the notorious exploitation of legal vacuums and uncertainties to justify a 'pick and choose' approach to international law underlines the importance of understanding and clarifying applicable law and the interrelationship between these areas of law in particular situations.

Many thanks to Marianna Leite and Nivedita S. for their assistance with publication, and to Claus Kress and as ever Fabricio Guariglia for insightful comments. This chapter reflects the author's views only.

[1] Perhaps the most notorious example of selective application of IHL (though there are others) was the decision to consider detainees enemy combatants for purposes of IHL but not to afford them the PoW rights that accompanied that status upon detention. The US government's recognition that the Geneva Conventions would be applied so far 'as appropriate' is another. See, e.g., Duffy, *The 'War on Terror' and the Framework of International Law* (Cambridge: Cambridge University Press, 2013 forthcoming), chs. 6 and 9. Challenges to the 'applicability' of human rights law in armed conflict situations or extra-territorially are noted below in this section.

While the question of the interrelationship between IHL and IHRL is not new,[2] it is in recent years that a range of courts and bodies, including the International Court of Justice and human rights bodies, have had reason to consider the nature of this relationship. Significant doctrinal discussion has also been dedicated to its theoretical underpinnings.[3] As will be seen, the 'co-application' of these areas of law in situations of armed conflict is now commonly accepted, but the issue of how that interrelationship works remains one of the more complex and controversial legal issues in the fight against terrorism. This chapter therefore sketches out broad approaches to the question of interrelationship and relevant international practice, before considering how this interplay might work in relation to particular controversial issues. These are the legal requirements concerning review of the lawfulness of detention, targeted killings and the investigation of violations and reparation of victims.

Section 1 looks at the applicability of each of international humanitarian law and international human rights law in the context of the fight against terrorism, as a necessary precursor to the more detailed consideration of the interplay between these branches of law. Section 2 considers various theoretical approaches to interplay, and the role of the International Court of Justice (ICJ) and human rights courts and bodies to date. Section 3 highlights a few of the many outstanding questions arising in respect of the interrelationship and the *lex specialis*

[2] See, e.g., language in the Martens Clause, I. Scobbie, 'Principle or Pragmatics? The Relationship between Human Rights Law and the Law of Armed Conflicts' (2010) *Journal of Conflict & Security Law*.

[3] See e.g. Droege, 'The Interplay between International Humanitarian Law and International Human Rights Law in Situations of Armed Conflicts' (2007) 40 *Israel Law Review* 310; Draper, 'Humanitarian Law and Human Rights' (1979) *Acta Juridica* 193; Schindler, 'Human Rights and Humanitarian Law: Interrelationship of the Laws' (1981) 31 *American University Law Review* 935; Lubell, 'Parallel Application of International Humanitarian Law and International Human Rights Law: An Examination of the Debate' (2007) 40 *Israel Law Review* 648; N. Prud'homme, '*Lex specialis*: Oversimplifying a More Complex and Multifaceted Relationship?' (2007) 40 *Israel Law Review* 355, 385; Matthew Happold, 'International Humanitarian Law and Human Rights Law', in Christian Henderson and Nigel White (eds.), *Research Handbook on International Conflict and Security Law* (2012); Marko Milanovich, 'Norm Conflict, International Humanitarian Law and Human Rights Law', in Orna Ben-Naftali (ed.), *International Humanitarian Law and International Human Rights Law* (2011), 95–128; Yuval Shany, 'Human Rights and Humanitarian Law as Competing Legal Paradigms for Fighting Terror' (*ibid.*, 13–33); Alejandro Lorite Escorhuela, 'Humanitarian Law and Human Rights Law: The Politics of Distinction', (2011) 19 Mich. St. J. Int'l L.299; K. Parker, 'Human Rights and Humanitarian Law' (1985) 7 *Whittier Law Review* 675.

notion in particular. Section 4 addresses the three issues that demonstrate the implications of these approaches to interplay in different situations and some of the questions they raise.

1 Applicability of IHL/IHRL in situations of armed conflict and the fight against terrorism

1.1 Applicability of IHL?

The elemental question upon which the applicability of IHL depends is of course whether there is an 'armed conflict'. This is an issue around which much legal and policy debate has revolved in recent years in the context of the 'war on terror' (WOT). As has been well rehearsed elsewhere,[4] a chasm of significant practical import separates the view, espoused by the US government that there is a potentially global armed conflict with al-Qaeda and related Islamic fundamentalist groups and the vast majority of international opinion which rejects the existence of such an 'armed conflict'.[5]

While much attention has been dedicated to this debate in the WOT context, it is worth recalling that to some extent this controversy is not unique or unusual. Controversy frequently surrounds the existence or acknowledgment of armed conflict, particularly in the context of non-international armed conflicts where insurgent groups are commonly referred to as 'terrorists' and prosecuted as such under domestic law, despite the fact that IHL may be applicable to the treatment of such persons. The test for the applicability of IHL is a legal one, depending on

[4] Duffy, '*War on Terror*', ch. 6.

[5] While Bush famously coined the phrase the 'global war on terror', the Obama administration continues to assert that it is at war with al-Qaeda and 'associated' groups. See e.g. B. Obama 'Remarks by the President on National Security', *The White House Office of the Press Secretary*, 21 May 2009, H. Koh, Legal Adviser, Department of State, 'The Obama Administration and International Law', Remarks at the Annual Meeting of the American Society of International Law (ASIL), 25 March 2010; E. Holder, Attorney General, Department of Justice, Address at Northwestern University School of Law, 5 March 2012; O. Brennan, 'Speech at the Woodrow Wilson 'International Center for Scholars: The Ethics and Efficacy of the President's Counterterrorism Strategy', 30 April 2012. This view has increasingly resoundingly been rejected on the international level in the course of the war on terror – see Duffy, '*War on Terror*'. The normative battle on whether there is or can be a global conflict with al-Qaeda, as opposed to a transnational criminal law enforcement challenge, shows no sign of ceding.

whether the facts meet the definition of 'armed conflict'[6] in international law, irrespective of the approach taken by parties to the conflict, or by parties to any related litigation.[7] Whatever the debate around a global 'war on terror' or not, it is uncontroversial that there have been and remain armed conflicts (such as that in Afghanistan) involving in one form or another individuals and groups linked with what is commonly referred to as 'terrorism', and that IHL is applicable to those conflicts.

In armed conflict, IHL is in principle applicable to conduct carried out as *part of* that conflict, as distinct from conduct that takes place in the broad *context* of a state in armed conflict without being 'associated' with it.[8] It may be particularly difficult to determine whether action that takes place far from the area of hostilities, such as much of the burgeoning practice of targeted drone killings, explored further below was in reality part of or 'associated' with an armed conflict. The onus ties with a state, if it seeks to justify action on the basis of the application of IHL that would not otherwise be permissible, to demonstrate the 'association' with the armed conflict and the relevance of IHL standards in the particular situation.[9]

[6] See *Prosecutor* v. *Tadić*, Appeal Judgment, Case No. IT-94-1-A, A.Ch., 7 May 1997. See e.g. C. Garraway and Y. Dinstein, 'The *Manual on the Law of Non-International Armed Conflict*: With Commentary' (2006) 36 *International Institute of Humanitarian Law* 71; and Chapter 14 in this volume.

[7] In practice, in litigation states may deny the application of IHL in order not to confer legitimacy on insurgents, applicants may not invoke it as it does not assist their case and it thus falls to the court to invoke IHL *propio motu* which it may be particularly reluctant to do. This poses challenges for human rights courts, the role of which is discussed further at section 2.4 below. See F. Hampson, 'The Relationship between International Humanitarian Law and Human Rights Law from the Perspective of a Human Rights Treaty Body' (2008) 90 *International Review of the Red Cross* 549.

[8] The nexus requirement is explored in most detail in relation to 'war crimes'. See ICC Elements of the Crimes document ('the conduct took place in the context of and was associated with an . . . armed conflict') and e.g. K. Dörmann, 'Preparatory Commission for the International Criminal Court: the Elements of War Crimes' (2000) 83 *International Review of the Red Cross* 771 and 'Preparatory Commission for the International Criminal Court: Part II: Other Serious Violations of Laws and Customs Applicable in International and Non-International Armed Conflict' (2001) 83 *International Review of the Red Cross*: '[t]he words "in the context of and was associated with" are meant to draw a clear distinction between war crimes and ordinary criminal behaviour . . . The words "in association with" were meant to reflect the jurisprudence of the ad hoc Tribunals which states that a sufficient nexus must be established between the offences and the armed conflict' (461).

[9] For one example of an onus on the state, see *Varnova* v. *Turkey*, para. 186, where the ECtHR made clear the onus on the state to demonstrate, in support of its case, that 'missing men were found dead or killed, in the conflict zone'.

While IHL is relevant to action taken in the fight against terrorism so far as the particular acts are part of or closely associated with a real armed conflict, for the vast majority of action against terrorism, IHL standards are not applicable and have no bearing. There is a danger that inflated resort to the war paradigm in relation to counter-terrorism over a period of years distorts our perception of the relevance of IHL, or indeed the significance of some of the questions around the interplay between IHL and human rights law. For most of the situations in which states act to meet the challenge of preventing and responding to terrorism, international human rights law provides the appropriate legal framework.

1.2 Applicability of international human rights law?

A substantial body of human rights law has been developed in response to the challenges posed by international terrorism across continents and over decades. So far as those acts of terrorism arise in relation to an armed conflict, both IHL and human rights law apply. It is now beyond reasonable controversy that human rights law continues to apply in times of armed conflict. While this is not universally accepted, with the US and Israeli states being the proposition's principal detractors,[10] it is supported by the overwhelming weight of international legal opinion and practice, having been affirmed by international courts,[11]

[10] See e.g. the US position in statements which entirely ignore the relevance of IHRL to matters such as Guantanamo detentions, extraordinary rendition or in Afghanistan, in large part on the basis of the purported existence of a global conflict with al Qaeda and associated groups to which IHL applies. See e.g. Koh ASIL Speech, above, which ignores IHRL, the US Second and Third Periodic Report to HRC; see the marginal shift of position in the Fourth Periodic Report to HRC, para. 507, where the US accepts that some human rights, apparently those that are not in any way connected to the conflict itself, may continue to apply, but not those issues mentioned above. See also U.N. Comm. Against Torture, Consideration of Reports submitted by State Parties Under Article 19 of the Convention Against Torture: United States of America, para. 14, U.N. Doc. CAT/C/USA/CO/2 (2006).

[11] *Legality of the Threat or Use of Nuclear Weapons*, Advisory Opinion of 8 July 1996 [1996] ICJ Rep. 226, para. 25 (with respect to the International Covenant of Civil and Political Rights); *Legal Consequences of the Construction of a Wall in the Occupied Palestinian Territory*, Advisory Opinion of 9 July 2004 [2004] ICJ Rep. 136, paras. 105–6 (with respect to human rights more broadly); *Armed Activities on the Territory of the Congo* (*Democratic Republic of Congo* v. *Uganda*), Judgment of 19 December 2005 [2005] ICJ Rep. 168, para. 216; *Bámaca Velásquez* v. *Guatemala*, Case No. 11/129 (Merits), IACtHR (Ser. C) No. 70 (2000), para. 207.

human rights treaty bodies and special procedures,[12] the International Committee of the Red Cross,[13] most states,[14] regional political bodies[15] and the United Nations Security Council and General Assembly.[16] So for those acts of terrorism that arise in relation to an armed conflict, therefore, both IHL and human rights law apply.

One of the key issues concerning the applicability of IHRL that has proved controversial is the extent of states' responsibility for human rights violations when operating outside their own territory.[17] Post-9/11 practice highlights the manipulation of the 'extraterritoriality' issue to avoid applicability of human rights law. In its most extreme manifestation the US starkly maintains before treaty bodies that its obligations under human rights treaties (ICCPR and CAT) did not or do not arise in respect of Guantánamo detentions, the CIA extraordinary rendition programme, and its actions in Afghanistan or Iraq for example, on the

[12] E.g., General Comment No. 29: States of Emergency (Article 4), UN Doc. CCPR/C/21/Rev.1/Add.11 (2001); General Comment No. 31, Nature of the General Legal Obligation on States Parties to the Covenant, UN Doc. CCPR/C/21/Rev.1/Add.13 (2004); Concluding Observations on: Democratic Republic of Congo, UN Doc. CCPR/C/COD/CO/3 (2006); *Las Palmeras* v. *Colombia*, Preliminary Objections, Judgment of 4 February 2000, IACtHR (Ser. C) No. 67 (2000), para. 33; *Request for Precautionary Measures Concerning the Detainees at Guantánamo Bay, Cuba*, IACHR, decision of 12 March 2002, 41 ILM 532 (2002), at www1.umn.edu/humanrts/cases/guantanamo-2003.html; African Commission on Human and Peoples' Rights, Resolution on Rwanda, Seventh Annual Activity Report, 1993–4, ACHPR/RPT/7th, Annex XII.

[13] J. Henckaerts and L. Doswald-Beck, *Customary International Humanitarian Law* (Geneva: ICRC, 2005), 303.

[14] Droege, 'Interplay', 324. See above on US and Israel.

[15] See, e.g., Peace and Security Council of the African Union statement on Libya, 23 February 2011, condemning 'the indiscriminate and disproportionate use of force against protesters in violations of human rights and international humanitarian law'.

[16] See, e.g., UN Doc. S/Res./1019 (1995) (Former Yugoslavia); UN Doc. S/Res./1653 (2006) (Great Lakes); UN Doc. A/Res./50/193 (1995) (Former Yugoslavia); UN Doc. A/Res./46/135 (1991) (Kuwait under Iraqi occupation); Commission on Human Rights Resolutions: UN Docs. E/CN.4/1992/84 (1992) (Iraq); E/CN.4/2003/77 (2003) (Afghanistan), A/E/CN.4/Res./2003/16 (2003) (Burundi); E/CN.4/Res./2001/24 (2001) (Russian Federation); E/CN.4/Res./2003/15 (2003) (Congo); OHCRH/STM/CHR/03/2 (2003) (Colombia); OHCHR/STM/CHR/03/3 (2003) (Timor-Leste).

[17] The ECHR and ACHR provide that states must secure the rights under the conventions to 'everyone within their jurisdiction', while the ICCPR refers to the state party's obligations to 'respect and ensure to all individuals within its territory and subject to its jurisdiction the rights recognized in the present convention'. But for both formulations it has become well established through jurisprudence that a state has obligations where it exercises sufficient authority and control abroad.

basis of *inter alia* the 'extraterritorial' nature of the state's action.[18] A narrow view of extraterritorial application has been mirrored elsewhere, albeit in slightly less caricatured form, such as in the dispute surrounding the applicability of the European Convention to the conduct of British troops in Iraq. The UK government argument, which was upheld by domestic courts, was that the ECHR did not apply to persons killed or injured by UK soldiers on the streets of Basra (but, somewhat anomalously, that persons held in UK custody in Iraq *were* covered by the Convention).[19] However in June 2011 the Grand Chamber of the European Court of Human Rights rejected this approach. In the *Al-Skeini* judgment, the Court clarified that the Convention applies extraterritorially where a state controls territory abroad, or where its agents violate rights abroad, noting that 'what is decisive in such cases is the exercise of physical power and control over the person in question'.[20] The approach of the *Al-Skeini* judgment brings ECtHR jurisprudence broadly into line with the long established view of other courts and human rights treaty bodies, which have emphasized that it would be 'unconscionable' to interpret treaty obligations as permitting a

[18] The US interprets the ICCPR as only applying within its own boundaries. Second and Third Periodic Report of the United States of America to the UN Committee on Human Rights Concerning the International Covenant on Civil and Political Rights, October 21, 2005, at www.state.gov/g/drl/rls/55504.htm and Annex I: Territorial Application of the International Covenant on Civil and Political Rights. For the Committee's response see UNHRC, Consideration of Reports Submitted by States Parties under Article 40 of the Covenant, Concluding Observations of the Human Rights Committee: United States of America, UN Doc. CCPR/C/USA/CO/3/Rev.1 (2006). The US submitted additional information: HRC, *Comments by the Government of the United States of America on the Concluding Observations of the Human Rights Committee* (UN Doc. CCPR/C/USA/CO/3/REV.1/ADD.1 (2008)). In its one-year follow-up report, it provided limited information on its position in respect of issues arising extraterritorially as 'a courtesy to the Committee while maintaining that the ICCPR does not apply'. In its 2011 4th periodic report to the HRC the US approach changed slightly, and it 'acknowledged' that its position on the extra-territorial effect of the treaty obligations is at odds with the position of the human rights treaty bodies and ICJ, though without apparently committing to bringing its position into line with international legal authority 4th period report, above.

[19] *Al-Skeini* v. *Secretary of State for Defence* [2007] UKHL 26, 13 June 2007. The case concerned six appellants, the first five of whom had been killed by UK 'patrols' in occupied Basra: while eating a family evening meal, during a raid on a family member's house or while driving a minibus while the sixth, Baha Mousa Baha, was tortured while in UK custody in Iraq. In its judgment of June 2007, the UK HL found the European Convention to apply only to the sixth as he was in UK custody at time of death.

[20] *Al-Skeini and others* v. *United Kingdom*, Judgment 7 July 2011, App. No. 55721/07, para. 136. See also *Al-Saadoon and Mufdhi* v. *United Kingdom*, Judgment of 2 March 2010 App. No. 61498/08 [2010] ECtHR.

state party to perpetrate violations on the territory of another state, which it could not do on its own territory.[21] While the issue of extra-territoriality and its fitful evolution is explored in more detail elsewhere in this volume,[22] it can be noted in sum that where the state exercises its effective control abroad, whether through control of territory or – through its agents – of individuals, the state's human rights obligations arise.

In conclusion, the applicability of HR law in time of peace or armed conflict and, in most scenarios, where the state operates inside or outside its own borders, is now well established. Despite this, one cannot be blind to the vast differences of approach between for example US and European states on issues of applicability of *either* area of law. As noted above, the United States does not accept the application of HRL at all in armed conflict or extraterritorially despite the current state of law whereas the weight of international opinion does not accept the war paradigm and the notion of al-Qaeda as per se a party to an armed conflict as framing the fight against Islamist extremism.[23] While the legally difficult issues may be those of interrelationship, to which the next section turns, in practice the vastly different views on applicability have constructed something of an intellectual and political Atlantic barrier which presents an important challenge to moving towards countering terrorism within an accepted and coordinated international rule of law framework.

1.3 Co-application and clarity: why it matters

As stated above, under the prevailing view, both IHRL and IHL co-apply in genuine armed conflict situations. More difficult are the questions as to how they interrelate and what that means in practice. Before addressing those issues of interplay, it may be worth recalling why it matters that we can identify, in relation to any particular issue whether IHRL and/or IHL applies, and if both, how they interact? The following factors highlight the significance of this determination.

[21] See e.g. *Lopez Burgos* v. *Uruguay* (Comm. No. 52/1979), Views of 29 July 1981, UN Doc. CCPR/C/13/D/52/1979, para. 12.

[22] See Chapter 16 in this volume; and Duffy, '*War on Terror*', ch. 7. The *Al-Skeini* case contrasts with the ECtHR's earlier *Banković and others* v. *Belgium and others*, Decision of 12 December 2001 [2001] ECHR (XII), 41 ILM 517, in which the Court's Grand Chamber suggested that control of territory was required for ECHR treaty obligations to take effect extra-territorially.

[23] See section 1.2 above.

1.3.1 Divergent standards?

As has often been pointed out, there is substantial overlap between IHL and HRL both in terms of the objectives pursued, underlying principles and areas of substantive coherence/similarity.[24] This is most obvious in respect of provisions on humane treatment or fair trial, where the development of IHL standards has drawn directly on human rights law, and further convergence on more controversial issues such as detention rights or the right to life (which will be explored later in this chapter).[25] Caution is however undoubtedly due not to overstate the 'convergence' of these areas of law. At least in some areas such as the scope of the right to life in hostilities or the lawfulness of certain grounds of detention (explored below), real substantive differences remain between the two regimes as regards starting points, processes – the questions that commanders must ask themselves about targeting and proportionality for example – and at least in some cases outcomes.[26]

1.3.2 Fora and remedies?

Significantly, even where the areas of law enjoy substantive coherence, they are characterized by a procedural imbalance. On the national level, access to courts may depend upon one or other applicable area of law.[27] But the imbalance is most apparent on the international level, where the

[24] See, e.g., Droege, 'Interplay'.

[25] See section 4 below, suggesting that even in respect of classically different issues such as the application of the right to life in conflict situations, while the starting points may be different, the end result is often the same. See also F. F. Martin, 'Using International Human Rights Law for Establishing a Unified Use of Force Rule in the Law of Armed Conflict' (2001) 64 *Saskatchewan Law Review* 347, 373; L. Doswald-Beck, 'The Right to Life in Armed Conflict: Does International Humanitarian Law Provide all the Answers?' (2006) 88 *International Review of the Red Cross* 881, 897.

[26] See below (section 4.2) on e.g. targeted killings as to whether the outcomes are necessarily different in all situations.

[27] An example is the *Al-Skeini* cases, where the object of the litigation was to compel the UK government to carry out an investigation into the alleged violations in Iraq as required by the ECHR, incorporated via the UK Human Rights Act. The government, opposing the applicability of its ECHR obligations to the lethal use of force abroad, argued in defence of its position that other international obligations including those under IHL continued to apply, but the effect was to escape judicial oversight; *R (Al-Skeini)* v. *Secretary of State for Defence* [2007] UKHL 26 [2007] 3 WLR 33 [2007] 3 All ER 685, paras. 11–25. See also refusal of the Italian Court to exercise jurisdiction in respect of violations of IHL by NATO forces in *Presidency of the Council of Ministers* v. *Markovic and others*, Application for preliminary order on jurisdiction, No. 8157; ILDC 293 (IT 2002), 8 February 2002, para. 117: Italian law implementing IHL treaties in

lack of an international complaints mechanism to give effect to IHL[28] contrasts with an intricate network of international and regional human rights courts and bodies charged with applying human rights law. Governments arguing that their human rights obligations do not apply in particular situations have relied on the continued application of IHL as negating any argument of legal vacuum.[29] Yet in practice one reason why the applicability of human rights treaties (or indeed by both IHRL and IHL) is important and perhaps in part why it is resisted, is that this triggers the jurisdiction of the human rights courts and bodies, which may provide victims with a complaints mechanism, and potentially their only prospect of access to a remedy.[30] This is particularly important where national remedies are blocked, due to for example state secrets, national security laws, immunities, all of which have come to the fore in attempts to litigate violations in the terrorism context.[31]

1.3.3 Actors and accountability

Also significant of course is the fact that HRL and IHL are at least on occasions directed at different actors. It remains generally the case that HRL binds states, despite developments in legal thinking, including on the possibility of holding terrorist groups accountable through human rights law.[32] This contrasts with IHL which is binding on both states and

question did not confer upon individuals the right to seek compensation for injuries caused by the unlawful conduct of the Italian state (para. 3).

28 The IHL supervisory system that comprises the Protecting Power mechanism, the enquiry procedure and the International Fact-Finding Commission envisaged in Art. 90 API have had little use in practice. The confidential supervisory role of the ICRC may be important in assisting victims of IHL violations such as detainees, but it is not an individual complaints procedure and ICRC communications with states are confidential. The ICC or ad hoc criminal tribunals are sorts of mechanisms of enforcement as regards acts amounting to war crimes, but inevitably have limited scope and capacity.

29 See government arguments relating to the applicability of IHL in support of the inadmissibility of the case before the Strasbourg court in the *Al-Skeini* v. *UK* case, para. 119, or the US government's response to the Inter-American Commission's *Request for Precautionary Measures in relation to Detainees at Guantánamo Bay*, denying the jurisdiction of the Commission in respect of acts covered by IHL.

30 On the applicability of international criminal law for war crimes, see 'accountability' below.

31 For a discussion of such obstacles see *e.g.* Duffy and Kostas, 'Extraordinary Rendition', in M. Salinas, K. Samuel and N. D. White (eds), *Counter-Terrorism Law and Practice* (Oxford: Oxford University Press, 2012), 539–78.

32 See Duffy, '*War on Terror*', ch. 3. For a more in-depth discussion of the responsibility of non-state actors, see A. Clapham, *Human Rights Obligations of Non-State Actors* (Oxford: Oxford University Press, 2006), 275–85.

non-states. The parties to an armed conflict co-applicability of IHL alongside IHRL may arguably provide a legal framework for the accountability of armed groups, alongside the provisions of criminal law.[33]

Co-application may in turn have implications for individual accountability. Notably isolated serious violations of IHL may amount to war crimes under international law, whereas violations of human rights law will generally only constitute crimes if they meet the threshold requirements of crimes against humanity. The extent of national implementing legislation incorporating the Geneva Conventions may mean that crimes can be prosecuted domestically, including according to principles of universal jurisdiction.[34] However, as discussed, further below, accountability obligations may well arise under either area of law, though standards have certainly been subject to greater elaboration under IHRL.[35]

1.3.4 Clarify for the person on the ground?

It is imperative that those bound by the law can conform their behaviour to it. The law needs to serve and protect potential victims but also members of armed forces on the ground, and it does so through being effective and, so far as possible, clear. Lack of clarity as to applicable rules may have implications for added vulnerability to harm on the ground, and to criminal sanction if the requirements of the law are not met. Those engaged in armed conflict or counter-terrorism need clear indications of what is required of them by the law and states are obliged to provide such a framework.[36]

[33] See e.g. Jann K. Kleffner, 'Section IX of the ICRC Interpretative Guidance on Direct Participation in Hostilities: The End of *Jus in Bello* Proportionality as We Know It?' (2012) 45 *Israel LR* 35, at 49. Though cited as support for applying IHL not IHRL, accountability under IHL also arises if both bodies of law co-apply.

[34] See e.g. K. Dörmann and R. Geiβ, 'The Implementation of Grave Breaches into Domestic Legal Orders' (2009) 7 *Journal of International Criminal Justice* 703. Incorporation of war crimes and crimes against humanity through implementation of the ICC Statute means both crimes may be in domestic laws. D. Fleck, 'Non-international armed conflict: legal qualifications and parties to the conflict', and M. Sassóli, 'Non-international armed conflict: qualification of the conflict and its parties', background papers presented at the 2003 San Remo Round Table on IHL.

[35] See Section 4.3 below.

[36] A. E. Cassimatis, 'International Humanitarian Law, International Human Rights Law, and Fragmentation of International' (2007) 56 *International and Comparative Law Quarterly* 623.

1.3.5 The rule of law

The law will not always be straightforward, and the quest for predetermined solutions to all scenarios may be legal folly.[37] Flexibility is an essential dimension of the application of any legal framework, particularly on the international level. But sufficiently accessible, clear and coherent parameters to applicable law are necessary for legal security and predictability and to provide essential protection against arbitrariness; in other words, such parameters are a prerequisite to the rule of law. At a minimum the co-application of the relevant areas of law should be pursuant to clear systemic objectives and principles.[38] This underlines the importance of attempting to at least clarify the undoubtedly complex issue around interrelationship in particular situations.

Co-application of IHL and IHRL, in genuine armed conflict situations, may serve the interest of justice and accountability together provide a comprehensive but flexible framework of rules. Clarity as to how that legal framework operates in particular situations is however essential for those implementing and affected by the law, and for the rule of law more broadly. The next part looks at how these two areas of law apply concurrently and how they intersect, and the practice of several courts and bodies in this respect.

2 Approaches to co-application: harmonious interpretation, *lex specialis* and beyond

2.1 Harmonious interpretation

The starting point for an assessment of the relationship between IHL and IHRL is what has been called the theory of complementarity, which emphasizes the scope for harmonious interpretation of the two bodies of law.[39] As one proponent of the view states: '[c]omplementarity means that human rights law and humanitarian law do not contradict each other but, being based on the same principles and values can influence and reinforce each other mutually.'[40]

An emphasis on harmonious interpretation is supported by the fact that, as the International Law Commission (ILC) has stated, '[i]n international

[37] See Scobbie, 'Principle or Pragmatics?'.

[38] In this respect the International Law Commission (ILC) notes: 'A weighing of different considerations must take must seek reference from what may be argued as the systemic objectives of the law, providing its interpretative basis and *milieu*.'

[39] Droege, 'Interplay', 337. [40] *Ibid.*

law, there is a strong presumption against normative conflict'.[41] This drives those applying the law to seek an interpretation whereby all applicable norms can be co-applied and understood not in conflict but in harmony. In some areas this approach is relatively straightforward, notably in these substantial areas of IHL and IHRL where there is normative similarity such as the prohibition on torture or requirements of fair trial. Each area of law can inform the substantially similar provisions of the other area of law.

The more difficult question is, of course, what role there can be for such a harmonious or complementary role where the norms appear to conflict. If the harmonious interpretative approach is to have real relevance or impact, it should not be seen as automatically abandonned in the face of by the existence of differing or even potentially conflicting norms. It may be that the two areas of law may be reconcilable despite 'apparent' conflict, if one takes the view that a certain 'adjustment' can and should be made to integrate conflicting obligations, without distorting the nature and substance of the norms. As the ILC has noted:

> Of course in such case, it is still possible to reach the conclusion that although the two norms seemed to point in diverging directions, after some adjustment, it is still possible to apply or understand them in such way that no overlap or conflict will remain ... [This] it may ... take place through an attempt to reach a resolution that integrates the conflicting obligations in some optimal way in the general context of international law.

However, there are 'definite limit[s] to harmonization'.[42] As one commentator put it, while this approach 'may resolve apparent conflicts; it cannot resolve genuine conflicts'.[43] The ILC report on fragmentation states that where 'the question of conflict arises regarding the fulfilment of the *objectives* (instead of the obligations) of the different instruments, little may be done to integrate the two and avoid conflict. In relation to certain issues even in face of conflict the question may well need to be addressed by way of contextual analysis of underlying purposes and principles'.[44] It is often noted that IHL and HR pursue similar but not

[41] ILC, *Fragmentation of International Law: Difficulties Arising from the Diversification and Expansion of International Law – Report of the Study Group of the International Law Commission*, finalized by Martti Koskenniemi, UN Doc. A/CN.4/L.682 (2006) [hereafter ILC Report 2006], para. 37. The report talks about interpretation as being about 'avoiding or mitigating conflict'.

[42] ILC Report 2006, para. 42.

[43] Borgen, 'Resolving Treaty Conflicts', 605–6 (ILC Report 2006).

[44] *Ibid.*, para. 33. See also treatment of conflict as arising from 'preventing the fulfillment of the other obligation or undermining its object and purpose' (*ibid.*, para. 130).

identical purposes, and reflect often overlapping but sometimes distinct principles (the principle of humanity and the principle of distinction being the most obvious examples of each). One of the questions in deciding whether particular norms are reconcilable is therefore whether the particular norms in fact pursue different purposes or reflect different principles.

It is in the face of irreconcilable conflicts in the substance or principles that the notion of *lex specialis* explored further below, comes into play.[45] As has been noted 'the *lex specialis* principle is assumed to apply if "harmonious interpretation" turns out to be impossible, that is, to overrule a general standard by a conflicting special one.'[46]

2.2 *Interpretative tool*

Even where such a conflict arises, and norms of *lex specialis* are identified, both sets of norms continue to be relevant and to have a role. It is a well-established principle that the interpretation and application of international legal rules should take into account other relevant norms of international law. This has its legal foundation in Article 31(3)(c) Vienna Convention on the Law of Treaties, which provides that in interpreting a treaty '[t]here shall be taken into account, together with the context ... any relevant rules of international law applicable in the relations between the parties.'[47] It reflects the increased focus on

[45] There is a difference of view as to whether *lex specialis* applies only where norms conflict, as opposed to also where one set of norms is more detailed and specific than the other. See e.g. ILC Report 2006; Expert Meeting on the Right to Life in Armed Conflict and Situations of Occupation, Geneva 1–2 September 2005, University Centre for International Humanitarian Law, at www.adh-geneve.ch/pdfs/3rapport_droit_vie.pdf [hereafter Expert Meeting], 19.

[46] ILC Report 2006, paras. 88–9; see also Art. 55 International Law Commission's Articles on State Responsibility. The ILC Commentary explains: 'For the *lex specialis* principle to apply it is not enough that the same subject matter is dealt with by two provisions; there must be some actual inconsistency between them, or else a discernible intention that one provision is to exclude the other.' Some suggest that *lex specialis* can be understood either as applying where two rules operate but one provides more specific content than the other, while it is more commonly thought that it applies only where two applicable norms conflict as set out above.

[47] 1969 VCLT 1155 UNTS 331, Art. 31(3)I. For example, in *Al-Adsani* v. *the United Kingdom*, No. 35763/97, Judgment of 21 November 2011: 'the Convention should be interpreted as far as possible in harmony with other principles of international law of which it forms part' (paras. 54–5).

seeing international law as a 'system' that is coherent and not fragmented[48] and the growing openness of courts and bodies, national or international, to look to other areas of law and practice (including those not necessarily themselves binding) to inform the exercise of their own jurisdiction.[49]

This cross referencing is closely related to the harmonious or complementary approach. The distinction between norms that govern as binding law and those that may be taken into account as tools in the interpretation of such norms must however be borne in mind. Whereas co-application through harmonious interpretation may make some adjustment as two sets of binding norms accommodate one another to enable consistent application, standards can also be used as 'interpretative tools' to inform the interpretation of binding norms. In practice, the range of norms and standards that are called upon as such tools is much broader and may indeed include standards that are not binding on the parties at all. Frequent reliance on human rights litigation to soft law instruments to interpret binding convention rights exemplifies this. For this reason it may be that the interpretative tool approach is not coterminous with the harmonious approach but suggests that even where harmony is impossible and a *lex specialis* rule is identified, there may well be a continuing role for provisions of the other area of law as tools in informing the interpretation of the *lex specialis* norm.[50] Thus, even where they do not avert conflict they may minimize its effects, ensuring that any exception to generally applicable law are no more than necessary, and contribute to greater cohesion.

2.3 The ICJ: lex specialis and beyond

The starting point for most discussions on the topic of the interrelationship between IHRL and IHL has been the *Nuclear Weapons* advisory opinion of the ICJ.[51] In that opinion, the ICJ held, in pertinent part, that

48 ILC Report 2006, para. 37–43; Droege, 'Interplay'.

49 Courts having regard to parallel approaches of other courts to similar issues is now commonplace. Examples from the author's practice include *Opuz* v. *Turkey* [2009] ECtHR 33401/02 (9 June 2009) on CEDAW's and other comparative approaches to domestic violence or *Hadijatou Mani Koraou* v. *The Republic of Niger*, 27 October 2008, ECW/CCJ/JUD/06/08 where the ECOWAS court drew on ICTY jurisprudence.

50 See, e.g., below on review procedures in non-international armed conflict where the question is asked whether, if IHRL provides *lex specialis*, the interpretation of that law should not seek to reflect principles of IHL.

51 *Nuclear Weapons.*

> [i]n principle, the right not arbitrarily to be deprived of one's life [codified in Article 6 of the International Covenant on Civil and Political Rights] applies also in hostilities. The test of what is an arbitrary deprivation of life, however, then falls to be *determined by the applicable lex specialis*, namely, the law applicable in armed conflict which is designed to regulate the conduct of hostilities. Thus whether a particular loss of life, through the use of a certain weapon in warfare, is to be considered an arbitrary deprivation of life contrary to Article 6 of the Covenant, *can only be decided by reference to the law applicable in armed conflict and not deduced from the terms of the Covenant itself.*[52]

While affirming the continued application of the IHRL rule in situations of armed conflict, the ICJ found that that application was realized through the *lex specialis* nature of IHL, which the Court then applied to the question at hand, terming IHL the 'directly relevant applicable law governing the question of which [the court] was seized'.[53] No further consideration of IHRL itself was considered necessary.

Eight years later, the Court developed its approach and considered how it might apply to a broader range of human rights treaty obligations. In its *Wall* Advisory Opinion, the ICJ held that there are

> three possible situations: some rights may be exclusively matters of international humanitarian law; others may be exclusively matters of human rights law; yet others may be matters of both these branches of international law. In order to answer the question put to it, the Court will have to take into consideration both these branches of international law, namely human rights law and, as *lex specialis*, international humanitarian law.[54]

The following year, however, in the first contentious case to address this issue, the ICJ did not invoke the *lex specialis* language, stating simply that 'both branches of international law, namely international human rights law and international humanitarian law, would have to be taken into consideration'[55] in its analysis of the alleged rights violations by the Ugandan military and its agents during hostilities in the Democratic Republic of Congo. Some have suggested that this might herald a retreat from the concept of *lex specialis* on the part of the ICJ.[56] At a minimum it suggests recognition that the interrelationship is more fluid than the ICJ's earlier formulation of the *lex specialis* model perhaps suggested,

[52] *Ibid.*, para. 25 (my emphasis). [53] *Ibid.*, para. 35. [54] *Israeli Wall*, para. 106.
[55] *Armed Activities*, para. 216. [56] Droege, 'Interplay', 338.

with a concurrent role for both areas of law which is ongoing even once a rule of *lex specialis* has been identified, as discussed further below.[57]

2.4 *The evolving approach of human rights bodies*

It is worth dedicating some attention to the specific approaches of human rights courts and bodies to the question of interplay between IHL and IHRL. Given their role and prolificity, and the absence of IHL equivalents, it is often before these bodies that these issues arise in practice. The approach of human rights bodies is shaped to a degree by their own jurisdictional limits; bodies inevitably focus on the application of the treaty from which their competence derives. But in the application of that instrument they must assess applicable law.[58] Courts are increasingly called upon to interpret IHL in order to give effect to human rights law as it applies in armed conflict situations, and the responses of human rights bodies to this call vary considerably.

The boldest approach has perhaps been that of the Inter-American Commission of Human Rights, the only body that has directly and explicitly 'applied' IHL and criticized states for violation of its terms.[59] In the *Abella* case[60] – concerning an attack by a group of individuals on military barracks at La Tablada, Buenos Aires in 1989 – the Commission reasoned that it was

[57] See above section 3, on some of the questions surrounding the meaning and effect of the *lex specialis* rule.

[58] Note the ILC 2006 Report: 'In debates about fragmentation and normative conflict, the suggestion is sometimes made that whatever the relations between legal rules and principles as conceived under *general international law*, those relations cannot be applied as such by treaty bodies or dispute-settlement organs whose jurisdiction is limited to or by the constituting instrument. A human rights body, for example, should have no business to apply a WTO covered agreement . . . a few remarks here will suffice. The jurisdiction of most international tribunals is limited to particular types of disputes or disputes arising under particular treaties. A limited jurisdiction does not, however, imply a limitation of the scope of the law applicable in the interpretation and application of those treaties' (paras. 44–5).

[59] As early as the 1970s it found states in violation of IHL, addressing the right to life as it applied to conflict-related casualties in Nicaragua: IACHR, *Report on the Situation of Human Rights in Nicaragua* (OEA/Ser.L/V/II.45, doc. 16 rev. 1 (1978), ch. 2). It found that the 'Nicaraguan National Guard not only used its firepower *indiscriminately* causing a great number of casualties and tremendous suffering to the *civilian population. . .violating a basic humanitarian norm*'.

[60] *Abella* v. *Argentina*, Case 11.137, IACHR., Report No. 55/97, OEA/Ser.L./V/II.98, doc. 6 rev. (1997), para. 1.

addressing a 'combat situation'[61] that 'none of the human rights instruments was designed to regulate',[62] and it concluded that it could not apply Article 4 on the right to life without regard to IHL rules.[63]

The approach in this case raises a number of questions.[64] One is the doubtful existence of an armed conflict in Argentina in the 1980s;[65] another whether resort to force by those attacking the barracks alone rendered it a 'combat situation' to which IHL is relevant, rather than a law enforcement operation in which there was (as is not uncommonly the case in the context of organized crime) resort to force. Also doubtful is the Commission's assessment – which may have coloured its approach – that IHL would provide 'greater protection for victims' in the particular case.[66]

Leaving aside the possible substantive overreach, the Commission was later found by the Inter-American Court to have overreached *jurisdictionally* in applying IHL directly. In *Las Palmeras* the Court called for a

[61] *Ibid.* The attack by 42 individuals precipitated a 30-hour armed confrontation with Argentine military personnel resulting in the deaths of 29 of the attackers and several state agents. The Commission found that 'several military uprisings' had occurred since the restoration of democracy in 1983.

[62] *Ibid.*, para. 158.

[63] '[The Commission] must necessarily look to and apply definitional standards and relevant rules of humanitarian law as sources of authoritative guidance in its resolution of this and other kinds of claims alleging violations of the American Convention in combat situations. To do otherwise would mean that the Commission would have to decline to exercise its jurisdiction in many cases involving indiscriminate attacks by State agents resulting in a considerable number of civilian casualties. Such a result would be manifestly absurd in light of the underlying object and purposes of both the American Convention and humanitarian law treaties' (*ibid.*, para. 161).

[64] For a critique of the case from a different perspective, see L. Zegveld, 'The Inter-American Commission on Human Rights and International Humanitarian Law: A Comment on the *Tablada* Case' (1998) 324 *International Review of the Red Cross* 505.

[65] *Ibid.* Arguably, had IHL only been used as an aid to interpretation in assessing right to life where individuals are fighting back, this might have mattered a little less. But it found that there was no violation as the individuals were legitimate targets, despite the fact that there was no apparent armed conflict at the time, though there certainly was an armed confrontation.

[66] *Abella* v. *Argentina*: 'the provisions of conventional and customary humanitarian law generally afford victims of armed conflicts greater or more specific protections than do the more generally phrased guarantees in the American Convention and other human rights instruments' (paras. 158–9). The Commission relied on the fact that the American Convention, like certain other human rights treaties, provides that the interpretation of the treaty should not limit any greater protection provided elsewhere in international law (1979 IACHR, 1144 UNTS 123, Art. 27 (1)). It is doubtful to what the application of IHL in this context is more human rights friendly to the victims in question (though it is also controversial to what extent this should be a relevant consideration).

more cautious approach on jurisdictional grounds, concluding that the Court's role is:

> to say whether or not that norm or that fact is compatible with the American Convention. The latter has only given the Court competence to determine whether the acts or the norms of the States are compatible with the Convention itself, and not with the 1949 Geneva Conventions.[67]

In subsequent cases the Court and the Commission have continued to have close regard to IHL, albeit to interpret and apply the American Convention.[68] They have emphasized the co-application of the two branches of law, with the Commission on occasion specifically suggesting that in some circumstances the relationship is one of IHL as *lex specialis*. For example in the Guantánamo Precautionary Measures case the Commission stated that:

> in certain circumstances . . . the test for evaluating the observance of a particular right, such as the right to liberty, in a situation of armed conflict may be distinct from that applicable in time of peace. In such situations, international law, including the jurisprudence of this Commission, dictates that it may be necessary to deduce the applicable standard by reference to international humanitarian law as the applicable *lex specialis*.[69]

Similarly a broad approach to *lex specialis* was evident in its 2002 *Report on Terrorism and Human Rights*.[70]

67 *Las Palmeras* v. *Colombia*.

68 Note though that in *Romero y Galdámez* v. *El Salvador*, Case 11.481, IACHR, Report No. 37/00, OEA/Ser.L./V/II.106, doc. 6 rev. (2000), paras. 56, 61–4 some ambiguity continues to be seen as it '*should also note* that the assassination of Monsignor Romero constitutes a grave infraction of the basic principles of international humanitarian law'. See also *Extrajudicial Executions and Forced Disappearances* v. *Peru*, Case 10.247 *et al.*, IACHR, Report No. 101/01, OEA/Ser.L./V/II.114 doc. 5 rev. at 563 (2001).

69 *Request for Precautionary Measures for Detainees in Guantánamo Bay*. See also *Coard et al* v. *United States*, Case No. 10.951, Report No. 109/99, Annual Report of the IACHR 1999, para. 59.

70 ACHR, *Report on Terrorism and Human Rights*, OEA/Ser.L./V/II.116, doc. 5 rev. 1, corr. (2002). It noted that IHL 'provide[s] specific standards against which to evaluate whether a deprivation of life occurring during an armed conflict was arbitrary and therefore unlawful. Such standards are used in distinguishing between civilians and combatants' (para. 112), and that 'international humanitarian law [should be incorporated] as the applicable lex specialis in interpreting and applying human rights protections in situations of armed conflict' (para. 2).

Where IHL has been invoked, it has been decisive to its determination of certain cases, but not in others.[71] In *Bámaca Velásquez* v. *Guatemala*, the IACtHR considered a petition regarding the capture, disappearance and death of a former guerrilla leader during a period when 'Guatemala was convulsed by an internal conflict',[72] and found that '*the relevant provisions of the Geneva Conventions may be taken into consideration as elements for the interpretation of the American Convention.*'[73] Interestingly, the Court relied in some detail on IHL standards in consideration of the right to life, while favouring an IHRL approach to issues related to detention, presumably reflecting the dearth of detailed IHL on detention in non-international conflict.

The Human Rights Committee in its General Comment and country reports has emphasized the role of IHL in the interpretation of the Covenant and the complementarity of IHL and IHRL. It rejects the idea of the displacement of HR standards,[74] noting that '[w]hile, in respect of certain Covenant rights, more specific rules of international humanitarian law may be specially relevant for the purposes of the interpretation of Covenant rights, both spheres of law are complementary, not mutually exclusive'.[75] While the Committee has therefore been forthright in asserting the need to have regard to IHL in armed conflict, its individual case law has focused on human rights standards without much regard to IHL, perhaps reflecting the circumstances of the particular cases. The *Guerrero* v. *Colombia* case for example concerned the lethal use of force against insurgents suspected of kidnapping in the

[71] For example, *Avilán* v. *Colombia*, Case 11.142, IACHR., Report No. 26/97, OEA/Ser.L./V/II.98, doc. 6 rev. (1997), paras. 131–42; 159–60; 166–78; 198–203 IACHR, *Third Report on the Human Rights Situation in Colombia*, ch. IV, 'Violence and Violations of International Human Rights Law and International Humanitarian Law' (OEA/Ser.L/V/II.102, doc. 9 rev. 1, 26 February 1999); *Prada González y Bolaño Castro* v. *Colombia*, Case 11.710, Report No. 63/01, OEA/Ser.L/V/II.111 doc. 20 rev. at 781 (2000); *Contreras et al. v. El Salvador*, Judgment, IACtHR. 24 November 2011 (Ser. C) No. 237.

[72] *Bámaca Velásquez* v. *Guatemala*, para. 121.

[73] *Ibid.*, paras. 207–8 [my emphasis; internal citations omitted].

[74] It has repeatedly reiterated that the ICCPR is not displaced by IHL during periods of conflict or occupation. See e.g. *Concluding Observations of the Human Rights Committee* (Israel, UN Doc. CCPR/C/79/Add.93, 18 August 1998, para. 10).

[75] Comment 31: Nature of the General Legal Obligation on States Parties to the Covenant, UN Doc. CCPR/C/21/Rev.1/Add.13 (2004), para. 11. See also General Comment 29: States of Emergency: 'During armed conflict, whether international or non-international, rules of international humanitarian law become applicable and *help, in addition to* the provisions in article 4 and article 5, para. 1, of the Covenant, to prevent the abuse of a State's emergency powers' (para. 3).

overall context of the NIAC in Colombia, but in the specific context of a house raid where the HRC adopted an essentially law enforcement approach.[76] The operation was deemed 'disproportionate to the requirements of law enforcement'.

The European Court of Human Rights has adopted an approach to IHL in conflict situations that may be described as at best reticent, at worst myopic, or perhaps simply opaque. It has been extremely reluctant to acknowledge explicitly any role for IHL in its interpretation and application of the Convention. In recent years it has addressed in detail issues of IHL in the particular contexts of cases concerning the legitimacy of prosecuting individuals for war crimes many years after the fact.[77] But in addressing a range of issues concerning detention or the right to life in live armed conflict situations, it has generally refused to even acknowledge the existence of IHL standards, and, where it has, to have close regard to then in its interpretation of the Convention determination of the case,[78] often emphasizing instead that absent derogation from Convention rights, the normal legal background continues to apply.[79]

It has been noted, however, that in some of the cases it may be that the Court has in fact had close regard to principles of IHL in reaching its conclusions, albeit not explicitly.[80] In respect of the use of force against individuals or small groups of persons allegedly engaged in terrorist activity, the Court has maintained a strict law enforcement approach requiring planning and carrying out operations to avoid the

[76] *Husband of Maria Fanny Suarez de Guerrero* v. *Colombia*, Communication No. R.11/45, UN Doc. Supp. No. 40 (A37/40) at 137 (31 March 1982) concerning the raid of a house in Bogotá to release a kidnap victim. The Committee found that '[i]n spite of the fact that Miguel de German Ribon was not found, the police patrol decided to hide in the house to await the arrival of the "suspected [guerrilla] kidnappers"'. Seven people who subsequently entered the house were shot dead by the police. See also Concluding Observations (Israel, UN Doc. CCPR/CO/78/ISR, 21 August 2003, para. 15).

[77] *Kononov* v. *Latvia*, App. No. 36376/04, Judgment of 24 July 2008; *Korbely* v. *Hungary*, Judgment 19 September 2008 [2008] ECHR. See also *Varnava and others* v. *Turkey*, Judgment 18 Sept. 2009 [2009] ECHR, para. 182.

[78] The Court has addressed cases in the context of several armed conflicts e.g. Turkey in Cyprus, Russia in Chechnya and Transnistria, the UK in Iraq.

[79] See e.g. *Isayeva and others* v. *Russia*, nos. 57947/00, 57948/00 and 57949/00, Decision of 19 December 2002, and *Isayeva* v. *Russia*, No. 57950/00, Judgment of 24 February 2005, para. 191.

[80] See e.g. W. Abresch, 'A Human Rights Law of Internal Armed Conflict: The European Court of Human Rights in Chechnya' (2005) 16 *European Journal of International Law* 741; Byron, 'A Blurring of the Boundaries: The Application of Inter-National Humanitarian Law by Human Rights Bodies' (2007) 47 *Virginia Journal of International Law* 839, 853.

use of force, using weapons that minimize suffering and giving warnings.[81] But so far as it has considered higher intensity armed confrontations in the context of armed conflict, it has reached conclusions much more closely reflective of IHL principles and language.

For example, the ECtHR held in both *Ergi* v. *Turkey* and *Özkan* v. *Turkey* concerning individuals caught in cross fire that the right to life requires states to 'take all feasible precautions in the choice of means and methods of a security operation mounted against an opposing group with a view to avoiding and, in any event, to minimizing, incidental loss of *civilian* life'.[82] This IHL standard[83] was reiterated in *Isayeva Yusupova and Bazayeva* v. *Russia*, concerning civilian deaths through aerial bombardment, where the court also found that the respondent state had failed to assess and prevent 'possible harm to civilians who might have been present . . . in the vicinity of what the military could have perceived as legitimate targets'.[84] This may serve to show how a context specific analysis of human rights law can lead to a substantially similar result as an analysis of IHL. Or the Court's reference to 'legitimate targets' may reflect that it did in fact have regard to IHL given the active conflict,[85] but the failure to explain its approach or acknowledge the relationship between IHRL and IHL makes meaningful assessment difficult.

There may however be indications of the willingness of the European Court to shift to a more overt relationship with IHL. This is consistent with its recognition in several cases of the importance of a coherent approach to the Convention consistent with other areas of international law.[86] More

[81] See *Oğur* v. *Turkey*, App. No. 21594/93, Judgment of 20 May 1999, Reports 1999-III; *Gül* v. *Turkey*, Appl. No. 22676/93, Judgment of 14 December 2000, Reports 2000-IV. See also *Suleymanova v. Russia*, no. 9191/06, §§ 78–87, 12 May 2010; *Abuyeva and others v. Russia*, no. 27065/05, §§ 196–203, 2 December 2010; *Esmukhambetou and others v. Russia*, no. 23445/03, §§ 140–51, 29 March 2011; *Kerimova and others v. Russia*, nos. 17170/04, 20792/04, 22448/04, 23360/04, 5681/05 and 5684/05, §§ 241–58, 3 May 2011; *Khamzayev and others v. Russia*, no. 1503/02, §§ 195–90, 3 May 2011; *Hamiyet Kaplan* v. *Turkey*, App. No. 36749/97, Judgment of 13 September 2005.

[82] *Ergi* v. *Turkey*, 1998-IV ECHR 1751, 1777 (my emphasis); *Ahmet Özkan and others* v. *Turkey*, App. No. 21689/93, Judgment of 6 April 2004, para. 297 (citing *Ergi* v. *Turkey*).

[83] Byron, 'A Blurring of the Boundaries', notes it has been noted that 'This phrase is taken almost faithfully from Article 57(2) (a)(ii) of Additional Protocol I merely substituting ["a security operation mounted against an opposing group"] for the word 'attack' in the Additional Protocol' (853). See also Abresch, 'Human Rights Law'.

[84] *Isayeva* v. *Russia*, para. 175.

[85] The Court's apparent insistence that in the absence of a derogation it would apply the 'normal legal background' sits uneasily with this (n. 74 above).

[86] E.g. *Al-Adsani* v. *UK*, *Varnava and others* v. *Turkey*, para. 185.

specifically, IHL has been referred to explicitly in later cases such as *Varnava* v. *Turkey*,[87] *Al-Skeini* v. *UK*,[88] *Al-Jedda* v. *UK*,[89] and *Finogenov* v. *Russian Federation*,[90] even if IHL was not critical to their outcome.[91] The pending cases relating to the Russian–Georgian conflict may further reveal the extent of any such shift to a more transparent and credible approach to the interplay of IHL and the Convention.[92]

Within the African system, the Commission has readily accepted that the Charter continues to apply in armed conflict situations, and in its Resolutions it has called on states to respect IHL in the context of conflicts on the continent.[93] However there has been relatively little regard to IHL in the Commission's individual decisions, in part the Commission suggests due to the lack of any mechanism for derogation from the Charter but perhaps also due to the violations that have come before the Commission, which have occasionally arisen in the context of an armed conflict but have not been associated closely with the conflict itself.[94] In the nascent African Court of Justice and Human Rights' first relevant decision – the Order for Provisional Measures against the Libyan state in February 2011 – the Court explicitly noted the situation of 'on-going conflict' and that the Peace and Security Council of the

[87] *Varnava and others* v. *Turkey*, para. 185; *Al-Skeini*, which upheld the duty to investigate in the context of armed conflict.

[88] *Al-Skeini*.

[89] *Al-Jedda* v. *the United Kingdom*, App. No. 27021/08, 7 July 2011, para. 107. Its approach to IHL, and the marginal significance afforded the right to detention for imperative reasons of security has been criticized. J. Pejic, 'European Court of Human Rights' Al-Jedda Judgment: The Oversight of International Humanitarian Law' (2011) 93 (883) *International Review of the Red Cross* 837–51.

[90] *Finogenov and others* v. *Russian Federation*, App. Nos. 18299/03 and 27311/03, 4 June 2012.

[91] See critique of the Court's refusal to acknowledge the lawful basis for detention in IHL in Pejic, '*Al-Jedda* Judgment', though the outcome of litigation is in part conditioned by the arguments of the parties, and the UK did not argue its cases based on a right to detain under IHL.

[92] *Georgia* v. *Russia No. 2*, App. No. 38263/08, found admissible 19 December 2011 and pending before the Grand Chamber.

[93] See e.g. Resolution on the Promotion and Respect of Humanitarian Law and the Charter on Human and Peoples Rights, 1994, adopted at 14th ordinary sessions, Addis 1993, and the African Commission Resolution on Rwanda, recognizing violations of IHL during the conflicts in Rwanda, 1994.

[94] The Commission has affirmed that: 'the African Charter unlike other human rights instruments does not allow for state parties to derogate from their treaty obligations during emergency situations. Thus even a civil war . . . cannot be used as an excuse by a state violating or permitting violations of rights in the Charter' (ACHPR, Decision regarding Communication 74/92, *Commission Nationale des Droits de l'Homme et de Libertés/Chad*, para. 21).

African Union had referred to 'violations of human rights and international humanitarian law', but made no reference to IHL in its decision. Instead it found that the state should 'refrain from any action that would result in loss of life or violation of physical integrity of persons, which could be a breach of this Charter or any other human rights instrument to which it is a party'.[95] It is unfortunate that the Court did not order the forces engaged by that stage in hostilities with rebel forces to observe applicable law, including IHL. It remains too early to assess what approach the Court will take with respect to these issues, and how it will contribute to the application of human rights law in armed conflict situations.

In conclusion, despite quibbles raised against the Inter-American Commission's approach at the beginning of this section, its plea to relevance was well heard.[96] The Inter-American Court has followed suit as has the Human Rights Committee, both emphasizing the role for IHL in interpreting human rights treaty obligations in conflict situations, and the continuing relevance of the human rights standards themselves. The European Court has been more reticent, while arguably, where it deemed necessary or appropriate, reaching decisions mindful of its terms.[97] Despite the divergent practice between bodies – with the ECtHR's reluctance to engage explicitly with IHL setting it apart – closer analysis may suggest that to some extent all have adopted context specific analyses of whether and to what extent particular sets of facts properly fell to be considered by reference to IHL alongside and/or in the interpretation of IHL (as in conduct of hostilities situations) or exclusively to IHRL (as in the hostage taking scenarios, or law enforcement operations, despite their arising in the broad context of armed conflict).

[95] *African Commission on Human Rights* v. *Great Socialist People's Libyan Arab Jamarihiya*, ACtHR, Case No. 004/2011, 25 March 2011, para. 25.

[96] In *Avilán* v. *Colombia* the Commission found that '[the] facts in this case *require* the application of humanitarian law if they are to be properly analyzed' (*Avilán* v. *Colombia*, Case 11.142, IACtHR, Report No. 26/97, OEA/Ser.L./V/II.98, doc. 6 rev. (1997), para. 169).

[97] A range of factors including political factors and capacity challenges may feed this reluctance. It is noted that particular challenges arise for adjudicative bodies in their determination of rights in conflict where for various reasons – political as well as substantive – neither party may argue the applicability of that area of law. See Hampson, 'Relationship between International Humanitarian Law and Human Rights Law'. The obligation rests on the court however to provide a viable assessment of applicable law.

3 *Lex specialis*: assumptions and controversies

Most courts, human rights bodies and commentators acknowledge some role for the notion of *lex specialis* in the interrelationship between IHL and IHRL, but there is much criticism of the concept and surprisingly little convergence or clarity as to the meaning and implications of the doctrine.[98] Critics have lavished criticism on the threefold elaboration provided in the *Wall* opinion as 'utterly unhelpful'[99] and rejection of it has been described as one of the few points of agreement between commentators on the subject.[100] Some of the myriad questions and controversies regarding how to determine when a rule is *lex specialis* and the implications are highlighted below.

A preliminary question of significant practical import is at what *level* the *lex specialis* relationship operates. There is perhaps an assumption in some of the debate around the interrelationship in the context of the 'war on terror' that IHL generally constitutes *lex specialis* in armed conflict situations.[101] Despite its attractive simplicity, this is a doubtful and dangerous proposition. IHL cannot be seen as monolithically constituting *lex specialis*, as normative conflict can only arise on the level of *particular norms*, not of legal regimes as a whole.[102] One commentator has noted '*lex specialis* is in some sense a contextual principle. It is difficult to use when determining conflicts between two normative orders *in abstracto*, and is, instead, more suited to the determination of relations between two norms in a

98 See by contrast M. Milanović, 'A Norm Conflict Perspective on the Relationship between International Humanitarian Law and Human Rights Law' (2009) 14(3) *Journal of Conflict and Security Law* 459–83, who claims the term should not be used at all. Most others note its limitations while recognizing its utility. See human rights bodies below.

99 Expert Meeting, 19.

100 Eden and Happold, 'Symposium: The Relationship between International Humanitarian Law and International Human Rights Law' (2009) 14(3) *Journal of Law and Security* 441–7.

101 The US approach is set out in e.g. its responses to human rights bodies, and generally consists of invoking IHL as the '*lex specialis*' in the purported conflict against al-Qaeda *et al*. A monolithic approach is evident in commentary, referred to in IHL as 'the *lex specialis* of armed conflict' in e.g. '*Lex Lacunae*: The Merging Laws of War and Human Rights in Counterinsurgency', Iain D. Pedden, *Valparaiso University Law Review* Volume 46 November 3 pp. 803–42. For discussion and an alternative view, see Hampson, 'Relationship between International Humanitarian Law and Human Rights Law', 560–1; M. Sassóli and L.M. Olson, 'The Relationship between International Humanitarian and Human Rights Law Where It Matters: Admissible Killing and Internment of Fighters in Non-International Armed Conflicts' (2008) 90 *International Review of the Red Cross* 599, 615; Duffy, '*War on Terror*', ch. 7B.

102 Milanović, 'Norm Conflict'; Sassóli notes that this is a neglected area of legal analysis ('Non-international armed conflict').

concrete case.'[103] The idea of regime-wide *lex specialis* effectively negates the applicability and role of IHRL in conflict, so widely endorsed in international practice as noted above.[104] This approach is demonstrated by US arguments in respect of detentions in Guantánamo and beyond or extraordinary rendition for example, to the effect that the existence of a 'war paradigm' means that IHRL does not apply. This approach is at odds with the more prevalent understanding that *lex specialis* must be determined on the basis of particular norms.

Another basic dispute is whether *lex specialis* governs the relationship between a general rule and a specific one, or arises only where there is some *conflict* between the two?[105] The ILC report suggests the latter; it is only where a norm requires the modification or overruling of another, that a general *lex specialis* situation arises.[106]

A related question is the criteria for determining when one rule would constitute *lex specialis* in respect of another. Here again the notion appears to be used in practice to embrace at least two broad aspects. These refer to the quite conceptually different ideas of contextual relevance or appropriateness on the one hand, and clarity and precision on the other. The first places the emphasis on the rules that are most closely directed to and better able to 'take account of particular circumstances', or 'regulate . . . the matter more effectively'.[107] The second way in which the term is used refers to the rules the content of which more 'concretely', 'definitely', 'directly' and 'with clarity' address the issue at hand.[108] Despite assumptions to the contrary,

[103] A. Lindroos, 'Addressing Norm Conflicts in a Fragmented Legal System: The Doctrine of *lex specialis*' (2005) 74 *Nordic Journal of International Law* 27; Scobbie, 'Principle or Pragmatics?'.

[104] See section 1 above.

[105] ILC Report: '(b) The two types of *lex specialis* reference 88. There are two ways in which law may take account of the relationship of a particular rule to general one. A particular rule may be considered an *application* of a general standard in a given circumstance. The special relates to the general as does administrative regulation to law in domestic legal order. Or it may be considered as a *modification, overruling* or a *setting aside* of the latter. The first case is sometimes seen as not a situation of normative conflict at all but is taken to involve the *simultaneous* application of the special and the general standard. Thus, only the latter is thought to involve the application of a genuine *lex specialis*.'

[106] *Ibid.*

[107] *Ibid.*, para. 60. Note also differences of view set out at Expert Meeting, 19–20: while some emphasized specificity in relation to the particular issue at stake, on one view 'a lex specialis need not necessarily be more detailed, more sophisticated or clearer than the rules that could be found in the lex generalis; the lex specialis need only have been designed for the given situation.'

[108] ILC Report 2006, notes that 'sensitivity to context, capacity to reflect State will, concreteness, clarity, definiteness' are all relevant to the assessment of and operation of the

IHL is not necessarily more specific in its content than IHRL. The two aspects may therefore compete.[109] Different conclusions regarding *lex specialis* may therefore arise from different understandings of whether the *lex specialis* stems from the more specific content of one norm or, as would seem to be the stronger and the predominant view, that the essence of what makes *lex specialis* is the specific context to which the norm is directed, or elements of both.[110]

Assumptions underlying superficial approaches to the *lex specialis* relationship are based on issues such as the right to life in the conduct of hostilities or security detentions in IAC, where IHL provides rules clearly directed to a particular objective inherently linked to the peculiarities of armed conflict. But the assumptions based on these (relatively) clear scenarios[111] are readily strained in situations of occupation for example where the nature of the functions, and the context in which they operate, may be more akin to the sort of situation IHRL was directed towards. They may not seem appropriate either, as the human rights bodies found, in addressing certain hostage taking scenarios, where the particular context of state control look, feel and smell more like law enforcement operations than the conduct of hostilities, despite the fact that they arise in the broader context of non-international armed conflicts. It would appear to be the case then that the issue of which norm is more appropriately specifically directed to the issue at hand depends on a broader range of contextual factors than simply the existence of armed conflict. The analysis of the *lex specialis* then has to be made on a situation-by-situation basis, taking into account the particular facts in context.

Particular questions arise as to the extent of IHL as *lex specialis* in *non-international conflicts* where it may not be clear whether there *is* an applicable norm of IHL at all. Assumptions of IHL as *lex specialis* tend to emanate from consideration of the sort of scenarios where there is conflict between HRL and IHL, and the latter provides a specific and relatively clear rule. Targeting, where the lethal use of force can be used against combatants based on a principle of distinction unknown in human rights law, or detention regimes in international armed conflict,

lex specialis principle, stating that '[n]o general, context-independent answers can be given to questions'.

109 Specific developed IHRL norms may conflict with less specific IHL. See e.g. the rules on review of detention or remedy in this section.

110 See also Art. 55 International Law Commission's draft articles on responsibility, setting out as a minority view holds that the *lex specialis* norm will be the one with 'more specific content'. Doctrine and cases emphasize the nature of the conflict as they are the key factor in determining *lex specialis* in this context.

111 See issues discussed in section 4 below.

are the paradigmatic examples. Far more doubtful are certain situations in non-international armed conflict, where the body of treaty law is more limited, and customary law is perhaps more open to question.[112] If there is no norm of IHL, there is presumably no normative conflict to be resolved and if so should IHRL not continue to apply?[113]

A related question on which legal thinking appears divided is whether both IHL and HRL can act as *lex specialis* to the other.[114] It has been suggested that in international law 'nothing indicates which of two norms is the lex specialis or the lex generalis, particularly between human rights law and humanitarian law'.[115] While IHL is directed more specifically towards hostilities, IHRL may be more specifically directed to particular types of operation within the broader conflict; its more elaborate nature and development through jurisprudence may provide the greater specificity on a particular issue that some see as associated with *lex specialis*. Whether one agrees with IHRL as potential *lex specialis* even in the armed conflict situations, or as the underlying *lex generalis*, there appears to be broad and growing recognition that in some situations associated with an armed conflict, particularly of the non-international variety, IHRL will provide the most relevant norms.

If, as assumed above and in much commentary elsewhere, the *lex specialis* rule can only operate on a rule by rule and context by context basis, how does this fit with requirements of legality and certainty?[116] What are the practical operational implications for those on the ground referred to above and how can attention be dedicated to meeting those challenges?

[112] See review of lawfulness of detention, below. J. Henckaerts, 'Study on Customary International Humanitarian Law: A Contribution to the Understanding and Respect for the Rule of Law in Armed Conflict' (2005) 857 *International Review of the Red Cross* 175, suggesting that many rules of IHL in NIAC are customary.

[113] For the view that human rights law then applies, as the *lex generalis* that continues in force until any particular norm of *lex specialis* takes effect, see review of detention below, though the application of IHRL even absent an applicable norm of IHL remains controversial.

[114] Droege, 'Interplay'; Prud'homme, '*Lex specialis*', 385. Another view, and an underlying assumption in the jurisprudence cited, is that while HRL can inform the interpretation of IHL, it is doubtful to what extent it can amount to *lex specialis* in armed conflict situations.

[115] Droege, 'Interplay', 338; she indicates that the concept has been misappropriated from the domestic law context, in which there is a clear hierarchy of norms, lacking in the international arena and as between these two sets of norms.

[116] See Scobbie on lawyers 'yearning for a legal system that is fully determined' in response to which he notes 'law is not like that' ('Principle or Pragmatics?)'. See also ILC Report 2006, para. 58; Droege, 'Interplay', 339.

A final broad group of questions relate to the effect of *lex specialis*. If one norm is *lex specialis*, does it provide the sole basis for determining the matter, with the other norm effectively displaced, or what if any is the ongoing role of the other body of norms? The basic theory common to for example the ICJ's approach in *Nuclear Weapons* or that of the Inter-American Commission in its early cases seemed to be that where IHL operates as *lex specialis*, the scope of the relevant IHRL was completely *defined* by the sister IHL provision(s). One need look no further than IHL to answer the relevant IHRL question.[117] But if the approach of the *Armed Activities* case, the human rights bodies or the majority of commentators is to be followed – whereby both bodies of law co-apply and interrelate – it would seem to be the case that even once the *lex specialis* is identified, there is still an ongoing dynamic interrelationship such that the binding norm can be applied by reference to the principles and provisions of the other area of law.[118] This approach helps to ensure that the human rights norms are not set aside to a greater extent than justified by the situation giving rise to the *lex specialis* relationship, meeting the objectives of not only avoiding but also minimizing and mitigating any conflict.[119]

By way of conclusion, it would appear that co-application requires that harmonious interpretation should be pursued where possible, without distorting the content of the norms or making them unworkable, which would serve the purpose of neither area of law. Where harmonious interpretation is impossible without distortion or ignoring real conflict, the *lex specialis – norm* more appropriately addressing or more precisely directed towards the conduct in question – may prevail. While in armed conflict situations that will often be IHL, particularly in conduct of hostilities situations which IHL was directed towards, and in international conflicts where a detailed normative framework may provide the clarity and specificity. But in other scenarios within an armed conflict this may not be the case, and in non-international armed conflict situations in particular IHL may well not provide binding norms, or ones that provide clear specific parameters for particular action. It

117 Expert Meeting, 19–20.

118 See, e.g., Sassóli and Olson, 'Relationship between International Humanitarian and Human Rights Law', who emphasize that the *lex generalis* 'still remains in the background. It must be taken into account when interpreting the lex specialis; to the extent possible, an interpretation of the lex specialis that creates a conflict with the lex generalis must be avoided, and, instead, an attempt to harmonize the two norms made' (354). Note in addition to the co-application of binding norms, the law continues to have a role as a tool of interpretation in the other norms (see section 2 above).

119 ILC 2006, para. 37.

would seem that careful analysis is required case by case and situation by situation to assess whether IHL does provide *lex specialis*, or whether IHRL should continue to apply. Whichever law binds as applicable law, it should not necessarily mean the end of the line for the relevance of the other area of law which continues to inform the interpretation of the principally applicable norm. The next section looks at how these theoretical questions arise in relation to real issues of current concern in the fight against terrorism.

4 Examples of issues of interplay and outstanding questions

This section highlights three issues that illustrate different aspects of the interrelationship between human rights and IHL and some of the outstanding challenges.

4.1 Review of lawfulness of detention in non-international armed conflict?

The question of the procedural safeguards to which 'security detainees' are entitled, particularly in non-international conflict, has been identified as raising particular challenges concerning the interplay of IHL/IHRL.[120] The question whether such detainees are entitled to review the lawfulness of detention, and specifically to *judicial* review as normally required by human rights law, has provoked serious controversy.[121] While the US Supreme Court found persons detained at Guantánamo Bay pursuant to a non-international armed conflict entitled to habeas corpus,[122] the application of habeas to detainees held in Afghanistan has thus far been denied.[123]

120 UNHRC 'Joint study on global practices is in relation to secret detention in the context of countering terrorism' (19 February 2010) UN Doc A/HRC/13/42. The power to detain is itself controversial but I focus here on the procedural guarantees. The US position is that there is no right to habeas for 'enemy combatants' held outside the US territory, as made clear in the course of litigation see e g. the UN joint study on global practices in relation to secret detention, 2010 on the right of all detainees to 'the possibility of resorting to legal procedures, including *habeas corpus*'.

121 On currently applicable review processes in Afghanistan, see R. Goodman, *Rationales for Detention: Security Threats and Intelligence Value* (forthcoming). See also Paust, 'Post-9/11 Overreaction and Fallacies Regarding War and Defense, Guantánamo, the Status of Persons, Treatment, Judicial Review of Detention, and Due Process in Military Commissions' (2003–4) 79 *Notre Dame Law Review* 1335.

122 *Lakhdar Boumediene et al., Petitioners* v. *George W. Bush, President of the United States et al.* 553 US. For a discussion of US and other litigation see cases; Duffy, '*War on Terror*'.

123 The US administration denies the applicability of habeas, invoking the 'law of war' paradigm as purported justification (without accepting that the standards of review under GC IV apply either). See the unfolding litigation, referred to further below in this

The approach of the US Courts to date has been instructive.[124] Petitions for habeas relief were brought in April 2009 by a Tunisian and two Yemenis who allege that they were captured outside Afghanistan, far from combat zones, mistakenly identified as terrorists and transferred for imprisonment to the Bagram Air Base military prison in Afghanistan.[125] The federal district court judge ruled that as these detainees were not captured in an area of war, they had the right to challenge their detention, although others captured in Afghanistan and held there did not. The federal appeals court for the District of Columbia overturned this decision however, finding that as the site of their *detention* was in an 'active theatre of military combat', and in light of 'pragmatic obstacles' stemming from the detention being within the sovereign territory of another state, detainees held at Bagram, regardless of where they were captured, have no constitutional right to challenge their detention in a US court.[126] The Supreme Court has declined to exercise its jurisdiction in respect of this decision.

The significance of these cases is their net effect: years after the Guantánamo cycle of litigation culminating in the Supreme Court judgment, there still exists a judicially endorsed void into which detainees captured anywhere in the world can be deposited to avoid judicial oversight.[127] But the District Court decision also shows the judiciary looking past the question of whether there is an armed conflict or not, to whether in reality the particular circumstances within that conflict precluded the application of certain guarantees or not. The Appeal Court, for its part, while denying the applicants rights to habeas, stated notably that its decision may have been different if the applicants had been transferred deliberately to preclude judicial oversight. The

section, e.g. *Al-Maqaleh et al.*, v. *Gates et al.*, *US Court of Appeals for District of Columbia*, Case No. 09-5265 decided 21 May 2010.

124 It also denies the applicability of GC IV guarantees. Goodman, *Rationales for Detention*.

125 The individuals allege they were captured in Thailand, Pakistan and another location beyond the Afghan border, all far from hostilities.

126 *Al-Maqaleh et al.* The Court stated that 'the *Boumediene* analysis has no application beyond territories that are, like Guantánamo, outside the *de jure* sovereignty of the United States but are subject to its *de facto* sovereignty.'

127 The Appeals Court noted 'the "speculation" as to the government avoiding oversight by using the base and the "importance" of the allegation but found it may have to be addressed in another case where such facts were established . . . the petitioners therefore presented a petition doing just that and the governments contests the relevance of allegations of manipulation' (25). See www.lawfareblog.com on *Al-Maqaleh* case.

applicants have proceeded to prove just that in subsequent, ongoing, litigation.[128]

As a matter of international law, according to which legal framework (and by reference to which approach to interrelationship) do we begin to answer the question of the extent of a detainee's entitlement to review under international law?[129] Is it IHRL with its clear right to challenge lawfulness before an independent court of law, or is there a conflicting norm of IHL? Given the dearth of treaty rules on review for NIAC, can IHL constitute the *lex specialis* here? If the conflict were international, there would be specific rules that one could readily see as potentially fitting within the *lex specialis* model, notably the specific provisions on PoW protections including limited review of their status by an Article 5 GC III tribunal, or periodic review of the detention of civilians for imperative reasons of security, including the right of appeal, under GC IV.[130] By providing for review by an 'appropriate court *or* administrative body', GC IV accepts that judicial review is neither required nor always appropriate or possible, while implicitly reflecting the importance of such review where the particular context made that possible or appropriate. But for non-international armed conflict,[131] while the prohibition on arbitrary detention in general has been described as customary law in either type of conflict,[132] there are no specific IHL rules on challenging lawfulness at all.

Where IHL makes no specific provision, a key question is what approach should be adopted? One approach that has been suggested is the application by 'analogy' of law applicable in international armed conflict.[133] This accords with the blurring of boundaries between norms

[128] *Al-Maqaleh*. See also www.lawfareblog.com.

[129] The key issue is whether the entitlement is to review by a court, thought fundamental in human rights law, by contrast to IHL's provisions (in international conflict only) on other forms of review.

[130] See e.g. Arts. 43 and 78 of GC IV. In neither IHL provision is there a right to judicial review but to review by and 'appropriate court *or* administrative body'. But appeal is attached to civilian internment to safeguard the process.

[131] NIAC is the most relevant scenario now in respect of Afghanistan for example (and more broadly if you take the difficult step of accepting the existence of a broader NIAC with al-Qaeda, as the Supreme Court seemed to do in *Hamdan*).

[132] Henckaerts and Doswald-Beck, *Customary International Humanitarian Law*, vol. I, 344. However, note that for the law applicable in non-international conflicts, it is human rights law and the fact that certain safeguards apply at all times that this commentary cites in support.

[133] Sassóli, 'Non-international armed conflict', 623; see Goodman, *Rationales for Detention*, on the application of GC IV review board in Afghanistan.

applicable in international and non-international conflicts, as developed through the work of the ad hoc criminal tribunals for example and reflected in the ICRC's work.[134] It is motivated by an understandable desire to ensure that applicable law is realistic and feasible and that it will ultimately be complied with.[135] But is there any principled legal basis for this approach in line with the harmonization, *lex specialis* or interpretative approaches to interrelationship outlined above? Absent assertions that a new norm of IHL has arisen, if there is no norm of IHL on one side and a norm of IHRL on the other, where is the normative conflict? In other words if human rights law is applicable in situations of conflict, is there a gap to be filled that might justify such application by analogy? Can binding law be displaced by principles applied by analogy, and would that be beneficial to the end of securing compliance in any event?

If we accept that IHRL applies in armed conflict, and there is no *lex specialis* to supersede IHRL, then the rules in that body of law should presumably apply. But despite the broad acceptance of co-application in principle, in practice the role of human rights law in conflict situations continues to meets real resistance. Essentially this stems from the view that respect for that framework is inappropriate or unrealistic in the context of armed conflict. This view should be treated with some caution first, as difficulties in meeting obligations do not render them inapplicable, though the legitimacy of any legal framework depends to a large extent on it being plausible, not merely aspirational.[136] Second, the question arises to what extent the IHRL framework itself can and does adequately accommodate the context specific considerations of armed conflict even without the, application of the IHL framework as *lex specialis*, or by analogy?

As is well known, the IHRL framework accommodates compromising security situations and the implications for the right to liberty in many ways. Most obviously it does so through derogation, where this is possible,[137] including of the right to liberty, providing certain

[134] J. Pictet (ed.), *Geneva Convention Relative to the Protection of Civilian Persons in Time of War: Commentary* (Geneva: ICRC, 1958), www.irrc.org; *Prosecutor* v. *Tadić*, Appeals Judgment, No. IT-94-1-A, A.Ch., 15 July 1999.

[135] Sassóli, 'Non-international armed conflict', 617–18.

[136] R. Provost, *International Human Rights and Humanitarian Law* (Cambridge: Cambridge University Press, 2002), 315.

[137] There is some question as to whether derogation is possible in respect of extra-territorial operations, as the threshold of an emergency threatening the life of the nation may not be met. The *Leiden Principles* highlight the importance of derogation being possible. The reality is that states rarely derogate even in armed conflict situations. The UK is the only state to have done so post 9/11.

requirements are met and the essence of the right is not set aside.[138] Certain principles of interpretation also inform the flexible and contextual application of human rights treaties, which are 'living instruments' that evolve over time and must be applied in light of their (protective) purpose as well as the principle of 'effectiveness', and holistically, as part of a broader body of international law.[139] Additionally, an inherently flexible rather than 'automatic' approach in the application of many rights leads human rights bodies to ask whether or not, for example, the overall effect of the 'totality' of proceedings rendered a trial fair or unfair. Likewise, with procedural guarantees in relation to the protection from *non-refoulement*, they may ask whether the proceedings afford a 'meaningful opportunity to challenge'.[140]

Human rights bodies have certainly indicated that judicial review of the lawfulness of detention is not a right that can be dispensed with, even in situations of emergency as prompt access is a safeguard against torture and ill-treatment as well as arbitrary detention. But it remains to be seen how human rights courts would respond to genuine battlefield detentions where the state provided independent but non judicial review on a temporary basis owing to a genuine lack of immediate access to regularly constituted courts. The reality is that contexts in which these issues arise, and in which courts have had to consider arbitrary detention have generally been quite different.

[138] See, e.g., the non-derogability of habeas corpus according to e.g. the IACtHR or the Human Rights Committee. IACtHR, Advisory Opinion OC-8/87, January 30, 1987, Ser. A, No. 9 (Advisory Opinion on Emergency Situations), HRC, General Comment 29, above note 28, para 16. UN Joint Study, A/HRC/13/42, 19 February 2010, para. 47. It permits restrictions on certain other related rights such as private or family life or expression on e.g. national security or public order grounds. Duffy, 'War on Terror', ch. 7A.

[139] Rights must be 'practical and effective not theoretical and illusory'. *Marckx v. Belgium*. Appl. No. 6833/74, ECtHR, 1979; *Barrios Altos*, cited above. The law should be capable of offering real protection or it will not be effective, conversely obligations that genuinely cannot be realized by states are unlikely to be considered effective either on the holistic approach *see, e.g., Al-Adsani v. The United Kingdom*, Appl. No. 35763/97, Judgment, EctHR, 21 November 2001, Murillo v. Costa Rica, IACHR, 27 Nov 2012.

[140] See, e.g., jurisprudence of the ECtHR in relation to fair trial, e.g., *Brogan* v. *UK*, Judgment of 29 November 1988, Ser. A, No. 145-B, where access to counsel was seen as an important component but the question was whether proceedings as a whole were adequate, or *Othman v. United Kingdom*, Application 8139/09, Judgment final on 9 May 2012. *Jabar Ahmad and others v. United Kingdom*, Applications 24027/07, 11949/08, 36742/08, 66911/09 and 67354/09, Judgment of 10 April 2012; *Saadi v. Italy*, Application 37201/06, Judgment of 28 February 2008.

If IHRL is applied by reference to IHL, to inform its interpretation, is open to question to what extent the realities of a high intensity conflict scenario would be taken into account, as one commentator suggested, to 'relax' the human rights requirements.[141] Conversely, if a Court were ever to look at IHL as the starting point for this analysis, would it not look at IHL standards in light of more developed standards of IHRL? In either case, where circumstances such as physical or temporal distance from the battlefield capture make judicial review possible, it may well be that at least at that point, such review should be provided.[142] A fortiori, where the individuals have been transferred *into* conflict situations by their captors, as in the *Baghram* cases referred to at the beginning of this section, it would seem highly unlikely that arguments concerning the exigencies of the situation would be viewed sympathetically. These cases perhaps serve as a reminder of the need for vigilance to ensure that illusory battlefield scenarios (particularly within an illusory war) do not provide a pretext for avoiding fundamental guarantees, oversight and accountability.

4.2 Targeted killing?

The classic scenario in which the *lex specialis* of IHL has been long recognized as applying is in relation to the lethal targeting of persons who are combatants or take a direct part in hostilities.[143] The rules of IHRL and IHL are different on this issue, as are the assumptions on which the rules are based, notably the fundamental principle of distinction that underpins IHL and is foreign to HRL, which emphasizes instead the universality of human rights protections and the principle of non-discrimination. In the context of the burgeoning practices of targeted killings by drones,[144] or special operations such as the bin Laden killing,[145] the importance of understanding the legal framework

[141] One commentator has suggested that in this way IHL may 'relax' the human rights requirements in some situations (Sassóli, 'Non-international armed conflict', 615).

[142] See *ibid.*, on 'harmonious' interpretation in this context.

[143] See Chapter 18 in this volume; D. Kretzmer, 'Rethinking the Application of International Humanitarian Law in Non-International Armed Conflicts' (2009) 42 *Israel Law Review* 1.

[144] See e.g. *Living under Drones: Death, Injury and Trauma to Civilians from US Drone Practices in Pakistan* (International Human Rights and Conflict Resolution Clinic, Standford Law School and Global Justice Clinic, New York University School of Law, 2012); Duffy, '*War on Terror*', chs. 6 & 7.

[145] See Duffy, '*War on Terror*', ch. 9.

and the roles of human rights and IHL are increased. What if anything is the continuing role of human rights law and the fore-mentioned principles regarding interrelationship in the interpretation of the law in this area?

The clearest manifestation of the tensions surrounding interplay in this area is the controversial question of whether there is an obligation in any circumstances to arrest rather than kill combatants or persons otherwise legitimately target of attack. The Israeli Supreme Court has provided the seminal case on point deciding that where arrest was in all the circumstances a feasible alternative to lethal killing and posed no risk to the opposing party, targeted killing would be unlawful.[146] More recently, the ICRC has adopted a broadly similar approach.[147] Reflections of the issue are seen in the debate around the lawfulness of drones, which preclude the possibility of capturing rather than killing where circumstances render this a feasible possibility, and some would say a matter of legal obligation.[148]

While the Israeli decision is often cited in support of mutual influence of IHRL and IHL, it is open to question to what extent these developments involve the co-application of IHRL and IHL in any real sense. One interpretation is that the Court was recognizing that even in armed conflict contexts there are certain factual scenarios more akin to the sort of context that IHRL was designed to regulate and where IHRL is more relevant to the interpretation of IHL: whatever the status of the individual, the different contexts of the supermarket and the battlefield can and should make a difference to lawful responses.[149] The Supreme Court certainly adopts language drawn over from the human rights world. But what is noteworthy is that the rationale for the decision by the Israeli Court, and certainly the ICRC approach, was predominantly principles enshrined in IHL itself – of military necessity and, in the ICRC commentary, of humanity – rather than express recognition of the importance of respecting human rights law as such.

[146] Public Committee against Torture in *Israel* v. *Government of Israel* (Supreme Court of Israel, HCJ 769/02, December 2006), at http://elyon1.court.gov.il/Files_fnG/02/690/007/a34/02007690.a34.HTM.

[147] N. Melzer, *Interpretative Guidance on the Notion of Direct Participation in Hostilities under International Humanitarian Law* (Geneva: ICRC, 2009).

[148] See Duffy, '*War on Terror*', ch. 6B.

[149] This reflects, e.g., *Guerrero* v. *Colombia* HRC, albeit the current case is more controversial as it concerns a clear rule of IHL on targeting combatants in IAC.

While it may be that human rights law was not applied as such, it was certainly relevant to interpreting these IHL principles. As cases before human rights courts referred to above have focused on violations arising from civilian casualties in conflict, not killing arguably legitimate targets in conflict, it remains to be seen whether, if this scenario comes before human rights courts they will in turn interpret the human rights conventions in light of IHL.[150] The Israeli Court's judgment suggests one approach whereby, even in respect of targeting in armed conflict, the outcome of the application of IHL in certain contexts might not be dissimilar to an application of IHRL. At a minimum, both the IHL developments highlighted above reflect the evolution and 'humanization' of that body of law, influenced by the parallel development of IHRL. So far as this approach continues to evolve the issue of normative conflict in this field should become less significant.

4.3 Investigation and reparation?

Over the past two decades, human rights law has experienced a tidal wave of development in respect of accountability norms. The result is a detailed body of law setting out the existence of obligations to investigate and prosecute serious violations of human rights law, and providing detail as to the content of these norms.[151] These duties have been held to be non-derogable in situations of emergency,[152] and to continue to apply in situations of armed conflict.[153]

IHL has of course not developed in the same way, due not least to the relative dearth of supervisory mechanisms and jurisprudential development. However, specific IHL treaty obligations reflect the principle of

[150] See The Evolving Approach of human rights bodies above, for examples of ECtHR cases on 'civilian' deaths.

[151] This includes the requirements that an investigation be thorough, effective and – critically – independent and the importance of individual accountability for serious violations. See e.g. *Cobzaru* v. *Romania*, App. No. 48254/99, Judgment 26 July 2007, para. 68; *Aydin* v. *Turkey*, App. Nos. 28293/95, 29494/95 and 30219/96, Judgment of 10 July 2001, para. 106; *Aksoy* v. *Turkey*, App. No. 21987/93, Judgment of 18 December 1996, para. 189; and *Cakiçi* v. *Turkey*, App. No. 23657/94, Judgment of 8 July 1999, para. 284. See also *Velasquez Rodríguez*, IACtHR, Ser. C., No. 4, Judgment of 29 July 1988; *Barrios Altos*, IACtHR, Ser. C, No. 75, Judgment of 14 March 2001; *Keremedchiev* v. *Bulgaria*, United Nations Committee against Torture, Merits, UN Doc. CAT/C/41/D/257/2004; *Chorzów Factory*, Judgment of 26 July 1927 PCIJ Rep., Ser. A, No. 9, 21.

[152] See, e.g., *Al-Skeini*, para. 162.

[153] *Ibid.*, para. 164, referring to a long line of cases that arose in the context of 'difficult security conditions, including in a context of armed conflict'.

investigation and accountability. Most notably, going further than human rights treaties which themselves set out no explicit obligations in this respect, the four Geneva Conventions specify the obligation to seek out and bring to justice those responsible for grave breaches.[154] Provisions also reflect obligations to investigate deaths of PoWs or civilian detainees.[155] In relation to both international and non-international conflicts, it has been suggested that a parallel obligation under customary law may also have emerged.[156]

IHL arguably therefore reflects the same rules, but does not provide the same level of detail as to the content of the norm. It may be that IHRL can help to clarify the precise nature of states' obligations to for example carry out a prompt, thorough, effective and independent investigation into serious violations of IHL.[157] Conversely, when IHRL is applicable, human rights jurisprudence makes clear that the existence of a conflict does not change the obligation to carry out a thorough, effective and impartial investigation, but it may well inform assessments as to the compliance by the state with these positive obligations by taking into account obstacles or concrete constraints that may affect the speed or nature of the investigation.[158] This situation is well encapsulated in the Report of the United Nations Special Rapporteur on Extrajudicial, Summary or Arbitrary Executions:

> Armed conflict and occupation do not discharge the State's duty to investigate and prosecute human rights abuses... It is undeniable that during armed conflicts circumstances will sometimes impede investigation. Such circumstances will never discharge the obligation to investigate – this would eviscerate the non-derogable character of the right to life – but they may affect the modalities or particulars of the investigation. In addition to being fully responsible for the conduct of their agents, in relation to the acts of private actors States are also held to a standard of due diligence in armed conflicts as well as peace. On a case-by-case basis a State might utilize less effective measures of investigation in response to

[154] Geneva Conventions, Arts. 49, 50, 129 and 146; API, Art. 85.

[155] GC IV, Arts. 121 and 131.

[156] C. Kress, 'Universal Jurisdiction over International Crimes and the Institut de Droit international' (2006) 4 *Journal of International Criminal Justice* 561 and 'War Crimes Committed in Non-International Armed Conflict and the Emerging System of International Criminal Justice' (2000) 30 *Israel Yearbook on Human Rights* (2000) 103, 171–4.

[157] Of these, greatest resistance attends the duty of independent investigation, which is not a [common] feature of military investigations to date.

[158] *Al-Skeini*, paras. 164–7.

> concrete constraints. For example, when hostile forces control the scene of a shooting, conducting an autopsy may prove impossible. Regardless of the circumstances, however, investigations must always be conducted as effectively as possible and never be reduced to mere formality.[159]

More complex is the question of the right to a remedy or to reparation. In IHRL, the right to a remedy in respect of violations of other rights is set out in human rights treaties, and the right to reparation for serious violations has been deemed inherent in the obligation to 'ensure' or 'secure' the protection of human rights through the evolution of jurisprudence.[160] In IHL, there are no general treaty provisions reflecting such a right,[161] though there are provisions that may incline in a similar direction. Notably the 1907 Hague Convention IV recognized in its Article 3 and Article 91 of Protocol I the obligation of a state that violates IHL to pay compensation.[162] This may be as IHL was not conceived as an 'individual rights paradigm'.[163] But so far as it is recognized that one of the functions of IHL is to enshrine 'rights applicable in armed conflict', then the concept of a remedy (as inherent in the notion of such right) should follow.[164] This corresponds with the push for IHL to reach the 'ultimate beneficiaries' of its protection.[165] In the establishment of the International Criminal Tribunal for the former Yugoslavia, the Security

159 P. Alston, *Civil and Political Rights, including the Question of Disappearances and Summary Executions: Extrajudicial, Summary or Arbitrary Executions* (UN Doc. E/CN.4/2006/53 (2006), para. 36).

160 Art. 13 ECHR, Art. 10 ACHR, Art. 21 ACHPR (compensation only in terms of property lost); *Velasquez Rodriguez* and *El Amparo* v. *Venezuela*, 1996 IACtHR (Ser. C) No. 28 (14 September 1996). Art. 75 ICC Statute reflects the importance of reparation for crimes under international law; 1998 Rome Statute for the International Criminal Court, 2187 UNTS 3.

161 L. Zegveld, 'Remedies for Victims of Violations of International Humanitarian Law' (2003) 85 *International Review of the Red Cross* 497.

162 Hague Convention (IV) Respecting the Laws and Customs of War on Land and Its Annex: Regulations Concerning the Laws and Customs of War on Land, 18 October 1907. Provost, *International Human Rights*, notes that this provision shows IHL was intended 'to benefit individuals as well states' and suggests that this provision reflects customary law: 'Despite some indicators in the *travaux préparatoires* of the 1907 Hague Convention IV that the obligation to compensate imposed by article 3 could have been intended to benefit individuals as well as states, subsequent practice indicates that the corresponding customary rule has evolved to envisage claims from states only' (45).

163 Matthew Happold, 'International Humanitarian Law and Human Rights Law' in Christian Henderson and Nigel White (eds), Research Handbook on International Conflict and Security Law, (2012) 21.

164 Zegveld, 'Remedies for Victims', citing Lord Denning's famous dicta 'a right without a remedy is no right at all', in *Gouriet* v. *Union of Post Office Workers*, AC, 1978, 435.

165 As one commentator put it, the purpose of IHL is to go 'beyond the interstate levels and [to reach] for the level of the real (or ultimate) beneficiaries of humanitarian protection,

Council recognized the right to compensation for serious violations of IHL[166] and the ICC Statute provisions on reparation are well known.[167] IHL also reflects the 'right of families to know the fate of their relatives' which has been regarded in IHRL as one aspect of reparation.[168] In relation to both international and non-international conflicts, the ICRC Study on customary law suggests that the obligations to provide reparations may have emerged under customary law.[169]

It may be concluded that while the practical challenges may be different, there is nothing in IHL that conflicts with the principle of reparation or remedy, and indeed there is growing indication of coherence in the underlying principles of the two bodies of law in this area. In these circumstances, despite the absence of specific treaty provisions of IHL, the right to remedy and reparation for violations of IHL and HR can be seen as an area ripe for harmonious interpretation, with IHRL and IHL being co-applied, and IHL interpreted by reference to the more specific guidance of IHRL.

This approach is reflected in the United Nations 'Basic Principles and Guidelines on the Right to a Remedy and Reparations for Victims of Violations of International Human Rights and Humanitarian Law' (hereafter 'UN Principles on the Right to a Remedy'), adopted by the United Nations Commission on Human Rights at its 64th session in 2005.[170] The Principles recognize the right of victims of violations of human rights and IHL with a right to a remedy. By clear reference to the development of human rights law they distinguish between five forms of

i.e. individuals and groups of individuals' (G. Abi-Saab, 'The Specificities of Humanitarian Law', in C. Swinarski (ed.), *Studies and Essays of International Humanitarian Law and Red Cross Principles in Honour of Jean Pictet* (The Hague: Martinus Nijhoff, 1984), 269).

166 UN Doc. S/Res./827 (1993) determines that 'the work of the Tribunal shall be carried out without prejudice to the right of victims to seek, through appropriate means, compensation for damages incurred as a result of violations of international humanitarian law.'

167 Rome Statute, Art. 75.

168 API, Art. 32 notes that 'In the implementation of this Section, the activities of the High Contracting Parties, of the Parties to the conflict and of the international humanitarian organizations mentioned in the Conventions and in this Protocol shall be prompted mainly by the right of families to know the fate of their relatives.'

169 Henckaerts and Doswald-Beck, *Henckaerts and Doswald-Beck, Customary International Humanitarian Law*, vol. I, 547. See also Kress, 'Universal Jurisdiction over International Crimes and the Institut de Droit International' (2006) 4 *Journal of International Criminal Justice* 561 and 'War Crimes Committed in Non-International Armed Conflict and the Emerging System of International Criminal Justice' (2000) 30 *Israel Yearbook on Human Rights* 103, 171–4.

170 Basic Principles and Guidelines on the Right to a Remedy and Reparation for Victims of Gross Violations of International Human Rights Law and Serious Violations of International Humanitarian Law (UN Doc. A/Res./60/147 (2005)).

reparation: restitution, compensation, rehabilitation, satisfaction, and guarantees of non-repetition. The Principles go on to provide that the content of this right includes access to justice, reparation for harm suffered and access to factual information concerning the violations.[171]

Just as the previous example on targeting saw the role of the courts in interpreting one area in light of the other, towards the development of a coherent international legal framework, this may be an example of the role that the United Nations can play in the cross fertilization between the two areas of law through the elaboration of (in this case soft law) standards.[172]

Interpreting IHL and IHRL obligations in this respect could have real practical import in enabling victims to secure their rights despite paradigm clashes. Momentum is gathering in several states around the need for thorough independent investigations of serious violations carried out in the name of counter-terrorism. Accountability has been slow and faltering, and obligation to provide reparations has been woefully neglected to date while attempts to seek remedies have been frequently hampered in domestic courts.[173] This in turn underscores the importance of regional or international human rights mechanisms which may provide the only potential vehicle for such redress. In this way '[t]he complementarity of human rights and humanitarian law . . . ensures that victims will not be left without a right to reparation for their injuries'.[174]

Reparation for victims, like effective investigation and where appropriate individual accountability, are legal imperatives rather than mere policy options. They should be presented and considered as such. Meeting the challenges to investigation, accountability and reparation in the context of international terrorism, however politically unattractive, may prove to be the litmus test for the rule of law in the fight against international terrorism.

[171] See Zegveld, 'Remedies for Victims', 488. See also Rome Statute, Art. 75.

[172] Mutual influence in the drafting of international standards is well recognized. For example, Art. 75 API is often cited as incorporating directly Art. 14 ICCPR fair trial standards, while the development of human rights law of forced disappearance including the Convention for the Protection of All Persons from Enforced Disappearance 2006, General Assembly Res. 61/177 (20 December 2006) has been cited as showing the influence of IHL standards on the right to information for example (see Droege, 'Interplay', 343).

[173] See, e.g., Duffy War on Terror Chapter 10 'Extraordinary Rendition' and Kostas above.

[174] Provost, *International Human Rights*, 49.

5 Conclusion

The co-application of IHRL and IHL in armed conflict situations, despite continuing resistance on policy grounds, is beyond reasonable dispute as a matter of international law co-application may potentially ensure that human rights can be protected to the greatest extent possible in armed conflict situations, where they are most vulnerable, but in a manner that is capable of responding to the realities of conflict scenarios. It may ensure that rights and obligations under both bodies of law can be given meaningful effect, with avenues for redress for victims and state and individual accountability. What this relationship means in practice, however, including in the context of controversial issues highlighted above, remain subject to much dispute and uncertainty, and will justifiably continue to occupy international attention for years to come.

What is clear is that the simplistic notion of IHL as *lex specialis* to human rights – as applying regime wide, rather than 'norm by norm', and to justify the wholesale displacement of HRL – has no legal basis. Where possible a harmonious approach to dual application should be explored, with the question of *lex specialis* arising in the event of conflict between particular norms, in light of their content and objectives, in particular situations. There is symbiotic relationship that must be determined norm by norm and situation by situation and which continues to inform the interpretation of applicable law even beyond the identification of a rule as *lex specialis*.

The dangers of the over-broad and rigid approach to *lex specialis* to exclude human rights law are illustrated by the lack of procedural guarantees for Baghram detainees, and the debate around whether the 'armed conflict' in Afghanistan has been used to justify the creation of (another) dumping ground for detainees beyond the reach of judicial oversight. By the same token, the myopic application of human rights law without recognizing the impact of certain armed conflict situations on applicable law, cannot give rise to the effective application of IHRL. In either case, rigid approaches to the application of one body of law to the exclusion of the other is no longer credible as a matter of international law, and undermines both the legitimacy and the effectiveness of the legal framework.

Conclusions and recommendations

(1) International human rights law applies at all times and is the body of international law most commonly applicable to counter-terrorist activity. States are bound by their human rights treaty obligations

whether they act at home or abroad. States and other actors should seek to give effect to and to clarify these principles through practice. Consideration of extraterritorial application as a customary rule deserves greater consideration, particularly given entrenched positions on the applicability of the ICCPR.

(2) The applicability of human rights law in situations of armed conflict, alongside IHL, is now beyond reasonable debate. Recent practice has been characterized by an unduly broad approach to armed conflict and to notions of 'association' with the conflict, coupled with an unduly narrow approach to the co-applicability of IHRL and IHL in armed conflict. Together they have undermined the complementary roles of human rights law and IHL.

(3) It should be recognized that norms of HRL and IHL co-apply, with an emphasis on harmonious interpretation where possible and *lex specialis* where necessary. There is symbiotic relationship that goes beyond the mere displacement of IHRL by IHL in situations of conflict that must be determined norm by norm and situation by situation. Whichever the predominant binding norm in relation to a particular situation, whether under IHL or IHRL, there remains an ongoing mutual regard between the two bodies of law that allows IHL to be interpreted in light of IHRL and vice versa, contributing to greater internal coherence in international law.

(4) A harmonious approach to interpretation is possible where the two areas have parallel purposes and principles, or where there are 'potential' conflicts that can be resolved through consistent interpretation. On most issues the principles do coincide or are complementary, as illustrated by the analysis of investigation and reparation for example. However, the limits of this approach should also be recognized. The operation of the *lex specialis* rule is important when there are norms of IHL directed to the particular situation that conflict with those of IHRL. This most obviously arises in relation to rules on the right to life and detention in international armed conflict.

(5) In non-international armed conflict, or otherwise where there are no clear norms of IHL in relation to a particular issue, there is no normative conflict and the applicable norms of IHRL bind states. These must be interpreted in a context sensitive manner and by reference to the principles of IHL, to ensure that the legal framework does not impose impossible burdens on states. It is noted however that a context sensitive application of IHRL and a human rights

informed application of IHL principles may not lead to greatly divergent standards on the vast majority of issues, and even potentially in relation to safeguards in detention as well as the targeted killings as discussed above.

(6) Attention should be paid to ensuring that all those charged with the implementation of IHL and IHRL understand and apply the relevant areas of law. Co-application and the 'norm-by-norm and case-by-case' approach bring with it a challenge to legal clarity and, while not a unique problem, attention should be directed to how to meet it. In particular, emphasis should be placed on the duties of states to provide guidelines to those on the ground to clarify applicable law, including the interrelationship of IHL and IHRL in relation to particular norms and situations, and as necessary support should be provided.

(7) Human rights courts bodies should be encouraged to engage with violations of human rights in armed conflict within their own jurisdictional limitations. Their increased engagement with such violations, including as appropriate by reference to IHL, provides victims with the prospect of a remedy, which may otherwise be elusive. However, these bodies have at times overreached in the application of IHL to violent exchanges not part of a conflict, and at others underreached in failing to have due regard to IHL in the determination of issues properly regulated by IHL in conflict situations. So far as human rights bodies determine matters properly regulated by IHL, the myopic application of IHRL standards as if there were no conflict threatens to undermine their own legitimacy and the force of applicable law. The future undoubtedly holds an increased volume of conflict-related violations before human rights courts and bodies (an immediate example is the thousands of cases pending before the European Court relating to the Russia–Georgian conflict). Barriers to the effective application of IHL alongside IHRL by these bodies should be overcome and effective measures of support should be considered, such as capacity building and guidance on matters of IHL.

(8) Accountability for serious crimes committed in the name of counter-terrorism should be seen as a legal imperative under IHL and IHRL, not a policy alternative. Investigation in face of credible allegations of serious violations of either IHL or IHRL should be thorough and independent in line with established international standards. The right to reparation of individual victims of violations

carried out in the name of fighting international terrorism should be recognized, as to other victims of violations. Principled recognition of the need for investigation, accountability and reparation is an important measure towards strengthening a rule of law framework weakened by the serious violations carried out in the name of the fight against terrorism.

17

The legal regime governing treatment and procedural guarantees for persons detained in the fight against terrorism

JELENA PEJIC AND CORDULA DROEGE

1 Introduction

The fight against terrorism has 'strained' many norms of international law, including those governing the treatment and procedural rights of persons detained[1] on suspicion of 'terrorist' activity. The term 'terrorist' has been marked by inverted commas not to downplay the extremely serious nature of terrorist acts, but to indicate that the designation has become almost legally meaningless. It is habitually used to cover both violent attacks directed against the general population in peacetime, which are prohibited by several bodies of law, as well as the use of force against legitimate military objectives in armed conflict, which are not prohibited under international humanitarian law (even though they remain prohibited under the domestic law of the detaining state).[2] Thus,

[1] For the purposes of this chapter, 'detained person' means any person deprived of personal liberty, whereas 'detention' means the condition of detained persons.

[2] See Chapter 20 in this volume. See also ICRC report, *International Humanitarian Law and the Challenges of Contemporary Armed Conflicts*, presented to the 30th International Conference of the Red Cross and Red Crescent held in Geneva in 2007, at www.icrc.org/Web/Eng/siteeng0.nsf/htmlall/p0892/$File/ICRC_002_0892.PDF: 'A recent challenge for IHL has been the tendency of States to label as "terrorist" all acts of warfare committed by organized armed groups in the course of armed conflict, in particular non-international armed conflict. Although it is generally agreed that parties to an international armed conflict may, under IHL, lawfully attack each other's military objectives, States have been much more reluctant to recognize that the same principle applies in non-international armed conflicts. Thus, States engaged in non-international armed conflicts have, with increasing frequency, labelled any act committed by domestic insurgents an act of "terrorism" even though, under IHL, such an act might not have been unlawful (e.g. attacks against military personnel or installations). What is being

any attempt to examine the legal framework governing the response to conduct colloquially labelled 'terrorist' must take into account the context in which it took place: peacetime or armed conflict? This chapter will attempt to briefly outline the rules governing the treatment of persons detained and their procedural rights based on this contextual distinction, with situations of armed conflict, i.e. international humanitarian law, serving as the starting point. As will be shown, in some cases the rules are the same regardless of the situation at hand, whereas in others they differ. The analysis will focus on: (1) the rules governing treatment; and (2) procedural safeguards applicable in detention, in particular security detention.

2 Treatment of persons detained in the fight against terrorism

Treatment is a very broad term which encompasses the entirety of the environment in which a detainee is held including, of course, the behaviour of the detaining authority towards him or her. The legal rules governing treatment in detention are therefore similarly broad and comprise both rules on adequate conditions of detention, which are beyond the scope of this chapter,[3] and rules safeguarding the physical and mental integrity of detained persons regardless of the specific detention setting (treatment in the narrow sense). It is in the latter sense that this term is used here, the examination being limited to legal and practical issues related to the prohibition of torture and other cruel, inhuman or degrading treatment.

overlooked here is that a crucial difference between IHL and the legal regime governing terrorism is the fact that IHL is based on the premise that certain acts of violence – against military objectives – are not prohibited. Any act of 'terrorism' is, however, by definition, prohibited and criminal. The need to differentiate between lawful acts of war and acts of terrorism must be borne in mind so as not to conflate these two legal regimes. This is particularly important in non-international armed conflicts, in which all acts of violence by organized armed groups against military objectives remain in any event subject to domestic criminal prosecution. The tendency to designate them additionally as "terrorist" may diminish armed groups' incentive to respect IHL, and may also be a hindrance in a possible subsequent political process of conflict resolution' (footnote omitted).

[3] Treatment in the narrow sense includes other prohibitions as well, such as the prohibition of arbitrary deprivation of life under human rights law, i.e. 'violence to life' (murder) under Common Article 3 to the Geneva Conventions. IHL also expressly prohibits a range of other acts, such as mutilation, medical experiments, etc., containing lists that are not replicated in the treaties of human rights law.

2.1 Preliminary remarks

Whatever the specific context in which a person is deprived of liberty (peacetime or armed conflict), and regardless of the purpose (questioning, security detention, criminal charges, etc.), the prohibition of torture and other forms of ill-treatment is absolute. While there are differences in the way human rights law and IHL provide for the prohibition due to the fact that IHL binds both state and non-state parties to an armed conflict, there is no doubt that humane treatment[4] is the underlying goal of both branches of the law. The concept is not limited to preserving physical or mental integrity, but is wider, and aims to preserve human dignity.

By way of reminder, the absolute prohibition of torture and other forms of ill-treatment is a bedrock provision of both international humanitarian and human rights law. Common Article 3 to the four Geneva Conventions forbids torture, cruel treatment and outrages upon personal dignity, in particular humiliating and degrading treatment.[5] Human rights law takes the same approach, prohibiting torture, cruel, inhuman or degrading treatment or punishment.[6] While there is a difference between the concepts of torture, cruel or inhuman and degrading treatment, it must be emphasized that all of these forms of ill-treatment are prohibited in equal measure; there is no situation in which torture would be prohibited but other forms of ill-treatment allowed. It is also clear that while the addressees of the obligation are different, the substantive content of the prohibited treatment is the same. In other words, the threshold for finding that an act constitutes torture or cruel, inhuman or degrading treatment is not higher in armed conflict than in peacetime.

In the context of the fight against terrorism, the absolute nature of the prohibition of torture and other forms of ill-treatment has been re-opened. While not calling the prohibition into question upfront, there has in some quarters been an attempt to circumvent its absolute nature by attempting to 'define out' of it a number of treatment methods.[7]

4 Common Article 3 to the Geneva Conventions, Art. 10 ICCPR.

5 Common Article 3(1)(a) and (c); torture and ill-treatment are also prohibited in many other provisions of IHL applicable in international and non-international armed conflicts: see, e.g., Art. 27 Fourth Geneva Convention, Arts. 50, 51, 130, 147 respectively of the four Geneva Conventions; Art. 75 API; Art. 4 APII.

6 See ICCPR, Art. 7.

7 See, e.g., J. Ross, 'Black Letter Abuse: The US Legal Response to Torture Since 9/11' (2007) 89 *International Review of the Red Cross* 561.

It is therefore important, in this article, to recall the meaning of the different legal concepts of ill-treatment as they have been developed in jurisprudence. Since the article focuses in particular on armed conflict situations, it draws in particular on IHL and on the jurisprudence of the International Tribunal for the Former Yugoslavia. The Tribunal itself has drawn inspiration for its jurisprudence from the case law of human rights bodies, which will not be repeated at length here, as the concepts are largely identical, with the caveat that IHL binds all parties to an armed conflict.[8]

The concepts of torture and other forms of ill-treatment are sometimes criticized for being too general, not amenable to clear interpretation. This has led on occasion to calls for lists of permissible behaviour, especially permissible interrogation methods, to avoid the difficulties of interpretation. Before entering into the definitions, two preliminary observations should be made in this respect.

First, it must be emphasized that the definitions of torture and cruel, inhuman or degrading treatment and outrages upon personal dignity are *necessarily* general as they must cover a wide range of situations. The Commentary to the Fourth Geneva Convention already acknowledged that it was impossible to draw up an exhaustive list of specifically prohibited behaviour. It states that: '[i]t seems useless and even dangerous to attempt to make a list of all the factors which make treatment "humane"'[9] and adds: '[i]t is always dangerous to try to go into too much detail – especially in this domain. However great the care taken in drawing up a list of all the various forms of infliction, it would never be possible to catch up with the imagination of future torturers who wished to satisfy their bestial instincts; and the more specific and complete a list tries to be, the more restrictive it becomes. The form of wording adopted in [Common Article 3] is flexible, and, at the same time, precise.'[10]

[8] See, *inter alia*, O. de Frouville, 'The Influence of the European Court of Human Rights' Case Law on International Criminal Law of Torture and Inhuman or Degrading Treatment' (2011) 9 *Journal of International Criminal Justice* 633; C. Droege, '"In Truth the Leitmotiv": The Prohibition of Torture and Other Forms of Ill-Treatment in International Humanitarian Law' (2007) 89 *International Review of the Red Cross* 515. A large part of the following section is based on the latter article.

[9] See J. Pictet, *The Geneva Conventions of 12 August 1949: Commentary IV Geneva Convention relative to the Protection of Civilians in Time of War* (Geneva: ICRC, 1958), 204.

[10] See *Commentary to Geneva Convention IV*, 39.

Second, it must also be acknowledged that the concepts of torture and cruel, inhuman or degrading treatment and outrages upon personal dignity evolve over time, and that acts that might not have been considered to be torture or ill-treatment in the past might be considered to be that nowadays.[11] Drawing up a list of behaviour, of interrogation methods for example, that would be deemed lawful regardless of the passage of time would therefore be inherently problematic.

2.2 *Torture*

2.2.1 Elements of the definition of torture

In human rights law, torture is explicitly defined in Article 1 1984 UN Convention against Torture and Other Cruel, Inhuman or Degrading Treatment or Punishment:[12]

> Any act by which severe pain or suffering, whether physical or mental, is intentionally inflicted on a person for such purposes as obtaining from him or a third person information or a confession, punishing him for an act he or a third person has committed or is suspected of having committed, or intimidating or coercing him or a third person, or for any reason based on discrimination of any kind, when such pain or suffering is inflicted by or at the instigation of or with the consent or acquiescence of a public official or other person acting in an official capacity. It does not include pain or suffering arising only from, inherent in or incidental to lawful sanctions.

While the treaties of IHL contain many references to torture, they do not provide a definition.[13] The ICTY, however, considers that the CAT

[11] See ECtHR, *Selmouni* v. *France*, Judgment of 28 July 1999: 'the Court considers that certain acts which were classified in the past as "inhuman and degrading treatment" as opposed to "torture" could be classified differently in future. It takes the view that the increasingly high standard being required in the area of the protection of human rights and fundamental liberties correspondingly and inevitably requires greater firmness in assessing breaches of the fundamental values of democratic societies' (para. 101).

[12] There are other similar definitions in human rights law, and human rights jurisprudence has broadly relied on this definition, i.e. intentional infliction of severe suffering at the hands of a state, inflicted for a purpose such as information, confession, punishment, etc. See Art. 1 Declaration on the Protection of All Persons from Being Subjected to Torture and Other Cruel, Inhuman or Degrading Treatment or Punishment; Art. 2 Inter-American Convention to Prevent and Punish Torture.

[13] The term torture is found, among others, in Common Article 3, Arts. 50, 51, 130, 147 four Geneva Conventions respectively, Arts. 17, 87 of GC III, Art. 32 of GC IV, Art. 75 API, Art. 4 APII.

definition reflects customary international law[14] and has adapted it for the purpose of international criminal law relating to armed conflicts. Furthermore, a large part of the Tribunal's interpretation draws on the jurisprudence of human rights bodies, in particular the European Court of Human Rights. While the Tribunal initially held that a perpetrator must be a public official,[15] it subsequently abandoned this requirement in order to ensure that non-state actors can also be held responsible for torture committed in non-international armed conflicts.[16] The Tribunal has retained the purposive element of the CAT definition, holding that this element and the level of severity of pain or suffering caused ('severe' rather than 'serious') are two factors that distinguish torture from inhuman treatment.[17] Based on the CAT, human rights jurisprudence, and on IHL case law, torture is defined in IHL as: (1) the infliction of severe mental or physical pain or suffering; (2) for a purpose such as obtaining information, confession, coercion, intimidation, humiliation, etc.

2.2.2 The need for a purpose as a constitutive element of torture

The purposes enumerated in the CAT are not exhaustive, as evidenced by the wording of Article 1 ('such purposes as') and the fact that a non-exhaustive list was likewise included in the Elements of Crime for the Rome Statute of the International Criminal Court.[18] The ICTY has held that the prohibited purpose 'need be neither the sole nor the main purpose of inflicting the severe pain or suffering'.[19] It is, however,

[14] *Prosecutor* v. *Zejnil Delalic and others*, Case No IT-96-21-T (Trial Chamber), 16 November 1998, para. 459.

[15] *Prosecutor* v. *Furundzija*, Case No IT-95-17/1 (Trial Chamber), 10 December 1998, para. 162 and Appeals Chamber Judgment, 21 July 2000, para. 111.

[16] *Prosecutor* v. *Kunarac and others*, Cases No IT-96-23 and IT-96-23/1 (Trial Chamber), 22 February 2001, para. 491; confirmed by the Appeals Chamber Judgment, 12 June 2000, para. 148; *Prosecutor* v. *Kvocka and others*, Case No IT-98-30/1-A (Appeals Chamber), 28 February 2005, para. 284.

[17] *Prosecutor* v. *Kunarac and others* (Appeals Chamber), para. 142; *Prosecutor* v. *Krnojelac*, Case No IT-97-5 (Trial Chamber), 15 March 2002, paras. 179, 180; *Prosecutor* v. *Brdjanin*, Case No IT-99-36-T (Trial Chamber), 1 September 2004, para. 486. This is in conformity with international human rights law, as reflected in Art. 1(2) Torture Declaration under which torture constitutes an aggravated and deliberate form of cruel, inhuman or degrading treatment or punishment.

[18] See Elements of Crime for Art. 8(2)(a)(ii) and Art. 8(2)(c)(i) Rome Statute.

[19] *Prosecutor* v. *Kvocka and others* (Trial Chamber), 2 November 2001, para. 153; *Prosecutor* v. *Kunarac and others* (Trial Chamber), para. 486 and (Appeals Chamber), para. 155.

generally accepted that an additional purpose, one not specifically enumerated in the CAT, would have to have 'something in common with the purposes expressly listed'.[20]

2.2.3 Severe physical or mental suffering

As regards the requirement of severity, human rights bodies[21] and the ICTY require a certain threshold of severity.

In this respect, there is an ongoing debate as to whether cruel or inhuman treatment on the one hand and torture on the other hand are distinct only by virtue of the purposive element required for torture or also by a higher degree of suffering. Without seeking to go into the detail of this controversial issue,[22] it is submitted that it is preferable to retain the ICTY's definition and differentiate between 'serious' and 'severe' injury or suffering in order to ensure that torture and cruel or inhuman treatment are distinguished not only based on the purpose of a prohibited treatment but also on the level of suffering inflicted. In this context it should be noted, however, that the Elements of Crime of the Rome ICC Statute define inhuman treatment as '*severe* physical or mental pain or suffering' (emphasis added),[23] thus adopting a higher threshold than that of *serious suffering* and eliminating the differentiation between torture and cruel or inhuman treatment. Even after the adoption of the Rome Statute, however, the ICTY has not abandoned the requirement that cruel or inhuman treatment or punishment constitute a 'serious' attack on human dignity.[24] It remains to be seen how the ICC will interpret the respective notions.

[20] J. H. Burger and H. Danelius, *The United Nations Convention against Torture* (Dordrecht: Martinus Nijhoff, 1988), 118.

[21] ECtHR, *Ireland* v. *the United Kingdom*, Judgment of 18 January 1978, Series A, No. 25, para. 162; IACtHR, *Caesar* v. *Trinidad and Tobago*, Judgment of 11 March 2005, Series C, No. 13, para. 68.

[22] See a thorough discussion of the question whether torture involves a degree of suffering that is higher than that of cruel or inhuman treatment in N. Rodley with M. Pollard, *The Treatment of Prisoners under International Law* (Oxford: Oxford University Press, 2009), 98–124. This chapter follows the approach outlined in Droege, '"In Truth the Leitmotiv"'.

[23] Emphasis added. All other elements, including the link to armed conflict and the *mens rea* are not addressed here as they are not relevant to interpreting the terms of common Art. 3 as such.

[24] See the cases *Prosecutor* v. *Blaskic* (Trial Chamber), 3 March 2000, para. 154–5; *Prosecutor* v. *Kordic and Cerkez*, IT-95-14/2-T (Trial Chamber), 26 February 2001, para. 256; *Prosecutor* v. *Naletilic and Martinovic*, Case No IT-98-34-T (Trial Chamber) 31 March 2003, para. 246.

The ICTY has over time developed its jurisprudence regarding the level of severity and a number of indicators can be found in its case law. The Tribunal, like human rights bodies, takes into account both general (i.e. 'objective') criteria, as well as criteria that pertain to the circumstances of a particular case (i.e. 'subjective').

Relevant factors include 'the nature and context of the infliction of pain', 'the premeditation and institutionalization of the ill-treatment', 'the manner and method used' and 'the position of inferiority of the victim'.[25] Moreover, the duration and forms of ill-treatment, its repetitiveness and severity are to be assessed as a whole.[26] The Tribunal has stressed that 'permanent injury is not a requirement for torture; evidence of the suffering need not even be visible after the commission of the crime'.[27] Further, 'factors such as the victim's age, sex, or state of health will also be relevant in assessing the gravity of the harm'.[28] The Tribunal has also held that 'in certain circumstances the suffering can be exacerbated by social and cultural conditions' and that 'the specific social, cultural and religious background of the victims [should be taken into account] when assessing the severity of the alleged conduct'.[29] In summary, the Tribunal does not 'specifically set the threshold level of suffering or pain required for the crime of torture', which 'consequently depends on the individual circumstances of each case'.[30] Torture may thus be the result of a single act or be the result of a combination or accumulation of several acts, which, taken individually and out of context, may appear harmless.

It is important to emphasize that *mental* suffering can be severe enough to amount to torture on its own. Indeed, psychological torture can cause suffering as severe as physical torture.[31] The ICTY has held that forcing a person to watch serious sexual attacks inflicted on an acquaintance constituted torture.[32] It has likewise held that death

[25] *Prosecutor* v. *Krnojelac* (Trial Chamber), para. 182. [26] *Ibid.*

[27] *Prosecutor* v. *Brdjanin* (Trial Chamber), para. 484; *Prosecutor* v. *Kvocka and others* (Trial Chamber), para.148.

[28] *Prosecutor* v. *Kvocka and others* (Trial Chamber), paras. 142–3. See also a similar formulation in ECtHR, *Kudła* v. *Poland*, Judgment of 26 October 2000, paras. 90–4; HRC, *Vuolanne* v. *Finland*, 2 May 1989, CCPR/C/35/D/265/1987, para. 9.2.

[29] *Prosecutor* v. *Limaj and others*, Case No. IT-03-66-T (Trial Chamber), 30 November 2005, para. 237.

[30] *Prosecutor* v. *Brdjanin* (Trial Chamber), para. 483.

[31] See H. Reyes, 'The Worst Scars Are in the Mind: Psychological Torture' (2007) 89 *International Review of the Red Cross* 591.

[32] *Prosecutor* v. *Kvocka and others* (Trial Chamber), para. 149.

threats, falsely informing a victim that his father had been killed[33] and obliging victims to collect the dead bodies of other members of their ethnic group amounted to torture.[34]

It should be noted that certain acts such as mock drowning or other forms of submersion in liquid, burns, electrical shocks, suspension, kneeling on sharp instruments,[35] flogging,[36] rape,[37] mutilation, the breaking of limbs, hyper-abduction (extreme stretching apart) of the legs, meet the threshold of severity per se, as they necessarily imply severe pain or suffering.

2.3 *Cruel or inhuman treatment*

While cruel treatment is prohibited in Common Article 3, inhuman treatment is not explicitly mentioned. It is, however, prohibited under the grave breaches provisions of the four Geneva Conventions – i.e. in Articles 50, 51, 130 and 147 respectively. Unlike torture, there is no treaty definition of cruel or inhuman treatment in either international humanitarian or human rights law. However, the contours of the definition are by now well established as a result of human rights jurisprudence and the case law of the International Criminal Tribunals.

2.3.1 Serious physical or mental suffering or serious attack on human dignity

As the ICRC Commentaries to the grave breaches provisions of Article 130 Third Geneva Convention and 147 Fourth Geneva Convention explain, inhuman treatment is a wider concept than an attack on physical integrity or health. It is intimately linked with the general rule that every person must be treated with respect for human dignity. According to the Commentary 'certain measures, for example, which might cut [prisoners of war or] civilian internees off completely from the outside world and in particular from their families, or which cause[d] grave

33 *Prosecutor* v. *Naletilic and Martinovic*, Case No IT-98-34-A (Appeals Chamber), 3 May 2006, paras. 294–5.

34 *Prosecutor* v. *Brdjanin* (Trial Chamber), para. 511.

35 For all of the preceding examples see the *Tokyo Judgment*, in Dr B. V. A. Röling and Dr C. F. Rüter (eds.), *The International Military Tribunal for the Far East, 29 April 1946–12 November 1948* (Amsterdam: APA University Press, 1977), vol. I, 406.

36 *Ibid.*, for all of the preceding examples.

37 *Prosecutor* v. *Brdjanin* (Trial Chamber), para. 485.

injury to their human dignity, could conceivably be considered as inhuman treatment'.[38]

This is also the ICTY's view. The Tribunal defines inhuman treatment as 'an intentional act or omission, that is an act which, judged objectively, is deliberate and not accidental, which causes *serious* mental or physical suffering or injury or constitutes a serious attack on human dignity' (emphasis added).[39] The Tribunal distinguishes the crime of inhuman treatment from the crime of 'causing great suffering or serious injury to body and health' by determining that attacks against human dignity, while included in the former, are not included in the latter, unless they caused serious mental or physical injury.[40]

2.3.2 Circumstantial criteria

For the ICTY the issue of 'whether particular conduct amounts to cruel treatment is a question of fact to be determined on a case by case basis'.[41] The Tribunal has likewise held that the duration of ill-treatment is not an element of the definition of the crime[42] and has found that conditions of detention, in particular, can amount to cruel or inhuman treatment.

The ICTY's case law echoes that of human rights bodies. According to the European Court of Human Rights, for example: '[i]ll-treatment must attain a minimum level of severity if it is to fall within the scope of Article 3 ECHR. The assessment of this minimum is, in the nature of things, relative; it depends on all the circumstances of the case, such as the nature and context of the treatment, the manner and method of its execution, its duration, its physical or mental effects and, in some instances, the sex, age and state of health of the victim.'[43] The Court has found treatment 'inhuman' because it was, *inter alia*, premeditated,

[38] See J. Pictet, *The Geneva Conventions of 12 August 1949: Commentary III Geneva Convention relative to the Treatment of Prisoners of War* (Geneva: ICRC, 1960), 627; see J. Pictet, *The Geneva Conventions of 12 August 1949: Commentary IV Geneva Convention relative to the Protection of Civilians in Time of War* (Geneva: ICRC, 1958), 598.

[39] *Prosecutor* v. *Delalic and others* (Trial Chamber), para. 543 (the emphasis is ours); *Prosecutor* v. *Naletilic and Martinovic* (Trial Chamber), para. 246; *Prosecutor* v. *Kordic and Cerkez* (Trial Chamber), para. 256; *Prosecutor* v. *Blaskic* (Trial Chamber), paras. 154–5. Note that the intent element is a function of criminal law and irrelevant for human rights or international humanitarian law violations.

[40] *Prosecutor* v. *Kordic and Cerkez* (Trial Chamber), para. 245.

[41] *Prosecutor* v. *Limaj and others* (Trial Chamber), para. 232.

[42] *Prosecutor* v. *Naletilic and Martinovic* (Appeals Chamber), para. 300.

[43] *Kudła* v. *Poland*, Judgment of 26 October 2000, paras. 90–4.

applied for hours at a stretch and caused either actual bodily injury or intense physical or mental suffering. It has, however, also consistently stressed that the suffering and humiliation inflicted must exceed the inevitable level of suffering or humiliation caused by a given form of legitimate treatment or punishment.[44]

The Human Rights Committee has similarly relied on 'all the circumstances of the case, such as the duration and manner of the treatment, its physical or mental effects as well as the sex, age and state of health of the victim' to determine whether a particular treatment could be characterized as cruel or inhuman.[45]

As with torture, it may be concluded that all the circumstances of a case have to be taken into account in order to assess whether the suffering caused by certain treatment meets the standard of seriousness. Relevant circumstances may include the manner and method or the institutionalization of the treatment, the environment in which the treatment takes place, its duration, the victim's isolation, his or her mental health or strength, the person's cultural beliefs and sensitivity, gender, age, social or political background, past experiences and the repetition or cumulative effect of several acts.

Similarly, as in the case of torture, there is no doubt that psychological effects in themselves can reach the threshold of seriousness such as to constitute ill-treatment. Prolonged incommunicado detention may, for example, amount to ill-treatment (or torture), because of the mental suffering caused to the victim as a result of his or her uncertainty about the length of detention, the accompanying social isolation and lack of communication with family and friends.[46] Similarly, prolonged solitary confinement can amount to ill-treatment (or torture).

2.4 *Outrages upon personal dignity, in particular humiliating and degrading treatment*

Outrages upon personal dignity have been defined in the Commentary to Article 75 of Additional Protocol I as 'acts which, without directly causing harm to the integrity and physical and mental well-being of

[44] *Ibid.* [45] *Vuolanne* v. *Finland*, 2 May 1989, CCPR/C/35/D/265/1987, para. 9.2.

[46] See HRC, General Comment 20 on Article 7, 10 March 1992, para. 11; Committee against Torture, UN Doc. A/52/44, para. 121(d); A/53/44, para. 135; and A 54/44, para. 182(a); Commission on Human Rights resolutions 2002/38, para. 14; 2003/32, para. 14; 2004/41, para. 8; 2005/39, para. 9.

persons, are aimed at humiliating and ridiculing them, even forcing them to perform degrading acts'.[47]

The ICTY has stated that the crime requires 'that the accused intentionally committed or participated in an act or an omission which would be generally considered to cause serious humiliation, degradation or otherwise be a serious attack on human dignity'.[48] Here too, it retained an objective,[49] as well as a subjective criterion. As regards the latter, the Tribunal has determined that '[t]he form, severity and duration of the violence, the intensity and duration of the physical or mental suffering, shall serve as a basis for assessing whether crimes were committed'.[50] It also determined that while the humiliation and degradation must be 'real and serious', it need not be lasting.[51] In addition, no prohibited purpose such as that required for an act to be characterized as torture is required.[52]

The Elements of Crime of the Rome Statute define the material element of outrages upon personal dignity as an act in which 'the perpetrator humiliated, degraded or otherwise violated the dignity of one or more persons' and 'the severity of the humiliation, degradation or other violation was of such degree as to be generally recognized as an outrage upon personal dignity'. The definition is, unfortunately, tautological. It nevertheless indicates that while the treatment does not have to entail the infliction of severe mental or physical pain, it must be significant enough if it is to be distinguished from a mere insult. Examples include: serious forms of racial discrimination;[53] not allowing a prisoner to change his soiled clothes;[54] refusal to provide timely medical treatment;[55] inappropriate conditions of confinement; forcing a prisoner to

[47] Y. Sandoz, C. Swinarski and B. Zimmermann (eds.), *Commentary on the Additional Protocols of 8 June 1977 to the Geneva Conventions of 12 August 1949* (Geneva: ICRC, 1987) [hereafter *Commentary to API*], paras. 3047ff.

[48] *Prosecutor* v. *Kunarac and others* (Appeals Chamber), para. 161. Considering the common element of attack on human dignity inherent in both the notions of cruel/inhuman treatment and outrages upon personal dignity, it will sometimes be difficult to distinguish between the two. Depending on the circumstances of a case treatment which is considered 'merely' degrading or humiliating could evolve into cruel and inhuman if it is repeated over a certain period of time or is committed against a particularly vulnerable person.

[49] *Prosecutor* v. *Kunarac and others* (Appeals Chamber), para. 162.

[50] *Prosecutor* v. *Aleksovski*, Case No. IT-95-14/1 (Trial Chamber), 25 June 1999, para. 57.

[51] *Prosecutor* v. *Kunarac and others* (Trial Chamber), para. 501.

[52] *Prosecutor* v. *Kvocka and others* (Trial Chamber), para. 226.

[53] *East African Asian* cases, 3 European Commission of Human Rights Reports 1973, 76.

[54] *Hurtado* v. *Switzerland*, Judgment of 28 January 1994, Series A No. 280-A, para. 12.

[55] *Ibid.*

relieve bodily functions in his or her clothing; enduring a constant fear of being subjected to physical, mental or sexual violence.[56]

2.5 *Practical challenges*

To reiterate what has been stated above: torture and other forms of ill-treatment are absolutely prohibited under both IHL and human rights law; also, the definitions of the proscribed acts overlap to a significant degree. Recent practice has nevertheless demonstrated that despite widely ratified treaty law and detailed case law the impact of the definitions remains tenuous because of lack of incorporation – or inadequate incorporation – into domestic law[57] and because of disregard for the prohibitions as such. It is probably fair to say that the fight against terrorism did not necessarily generate an increase in the incidence of torture worldwide (given that torture and other forms of ill-treatment remain rampant),[58] but has shed significantly more light on the legal questions arising from this practice. It is beyond the purview of this article to address the myriad domestic court cases, particularly in countries such as Israel, the UK or the US, and the other ways in which efforts to prevent or punish torture, cruel, inhuman or degrading treatment are being undertaken. Mentioned below are two issues which arguably remain insufficiently understood or regulated by international and/or domestic law and/or remain a protection concern in practice: the first concerns the practice of solitary confinement, the second the use of evidence obtained as a consequence of torture or other forms of ill-treatment.

2.5.1 Solitary confinement

While solitary confinement has been widely used in the fight against terrorism (and outside this context as well), it is submitted that the pernicious effects[59] of this often unlawful practice have not attracted

[56] *Prosecutor* v. *Kvocka and others* (Trial Chamber), para. 173.

[57] See the US Military Commissions Act of 2006, para. 950v (b)(11) and (12), at http://frwebgate.access.gpo.gov/cgi-bin/getdoc.cgi?dbname=109_cong_bills&docid=f:s3930enr.txt.pdf.

[58] See *Amnesty International Report 2009: State of the World's Human Rights*, at http://thereport.amnesty.org/en/facts-and-figures.

[59] A must-read account on solitary confinement and its effects was published in the *New Yorker* magazine. See 'Hellhole', by Atul Gawande, March 30, 2009, at www.newyorker.com/reporting/2009/03/30/090330fa_fact_gawande. See also Stuart Grassian

sufficient public attention.[60] This is partly because solitary confinement is not unlawful as such and because jurisprudence has not been sufficiently consistent to allow a more precise delineation of when it must be considered abusive.

The *Istanbul Statement on the Use and Effects of Solitary Confinement* defines solitary confinement as: '[T]he physical isolation of individuals who are confined to their cells for twenty-two to twenty-four hours a day. In many jurisdictions prisoners are allowed out of their cells for one hour of solitary exercise. Meaningful contact with other people is typically reduced to a minimum. The reduction in stimuli is not only quantitative but also qualitative. The available stimuli and the occasional social contacts are seldom freely chosen, are generally monotonous, and are often not empathetic.'[61]

In practice, solitary confinement is either the consequence of unlawful or incommunicado detention or enforced disappearance, or is applied in administrative and criminal detention (in the latter case either in pre-trial or upon conviction). Its harmful effects are fairly well documented: solitary confinement gives rise to a specific psychiatric syndrome which in severe cases is associated with agitation, self-destructive behaviour and overt psychotic disorganization.[62] Solitary confinement also 'often results in severe exacerbation of a previously existing mental condition, or in the appearance of a mental illness where none had been observed before'.[63] Just as important, although many of the acute symptoms linked to solitary confinement usually disappear when it ends, many persons subjected to this type of detention suffer permanent harm as a result.[64]

An overview of soft-law standards and jurisprudence confirms that solitary confinement is not seen as unlawful per se, but as in principle

'Psychopathological Effects of Solitary Confinement' in *American Journal of Psychiatry* 140 (1983), 1450–4.

60 The UN Special Rapporteur on Torture has contributed to reversing this state of affairs by recently publishing an interim report submitted to the UN General Assembly devoted entirely to the issue of solitary confinement. See Interim Report of the Special Rapporteur of the Human Rights Council on Torture and Other Cruel, Inhuman or Degrading Treatment or Punishment (UN Doc. A/66/268, 5 August 2011).

61 The Istanbul Statement on the Use and Effects of Solitary Confinement, adopted on 9 December 2007 at the International Psychological Trauma Symposium, Istanbul, at www.solitaryconfinement.org/istanbul.

62 Stuart Grassian, *The Psychiatric Effects of Solitary Confinement*, redacted version of a Declaration submitted in September 1993 in *Madrid* v. *Gomez*, 889 F. Supp.1146, p. 1 (on file with the authors).

63 *Ibid.*, 2. 64 *Ibid.*, 3.

undesirable and only a measure to be imposed as a last resort, and only if sufficient safeguards are in place.

Principle 7 of the *Basic Principles for the Treatment of Prisoners*[65] indicates that solitary confinement is in principle undesirable: '[e]fforts addressed to the abolition of solitary confinement as a punishment, or to the restriction of its use, should be undertaken and encouraged'.

The *Standard Minimum Rules for the Treatment of Prisoners*[66] do not address solitary confinement in general, but impose specific prohibitions and restrictions. They prohibit, in particular, 'punishment by close confinement . . . unless the medical officer has examined the prisoner and certified in writing that he is fit to sustain it' and subject to the limitation that 'corporal punishment, punishment by placing in a dark cell, and all cruel, inhuman or degrading treatment shall be completely prohibited as punishment for disciplinary offences'.[67] Similarly, the *European Prison Rules* prohibit placement in a dark cell, and all other forms of inhuman or degrading punishment.[68] Pursuant to the *Rules*, solitary confinement shall be imposed 'only in exceptional cases and for a specified period of time, which shall be as short as possible'.[69]

International human rights bodies have followed the same approach. They have not considered solitary confinement to amount to cruel, inhuman or degrading treatment, unless used for an excessive amount of time or accompanied by other restrictions that are so harmful to the individual that they may, taken together, be considered to have reached the requisite threshold.

65 Adopted by UN General Assembly resolution 45/111 of 14 December 1990.

66 Approved by UN ECOSOC resolutions 663 C (XXIV) of 31 July 1957 and 2076 (LXII) of 13 May 1977.

67 Principles 32(1) and 31. This could be understood as excluding this type of treatment only as disciplinary punishment, but not as punishment for criminal offences. However, that interpretation cannot be right as it would mean that cruel, inhuman or degrading treatment is allowed as a criminal sanction, which is incompatible with its non-derogable nature.

68 Rule 60.3.

69 Rule 60.5. Also, the footnote to Principle 6 of the *Body of Principles for the Protection of All Persons under Any Form of Detention or Imprisonment*, which prohibits torture or cruel, inhuman or degrading treatment or punishment, explains that: 'The term "cruel, inhuman or degrading treatment or punishment" should be interpreted so as to extend the widest possible protection against abuses, whether physical or mental, including the holding of a detained or imprisoned person in conditions which deprive him, temporarily or permanently of the use of any of his natural senses, such as sight or hearing, or of his awareness of place and the passing of time.'

The European Court of Human Rights (and previously the European Commission of Human Rights)[70] decided a number of cases involving solitary confinement. The Court rejects 'complete sensory deprivation, coupled with total social isolation', as it destroys the personality and constitutes inhuman treatment.[71] However, it does not consider that prohibition of contact with other prisoners for reasons relating to security, discipline or protection constitutes inhuman treatment in itself. To determine whether a certain detention regime amounts to inhuman or degrading treatment or torture, the Court relies on its established case law. It has, for instance, found that a prisoner who was kept in solitary confinement for over eight years with no contact with his family, other prisoners or the wardens had not been subjected to ill-treatment, because he had been frequently visited by his lawyer, doctors and others, and had had a TV, access to newspapers and books and could walk around a small enclosed yard for two hours a day.[72] In another case the Court did not find a violation of Article 3 in the case of the solitary confinement of a mafia member since he was not completely isolated: while there were restrictions on his activities, exercise and food and he had no contact with other prisoners, he could see his family from time to time.[73] In other words, the Court appears to be rather cautious to condemn solitary confinement as ill-treatment.

The European Committee for the Prevention of Torture and Inhuman or Degrading Treatment or Punishment (CPT) takes a similar approach,[74] but appears to be more inclined to criticize solitary confinement regimes than the European Court. It considers that there should be an absolute upper limit to the length of solitary confinement and that persons held in this form of detention should continue to be allowed activities and 'appropriate human contact'.[75] The Committee criticized the use of a so-called calming-down cell measuring less than 6 m^2, whose walls and floor were covered with padded black fabric, which had no furniture, and no access to natural light (there being no window), but

[70] See the cases of ECtHR, *Ensslin, Baader and Raspe* v. *Germany*, Decision on the admissibility of the application of the 28 May 1975, and European Commission of Human Rights, *Kröcher and Möller* v. *Switzerland*, *European Commission of Human Rights Reports*,16 December 1982, DR 34.

[71] *Ramirez Sanchez* v. *France*, Judgment of 27 January 2005, para. 100.

[72] *Ibid.*, para. 65. Three judges dissented from the judgment and considered that the solitary confinement of the applicant amounted to inhuman and degrading treatment.

[73] *Bastone* v. *Italy*, Decision of 18 January 2005, 5.

[74] *The CPT Standards*, CPT/Inf./E (2002) 1 – Rev. 2004, 17, para. 56.

[75] *Report on Norway*, 11 April 2006, CPT/Inf. (2006) 14, paras. 52, 56.

only dim artificial lighting. It held that '[p]lacing an aggressive and/or agitated prisoner in such oppressive facilities is unacceptable'.[76] In other words, whether solitary confinement amounts to an unacceptable measure will depend on the length of time, on the confinement facility and on other additional restrictions.[77] The Committee has also paid attention to the kind of outdoor exercise available to the prisoner and whether it could afford appropriate relief.[78]

For the UN Human Rights Committee, like the European Court of Human Rights and the CPT, solitary confinement does not in itself constitute cruel, inhuman or degrading treatment or torture, but 'prolonged solitary confinement' may amount to such treatment.[79] In assessing whether a violation of the prohibition of torture or cruel, inhuman or degrading treatment has occurred, the Committee relies on 'all the circumstances of the case, such as the duration and manner of the treatment, its physical or mental effects as well as the sex, age and state of health of the victim'.[80]

[76] *Report on Lithuania*, 23 February 2006, CPT/Inf. (2006) 9, para. 107; see also *Report on Azerbaijan*, 7 December 2004, CPT/Inf. (2004) 36, para. 133; *Report on Belgium*, 17 October 2002, CPT/Inf. (2002) 25, paras. 92, 95.

[77] *Report on Belgium*, 17 October 2002, CPT/Inf. (2002) 25, para. 116 for an 'adequate' isolation cell.

[78] 'On a more positive note, the delegation was satisfied that prisoners placed in disciplinary isolation cells were allowed 1 hour of outdoor exercise per day. However, the outdoor exercise facilities left much to be desired. Two of the so-called "exercise yards" . . . were in fact cages measuring some 3 m^2; such facilities are totally inappropriate for outdoor exercise' (*Report on the Russian Federation*, 30 June 2003, CPT/Inf. (2003) 30, para. 118).

[79] HRC, General Comment 20 on Article 7, 13 March 1992 (UN Doc. HRI/GEN/1/Rev.7/Add.1, para. 6).

[80] *Vuolanne* v. *Finland*, 2 May 1989, CCPR/C/35/D/265/1987, para. 9.2. In that same case the applicant was held day and night in a cell of 2 x 3 m for ten days. He was allowed to leave his cell only for purposes of eating, going to the toilet and taking air for half an hour a day. He was prohibited from talking to other detainees and from making any noise in his cell. His correspondence and personal notes were interfered with. The Committee did not find a violation of Arts. 7 or 10 ICCPR. In another case the complainant was 'detained in solitary confinement on death row for a period of five years in a cell measuring 6 by 9 feet, with no sanitation except for a slop pail, no natural light, being allowed out of his cell only once or twice a week during which he was restrained in handcuffs, and with wholly inadequate food that did not take into account his particular dietary requirements.' The Committee considered that these conditions of detention, taken together, amounted to a violation of Art. 10. (See *Kennedy* v. *Trinidad and Tobago*, 5 May 2003, CCPR/C/77/D/908/2000, para. 6.4.) In a case where a political prisoner was held in total isolation for a period of a year and was denied visits from or correspondence with his family, the Committee found that this constituted inhuman treatment in

Lastly, it should be mentioned that the Istanbul statement makes several useful recommendations in relation to solitary confinement: 'As a general principle solitary confinement should only be used in very exceptional circumstances, for as short a time as possible and only as a last resort.'[81] The statement stresses that the 'use of solitary confinement should be absolutely prohibited in the following circumstances: for death row and life-sentenced prisoners by virtue of their sentence, for mentally ill prisoners and for children under the age of 18'.[82] It is submitted that these recommendations should be relied on as minimum standards in assessing any regime of solitary confinement.

2.5.2 Evidence obtained as a result of torture or ill-treatment

The second legal and practical challenge to the absolute prohibition of torture and other forms of ill-treatment is the use of evidence obtained in contravention of the prohibition in criminal proceedings against persons suspected of terrorism. Two issues are of particular importance: whether the exclusion of evidence obtained by means of torture also includes evidence obtained through other forms of ill-treatment, and whether the duty to exclude evidence extends to so-called derivative evidence. While the law is silent, non-binding interpretation is evolving.

Under Article 15 Convention against Torture: 'Each State Party shall ensure that any statement which is established to have been made as a result of torture shall not be invoked as evidence in any proceedings, except against a person accused of torture as evidence that the statement was made.' Even though the wording does not explicitly extend the obligation to exclude evidence obtained by other forms of ill-treatment, the Committee against Torture has stressed that the 'obligation to prevent ill-treatment in practice overlaps with and is largely congruent with the obligation to prevent torture'.[83] It has specifically opined that '[A]rticles 3–15 are likewise obligatory as applied to both torture and ill-treatment'.[84] Moreover, Article 16 CAT (which provides that certain

violation of Arts. 7 and 10 ICCPR. (See *Polay Campos* v. *Peru*, 9 January 1998, CCPR/C/61/D/577/1994, para. 8.6.) In a case where someone was 'repeatedly subjected to solitary confinement and was held in the coldest part of the prison ... plagued with severe rheumatism in his spine which often prevented him from leaving his cell for a few minutes exercise when allowed', the Committee found a violation of Art. 7. (See *Conteris* v. *Uruguay*, 17 July 1985, CCPR/C/25/D/139/1983, para. 1.6.)

[81] Istanbul Statement, section entitled 'Policy Implications'. [82] *Ibid.*

[83] Committee against Torture, General Comment 2, Implementation of Art. 2 by States Parties (UN Doc. CAT/C/GC/2/CRP.1/Rev. 4 (2007), para. 3).

[84] *Ibid.*, para. 6.

state obligations related to torture also extend to ill-treatment) is not exhaustive; the inference may thus be made that the obligation to exclude evidence may be interpreted to apply equally to evidence obtained by means of torture and by means of cruel, inhuman or degrading treatment.

For its part, the Human Rights Committee has drawn a link between the absolute prohibition of torture and other forms of ill-treatment (under ICCPR, Article 7) and the right of a person not to be compelled to testify against him or herself or to confess guilt in criminal proceedings (ICCPR, Article 14(3)(g)). The Committee has stated that: 'It is important for the discouragement of violations under Article 7 that the law must prohibit the use or admissibility in judicial proceedings of statements or confessions obtained through torture or other prohibited treatment.'[85]

The prohibition on cruel, inhuman and degrading treatment in Common Article 3 to the Geneva Conventions, as well as in other articles of the treaties and in Article 75 of Additional Protocol I (which also contains the prohibition of coerced statements in criminal trials) may, it is submitted, be relied on to come interpretatively to a similar conclusion. Since Common Article 3 is a minimum standard of treatment, any act that could constitute an incitement to violate its prohibitions must be rejected. In other words, to prohibit cruel, inhuman or degrading treatment but to interpret the Article as allowing the use in evidence of statements obtained by such means would undermine the prohibitions. Not only would the perpetrator not be sanctioned for committing cruel, inhuman or degrading treatment, but the acts might indirectly be condoned by a court of law which would accept the direct fruit of prohibited conduct.

It is thus submitted that the use as evidence of any statement made under cruel, inhuman or degrading treatment, whether in peacetime or in a situation of armed conflict, must be prohibited. This applies not only to confessions made by the accused, but also to statements made by witnesses, as well as to statements by co-defendants or any other third person.[86]

[85] Human Rights Committee, General Comment 20 on Article 7, para 12, at www.unhchr.ch/tbs/doc.nsf/0/6924291970754969c12563ed004c8ae5?Opendocument.

[86] With respect to Art. 15 CAT, the UN Committee against Torture has criticized legislation which allowed statements by third parties: *Concluding observations, United Kingdom* (UN Doc. CAT/C/CR/33/3, 10 December 2004, para. 4(a)(i)); *Concluding*

The issue of the use of so-called derivative information or evidence, i.e. evidence obtained as a result of following leads given in statements made as a result of torture is trickier, for a variety of reasons. First, Article 15 CAT explicitly prohibits the use of *statements* (emphasis added) made under torture, not of other forms of evidence, especially not derivative evidence.[87] There is likewise no explicit prohibition on the use of derivative evidence in any treaty-based or customary law provision aimed at prohibiting torture or cruel, inhuman or degrading treatment. Second, a comparative analysis shows that national systems deal with the issue quite differently. While the doctrine of 'fruit of the poisonous tree' is well established in US jurisprudence,[88] other common law countries do not follow the same approach,[89] and in continental law systems the admissibility of derivative evidence will, broadly speaking, depend on the gravity of the error made in evidence gathering.

Third, several arguments can be made *pro et contra* the use of derivative evidence, of which only one set will be mentioned here. It is valid to say that to allow evidence which would have never seen the light of day had it not been for an act of torture is an incentive for torture. It is also valid to say that if the derivative evidence as such is reliable (e.g. bank statements, weapons caches, etc.) the common good is better served if a person suspected of terrorism is brought to justice. Whichever position one prefers, it is likely that the issue of the admissibility of derivative evidence, particularly in criminal proceedings, including those involving the cooperation of two or more states in the transfer of evidence, will become increasingly important.

3 Procedural guarantees for persons detained in the fight against terrorism

Procedural guarantees is a broad term that may be used to designate due process rights in both criminal and administrative proceedings.

observations, Spain (UN Doc. A/53/44, paras. 119–36, 27 November 1997, para. 132); *Concluding observations, Chile* (UN Doc. CAT/C/CR/32/5, 14 June 2004, para. 6(j)).

87 The Committee against Torture has sometimes criticized the use of derivative evidence obtained as a consequence of unlawfully extracted confessions. See Committee against Torture, *Concluding observations, United Kingdom* (UN Doc. A/54/44, paras. 72–7, 17 November 1998, para. 76(d)); *Concluding observations, Israel* (UN Doc. A/57/44, paras. 47–53, 25 September 2002, para. 6(k)).

88 For a recent update see J. Hochberg, 'Dining in Good Faith on Poisonous Fruit' (2009) 15 *Widener Law* 301, at http://widenerlawreview.org/files/2009/09/Microsoft-Word-07-HOCHBERG-FINAL.pdf.

89 See, e.g., in the UK *A and others* v. *the Secretary of State for the Home Department*, House of Lords [2005] UKHL 71, para. 16.

Fair trial guarantees in criminal proceedings, whether governed by humanitarian or human rights law, are essentially the same. The issue will not be dealt with further in this chapter except to point out that fair trial guarantees represent an area in which IHL and human rights law are complementary: on the one hand, the right to a fair trial is expressly protected under IHL,[90] which means that no derogation to the corresponding right under the ICCPR could be accepted as valid in a situation of armed conflict.[91] On the other hand, human rights law[92] may be relied on to inform the content and interpretation of IHL fair trial standards which, as just noted, are almost identical to the human rights catalogue.

The rules governing detention without criminal charge under human rights law are dealt with by other contributors to this volume and will be given only the briefest mention here.[93] In peacetime, criminal detention is the rule, while administrative detention a mostly infrequent exception. Where administrative detention is allowed, it must in all circumstances be supervised by a judicial body to which the person affected must have prompt recourse (habeas corpus or equivalent rights).[94] The relevant court must be able to order release if it determines that detention is unlawful, and the person involved must be able to seek compensation for wrongful deprivation of liberty.[95] It is fairly clear that a state would be obliged to derogate from the right to liberty under ICCPR Article 9 if it were to entrust the review of lawfulness of detention to a non-judicial body.[96] (It is somewhat less clear whether the obligation to derogate would exist where the state detains a large number of persons on security grounds in a non-international armed conflict while providing judicial review, but without pressing criminal charges for the same behaviour.)

It must be stressed that, regardless of the law, de facto derogations from the right to habeas corpus are frequent in practice, outside situations of armed conflict, and a number of anti-terrorism laws provide for long detention periods without any form of court supervision.[97]

90 See Common Article 3(1)(d), API, Art. 75(4).

91 Under ICCPR Art. 4(1), a derogation may not be 'inconsistent' with a state party's 'other obligations under international law' which, of course, include the Geneva Conventions and therefore Common Article 3. The Conventions have achieved universal ratification.

92 ICCPR, Art. 14. 93 See Chapter 15 in this volume. 94 ICCPR, Art. 9(4).

95 *Ibid.*, Art. 9(5). 96 See Chapter 15 in this volume.

97 See 'Malaysia's Internal Security Act: A Human Rights Watch Backgrounder', at www.hrw.org/legacy/backgrounder/asia/malaysia-bck-0513.htm. See also Pakistan Anti-Terrorism Ordinance (Ordinance No. XXI of 2009) amending the Anti-Terrorism Act of 1997, published in the Gazette of Pakistan, Extraordinary, Part-I, dated 1 October 2009, www.na.gov.pk/ordinances/ord2010/anti_terrorism_amendment_ord2009_250110.pdf.

However, it is the process due to persons interned/administratively detained in relation to an armed conflict who are deemed to pose a serious security threat, that has topped the list of controversial issues over the past few years. Outlined below are the basic rules governing wartime internment, the gaps in procedural protection with recommendations on how to fill them, as well as an overview of several practical challenges.

3.1 Internment in international armed conflict

By way of reminder, there are two types of armed conflicts under IHL: international armed conflicts are those waged between states,[98] while non-international armed conflicts are those waged between states and organized non-state armed groups or between such groups themselves. There is no doubt that internment is a lawful incidence of armed conflict, as reflected in the considerable number of rules devoted to this form of deprivation of liberty.

PoW status – and therefore PoW internment – exists only in international armed conflict.[99] Prisoners of war[100] are essentially combatants captured by the adverse party, who may not be criminally prosecuted for lawful acts of war, but only for war crimes, or other crimes under international law. In case of doubt about the entitlement to PoW status of a captured belligerent, Article 5 Third Geneva Convention provides that such person shall be protected by the Convention until his status has been determined by a competent tribunal.[101] It is uncontroversial that the Third Geneva Convention provides a sufficient legal basis for PoW internment and that the detaining state is not obliged to provide any review, judicial or other, of the lawfulness of PoW internment. PoW internment must cease and PoWs must be released at the cessation of active hostilities[102] (unless they are subject to criminal proceedings or are serving a criminal sentence).[103] They may also be released earlier on medical grounds[104] or on their own cognizance.[105]

Internment of civilians is defined as a deprivation of liberty that has been ordered by the executive branch – not the judiciary – without

98 See Common Article 2 to the Geneva Conventions. See also API, Art. 1.

99 The retention of religious and medical personnel provided for in the First and Second Geneva Conventions is outside the scope of this article.

100 Third Geneva Convention, Art. 4. 101 *Ibid.*, Art. 5. 102 *Ibid.*, Art. 118.

103 *Ibid.*, Art. 119. 104 *Ibid.*, Arts. 109(1) and 110. 105 *Ibid.*, Art. 21.

criminal charges being brought against the individual concerned.[106] Under IHL, internment (and assigned residence) are the most severe 'measures of control' that a detaining authority may take with respect to persons against whom no criminal proceedings are initiated.[107] Internment of civilians in international armed conflict is provided for in the Fourth Geneva Convention. The scope of persons protected by the Convention is defined in Article 4; it should be noted that the Convention does not apply to civilians who are nationals of the detaining state. There is some debate among legal scholars whether, on its own, the Fourth Convention constitutes a sufficient legal basis for the detention of civilians in IAC or whether it must be accompanied by domestic legislation. It is submitted that the former is the case.

The Fourth Convention provides different standards in terms of permissible grounds for internment depending on whether an internee is held in a state's own territory ('if the security of the Detaining Power makes it absolutely necessary')[108] or is held in occupied territory ('imperative reasons of security').[109] It has been suggested that the difference in wording simply indicates that internment in occupied territory should in practice be even more exceptional than it is inside the territory of the parties to the conflict.[110] The issue of grounds for internment will be dealt with further below.

The internment review process in the two international armed conflict scenarios above would appear to differ somewhat: for example, in a state's own territory internment review is to be carried out by 'appropriate court or administrative board',[111] while in occupied territory the Convention refers to a 'regular procedure' that is to be administered by a 'competent body'.[112] Despite these and other textual differences in the relevant provisions, it is well established that, in essence, the rules are the same: a person interned in an IAC has the right to submit a request for review of the decision on internment (to challenge it), the review may be conducted either by a court or an administrative board, and periodic review is thereafter to be automatic, on a six-monthly basis.[113] According to the general IHL rule, internment in IAC must cease as

[106] See *Commentary to API*, para. 3063.
[107] Fourth Geneva Convention, Arts. 41(1) and 78(1). [108] *Ibid.*, Art. 42(1).
[109] *Ibid.*, Art. 78(1). [110] See Pictet, *Commentary to Geneva Convention IV*, 367.
[111] Fourth Geneva Convention, Art. 43(1). [112] *Ibid.*, Art. 78(2).
[113] See J. Pictet, *Commentary to Geneva Convention IV*, 261 and 368–9.

soon as the reasons which necessitated it no longer exist.[114] Internment must in any event cease 'as soon as possible after the close of hostilities'.[115]

3.2 *Internment in non-international armed conflict*

While treaty rules on procedural safeguards for internment in IAC are rudimentary, IHL applicable in non-international armed conflict is even more sparse. Common Article 3 does not mention internment and the relevant customary law rule (applicable in both IAC and NIAC) is that: 'Arbitrary deprivation of liberty is prohibited'.[116] Additional Protocol II mentions internment in Articles 5 and 6 and provides guidance on certain aspects of an internment regime, but does not elaborate on the process due.

Lack of sufficient procedural rules in NIAC has become a legal and protection issue over the past several years because of the increased incidence of different types of non-international conflicts. Most pertinent for the purposes of this chapter is the classification, as an NIAC, of an armed conflict in which the forces of one or more states are assisting a 'host' government in fighting an organized non-state armed group (or groups) in its territory (hereafter 'multinational NIAC'): e.g. the current situations in Afghanistan and Iraq. These two contexts have been classified by a range of international organizations and scholars as having been international in nature between October 2001 and mid-2002 (Afghanistan) and between March 2003 and mid-2004 (Iraq), when the hostilities were interstate. At present, they are not of an international character because they involve a group of states, on one side, and non-state armed groups, on the other (in the Afghan case the Taliban, al-Qaeda and other organized armed groups; in the Iraq case a range of organized armed groups).

The paucity of clear IHL treaty rules governing internment in NIAC, as well as the already mentioned rudimentary nature of procedural safeguards in situations of IAC, led the ICRC to develop a legal/policy paper[117] on the minimum procedural rules that should be applied in all

[114] Fourth Geneva Convention Art. 132; API, Art. 75(3).

[115] *Ibid.*, Arts. 46 and 133(1).

[116] J.-M. Henckaerts and L. Doswald-Beck (eds.), *Customary International Humanitarian Law* (Cambridge: Cambridge University Press, 2005), vol. I, Rule 99, 344–52.

[117] See J. Pejic, 'Procedural Principles and Safeguards for Internment/Administrative Detention in Armed Conflict and Other Situations of Violence' (2005) 87 *International Review of the Red Cross* 375. It was published as Annex 1 to an ICRC report, *International Humanitarian Law*, see www.icrc.org/Web/Eng/siteeng0.nsf/htmlall/p0892/$File/ICRC_002_0892.PDF.

situations of internment/administrative detention,[118] whether in or outside of armed conflict. The rules are based on law and policy and are meant to be implemented in a manner that takes into account the specific situation at hand. Provided below is a list of the rules that are formulated as 'general principles' and as specific 'procedural safeguards':

General principles applicable to internment/administrative detention:

- internment/administrative detention is an exceptional measure;
- internment/administrative detention is not an alternative to criminal proceedings;
- internment/administrative detention can only be ordered on an individual case-by-case basis, without discrimination of any kind;
- internment/administrative detention must cease as soon as the reasons for it cease to exist; and
- internment/administrative detention must conform to the principle of legality.

Procedural safeguards:

- right to information about the reasons for internment/administrative detention;
- right to be registered and held in a recognized place of internment/administrative detention;
- foreign nationals in internment/administrative detention (right to consular access);
- a person subject to internment/administrative detention has the right to challenge, with the least possible delay, the lawfulness of his or her detention;
- review of the lawfulness of internment/administrative detention must be carried out by an independent and impartial body;
- an internee/administrative detainee should be allowed to have legal assistance;
- an internee/administrative detainee has the right to periodical review of the lawfulness of continued detention;
- an internee/administrative detainee and his or her legal representative should be able to attend the proceedings in person;
- an internee/administrative detainee must be allowed to have contacts with – to correspond with and be visited by – members of his or her family;

[118] The terms 'internment' and 'administrative detention' are used interchangeably.

- an internee/administrative detainee has the right to the medical care and attention required by his or her condition;
- an internee/administrative detainee must be allowed to make submissions relating to his or her treatment and conditions of detention; and
- access to persons interned/administratively detained.

Multinational forced internment in a 'host' country poses significant legal and practical challenges, which can only be addressed on a case-by-case basis. Certain legal and practical issues have nevertheless emerged as common and are briefly outlined below.

3.2.1 Legal basis for internment in a multinational NIAC

The fact that Article 3 common to the Geneva Conventions neither expressly mentions internment, nor elaborates on permissible grounds or process, has become a source of different positions on the legal basis for internment in non-international armed conflict, and in multinational NIAC in particular.[119]

One view is that a legal basis for internment would have to be explicit, as it is in the fourth Geneva Convention; in the absence of such a rule, IHL as a generally restrictive rather than permissive body of law in nature and structure cannot provide it implicitly. Another view – the ICRC's, for instance – is that both customary and treaty IHL contain an inherent power to intern and may thus be said to provide a legal basis for internment in NIAC. This position is based on the fact internment is a form of deprivation of liberty which is an inevitable and lawful incidence of armed conflict and that Additional Protocol II (which has been ratified by 165 states), refers explicitly to internment in Articles 5 and 6.

Whichever view one adopts, it is submitted that in the absence of any specific provision of Common Article 3 or of Additional Protocol II on the grounds for internment or on the process to be followed, an international agreement (treaty) between the multinational force(s) and the 'host' state should be concluded, or domestic law adopted, specifying grounds and process for internment in keeping with the principle of legality. In the latter case the domestic law basis should be provided by the 'host' state or, in exceptional circumstances, by the state(s) to which the multinational forces belong. Standard operating procedures of a

[119] See Report on the ICRC-Chatham House Expert Meeting *Procedural Safeguards for Security Detention in Non-International Armed Conflict*, London, 22–3 September 2008, at www.icrc.org/Web/eng/siteeng0.nsf/htmlall/security-detention-report-091209/$File/security-detention-chatham-ICRC-report-091209.pdf.

multinational force do not provide a sufficient legal basis for internment as they do not have the force of law.

Arguably, a UN Security Council resolution adopted under Chapter VII of the UN Charter[120] would also provide a legal basis for internment, although legal experts differ as to whether such a resolution must expressly authorize internment or whether the standard formula of authorization to use 'all necessary means' (to accomplish a mission) is sufficient. It is submitted that more specific rules on grounds and process for internment would be preferable.

3.2.2 Grounds for internment

IHL applicable in NIAC does not specify permissible grounds for internment. It is submitted that 'imperative reasons of security' is the minimum legal standard that should inform internment decisions in NIAC. This policy choice – drawn from the identical language in the Fourth Geneva Convention[121] – is recommended because, as explained above, the wording was meant to emphasize the exceptional nature of internment in situations of occupation where a state is responsible for the internment of non-nationals abroad. The proposed legal standard seems to be particularly appropriate in a multinational NIAC where foreign forces are likewise detaining non-nationals in the territory of a third ('host') state. It is believed that the 'imperative reasons' threshold strikes a workable balance between the need to protect personal liberty and the detaining authority's need to protect against activity seriously prejudicial to its security.

The exact meaning of 'imperative reasons of security' has not been sufficiently elaborated in international or domestic law to enable a determination of the specific types of conduct that would meet that threshold. As noted in the Commentary to the Fourth Geneva Convention: 'It did not seem possible to define the expression "security of the State" in a more concrete fashion. It is thus left very largely to Governments to decide the measure of activity prejudicial to the internal or external security of the State which justifies internment or assigned residence.'[122] The Commentary nevertheless adds that: 'In any case such

[120] For example, UNSC resolution 1546 of 8 June 2004 on Iraq: 'Decides that the multinational force shall have the authority to take all necessary measures to contribute to the maintenance of security and stability in Iraq' (UN Doc. S/Res./1546 (2004)).

[121] GC IV, Art. 78(1). [122] See *Commentary to Geneva Convention IV*, 257.

measures can be ordered for real and imperative reasons of security, their exceptional character must be preserved.'[123]

While states are therefore left a margin of appreciation in deciding on the specific activity deemed to represent a serious security threat, there are pointers in terms of what activity would or would not meet that standard.

It is uncontroversial that direct participation in hostilities is an activity that would meet the imperative reasons of security standard.[124] Conversely, internment cannot be resorted to for the sole purpose of interrogation or intelligence gathering, unless the person in question is deemed to represent a serious security threat based on his or her own activity. Similarly, internment cannot be resorted to: (1) to punish a person for past activity; or (2) to act as a general deterrent to the future activity of another person.[125] In addition, where sufficient criminal evidence exists prosecution should take place so that the person in question is given an opportunity to prove his or her innocence.

In sum, the 'imperative reasons of security' standard includes direct participation in hostilities, as well as other acts that are deemed to reach the requisite threshold. The standard is, however, necessarily high and careful evaluation of whether it has been met must take place in each individual case.

3.2.3 The internment review process

As mentioned above, the Fourth Geneva Convention provides a basic outline of the process of internment review in IAC. It stipulates that an internee has the right to request that an internment decision be reconsidered/appealed,[126] that such review may be carried out by a court or administrative board,[127] and that there must be automatic, periodic review of internment if the initial decision is maintained on appeal.[128]

The fact that IHL applicable in NIAC does not provide details on the internment review *inter alia* gave rise to the need to develop the

[123] See *Commentary to Geneva Convention*, 368.

[124] For the ICRC's interpretation of the notion of direct participation in hostilities, see N. Melzer, *Interpretive Guidance on the Notion of Direct Participation in Hostilities under International Humanitarian Law* (Geneva: ICRC, 2009), at www.icrc.org/web/eng/siteeng0.nsf/htmlall/p0990?opendocument.

[125] See Supreme Court of Israel (sitting as the Court of Criminal Appeals), Judgment in A and B versus the State of Israel, 30 June 2008, at http://elyon1.court.gov.il/files_eng/06/590/066/n04/06066590.n04.htm.

[126] GC IV, Arts. 43(1) and 78(2). [127] *Ibid.*, Art. 43(1). [128] *Ibid.*, Arts. 43(1) and 78(2).

legal/policy paper on procedural guarantees for internment mentioned above.[129] Among them is the requirement that an internee be informed promptly, in a language he or she understands, of the reasons for internment. Its fulfilment[130] has proven to be particularly problematic in practice. The reasons for detention provided by detaining authorities are usually of the most general nature, thus preventing the internee both from knowing the specifics of the activity alleged and from being able to effectively contest them in the internment review process. While the detaining authority's need to ensure operational security must be recognized, security concerns cannot trump its obligation to adequately inform a detainee of why he or she is being held.

The procedural guarantees text also posits that a person subject to internment has the right to challenge, with the least possible delay, the lawfulness of his or her detention (in Fourth Geneva Convention terms, to request 'reconsideration' or to 'appeal' the internment decision). The purpose of the challenge is to enable the review body to determine whether the person was deprived of liberty for valid reasons and to order his release if that was not the case. Mounting an effective challenge presupposes the fulfilment of several procedural and practical steps, including the following: (1) providing the internee with sufficient information about the reasons for detention, as mentioned above; (2) providing the internee with evidence supporting the allegations against him so as to enable him to rebut them; (3) ensuring that procedures are in place to enable a detainee to seek and obtain evidence on his behalf, with such procedures being explained; and (4) making the internment review process and its various stages known and understood.

Automatic, periodical review of internment is a further procedural safeguard identified.[131] Periodical review obliges the detaining authority to ascertain whether the detainee continues to pose an imperative threat to security and to order release if that is not the case. The safeguards that apply to initial review are also to be applied at periodical review.

For reasons of protection, internees should benefit from expert assistance in the internment review process. While assistance of counsel of choice is preferable and should be allowed or provided whenever

[129] See note 119 above.

[130] The right to information of the reasons for internment is provided for in Art. 75(3) API. The right to information of any person detained is also an obligation under human rights law, i.e. Art. 9 ICCPR.

[131] Periodical review is provided for in GC IV with respect to internees in a state's own territory and in occupied territory. See Arts. s 43(1) and 78(2), respectively.

possible, there is a range of other modalities that can also be explored, such as the appointment of personal representatives, detainee representatives, special advocates, etc.

Internment review must be carried out by an independent and impartial review body (which must be distinct from the authority that initially deprived the person involved of liberty, if the challenge is to be effective.) Where internment review is administrative rather than judicial in nature, ensuring the requisite independence and impartiality of the review board represents a particular challenge. Elements relevant to safeguarding independence and impartiality include: i) the composition of the review board, including the process of selection and appointment of its members, ii) board members' qualifications and training, iii) the terms and tenure of their function, iv) their insulation from outside influence and vi) their decision-making authority.

3.2.4 Judicial review of internment

While in international armed conflict internment review may be carried out either by a court or an administrative board, IHL is silent as to the nature of the review body in an NIAC. It is, nevertheless, fairly uncontroversial that judicial review of detention would be mandatory under human rights law in situations of 'classical' civil wars, unless the right to habeas corpus had been derogated from. The legal requirement of judicial review in situations of battlefield detention by multinational forces in a 'host' state is not established and would in many instances be unworkable in reality for a variety of reasons. There is thus a range of conflicting state practice and legal and scholarly opinion on this issue. It was this lack of clarity and the unresolved issues of interplay between various branches of international law that led the ICRC to identify, as a minimum standard, the requirement that internment review be carried out by an independent and impartial body (along with the other safeguards outlined above). The form of process that would satisfy this standard is to be assessed on a case-by-case basis, having in mind the legal obligations that exist.

3.2.5 End of internment

No body of international law permits indefinite internment as such. As already noted, the general IHL rule governing the duration of internment is that internment must end as soon as the reasons justifying it cease to exist. In view of the rapid progression of events in armed conflict, a person considered to be a threat at the time of capture might not pose the same threat after a change of circumstances on the ground. Thus, the longer the internment lasts, the greater the burden on the detaining authority to show that the concerned person remains an imperative threat to security. As regards the outer temporal limit of internment, the general IHL rule is that internment must end after the close of active hostilities in the armed conflict in relation to which a person was interned. The close of hostilities is a factual matter that is determined on a case-by-case basis.

Given the often voiced question of when the detention of persons captured in what has been called the 'global war on terror' could end, it must be emphasized that current facts do not support the proposition that there is (or was) a 'global battlefield', but rather a multifaceted fight against terrorism. When acts of violence and the responses thereto reach the level of armed conflict, international or non-international, IHL will be applicable. Outside armed conflict, the status and rights of persons detained will be governed by human rights and domestic law.

4 Conclusion

Whether the treatment of persons detained in the fight against terrorism is governed by international humanitarian law or human rights law the end result is the same. Both bodies of law absolutely prohibit torture and other forms of ill-treatment, regardless of the reasons for, circumstances of or type of detention. One of the more pernicious effects of the fight against terrorism has been the attempt to calibrate legal interpretations to different categories of detainees, based on the implied understanding that certain persons are not deserving of the full protection of the law. This approach is clearly unlawful, violates the notion of the inherent humanity of every person and has proven to be counterproductive in practice. The abiding challenge as regards standards of treatment is to ensure they are applied in keeping with the letter and spirit of the law, without distinctions of any kind. Specific challenges that have arisen or have been exacerbated by the fight against terrorism relate to interrogation methods (a check list approach cannot suffice), to the use of solitary confinement (it may only be used as a last resort for a very short period of time) and to the use of evidence in judicial proceedings obtained by means of torture or other ill-treatment (direct evidence must, at a minimum, be excluded).

The procedural rights of persons detained in the fight against terrorism have been more controversial both under human rights and humanitarian law, this issue being also a point of divergence between the two bodies of law. While human rights law allows administrative detention only under very strict conditions, including the obligation to derogate if judicial review is suspended, IHL regulates a different reality, in which the *raison d'être* of detention, and thus the rules, are different. Regardless of the divergence in legal regimes, administrative detention in peacetime and internment in armed conflict are often practiced without regard for the rules such as they exist. Rules or guidelines on detention for security reasons without criminal charge should be elaborated at the international level, at least for situations of non-international armed conflict, in order to properly establish the procedural rights of detainees. In the interim, it is suggested that legal/policy recommendations, such as those developed by the ICRC, may be relied on as a means of ensuring basic procedural guarantees in practices.

18

The legal regime governing the use of lethal force in the fight against terrorism

DAVID KRETZMER

1 Introduction

The case study that forms the starting point for this analysis involves use of lethal force by one State (A) against a non-state actor who is currently in the territory of another State (B). State A claims that the said non-state actor is involved in terrorist activities directed against it or its citizens, and that State B has failed to take action to apprehend him and put an end to his terrorist activities, because it is either unwilling or incapable of doing so. The question for discussion is which regime of international law applies to the action of State A.

In analysing this question it is important to distinguish between two separate, though connected, issues:

(1) legality of using force in the territory of another state;
(2) the right to life of the individual concerned.

1.1 Legality of using force in territory of another state

Article 2(4) UN Charter obliges members to 'refrain in their international relations from the threat or use of force against the territorial integrity or political independence of any state'. There are, of course, exceptions to this prohibition. First and foremost among these is use of force in exercise of the inherent right of a state to self-defence, recognized in Article 51 of the Charter.

The first issue in analysing our question is whether use of force against a person who is in the territory of another state involves violation of

Article 2(4). This issue is analysed in other chapters in this collection,[1] and shall not be discussed in this chapter.

1.2 The right to life of the individual concerned

This is the issue that shall be discussed in this chapter. It raises questions which are quite different from those that arise in issue 1.

The fact that a state has acted lawfully in interstate relations does not necessarily imply that its act is lawful vis-à-vis the individual concerned. Thus, for example, if State B agrees in advance to the actions of State A in its territory, those actions will not constitute a violation of State A's obligation under Article 2(4) of the Charter. This does not necessarily mean that the targeting of the individual concerned will be lawful. Contrarily, the fact that the act concerned is unlawful in relation to the state on whose territory the attack takes place does not necessarily mean that the act involves unlawful violation of the right to life of the individual concerned. Thus, for example, if the attack is against a person who is about to fire a rocket into a town in State A's territory, the act might involve justified use of lethal force against that person, even though it might still amount to use of force against the territorial integrity of State B.

There are four conceivable variations to the relationship between the lawfulness of the force vis-à-vis the other state and its lawfulness vis-à-vis the targeted individual: (1) the use of lethal force involves violation of the obligations to respect both the territorial integrity of state B and the right to life of the targeted individual; (2) it does not involve violation of either of these two obligations; (3) it involves violation of the right to territorial integrity of State B, but not of the right to life of the individual; (4) it involves violation of the right to life of the individual, but not of the territorial integrity of State B.

1.3 Two legal regimes

The use by state agents of lethal force against an individual may conceivably be assessed under two competing legal regimes:

(1) criminal justice/law enforcement regime;
(2) armed conflict/hostilities regime.

[1] See in Chapters 11–13 in this volume. Also see N. Lubell, *Extraterritorial Use of Force against Non-State Actors* (Oxford: Oxford University Press, 2010), chs. 1–3.

The difference between these two regimes is crucial. Whether employment of lethal force by state agents is lawful or not under international law will in many cases depend on the applicable legal regime. Under the law enforcement regime, the primary obligation of the state involved is to respect the right to life of every individual subject to its jurisdiction. Intentionally taking the life of an individual by state agents will normally involve violation of this obligation. The exceptions to this principle are narrow, and have to be proved on the facts of each individual case. In the case under discussion here the exception that could be relevant is that employment of lethal force may be justified when absolutely necessary in order to protect others against unlawful violence. This is generally taken to mean that lethal force may be used only when the anticipated unlawful violence is imminent, leaving no time for choice of means or use of other law enforcement measures to prevent it.[2] Under the armed conflict regime, whether lethal force is lawful or not will generally (but not solely) depend upon the status of the targeted individual. If that individual is a combatant (or fighter), it will be lawful to target him (unless he is *hors de combat*) even if he presents no imminent danger to others; if he is not a combatant it will be unlawful to target him, unless he is at the time taking a direct part in hostilities.

The rest of this chapter will be devoted to discussing which of these two legal regimes applies in the kind of case under discussion here. Inevitably there is considerable overlap with topics that are discussed in other chapters in this collection. I have touched upon extraterritorial application of human rights obligations, parallel application of IHL and human rights law and the notion of a transnational armed conflict between a state and an organized armed group. However, as these issues are the focus of other chapters[3] I have not gone into the questions in much detail.

2 Current legal position

2.1 *Guiding principle*

The general legal regime that applies to use of force by state authorities is the law enforcement regime. Such a regime must comply with the standards laid down in international human rights law. In cases of hostilities

[2] See G. Nolte, 'Preventive Use of Force and Preventive Killings: Moves into a Different Legal Order' 5 (2004) *Theoretical Inquiries in Law* 111.

[3] See in Chapters 14–15 in this volume.

that are part of an armed conflict, the law of armed conflict, often referred to today as international humanitarian law, becomes the *lex specialis*, and the lawfulness of lethal force will be assessed under its principles and rules.[4]

The answer to our question – which legal regime applies to targeting of suspected terrorists who are in the territory of another state? – is therefore: it all depends. *If* the use of lethal force has a nexus to hostilities that are part of an ongoing armed conflict, the LOAC will apply; if not, the law enforcement principles of international human rights law will apply.

2.2 LOAC

The law of armed conflict distinguishes between international armed conflicts and non-international conflicts. Under customary international law and IHL conventions IACs are interstate conflicts. Additional Protocol I to the Geneva Conventions provides that armed conflicts in which peoples are fighting against 'colonial domination and alien occupation and against racist regimes in the exercise of their right of self-determination' shall also be regarded as IACs. The classic type of NIAC is an armed conflict between state authorities and an organized armed group taking place in the territory of that state. There is some disagreement whether a conflict between a state and an organized armed group that transcends the borders of that state may ever be regarded as a non-international armed conflict that is covered by prevailing norms of international humanitarian law.[5]

Protracted armed violence between the forces of a state and members of an organized armed group could take place in the course of hostilities that constitute an IAC between two or more states. Such violence could also amount to an NIAC between that state and the organized armed group. Finally, the violence could amount to an NIAC which is taking place in a territory in which an IAC is also taking place, thereby creating a mixed

[4] I stress the point here that we are talking of hostilities that are part of an armed conflict, and not merely of an armed conflict. The reason is that within the context of an armed conflict there may be situations in which a law enforcement model would be the applicable legal regime. This would be the case, for example, in the maintenance of law and order by an army in occupied territory. See N. Melzer, *Targeted Killing in International Law* (Oxford: Oxford University Press, 2008), 241–78; K. Watkin, 'Maintaining Law and Order During Occupation: Breaking the Normative Chains' (2008) 41 *Israel Law Review* 175.

[5] For further discussion of this issue, see Chapter 14 in this volume.

armed conflict, which has both international and non-international aspects. Each one of these possibilities requires separate consideration.

2.2.1 International armed conflict

An international armed conflict is either an interstate conflict, or a conflict between a state that is party to API and the armed forces of a people fighting against colonial domination, alien occupation or a racist regime in the exercise of its right of self-determination. A distinction must be made between these two types of IAC.

Interstate armed conflict The classic IAC is an interstate conflict. According to the view of the ICTY Appeals Chamber in the *Tadić* case, an international armed conflict exists whenever 'there is a resort to armed force between States'.[6]

In IACs there is a fairly clear definition of combatants. Anyone who is not a combatant is, by definition, a civilian. Combatants may be attacked unless they are *hors de combat*. Under the principle of distinction, civilians may not be the object of an attack, unless and for such time as they take direct part in hostilities.

How do suspected terrorists fit into this picture? *We shall assume that such terrorists do not belong to the armed forces of one of the states involved in the conflict*. If they do, they may be the object of an attack at any time and place. However, what is the position on the basis of our assumption that they do not?

Article 4 Geneva Convention III Relative to the Treatment of Prisoners of War, 1949, defines which persons are entitled to the status of POWs. While this definition is seemingly relevant only for that purpose, Article 50(1) Additional Protocol I adopts the criteria of Article 4 in defining combatants for the purposes of the principle of distinction.[7] This creates some problems.

Article 4(A)(2) GC III provides that besides members of the armed forces of a state, persons entitled to POW status shall include:

> Members of other militias and members of other volunteer corps, including those of organized resistance movements, belonging to a Party to the

[6] *Prosecutor* v. *Tadić*, Case No. IT-94-1-A, Decision on the Defence Motion for Interlocutory Appeal on Jurisdiction, A Ch., 2 October 1995, para. 70.

[7] According to Art. 50, combatants are members of the armed forces of a state that is involved in the IAC, members of militia who fulfil the conditions of Art. 4(A)(2) and inhabitants of a territory who rise levée en masse to resist an invading force.

> conflict and operating in or outside their own territory, even if this territory is occupied, provided that such militias or volunteer corps, including such organized resistance movements, fulfil the following conditions:
>
> (a) that of being commanded by a person responsible for his subordinates;
> (b) that of having a fixed distinctive sign recognizable at a distance;
> (c) that of carrying arms openly;
> (d) that of conducting their operations in accordance with the laws and customs of war.

It is unlikely that members of a terrorist group could meet the conditions for recognition as combatants entitled to POW status under this provision. First, the provision refers to a militia, corps or movement *belonging* to a party to the conflict.[8] Admittedly this does not mean that there has to be a formal agreement between the state and that group. Informal or de facto arrangements may be sufficient.[9] Thus, for example, if members of an organized armed group are fighting alongside the armed forces of a state involved in an IAC, they will be regarded as belonging to that state party.[10] On the other hand, the mere fact that a state harbours a terrorist group, even allowing it to carry out activities from its territory, does not imply that the group belongs to that state. The US claim that the Taliban regime, which, at the time of 9/11 was the de facto government of Afghanistan, was harbouring al-Qaeda and allowing it to operate from the territory of Afghanistan, did not of itself mean that al-Qaeda was at that time a militia belonging to Afghanistan, although the position probably changed once the war started and al-Qaeda was fighting alongside the Taliban.[11] Second, even if it is argued that the terrorist group belongs to one of the states involved in the IAC, it will generally not meet the conditions of Article 4(A)(2). If the group is indeed a terrorist group

[8] See Pictet (ed.), *Commentary on the Third Geneva Convention Relative to the Treatment of Prisoners of War* (Geneva: ICRC, 1960), 57; *Military Prosecutor* v. *Kassem*, decision of Israel Military Court sitting in Ramallah of 13 April 1969, 42 *International Law Reports* 470 (1971).

[9] Pictet, *Commentary*; N. Melzer, *Interpretative Guidance on the Notion of Direct Participation in Hostilities under International Humanitarian Law* (Geneva: ICRC, 2009), 23 [hereafter, *Interpretive Guidance*], at www.icrc.org/Web/eng/siteeng0.nsf/htmlall/direct-participation-report_res/$File/direct-participation-guidance-2009-icrc.pdf.

[10] See D. Jinks, 'The Laws of War: Past, Present, and Future: Article: The Applicability of the Geneva Conventions to the "Global War on Terrorism"' (2005) 46 *Virginia Journal of International Law* 165, 181–2.

[11] *Ibid.*

whose members routinely carry out terrorist attacks, namely attacks against civilians for the purpose of terrorizing the population, the group will not fulfil the final condition of this provision: conducting its operations in accordance with the laws and customs of war, which prohibit making civilians the object of an attack. Furthermore, members of terrorist groups generally do not have distinctive signs recognizable from a distance. Nor do they carry their arms openly.

The notion, flowing from the approach adopted in Article 50 API, that members of organized armed groups that fight alongside a state party in an IAC but do not meet the conditions in Article 4(A)(2) Geneva Convention III are not combatants leads to an anomaly. Blindly following this approach would imply that by systematically violating the laws and customs of war, members of such groups would become civilians, who enjoy protection against attack not enjoyed by combatants. In order to avoid this anomaly, the recent ICRC *Interpretive Guidance on Direct Participation in Hostilities* takes the position that, *for the purpose of the principle of distinction*, members of armed groups that belong to a state that is a party in an IAC are considered combatants even if they do not comply with the four conditions in Article 4(A)(2) Geneva Convention III.[12] While the *Interpretive Guidance* refrains from using the terms 'unprivileged' or 'unlawful' combatants, the implications of the approach taken therein is that if the members of the armed group meet the conditions in Article 4(A)(2) they will enjoy the privileges of combatants; if not, they will de facto be 'unprivileged' or 'unlawful' combatants.[13]

What is the position of members of an organized terrorist group who take a direct part in an IAC, without belonging to a state that is one of the

[12] *Interpretive Guidance*: 'it would contradict the logic of the principle of distinction to place irregular armed forces under the more protective legal regime afforded to the civilian population merely because they fail to distinguish themselves from that population, to carry their arms openly, or to conduct their operations in accordance with the laws and customs of war' (22). Clearly this does not imply that such persons will be entitled to PoW status. In order to achieve such status the armed group must meet all the conditions in Art. 4(A)(2).

[13] *Ibid.* I am not going to discuss the question whether the demands of Art. 4(A)(2) are collective or individual. For differing views on this question see Y. Dinstein, *The Conduct of Hostilities under the Law of International Armed Conflict* (Cambridge: Cambridge University Press, 2004), 43; and K. W. Watkin, 'Combatants, unprivileged belligerents and conflicts in the 21st century', paper presented at Informal High-Level Expert Meeting on the Reaffirmation and Development of International Humanitarian Law, Cambridge, 27–9 January 2003, 9–10, at www.hpcrresearch.org/sites/default/files/publications/Session2.pdf.

parties involved in that conflict? Unless there is a separate armed conflict going on between one of the states and this armed group (a possibility discussed below), such persons will be regarded as civilians taking a direct part in hostilities.[14] The implications are that they may be targeted only for such time as they are taking a direct part in hostilities.

Some experts include within the term 'unlawful combatants' or 'unprivileged belligerents' all persons who are not entitled to POW status under the GC III but who take a direct part in hostilities in an IAC.[15] Under this view the term includes both civilians who take a limited, sporadic, part in hostilities, and persons who fulfil a continuous combat function, such as members of organized armed groups fighting alongside one of the states who do not meet the criteria of Article 4(A)(2) GC III. It seems that it would be preferable to confine the term 'unprivileged' or 'unlawful' combatants to those who fulfil a continuous combat function as part of an organized armed group taking part in the conflict. Persons who do not belong to the armed forces of a state or an organized armed group belonging to the state should simply be regarded as civilians taking a direct part in hostilities.

The difference between civilians who take a direct part in hostilities and 'unprivileged combatants' is not purely semantic. Civilians who take a direct part in hostilities lose their protection as civilians only for such time as they are taking such a part; under the prevailing legal view,

[14] *Interpretive Guidance*, 27. And cf. HCJ 769/02, *The Public Committee against Torture in Israel* v. *Government of Israel*, at http://elyon1.court.gov.il/files_eng/02/690/007/A34/02007690.a34.pdf. The Supreme Court of Israel held that the ongoing armed conflict in the Occupied Territories is an international armed conflict. However, since members of Palestinian armed groups involved in hostilities against Israel do not meet the definition of combatants entitled to POW status under Art. 4(A)(2) Geneva Convention III they must be regarded as civilians. The Court rejected the argument that under customary international law there is a separate category of 'unprivileged' or 'unlawful' combatants. It would seem that the Court could have reached the same result had it taken the position of the ICRC in *Interpretive Guidance*, namely that since the armed groups did not belong to a state involved in an international armed conflict they could not be combatants in such a conflict. But this would have required consideration of a question ignored by the Court: who are the parties to the international armed conflict that, according to the Court's decision, was taking place in the Occupied Territories? The original parties to the conflict which led to the occupation of these territories, Egypt and Jordan, have signed peace treaties with Israel. And Israel is not a party to API; hence it is not bound by its provisions that a conflict between an occupying power and a people struggling against an occupation is an international armed conflict.

[15] See K. Dörmann, 'The Legal Situation of 'Unlawful/Unprivileged Combatants'' (2003) 85 *International Review of the Red Cross* 45.

for the purposes of the principle of distinction, 'unprivileged combatants' may be targeted at any time, so long as they are not *hors de combat*..[16]

API IACs In situations where armed groups belong to a people fighting against colonial domination, alien occupation or a racist regime in the exercise of its right of self-determination against a state that is party to API, members of those groups will be regarded as combatants. While the main object of API in recognizing such persons as combatants was to grant them POW status if apprehended by the forces of the state involved in the conflict,[17] their combatant status also makes them legitimate targets, as long as they are not *hors de combat*.

How does the terrorist nature of the acts of such groups affect the status of their members? Acts of terrorism are by their very nature contrary to the laws and customs of war. Does this mean that members of such groups will forfeit their combatant status? Under GC III, if such a group belongs to a state which is a party in an international armed conflict, the fact that its methods of fighting are contrary to the laws and customs of war means that its members are not entitled to combatant status. Under API the position is different. While Article 43 demands that armed forces of peoples fighting against colonial domination etc. enforce compliance with the rules of international law applicable in armed conflicts, under Article 44(2) violation of these rules does not deprive a person of his right to be a combatant or, if he falls into the power of an adverse party, to be a POW. Thus, even if such groups systematically employ terrorism, their members shall retain their combatant status. While API is concerned with the rights or privileges of a person as a combatant, these rights and privileges come burdened with the vulnerability of combatants as legitimate targets. Members of groups

[16] It must be stressed that the category of 'unlawful combatants' or 'unprivileged combatants' is important only for the principle of distinction. When it comes to detention, persons who are not entitled to POW status must be treated as civilians, who may only be detained according to the provisions of Geneva Convention IV. See J. Pejic, '"Unlawful/Enemy Combatants": Interpretations and Consequences', in M. Schmitt and J. Pejic (eds.), *International Law and Armed Conflict: Exploring the Faultlines. Essays in Honour of Yoram Dinstein* (Leiden: Martinus Nijhoff, 2007), 335 and Chapter 17 in this volume. Below I discuss the view that targeting combatants is subject to the principle of military necessity.

[17] See *Commentary on API*, para. 1671.

who enjoy the privileges of combatants may be targeted as long as they are not *hors de combat.*[18]

2.2.2 NIACs

In the absence of an international armed conflict, a conflict between a terrorist group and the forces of a state could conceivably constitute a non-international armed conflict.[19] I emphasize the words 'could conceivably constitute' in order to make it quite clear that the mere existence of violence between a terrorist group and a state does not mean that an armed conflict exists.[20] The big question is, of course, when the struggle between a state and a terrorist group becomes an armed conflict, to which the rules of international law relating to non-international armed conflicts apply.

It is beyond the scope of this chapter to go into a detailed analysis of the criteria for categorizing a situation of conflict as a non-international armed conflict rather than one of disturbances, riots, domestic strife or criminal violence.[21] I will therefore only touch on the issue briefly.

In the *Tadić* case the Appeals Chamber of the ICTY held that a non-international armed conflict exists when there is 'protracted armed violence between governmental authorities and organized armed groups or between such groups within a State'.[22] While the protracted nature of the armed violence is certainly one factor to be considered, it is neither a condition *sine quo non*, nor determinative when present.[23] Two principal conditions must be fulfilled in order for internal strife to constitute an armed conflict covered by Common Article 3 of the Geneva Conventions: the intensity of the violence and the level of organization behind it.[24] Given the amorphous

[18] As pointed out in n. 12 above, and the text accompanying it, the position would hardly be different even if members of such groups would lose their right to POW status by violating the laws and customs of war.

[19] See *Prosecutor* v. *Boškoski*, Case No. IT-04-82, Trial Judgment, T.Ch.II, 10 July 2008, paras. 184–92.

[20] See Jelena Pejic, 'Armed Conflict and Terrorism: There Is a (Big) Difference', in Ana María Salinas de Frías, Katja L. H. Samuel and Nigel D. White (eds.), *Counter-Terrorism: International Law and Practice* (Oxford: Oxford University Press, 2012), 171.

[21] On the essential distinction between these two possible situations, see Chapter 14 in this volume; Lubell, *Extraterritorial Use of Force*, 105–11.

[22] *Tadić*, Decision on Defence Motion for Interlocutory Appeal on Jurisdiction, para. 70.

[23] See Melzer, *Targeted Killing*, 257.

[24] 'How is the Term "Armed Conflict" Defined in International Humanitarian Law?' ICRC Opinion Paper, March 2008; *Prosecutor* v. *Limaj*, Case No. IT-03-66-T, Trial Judgment, T.Ch.II, 30 November 2005, paras. 83–174; *Boškoski*, paras. 175–206.

nature of these requirements, there is obviously room for differences of opinion on whether the violence in a given situation meets the minimum demands in order to be regarded as an NIAC. Thus, for example, after violence broke out in the Occupied Territories between Israeli forces and members of Palestinian armed groups, the Israeli authorities claimed that the situation was one of active armed conflict.[25] Others thought otherwise.[26]

Article 1(1) APII provides that APII shall apply to those armed conflicts 'which take place in the territory of a High Contracting Party between its armed forces and dissident armed forces or other organized armed groups which, under responsible command, exercise such control over a part of its territory as to enable them to carry out sustained and concerted military operations and to implement this Protocol'. This sets a higher threshold than cases covered only by Common Article 3, encompassed in the demand for control over part of the territory of the state concerned and the ability to carry out sustained and concerted military operations.[27]

Whatever the threshold of violence required for a situation of conflict to be regarded as a non-international armed conflict, one other factor must also be present: the organized armed group or groups involved in such a conflict must be identifiable.[28] The nature of the parties determines whether a conflict is of an international or non-international character. Just as an international armed conflict is a conflict between specific states, a non-international armed conflict is between a state and an identifiable organized group of non-state actors (or between two such groups). There cannot be an armed conflict between a state and 'terror' or 'terrorists'.

Both Common Article 3 and APII refer to an armed conflict occurring 'in the territory of a High Contracting Party'. Relying on this stipulation the argument has been made that there is no such thing as a transnational NIAC, or a conflict between a state and a group of non-state actors that transcends the territory of that state.[29] According to this view, there

[25] See *Sharm el-Sheikh Fact-Finding Committee Report* (*Mitchell Report*), citing from statements submitted by the government of Israel, at www.mideastweb.org/mitchell_report.htm; government brief submitted in HC 769/02 (on file with the author).

[26] See, e.g., 'Legal Consequences of Israel's Construction of a Separation Barrier in the Occupied Territories', International Law Opinion *by Oxford Public Interest Lawyers*, February 2004 (on file with author), para. 115.

[27] See Chapter 14 in this volume.

[28] See Melzer, *Targeted Killing*, 266.

[29] See, e.g., discussion forum of *European Journal of International Law*: Attack on the WTC: legal responses' (Pellet, 'No, this is not war'; Gaga, 'In what sense was there an

cannot be an armed conflict between a state and a terrorist group that is not confined to the territory of that state. This view is taken by Professors Schmitt, Dinstein, Garraway in their draft *Manual on the Law of Non-International Armed Conflict*. These authors define non-international armed conflicts as 'armed confrontations occurring within the territory of a single State and in which the armed forces of no other State are engaged against the central government'.[30]

There are a number of counter-arguments. On the formal level it may be argued that the term 'in the territory of a state party' simply means that the Geneva Conventions apply to state parties.[31] Furthermore, as Marco Sassòli argues, if conflicts extending beyond the borders of a single state were not non-international armed conflicts, 'there would be a gap in protection, which could not be explained by states' concerns about their sovereignty'.[32] Sassòli and others draw the conclusion that even a transnational conflict may be a non-international armed conflict to which LOAC applies.[33] In judging whether a conflict between an organized armed group and a given state that transcends the boundaries of that state is indeed an armed conflict the criteria will be the

"armed attack"?'), at www.ejil.org/forum_WTC/index.html; R. Kolb and R. Hyde, *An Introduction to the International Law of Armed Conflicts* (Oxford: Hart, 2008), 106. Also see T. Franck, 'Editorial Comments: Terrorism and the Right of Self-Defence' (2001) 94 *American Journal of International Law* 839; who mentions that this view was advanced at a conference of primarily German international lawyers. And cf. R. Goldman, 'Certain Legal Questions and Issues Raised by the September 11th Attacks' (2001) 9 *Human Rights Brief* 2, arguing that there may be a transnational armed conflict between a state and an organized armed group. For an excellent presentation of the differing views on this issue, see Roy S. Schondorf, 'Extra-State Conflicts; Is There a Need for a New Legal Regime?' (2005) 47 *New York University Journal of International Law and Politics* 1.

30 M. Schmitt, C. Garraway and Y. Dinstein (eds.), *The Manual on the Law of Non-International Armed Conflict with Commentary* (Leiden: Martinus Nijhoff, 2006), para. 1.1.1. a, at www.michaelschmitt.org/images/Manual%5B1%5D.Final.Brill.pdf. The draft *Manual* was also printed as a supplement in *Israel Yearbook on Human Rights*, 36 (2006). In a commentary to their draft *Manual* the authors state expressly that NIACs do not 'encompass conflicts extending to the territory of two or more States'.

31 See M. Sassòli, 'Transnational Armed Groups and International Humanitarian Law', *Program on Humanitarian Policy and Conflict Research, Harvard University, Occasional Article Series*, winter 2006.

32 Sassòli, 'Transnational Armed Groups'. Also see D. Jinks, 'September 11 and the Laws of War' (2003) 28 *Yale Journal of International Law* 16 and 'The Laws of War: Past, Present, and Future: Article: The Applicability of the Geneva Conventions to the "Global War on Terrorism"' (2005) 46 *Virginia Journal of International Law* 165, 188–9.

33 Sassòli, 'Transnational Armed Groups'. Also see Jinks, 'Laws of War'; Schondorf, 'Extra-State Conflicts'; Melzer, *Targeted Killing*, 257–61; Lubell, *Extraterritorial Use of Force*, 99–104.

same as those to assess whether an internal armed conflict exists, namely the intensity of the violence, its protracted nature and the degree of organization behind the activities of the armed group. Thus, according to Nils Melzer, 'the modern concept of non-international armed conflict includes all situations of sufficiently intense or protracted armed violence between identifiable and organized armed groups regardless of where they occur, as long as they are not of an interstate character.'[34]

In summary: there is disagreement whether a conflict between a state and an organized armed group whose activities are not confined to the territory of that state could constitute a non-international armed conflict. The majority opinion would seem to be that if such a conflict meets the criteria for existence of an NIAC, the fact that it transcends the borders of one state should not mean that it cannot be categorized as an NIAC. Such categorization does not imply that the state involved in the conflict is free to ignore the territorial integrity of other states from whose territory the organized armed group carries out its activities. Whether it may do so or not will depend on questions which are not the topic of this chapter. These include the legality of using force against members of such an armed group who are in 'neutral' states, in states that harbour the group, in states that grant them active support and in failed states.

Assuming that there is an ongoing non-international armed conflict between State A and an organized group of terrorists, what is the status of the members of that group? International law relating to NIACs does not recognize that fighters in such conflicts should enjoy the privileges of combatants in IACs: immunity from prosecution for fighting and POW status if apprehended by the enemy. Hence it does not mention the terms 'combatant' or 'fighter', and consequently obviously does not make one's classification as a combatant or fighter dependent on compliance with certain conditions, such as wearing a uniform during military operations. Some experts reach the rather extreme conclusion that the law of NIAC does not include a category of fighters, but merely civilians who take part in activities.[35]

While international conventions dealing with non-international armed conflicts do not refer to combatants or fighters, they do refer to civilians. Thus Article 13(2) Additional Protocol II to the Geneva

[34] Melzer, *Targeted Killing*, 261.

[35] See University Centre for International Humanitarian Law, Geneva, Expert Meeting on the Right to Life in Armed Conflicts and Situations of Occupation (2005), 36–7, at www.adh-geneve.ch/pdfs/3rapport_droit_vie.pdf.

Conventions states that '[t]he civilian population as such, as well as individual civilians, shall not be the object of attack'. It has always seemed to the present writer that the very mention of the term civilians in the context of non-international armed conflicts rests on the assumption that in such conflicts there must also be non-civilians, namely fighters or combatants.[36] This view was adopted in the ICRC *Interpretive Guidance on Direct Participation in Hostilities*.[37] While not using the term 'fighter' or 'combatant' the ICRC distinguishes between persons who fulfil a continuous combat function and civilians who take a one-time or sporadic part in hostilities. The former are in effect combatants who may be targeted at any time. This follows the position in the ICRC Commentary on APII that those 'who belong to armed forces or armed groups may be attacked at any time'.[38]

2.2.3 Mixed conflict

I have presented the question above as dichotomous. If there is an armed conflict at all, it is either an IAC or an NIAC. In the former case, members of terrorist groups are either unprivileged combatants belonging to one of the states involved or civilians. In the latter case, members of such groups may be fighters, or persons who play a continuous combat role. Individual terrorists who do not belong to an armed group that is a party in the conflict must be regarded as civilians.

There is, however, a third possible scenario: that in the same territory there are two conflicts taking place simultaneously, one international, and the other non-international. In this scenario, the conflict between the states involved (e.g., Serbia and Bosnia, or US and Afghanistan) is an IAC; the conflict between one of the states involved in the IAC and the members of an organized armed group (e.g., Bosnia and the Bosnian Serb rebel forces, or the US and al-Qaeda) is an NIAC.[39] The legal regime applying to the non-state actors involved in the conflict will be the NIAC regime.

36 For a similar view see Watkin, 'Combatants'.

37 See *Interpretive Guidance*: 'In non-international armed conflict, organized armed groups constitute the armed forces of a non-State party to the conflict and consist only of individuals whose continuous function it is to take a direct part in hostilities ("continuous combat function")' (17).

38 *Commentary on Protocol Additional to the Geneva Conventions of 12 August 1949, and relating to the Protection of Victims of International Armed Conflicts (Protocol I), 8 June 1977*, para. 4789. But see below for discussion of the principle of military necessity and its effect on this position.

39 This was the view taken by the ICTY Appeals Chamber in the *Tadić* case: *Tadić*, Decision on the Defence Motion for Interlocutory Appeal on Jurisdiction, para. 72. Similarly, in

2.3 *Law enforcement*

The law of armed conflict is *lex specialis*: a special regime of law that applies only when given conditions exist, namely an armed conflict. Unless these conditions pertain, the general law that applies to use of state power will be the relevant regime. As regards the question which interests us here, the intentional killing of an individual by state authorities, the general legal regime of international law is international human rights law. This law is to be found in universal and regional human rights conventions. Many of its norms have also become part of customary international law, which apply even to states that are not party to the relevant human rights conventions and in situations in which a specific human rights convention may not apply. There is wide-scale agreement that the norm which lies at the centre of our discussion – the duty of a state to respect the right to life of individuals – has become part of customary international law.[40]

In addressing application of international human rights law to our question a preliminary question must be discussed: does the human rights regime apply to the actions of a state against persons who are not in its territory? This discussion must be divided into two parts: (1) application of human rights treaties to actions of state parties in the territory of other states; (2) application of customary international human rights law to such actions.

2.3.1 Extraterritorial application of human rights conventions[41]

The scope of application of a human rights convention is a function of the terms of that convention. On this issue there are some differences between the four conventions that are most relevant to our discussion: the International Covenant on Civil and Political Rights, 1966; the European Convention for the Protection of Human Rights and Fundamental

the *Case Concerning Military and Paramilitary Activities in and against Nicaragua* the International Court of Justice held that the conflict between the Nicaraguan forces and the *contras* was a conflict of a non-international character, while the conflict between Nicaragua and the US was an IAC (26 ICJ Reps, 1986 3, 114). And see C. Greenwood, 'International Humanitarian Law and the *Tadić* Case' (1996) 7 *European Journal of International Law* 265.

[40] See Y. Dinstein, 'The Right to Life, Physical Integrity, and Liberty', in L. Henkin (ed.), *The International Bill of Rights: The Covenant on Civil and Political Rights* (New York: Columbia University Press, 1981), 114, 115; Gormley, 'The Right to Life and the Rule of Non-derogability: Peremptory Norms of *Jus Cogens*', in B. G. Ramcharan (ed.), *The Right to Life in International Law* (Dordrecht: Martinus Nijhoff, 1985), 120; N. Rodley, *The Treatment of Prisoners under International Law* (Oxford: Oxford University Press, 1999), 178–9.

[41] This issue is discussed in detail in Chapter 15 of this volume.

Freedoms, 1950; the American Convention on Human Rights, 1969, and the African (Banjul) Charter on Human and Peoples' Rights, 1981.

The ICCPR provides that a state party undertakes to respect and ensure the rights enshrined therein 'to all individuals within its territory and subject to its jurisdiction'. Under the ECHR the duty of states parties is to secure the rights therein to everyone within their jurisdiction. The ACHR obligates states parties 'to respect the rights and freedoms recognized herein and to ensure to all persons subject to their jurisdiction the free and full exercise of those rights and freedoms'. The ACHPR requires states parties to respect the rights therein and to adopt legislative or other measure to give them effect. No express attempt is made to restrict this obligation towards certain persons (such as those within the jurisdiction of the state involved).

When judged on the basis of their formal wording the ACHPR would seem to have the widest berth of application, while the ICCPR's field of application would appear to be narrowest, applying only to those within the territory of a state and subject to its jurisdiction. The ECHR and ACHR would seem to be somewhere in the middle.

The extraterritorial application of the ICCPR has proved to be a bone of contention between some states parties and the Human Rights Committee, which monitors implementation of the Covenant. The Committee has consistently taken the position that the Convention may apply to acts of a state committed outside its national borders. It has opined that the word 'and' in the phrase 'individuals within its territory and subject to its jurisdiction' should be read in a disjunctive rather than conjunctive manner. In the Committee's view, the phrase really means that a state must respect the rights both of individuals within its territory and individuals subject to its jurisdiction.[42] Furthermore, the term 'jurisdiction' must not be taken so as to imply the sovereign territory of the state. Any person over whom a state exercises actual control, is, for the purposes of that control, subject to the state's jurisdiction.[43] This means that if a state has the power to intentionally kill a person, for the purposes of the duty to respect that person's right to life he/she is subject to that state's jurisdiction.

This view has been rejected by the US, which maintains that the ICCPR does not have extraterritorial application.[44] Relying, *inter alia*,

[42] HRC, General Comment No. 31, Nature of the General Legal Obligation Imposed on States Parties to the Covenant, UN Doc. CCPR/C/21/Rev.1/Add.13, 26 May 2004, para. 10.

[43] *Ibid.*

[44] See *US Responses to Selected Recommendations of the Human Rights Committee*, 10 October 2007, and documents cited by Melzer, *Targeted Killing*, 79.

on the *travaux préparatoires* of the Covenant the US government has argued that in order to be covered by the Covenant an individual must be both in the sovereign territory of a state party and subject to that state party's jurisdiction. According to this view, the ICCPR does not apply to US actions in a place outside its sovereign territory even when its authorities exercise de facto control over persons' liberty and lives.[45]

Application of the ECHR outside the territory of the state party concerned has raised other problems. As noted above, the ECHR does not require that the individual whose rights are violated by the state be in that state's territory, but only that he/she be within its jurisdiction. The ECtHR has vacillated in its interpretation of the term 'jurisdiction'. On the one hand, it has made it clear that persons may be within the jurisdiction of a state even when they are not in its sovereign territory, if they are under the effective control of the agents of that state operating in the territory of another. Thus, for example, persons in occupied territory are within the jurisdiction of the occupying power.[46] On the other hand, in the *Banković* case the Court refused to accept the wide, cause and effect, view of the Human Rights Committee, according to which if a state is capable of intentionally killing a person, for the purposes of the right to respect that person's life he/she is within the jurisdiction of that state.[47] In that case the Court also intimated that whether the ECHR applies to the actions of a state party in the territory of another may depend on whether the latter state is also party to the Convention.[48] In the *Issa* case the Court seems to have backtracked on this view.[49] In this case the Court stated that

[45] See M. J. Dennis, 'Application of Civil and Political Rights Treaties Extraterritorially During Times of International Armed Conflict' (2007) 40 *Israel Law Review* 453.

[46] *Loizidou* v. *Turkey*, Judgment on Preliminary Objections of 23 March 1995 [1995] ECHR (Ser. A).

[47] *Banković and others* v. *Belgium and others*, Decision on Admissibility of 12 December 2001 [2001] ECHR XII, para. 333.

[48] *Ibid.* For criticism of the idea that this judgment restricts jurisdiction of states to the *espace jurisdique* of the Convention, see R. Wilde, 'The "Legal" Space or "*Espace Juridique*" of the European Convention on Human Rights: Is It Relevant to Extraterritorial State Action?' (2005) 10 *European Human Rights Law Review* 115; T. Thienel, 'The Judgment of the House of Lords in *R (Al-Skeini) v. Secretary of State for Defence*' (2008) 6 *Journal of International Criminal Justice* 115.

[49] *Issa and others* v. *Turkey*, Judgment of 16 November 2004, App. No. 31821/96. For analysis of ECtHR jurisprudence on the issue of extraterritorial application of the Convention, see Michal Gondek, 'Extraterritorial Application of the European Convention on Human Rights: Territorial Focus in the Age of Globalization?' (2005) 52 *Netherlands International Law Review* 349.

> a State might also be held accountable for violation of the Convention rights and freedoms of persons who are in the territory of another State but who are found to be under the former State's authority and control through its agents operating – whether lawfully or unlawfully – in the latter State. Accountability in such situations stemmed from the fact that Article 1 of the Convention could not be interpreted so as to allow a State party to perpetrate violations of the Convention on the territory of another State, which it could not perpetrate on its own territory.[50]

In the *Al-Skeini* case the House of Lords followed the narrow view of the term 'within its jurisdiction' adopted by the ECtHR in the *Banković* case. The Lords refused to accept that the view expressed by the ECtHR in the *Issa* case should be seen as overruling the *Banković* decision. Consequently the House of Lords held that in parts of Iraq which were at the time occupied by UK forces, only persons being detained by the British forces were within UK jurisdiction, while persons killed by British forces in the course of security operations were not within that jurisdiction.[51] The applicants in this case took the matter to the ECtHR, which delivered its judgment in the case in July 2011.[52] While not overruling its *Banković* decision, the Court held that when a state party to the ECHR exercises 'public powers' outside its own territory, persons within the area in which it exercises such powers are within that state's jurisdiction. Consequently, the Court held that all the persons killed by British forces in the Basra area of Iraq during the period that British troops were responsible for law and order there were subject to UK's jurisdiction. The UK had a duty to ensure their right to life and had violated this duty by not holding an independent inquiry into the circumstances and legality of the actions that led to the death not only of the applicant who was detained but also of the other applicants who were allegedly killed during British security operations.

What does all this imply for the case under discussion here? Do the treaty obligations of State A to respect the right to life apply to individuals who are in the territory of State B over which State A does not exercise effective control? Or, to put the matter slightly differently, does the intentional killing by State A of a person who is in the territory of

[50] *Issa*.

[51] *R* (*Al-Skeini*) v. *Secretary of State for Defence* [2007] UKHL 26 [2007] 3 WLR 33 [2007] 3 All ER 685, at www.bailii.org/uk/cases/UKHL/2007/26.html.

[52] *Al-Skeini and others* v. *United Kingdom*, Judgment of 7 July 2011, App. No. 5572/07, at http://cmiskp.echr.coe.int/tkp197/view.asp?item=1&portal=hbkm&action=html&highlight=Al-Skeini&sessionid=77278065&skin=hudoc-en.

State B of itself imply that State A had the kind of control over that individual which is sufficient for its human rights treaty obligations to apply?

As far as the ICCPR goes, the jurisprudence of the Human Rights Committee on this question is quite clear. The very ability of State A to target an individual implies that for the purposes of its duty to respect that individual's right to life he or she is subject to the jurisdiction of State A.[53] Consequently, by intentionally killing that individual State A might be liable for violation of its Covenant obligations. This view is not accepted by all state parties to the ICCPR.

When it comes to the ECHR the answer is less clear. While the ECtHR's judgment in the *Al-Skeini* case extends the situation in which a state party's Convention obligations apply extraterritorially, that judgment falls short of adopting the line of the Human Rights Committee.[54] As the ECtHR's case law stands at present, absent some form of control over the territory in which the killing takes place, the persons killed will not be regarded as being within that state's jurisdiction. In a concurring opinion in the *Al-Skeini* case, Judge Bonello was highly critical of this position. In his view, when it is in the power of a state to observe or breach any of the actions required for observance of the rights protected under the Convention, that state has jurisdiction for the purposes of the Convention. For the moment, at least, this remains the minority view.

2.3.2 Customary international law

It is not necessary in this chapter to discuss the scope of human rights which have become part of customary international law. For there seems to be wide consensus that the right to life of individuals is certainly one of the rights protected under customary law.[55] While states may not have the duty to protect and ensure the lives of persons who are not in their territory, or other territory under their control, they do have the duty to respect the lives of such persons. By intentionally depriving an individual

53 See the Communication R. 12/52, *Burgos* v. *Uruguay* (1981), A/36/40, in which the HRC declared that 'it would be unconscionable to so interpret the responsibility under article 2 of the Covenant as to permit a State party to perpetrate violations of the Covenant on the territory of another State, which violations it could not perpetrate on its own territory' (176).

54 See M. Milanović, '*Al-Skeini* and *Al-Jedda* in Strasbourg' (2012) 23 *European Journal of International Law*, 121.

55 See Dinstein, 'Right to Life'; Gormley, 'Right to Life'; Rodley, *Treatment of Prisoners*; Melzer, *Targeted Killing*, 177–211.

of his life a state could be liable for violation of its obligations under customary international law, no matter where that individual happened to be at the time. Arbitrarily depriving a person of his or her life by state agents would therefore involve a violation of customary international law by the state involved, no matter where the individual was when he or she was killed.

2.4 *Summary*

(1) The normal international law regime that applies to targeting of suspected terrorists is the human rights regime, based both on conventions and norms of customary international law. There is some disagreement whether and when human rights conventions apply to the intentional actions of one state against persons who are in the territory of another state. Whether or not a specific human rights convention applies to the actions of a state in a given situation or not, under customary international law it is forbidden for a state to arbitrarily deprive an individual of his or her life wherever that individual may be.

(2) In a situation of hostilities that are part of an armed conflict, LOAC will apply to targeted killings that have a nexus to those hostilities.

(3) If the armed conflict is an IAC, the question of whether suspected terrorists may be targeted will depend first and foremost on whether those terrorists are combatants. Members of organized terrorist groups fighting alongside the forces of a state that is involved in the IAC will be regarded as 'unprivileged combatants'.

(4) If the members of a terrorist group are not fighting alongside one of the states that is a party to the IAC they will not be regarded as combatants in that conflict. Unless there is a separate NIAC taking place between the group and the state involved, their status will be that of civilians, who are protected against being the object of attack unless and for such time as they take a direct part in hostilities.

(5) Armed violence between a state and an organized terrorist group may become a non-international armed conflict. Whether it does so will depend on the intensity of the violence, its protracted nature and the level of organization involved. If such an armed conflict is taking place members of an organized terrorist group who fulfil a continuous combat function may be targeted. If they do not fulfil a continuous combat function suspected terrorists may be targeted only while taking a direct part in hostilities.

(6) There is a division of opinion whether a transnational conflict between a state and an organized terrorist group may constitute a non-international armed conflict that is regulated by the international norms that apply to such conflicts. The majority opinion would seem to be that if such a conflict meets the criteria of a non-international armed conflict (namely, intensity of armed violence, its protracted nature and the level of organization behind the violence), it may become a non-international armed conflict. This does not mean that the state involved is free to attack members of the armed group wherever they happen to be.

(7) In some situations there may be both an IAC and an NIAC taking place in the same territory. In such a mixed situation, whether a suspected terrorist may be targeted will depend on the place of the group to which he belongs in those conflicts. Unless he is either a combatant in the IAC, or fulfils a continuous combat function in the NIAC, he may only be targeted while taking a direct part in hostilities.

3 Practical challenges and outstanding legal issues

The existing legal framework of two competing legal regimes creates challenges on a number of levels. I shall consider challenges that relate to the following questions:

(1) scope of protection of the right to life under the two regimes;
(2) attempts to deal with armed conflict hostilities under a human rights regime;
(3) the indeterminate nature of the criteria for application of the *lex specialis*;
(4) lack of definition of 'combatants' in NIACs; and
(5) proportionality.

3.1 Right to life under the two competing regimes

The assumption in the above discussion has been that there is a clear divergence between protection of the right to life of suspected terrorists under human rights and armed conflict legal regimes. The conventional wisdom, presented above, is that under a human rights regime it is lawful to target a suspected terrorist only when necessary to frustrate an imminent attack on others. In an armed conflict regime, on the other hand, it is lawful to target a combatant as long as he is not *hors de combat*. Hence an attack against a suspected terrorist may be lawful even if he is not about to place a bomb or commit another act of unlawful violence.

If we challenge the premises on which the above analysis rests the disparity between the two regimes may be narrowed. Despite the accepted notion that under LOAC combatants may be attacked at any time, it has been argued that any decision to target a person is subject to the overriding principle of military necessity.[56] This is the approach taken in the ICRC *Interpretive Guidance on Direct Participation*.[57] Chapter IX of the *Guidance* pursues the line that 'the kind and degree of force which is permissible against persons not entitled to protection against direct attack must not exceed what is actually necessary to accomplish a legitimate military purpose in the prevailing circumstances'.[58] This 'does not necessarily imply a legal obligation to capture rather than kill regardless of the circumstances'.[59] However, when it is feasible to apprehend a combatant, or to use non-lethal means to accomplish a military objective, use of lethal force would be incompatible with the principle of military necessity.[60]

Even if we accept this view, lethal force in an armed conflict situation is not confined to the case of an imminent threat to life, since the risk to the forces involved or other factors, such as their lack of power and authority to apprehend a person who is in the territory of another state, may make apprehending the suspected combatant unfeasible.[61] In such a case the combatant may be targeted even if he does not pose an imminent danger. Nevertheless, subjecting use of lethal force to a military necessity test could go some way towards narrowing the discrepancy between the two regimes.

It should also be noted that the implications of subjecting attack on combatants to a test of military necessity are not confined to the duty to apprehend rather than to use lethal force where apprehension is feasible. The mere fact that a person may be the object of an attack does not necessarily imply that there will be a military advantage in attacking him. There could conceivably be cases in which targeting members of terrorist groups provides no military advantage to the state

[56] Melzer, *Targeted Killing*, 278–99. [57] *Interpretive Guidance*, ch. IX. [58] *Ibid.*, 82.
[59] *Ibid.*, 78. [60] *Ibid.* Also see Melzer, *Targeted Killing*, 397–9.
[61] The *Interpretive Guidance* states that the duty to detain a combatant rather than attacking him would arise if he could be detained 'without additional risk to the operating forces or the surrounding civilian population' (81).

involved. In such cases, use of lethal force may not meet the military necessity test.

The accepted notion that under a law enforcement regime use of lethal force will be regarded as 'absolutely necessary' only when needed to frustrate an imminent attack rests on the assumption that unless the attack is imminent law enforcement authorities have the power and capability of using other law enforcement measures. In our case this assumption is generally not valid, since the suspected terrorist is not within the jurisdiction of the law enforcement authorities of the state towards whose citizens the feared unlawful violence is directed. If the host state is either unwilling or incapable of preventing the terrorists' activities, arrest is not available as an alternative to use of force. The question for discussion must therefore be whether the demand that lethal force be used only when an attack is imminent remains valid in all circumstances. Might it be possible to argue that in certain circumstances use of lethal force could be absolutely necessary even when the unlawful violence by the suspected terrorist is not imminent? This may be the situation, for example, when a window of opportunity exists of using force against a person who is actively involved in directing or carrying out terrorist actions and who has in the past eluded apprehension. If there is a high risk that unless the person is targeted he will direct and carry out further terrorist acts, it may be argued that use of lethal force may be absolutely necessary to protect others against those acts.

The view that lethal force may not be employed even during an armed conflict if there is a non-lethal alternative may also rest on the idea of parallel application of the two legal regimes under consideration here. While the lawfulness of a targeted killing that takes place in the course of an armed conflict will be assessed under the *lex specialis*, namely LOAC, certain aspects of the law enforcement regime may still be applicable. Rather than resting the demand for arrest on the lack of military necessity when apprehension of a combatant is feasible, it may rest on a model of parallel application of LOAC and human rights law. Under this model the demand for use of lethal force only as a last resort does not fall away simply because an armed conflict exists.[62]

[62] I have developed this argument elsewhere: see D. Kretzmer, 'Targeting Killing of Suspected Terrorists: Extra-Judicial Executions or Legitimate Means of Defence?' (2005) 16 *European Journal of International Law* 171.

3.2 *Armed conflicts under a human rights regime*

There are institutional reasons why attempts may be made to place armed conflict situations in a law enforcement framework which rests on international human rights rather than LOAC norms. As there are no international tribunals with jurisdiction to entertain individual suits against states for violations of LOAC, victims of such alleged violations or family members of such victims have invoked the jurisdiction of human rights tribunals. There is a growing body of jurisprudence both of the ECtHR and the Inter-American Court of Human Rights that deals with situations of hostilities. While the Inter-American Commission on Human Rights has been prepared to apply LOAC norms,[63] and the Inter-American Court of Human Rights considers such norms in interpreting the ACHR,[64] the ECtHR has remained within the confines of the ECHR, dealing with lethal force in armed conflict situations under a human rights regime, rather than a LOAC regime. In doing so it seems to have relaxed some of the assumptions regarding use of lethal force under a human rights regime so as to cater for the special conditions of organized armed violence.[65]

The Court's decisions in some of these cases reveal that in situations of armed conflict the Court is prepared to accept that use of lethal force may be considered absolutely necessary even when the risk of unlawful violence against which it protects is not imminent.[66] The clearest

[63] See *Case of Juan Carlos Abella* (Argentina) (*La Tablada* Case), IACtHR, Case 11.137 (1997).

[64] See *Las Palmeras Case*, Judgment on Preliminary Objections of 4 February 2000, IACtHR (Ser. C) No. 67 (2000); *Bámaca Velásquez Case*, Judgment of 22 February 2002, IACtHR (Ser. C) No. 91 (2002). In the latter case the Court declared: 'Although the Court lacks competence to declare that a State is internationally responsible for the violation of international treaties that do not grant it such competence, it can observe that certain acts or omissions that violate human rights, pursuant to the treaties that they do have competence to apply, also violate other international instruments for the protection of the individual, such as the 1949 Geneva Conventions and, in particular, common Article 3' (para. 208).

[65] For consideration of the Court's decisions in these cases, see H.-J. Heintze, 'The European Court of Human Rights and the Implementation of Human Rights Standards During Armed Conflicts' (2006) 45 *German Year Book International Law* 60; W. Abresch, 'A Human Rights Law of Internal Armed Conflict: the European Court of Human Rights in Chechnya' (2005) 16 *European Journal of International Law* 741; G. Gaggioli and R. Kolb, 'A Right to Life in Armed Conflicts: The Contribution of the European Court of Human Rights' (2007) 37 *Israel Year Book Human Rights* 115; Melzer, *Targeted Killing*, 382–93.

[66] See Melzer, *Targeted Killing*, 389.

expression of this is a dictum in the case of *Isayeva et al* v. *Russia*. In that case the Court considered an aerial attack on a convoy of Chechnyan fighters. While there was no evidence that the attack was needed to thwart an imminent use of unlawful violence, the Court declared that given the context of the conflict in Chechnya at the time it would assume 'that the military reasonably considered that there was an attack or a risk of an attack from illegal insurgents, and that the air strike was a legitimate response to that attack'.[67]

In light of the judgments of the ECtHR in armed conflict cases, Nils Melzer has argued that while formally examining the cases under the norms of the ECHR the Court has in fact used a paradigm of hostilities.[68] It must be remembered, however, that in none of the cases did the state involved argue that an armed conflict was taking place and that its actions should be assessed by LOAC. On the contrary, even when the applicants and NGOs whose briefs were submitted tried to base their complaints on LOAC norms, the respondent state attempted to justify its actions under Article 2 ECHR, as being absolutely necessary to protect persons against unlawful violence.[69] In the one judicial decision dealing directly with targeted killing of suspected terrorists – that of the Supreme Court of Israel in the *PCATI* case[70] – the Court was not institutionally confined to either human rights law or LOAC. It accepted the government argument that the relevant legal regime was the LOAC regime, although in describing the applicable norms it incorporated certain norms that are part of a law enforcement regime.[71]

3.3 *Indeterminacy of applicable regime*

While the conditions for existence of an interstate conflict are clear, those for the existence of a non-international armed conflict are

[67] *Isayeva et al.* v. *Russia*, Judgment of 24 February 2005, App. Nos. 57947/00, 57948/00 and 57949/00, para. 181.

[68] Melzer, *Targeted Killing*, 392–3. Support for this view is the frequent reference by the Court to the failure of the authorities to take precautions to avoid harm to civilians, a term that belongs to the realm of armed conflict and has no relevance in a pure human rights or law enforcement approach, which steers away from distinctions between individuals on the basis of their status or group membership.

[69] See, e.g., *Isayeva et al.* v. *Russia*; *Isayeva* v. *Russia*, Judgment of 24 February 2005, App. No. 57950/00.

[70] HCJ 769/02.

[71] See R. S. Schondorf, 'The *Targeted Killings* Judgment: A Preliminary Assessment' (2007) 5 *Journal of International Criminal Law* 301.

indeterminate. Hence, there is often room for disagreement whether such a conflict is taking place or not. The uncertainty whether a given situation may indeed be classified as a non-international armed conflict revolves around two questions: (1) evaluation of the facts in a given context, namely whether the intensity of armed violence and degree of organization justify categorizing the situation as one of armed conflict, rather than criminal activity, riots or disturbances; and (2) disagreement on the legal question of whether a transnational conflict between a state and a terrorist group may ever be regarded as a non-international armed conflict. These are both issues that require further discussion.

It seems to me that this discussion must attempt to clarify a number of points:

(1) As mentioned above, categorization of a conflict with a transnational terrorist group as an armed conflict does not imply that the state involved in that conflict is free to attack members of that group, wherever they may be. What needs to be considered is an integrative approach that considers the two questions – the right to use force against the territorial integrity of another state and the right to attack members of the terrorist group – together, and forges an accepted legal framework for use of state force against terrorists who are outside the territory of the state involved.[72]

(2) Is it possible to forge more determinate criteria for deciding whether a given situation meets the conditions required to classify it as an armed conflict situation of a non-international character? Given the serious implications of moving from a law enforcement to an armed conflict model, I have argued elsewhere that the threshold of violence and organization should be high.[73] Even if we accept this view it would be helpful if we were to develop fairly clear parameters for the existence of a non-international armed conflict.

(3) There is some disagreement when an international armed conflict ends. The position in non-international conflicts is especially complex. As the very existence of such a conflict depends on an assessment of the intensity of the violence and level of organization involved, what happens when the intensity or level are reduced?

[72] For a recent attempt to forge such an integral approach, see T. Reinold, 'State Weakness, Irregular Warfare, and the Right to Self-Defense Post-9/11' (2011) 105 *American Journal of International Law* 244.

[73] See D. Kretzmer, 'Rethinking the Application of IHL in Non-International Armed Conflicts' (2009) 42 *Israel Law Review* 1.

Does this mean that the situation is no longer one of armed conflict, and must be treated as a law enforcement situation? Or do we draw a parallel to the criteria of Geneva Convention IV dealing with international armed conflicts, according to which IHL ceases to apply only on general close of hostilities? If the latter, the state involved would be allowed to employ the hostilities paradigm, with all that it implies vis-à-vis the right to use lethal force against members of the terrorist group, even when law enforcement mechanisms would seem to be adequate. If the former, the situation could fluctuate between armed conflict and law enforcement regimes, thus heightening the legal uncertainty at any given time.

3.4 'Combatants' in NIACs

The principle of distinction is the linchpin of international humanitarian law. Combatants are legitimate targets; non-combatants, or civilians, are not. This principle applies both in international and non-international armed conflicts. The problem is, of course, that international conventions relating to non-international armed conflicts do not recognize a category of combatants or fighters and consequently they do not require that non-civilians wear uniforms or recognizable insignia.

We have seen above that notwithstanding this lacuna in the international conventions, members of organized armed groups who fulfil a continuous combat function in an NIAC may be targeted at any time.[74] This raises serious issues of identification. On what basis may the state involved in the armed conflict decide that a certain individual is indeed a fighter? In many cases the answer is intelligence information. But such information may often be wrong. And like all other intelligence information it suffers from an inherent lack of transparency. Hence, one of the pitfalls of the armed conflict regime in the context of the fight against a terrorist group is that in practice it legitimizes use of lethal force by state authorities against persons whom they have labelled as terrorists or members of organized armed groups. Unless a system of accountability is set in place, there is a serious danger that this power of the state will be misused or abused.

There are a number of ways to mitigate this danger, which is inherent in any non-international armed conflict situation, but may well be

[74] As stated above, according to the *Interpretive Guidance* this is subject to the overriding principle of military necessity.

aggravated in situations of organized terrorist groups operating from the territory of another state. First, even if we accept the view that in a normal armed conflict situation it is not incumbent on belligerents to attempt to apprehend enemy combatants before using lethal force against them, in the murky situation of suspected terrorist groups states should face such a duty. In its judgment in the *PCATI* case, the Supreme Court of Israel accepted this, although it refrained from explaining the legal basis for the said duty.[75] As we have seen above, this duty could be based on one or both of two legal grounds: lack of military necessity when apprehension of the suspected terrorist is feasible, and parallel application of human rights norms which require that use of lethal force should be a last resort, to be employed only when other means are unavailable.[76]

A second mechanism for mitigating the dangers inherent in allowing a state to target suspected terrorists is the requirement for an investigation after every such targeting so as to ensure that the targeting decision did indeed rest on credible information and a reasonable assessment that apprehending the targeted individual was not a feasible alternative. The demand for such an investigation rests on well-developed jurisprudence of the ECtHR and the Human Rights Committee that state authorities have a duty to carry out an investigation in cases in which persons have been killed by law enforcement authorities.[77] In armed conflict situations there is no general demand for an investigation based purely on the lethal consequences of state action. Rather such demand exists only when there is prima facie evidence that a grave violation of LOAC has been committed. Given the mixed and problematical nature of targeted killings of

[75] HCJ 769/02.

[76] These two legal grounds do not necessarily lead to the same result in concrete circumstances. Under a law enforcement regime the use of lethal force must be 'absolutely necessary', thus implying that law enforcement authorities have to face a certain amount of risk before resorting to lethal force. Under the military necessity doctrine, the forces of one side do not have to take risk to themselves in order to apprehend a combatant rather than using lethal force against him. This is conceded in the *Interpretive Guidance*.

[77] See, e.g., *Güleç* v. *Turkey*, Judgment of 27 July 1998 [1998] ECHR IV; *McKerr* v. *United Kingdom*, Judgment of 4 May 2001 [2001] ECHR III; *Jordan* v. *United Kingdom*, Judgment of 4 May 2001, App. No. 24746/94; *Kelley and others* v. *United Kingdom*, Judgment of 4 May 2001, App. No. 30054/96; *Shanaghan* v. *United Kingdom*, Judgment of 4 May 2001, App. No. 37115/97; *Isayeva* v. *Russia*; *Khamila Isayeva* v. *Russia*, Judgment of 15 November 2007, App. No. 6846/02; *Al-Skeini*. For views of the HRC, see, e.g., HRC, *Herrera Rubio* v. *Colombia*, Views of 2 November 1987 Communication No. 161/1983 (UN Doc. CCPR/C/31/D/161/1983, 2 November 1987, para. 11) and General Comment No. 31, para. 8.

suspected terrorists this demand should be valid no matter which legal regime applies. This was accepted by the Supreme Court of Israel in its decision in the *PCATI* case.[78]

3.5 *Proportionality*

Like every other attack on a legitimate military target, use of lethal force against a member of an organized armed group involved in an armed conflict with a state is subject to the principle of proportionality. Thus, if civilians are likely to be harmed in the attack it will be unlawful if the expected harm is excessive in relation to the anticipated direct military advantage involved in targeting the member of the armed group.

It is notoriously difficult to decide how this proportionality test is to be applied in concrete circumstances. There will inevitably be differences of opinion on this question between human rights NGOs and military officers or other officials involved in counter-terrorist action. It is not possible to provide guidelines that will help in weighing expected harm against anticipated direct military advantage. Nevertheless, it is suggested that there should be a presumption that death or serious wounding of civilians would normally be excessive in relation to the anticipated direct military advantage in targeting an individual member of an armed group. In order to refute the presumption evidence would be needed on the concrete military advantage anticipated from targeting the specific individual member of the armed group.

4 Recommendations

The existence of two competing legal regimes which could conceivably apply to targeted killing of suspected terrorists leads to confusion and to self-serving uses of law. While in the past it was generally assumed that states would be reluctant to invoke IHL or LOAC in conflicts with non-state actors, the rise of transnational terrorism has led some states involved to invoke the 'war model' in their fight against terrorism. They have done so, of course, because of their perception that such a model frees them from the constraints of law enforcement, allowing them to use lethal force against suspected terrorists even when that force is not required to frustrate an imminent terrorist attack. As suspected terrorists are either 'unprivileged combatants' in an IAC, or

[78] HCJ 769/02.

fighters in an NIAC who do not enjoy the privileges of combatants in an IAC, use of this model is largely costless for the state.

The strategic and self-serving use of the armed conflict, rather than the law enforcement regime, exposes the inherent difficulties of the law of armed conflict in non-symmetrical armed conflict. It is all too easy, however, to simply dismiss the armed conflict regime as irrelevant and to argue that all anti-terrorist activities must conform to the law enforcement model. The case under discussion illustrates that point well. When terrorists are operating out of a host state that cannot or will not take effective action to curb their activities, restricting the 'victim state' to the law enforcement regime may amount to saying that it is prevented from taking effective action to protect its citizens and residents from violence.

Thus it is essential to clarify the borders between the law enforcement and armed conflict regimes. In this paper I have tried to point to the different possibilities and the criteria for distinguishing between organized armed groups who belong to a party to an IAC, organized armed groups who are involved in an NIAC with a state, mixed armed conflict situations that have both an international and non-international character, situations of violence by organized armed groups that do not constitute an armed conflict, and actions by individual terrorists which can never fit into an armed conflict paradigm. While some cases are by nature indeterminate, the principled borders between the various situations must be maintained. In any given situation a serious analysis must be demanded to determine which legal regime applies.

As seen above, given the absence of privileged combatants in NIACs there is disagreement over the very existence of a special category of 'fighters', 'combatants' or 'non-civilians'. The ICRC *Interpretative Guidance* is helpful in resolving this controversy. The approach taken there that distinguishes in NIACs between persons fulfilling a continuous combat function and others is a helpful approach that should be accepted.

19

The legal regime governing transfer of persons in the fight against terrorism

MARGARET L. SATTERTHWAITE

1 Introduction: formal and informal transfer in the context of counter-terrorism

Crimes of terrorism are frequently committed by individuals and groups in countries other than those they target. Even when 'home-grown' terrorists are responsible for violent acts, they often flee across borders to evade justice. States seeking to punish acts of terrorism therefore regularly need to obtain custody of individuals accused of committing such acts.[1] They

Parts of this chapter draw on a series of articles I have published on the topic of rendition, including CHRGJ/Margaret Satterthwaite, 'Minimum Standards for Transfer: International Law Concerning Rendition in the Context of Counter-Terrorism' (2009) (CHRGJ at: http://chrgj.org/up-content/uploads/2012/10/legaladvisory-detainess-2009.pdf); M. Satterthwaite, 'Rendered Meaningless: Extraordinary Rendition and the Rule of Law' (2007) 75 *George Washington Law Review* 1333; M. Satterthwaite, 'Extraordinary Rendition and Disappearances in the "War on Terror"' (2006) 10 *Gonzaga Journal of International Law* 70; and M. Satterthwaite and A. Fisher, 'Tortured Logic: Renditions to Justice, Extraordinary Rendition, and Human Rights Law' (2006) 6 *Long Term View* 52. Work on this chapter was supported by the Filomen D'Agostino Research Fund at New York University School of Law. Many thanks to those with whom I have puzzled through these issues in the past few years, in particular Jayne Huckerby, Julia Hall, and Wendy Patten. Thanks to Jelena Pejic, Zoe Salzman and the members of the January 2010 expert meeting in The Hague for invaluable comments on an earlier draft. Some of the core ideas set out here began as an *amicus curiae* brief that I worked on with Jayne Huckerby, Zoe Salzman and Junko Tadaki; I am indebted to them. I am grateful to Niran Anketell (NYU LLM 2010), Valerie Brender (NYU JD 2012), Tamar Feldman (NYU LLM 2008), Ryan Gee (NYU JD 2010), and Tafadzwa Pasipanodya (NYU JD 2008) for impeccable research assistance.

[1] States that have ratified international counter-terrorism conventions have obligations to prohibit certain acts of terrorism as crimes and to prosecute or extradite individuals found on their territory who are suspected of committing such crimes. Still, no international body has jurisdiction over crimes of terrorism, so punishing such acts is left to states. See (1) Convention on the Prevention and Punishment of Crimes Against Internationally Protected Persons, Including Diplomatic Agents, Art. 7; (2) International Convention against the Taking of Hostages, Art. 8; (3) International Convention on the Suppression of Terrorist Bombings,

may do so by requesting the extradition or deportation of a suspect from a state where the individual is found. States also directly apprehend suspected terrorists in other countries and deliver them to justice before their own or third states' courts through 'rendition to justice'. Finally, when terrorism occurs in the context of armed conflict, states may move suspects from one state to another through wartime processes such as the transfer of prisoners of war. In short, states use both formal and informal processes when transferring individuals suspected of terrorist crimes.

The practice of rendition – the involuntary transfer of an individual across borders without recourse to extradition or deportation proceedings – is not new. Indeed, the practice has been used by governments for more than a century. Famous renditions include that of Nazi war criminal Adolf Eichmann from Argentina to Israel, and terrorist Carlos 'the Jackal' (Ilich Ramirez Sanchez) from Sudan to France. Although such renditions have been controversial in human rights circles, they have been celebrated by many as crucial in the fight against impunity for grave crimes and are sometimes called 'rendition to justice'.[2]

The administration of former US President George W. Bush was criticized for the new[3] practice of 'extraordinary rendition' – the transfer

Art. 8; (4) International Convention for the Suppression of Financing of Terrorism, Art. 10; (5) International Convention for the Suppression of Acts of Nuclear Terrorism, Art. 11; (6) Convention on the Suppression of Unlawful Seizure of Aircraft, Art. 7; (7) Convention for the Suppression of Unlawful Acts against the Safety of Civil Aviation, Art. 7; (8) Convention on the Physical Protection of Nuclear Material, Art. 10; (9) Convention for the Suppression of Unlawful Acts against the Safety of Maritime Navigation, Art. 10; (10) Convention for the Suppression of Unlawful Acts against the Safety of Civil Aviation, signed at Montreal, Art. 3; at: http://treaties.un.org/Pages/DB.aspx?path=DB/studies/page2_en.xml.

2 For a defence of rendition to justice, see G. S. McNeal and B. J. Field, 'Snatch and Grab Ops: Justifying Extraterritorial Abduction' (2007) 16 *Transnational Law & Contemporary Problems* 491. For an additional defence of rendition, alongside some recommendations for changes in the procedure to make it more 'regular', see A. J. Radsan, 'A More Regular Process for Irregular Rendition' (2006) 37 *Seton Hall Law Review* 1; see also D. B. Rivkin, Jr. and L. A. Casey, 'Europe's runaway prosecutions, *Washington Post*, 28 February 2007, 19.

3 The US practice of extraordinary rendition was a new form of an older practice. 'Rendition to justice', in which a suspect is apprehended and transferred to the United States for criminal prosecution, was approved and formalized by President Ronald Reagan and expanded by President George H. W. Bush. US courts approved of the practice in a series of cases that culminated in the 1992 Supreme Court case *US* v. *Alvarez-Machain* 504 US 655 (1992). President Bill Clinton altered the practice by initiating the transfer of suspects from one country to another, placing them into foreign legal processes rather than bringing them into the US legal system. For a discussion of this history, see M. Satterthwaite and A. Fisher, 'Tortured Logic: Renditions to Justice, Extraordinary Rendition, and Human Rights Law' (2006) 6 *Long Term View* 52.

of suspects to countries known for the systematic use of torture.[4] US officials at the time defended the practice, relying on justifications developed to support 'rendition to justice' and arguing that the practice was legal.[5] Despite these justifications, international human rights bodies and intergovernmental bodies including the Council of Europe, the European Union and human rights bodies of the United Nations have determined that the extraordinary form of rendition is unlawful under human rights law.[6] Although individuals have faced significant legal hurdles in fighting the practice in the US legal system (most prominently in the form of the state secrets doctrine),[7] there is little doubt among international law experts that extraordinary rendition is prohibited.[8] Despite this consensus, the

[4] For a discussion of these criticisms, see M. Satterthwaite, 'Rendered Meaningless: Extraordinary Rendition and the Rule of Law' (2007) 75 *George Washington Law Review* 1333.

[5] See Condoleezza Rice, US Secretary of State, US Department of State, Remarks upon her departure for Europe (5 December 2005), www.state.gov/documents/organization/132592.pdf (in which Secretary Rice defends the US use of rendition); Michael Hayden, *Charlie Rose Show*, interview with Director Michael Hayden (PBS television broadcast 22–3 October 2007) (transcript at https://www.cia.gov/news-information/press-releases-statements/press-release-archive-2007/interview-with-charlie-rose.html) (in which CIA Director Michael Hayden explains the continuation of the US Program of rendition and CIA detention).

[6] See UN Committee against Torture, Consideration of Reports Submitted by States Parties Under Article 19 of the Convention: Second Periodic Reports of States Parties Due in 1999: Addendum: United States of America, UN Doc. CAT/C/48/Add.3 (2005), 5 (considering US report submitted 6 May 2005); UNHRC, Concluding Observations of the Human Rights Committee: United States of America, UN Doc. CCPR/C/USA/CO/3/Rev.1 (2006); Report on the Alleged Use of European Countries by the CIA for the Transportation and Illegal Detention of Prisoners, Eur.Parl.Doc. A6-0020/2007(2007), at www.europarl.europa.eu/comparl/tempcom/tdip/final_report_en.pdf; Draft Interim Report on the Alleged Use of European Countries by the CIA for the Transportation and Illegal Detention of Prisoners, Eur.Parl.Doc. A6-0213/2006 (2006), at http://assembly.coe.int/CommitteeDocs/2006/20060124_Jdoc032006_E.pdf; Eur. Parl. Ass. Comm. on Legal Affairs and Human Rights, Alleged Secret Detentions in Council of Europe Member States, Doc. No. AS/Jur. (2006), at http://assembly.coe.int/main.asp?link=/committeedocs/2006/20060124_jdoc032006_e.htm [hereafter *Council of Europe January 2006 Report*]; Eur. Parl. Ass. Comm. on Legal Affairs and Human Rights, Secret Detentions and Illegal Transfers of Detainees Involving Council of Europe Member States: Second Report, 64, Doc. No. 11302 rev. (2007), at www.coe.int/T/E/Com/Files/Events/2006-cia/ [hereafter *Council of Europe June 2007 Report*].

[7] One of the most famous extraordinary rendition cases, that of German citizen Khalid El-Masri, was thrown out on the grounds that defending against the case would require the exposure of state secrets. See M. Satterthwaite, 'Human Rights and Humanitarian Law in the "War on Terror": The Story of El Masri v. Tenet', in D. Hurwitz and M. L. Satterthwaite, with D. Ford (eds.), *Human Rights Advocacy Stories* (New York: Foundation Press, 2009).

[8] For legal analyses of the prohibitions relevant to extraordinary rendition, see Satterthwaite and Fisher, 'Tortured Logic'; Satterthwaite, 'Rendered Meaningless';

United States is not the only country that appears to have used the practice in the context of counter-terrorism. Reports indicate that governments in East Africa and the Horn of Africa have conducted extraordinary renditions in recent years. Ethiopia has been criticized for allegedly 'abducting terrorism suspects from other countries' and subjecting them to torture and secret detention,[9] and Kenya has been accused of abducting and transferring suspects to the custody of Uganda, Somalia and Ethiopia, where they have been subjected to torture or cruel, inhuman or degrading treatment.[10]

There is no consensus concerning the practice of informal transfers – renditions of the non-'extraordinary' kind – more generally in the context of counter-terrorism efforts. In part this lack of consensus comes from the varied contexts in which informal transfers occur. Such transfers include the movement of individuals captured on the battlefield in Afghanistan to the detention facility at Guantánamo, the transfer of individuals captured in a variety of settings to secret offshore detention centres, the transfer of individuals detained by one state to the custody of their own state of nationality (sometimes for trial, but often simply for detention), and the transfer of individuals to the territory of the transferring state to stand trial before a regular criminal court.

Soon after US President Barack Obama was inaugurated in January 2009, he promised to end the most severe human rights violations carried out by the US government in the name of fighting terrorism, including the use of torture and secret detention facilities.[11] Although he signed Executive Orders ending the use of such practices, he did not order the cessation of rendition, defined as the transfer of an individual without the benefit of judicial or administrative proceedings. Instead, he formed a Task Force to examine the issue and to compile recommendations about how the process could be brought back in line with US law and international obligations.[12] In July 2009, this Task Force recommended some improvements in the use of diplomatic assurances – promises from countries receiving detainees

Satterthwaite, 'Human Rights and Humanitarian Law'; D. Weissbrodt and A. Bergquist, 'Extraordinary Rendition: A Human Rights Analysis' (2006) 19 *Harvard Human Rights Journal* 123, 'Extraordinary Rendition and the Torture Convention' (2006) 46 *Virginia Journal of International Law* 585 and 'Extraordinary Rendition and the Humanitarian Law of War and Occupation' (2007) 47 *Virginia Journal of International Law* 295.

9 UN Committee Against Torture, Conclusions and Recommendations of the Committee against Torture: Ethiopia (2011), para. 20.

10 See Dominic Casciani, 'High Court rejects Kenyan terror trial intervention', BBC News, 26 August 2011; Amnesty International, 'Horn of Africa: Unlawful Transfers in the "War on Terror"', AI Index: AFR 25/006/2007; Redress and Reprieve, *Kenya and Counter-Terrorism: A Time for Change* (2009).

11 See Exec. Order No. 13,491, 74 Fed. Reg. 4893 (22 January 2009).

12 See *ibid.*

upon which the United States has relied when transferring individuals to states where they may face a risk of torture.[13] However, the Task Force did not recommend any significant reform of rendition itself.[14] The US practice of rendition has continued, and along with it controversy over the practice, since many governments have critiqued the US use of rendition while failing to formulate clear policies for their own actions in connection with the transfer of terrorism suspects.[15]

Indeed, European governments and Canada have endured critique for the transfer of detainees held by their armed forces in Afghanistan and Iraq to the custody of the home state or to the United States.[16] Although many governments have engaged in discussion aimed at clarifying the legal status of such transfers,[17] confusion has continued, and the governments of Denmark and Canada, as well as the United States, have faced

[13] Press release, US Department of Justice, Special Task Force on Interrogations and Transfer Policies Issues Its Recommendations to the President (24 August 2009), at www.justice.gov/opa/pr/2009/August/09-ag-835.html. The recommendations themselves have not been made public.

[14] *Ibid.*

[15] For example, European governments have taken a series of initiatives aimed at clarifying their policies concerning the transfer of individuals suspected of terrorist offenses. Some of these initiatives have been bilateral and aimed at withdrawing assistance for transfers conducted outside normal detainee transfer rules. Other initiatives have been multilateral, such as the actions by the Council of Europe to investigate European involvement in the US rendition programme and recommend changes to policies concerning the conduct of foreign intelligence services on European soil. See Eur. Parl. Ass., Comm. on Legal Affairs and Human Rights, *Alleged Secret Detentions in Council of Europe Member States*, Doc. No. AS/Jur. (2006) 03 rev. (2006), at http://assembly.coe.int/main.asp?link=/committeedocs/2006/20060124_jdoc032006_e.htm, and Eur. Parl. Ass., Comm. on Legal Affairs and Human Rights, *Secret Detentions and Illegal Transfers of Detainees Involving Council of Europe Member States: Second Report*, para. 64, Doc. No. 11302 rev. (2007), at http://assembly.coe.int/Documents/WorkingDocs/Doc07/edoc11302.pdf. See also Council of Europe Parliamentary Assembly, Res. 1507 (2006), 'Alleged secret detentions and unlawful inter-state transfers of detainees involving Council of Europe member states', at http://assembly.coe.int/Main.asp?link=/Documents/AdoptedText/ta06/ERES1507.htm.

[16] See, e.g., Amnesty International, Afghanistan: Detainees Transferred to Torture: ISAF Complicity?, AI Index ASA 11/011/2007, at www.amnesty.org/en/library/info/ASA11/011/2007 (critiquing the transfer activities of European, US and Canadian forces in Afghanistan under the rubric of ISAF forces and calling for a temporary halt of such transfers to ensure ISAF countries were living up to their international obligations pertaining to transfer).

[17] For example, European governments, led by the government of Denmark, participated alongside the United States in the Copenhagen Process, a five-year multilateral process that sought to clarify the 'legal, political, operative, and practical challenges relating to detainees in international military operations', particularly those in Afghanistan. One of the main issues for discussion was the legal rubric governing the transfer of detainees.

litigation by individuals and groups challenging the legality of certain battlefield transfers.[18] The European Court of Human Rights has clarified the legal picture through its decision in the case of *Al-Saadoon and Mudfhi* v. *United Kingdom*, in which individuals detained by UK forces in Iraq challenged their transfer to Iraqi authorities on the basis that they could be subjected to the death penalty after their transfer.[19] The Court found that the individuals facing transfer were protected by the *non-refoulement* norm enshrined in the European Convention on Human Rights since they had been brought into the jurisdiction of the UK government through arrest and detention.[20] In 2012, the UK

See, e.g., Legal Department, Ministry of Foreign Affairs of Denmark, Copenhagen Conference, The Handling of Detainees in International Military Operations, Non-Paper on Legal Framework and Aspects of Detention, 4 October 2007, at www.ambottawa.um.dk/NR/rdonlyres/F5364962-DC30-4333-9EFC-1B612B43DC28/0/NonpaperCopenhagenConference.pdf. The process concluded in October 2012 with the publication of a set of 'Principles and Guidelines' that have been endorsed by many of the more than twenty countries and several international organizations that participated in the process. One of the sixteen principles addresses the transfer of detainees but it does no more than restate existing law by affirming that 'A state or international organization will only transfer a detainee to another state or authority in compliance with the transferring state's or international organizations' international law obligations'. The Copenhagen Process, 'Principles and Guidelines', Art. 15 (2012), at http://inprol.org/sites/default/files/news_room/naecrra_in_the_news/2012/copenhangen_process_principles_and_guidelines_3.pdf

18 Denmark was sued by a former Afghan detainee who was handed over by Danish forces to the US military, in whose detention he alleged he was tortured. See 'Afghan ex-prisoner sues Denmark over torture', *Swedish Wire*, 9 September 2009. Similarly, the United States was sued by two US citizens held by the US military in Iraq who alleged that they would be abused if transferred to Iraqi custody, where they faced criminal charges. The US Supreme Court threw out the case, ruling that although the US courts could hear the case, the Court would not interfere with the decision of the military to transfer them to a foreign government that planned to try them. See *Munaf* v. *Geren*, 128 S. Ct. 2207 (Supreme Court of the United States, 12 June 2008). Amnesty International Canada and the British Columbia Civil Liberties Association sued the government of Canada, alleging that Canadian forces operating in Afghanistan had a policy and practice of transferring detainees to the Afghan government, where they were at risk of torture. See P. Koring, 'Amnesty slams Canada over Afghan detainees: rights groups seek to argue before court that transfer of captives violates law', *Globe and Mail* (Canada), 21 February 2007, A16. The case was ultimately dismissed on the grounds that the Canadian Charter of Rights and Freedoms did not extend to the actions in question; Canada temporarily halted prisoner transfers during the suit, but resumed after it concluded an agreement with the Afghan government concerning detainee treatment. See J. Tibbetts, 'Supreme Court rejects Charter protection for Afghan detainees', *National Post*, 21 May 2009, and *Decision on Charter Applicability/Dismissing Application* (03/12/08) (Supreme Court of Canada, 21 May 2009).

19 *Al-Saadoon and Mudfhi* v. *United Kingdom*, App. No. 61498/08 (2010).

20 *Ibid.*, para. 140.

government announced that it halted transfers of detainees held by its forces in Afghanistan to the custody of the Afghan government due to concerns over ill-treatment.[21]

Because they are carried out in a wide variety of settings, the question of which legal regime applies to the transfer of terrorism suspects raises difficult and complex issues.[22] A careful examination of relevant rules of international human rights and humanitarian law is therefore needed. This chapter examines the legal norms governing such transfers and sets out a minimum standard that must be upheld in all settings. This standard is most relevant for informal transfers, since they are almost always accomplished without regard to the full set of protections due to the individual being transferred. To the extent that formal transfers in the context of counter-terrorism also fail to duly protect individual rights, the minimum standard will be a useful reference.[23] Although some background will be provided in the next section concerning formal regimes of transfer, the remainder of this chapter focuses on the minimum rules required when states transfer individuals outside of deportation or extradition proceedings.

[21] See Amnesty International, 'UK holds off on detainee transfers to Afghan authorities' (30 Nov. 2012), at http://www.amnesty.org.au/news/comments/30611/?utm_source=feedburner&utm_medium=feed&utm_campaign=Feed%3A+AmnestyInternationalAustraliaNews+Amnesty+International+Australia+News#when:00:19:48z.

[22] The confusion was evident in the way the US Special Task Force on Interrogations and Transfer Policies understood the various forms of transfer carried out by the United States. Commenting on the Task Force's recommendations, the US Attorney General explained that the Task Force 'considered seven types of transfers conducted by the U.S. government: extradition, transfers pursuant to immigration proceedings, transfers pursuant to the Geneva Conventions, transfers from Guantánamo Bay, military transfers within or from Afghanistan, military transfers within or from Iraq, and transfers pursuant to intelligence authorities' (see Task Force press release). This list of types of transfer betrays a mix of categories: some transfers are described based on the legal regime underlying them, others are described according to which agency carries them out, and others are defined according to which domestic legal authorities allow for the transfer.

[23] Many states have altered their immigration rules to create stricter regimes for expelling or excluding individuals suspected or convicted of committing crimes of terrorism. Some reforms were called for by the SC, which called on states to 'ensure . . . that refugee status is not abused by the perpetrators, organizers, or facilitators of terrorist acts' (UN Doc. S/Res./1373 (2001)). The new rules in many countries, however, have been challenged under human rights law. For a discussion of these issues, see, e.g., C. Warbrick, 'The European Response to Terrorism in An Age of Human Rights' (2004) 15 *European Journal of International Law* 989 (discussing laws in the UK), P. Margulies, 'Uncertain Arrivals: Immigration, Terror, and Democracy After September 11' (2002) 17 *Brooklyn Journal of International Law* 447 (discussing laws in the US), I. Nazarova, 'Alienating "Human" from "Right": US and UK Non-Compliance with Asylum Obligations Under International Human Rights Law' (2002) 25 *Fordham International Law Journal* 1335.

The chapter will also discuss questions left unanswered by the existing law. It will conclude with recommendations for states seeking to comply with international human rights and humanitarian law when transferring individuals suspected of terrorism.

2 Background and current legal position

2.1 Formal and informal transfer

Rendition is a term that is defined in many ways by what it is not: it is not extradition and it is not deportation, two formal means through which governments transfer individuals across international borders.[24] Extradition is a 'formal process by which a person is surrendered by one state to another'.[25] It is the usual method for transfer of criminal suspects and fugitives, and it is designed to protect the sovereignty of the nation where the suspect has taken refuge (the 'host state'), safeguard basic individual rights, and allow the requesting state to obtain jurisdiction over an individual who is either suspected of committing or has been convicted of committing a crime subject to its criminal jurisdiction.[26] Most of the key international counter-terrorism treaties contain extradite or prosecute clauses, meaning that states parties to the conventions must either prosecute individuals within their jurisdiction who are accused of committing acts of terrorism, or extradite them to a state that is willing and able to prosecute them.[27]

[24] Some scholars use the term 'rendition' to cover all forms of transfer – formal and informal. See, e.g., J. F. Murphy, *Punishing International Terrorists: The Legal Framework for Policy Initiatives* (Totowa, NJ: Rowman & Allanheld, 1985), 36. This chapter uses the term to encompass only informal transfers.

[25] M. C. Bassiouni, *International Extradition: United States Law and Practice* (Oxford: Oxford University Press, 2007), vol. I.

[26] V. Epps, 'The Development of the Conceptual Framework Supporting International Extradition' (2003) 25 *Loyola of Los Angeles International and Comparative Law Review* 369, 371–2.

[27] See (1) Convention on the Prevention and Punishment of Crimes Against Internationally Protected Persons, Including Diplomatic Agents, Art. 7; (2) International Convention Against the Taking of Hostages, Art. 8; (3) International Convention on the Suppression of Terrorist Bombings, Art. 8; (4) International Convention for the Suppression of Financing of Terrorism, Art. 10; (5) International Convention for the Suppression of Acts of Nuclear Terrorism, Art. 11; (6) Convention on the Suppression of Unlawful Seizure of Aircraft, Art. 7; (7) Convention for the Suppression of Unlawful Acts against the Safety of Civil Aviation, Art. 7; (8) Convention on the Physical Protection of Nuclear Material, Art. 10; (9) Convention for the Suppression of Unlawful Acts against the Safety of Maritime Navigation, Art. 10; (10) Convention for the Suppression of Unlawful Acts against the Safety of Civil Aviation, signed at Montreal, Art. 3, at http://treaties.un.org/Pages/DB.aspx?path=DB/studies/page2_en.xml.

Although the exact procedures for extradition vary according to domestic law, the general practice follows a similar pattern. Extradition usually arises under a bilateral or multilateral treaty and begins with a request from the representative of a foreign state for the transfer of a named individual who is present on the territory of the host state.[28] The request is followed by apprehension and a proceeding in which a judicial officer determines whether the individual is extraditable; this requires a showing that the crime is one covered by a valid extradition treaty (and is an act criminalized in both jurisdictions), and a sufficient quantum of evidence to satisfy the relevant legal standard for extradition.[29] Once these prerequisites are satisfied, the judicial officer determines that the individual is extraditable and the decision concerning whether to extradite or not passes to an executive officer[30] who must then decide whether to surrender the alleged fugitive to the requesting foreign state.[31] Many treaties authorizing extradition include clauses allowing host states to refuse to extradite individuals who would be at risk of persecution or unfair treatment in the receiving state.[32] In addition, in states that have ratified major human rights treaties, the determination of whether to extradite an individual usually includes a consideration of any risk of torture or grave ill-treatment the individual may face upon transfer.[33] Individuals facing extradition may also seek asylum from persecution, though there may be separate procedures for obtaining such protection under the relevant domestic law.[34] Certain individuals suspected of, or who have been convicted of, terrorist crimes may be excluded from

For a discussion of the extradite or prosecute obligation in the context of terrorism, see Chapter 3 in this volume.

28 See generally G. Gilbert, *Transnational Fugitive Offenders in International Law: Extradition and Other Mechanisms* (Leiden: Martinus Nijhoff, 1998), 59–146. For the relevant US law, see 18 USC, para. 3184 (2006).

29 Gilbert, *Transnational Fugitive Offenders*. For a discussion of relevant US law, see *Quinn* v. *Robinson*, 783 F.2d 776, 787 (9th Cir. 1986).

30 Gilbert, *Transnational Fugitive Offenders*. In the United States, the relevant executive officer is the Secretary of State. See 18 USC, para. 3184.

31 Gilbert, *Transnational Fugitive Offenders*. For relevant US law, see 18 USC, paras. 3184, 3186; see also 22 CFR, para. 95.2(b) (1999).

32 See, for example, 1979 International Convention against the Taking of Hostages, 1316 UNTS 205, Art. 9 and UN Model Treaty on Extradition, UN Doc. A/Res./45/116 (1990), Art. 3.

33 Gilbert, *Transnational Fugitive Offenders*, ch. 4. This obligation is explicitly contained in Art. 3 Convention against Torture and Other Cruel, Inhuman or Degrading Treatment or Punishment and implicitly in Art. 7 ICCPR. See 1984 United Nations Convention against Torture and Other Cruel, Inhuman or Degrading Treatment or Punishment, 1465 UNTS 85 [hereafter CAT or Convention against Torture]; and 1966 United Nations International Covenant on Civil and Political Rights, 999 UNTS 171.

34 See Bassiouni, *International Extradition*, vol. I, 193–202 ('Interrelationship between Asylum and Extradition'). Because extradition, asylum and withholding of deportation are separate

the protection against *refoulement* set out in refugee law. However, the *non-refoulement* rule relating to torture is absolute under human rights law, so individuals facing a substantial risk of torture are protected against extradition even when they are excluded from refugee protection.[35] In addition to these human rights protections, many extradition treaties include exceptions allowing host states to refuse extradition if the individual sought is a national of the requested state, or if the crime for which he is sought is of a 'political' nature. Key states argue that these exceptions have proven to be obstacles to extraditing terrorism suspects.[36]

Deportation and exclusion are general terms for the multiple legal processes a country may use to expel an individual who has entered its territory, or to prevent an individual from entering that territory at the outset.[37] Under international law, states have the right to restrict access to their territory by non-nationals through immigration procedures. These procedures are regulated by law, and the individual subject to them is guaranteed certain rights,[38] though these rights have been severely restricted in some circumstances (such as in the case of admission and removal of individuals suspected of terrorist activity or connections).[39] Under human rights and refugee law, individuals facing

legal claims with different procedural and substantive requirements, the decision as to one claim is not dispositive of the other. This can create anomalous results (see *ibid.*).

35 Convention against Torture; 1951 United Nations Convention Relating to the Status of Refugees, 187 UNTS 6259, Art. 33; 1967 Protocol Relating to the Status of Refugees, 606 UNTS 627. The Refugee Convention prohibits states from expelling or returning a refugee to a country 'where his life or freedom would be threatened on account of his race, religion, nationality, membership of a particular social group or political opinion' (6276). These issues are discussed further below.

36 For a discussion of these issues, see S. Borelli, 'The Rendition of Terrorist Suspects to the United States', in A. Bianchi (ed.), *Enforcing International Law Norms Against Terrorism* (Oxford: Hart, 2004). Despite these arguments, Borelli finds that the political offence exception has declined so much as to not pose a significant hurdle to extradition for crimes of terrorism.

37 See Murphy, *Punishing International Terrorists*, 81–2.

38 Under human rights law, individuals lawfully on the territory of a state are guaranteed a wide variety of rights and cannot be summarily expelled. See ICCPR: 'An alien lawfully in the territory of a State Party to the present Covenant may be expelled therefrom only in pursuance of a decision reached in accordance with law and shall, except where compelling reasons of national security otherwise require, be allowed to submit the reasons against his expulsion and to have his case reviewed by, and be represented for the purpose before, the competent authority or a person or persons especially designated by the competent authority' (Art. 13).

39 See, e.g., M. Scaperlanda, 'Are We that Far Gone? Due Process and Secret Deportation Proceedings' (1996) 7 *Stanford Law and Policy Review* 23 (describing US legal regime for deportation of 'terrorists'); S. H. Legomsky, 'Immigration Law and Human Rights: Legal Line Drawing Post September 11: Symposium Article: The Ethnic and Religious Profiling of Non-Citizens: National Security and International Human Rights' (2005) 25 *Boston College Third World Law Journal* 161, 162–77.

transfer away from the territory of a country through immigration proceedings – like those facing transfer through extradition processes – may forward claims that their transfer should be prohibited since it would place them at risk of persecution, torture or grave ill-treatment.

Disguised extradition is a term used to describe the reliance by a state on its immigration procedures such as exclusion, deportation, and removal to effect the transfer of an individual to the custody of another state for the purpose of punishment.[40] It is used in cases where extradition is impossible or deemed to be unlikely, or where extradition has been pursued but refused.[41] A number of states, including the United States, France, the UK and South Africa, have used disguised extradition with some frequency.[42] Individuals facing disguised extradition can use immigration proceedings to claim protection from potential persecution or torture in the same way that others facing deportation or exclusion may forward such claims.[43] However, since the process is one designed to deal with immigration control and not criminal matters, the

[40] See *Bassiouni, International Extradition*, vol. I, 204, 203–4 ('Disguised Extradition: The Use of Immigration laws and Alternatives to Extradition: Introduction').

[41] *Ibid.* The expulsion of Klaus Barbie, who was convicted *in absentia* in France for crimes committed while he was an SS officer during the Second World War, from Bolivia to French Guyana, is a famous case of disguised extradition. The Bolivian Supreme Court had denied a French request for extradition prior to Barbie's expulsion (see *ibid.*, 211).

[42] See *ibid.*, 203–4, 209–11. For an overview of disguised renditions carried out by the United States during the first half of the twentieth century, see A. Evans, 'Acquisition of Custody Over the International Fugitive Offender: Alternatives to Extradition: A Survey of United States Practice' (1966) 40 *British Yearbook of International Law* 77. For information about disguised extradition in South Africa, see M.C. Cowling, 'Unmasking "Disguised" Extradition: Some Glimmer of Hope' (1992) 109 *South African Law Journal* 242. Two cases in which France allegedly used disguised extradition to obtain jurisdiction over an individual sought for criminal matters were found by the European Commission on Human Rights not to have amounted to a human rights violation. See *Ilich Sánchez Ramirez* v. *France*, App. No. 28780/95 (1996), 162 ('even assuming the circumstances in which the applicant arrived in France could be described as a disguised extradition, this could not, as such, constitute a breach of the Convention'); *Klaus Altmann (Barbie)* v. *France*, App. No. 10689/83 (1984), 233 ('even if the applicant's extradition could be described as a disguised extradition, this would not, as such, constitute a breach of the Convention'). Another disguised extradition was found to amount to a violation of human rights by the ECtHR in large part because it was carried out in violation of domestic law (*Bozano* v. *France* [1986] 9 EHRR 297 (1986) 9 EHRR 297, 9 EHRR 297 [1986] ECHR 16 (1987) 9 EHRR 297, para. 60).

[43] These protections derive from international conventions such as the Convention against Torture. Individuals facing disguised extradition will not have the opportunity for review of any other claims pertaining to the procedures that may face them in the country that seeks custody of them, since the exchange of custody is not a formal part of the legal proceeding.

safeguards built into the extradition process – such as the requirement that the requesting state bring forward sufficient evidence to justify extradition and the requirement that the crime for which the individual is sought is one specified in a valid treaty – are missing from disguised extradition.[44]

In the context of armed conflict, the rules of international humanitarian law both prohibit and require certain forms of transfer. Relevant here are rules concerning transfer, repatriation and release of individuals deprived of their liberty during armed conflict. Like other forms of international transfer regulated by law, the rules concerning transfer in the context of armed conflict include protections against persecution: prisoners of war may only be transferred to countries that will uphold their rights[45] and it is prohibited to transfer a protected person to a country 'where he or she may have reason to fear persecution for his or her political opinions or religious beliefs'.[46] Concerning repatriation, states must repatriate prisoners of war without delay once active hostilities have ended[47] and civilians interned by belligerents in international armed conflict must likewise be promptly released once the reasons for their detention have resolved themselves, or – at the latest – at the close of active hostilities.[48] Practice has evolved to protect those subject to such transfers from involuntary transfer if they fear persecution upon return.[49]

International rendition is the transfer of an individual from the custody of one state to another without the benefit of any process – whether extradition or deportation – by the rendering country. Such renditions may be used by a country aiming to deliver an individual to another country or to an international court, or they may be used by a country that is itself seeking custody of an individual. There is

[44] Murphy explains: '[Immigration proceedings] are not designed for the purpose of cooperation in furthering the international criminal justice system. Rather, both exclusion and deportation are civil processes, designed for immigration control and dominated by the executive. As a consequence, exclusion and deportation proceedings utilized for [disguised extradition] purposes do not apply criminal justice standard, either with respect to the interests of the states involved or to the protection of the accused' (*Punishing International Terrorists*, 219).

[45] See 1949 Geneva Convention Relative to the Treatment of Prisoners of War, 75 UNTS 135, Art. 12 [hereafter GC III].

[46] See 1949 Geneva Convention Relative to the Protection of Civilian Persons in Time of War, 75 UNTS 287, Art. 45 [hereafter GC IV].

[47] See GC II, Art. 118. [48] See GC IV, Arts. 132–3.

[49] See J. Henckaerts and L. Doswald-Beck, Customary International Humanitarian Law (Cambridge: Cambridge University Press, 2005), vol. I, Rule 128.

continuing controversy over the legality of such renditions (discussed below), and the absence of formal procedures means that individuals subject to such transfers cannot avail themselves of the usual human rights protections. Notwithstanding such controversy, the rendition of terrorism suspects has been common in recent years.[50]

In sum, formal processes for transferring individuals across borders generally include procedures aimed at protecting those being transferred from grave human rights abuse such as the risk of torture or persecution.[51] While the protections afforded individuals in the different proceedings have in the past varied significantly, there has been a convergence of norms in recent years. This convergence can be understood to have produced a basic core of rights that must be upheld in relation to all transfers – formal and informal.[52] Although there is a well-developed case law concerning formal transfer, domestic and international bodies have had limited opportunities to review informal transfers and to opine on the norms applicable to such procedures. Despite this, the contents of the basic core rights that apply to all transfers can be discerned and should be upheld by states when transferring terrorism suspects. The next section of this chapter will set out these core rights.

2.2 Current legal position concerning the transfer of terrorists: a minimum standard

Several bodies of international law set out rules relevant to the transfer of individuals from the custody of one state to another in the context of

[50] One prominent national security expert asserts that 'In the national security area, extraordinary renditions are not extraordinary at all. Informal processes of transfer are the prevalent method for obtaining custody over fugitives abroad. This reflects the security risk inherent in initiating formal extradition requests. It also permits governments who are either unwilling or unable to transfer fugitives publicly via extradition to do so through quiet means' (J. E. Baker, *In the Common Defense: National Security Law for Perilous Times* (Cambridge: Cambridge University Press, 2007), 165). This is in contrast to the assessment of an earlier commentator, who explained that 'illegal methods of rendition – that is, abduction and unlawful seizure – have apparently not yet been utilized with respect to international terrorists' (Murphy, *Punishing International Terrorists*, 81).

[51] For an additional discussion of these protections, see Borelli, 'Rendition of Terrorist Suspects', 338–50.

[52] C. Droege also argues that *non-refoulement* protections should be applied to all forms of transfer since such norms were developed to apply across the spectrum of transfer processes (see 'Transfers of Detainees: Legal Framework, Non-Refoulement, and Contemporary Challenges' (2008) 90 *International Review of the Red Cross* 669, 677).

counter-terrorism operations. International refugee law, international human rights law, and international humanitarian law are the most relevant frameworks. These regimes of law, as a general rule, apply extraterritorially and concurrently.[53] International humanitarian law was designed to apply extraterritorially and thus its application in such circumstances is uncontroversial. Although there have been debates over the circumstances in which international human rights treaties have extraterritorial effect, human rights bodies have found that such norms apply whenever states have effective control over territory or when they exercise effective control over an individual.[54] An individual facing transfer is plainly within the control of the state conducting the transfer so the application of human rights law to such transfers should be less controversial than the general extension of such norms to territory outside the state. The applicability of the protections to transfers of custody from one state to another in the context of armed conflict in which states are cooperating pursuant to collective defence regimes or peacekeeping operations within the borders of a single state have been subject to intense debate, but recent decisions by human rights bodies affirm that because international law protects individuals within the effective control of a state or its agents regardless of the location of that custody, the protections of human rights law apply to any handover of an individual from the jurisdiction of one state to another.[55]

[53] On the concurrent application of international humanitarian law and international human rights law, see *Legality of the Threat or Use of Nuclear Weapons*, Advisory Opinion of 8 July 1996 [1996] ICJ Rep. 226, para. 25 (holding that international human rights law continues to apply in times of armed conflict). For a discussion of the concurrent application of international humanitarian law and international refugee law, see S. Jaquemet, 'The Cross-Fertilization of International Humanitarian Law and International Refugee Law' (2001) 83 *International Review of the Red Cross* 651.

[54] For a discussion of the extraterritorial application of human rights treaties to transfers, see Chapter 15 in this volume, and Satterthwaite, 'Rendered Meaningless' and 'Human Rights and Humanitarian Law'. See, e.g., *Legal Consequences of the Construction of a Wall in the Occupied Palestinian Territory*, Advisory Opinion of 9 July 2004 [2004] ICJ Rep. 136, para. 109; and UNHRC, General Comment No. 31: The Nature of the General Legal Obligation Imposed on States Parties to the Covenant (UN Doc. CCPR/C/21/Rev.1/Add.13 (2004), para. 12). The *non-refoulement* obligation under international refugee law has also been found to apply extraterritorially. See UN High Commissioner for Refugees, Advisory Opinion on the Extraterritorial Application of Non-Refoulement Obligations under the 1951 Convention relating to the Status of Refugees and its 1967 Protocol (2007).

[55] See *Al-Saadoon and Mufdhi v. United Kingdom*. The UN Committee against Torture has found that the Convention against Torture applies to transfers carried out by a state's troops abroad. See UN Committee against Torture, Conclusions and Recommendations of the Committee against Torture: United States of America (UN Doc. CAT/C/USA/

As a general rule, the *lex generalis* of international human rights law sets out basic norms that apply in all situations, including during armed conflict.[56] Where there is a direct conflict of norms during armed conflict, the *lex specialis* of international humanitarian law may displace or

CO/2 (2006), para. 20), calling on the US government to 'apply the *non-refoulement* guarantee to all detainees in its custody', and UN Committee against Torture, Conclusions and Recommendations of the Committee against Torture: Sweden (UN Doc. CAT/C/SWE/CO/5 (2008), para. 14), clarifying, in the context of the transfer of prisoners in Afghanistan by Swedish military personnel, that 'it is the Committee's constant view, as reiterated in its General Comment on article 2 of the Convention (CAT/C/GC/2) that article 3 of the Convention and its obligation of non-refoulement apply to a State party's military forces, wherever situated, where they exercise effective control, de jure or de facto, over an individual. With regard to the possible transfer of detainees within a State party's effective custody to the custody of any other State, the State party should ensure that it complies fully with article 3 of the Convention in all circumstances.' See also Droege 'Transfers of Detainees', 677 and 682–3, who argues that *non-refoulement* rules should apply to all transfers from the effective control of one state to another, whether they take place within or across borders, since 'it is the only interpretation compatible with the very object and purpose of the *non-refoulement* principle'. The UN Committee against Torture has also repeatedly emphasized that the Convention's protections against *refoulement* apply to individuals in the custody of state agents regardless of their participation in a multilateral operation. See UN Committee against Torture, Conclusions and Recommendations of the Committee against Torture: Denmark (UN Doc. CAT/C/DNK/CO/5 (2007), para. 13). 'The Committee recalls its constant view . . . that article 3 of the Convention and its obligation of non-refoulement applies to a State party's military forces, wherever situated, where they exercise effective control over an individual. This remains so even if the State party's forces are subject to operational command of another State. Accordingly, the transfer of a detainee from its custody to the authority of another State is impermissible when the transferring State was or should have been aware of a real risk of torture.' For a discussion of the obligations of international organizations for transfers carried out by troops under its command, see Droege, 'Transfers of Detainees', 683–7. The HRC has also emphasized that the Covenant applies to the actions of troops abroad, including when they are part of a peacekeeping mission. See HRC, General Comment No. 31: The Nature of the General Legal Obligation Imposed on States Parties to the Covenant (UN Doc. CCPR/C/21/Rev.1/Add.13 (2004), para. 10). The Covenant applies 'to those within the power or effective control of the forces of a State Party acting outside its territory, regardless of the circumstances in which such power or effective control was obtained, such as forces constituting a national contingent of a State Party assigned to an international peace-keeping or peace-enforcement operation'.

56 This general rule is relevant to those rights considered to be non-derogable under human rights law. Such non-derogable rights include, *inter alia*, the right to be free from torture and cruel, inhuman or degrading punishment and the right to life. See, e.g., ICCPR, Art. 4. See also *Legality of the Threat or Use of Nuclear Weapons, Advisory Opinion*, para. 25. 'The Court observes that the protection of the International Covenant of Civil and Political Rights does not cease in times of war, except by operation of Article 4 of the Covenant whereby certain provisions may be derogated from in a time of national emergency. Respect for the right to life is not, however, such a provision.' See also *Israeli Wall* opinion, para. 106, explaining that some rights are regulated by either

modify a particular rule of human rights law. Relevant here, international humanitarian law contains provisions regulating or entirely prohibiting the transfer of specific categories of persons. Because these specific protections are consistent with – though often more protective than – the *lex generalis* of human rights law, the norms complement the generally applicable human rights rules on transfer.[57]

Examining human rights, refugee law and humanitarian law norms together therefore allow for the identification of a minimum baseline standard to be applied whenever states carry out the transfer of an individual within their effective control.[58] The *lex specialis* rule in this context means that while certain individuals facing transfer have greater protections than those set out here, no individual would have less protection. Individuals entitled to specific guarantees must be given those protections as well.[59] This will be the case not only where *lex specialis* so dictates, but also where relevant states have ratified conventions with rules that are more protective than those set out in the minimum standard.

The minimum standard is derived from both procedural and substantive norms set out in the major international human rights treaties. The relevant substantive norms concern protections from transfer to a risk of certain types of grave human rights violations, including torture or cruel, inhuman or degrading treatment, enforced disappearance, persecution, arbitrary deprivation of life, as well as specific rules concerning wartime transfers. Relevant procedural norms have been articulated in the context of detention and formal transfer as well as in relation to the substantive norms concerning transfers to a risk of grave abuse.

The status of customary international law rules concerning informal transfer *qua* transfer is hard to decipher with precision. This is in part

human rights or humanitarian law while 'others may be matters of both these branches of international law'. For a discussion of the relationship between human rights law and international humanitarian law in the context of terrorism, see Chapter 16 in this volume.

57 Droege, 'Transfers of Detainees', 676 similarly argues that the *non-refoulement* rules of human rights law complement international humanitarian law and should be applied in conjunction with such rules.

58 See *ibid.*, for a similar argument and set of complementary norms. The transfers to which this minimum standard applies include, for example, 'renditions to justice' to the territory of the transferring state or a third state; renditions pursuant to an international arrest warrant; transfers carried out at the close of hostilities in the context of armed conflict (i.e. repatriations of prisoners of war or security detainees); and transfers of individuals detained in the context of armed conflict.

59 See discussion of those rules below.

due to the difficult practical situation facing many individuals who have been subject to informal transfers – only a subset of whom will ever have the opportunity to challenge their treatment in court – and in part due to the very different approaches taken by domestic and international courts when faced with questions concerning the informal transfer of criminal suspects to regular criminal processes ('rendition to justice').[60] The domestic courts of countries that have examined rendition to justice have usually done so in the context of challenges to their ability to exercise adjudicatory jurisdiction over an individual who alleges to have been unlawfully transferred, rather than human rights-based challenges to the transfer itself. In so doing, they have generally come to one of two opposite conclusions, relying on different Latin maxims: *male captus, bene detentus*, according to which a court will not inquire into the manner by which an individual comes before it so long as it can otherwise properly adjudicate the case, and *ex injuria ius non oritur*, according to which the court must not allow an egregiously illegal action to lead to conviction, even if the individual may indeed be guilty of the crime of which he is accused.[61] Some systems have adopted rules that essentially use the two maxims as opposite ends of a continuum.[62] In the face of such contradictory results, state practice cannot be said to have coalesced around a particular norm concerning domestic courts' ability to exercise jurisdiction following rendition.[63]

International courts have recently weighed in on the issue, seeming to adopt the *male captus, bene detentus* rule, with some modification, for the purpose of their exercise of jurisdiction over individuals accused of grave international crimes. Most importantly, the Appeals Chamber of the International Criminal Tribunal for the former Yugoslavia (ICTY)

[60] R. J. Currie, 'Abducted Fugitives before the International Criminal Court: Problems and Prospects' (2007) 18 *Criminal Law Forum* 349.

[61] For a discussion of domestic case law, see *ibid.* See also J. Cazala, 'L'adage male captus bene detentus face au droit international' (2007) 134 *Journal du droit international* 837, examining the use of the adage and finding the number of cases where it was actually relied upon to justify the exercise of jurisdiction to be very limited; Borelli, 'Rendition of Terrorist Suspects', 353–62, finding that the *male captus* rule has been in decline in national courts in recent years; McNeal and Field, 'Snatch and Grab Ops', 510–19.

[62] The courts of the United States, including the Supreme Court, have embraced the *male captus* doctrine, but have also stated – largely in *obiter dictum* – that egregious abuses could lead to divestment of jurisdiction to try the individual. See A. Fisher and H. Shamshi, 'Torture by Proxy: International and Domestic Law Applicable to "Extraordinary Renditions"' (2004), at www.chrgj.org/docs/TortureByProxy.pdf.

[63] Currie, 'Abducted Fugitives', 360; Borelli, 'Rendition of Terrorist Suspects', 361–2.

held in the case of Dragan Nikolić, that the Tribunal would not be divested of jurisdiction over an accused unless his transfer entailed 'serious' human rights violations akin to torture or cruel, inhuman or degrading treatment.[64] Nikolić had been transferred to the ICTY by Stabilization Forces after they took custody of him in Bosnia following his kidnapping in Serbia and Montenegro. Examining domestic case law, the Appeals Chamber found that breach of sovereignty was not a bar to the exercise of the Court's jurisdiction over an individual.[65] Concerning human rights, the Chamber first stated, in *obiter dictum*, that 'certain human rights violations are of such a serious nature that they require that the exercise of jurisdiction to be declined'.[66] In making this observation, the Appeals Chamber referred to an ICTY Trial Chamber case and an ICTR Appeals Chamber case in which the principle that the tribunals should decline jurisdiction due to egregious human rights violations were set out.[67] The Appeals Chamber then determined that since no such egregious violations were present in the case at hand, the Tribunal could properly exercise jurisdiction over Nikolić. In coming to this conclusion, the Chamber emphasized the importance of striking a balance 'between the fundamental rights of the accused and the essential interests of the international community in the prosecution of persons charged with serious violations of international humanitarian law'.[68]

International human rights bodies have viewed the issue of rendition differently, since the individuals challenging informal transfers before such forums are in a very different posture than defendants seeking relief before domestic and international criminal courts. While such defendants seek the specific remedy of dismissal of jurisdiction to adjudicate, petitioners to human rights bodies seek vindication of the full range of their human rights. The HRC's earliest jurisprudence concerning the

[64] *Prosecutor* v. *Dragan Nikolić*, Decision on Interlocutory Appeal Concerning Legality of Arrest, Case No. IT-94-2-PT, A.Ch., 5 June 2003, paras. 11–12.

[65] *Ibid.*, paras. 9–10. To reach this conclusion, the Court examined domestic courts' treatment of the issue and concluded that they tended to exercise jurisdiction in two circumstances notwithstanding international law violations: where 'Universally Condemned Offences' were concerned, and where the state of refuge refrained from lodging a complaint. Since both principles were at play in *Nikolić*, the Chamber reasoned, breaches of state sovereignty should not bar the ICTY's exercise of jurisdiction over the defendant.

[66] *Ibid.*, para. 11.

[67] *Ibid.*, para. 1, citing *Prosecutor* v. *Dokmanovic*, Case No. IT-95-13a-PT and *Barayagwiza* v. *Prosecutor*, Case No. ICTR-97-19-AR72.

[68] *Ibid.*, para. 12.

extraterritorial reach of the International Covenant on Civil and Political Rights (ICCPR) related to the abduction of individuals by officials of Uruguay in Argentina and Brazil. These abductions, followed by detention and mistreatment on foreign and Uruguayan soil, were found to violate the Convention in numerous respects.[69] The abductions themselves, which Uruguay sought to justify on security grounds, were found to constitute arbitrary arrest and detention.[70] The HRC found the alleged consent of the host state irrelevant in assessing the violations: the Covenant's jurisdictional article 'does not imply that the State party concerned cannot be held accountable for violations of rights under the Covenant which its agents commit upon the territory of another State, whether with the acquiescence of the Government of that State or in opposition to it'.[71] In contrast, the European Court of Human Rights has accepted informal transfers in the counter-terrorism context when they are carried out with the consent of the host state and in conformity with the transferring state's domestic law. In the case of *Öcalan* v. *Turkey*, the Court examined the case of an individual suspected of crimes of terrorism who was apprehended informally in Kenya and handed to Turkish officials, who then flew him to Turkey and placed him into criminal proceedings.[72] The Court accepted as valid the 'cooperation' between Turkey and Kenya, and emphasized the importance of the host state's consent in the operation: 'An arrest made by the authorities of one State on the territory of another State, without the consent of the latter, affects the person concerned's individual rights to security.'[73]

In contrast to the conflicting case law concerning the propriety of informal transfer to regular criminal proceedings, the rules pertaining to transfers to a risk of grave abuse have been consistent and increasingly protective.[74] Since most states conducting informal transfers of the type examined in this chapter are parties to the relevant human rights treaties, customary international law will not be examined in depth. Instead, the

69 See HRC, *Communication No. R.12/52: Burgos* v. *Uruguay*, 12.3, 176, Supp. No. 40 (UN Doc. A/36/40 (1981)) [hereafter HRC, *Burgos* v. *Uruguay*]; HRC, Communication No. 56/1979: *Celiberti de Casariego* v. *Uruguay*, 10.3, 92 (UN Doc. CCPR/C/13/D/56/1979 (1981)) [hereafter HRC, *Celiberti de Casariego* v. *Uruguay*].

70 *Burgos* v. *Uruguay*, para. 13; *Celeberti de Casariego* v. *Uruguay*, para. 11.

71 *Burgos* v. *Uruguay*, para. 12.3; *Celiberti de Casariego* v. *Uruguay*, para. 10.3.

72 *Öcalan* v. *Turkey*, 41 Eur. HR Rep. 985 (2005). See also *Sánchez Ramirez* v. *France*, Eur. Commission on Human Rights, No. 28780/95 (1996), 162 (noting the importance of cooperation among states in terrorism cases).

73 *Ibid.* 74 For a similar view, see Borelli, 'Rendition of Terrorist Suspects', 342.

chapter will focus mostly on relevant human rights and humanitarian treaty law.[75]

The minimum standard is based on jurisprudence, commentary and doctrine in the fields of international human rights law, humanitarian law and refugee law, and it draws especially on the norms set out in international human rights conventions, especially the ICCPR and the Convention against Torture and All Forms of Cruel, Inhuman or Degrading Treatment. Regional jurisprudence is drawn on where relevant, though a comprehensive examination of regional law is not included. While the analysis is meant to be a fair description of law at the time of drafting, international human rights bodies have not had the opportunity to comprehensively set out the rules pertaining to the informal transfer of an individual from the custody of one state to the custody of another.[76] In some respects, therefore, the minimum standard may reflect a progressive view of the law.

2.2.1 Threshold principles

Formal procedures may not be intentionally bypassed Extradition, deportation and other formal processes were designed to protect basic international law norms such as territorial sovereignty and equality, the principle of legality and the essential rights of the person. Notwithstanding domestic jurisprudence to the contrary, international legal norms require that, where they exist, formal procedures must not be

[75] It should be observed nonetheless that the main components of the norms set out here are protected by customary international law. For a discussion of the status of these norms under customary law, see Sir E. Lauterpacht and D. Bethlehem, 'The Scope and Content of the Principle of Non-Refoulement', in E. Feller, V. Türk and F. Nicholson (eds.), *Refugee Protection in International Law: UNHCR's Global Consultations on International Protection* (Cambridge: Cambridge University Press, 2003), 155–64.

[76] The former UN Special Rapporteur on Promoting and Protecting Human Rights and Fundamental Freedoms While Countering Terrorism, Professor Martin Scheinin has made the following statement about rendition: 'The transfer of a person from one jurisdiction to another (or from the custody and control of one State to another) can occur by various means, including: rendition under established extradition rules; removal under immigration law; resettlement under refugee law; or "rendition to justice", where a person is outside formal extradition arrangements but is nevertheless handed to another State for the purpose of standing trial in that State. As long as there is full compliance with the obligation of non-refoulement, these mechanisms may be lawful, although it should be noted that the particular circumstances in which a person is "rendered to justice" may involve an unlawful detention' (Report of the Special Rapporteur on the Promotion and Protection of Human Rights and Fundamental Freedoms While Countering Terrorism, Addendum: Mission to the United States of America, UN Doc. A/HRC/6/17/Add.3 (2007)).

intentionally bypassed.[77] Where formal procedures may be unavailable or have become impossible, to ensure the rights of the individual are respected, notice must be given to the host state and cooperation – or at a minimum, consent – must be sought in apprehending the individual.[78] Although the original purpose of rules requiring the consent of the host state was to protect the sovereign integrity of the state,[79] sovereignty has become a human rights issue in so far as every individual within the jurisdiction of a state is protected by human rights law vis-à-vis that state; abductions that take the individual forcibly out of the host state may deprive the individual of the ability to avail himself of the state's legal system and other protections. To ensure that interstate cooperation does not amount to collusion in the violation of the individual's rights, the host state and transferring state should ensure that the minimum procedural and substantive standards applicable to transfer are guaranteed and that the transferring state is not, by consenting to such a transfer, otherwise infringing the individual's human rights.[80] This

[77] In its *Legal Opinion on the Decision of the Supreme Court of the United States of America* critiquing the US Supreme Court's decision in *United States* v. *Alvarez-Machain* (in which the US abducted an individual in Mexico despite the existence of an extradition treaty), the Inter-American Juridical Committee underscored the requirement that states uphold extradition treaties in good faith. See Organization of American States Permanent Council, *Legal Opinion on the Decision of the Supreme Court of the United States of America*, 4 Crim. LF 119, 131 (1993). Similarly, Bassiouni explains that when a state uses informal transfer in a case where formal methods exist, the transfer 'circumvents the intent of states who enter into extradition treaties for the specific purpose of avoiding disguised extradition' and as a result, 'detrimentally affects the international rule of law' (*International Extradition*, vol. IV, 29).

[78] *See Öcalan* v. *Turkey*, 41 Eur. HR Rep. 985 (2005) (noting that 'An arrest made by the authorities of one State on the territory of another State, without the consent of the latter, affects the person concerned's individual rights to security under Article 5 § 1 [of the European Convention]' (*Sánchez Ramirez* v. *France*, 162, noting the importance of cooperation among states in terrorism cases).

[79] As the SC underscored following Israel's abduction of Adolf Eichmann in Argentina, 'the violation of the sovereignty of a Member State is incompatible with the Charter of the United Nations' (UN Doc. S/4349 (June 23, 1960), entitled *Question Relating to the Case of Adolf Eichmann*).

[80] The IACHR has explained, in the context of counter-terrorism, that 'As with all acts and omissions attributable [to] a state and its agents, these human rights protections oblige states to refrain from supporting or tolerating methods of inter-state cooperation that fail to conform with their international human rights commitments.' The Commission cites as an example of such cooperation 'extraterritorial abduction or kidnapping of a subject present in one state for prosecution in another state' (IACHR, *Report on Terrorism and Human Rights*, OEA/Ser.L/V/II.116 (2002), 159). Depending on the circumstances, the individual may have rights under domestic law or additional rights

may be difficult in circumstances where individuals are either nationals of the host state or are aliens lawfully within the territory of the host state, since such individuals have heightened protections against expulsion under human rights law.[81] It may also be difficult – if not impossible – in some states that have ratified human rights conventions that would make apprehensions and transfers outside of formal procedures unlawful.[82] The consent of a host state to an informal transfer in such circumstances will need to be carefully scrutinized, since the state conducting the transfer may have derivative liability under the rules of state responsibility if its actions amount to assistance in the host state's violation of the rights of the transferee.[83]

In practice, then, states with functioning legal systems must – before consenting to the apprehension – at a minimum ensure that the transferring state has a valid basis for apprehension and detention, and that the procedural rights due the individual will be respected.[84] In countries without an effective government or functioning judicial system, it may be lawful to conduct a transfer without the consent of the state without such action amounting to the deprivation of rights vis-à-vis that state so

under international human rights law (such as rights accruing to aliens lawfully in the territory of the state).

81 Note, however, that with respect to aliens, such protections have national security exceptions. See, e.g., Art. 13, ICCPR (guaranteeing aliens lawfully within the territory of a state the ability to challenge the decision to expel them 'except where compelling reasons of national security otherwise require').

82 This may be the case for all European states. The Venice Commission has stated that 'There are only four legal ways for Council of Europe member States to transfer a prisoner to foreign authorities: deportation, extradition, transit and transfer of convicts for the purpose of their serving the sentence in another country. Extradition and deportation proceedings must be defined by the applicable law, and the prisoners must be given access to the competent authorities' (European Commission for Democracy through Law (Venice Commission), *Draft Opinion on the International Legal Obligations of Council of Europe Member States in Respect of Secret Detention Facilities and Inter-State Transport of Detainees*, Opinion No. 363/2005 (8 March 2006), Doc. No. CDL-DI(2006)001rev, para. 160(f)).

83 Art. 16 of the Articles of State Responsibility provide that 'A State which aids or assists another State in the commission of an internationally wrongful act by the latter is internationally responsible for doing so if (a) that State does so with knowledge of the circumstances of the internationally wrongful act; and (b) the act would be internationally wrongful if committed by that State.' The ILC gave as an example of this form of responsibility 'facilitating the abduction of persons on foreign soil' (see Crawford, *International Law Commission's Articles on State Responsibility*, 148–51).

84 Another way of viewing the host state's human rights obligations would be to conclude that only individuals who have been found by a local court to be deportable or excludable are eligible for informal transfer, since informal apprehension would not thereby deprive the individual of the opportunity to avail himself of the protection of local law.

long as the human rights of the individual are otherwise protected by the transferring authority.[85]

The transferring state must have a valid legal basis for apprehending the individual in contemplation of transfer Human rights law – through the right to be free from arbitrary detention – requires that states have a valid basis for apprehending an individual in contemplation of transfer. Such bases must be set out in existing law and must be valid under international norms concerning arrest and detention.[86] The substance of the norms governing the legality of the detention will depend on whether the transfer occurs within or outside the context of armed conflict. Detaining individuals for the purpose of interrogation without another basis for detention amounts to arbitrary detention and thus is unlawful under human rights law.[87]

[85] See, e.g., D. C. Findlay, 'Abducting Terrorists Overseas for Trial in the United States: Issues of International and Domestic Law' (1988) 23 *Texas Journal of International Law* 1, 16–17. In addition to the potential acceptability of transfers from failed states, some authors and policy-makers argue that the consent of the host state is not required in two other circumstances: (a) when the host state has failed to either prosecute or extradite an individual suspected of committing a grave international crime (see, e.g., B. Izes, 'Drawing Lines in the Sand: When State-Sanctioned Abductions of War Criminals Should Be Permitted' (1991) 31 *Columbia Journal of Law & Social Problems* 1, 18); and (b) where the host state is knowingly harbouring international terrorists (see, e.g., D. Benjamin, 'Rendition to Torture: The Case of Maher Arar', testimony before the US House of Representatives Committee on Foreign Affairs Subcommittee on International Organizations, Human Rights and Oversight (18 October 2007), at www.brookings.edu/testimony/2007/1018rendition.aspx.

[86] Under human rights law, no one may be deprived of their liberty 'except on such grounds and in accordance with such procedure as are established by law' (ICCPR, Art. 9(1)). The HRC has made clear that the substantive and procedural aspects of Art. 9(1) apply to all deprivations of liberty by the state. See UNHRC, General Comment No. 8: Right to Liberty and Security of Persons (UN Doc. CCPR/30/06/82 (1982), para. 1, referring to 'all deprivations of liberty', including those for 'immigration control') [hereafter General Comment No. 8]. States may not detain individuals 'to repress the exercise of fundamental freedoms, such as freedom of religion, freedom of opinion, freedom of association'. See UN Working Group on Arbitrary Detention, Report of the Working Group on Arbitrary Detention (UN Doc. A/HRC/4/40 (2007)). Counter-terrorism laws that criminalize such freedoms may not be relied upon as a valid basis for apprehension in contemplation of transfer.

[87] The goal of intelligence gathering rather than prosecution has been one of the hallmarks of recent rendition operations in the context of counter-terrorism. See International Commission of Jurists, *Assessing Damage, Urging Action: Report of the Eminent Jurists Panel on Terrorism, Counter-Terrorism and Human Rights* (Geneva: International Commission of Jurists, 2009), 78–90, at www.ifj.org/assets/docs/028/207/3e83f1c-fbfc2cf.pdf.

Outside the context of armed conflict, states conducting transfers to their soil may rely on lawful bases such as an arrest warrant duly executed under their domestic law[88] or a prison sentence imposed following a trial in accordance with due process.[89] The basis for apprehension and detention by one state in contemplation of transfer to another state is more complex. States are permitted – and in some circumstances, mandated – to assist one another in the fight against terrorism. This does not mean, however, that they may resort to unlawful measures.[90] States assisting other states by transferring individuals to the receiving state's custody must therefore ensure that their cooperative efforts are permissible by determining that the receiving state has a lawful basis for apprehension and detention such as an arrest warrant or certification that the individual is sought to serve a prison sentence following fair trial. Both of these bases for apprehension must be accompanied by a request for legal assistance to the transferring state.[91] All

[88] See *Sánchez Ramirez* v. *France*, 162 (holding that the applicants' rights were not violated when he was transferred to France from Sudan via cooperative efforts between the two governments; the fact that the underlying French arrest warrant was valid only inside France did not give rise to a human rights violation so long as the domestic courts had determined that the arrest was legal); *Klaus Altmann* (*Barbie*) v. *France*, 234–5 (finding no human rights violation where the domestic courts found the arrest of the applicant, which allegedly occurred by disguised extradition, to be valid under French law).

[89] Arrest warrants and criminal sanctions must be for acts that are lawfully proscribed under international law. This means that not only may such warrants or convictions not be for the exercise of protected freedoms, but they must also be sufficiently precise and established to ensure that the rule of *nullum crimen sine lege* is not violated. This is especially important in the context of counter-terrorism, where states have used imprecise definitions of crimes of terrorism to repress legitimate forms of protest. For a discussion of these issues, see R. Kolb, 'The Exercise of Criminal Jurisdiction over International Terrorists', in Bianchi, *Enforcing International Law*, 227–81.

[90] Indeed, doing so will not only constitute unlawful action by the transferring state, but may also amount to the assistance by the transferring state in the wrongful act of the receiving state under the law of state responsibility.

[91] *See Öcalan* v. *Turkey*, para. 89 (as the ECtHR explained, 'Subject to it being the result of cooperation between the States concerned and provided that the legal basis for the order for the fugitive's arrest is an arrest warrant issued by the authorities of the fugitive's State of origin, even an atypical extradition cannot as such be regarded as being contrary to the Convention'). While it may seem that the nationality of Öcalan was a crucial factor in the Court's holding here, the court cites the case of *Sánchez Ramirez* v. *France*, 162, in which a state issuing the arrest warrant underlying the transfer was not the state of nationality of the transferee. In that case, the European Commission underlined the relevance of interstate cooperation in counter-terrorism measures to human rights analysis: 'It does not appear to the Commission that any cooperation which occurred in this case between the Sudanese and French authorities involved any factor which could raise problems from the point of view of Article 5 of the Convention, particularly in the field of the fight

warrants or requests for surrender must have been obtained in accordance with international due process standards[92] as well as rules concerning the permissible exercise of jurisdiction by states.[93]

In the context of international armed conflict, prisoners of war may be lawfully detained by a party to an international armed conflict and transferred to another detaining power that will uphold their Geneva rights.[94] As discussed earlier, prisoners of war who are lawfully detained must be released and repatriated (transferred) at the close of active hostilities.[95] Certain protected persons in the territory of a party to an armed conflict may be permissibly subject to internment during international armed conflict and may be transferred to another power that will uphold their Geneva rights.[96] Civilians who are lawfully interned must be transferred or repatriated once the reasons for their internment no longer obtain, or as soon as possible after the close of hostilities.[97] Detentions in the context of a 'classical' non-international armed conflict – i.e. between a state and a rebel group on the territory of that state – must have a valid basis set out in domestic law and must not amount to violations of Common Article 3 to the Geneva Conventions or applicable human rights standards.[98]

against terrorism, which frequently necessitates cooperation between States.' The Court has not addressed the question of whether a state may consent to the transfer of a detainee through cooperation (i.e. rendition) if it is relying on an arrest warrant issued by the receiving state and not one its own authorities have issued.

92 Substantial violations of due process render the subsequent detention arbitrary under international human rights law. See, e.g., *Jacobo Silva Nogales et al.* v. *Mexico*, Working Group on Arbitrary Detention (UN Doc. E/CN.4/2002/77/Add.1, 28 (2000)).

93 For a discussion of the permissible bases of jurisdiction for crimes of terrorism, see Kolb, 'Exercise of Criminal Jurisdiction'.

94 Art. 4 GC III allows states to detain as prisoners of war certain specified categories of individuals, and Art. 12 GC III provides that prisoners of war may 'only be transferred by the Detaining Power to a Power which is a party to the Convention and after the Detaining Power has satisfied itself of the willingness and ability of such transferee Power to apply the Convention'.

95 Art. 118 GC III requires detaining powers to release and repatriate prisoners of war at the close of active hostilities.

96 Art. 45 GC IV states that 'Protected persons may be transferred by the Detaining Power only to a Power which is a party to the present Convention and after the Detaining Power has satisfied itself of the willingness and ability of such transferee Power to apply the present Convention.' Note, however, that protected persons may not be transferred out of occupied territory (*ibid.*, Art. 49).

97 Art. 132 GC IV requires detaining powers to release and transfer internees as soon as the reasons for the detention cease to exist and Art. 133 GC IV requires the release of internees as soon as possible after the close of hostilities.

98 The legal bases for detention in 'multinational' non-international armed conflict are more complex; see Chapter 17 in this volume. The question of whether a state that is not

The question of whether a state may apprehend an individual in order to transfer the person for preventive detention outside the context of armed conflict is a complex one that has not been comprehensively addressed by human rights bodies. 'Preventive' or 'administrative' detention for reasons of national security without trial is only allowed in very rare circumstances where the country has officially derogated from normal human rights norms and when such schemes still comply with the essential rights regarding liberty and freedom from arbitrary detention.[99] Apprehension in contemplation of transfer to such detention schemes must therefore also be limited to circumstances in which the state has officially derogated from the usual protections and where the preventive detention scheme is otherwise in accord with human rights norms.

In addition to these bases, a state may lawfully apprehend and detain an individual pursuant to an international arrest warrant or request for arrest and surrender from an international court, though these bases are rarely relevant in the context of terrorism.[100] Regarding the permissible

engaged in an armed conflict may transfer an individual considered by the requesting state to be an individual subject to its detention under the laws of armed conflict (as a prisoner of war or a security detainee, for example) is complex. Some would argue that under public international law, the requesting state may request cooperative measures – i.e. assistance by the requested state in transferring the individual to its custody – on the basis that the individual is detainable under the laws of war rather than on suspicion of criminal activity. In such cases, however, the requested state must assess whether the detention would be lawful.

[99] Human rights bodies have frequently critiqued the use of 'administrative' or 'preventive' detention schemes and have made clear that such arrangements must still comply with the basic, non-derogable aspects of the right to liberty and security. For example, the UN Working Group on Arbitrary Detentions has concluded that administrative detention for those suspected of crimes of terrorism is 'inadmissible' under human rights law. See UN Working Group on Arbitrary Detention, Report of the Working Group on Arbitrary Detention (UN Doc. A/HRC/10/21 (2009), para. 54). See H. Duffy, *The War on Terror and the Framework of International Law* (Cambridge: Cambridge University Press, 2005), 315–16, 404–7; and OSCE/ODIHR, 'Protecting the Rights of Victims of Terrorist Attacks', in *Countering Terrorism, Protecting Human Rights: A Manual* (Warsaw: OSCE/ODIHR, 2007), 156–7.

[100] For example, the ad hoc criminal tribunals may request the surrender of individuals sought for trial; these requests are understood to be mandatory on member states of the United Nations since the courts were created by the SC acting under Chapter VII of the UN Charter. See Statute of the ICTY, Art. 29 (directing states to cooperate with the ICTY by complying with requests to 'arrest' and 'surrender or transfer' individuals sought by the Court); the Report of the Secretary General analysing the proposed statute at the time of the ICTY's creation explained that 'an order by a Trial Chamber for the surrender or transfer of persons to the custody of the International Tribunal shall be considered to be the application of an enforcement measure under Chapter VII

duration of detention prior to transfer, although there is not a great deal of jurisprudence on the issue, existing norms suggest that an individual can only be held for a reasonable period needed to effect the transfer; detention in excess of this period or when transfer becomes impossible becomes arbitrary.[101]

2.2.2 Substantive guarantees: *non-refoulement*

Taken together, international humanitarian law, international refugee law and human rights law require states to refrain from transferring any individual to the custody of a state where he is at a real risk[102] of: torture or ill-treatment; persecution; enforced disappearance; and arbitrary deprivation of life.[103] This is the principle of

of the Charter of the United Nations' (*Report of the Secretary General Pursuant to Paragraph 2 of Security Council Resolution 808*, UN Doc. S/25704 (1993), para. 126). The regime for apprehension and surrender under the ICC Statute is less robust and not mandatory on states that are not parties to the Statute, in part because the Court was created by multilateral treaty and not the SC. See Rome Statute of the International Criminal Court, Art. 89 (Surrender of Persons to the Court) (providing that state parties shall comply with requests in accordance with the statute and procedures established under national law). For a discussion, see G. Sluiter, 'The Surrender of War Criminals to the International Criminal Court' (2003) 25 *Loyola of Los Angeles International and Comparative Law Review* 605.

101 See, for example, UN Working Group on Arbitrary Detention, *Report of the Working Group on Arbitrary Detention* (UN Doc. A/HRC/10/21 (2009), para. 67); ECtHR, *Shamsa* v. *Poland*, Decision of 27 November 2003, App. No. 45355/99, 45357/99, paras. 48–60 (holding that detention in contemplation of deportation could not be justified if the deportation proved to be impossible and there was no other basis for detention under domestic law); HRC, Concluding Observations of the Human Rights Committee: Belgium, para. 17 (2004) (finding that detention of individuals awaiting deportation for several months in transit area of airport were 'akin to arbitrary detention' and should cease).

102 The various *non-refoulement* rules articulated in different treaties contain different threshold standards for the level of risk triggering the prohibition on transfer. For sake of brevity, the term 'real risk' is used in this chapter to encompass these varying thresholds. For a discussion of the differing standards, see E. Gillard, 'There's No Place Like Home: States' Obligations in Relation to Transfers of Persons' (2008) 90 *International Review of the Red Cross* 703, 725.

103 In addition to these guarantees, emerging principles suggest that states should not transfer persons to countries where they will face arbitrary detention or an unfair trial. See Report of the Working Group on Arbitrary Detention (UN Doc. A/HRC/4/40 (2007), paras. 47–49 (concerning transfer to a risk of arbitrary detention)); and Borelli, 'Rendition of Terrorist Suspects', 349–50 (concerning transfer to a risk of unfair trial). These emerging principles are not discussed in this chapter, except to the extent that a transferring state must satisfy itself that the receiving state has a valid basis for detention. Further, to the extent that extreme forms of arbitrary detention may amount to cruel, inhuman and degrading treatment, transfers to a risk of such detention are unlawful (see *ibid.* para. 48).

non-refoulement.[104] International humanitarian law provides additional guarantees to protected persons with specific statuses in times of international armed conflict.

No transfers to a risk of torture or cruel, inhuman or degrading treatment The Convention against Torture and Other Cruel, Inhuman or Degrading Treatment or Punishment (explicitly, in Article 3) and the ICCPR (implicitly, through Article 7) require that states refrain from transferring persons under their effective control to the custody of another state if the transfer would put the individual at a real risk of torture or cruel, inhuman or degrading treatment or punishment.[105] Indeed, the protection against transfer to a risk of torture or cruel treatment is understood to be so essential to the norm against such treatment that it is not considered to be a separate rule at all.[106] Human rights bodies have repeatedly underscored the importance of upholding the prohibition on transfers to a risk of torture with respect to individuals suspected of crimes of terrorism since such persons are often at risk of ill-treatment.[107] The norm against torture is a *jus cogens* norm, and the prohibition on ill-treatment is non-derogable.[108] In the context of

[104] For two excellent summaries of the *non-refoulement* obligations relevant to states when transferring individuals, see Gillard, 'No Place Like Home'; Droege, 'Transfers of Detainees'.

[105] See CAT, Art. 3; ICCPR, Art. 7, as interpreted in General Comment No. 20. See HRC, General Comment No. 20, Prohibition of Torture, Cruel, Inhuman or Degrading Treatment or Punishment, para. 9 (1992). See also *Byahuranga* v. *Denmark* (UN Doc. CCPR/C/82/D/1222/2003 (15 August 2003) (finding that the transfer of an individual to a risk of treatment contrary to Art. 7 was a violation of the ICCPR)).

[106] See Report of the Special Rapporteur on torture and other cruel, inhuman or degrading treatment or punishment (UN Doc. A/59/324 (2004), para. 28). See also *Soering* v. *United Kingdom*, 161 ECtHR (Ser. A) (1989), para. 91 (finding that protection against transfer to a real risk of torture or cruel treatment was inherent in Art. 3 ECHR).

[107] See, e.g., UN Committee against Torture, *Communication No. 39/1996: Paez* v. *Sweden*, para. 14.5 (UN Doc. CAT/C/18/D/39/1996) ('the text of article 3 is absolute . . . The nature of the activities in which the person concerned engaged cannot be a material consideration when making a determination under article 3 of the Convention'); *Saadi* v. *Italy*, App. No. 37201/06 (2008), para. 137 ('The Court notes first of all that States face immense difficulties in modern times in protecting their communities from terrorist violence . . . It cannot therefore underestimate the scale of the danger of terrorism today and the threat it presents to the community. That must not, however, call into question the absolute nature of Article 3'). The ECtHR has also emphasized that the determination of a *non-refoulement* claim must be decided independently of consideration of national security concerns (see ECtHR, *Chahal* v. *The United Kingdom* (1996)).

[108] For a discussion of the nature of the prohibition on torture in the context of transfer, see Borelli, 'Rendition of Terrorist Suspects', 343–5. Some authors consider the

armed conflict – both international and non-international – these human rights protections continue to apply and are also found in Article 3 common to the four Geneva Conventions of 1948 ('Common Article 3'), which forbids 'cruel treatment and torture' of anyone in the custody of a party to the conflict.[109] In light of the humanitarian nature of the norm and the interpretations of similar provisions under human rights law, Common Article 3 should be understood to include protection against transfers to such treatment.[110]

No transfers to a risk of persecution The 1951 Convention Relating to the Status of Refugees ('Refugee Convention') and the Geneva Conventions of 1948 prohibit states from transferring individuals to countries where they face a risk of persecution. Article 33(1) Refugee Convention prohibits states from transferring an individual to a country where his or her 'life or freedom would be threatened on account of his race, religion, nationality, membership of a particular social group or political opinion'. Article 33(2) Convention Relating to the Status of Refugees excludes from the protection of Article 33(1) individuals about 'whom there are reasonable grounds for regarding as a danger to the security of the country in which he is, or who, having been convicted by a final judgement of a particularly serious crime, constitutes a danger to the community of that country'. These exclusion clauses must be construed narrowly,[111] and even when they are applicable, individuals retain

non-refoulement rule itself to be a *jus cogens* norm. See R. Bruin and K. Wouters, 'Terrorism and the Non-derogability of Non-refoulement' (2003) 15 *International Journal of Refugee Law* 1, 25–6; J. Allain, 'The *jus cogens* Nature of *Non-refoulement*' (2001) 13 *International Journal of Refugee Law* 533.

[109] Common Article 3 has been found to 'constitute a minimum yardstick' applicable to both international and non-international armed conflict. *Military and Paramilitary Activities in and against Nicaragua* (*Nicaragua* v. *United States of America*), Merits, Judgment of 27 June 1986 [1986] ICJ Rep. 14, para. 218.

[110] This is consistent with the way that authoritative bodies have interpreted the prohibition on torture and cruel treatment set out in human rights instruments. See, e.g., HRC, General Comment No. 31, Nature of the General Legal Obligation Imposed on State Parties to the Covenant, para. 12 (2004) (interpreting Art. 7 ICCPR); *Soering* v. *United Kingdom*, paras. 86–91 (interpreting Art. 3 ECHR). Droege, 'Transfers of Detainees', 675 also makes this argument concerning Common Article 3.

[111] See A. Farmer, '*Non-refoulement* and *jus cogens*: Limiting Anti-Terror Measures that Threaten Refugee Protection' (2008) 23 *Georgia Immigration Law Journal* 1 (arguing that 'we must insist on strict limits to the exceptions to non-refoulement articulated in the 1951 Convention on the Status of Refugees, given current state obligations under international law. There is great potential for refugee-receiving states to rely heavily on the exceptions to non-refoulement in enacting anti-terrorism policies, to the detriment of refugee protection. And yet, non-refoulement – the doctrine central to refugee

the protection against *refoulement* to other risks, including the risk of torture and cruel treatment under international human rights law, which contains no exclusions.[112]

In the context of international armed conflict, as stated above, Article 45 Geneva Convention IV specifies that no protected person may be transferred 'to a country where he or she may have reason to fear persecution for his or her political opinions or religious beliefs'. State practice and *opinio juris* demonstrates the existence of an emerging customary international humanitarian law norm requiring states to protect those repatriated or released at the close of hostilities (such as prisoners of war and civilian internees) from transfers to a risk of persecution.[113] With respect to persons detained in connection with

protection that prohibits return of an individual to a country in which he or she may be persecuted – is emerging as a new *jus cogens* norm.'

[112] Under the Convention, individuals who have committed war crimes, crimes against humanity, serious non-political crimes, or acts contrary to the purposes of the United Nations may not qualify as refugees (1951 Convention Relating to the Status of Refugees, 189 UNTS 137, Art. 1(F)). Even those who count as refugees are not protected by the Convention's *non-refoulement* rule if 'there are reasonable grounds for regarding [them] as a danger to the security of the country'; or if they 'constitute . . . a danger to the community' because they have been convicted of a 'particularly serious crime' (*ibid.*, Art. 33). Individuals who have committed certain terrorist crimes may fall within these exclusions; indeed, the Convention includes the exclusion to ensure that refugee status would not serve as a vehicle of safe haven for certain criminals. See J. Fitzpatrick, 'Rendition and Transfer in the War against Terrorism: Guantánamo and Beyond' (2003) 25 *Loyola of Los Angeles International & Comparative Law Review* 457, 472. Not all terrorism suspects will fall within these categories, however, and refugee law requires safeguards to ensure that individuals have the opportunity to forward a claim for protection on the basis of the Convention (see *ibid.*, 471–6, discussing substantive and procedural obstacles for terrorism suspects); Bruin and Wouters, 'Terrorism'; Lauterpacht and Bethlehem, 'Scope and Content of the Principle of Non-Refoulement', 134–8, analysing the national security exception. Unlike Art. 33 Refugee Convention, the *non-refoulement* obligation in the CAT is subject to no exclusions; even individuals who committed the gravest crimes have protection against the return to countries where they may be maltreated. The Committee against Torture made this clear in the 1997 case *Paez* v. *Sweden*, where it held that '[t]he nature of the activities in which the person concerned engaged cannot be a material consideration when making a [*non-refoulement*] determination under Article 3 of the Convention' (*Communication No. 39/1996: Paez* v. *Sweden*, para. 14.5, UN Doc. CAT/C/18/D/39/1996 (28 April, 1997)). The Committee's finding echoed the holding of the ECtHR, in *Chahal* v. *United Kingdom*, 23 ECtHR (Ser. A) 413, 457, para. 80 (1996), which found that 'the activities of the individual in question, however undesirable or dangerous, cannot be a material consideration' in determining whether an expulsion would be legal under Art. 3 ECHR.

[113] See *Customary International Humanitarian Law*, Rule 128; H. Gasser, 'Protection of the Civilian Population', in D. Fleck (ed.), *The Handbook of International Humanitarian Law* (Oxford: Oxford University Press, 2008), 237, 323; H. Fisher, 'Protection of Prisoners of War', in *ibid.*, 367, 416–17.

non-international armed conflict, the International Committee of the Red Cross (ICRC) has found that practice establishes that all individuals subject to repatriation or release have protection from such repatriation or release if they fear persecution.[114] Furthermore, in the context of US 'war on terror' repatriations, where the ICRC has had access to detainees, it interviews them prior to repatriation 'to ensure [the detainee] agrees to be repatriated'.[115] Finally, the UN High Commissioner for Refugees (UNHCR) has recently become more involved in protecting former detainees when they are repatriated or released in situations of armed conflict. The UNHCR has worked with states to assist individuals who fear persecution should they be returned to their country of nationality to find alternative settlement options.[116] Even absent such protections under humanitarian law, international refugee law continues to apply in the context of armed conflict to prevent transfers to a risk of persecution.[117]

No transfers to a risk of enforced disappearance An enforced disappearance is the deprivation of liberty of an individual by a state that either refuses to acknowledge the detention or conceals the fate and whereabouts of the detainee, placing the individual outside the

114 See *Customary International Humanitarian Law*, Rule 128: 'practice since 1949 has developed to the effect that in every repatriation in which the ICRC has played the role of neutral intermediary, the parties to the conflict, whether international or non-international, have accepted the ICRC's conditions for participation, including that the ICRC be able to check prior to repatriation (or release in case of a non-international armed conflict), through an interview in private with the persons involved, whether they wish to be repatriated (or released)'; H. Gasser, 'Protection of the Civilian Population', 237, 323, explaining that the refusal of transfer by a former internee to a country where he or she faces persecution 'must at all times be respected'; H. Fisher, 'Protection of Prisoners of War', 367, 416–17, concluding that although practice is mixed, the duty to repatriate POWs has in recent practice been modified by need to assess, on an individual basis, whether former POWs fear persecution upon repatriation.

115 See ICRC, Operational Update: Guantánamo Bay: Overview of the ICRC's Work for Internees (30 January 2004), at www.icrc.org/eng/resources/documents/misc/5qrc5v.htm.

116 For example, the UNHCR has worked with the United States to find settlement options for individuals set for release from detention at Guantánamo Bay.

117 See, e.g., Executive Committee, UN High Commissioner for Refugees, *Conclusion No. 94* (2002) ('Respect for the right to seek asylum, and for the fundamental principle of *non-refoulement*, should be maintained at all times.')

protection of the law.[118] Enforced disappearances are considered to be violations in themselves,[119] as well as amounting to cruel, inhuman and degrading treatment and – depending on the circumstances – possibly torture and a deprivation of the right to life under international human rights law.[120] As such, transfers to a risk of enforced disappearance – like

[118] Art. 2, International Convention for the Protection of All Persons from Enforced Disappearance, and the Inter-American Convention on Forced Disappearance of Persons. The Rome Statute establishing the International Criminal Court defines the crime of enforced disappearance more stringently, requiring intent to remove the victim from the protection of the law 'for a prolonged period of time' (Art. 7(2)(i)).

[119] Human rights bodies have found disappearances to be composite violations (citing to, among others, the rights to be free from arbitrary detention, the right to security of the person, the right to be free from torture or ill-treatment, the right to due process, and the right to life). The HRC has found disappearances to constitute violations of the ICCPR. See, e.g., *Mr S. Jegatheeswara Sarma* v. *Sri Lanka*, Communication No. 950/2000 (UN Doc. CCPR/C/78/D/950/2000 (2003), para. 9.3). The Committee against Torture has determined that secret detention is a 'per se' violation of the Convention against Torture. See Committee against Torture, Consideration of Reports Submitted by States Parties Under Article 19 of the Convention: Conclusions and Recommendations of the Committee Against Torture; United States of America (UN Doc. CAT/C/USA/CO/2 (2006), finding that enforced disappearances constitute a 'per se' violation of the Convention). The IACtHR has held that enforced disappearances violate the ACHR. See, e.g., *Velásquez Rodríguez Case*, IACtHR (Ser. C) No. 4 (1988), para. 155. The ECtHR has held that enforced disappearances constitute violations of the ECHR. See, e.g., ECtHR, *Kurt* v. *Turkey* (15/1997/799/1002) (1998). The African Commission on Human and Peoples' Rights has determined that enforced disappearances are a violation of the African Charter of Human and Peoples' Rights. See, e.g., *Mouvement Burkinabé des Droits de l'Homme et des Peuples* v. *Burkina Faso*, African Commission on Human and Peoples' Rights, Comm. No. 204/97 (2001). Enforced disappearance is also expressly prohibited by a number of international conventions. See, e.g., the International Convention for the Protection of All Persons from Enforced Disappearance; Inter-American Convention on Forced Disappearance of Persons.

[120] The HRC has determined that being disappeared amounts to cruel and inhuman treatment, and may also amount to torture, depending on the duration and circumstances. For example, the Committee found that 'being subjected to prolonged incommunicado detention [for three years] in an unknown location' amounts to 'torture and cruel and inhuman treatment, in violation of articles 7 and 10, paragraph 1' of the ICCPR. *El-Megreisi* v. *Libyan Arab Jamahiriya*, Communication No. 440/1990, UN Doc. CCPR/C/50/D/440/1990 (1994), para. 5.4. In another case, the Committee held that being abducted and denied contact with the outside world amounted to cruel and inhuman treatment. *Basilio Laureano Atachahua* v. *Peru*, Communication No. 540/1993, UN Doc. CCPR/C/56/D/540/1993 (1996), para. 85. The HRC has also repeatedly emphasized that, where the victim dies, enforced disappearances often amount to violations of the right to life. See, e.g., *Elcida Arévalo Perez et al.* v. *Colombia*, Communication No. 181/1984, UN Doc. CCPR/C/37/D/181/1984 (1989), para. 10 (noting that enforced disappearances may amount to a violation of the right to life). Similarly, the IACtHR has held that 'prolonged isolation and deprivation of

transfers to a risk of other forms of cruel treatment – are prohibited under binding human rights law.[121]

In addition to these protections, which are non-derogable and apply at all times, in the context of international armed conflict, prisoners of war and aliens in the territory of a state party may not be transferred to a country that is unwilling or unable to ensure that all the protections owed to such persons under the Geneva Conventions are upheld.[122] Enforced disappearance is understood as forbidden by the Geneva Conventions (via provisions of Geneva Conventions III and IV concerning registration of persons detained and provision of access by the ICRC to detainees[123] and by customary international law),[124] meaning that prisoners of war and protected persons may not be transferred to a risk of secret detention during international armed conflict. With respect to non-international armed conflict, both international human rights norms, which continue to apply, and customary international humanitarian law applicable to such conflicts, prohibit enforced disappearance.[125] In so far as disappearance amounts to torture or cruel treatment, transfers to a risk of such treatment should be understood to be prohibited by customary international humanitarian law.

No transfers to a risk of arbitrary deprivation of life Article 6 ICCPR prohibits the arbitrary deprivation of life. This provision, along with the general obligations set out in Article 2 to respect and ensure the rights set

communication are in themselves cruel and inhuman treatment, harmful to the psychological and moral integrity of the person and a violation of the right of any detainee to respect for his inherent dignity as a human being' (*Velásquez Rodríguez Case*, para. 156). The ECtHR has viewed this issue differently, declining to find inherent in disappearances violations of the detainee's right to be free from torture and cruel treatment. See, e.g., ECtHR, *Orhan* v. *Turkey* (App. No. 25656/94) (2002).

121 In addition, Art. 16 International Convention for the Protection of All Persons from Enforced Disappearance includes an explicit prohibition of transfers to a risk of enforced disappearance.

122 Art. 12, GC III; Art. 24, GC IV.

123 See Arts. 122, 123, 125 and 126 GC III (concerning prisoners of war), and Arts. 136, 140, 142 and 143 of GC IV (concerning enemy aliens and civilian internees). See also report submitted by Mr Manfred Nowak, independent expert charged with examining the existing international criminal and human rights framework for the protection of persons from enforced or involuntary disappearances, pursuant to para. 11 of Commission resolution 2001/46, E/CN.4/2002/71 at para. 56 (explaining that 'While international humanitarian law does not utilize the term "enforced disappearances" as such, there is no doubt that many of its provisions are aimed at preventing enforced disappearances in the context of armed conflict').

124 See *Customary International Humanitarian Law*, Rule 98.

125 *Ibid.*

out in the Covenant imposes an obligation on states not to transfer individuals to a risk of arbitrary deprivation of life.[126] This includes non-transfer to extrajudicial executions and the imposition of the death penalty in circumstances where basic procedural guarantees have not been observed.[127] States that have abolished the death penalty may not transfer individuals to countries that retain it unless they obtain firm assurances that the transferee will not be subject to capital punishment.[128]

While the right to life is non-derogable,[129] in the context of armed conflict, the *lex specialis* of international humanitarian law modifies the right to life as protected by the *lex generalis* of human rights law through rules concerning, *inter alia*, permissible targeting.[130] In both international and non-international armed conflict, persons deprived of their

[126] See HRC, General Comment No. 31, Nature of the General Legal Obligation Imposed on State Parties to the Covenant, para. 12 (2004).

[127] See HRC, General Comment No. 6, The Right to Life, para. 7 (1982). The HRC has held, in *Kindler* v. *Canada*, that a state would violate the right to life as protected by the ICCPR if it transferred an individual within its jurisdiction to the custody of a state where the individual faced a real risk of having his or her right to life violated. *See Kindler* v. *Canada* (UN Doc. CCPR/C/48/D/470/1991 (1993), para. 14.3). This includes transfer to a real risk of the imposition of the death penalty in circumstances where procedural guarantees are not upheld and no appeal is possible, or where the method of execution itself amounts to torture or cruel, inhuman or degrading treatment. See *Wright* v. *Jamaica* (UN Doc. CCPR/C/55/D/459/1991 (1995), para. 0.6); and *Ng* v. *Canada* (UN Doc. CCPR/C/49/D/469/1991 (1994), para. 16.4). While the ECtHR has determined that capital punishment carried out following unfair trial amounts to a violation of the right to life, it has not had the opportunity to rule on the issue of protections against transfer to a risk of such treatment. See Droege, 'Transfers of Detainees', 673.

[128] This rule has been set out most clearly by the ECtHR. See, e.g., *Soering* v. *UK*, para. 98; *Al-Saadoon*, paras. 141–5. The Council of Europe has emphasized this obligation in its *Guidelines on Human Rights and the Fight against Terrorism*; see Guideline XIII on Extradition. See Borelli, 'Rendition of Terrorist Suspects', 346–9, for a discussion of this issue.

[129] See, e.g., ICCPR, Art. 4.

[130] See Article 3 Common to the Geneva Conventions of 1949; Art. 46, GC I; Art. 47, GC II; Art. 13, GC III; Art. 33, GC IV. For a discussion of the distinction between permissible targeting and unlawful killings in the context of counter-terrorism, see Melzer, *Targeted Killing*, 396 (explaining that targeted killings cannot be analysed under the laws of war unless they are part of the conduct of hostilities and characterizing as a 'misconception by the US government' that its 'large-scale counter-terrorism campaign' is 'an actual war, the so-called 'war on terrorism' . . . this misleading rhetoric conflates diplomatic efforts, economic measures, law enforcement operations, international and non-international armed conflicts in a manner that does not withstand juridical scrutiny'); Duffy, *War on Terror*, 340–4.

liberty, civilians taking no active part in the hostilities, and those otherwise *hors de combat* are protected against 'violence to life and person, in particular murder of all kinds'.[131] Applying human rights law concurrently with the *lex specialis* of targeting rules, states are prohibited from transferring any person to a risk of acts that would constitute arbitrary deprivation of life in the context of armed conflict.[132]

Specific guarantees for protected persons in the context of international armed conflict In addition to the protections discussed above, states must observe additional norms in relation to particular categories of persons; such norms are not thoroughly examined in this chapter.[133] By way of example, in the context of international armed conflict, humanitarian law identifies particular requirements and bars certain transfers. Article 12 Geneva Convention III provides that prisoners of war may 'only be transferred by the Detaining Power to a Power which is a party to the Convention and after the Detaining Power has satisfied itself of the willingness and ability of such transferee Power to apply the Convention'. Article 45 Geneva Convention IV includes an almost identical provision concerning aliens in the territory of a party to an international armed conflict. These provisions mean that a state may not transfer prisoners of war or aliens to states that will not, in practice, apply all of the provisions of the Geneva Conventions relevant to those persons.[134] Such provisions include a wide variety of requirements concerning, *inter alia*, humane and fair treatment. In addition to these protections, Article 49 Geneva Convention IV categorically bars transfers of protected persons out of occupied territory, and Article 147 makes such transfers a grave breach of the Convention.[135] Individuals who are not covered by these protections set out in Geneva Conventions III and IV must nonetheless be protected against transfer to a situation in which the fundamental guarantees set out in Article 75 Additional Protocol I to

[131] See Art. 3 Common to the Geneva Conventions of 1949.

[132] Applying human rights law concurrently with the *lex specialis* of targeting rules, states should be understood to be prohibited from transferring any person to a risk of arbitrary deprivation of life in the context of armed conflict – i.e. to a country where they may be at a risk of unlawful targeted killing.

[133] For a discussion of these protections, see Gillard, 'No Place Like Home'.

[134] The Geneva Conventions also impose on the transferring state the obligation to 'take effective measures to correct the situation or shall request the return' of the prisoners of war or protected persons. Art. 12, GC III; Art. 45, GC IV.

[135] Exceptions are made for evacuations from specific areas for the security of the population; individual transfers are not countenanced in this formulation. Art. 147, GC IV.

the Geneva Conventions, which reflects customary international law, would be violated.[136]

Procedural guarantees: right to challenge transfer in advance before an independent decision-maker Formal processes for the transfer of individuals such as extradition and deportation are structured to include basic human rights guarantees and to respect the sovereignty of states. These procedures generally include mechanisms that allow individuals to challenge their transfer in advance. This right to challenge has been understood to be an aspect of the substantive guarantee of *non-refoulement*, and has also been considered as part of the right to an effective remedy, and inherent in the right to due process of law.[137] Individuals subjected to transfers outside these procedures must similarly be afforded the opportunity to challenge their detention and potential transfer.[138] As the Inter-American Juridical Committee has stated,

[136] Droege, 'Transfers of Detainees', 675 argues that the protective principles concerning transfer applicable in international armed conflict should also apply in situations of non-international or internationalized armed conflict. Droege also points out that Art. 5(4) APII to the Geneva Conventions requires that detaining powers should 'ensure [the] safety' of persons being released after detention; this rule is relevant to transfers in the context of non-international armed conflict (*ibid.*)

[137] See, e.g., ECtHR, *Chahal* v. *The United Kingdom*, para. 80 (holding that independent review of a decision to transfer in the face of a claim of *refoulement* must be independently scrutinized); UN Committee Against Torture, *Agiza* v. *Sweden*, Communication No. 233/2003 (2005), para. 13.5 (finding that 'the right to an effective remedy contained in article 3 requires, in this context, an opportunity for effective, independent and impartial review of the decision to expel or remove, once that decision is made, when there is a plausible allegation that article 3 issues arise'); HRC, *Mansour Ahani* v. *Canada*, Communication No. 1051/2002 (2006), paras. 106–8 ('the closest scrutiny should be applied to the fairness of the procedure applied to determine whether an individual is at substantial risk of torture').

[138] See IACHR, *Extension of Precautionary Measures (No. 259) regarding Detainees in Guantánamo Bay, Cuba* (2005) (finding that the right to determination of protection from *refoulement* applies to individuals held by the United States at Guantánamo and requesting that the United States provide to detainees facing transfer 'an adequate, individualized examination of their circumstances through a fair and transparent process before a competent, independent and impartial decision-maker'). The UN Committee against Torture has found that the *non-refoulement* provision of the Convention was violated when an individual was transferred informally by French authorities to Spanish police officers. The Committee stressed 'its concern at the practice whereby the police hand over individuals to their counterparts in another country . . . without the intervention of a judicial authority . . . That meant that a detainee's rights had not been respected and had placed the author in a situation where he was particularly vulnerable to possible abuse' (*Arana* v. *France*, Communication No. 63/1997, UN Doc. CAT/C/23/D/63/1997 (2000), 11.5 and

there is an inherent 'incompatibility of the practice of extraterritorial abduction with the rights of due process to which every person is entitled, no matter how serious the crime they are accused of, a right protected by international law'.[139] The minimum requirements for challenges to apprehension and transfer are set out below. Although some procedural rights guaranteed under human rights law may be subject to derogation in times of emergency that threaten the life of a nation, certain essential procedural guarantees may not be restricted even in times of great strife.[140] I argue that in the context of transfer, the rights set out below should be understood to be such non-derogable procedural rights because without them, the substantive guarantee of *non-refoulement* would lose meaning. Finally, the practice in recent years of obtaining 'diplomatic assurances' – promises by states receiving individuals that they will not subject the transferee to torture or cruel treatment – is subject to stringent procedural requirements; these requirements apply to all forms of transfer where such assurances are used.

Ability to challenge transfer on basis of fear of *refoulement* to any of the risks protected against by international law The most commonly – and clearly – set out procedural obligation in the context of transfer is the requirement that states provide individuals being transferred with the opportunity to challenge the transfer on the basis that they fear mistreatment in the receiving country. This procedural requirement has been understood to be inherent in the various norms of *non-refoulement* set out earlier in this chapter.[141] This is because *non-refoulement* standards

n. 12). For a discussion of how rendition violates procedural guarantees, see OSCE/ODIHR, 'Protecting the Rights', 143–5.

[139] Inter-American Juridical Committee, Legal Opinion Regarding the Decision of the Supreme Court of the United States of America CJI/Res./II/15/91.

[140] The HRC has made clear that states may not derogate from the right to challenge the basis of detention – even in the context of administrative detention imposed as a counter-terrorism measure. See UNHRC, General Comment No. 29, States of Emergency (UN Doc. CCPR/C/21/Rev.1/Add.11, para. 16 and n. 9, citing concluding comments concerning Israel's administrative detention scheme). Further, the *non-refoulement* obligation is non-derogable and has been found to include the right to challenge transfer on a basis of a fear of *refoulement*. See discussion below.

[141] *Chahal* v. *The United Kingdom*; *Agiza* v. *Sweden*; *Mansour Ahani* v. *Canada*. See also UN Committee against Torture, Conclusions and Recommendations of the Committee Against Torture: United States of America, para. 20 (finding that 'The State party should always ensure that suspects have the possibility to challenge decisions of *refoulement*' (2006)).

have both a subjective and an objective element: the individual must demonstrate his or her fear of mistreatment, and an official of the state considering transfer must objectively weigh this fear in light of relevant evidence.[142] This requires a process that allows the individual the opportunity to make out his or her claim, and to challenge the evidence brought forward by the state proposing transfer. Any process whereby the transferring state purports to make the *non-refoulement* assessment on its own and without the participation of the individual facing transfer is therefore impermissible under relevant international law.[143]

Ability to challenge transfer must take place prior to transfer and before an independent decision-maker To make real the substantive protections of international human rights law set out above, individuals facing transfer must have the opportunity to mount a pre-transfer challenge on the basis of any fear of *refoulement*.[144] Although human rights bodies have not held unequivocally that such a challenge must be heard by a court,[145] the review must be by an independent

[142] See, e.g., Art. 1, Convention Relating to the Status of Refugees. See also Lauterpacht and Bethlehem, 'Scope and Content of the Principle of Non-Refoulement', 128.

[143] For example, in the case of *US Interdiction of Haitians on the High Seas*, the IACHR found that the United States violated the rights of individuals it interdicted at sea when it transferred them to their country of origin without a hearing concerning their fear of *refoulement*. See *Haitian Centre for Human Rights et al.* v. *United States* (*US Interdiction of Haitians on the High Seas*), Case 10.675, IACtHR, Report No. 51/96, OEA/ser. L/V.II. 95 doc. 7 rev. paras. 167–71 (1997).

[144] *Chahal* v. *The United Kingdom*; *Agiza* v. *Sweden*; *Mansour Ahani* v. *Canada*. In its critique of the US practice of 'rendition of suspects', the UN Committee against Torture has called on the US to provide *non-refoulement* protections to individuals subject to transfer, end transfers to a risk of torture, and 'always ensure that suspects have the possibility to challenge decisions of *refoulement*' (Conclusions and Recommendations of the Committee against Torture: United States of America (2006), para. 20). The HRC has emphasized that 'By the nature of refoulement, effective review of a decision to expel to an arguable risk of torture must have an opportunity to take place prior to expulsion, in order to avoid irreparable harm to the individual and rendering the review otiose and devoid of meaning' (*Alzery* v. *Sweden*, Communication No. 1416/2005, HRC, UN Doc. CCPR/C/88/D/1416/2005 (2005), para. 11.8). Similarly, the ECtHR has held that a state violates the rights of a transferee if it does not afford the transferee the opportunity to challenge the transfer on the basis of a fear of torture (see *Shamayev* v. *Georgia and Russia*, No. 36378/02 (12 April 2005)).

[145] See Droege, 'Transfers of Detainees', 680. The issue of whether a court is required or not depends in part on whether human rights bodies construe a pre-transfer process as more akin to a deportation hearing, a criminal proceeding, or an extradition hearing. Different standards have been applied to these different procedures by various human rights bodies. For example, the HRC has held that all detainees challenging the legality

decision-maker[146] with the power to suspend the transfer during the pendency of review.[147]

Specific requirements regarding the use of diplomatic assurances A number of countries have developed a practice of seeking diplomatic assurances when they extradite, deport, or expel an individual to a country where the individual may be at risk of torture.[148] In the aftermath of the events of September 11, 2001, countries including Austria, Canada, the Netherlands, Sweden, Turkey, the United Kingdom and the United States have sought and accepted assurances concerning torture and ill-treatment in the context of legally regulated transfers from the territory of the country; legal challenges concerning the permissibility, form, and

of their detention should have access to a court for such determination (OSCE/ODIHR, 'Protecting the Rights', 160–1).

146 See UN Committee against Torture, *Agiza* v. *Sweden*. See also ECtHR, *Jabari* v. *Turkey*, App. No. 40035/98 (2000), para. 50 (stressing that the prohibition on *refoulement*, combined with the right to a remedy requires 'independent and rigorous scrutiny of a claim that there exist substantial grounds for fearing a real risk of treatment contrary to Article 3').

147 See ECtHR, *Gebremedhin* v. *France* (2007) para. 66 ('In view of the importance which the Court attaches to Article 3 of the Convention and the irreversible nature of the damage which may result if the risk of torture or ill-treatment materializes . . . [the right to a remedy] requires that the person concerned should have access to a remedy with automatic suspensive effect'). See also ECtHR, *Chahal* v. *The United Kingdom* (1996), para. 80; ECtHR, *Conka* v. *Belgium* (2002); UN Committee against Torture, *Agiza* v. *Sweden*, para. 13.5; IACHR, *Extension of Precautionary Measures (No. 259) regarding Detainees in Guantánamo Bay, Cuba* (2005). See also Report of the Special Rapporteur on torture and other cruel, inhuman or degrading treatment or punishment, para.29, UN Doc. A/59/324 (2004), at www.ohchr.org/EN/Issues/Torture/SRTorture/Pages/SRTortureIndex.aspx ('in cases where the risk of torture and ill-treatment is elevated, it is particularly important that proceedings leading to expulsion respect appropriate legal safeguards, at the very least a hearing before a judicial instance and the right to appeal'). The UNCHR has stressed that 'judicial oversight and review must be available prior to any transfer' of a terrorism suspect. See UNCHR, *Report of the United Nations High Commissioner for Human Rights on the Protection of Human Rights and Fundamental Freedoms while Countering Terrorism* (UN Doc. A/HRC/4/88 (2007)). On the requirement that transfer be suspended during review of the decision to transfer, see ECtHR, *Jabari* v. *Turkey* (2000), para. 50 (holding that the right to a remedy in the context of *non-refoulement* requires the suspension of transfer during review of a claim of *refoulement*), HRC, *Concluding Observations of the Committee Against Torture: Australia* (UN Doc. CAT/C/AUS/CO/3 (2008), para. 17, expressing concern that transfer was not automatically stayed pending review of a claim of *refoulement*).

148 Historically used in relation to promises not to use capital punishment, assurances have been accepted when used to obtain promises from a country seeking custody over a fugitive who could face the death penalty if transferred. Human rights bodies' acceptance of assurances in the death penalty context has not translated into their acceptance in the torture and ill-treatment context.

procedure for using such assurances have been mounted in each country with differing results.[149] In the face of this state practice, human rights bodies have developed an emerging rule concerning the use of diplomatic assurances against torture and ill-treatment. This rule begins with the bedrock principle that the norm of *non-refoulement* is a direct outgrowth of the prohibition of torture, and is absolute, applying to everyone in all circumstances.[150] In this context, UN human rights bodies have set out minimum procedural rules governing any use of assurances against torture. Assurances not meeting this threshold are considered by UN bodies to be violations of the sending state's human rights obligations. According to the HRC and the Committee against Torture, there are three basic requirements for the use of assurances to counter a risk of torture:[151]

(1) Assurances must be obtained using 'clear' and established procedures.[152]
(2) Assurances must be subject to judicial review.[153]

[149] See *Still at Risk: Diplomatic Assurances No Safeguard against Torture*, 17 *Human Rights Watch*, April 2005, 47–57 (Canada); 57–66 (Sweden); 67–72 (United Kingdom); 72–6 (The Netherlands); 75–9 (Austria); and 79 (Turkey). For an outstanding review of US practice, see Columbia Law School Human Rights Institute, *Promises to Keep: Diplomatic Assurances against Torture in US Terrorism Transfers* (2010), at http://web.law.columbia.edu/human-rights-institute/diplomatic-assurances/promises-keep.

[150] See, e.g., CAT Committee, *Conclusions and Recommendations of the Committee against Torture, Canada* (UN Doc. CAT/C/CR/34/CAN (2005) ('Given the absolute nature of the prohibition against refoulement contained in article 3 of the Convention, the State party should provide the Committee with details on how many cases of extradition or removal subject to the receipt of "diplomatic assurances" or guarantees have occurred since 11 September 2001').

[151] These specific requirements concerning assurances draw upon the CAT Committee's and the Human Rights Committee's recent statements which support a more general procedural right to appeal a state's decision to transfer an individual. See nn. 180–181 below. The ECtHR has also emphasized that the review of assurances must be on a case-by-case basis, taking into account the 'circumstances prevailing at the material time' (*Saadi* v. *Italy*, paras. 147–8).

[152] See HRC, *Concluding Observations of the UN Human Rights Committee, United States of America* (UN Doc. CCPR/C/USA/CO/3/Rev.1 (2006)) [hereafter HRC, *US Concluding Observations*]; see CAT Committee, *Conclusions and Recommendations of the Committee against Torture: United States of America*, 21 (UN Doc. CAT/C/USA/CO/2 (2006)) [hereafter CAT Committee, *US Conclusions*].

[153] See HRC, *US Concluding Observations*, 16; HRC, *Concluding Observations of the UN Human Rights Committee, Sweden* (UN Doc. CCPR/C/SWE/CO/6 (2009)) [hereafter HRC, *Concluding Observations: Sweden*]. The availability of judicial review was also suggested by the CAT Committee's findings in the *Agiza* case against Sweden. See CAT Committee, *Agiza* v. *Sweden*, 13.4. See *Manickavasagam Suresh* v. *Minister of*

(3) Assurances must be followed by effective post-return monitoring of the treatment of the individual returned subject to assurances.[154]

In addition to the procedural requirements set out above, the CAT Committee has also indicated that assurances may not be relied upon when transferring an individual to a country that systematically violates the Torture Convention.[155] While the HRC has not categorically rejected the use of assurances in relation to such countries, it has indicated that assurances are unlikely to mitigate the risk of torture upon return, thus indicating that they will rarely enable permissible transfers to such countries by states that have ratified the ICCPR.[156] The Special Rapporteur on Torture has set out a more stringent rule, suggesting that *any* use of diplomatic assurances to protect against torture and ill-treatment is impermissible:

> It is the view of the Special Rapporteur that diplomatic assurances are unreliable and ineffective in the protection against torture and ill-treatment: such assurances are sought usually from States where the practice of torture is systematic; post-return monitoring mechanisms have proven to be no guarantee against torture; diplomatic assurances are not legally binding, therefore they carry no legal effect and no accountability if breached; and the person whom the assurances aim to

Citizenship and Immigration and the Attorney General of Canada, 2002 SCC 1. (11 January 2002), at www.unhcr.org/refworld/country,,CAN_Se,,LKA,,3c42bdfa0,0.html. In that case, the Court examined the adequacy of procedural safeguards in the context of the *non-refoulement* obligation set out in Art. 3 CAT. The court held that '[g]iven Canada's commitment to the CAT, we find that ... the phrase "substantial grounds" raises a duty to afford an opportunity to demonstrate and defend those grounds' (*ibid.*, para. 119). The Court added that '[w]here the Minister is relying on written assurances from a foreign government that a person would not be tortured, the refugee must be given an opportunity to present evidence and make submissions as to the value of such assurances' (*ibid.*, para. 123).

154 See HRC, *Concluding Observations of the UN Human Rights Committee, United States of America*, para. 16 (UN Doc. CCPR/C/USA/CO/3/Rev.1 (2006)); *Alzery* v. *Sweden*, Communication No. 1416/2005, HRC (UN Doc. CCPR/C/88/D/1416/2005 (2005), 11.5, post-return monitoring must meet 'key aspects of international good practice').

155 See CAT Committee, US Conclusions, 21; HRC, *Concluding Observations: Sweden*, 16 ('the more systematic the practice of torture or cruel, inhuman or degrading treatment, the less likely it will be that a real risk of such treatment can be avoided by diplomatic assurances, however stringent any agreed follow-up procedure may be'). The ECHR has recently accepted assurances given by a state where torture was 'Widespread and Routine' *Othman (Abu Qatada)* v. *the United Kingdom*, App. No. 8139/09, para. 191; *Saadi* v. *Italy*, para. 237.

156 See HRC, *US Concluding Observations*, para. 16 (reminding the US that 'the more systematic the practice of torture or cruel inhuman or degrading treatment or punishment, the less likely it will be that a real risk of such treatment can be avoided by such assurances, however stringent any agreed follow-up procedures may be').

> protect has no recourse if the assurances are violated. The Special Rapporteur is therefore of the opinion that states cannot resort to diplomatic assurances as a safeguard against torture and ill-treatment where there are substantial grounds for believing that a person would be in danger of being subjected to torture or ill-treatment upon return.[157]

The acceptance of diplomatic assurances by third states that seek to ensure that their territory or facilities – such as airports – are not used to facilitate informal transfers that breach human rights law presents a different set of issues.[158] In such cases, third states seek assurances from the transferring state concerning the propriety of the transfer in order to comply with their positive obligations to prevent abuses under human rights law and to ensure they do not incur derivative liability under the rules of state responsibility. Human rights bodies have not yet addressed the standard to be used in such circumstances to assess such assurances, though they have recommended that third states undertake investigations in cases where the circumstances placed the credibility of the promises in doubt.[159]

[157] M. Nowak, Special Rapporteur of the Commission on Human Rights on Torture and Other Cruel, Inhuman or Degrading Treatment or Punishment, Report of the Special Rapporteur on Torture and Other Cruel, Inhuman or Degrading Treatment or Punishment, 51 (UN Doc. A/60/316 (2005)). This approach has been underlined in relation to specific country practices. See, e.g., Special Rapporteur of the Commission on Human Rights on Torture and Other Cruel, Inhuman or Degrading Treatment or Punishment, Report of the Special Rapporteur on Torture and Other Cruel, Inhuman or Degrading Treatment or Punishment (UN Doc. A/HRC/10/44/ADD.2 (2009)). This approach is more stringent than that adopted by the previous Special Rapporteur, Theo van Boven, who set out the following 'essential requirements for diplomatic assurances' in 2004: '[A]ssurances should as a minimum include provisions with respect to prompt access to a lawyer, recording (preferably video-recording) of all interrogation sessions and recording the identity of all persons present, prompt and independent medical examination, and forbidding incommunicado detention or detention at undisclosed places. Finally, a system of effective monitoring is to be put in place so as to ensure that assurances are trustworthy and reliable. Such monitoring should be prompt, regular and include private interviews. Independent persons or organizations should be entrusted with this task and they should report regularly to the responsible authorities of the sending and receiving States' (Special Rapporteur of the Commission on Human Rights on Torture and Other Cruel, Inhuman or Degrading Treatment or Punishment, Report of the Special Rapporteur on Torture and Other Cruel, Inhuman or Degrading Treatment or Punishment (UN Doc. A/58/324 (2005), prepared by Theo van Boven; internal citation omitted).

[158] For a discussion of such issues, see F. de Londras, 'Ireland's Potential Liability for Extraordinary Renditions Through Shannon Airport' (2007) 25 *Irish Law Times* 106.

[159] The HRC has recommended that Ireland investigate potential cases of extraordinary rendition by the United States that stopped at an Irish airport despite the use of diplomatic assurances. See HRC, *Concluding Observations of the Human Rights Committee: Ireland*

3 Practical challenges and outstanding legal issues

3.1 *Outstanding legal issues*

Existing jurisprudence and authoritative interpretations of human rights, humanitarian law and refugee law do not answer all of the legal questions pertaining to the interstate transfer of individuals suspected of terrorism. Some significant questions remain open to debate. Perhaps the most important is whether the full panoply of procedural protections are required in cases where an individual is apprehended on foreign territory by a single state and brought back to that same state for a regular criminal proceeding. Are such 'renditions to justice' lawful when the host state consents to the apprehension, even without a pre-transfer hearing? With respect to the transferring state, and under the case law of the European Court of Human Rights, the answer may be yes, so long as the transferring state abides by the substantive protections concerning basis for arrest and *non-refoulement*.[160] But what about the individual's rights vis-à-vis the host state? The host state's consent will contribute to relieving the transferring state of any wrongfulness for the apprehension and transfer under existing case law,[161] but it is not clear whether this has an impact on its own human rights obligations.[162]

Under human rights law, the host state may be liable for violating the suspect's rights if the individual would normally have had the opportunity to avail himself of the protection of domestic law before expulsion. Thus, while the transferring state may be able to design a regime through which it would not directly violate the individual's human rights, such

(UN Doc. CCPR/C/IRL/CO/3/ (2008)) [hereafter HRC, *Concluding Observations: Ireland*]. De Londras identifies three criteria from human rights jurisprudence for the acceptable use of diplomatic assurances by third states: '(i) the promise must be adequate; (ii) the matter in relation to which the promisee is made must be within the control of the promisor; and (iii) the promisor must enjoy credibility in relation to the matter at hand and in relation to the promise state' ('Ireland's Potential Liability').

160 See, e.g., *Öcalan*; *Barbie*; *Ilich Sánchez Ramirez*, accepting rendition to justice and disguised extradition.

161 See, e.g., *Öcalan* (noting with approval that the host and transferring states had cooperated in informal transfers).

162 The cases most often addressed by human rights bodies have not presented the question of the human rights obligations of the host state for informal transfers to which it has consented in the absence of a risk of torture or ill-treatment. For example, the ECtHR has either addressed the obligations of host states carrying out formal transfers (i.e. deportation and extradition from European states) or the obligations of receiving states following informal transfers (i.e. renditions to justice in European states). The 2012 case of *El-Masri* v. *Macedonia* can be distinguished as it involved a transfer to a manifest risk of torture and ill-treatment.

careful planning may not alone ensure that the individual's rights would not be violated during the transfer. To achieve an entirely rights-protecting transfer scheme, the transferring state must ensure that its actions do not amount to collusion with the host state in violation of the individual's rights in that jurisdiction.[163] Thus, the consent of the host state should be understood as necessary but not sufficient to protect the rights of the individual.[164]

In addition to these issues, additional questions remain under human rights law concerning the procedural rights of the individual facing transfer. For example, does the individual have a right to counsel during the pre-transfer hearing? Would he also have a right to appeal the decision of the independent decision-maker? Is the state conducting the transfer required to open such procedures to the public? Could it use classified materials or withhold evidence from the individual and/or his attorney? These questions need further clarification and depend, in part, on whether human rights bodies would view a pre-transfer proceeding as more akin to a criminal proceeding, a deportation hearing, or an extradition procedure, since different rules have been developed for these settings. Certain key human rights principles such as the principle of legality and due process would apply to these proceedings regardless of their form, meaning that any state that constructs a transfer regime must ensure that the procedures are set out clearly in domestic law and that the individual facing transfer is guaranteed a fair hearing.

Another set of legal issues that need further clarification are the responsibilities of third states to ensure that their actions do not either breach their own direct obligations or amount to assistance in the human rights violations of the transferring state.[165] In particular, the

[163] The test for such collusion would be the standard set out in the ILC's Articles on State Responsibility. See discussion above.

[164] The host state may not waive individual rights such as those to seek the protection of the law in its courts. While under general public international law the host state's consent may be sufficient to obviate the wrongfulness of a transferring state's actions on its territory, from a rights perspective this consent may instead amount to a violation. On the other hand, human rights law should not be allowed to prohibit transfers from failed and weak states if such states harbour suspected terrorists. Although the issue has not been squarely addressed in the case law, states lacking functioning judicial systems and effective legal protections for individuals facing expulsion should not be able to block rendition through failure to consent to a transfer. If recourse to domestic law in such situations would be meaningless, it should be understood to be unnecessary.

[165] For an excellent discussion of this issue, see J. Huckerby, 'Enabling Torture: International Law Applicable to State Participation in the Unlawful Acts of Other States' (2006), at www.chrgj.org/docs/BriefingPaperEnablingTorture.pdf.

responsibility of states that are used for stopovers, refuelling and fly-over need to be clearly articulated. Under human rights law, states have positive obligations to prevent and investigate human rights violations.[166] With respect to torture or cruel treatment, states are required to investigate acts of torture and cruel treatment or participation or conspiracy in such acts by individuals within their jurisdiction.[167] These obligations mean that when there is credible evidence that transfers involving *refoulement* are occurring that rely on the assistance of a state, that state must take action to investigate the allegations and withdraw its support.[168] The exact level of information required to trigger this obligation needs further elaboration. In addition to these direct obligations, states may attract derivative liability if their actions amount to assistance in the wrongful acts of the transferring state. Under the rules of state responsibility, states will be responsible for the acts of other states if they knowingly assist in the commission of a wrongful act that would be wrongful had the state carried out the act itself.[169] These elements are present in the case of stopovers, refuelling and even overflight, so long as the state providing such assistance did so knowing of the wrongful act. States will often be aware of informal transfers; the difficult questions concern the level of knowledge about the wrongful act – i.e. *refoulement* – required.[170] Also in need of clarification is the standard

[166] These obligations are both explicitly laid out in the text of human rights conventions and have been understood as part of the substantive prohibitions on torture and ill-treatment. For a discussion of these obligations in the context of extraordinary rendition, see Huckerby, 'Enabling Torture'.

[167] For a discussion of these obligations, see *ibid.*, 10–12.

[168] The HRC has called on European states to investigate allegations that their territory was being used for extraordinary rendition. See HRC, *Concluding Observations of the Human Rights Committee: United Kingdom of Great Britain and Northern Ireland* (UN Doc. CCPR/C/GBR/CO/6 (2008)). 'The State party should investigate allegations related to transit through its territory of rendition flights and establish an inspection system to ensure that its airports are not used for such purposes'. See also HRC, *Concluding Observations of the Human Rights Committee: Denmark* (UN Doc. CCPR/C/DNK/CO/6 (2008)); HRC, *Concluding Observations: Ireland*, calling on Ireland to 'establish a regime for the control of suspicious flights and ensure that all allegations of so-called renditions are publicly investigated'.

[169] See Huckerby, 'Enabling Torture', for a discussion of this issue in the context of extraordinary rendition.

[170] Jayne Huckerby cogently explains the test this way: 'the question of whether a State is responsible for complicity in the wrongful acts of Extraordinary Renditions and Disappearances requires a fact-intensive inquiry into exactly what it is that a State(s) is aware of with respect to the use of its territory for human rights violations. This

that should be used to assess the reliance by third states on diplomatic assurances from transferring states that use their facilities or air space.[171]

In addition to these issues, open questions relevant to all counter-terrorism operations – such as when and to what extent international humanitarian law applies to counter-terrorism measures and thus which regime of law applies to various transfers – are relevant to the transfer of terrorism suspects but are too broad to be examined here. Additional – more finite and limited – legal issues are addressed in the text and footnotes above.[172] Like all legal issues that have not been adequately presented to a court or authoritative human rights body, a wide range of additional legal issues could arise when applying the legal principles set out above to the complex facts presented in the context of counter-terrorism.

3.2 *Practical challenges*

National courts have often taken significantly more conservative approaches to the legal questions analysed in this chapter. To cite a single example, courts in the United States have rejected the extraterritorial application of refugee law, dismissed the ability of courts to halt the transfer of individuals held by US forces abroad on the basis of a fear of ill-treatment; and declined to reject the use of diplomatic assurances in some cases where individuals fear torture upon transfer.[173] The most pressing practical challenge, therefore, is how to ensure that domestic

inquiry will take place in the context of what has been described by the UN Committee Against Torture in *Agiza* v. *Sweden* as "progressively wider discovery of information as to the scope of measures undertaken by numerous States to expose individuals suspected of involvement in terrorism to risks of torture abroad"' ('Enabling Torture', 13).

171 For a discussion of these issues, see de Londras, 'Ireland's Potential Liability'.

172 For example, it is not clear whether access to a court is required for the procedural rights of the individual to be protected or if another type of independent body may be acceptable (see *ibid.*).

173 See *Sale* v. *Haitian Centers Council*, 509 US 155 (1993) (US Supreme Court held that Art. 33, the provision of the Refugee Convention concerning *non-refoulement*, does not apply outside the United States); *Munaf* v. *Geren* (US Supreme Court held that detainees held by US forces in Iraq could not obtain relief from a US court on the grounds that their transfer to Iraqi authorities would place them at risk of torture); and *Sameh Sami S. Khouzam* v. *Attorney General et al.*; *Sameh Sami S. Khouzam* v. *M Chertoff, Secretary of Department of Homeland Security et al.*, Nos. 07-2926 and 08-1094 (US Court of Appeals for the Third Circuit, 2008), holding that while diplomatic assurances may be used, an individual facing transfer on the basis of their existence must have the chance to challenge them.

courts, legislatures and executive authorities will integrate the more protective norms into national practice.

Even with respect to states that actively seek to ensure that their policies are compliant with humanitarian, refugee, and human rights law, a wide range of practical challenges remain. Some examples include:

- What should be done with individuals suspected of crimes of terrorism who cannot be transferred due to *non-refoulement* concerns and who also cannot be tried due to the host state's lack of evidence? This scenario is not unlikely, since the quantum of evidence needed to justify apprehension and transfer is significantly below that needed for criminal conviction.
- Could a transfer process that upholds the rights of the individual be sufficiently quick to ensure that individuals suspected of planning crimes of terrorism can be apprehended before plots are carried out? Rendition has often been justified by its relative celerity in comparison with extradition or even deportation. Would formalized processes allow states to apprehend terrorism suspects quickly enough to thwart plots?[174]
- Could rendition processes be designed to avoid common legal problems such as the bar on extradition of nationals,[175] the absence of dual criminality,[176] and the failure of key states to agree to extradition treaties? What about common political problems, such as the need for a host state to be seen as protecting its nationals or the desire on the part of host state politicians to avoid overtly cooperating with the transferring state?[177]
- How can transferring states comply with procedural guarantees extraterritorially? What forum would be used to allow the suspect to challenge his transfer? Where would the detainee be held during this process, and for how long?

[174] See Borelli, 'Rendition of Terrorist Suspects', 338. See also L. Wright, *The Looming Tower: Al Qaeda and the Road to 9/11* (New York: Vintage, 2007), 231–4, describing a rendition to the United States and how it was designed to get around logistical problems with extradition.

[175] This is a common bar to extradition.

[176] This would occur, for example, when a state has not adequately criminalized all acts of terrorism.

[177] See McNeal and Field, 'Snatch and Grab Ops', 492–3, citing examples of instances in which the United States tried to get custody of an individual suspected of terrorism but could not due to the non-cooperation of foreign states or a failed state.

- If the transfer rules apply to situations of collective self-defence, assistance in peacekeeping, or other lawful collective military operations, how can the international community avoid creating a situation where the detaining power is permanently responsible for those it detains when the local authorities cannot credibly guarantee the individual will not be subject to ill-treatment?[178]
- What kind of information, and in what form, should third states require from transferring states to ensure that they are not facilitating wrongful acts by allowing the use of their airspace, airports or other facilities?
- How can the international community ensure that procedural protections for individuals suspected of terrorism do not create perverse incentives – such as the incentive to kill a suspected terrorist instead of detaining and transferring him?[179]

4 Recommendations

To ensure that human rights, humanitarian law and refugee law are upheld in the transfer of individuals suspected of crimes of terrorism, the following recommendations are offered.

4.1 Recommendations to transferring states

- Transferring states should use all available formal processes of transfer, such as deportation or extradition and may not intentionally bypass them. States seeking individuals for crimes of terrorism should pursue formal arrangements such as bilateral or multilateral extradition treaties with the widest possible range of states, and should

[178] See Droege, 'Transfers of Detainees', 693. 'Clearly, if states are present in situations of armed conflict, it is foreseeable that they will have to take people into their effective control, in which case they will be responsible for those persons' well-being.' Droege also offers a potential solution: 'states have sometimes found alternative solutions, such as prolongation of temporary detention; release of individuals who do not pose a serious risk, accompanied by surveillance measures and regular appearances before government authorities; transfers to third states; or transfers limited to specific detention facilities where the person does not run a risk or specifically excluding detention facilities where he or she would run a risk' (*ibid.*, 693–4).

[179] This scenario could arise when a transferring state asserts the right under international humanitarian law to lawfully target a suspected terrorist (for example, when the individual is directly participating in hostilities against it or is a member of an irregular armed force) and does not wish to prosecute the individual criminally. For more on targeted killings in the context of counter-terrorism, see Chapter 18 in this volume.

address the practical and political obstacles to their use. States contemplating transfer should consider alternative means, such as cooperation with the judicial authorities of the host state in prosecuting the individual.

- Transferring states should seek the consent of the host state if contemplating a transfer and should not accept that consent where it would amount to assistance in violating the rights of the individual sought (for example, if the suspect has valid rights to assert in the host state's courts).
- Transferring states must have a valid legal basis for apprehending the individual in contemplation of transfer. They must not rely on overly broad conceptions of terrorism or armed conflict to justify detentions that would otherwise be arbitrary.
- Transferring states may not transfer individuals to a risk of: torture or cruel, inhuman or degrading treatment; persecution; enforced disappearance; or arbitrary deprivation of life.
- Transferring states must extend the right to challenge the basis for the transfer and any fear of *refoulement* in advance before an independent decision-maker.
- Transferring states may only rely on diplomatic assurances if they are obtained using 'clear' and established procedures, subject to judicial review, and followed by effective post-return monitoring of the treatment of the individual returned subject to assurances. Assurances from states that systematically violate the prohibition on torture or ill-treatment must be subject to searching inquiry and may not be permissible.

4.2 *Recommendations to host states*

- States that have not ratified the major international conventions on terrorism should do so.
- All states should ensure that crimes of terrorism are established in domestic law.
- States should work to eliminate the practical obstacles to prosecution by establishing judicial cooperation agreements.
- States should actively pursue prosecution of individuals present on their territory who are suspected of crimes of terrorism, including through legal cooperation regimes and the sharing of evidence. Where it is not possible to prosecute such individuals, they should be subject to extradition to a state capable of prosecuting them.
- States should not harbour individuals sought for crimes of terrorism by failing to prosecute or extradite.

- States should work to eliminate the legal obstacles to extradition:
  - states should eliminate the rule against extraditing nationals; and
  - states should ensure that the political offence exception does not apply to crimes of terrorism.
- A host state should not consent to a transfer from its territory until it has satisfied itself that the transferring state will comply with the minimum substantive and procedural guarantees owed to an individual subject to transfer:
  - to do so, host states should require documentation confirming the legal basis for any transfer that would be initiated from its territory; and
  - states should not consent to transfers from their territory when doing so would otherwise violate the human rights of that individual.
- Host states should exercise due diligence to ensure that foreign agents do not violate the human rights of individuals on their territory or in their effective control:
  - states should not tacitly consent to apprehensions and transfers that would involve human rights violations; and
  - states should seek information about the activities of foreign agents on their soil and should, where credible allegations arise, initiate investigations into violations by such agents.

4.3 Recommendations to third states

- Third states should ensure that their actions in allowing transit, refuelling or other logistical assistance, do not amount to the aid or assistance in acts that are wrongful under international law:
  - third states should require explicit assurances that any aircraft used by a state that will transit through its airspace or use its facilities is doing so in full respect of human rights; and
  - third states should require documentation confirming the status and legal basis for the transport of any detainees through its airspace or territory.
- States should take prompt action to investigate whenever credible allegations arise that their airports, airspace, or other territories have been used to transfer individuals contrary to human rights protections.
  - In such cases, the establishment of inspection systems at airports or other positive measures may be required.

20

Terrorism as a crime in international and domestic law: open issues

CLAUDIA MARTIN

1 Introduction

There are thirty instruments adopted within the universal and regional level pertaining to the fight against international terrorism.[1] At the universal level, four treaties refer to the prohibition of terrorism in the context of civil aviation,[2] one refers to the prevention and punishment of crimes against internationally protected persons,[3] one refers to the prohibition of taking of hostages,[4] five refer to the prevention and protection against the use of bombs and nuclear materials,[5] four refer to the suppression of terrorist acts against maritime navigation and fixed platforms[6] and one refers to the suppression of the financing of

[1] Extract from the Report of the Secretary-General on Measures to Eliminate International Terrorism (UN Doc. A/64/161(2009)). According to the report, 16 instruments are universal (13 conventions and 3 amendments) and 14 are regional treaties.

[2] 1963 Convention on Offences and Certain Other Acts Committed on Board Aircraft, 704 UNTS 220; 1970 Convention for the Suppression of Unlawful Seizure of Aircraft, 860 UNTS 106; 1971 Convention for the Suppression of Unlawful Acts against the Safety of Civil Aviation, 974 UNTS 178; and 1988 Protocol for the Suppression of Unlawful Acts of Violence at Airports Serving International Civil Aviation, supplementary to the Convention for the Suppression of Unlawful Acts against the Safety of Civil Aviation, 1589 UNTS 474.

[3] 1973 Convention on the Prevention and Punishment of Crimes against Internationally Protected Persons, including Diplomatic Agents, 1035 UNTS 167.

[4] 1979 International Convention against the Taking of Hostages, 1316 UNTS 205.

[5] 1980 Convention on the Physical Protection of Nuclear Materials, 1458 UNTS 125; 2005 Amendment to the Convention on the Physical Protection of Nuclear Materials; 1991 Convention on the Marking of Plastic Explosives for the Purpose of Detection, 2212 UNTS 359; 1997 International Convention for the Suppression of Terrorists Bombings, 2149 UNTS 256; and 2005 International Convention for the Suppression of Acts of Nuclear Terrorism, 2445 UNTS 89.

[6] 1988 Convention for the Suppression of Unlawful Acts against the Safety of Maritime Navigation, 1678 UNTS 222; 2005 Protocol to the Convention for the Suppression of

terrorism.[7] At the regional level, in general, all the anti-terrorist instruments gear towards the overall suppression and combating of terrorism.[8] These treaties have created a complex web of international obligations defined by some as 'a sort of evolving code of terrorist offences'.[9] However, a comprehensive definition of terrorism as an international crime has not been provided.

Lack of consensus in the international community regarding the scope of the crime of terrorism coupled with the need to react against specific acts considered 'terrorist' prompted the so-called 'piecemeal approach', which lead to the adoption of several counter-terrorist conventions at the universal level. Adoption of these 'sectoral' conventions, however, was considered insufficient to address the phenomenon of terrorism. In 1999 the General Assembly of the United Nations decided that the elaboration of a Comprehensive Convention on International Terrorism ('Draft Terrorism Convention') was required to provide a framework to the fight against international terrorism and entrusted this task to two bodies: an Ad Hoc Committee and a Working Group of the General Assembly's Six Committee.[10] Though some progress on the negotiation of the Convention is reflected in the adoption of a draft text, final adoption of a comprehensive treaty has remained stalled as a result of divergent views on the scope of the definition of terrorism.[11]

In the aftermath of September 2001, the UN Security Council adopted several Resolutions under its Chapter VII powers imposing upon state members a number of general obligations to combat international terrorism.[12] Due to the need for immediate action, the inexistence of a comprehensive treaty on international terrorism, and the insufficiency

Unlawful Acts against the Safety of Maritime Navigation; 1988 Protocol for the Suppression of Unlawful Acts against the Safety of Fixed Platforms Located on the Continental Shelf, 1678 UNTS 304; 2005 Protocol to the Protocol for the Suppression of Unlawful Acts against the Safety of Fixed Platforms Located on the Continental Shelf.

7 1999 International Convention for the Suppression on the Financing of Terrorism, 2178 UNTS 179.

8 See, generally, Extract from the Report of the Secretary-General on Measures to Eliminate International Terrorism.

9 D. O'Donnell, 'International Treaties against Terrorism and the Use of Terrorism during Armed Conflict and by Armed Forces' (2006) 88 *International Review of the Red Cross* 864, 855.

10 M. Hmoud, 'Negotiating the Draft Comprehensive Convention on International Terrorism: Major Bones of Contention' (2006) 4 *Journal of International Criminal Justice* 1031, 1031–2.

11 *Ibid.*

12 See generally UN Doc. S/Res/1373 (2001), UN Doc. S/Res/1540 (2004) and UN Doc. S/Res./1566 (2004).

of the 'sectoral' treaties, the Security Council was prompted to take up the role of a 'law-making' body.[13] In Resolution 1373, the Security Council urged states, *inter alia*, to prevent and suppress the financing of terrorism; refrain from providing any support to individuals or entities involved in terrorism; deny safe haven to those who plan, support or carry out terrorist acts; make terrorism a serious crime in domestic legislation with commensurate punishment; cooperate with other states to prevent and suppress terrorism; and ratify international anti-terrorist treaties.[14] Also, this resolution set up the Counter-Terrorism Committee to monitor compliance with the obligations imposed upon states.[15] In Resolution 1566, the Security Council condemned all acts of terrorism as one of the most serious threats to peace and security and reaffirmed a number of the obligations stated in previous resolutions regarding cooperation and the ratification of treaties.[16] In subsequent Resolution 1624, not adopted in the framework of Chapter VII,[17] the Security Council called upon states to adopt all necessary measures to prohibit, prevent, and deny safe haven to those who incite others to commit terrorist acts. Though this resolution is not technically binding, the Security Council directed the Counter-Terrorism Committee to monitor states' efforts to implement it. Despite the binding obligations imposed upon states, the Security Council resolutions failed to provide for a clear definition of terrorism. The only exception is the definition attempted in Resolution 1566 which states that certain criminal acts committed with intent to cause death or serious bodily injury, or taking hostages, with the purpose of provoking a state of terror in the population or compelling a government or an international organization to do or abstain from doing an act, which constitute an offence within the anti-terrorist conventions, embody the notion of terrorism.[18] Even if this definition may contribute in developing a more consistent approach to the work carried out by the Security Council, its scope does not appear to be fully in line with the one debated at the negotiations of the Draft Terrorism Convention.

The existing anti-terrorist conventions, the negotiations on a Draft Terrorism Convention to combat international terrorism and the

[13] A. Bianchi, 'Security Council's Anti-Terror Resolutions and Their Implementation by Member States: An Overview' (2006) 4 *Journal of International Criminal Justice* 1044, 1047.

[14] UN Doc. S/Res./1373 (2001), paras. 2–3. [15] *Ibid.*, paras. 6–7. [16] Res. 1566.

[17] UN Doc. S/Res./1624 (2005). [18] UN Doc. S/Res./1566, para. 3.

Resolutions adopted by the UN Security Council in the aftermath of September 11 have created a patchwork of norms that lack a cohesive approach in articulating acts that constitute terrorism in current international law. The recent judgment of the Special Tribunal of Lebanon holding that there is sufficient evidence to conclude that an international crime of terrorism in times of peace has evolved into a rule of customary international law does not seem to resolve this problem.[19] The Special Tribunal found that existing anti-terrorism treaties, UN Resolutions, and the legislative and judicial practice of states showed 'the formation of a general *opinio juris* in the international community, accompanied by a practice consistent with such *opinion*, to the effect that a customary rule of international law regarding the international crime of terrorism, at least in time of peace, has indeed emerged'.[20] This conclusion, however, has been contested by a number of experts who considered that the evidence used by the Special Tribunal to support its holding was scant and failed to demonstrate any existing consensus as to the scope of such international crime.[21] Moreover, the ongoing inability of states to complete the Draft Terrorism Convention is considered as a very persuasive reason to challenge the actual existence of a rule of customary international law.[22]

Furthermore, despite the arguments that the definition provided in Security Council Resolution 1566 constitutes an adequate starting point for purposes of combating international terrorism,[23] uncertainty still

[19] Special Tribunal for Lebanon, Interlocutory Decision on the Applicable Law: Terrorism, Conspiracy, Homicide, Perpetration, Cumulative Charging, STL-11-01/I, A.Ch., 16 February 2011 [hereafter STL Decision]. See also on this issue, A. Cassese, 'The Multifaceted Criminal Notion of Terrorism in International Law' (2006) 4 *Journal of International Criminal Justice* 933, 935.

[20] STL Decision, para. 85. With respect to the scope of the definition of terrorism under customary international law, the Tribunal held that it involved three key elements: (1) the perpetration of a criminal act (murder, kidnapping, hostage-taking, arson, among others), or threatening such act; (2) the intent to spread fear among the population or directly or indirectly coerce a national or international authority to take some action or refrain from it; (3) when the act involves a transnational element.

[21] See, in general, B. Saul, 'Legislating from a Radical Hague: The United Nations Special Tribunal for Lebanon invents an International Crime of Transnational Terrorism' (2011) 24 *Leiden Journal of International Law* 677. Also, K. Ambos, 'Judicial Creativity at the Special Tribunal for Lebanon: Is There a Crime of Terrorism under International Law?' (2011) 24 *Leiden Journal of International Law* 655.

[22] Saul, 'Legislating from a Radical Hague', 694.

[23] See generally Report of the Special Rapporteur on the promotion and protection of human rights and fundamental freedoms while countering terrorism (UN Doc. E/CN.4/2006/98 (2005)).

remains regarding crucial aspects of this offence that makes a consistent application of the term very challenging and, consequently, ineffective for the overall success of the fight against this crime. Therefore, reaching an agreement on a comprehensive definition of terrorism at the international level seems to be the next unavoidable step forward.

The goal of this chapter is to explore two issues that remain unresolved as a result of the lack of definition of terrorism in international law and that have become either an obstacle for combating this crime or have adversely impacted the respect of other rules of international law, especially human rights and humanitarian law principles. The first of these issues involves the blurring between the notion of terrorism and armed conflict. The second aspect explores the impact that the failure to articulate a definition of terrorism coupled with the obligations arising out of UN Security Council Resolutions and other anti-terrorist treaties have had on the protection of human rights in the domestic jurisdiction of states. Consideration is also made on the impact that the lack of a definition of terrorism has on the international judicial cooperation of states for purposes of prosecuting alleged terrorists.

2 The blurring between the notion of international terrorism and armed conflict

The perpetration of acts of violence against civilians and civilian targets has taken place in the context of armed conflicts and in peacetime. The lack of a clear definition distinguishing international terrorism from acts of warfare, however, has provided fertile terrain for conflating the notion of international terrorism and armed conflict. Whereas language in existing anti-terrorist international conventions and Security Council resolutions adopted to combat terrorism have not contributed to the resolution of this matter, negotiations on the Draft Terrorism Convention remain stalled as a consequence of a lack of agreement regarding whether acts committed in armed conflict should be excluded from the scope of that offence.[24]

Four of the anti-terrorist conventions adopted at the international level have provisions excluding application of the treaty in certain situations of armed conflict or when international humanitarian law becomes the applicable law in a particular context. The language of these instruments, however, does not provide for a consistent approach

[24] Hmoud, 'Negotiating the Draft Comprehensive Convention'.

on whether or under which circumstances the crime of terrorism would not be applied in armed conflict. First, Article 12 International Convention against the Taking of Hostages ('Convention against Taking Hostages') declares that an act of hostage-taking would be excluded from the application of this treaty if it were committed in an armed conflict as defined by the Geneva Conventions and the Additional Protocols, provided that those conventions and protocols impose upon the states parties thereto to prosecute or extradite the hostage-taker.[25] Regardless of the fact that hostage taking is prohibited by several provisions of international humanitarian law,[26] the application of the anti-terrorist convention would prevail even in a situation of armed conflict if it cannot be established that the Geneva Conventions or the Protocols created an obligation to prosecute or extradite.[27]

Second, Article 19 International Convention on the Suppression of Terrorist Bombings ('Convention on the Suppression of Terrorist Bombings') provides that this treaty does not affect other rights or obligations of states and individuals under international law, in particular those arising under international humanitarian law.[28] Next, it excludes from the application of the Convention 'the activities of armed forces during an armed conflict, as those terms are understood under international humanitarian law, which are governed by that law'.[29] Thus, the precise definition of what constitutes armed forces and armed conflict are essential for characterizing a particular act as a terrorist act or not under this Convention. As the debate on 'unprivileged combatants' and the so-called 'war on terror' shows, the scope of 'armed forces' and 'armed conflict' continues to present challenges for their application.

Third, Article 2 International Convention for the Suppression of the Financing of Terrorism ('Convention for the Suppression of the Financing of Terrorism') does not include a provision excluding application of this treaty in situations of armed conflict. However, it states

[25] International Convention against the Taking of Hostages.

[26] 1949 Geneva Conventions, 75 UNTS 32, Common Article 3; 1949 Convention Relative to the Protection of Civilian Persons in Time of War, 75 UNTS 288, Arts. 34 and 147; 1977 Protocol Additional to the Geneva Convention of 12 August 1949 and Relating to the Protection of Victims of Internal Armed Conflict, 1125 UNTS 4, Art. 75(2); and 1977 Protocol Additional to the Geneva Convention of 12 August 1949 and Relating to the Protection of Victims of Non-International Armed Conflict, 1125 UNTS 610, Art. 4(2)(c).

[27] O'Donnell, 'International Treaties', 864.

[28] 1997 International Convention for the Suppression of Terrorists Bombings.

[29] *Ibid.*

that a person would commit the offence of financing terrorism if he or she provides or collects funds intended to be used to carry out, *inter alia*, death or serious bodily injury 'to a civilian, or to any other person not taking an active part in the hostilities in a situation of armed conflict' when the motive is to intimidate a population or compel a government or international organization to do or abstain from doing any act.[30] The language of this provision poses a number of questions if applied in the context of an armed conflict. The first question is whether the provision implies that the financing of acts carried out in violation of the principle of distinction under international humanitarian law constitute acts of terrorism that trigger the application of the Convention. The second question is whether, as a consequence of the previous question, the financing of all acts considered lawful under international humanitarian law remain excluded from the Convention's reach. Finally, the need to show motive in carrying out an act proscribed by the Convention would be in principle determinant for its application. Thus, financing acts of terror against the civilian population or of those not participating in a conflict for a motive different from terrorizing the population appear not to fall within the scope of the treaty.

Finally, Article 4 of the most recent anti-terrorism Convention adopted in the framework of the United Nations, the International Convention for the Suppression of Acts of Nuclear Terrorism follows a similar approach to Article 19 of the Convention on the Suppression of Terrorist Bombings and excludes application of the treaty to the activities of the armed forces during an armed conflict as these terms are governed under international humanitarian law.[31]

The resolutions adopted by the Security Council in the aftermath of September 11 have also failed, at least expressly, to consider whether the obligations they are imposing upon states apply in a context of armed conflict. Resolutions 1373 and 1540 only state that the fight against terrorism must be carried out in accordance with the Charter of the United Nations.[32] Resolutions 1566 and 1624, on the other hand, go further in clarifying states' obligations when they assert that states must implement the duties arising from these resolutions in compliance with

30 1999 International Convention for the Suppression on the Financing of Terrorism.

31 2005 International Convention for the Suppression of Acts of Nuclear Terrorism. The European Union Framework Decision on Combating Terrorism also includes a similar saving clause in its preamble. The OAS Convention only includes a general clause.

32 See UN Doc. S/Res./1373 (2001), preamble and UN Doc. S/Res./1540 (2004), preamble.

their obligations under international humanitarian law.[33] Furthermore, Resolution 1566 appears to include within its definition of terrorism acts intended to cause death or serious bodily injury perpetrated against civilians, without any qualification as to the context in which the act needs to occur.[34] Ultimately, the resolutions underlined that all acts of terrorism, regardless of their motive and whoever is the perpetrator constitute serious threats to peace and security.[35] This language has been understood by some experts as a trend towards decoupling or toning down the position of the principle of self-determination in relation to terrorism.[36]

The Draft Terrorism Convention position on whether acts committed in armed conflict should be excluded from the notion of terrorism and to what extent remains subject to intense negotiation. The initial draft submitted by India closely followed the language of Article 19 Convention on the Suppression of Terrorist Bombings and stated that 'activities of the armed forces during an armed conflict, as those terms are understood under international law, which are governed by that law' would be excluded from the scope of the Draft Terrorism Convention.[37] This language was challenged by states representing the Organization of Islamic Conferences (OIC) arguing that the language was not sufficiently protective of peoples struggling against foreign occupation, aggression or colonialism under the principle of self-determination.[38] The OIC member states proposed alternative language replacing 'armed forces' for 'parties' and adding 'including situations of foreign occupation' as part of the notion of armed conflict.[39] Since a narrow interpretation of 'armed forces' could restrict its meaning only to armed forces of the state, the goal of the OIC proposal was to ensure that by using the word 'parties' the acts of other combatants such as armed forces of organized resistance and liberation movements in situations of occupation in international armed conflicts or insurgents in non-international armed conflicts would not fall within the notion of terrorism.[40] The reasons

[33] See UN Doc. S/Res./1566, preamble; and UN Doc. S/Res./1624, preamble and para. 4.

[34] See UN Doc. S/Res./1566, para. 3.

[35] See UN Doc. S/Res./1566, para. 1; and UN Doc. S/Res./1624 (2005), preamble.

[36] E. Johannes Husabø and I. Bruce, *Fighting Terrorism through Multilevel Criminal Legislation: Security Council Resolution 1373, the EU Framework Decision on Combating Terrorism and their Implementation in Nordic, Dutch, and German Criminal Law* (Leiden: Martinus Nijhoff, 2009).

[37] Hmoud, 'Negotiating the Draft Comprehensive Convention'. [38] *Ibid.* [39] *Ibid.*

[40] *Ibid.*

behind adding the phrase 'situations of foreign occupation' are less clear and have triggered different interpretations by experts in the field. Some authors have considered that the purpose of the amendment is to exclude from the scope of the future convention acts transpiring during occupation in the absence of armed conflict.[41] As of the last reported meeting of the Ad Hoc Committee in charge of the treaty negotiations, there was no consensus to resolve this sensitive issue.[42]

The recent judgment of the Special Tribunal for Lebanon (STL) has suggested that an incipient rule of customary international law may be emerging regarding the application of the notion of international terrorism during times of armed conflict. The Tribunal cited the extensive state ratification of the Convention for the Suppression of Financing Terrorism without reservation to the provision which makes this treaty applicable to armed conflict as evidence of a consensus in the international community that international terrorism should criminalize acts which occur both in peacetime and in armed conflict. Ultimately, however, the STL concluded that the rule was not in existence yet and that only a definition of terrorism applicable in peacetime has crystallized into a rule of customary international law.[43]

In sum, the existing anti-terrorism legal framework shows an overlapping between acts falling within the notion of terrorism and acts of war regulated under international humanitarian law that does not benefit a consistent application of these two areas of law.[44] The best approach to resolve this situation would be to avoid blurring international terrorism with acts of warfare and assert the authority of international humanitarian law to regulate situations of armed conflict in its entirety. International humanitarian law is the corpus of law governing the conduct of the parties in an armed conflict and is comprised of both treaty law and customary international law. Though 'armed conflict' is not clearly defined under international humanitarian law, both international and non-international conflicts trigger application of this body of law. Article 2 Protocol II to the Geneva Conventions excludes from the notion of armed conflict 'situations of internal disturbances and

[41] O'Donnell, 'International Treaties', 877.

[42] See, generally, Report of the Ad Hoc Committee established by General Res. 51/210 of 17 December 1996 (UN Doc. A/64/37 (2011)).

[43] STL Decision, paras. 107–10.

[44] For a detailed examination of the issues of armed conflict and terrorist organizations, see Chapter 14 of this volume.

tensions, such as riots, isolated and sporadic acts of violence and other acts of a similar nature'.[45]

Acts considered as terrorist in many of the existing international definitions of terrorism are similarly prohibited under international humanitarian law when occurring in the context of an armed conflict.[46] First, the principle of distinction between civilians and combatants and between civilian objectives and military objectives is a core principle of international humanitarian law codified in the Geneva Conventions Protocol I and Protocol II thereto, as well as in other related treaties.[47] Moreover, the principle of distinction is considered a rule of customary international law applicable in both international and non-international armed conflicts.[48] The two core prohibitions that derive from the principle of distinction are the prohibition on directing attacks against civilians and civilian objects and the prohibition on indiscriminate attacks. Other rules governing the conduct of hostilities which main purpose is to prevent unnecessary harm to civilians and civilian objects include the prohibition of using 'human shields' as well as the principle of precautions in attack.[49] Finally, the taking of hostages is prohibited by Common Article 3 of the Geneva Conventions, the Fourth Geneva Convention and Protocols I and II.[50]

Moreover, several provisions from the Geneva Conventions and its Protocols specifically prohibit the use of measures of terrorism or acts of terrorism against persons in the power of a party to the conflict.[51] In particular, Articles 51(2) of Additional Protocol I and 13(2) of Additional Protocol II prohibit 'acts or threats of violence the primary purpose of which is to spread terror among the civilian population' during the conduct of hostilities. These rules are also considered customary international law applicable in international and non-international armed conflicts.[52]

[45] See APII, Art. 2.

[46] *International Humanitarian Law and the Challenges of Contemporary Armed Conflicts* (ICRC Doc. 301C/07/8.4 (2007), 5). See also generally, S. Jodoin, 'Terrorism as a War Crime' (2007) 7 *International Criminal Law Review* 77.

[47] See API, Arts. 48, 51(2) and 52(2) and APII, Art. 13(2).

[48] J. M. Henckaerts and L. Doswald-Beck, *Customary International Humanitarian Law* (Cambridge: Cambridge University Press, 2005), 3.

[49] *International Humanitarian Law and the Challenges of Contemporary Armed Conflicts.*

[50] GC, Common Article 3; GC IV, Arts. 34 and 147; API, Art. 75(2); APII, Art. 4(2)(c).

[51] Henckaerts and Doswald-Beck, *Customary International Humanitarian Law*, 8–9.

[52] *Ibid.*, 8.

As the International Committee of the Red Cross and several experts have stated, once the threshold of an armed conflict has been reached, there is little added value in designating acts of violence against civilians or civilian objects as 'terrorists'.[53] First, applying humanitarian law principles to acts of violence against civilians or civilian objects in an armed conflict does not imply that these acts cannot be punished. In fact, directing attacks against the civilian population and civilian objects in international armed conflict is considered a war crime under the Statute of the International Criminal Court[54] and a grave breach under Additional Protocol I.[55] Also, making the civilian population the object of attack in a non-international armed conflict is considered a war crime under the Statute of the International Criminal Court.[56] Moreover, under the same statute, directing attacks against civilian objects in non-international armed conflicts could be, under certain circumstances, a war crime as well.[57] Furthermore, the taking of hostages is considered a grave breach under the Geneva Conventions[58] and a war crime under the Statute of International Criminal Court regardless if it was committed in international or non-international armed conflict.[59]

Additionally, 'acts of terrorism' have been considered as war crimes under the Statutes of the International Criminal Tribunal for Rwanda and the Special Court for Sierra Leone.[60] Finally, the International Criminal Tribunal of the former Yugoslavia in the *Galić* case found that the shelling and sniping to kill, maim, wound and terrorize civilians constituted the crime of terrorizing the civilian population in violation of the laws and customs of war.[61] Perpetrators of war crimes bear individual criminal responsibility and may be prosecuted by states or international courts under different bases of jurisdiction. If the crimes are considered grave breaches under the Geneva Convention or Protocol I,

[53] *International Humanitarian Law and the Challenges of Contemporary Armed Conflicts*, 5.

[54] 1998 Rome Statute for the International Criminal Court, 2187 UNTS 3, Art. 8(2)(b)(1).

[55] API, Art. 85(3)(a). [56] Rome Statute, Art. 8(2)(e)(i)

[57] Henckaerts and Doswald-Beck, *Customary International Humanitarian Law*, 7.

[58] GC IV, Arts. 34 and 147. [59] Rome Statute, Art. 8(2)(a)(viii) and (c)(iii).

[60] Statute of the International Criminal Tribunal for Rwanda (UN Doc. S/Res./955 (1994), Art. 4(d)); Statute of the Special Court for Sierra Leone, S/Res./1315 (2000), Art. 3(d).

[61] *Prosecutor* v. *Stanislav Galić*, Judgment, Case No. IT-98-29-T, T.Ch.I, 5 December 2003, para. 160. See also D. Kravetz, 'The Protection of Civilians in War: The ICTY's *Galić* Case' (2004) 17 *Leiden Journal of International Law* 521.

they must be prosecuted by states under the obligations arising out of those treaties.[62]

Furthermore, labelling acts of warfare carried out by parties in a conflict not falling within the traditional notion of 'armed forces' as terrorism and the members of those groups as 'terrorists' may lead to an erosion in compliance with the principles of international humanitarian law and ultimately endanger the peaceful resolution of conflicts.[63] As described before, several anti-terrorist conventions and the draft comprehensive convention on terrorism only exclude from the notion of terrorism actions by armed forces during armed conflict. 'Armed forces' under Article 43 Protocol I, considered also a rule of customary international law, comprises members of a party's regular forces, members of militias or volunteer corps, paramilitary and armed law enforcement agencies.[64] Thus, an interpretation in light of that rule would exclude the so-called 'unprivileged combatants' in international armed conflict and members of 'dissident armed forces or other organized armed groups ... under responsible command' in non-international armed conflict. These two parties in a conflict would be characterized as terrorists despite the fact that, under international humanitarian law, attacks mounted by them against military objectives as part of the conduct of hostilities are not unlawful.[65]

Arguments advanced in support of this interpretation assert that since civilians who take direct part in the hostilities in international armed conflict and insurgents in non-international conflicts do not enjoy immunity for their involvement in the conflict, they still may be subject to prosecution for lawful acts of warfare under domestic national laws. This argument, however, is not sufficient to support the need to characterize these 'combatants' as terrorists under international law because the crimes they may face for their participation in the conflict are established in the domestic legislation of a particular state and are applied upon the discretion of the national authorities within the needs of a national context. Moreover, characterizing insurgents in

[62] See, for example, GC IV, Art. 14; API, Art. 86.

[63] *International Humanitarian Law and the Challenges of Contemporary Armed Conflicts*, 7.

[64] This provision has relaxed the more strict rules under Art. 4 GC III requiring that to be considered a combatant the members of militias or volunteer corps carry arms openly and conduct their operations in accordance with the laws of war.

[65] *International Humanitarian Law and the Challenges of Contemporary Armed Conflicts*, 50.

non-international armed conflict as terrorists under international law curtails states' power to offer an amnesty to those persons involved in a non-international armed conflict, who have not perpetrated genocide, war crimes or crimes against humanity.[66] According to Article 6(5) Additional Protocol II, authorities in power at the end of hostilities in a non-international armed conflict must endeavour to grant the broadest possible amnesty to persons who have participated in the armed conflict. Though this provision does not entail an absolute obligation for states to issue an amnesty in every case, states are required to give this option careful consideration and endeavour to adopt that measure if possible.[67]

In sum, efforts at the international level to agree on a comprehensive definition on international terrorism should focus on making illegal acts of violence that only occur in peacetime. Acts that transpired in an international or non-international armed conflict should be regulated in their entirety by the principles of international humanitarian law. Blurring the notion of terrorism and acts of warfare does not appear to bring any benefit to the punishment of terrorism. First, violent acts directed against civilians and civilian objects in an armed conflict are already considered war crimes under treaty and customary international humanitarian law. As such they entail the individual criminal responsibility of the perpetrators who may be prosecuted by national and international courts under different bases of jurisdiction, including universal jurisdiction if they constitute grave breaches. Second, designating certain parties in a conflict as 'terrorist' despite the fact that their acts of warfare are lawful under international humanitarian law could contribute to a process of eroding compliance with these rules by all parties in a conflict. Also, it may endanger the peaceful solution of armed conflicts, particularly at the domestic level, by restricting states' power to grant a broad amnesty to those who participated in the conflict and were not involved in the perpetration of genocide, war crimes or crimes against humanity.

[66] See generally M. Sassòli, 'Terrorism and War' (2006) 4 *Journal International Criminal Justice* 959, 970–1; L. M. Olson, 'Prosecuting Suspected Terrorists: The "War on Terror" Demands Reminders about War, Terrorism and International Law' (2010) 24 *Emory International Law Review* 479, 488–9.

[67] *International Humanitarian Law and the Challenges of Contemporary Armed Conflicts*, 50–1.

3 The interplay between the international and domestic notions of terrorism

Most of the existing anti-terrorist treaties apply only to acts that have an international scope. The Convention against Taking Hostages specifically provides that this treaty will not apply 'where the offence is committed within a single state, the hostage and the alleged offender are nationals of that state and the alleged offender is found in the territory of that state.'[68] Likewise, the Convention for the Suppression of Terrorists Bombings and the Convention for the Suppression of the Financing of Terrorism limit their scope of application to offences that have an international dimension.[69] The Draft Terrorism Convention also includes a provision excluding from its scope acts that are perpetrated within the jurisdiction of a state, where the perpetrator and the victims are nationals of that state, and the offender resides in that state.[70]

In the wake of the September 11 attacks, however, some of the counter-terrorism resolutions adopted by the UN Security Council imposing general obligations to combat terrorism have blurred the distinction between the international and domestic notions of this offence. Since the early 1990s and until September 2001, the UN Security Council Resolutions adopted to condemn terrorism asserted that particular acts of international terrorism threatened international peace and security.[71] Resolution 1373 represents a departure from that approach.[72] Even if in that resolution the Security Council still condemns acts of international terrorism as a threat to international peace and security, for the first time this assertion was made as a declaration with no connection to specific acts or contexts.[73] Moreover, the resolution declared that 'acts, methods, and practices of terrorism are contrary to the purposes and principles of the United Nations and that knowingly financing, planning and inciting terrorist acts are also contrary to the

[68] 1979 International Convention against the Taking of Hostages, Art. 13.

[69] 1997 International Convention for the Suppression of Terrorists Bombings, Art. 3; 1999 International Convention for the Suppression of the Financing of Terrorism, Art. 3.

[70] See Draft Comprehensive Convention on Terrorism, UN Doc. A/57/37 (2002), Art. 3.

[71] B. Saul, 'Definition of "Terrorism" in the UN Security Council: 1985–2004' (2005) 4 *Chinese Journal of International Law* 1, 2.

[72] *Ibid.*, 18–20.

[73] *Ibid.* Also, see Report of the Special Rapporteur on the promotion and protection of human rights and fundamental freedoms while countering terrorism (UN Doc. A/65/258 (2010), para. 34).

purposes and principles of the United Nations'.[74] In subsequent resolutions,[75] the Security Council went further in affirming that 'terrorism in all its forms and manifestations constitutes one of the most serious threats to peace and security'[76] and condemning 'in the strongest terms all acts of terrorism irrespective of their motivation, whenever and by whomsoever committed, as one of the most serious threats to peace and security'.[77] By using 'all forms' and 'all acts', the Security Council resolutions suggested that their scope of application reaches beyond the international sphere to cover also domestic acts of terrorism.[78] This interpretation finds additional support in several Security Council Resolutions condemning domestic acts of terrorism in which the Council expressly stated that those circumstances threatened international peace and security.[79]

Ascertaining that acts of terrorism constitute a threat to international peace and security triggered the Security Council's power to act under Chapter VII of the UN Charter and call upon states to adopt a number of unprecedented measures to prevent terrorism and punish alleged offenders.[80] Among those measures, states have been called upon to criminalize the financing, planning, preparation or perpetration of terrorist acts as serious offences in domestic laws; deny refugee status to those suspected of having participated in the commission of terrorist acts; bring to justice on the basis of the principle of extradition or prosecution those responsible for the perpetration of terrorist acts; freeze the financial assets of those financing or participating in acts of terrorism; and prohibit by law incitement to commit a terrorist act or acts.[81] Compliance with these measures has been closely monitored by a Counter-Terrorism Committee[82] and a Counter-Terrorism Committee

[74] Res. 1373, para. 5 [75] See esp. Res. 1566. [76] *Ibid.*, preamble.

[77] *Ibid.*, para. 1. This language was also incorporated in the General Assembly Resolutions adopting the United Nations Global Counter-Terrorism Strategy and reaffirming states' commitment to implement the actions proposed in that plan. See, *inter alia*, UN Doc. A/Res./60/288 (2006).

[78] Report of the Special Rapporteur on the promotion and protection of human rights and fundamental freedoms while countering terrorism, para. 34.

[79] Saul, 'Definition of "Terrorism"', 25–6.

[80] Report of the Special Rapporteur on the promotion and protection of human rights and fundamental freedoms while countering terrorism, para. 34. The Rapporteur has considered that the SC's prerogative to impose a number of permanent measures, not linked to a particular geographical situation or limited to a specific time, could be challenged since arguably it does not have the power to establish new binding rules of international law.

[81] See in particular Res. 1373. [82] *Ibid.*, para. 6.

Executive Directorate,[83] created to assist the latter, through the analysis of periodic reports submitted by states. As discussed previously, in spite of the binding nature of the obligations imposed by the Security Council to fight terrorism, these resolutions have failed to provide a generally accepted international definition of terrorism. The Special Rapporteur on the Promotion and Protection of Human Rights and Fundamental Freedoms while Countering Terrorism ('Special Report on Counter-Terrorism') has found the binding measures of the Security Council problematic since they are imposed on all state members 'on the basis of hypothetical future acts falling under such a controversial and internationally undefined notion as terrorism'.[84]

Blurring the notions of international and domestic terrorism and bringing the regulation of this offence within the purview of international law without defining its scope has had adverse consequences for the protection of certain human rights.[85] Civil society organizations, universal and regional international monitoring mechanisms and scholars have expressed concerns that some states have taken advantage of the inexistence of a definition of terrorism coupled with the obligations imposed by the Security Council to enact sweeping counter-terrorism legislation punishing political dissent and other forms of violence that cannot be characterized as acts of terrorism.[86] The Special Rapporteur

[83] See UN Doc. S/Res./1535 (2004) creating the Counter-Terrorism Committee Executive Directorate.

[84] Report of the Special Rapporteur on the promotion and protection of human rights and fundamental freedoms while countering terrorism, para. 37.

[85] Even the Counter-Terrorism Committee Executive Directorate has acknowledged that in all regions of the world, 'States have continued to face challenges in ensuring the compliance of their counter-terrorism measures with all their obligations under international law, including international human rights law, refugee and humanitarian law.' See *Global Survey of Implementation of Security Council Resolution 1373* (2001) *by Member States* (UN Doc. S/2011/463 (2011), para. 18.

[86] See, for example, the use of antiterrorist legislation to prosecute members of the Mapuche indigenous group who were involved in demonstrations against the government in Chile. This measure was criticized by the UN Committee for the Elimination of Racial Discrimination (Concluding Observations of the Committee for the Elimination of Racial Discrimination, Chile, UN Doc. CERD/C/CHL/CO/15–18 (2009), para. 15) and the UN Rapporteur on Indigenous People (*Informe del Relator Especial sobre la situación de los derechos humanos y las libertades fundamentales de los indígenas, James Anaya* (UN Doc. A/HRC/12/34/Add.6 (2009), para. 61)). Another example is the prosecution of demonstrators protesting the *coup d'état* in Honduras who were charged with terrorism. See IACHR, Honduras: Human Rights and the Coup d'État, Doc. OEA/Ser.L/V/II. Doc. 55 (2009), para. 359. Also, see generally International Commission of Jurists, *Assessing Damage, Urging Action: Report of the Eminent Jurists Panel on*

on Countering Terrorism has admonished that resort to terrorism to stigmatize political, ethnic, regional or other movements have become the new trend since September 2001.[87] According to international reports, the human rights affected by domestic counter-terrorism legislation involve the principle of legality, the right to freedom of expression, the right to freedom of association, the right to fair trial, the right to property and the right to a remedy, among other rights.[88] In this chapter, however, we will only focus on the principle of legality, freedom of expression and freedom of association because it is easily demonstrable that infringements of these rights are linked to the existent legal vacuum regarding the scope of the crime of terrorism in international law.

As a consequence of the lack of precision regarding the conduct that states are obliged to criminalize, many domestic legislations enacted to incorporate the crime of terrorism in the national jurisdiction have been criticized for their vagueness and/or overbreadth and, consequently, considered in violation of the principle *nullum crimen sine lege* or principle of legality. The Human Rights Committee under the International Covenant on Civil and Political Rights, for example, has consistently recommended states to either amend their definitions of terrorism or incorporate definitions that are in line with the grave nature of the offence and respect the rights protected in that treaty. In the last few years, the Human Rights Committee has identified shortcomings in the counter-terrorism legislation of Ethiopia,[89] Jordan,[90] Hungary,[91] the Russian Federation,[92] Tanzania,[93] Australia,[94] Ireland,[95] the United Kingdom[96] and Chile[97] as part of the review process of periodic reports presented by those states under Article 40 ICCPR. Likewise, the

Terrorism, Counter-Terrorism and Human Rights (Geneva: International Commission of Jurists, 2009), ch. 6.

87 Report of the Special Rapporteur on the promotion and protection of human rights and fundamental freedoms while countering terrorism, paras. 26–7.

88 See, *inter alia*, IACHR, Report on Terrorism and Human Rights, OEA/Ser.L/V/II.116 Doc. 5 rev. 1 corr. (2002) at www.cidh.oas.org/Terrorism/Eng/toc.htm, and *Assessing Damage, Urging Action.*

89 HRC, Concluding Observations (UN Doc. CCPR/C/ETH/CO/1 (2011)).

90 HRC, Concluding Observations (UN Doc. CCPR/C/JOR/C/4 (2010)).

91 HRC, Concluding Observations (UN Doc. CCPR/C/HUN/C/5 (2010)).

92 HRC, Concluding Observations (UN Doc. CCPR/C/RUS/CO/6 (2009)).

93 HRC, Concluding Observations (UN Doc. CCPR/C/TZA/CO/4 (2009)).

94 HRC, Concluding Observations (UN Doc. CCPR/C/AUS/CO/5 (2009)).

95 HRC, Concluding Observations (UN Doc. CCPR/C/IRL/CO/3 (2008)).

96 HRC, Concluding Observations (UN Doc. CCPR/C/GBR/CO/6 (2008)).

97 HRC, Concluding Observations (UN Doc. CCPR/C/CHL/CO/5 (2007)).

Committee against Torture under the Convention against Torture has shown concern for the overly broad definition of terrorism in the domestic legislation of Monaco and the Philippines, among others, and recommended those states to bring them into conformity with international human rights standards.[98] Furthermore, the Survey of the Implementation of Security Council Resolution 1373 (2001) by member states compiled by the Counter-Terrorism Committee published in December 2009 underlined that one issue of continuing concern in the implementation of this resolution was that definitions of terrorism in some states remained vague or overbroad.[99] Most recently, the Venice Commission has warned against situations in which definitions of terrorism in certain countries are so broad that they encompass a wide range of activity representing different levels of gravity.[100]

The adoption of overbroad definitions of terrorism leaves ample opportunity for state deliberate misuse and, as a consequence, for more extended human rights abuses.[101] In recent times, non-governmental organizations have pointed to two clear situations where the adoption of overly broad and vague definitions of terrorism have resulted in massive human rights abuses, including detention, forced disappearances, extra-judicial executions and torture. The first example refers to the application of the anti-terrorist legislation in Turkey that has been used to repress the political views of those associated with the Kurdish movement in that country.[102] The other example refers to the counter-terrorism laws adopted in India which have resulted in abuse of terrorism suspects and the breach of basic due process rights.[103] Another interesting example is the *Case of Norin Catriman et al.* v. *Chile*, currently under consideration by the Inter-American Court of Human

[98] Committee against Torture, Concluding Observations (UN Doc. CAT/C/MCO/Co/4–5 (2011)) and Committee against Torture, Concluding Observations (UN Doc. CAT/C/PHL/CO/2 (2009)).

[99] See, generally, UN Doc. S/2009/620 (2009).

[100] European Commission for Democracy through Law (Venice Commission), *Report on Counter-Terrorism Measures and Human Rights* (Study 500/2008, CDL-AD (2010)022, 5 July 2010, paras. 29–30).

[101] Report of the Special Rapporteur on the promotion and protection of human rights and fundamental freedoms while countering terrorism (UN Doc. A/HRC/16/51 (2010), paras. 11–2).

[102] See in this regard HRW, *Protesting as a Terrorist Offence: The Arbitrary Use of Terrorism Laws to Prosecute and Incarcerate Demonstrators in Turkey* (2010), at www.hrw.org/reports/2010/11/01/protesting-terrorist-offense-0.

[103] HRW, *Back to the Future: India's 2008 Counterterrorism Laws* (2010), at www.hrw.org/reports/2010/07/28/back-future-0.

Rights.[104] The victims in the case are leaders of the Lonkos and Mapuches indigenous peoples. They were prosecuted and convicted for terrorist offences in application of the anti-terrorist legislation in Chile for the commission of several acts of arson perpetrated in the context of a social conflict between the indigenous groups and private land owners. The characterization of the crimes as terrorist offences triggered the application of serious consequences stipulated in the anti-terrorist legislation, including a more severe punishment, restrictions to political rights, longer periods of detention, telephone wiretapping, as well as the secrecy of the proceedings for up to six months. The petitioners have claimed violations of the principle of legality as a result of the overly broad definition of terrorism and terrorist activities in the Chilean legislation, among other breaches of the American Convention on Human Rights.[105] In light of this situation and given the lack of a common definition of international terrorism, the Special Rapporteur on Counter-Terrorism has concluded that the main framework of reference remains human rights law, in particular Article 15 ICCPR that protects the non-derogable principle of legality.[106] According to that principle, any terrorism offence must be prescribed by law, in other words, it must be adequately accessible and formulated with sufficient precision so that individuals can regulate their conduct in light of the existence of that crime.[107] Also, it must respect the principle of non-discrimination and equality before the law and cannot be applied retroactively.[108]

Another area in which the lack of a definition on terrorism has resulted in the encroachment upon human rights concerns freedom of

[104] See IACHR press release, IACHR takes case involving Chile to Inter-American Court (2011), at www.cidh.oas.org/Comunicados/English/2011/94-11eng.htm.

[105] See, IACHR, *Case of Aniceto Norin Catriman and Pascual Pichun Paillalao* v. *Chile*, Petition 619-03, Admissibility (2006), at www.cidh.oas.org/annualrep/2006eng/CHILE.61.03eng.htm.

[106] Report of the Special Rapporteur on the promotion and protection of human rights and fundamental freedoms while countering terrorism, para. 45. Art. 15 ICCPR reads: 'No one shall be held guilty of any criminal offence on account of any act or omission which did not constitute a criminal offence, under national or international law, at the time when it was committed. Nor shall a heavier penalty be imposed than the one that was applicable at the time when the criminal offence was committed. If, subsequent to the commission of the offence, provision is made by law for the imposition of the lighter penalty, the offender shall benefit thereby.'

[107] Report of the Special Rapporteur on the promotion and protection of human rights and fundamental freedoms while countering terrorism, paras. 46–7.

[108] *Ibid.*, paras. 48–9.

expression and freedom of association. Security Council Resolution 1624 has called upon states to prohibit by law and prevent incitement to commit terrorist acts without elaborating on what constitutes 'incitement to terrorism.'[109] The resolution, however, stressed that states must ensure that any measures enacted to comply with its provisions comply with all their obligations under international human rights law.[110] Moreover, in the preamble, the resolution acknowledged the right to freedom of expression and the need that restrictions to this right are provided by law, pursue a legitimate aim and are proportional to the necessity of the situation as required by Article 19 ICCPR.[111] Finally, the resolution directs states to report to the Counter-Terrorism Committee on the implementation of its terms.[112] It also directs the Counter-Terrorism Committee to engage with states to assist in their efforts to comply with the resolution and to report back to the Security Council with the results of that process.[113] In practice, however, the role of the Counter-Terrorism Committee appears to have been limited to the issuance of reports recounting in general terms the wide array of measures that states have reported to implement the prohibition and prevention of incitement to commit terrorist acts, without assessing whether the implementing measures were in compliance with international human rights law.[114] Even in situations in which the reports indicate that certain states have criminalized incitement to include 'glorification' or 'apology', the Committee has not addressed the risks that such definitions may pose for the protection of fundamental human rights.[115] Consequently, the work of the Committee has not provided states with concrete guidance as to the implementation of the crime of incitement to terrorism and states have enjoyed a wide discretion and flexibility to translate such prohibition into domestic law and practice.

Many states have used this discretion to define 'incitement' as involving the praising, glorification, indirect encouragement, public justification, or

[109] Para. 1 Res.1624 calls upon 'all States to adopt such measures as may be necessary and appropriate and in accordance with their obligations under international law to: (a) Prohibit by law incitement to commit a terrorist act or acts; (b) Prevent such conduct; and (c) Deny safe haven to any persons with respect to whom there is credible and relevant information giving serious reasons for considering that they have been guilty of such conduct' (UN Doc. S/Res./1624 (2005)).

[110] *Ibid.*; preamble of the resolution. [111] *Ibid.* [112] *Ibid.*, para. 5.

[113] *Ibid.*, para. 6.

[114] Report of the Special Rapporteur on the promotion and protection of human rights and fundamental freedoms while countering terrorism, para. 46.

[115] *Ibid.*

promotion of terrorist acts.[116] Moreover, they have also included in the notion of incitement the dissemination, publication and possession of materials related to organizations considered as 'terrorists'.[117] A closer look to these definitions of incitement show that they create a risk of arbitrary and discriminatory application and, therefore, leave room to stifle opposition groups, minorities, religious groups and others who do not share the views of those in power.[118] The Special Rapporteur on Counter-Terrorism, for example, concluded in his report on Turkey that a number of provisions in the anti-terrorist legislation and criminal legislation of that country imposed undue restrictions on the right to freedom of expression.[119] Also, the Report of the Eminent Jurists Panel on Terrorism, Counter-Terrorism and Human Rights provides a good description of domestic provisions enacted in the aftermath of September 2001 criminalizing incitement to terrorism.[120] Furthermore, the report *Speaking of Terror: A Survey of the Effects of Counter-Terrorism Legislation on Freedom of the Media in Europe*, published by the Council of Europe describes how anti-terrorist provisions have restricted the right to freedom of expression in Europe.[121] Most recently, the HRC has called upon states to

[116] See, for example, the case of Spain at Special Rapporteur on the promotion and protection of human rights and fundamental freedoms while countering terrorism, Addendum: Mission to Spain (UN Doc. A/HRC/10/3/Add.2 (2008), para. 11). On 25 April 2011, the Supreme Court of Spain found that the exhibition of pictures of ETA detainees on a public board during local celebrations constituted glorification of terrorism since through these actions the accused praised convicted terrorists. Sentencia del Tribunal Supremo, Sala de lo Penal, No. de Resolución 299/2011, 25 April 2011, at www.icj.org/img/SpainSC.pdf.

[117] The ECtHR has found in several judgments that the anti-terrorist legislation in Turkey as applied in cases of alleged dissemination or propaganda of terrorism violated Art. 10 ECHR. See, in this regard, *Fatih Tas v. Turkey*, Judgment of 25 April 2011, App. No. 36635/08,; *Gözel and Özer* v. *Turkey*, Judgment of 6 July 2010, App. No. 43453/04 and 31098/05; *Turgay and others* v. *Turkey*, Judgment of 15 June 2010, App. Nos. 8306/08, 8340/08 and 8366/08.

[118] See, for example, the situation in Ethiopia where a number of journalists and opposition activists have been tried for the crime of 'encouragement of terrorism' under the Anti-Terrorism Proclamation of 2009. HRW, 'Ethiopia: Stop Using Anti-Terror Law to Stifle Peaceful Opposition', 21 November 2011, at www.hrw.org/news/2011/11/21/ethiopia-stop-using-anti-terror-law-stifle-peaceful-dissent and 'Analysis of Ethiopia's Draft Antiterrorist Law', 30 June 2009 at www.hrw.org/node/84132.

[119] Report of the Special Rapporteur on the promotion and protection of human rights and fundamental freedoms while countering terrorism, Addendum: Mission to Turkey (UN Doc. A/HRC/4/26/Add.2 (2006)).

[120] *Assessing Damage, Urging Action.*

[121] *D. Banisar, *Speaking of Terror: A Survey of the Effects of Counter-Terrorism Legislation on Freedom of the Media in Europe*, Strasbourg, Media and Information Society

ensure that counter-terrorism measures are compatible with Article 19 ICCPR.[122] In that respect, the HRC has stated that offences such as 'encouragement of terrorism', 'extremist activity', 'praising', 'glorifying' or justifying terrorism 'should be clearly defined to ensure that they do not lead to an unnecessary or disproportionate interference with freedom of expression'.[123]

In addition, incorporation in domestic laws of the obligations arising out of Security Council Resolution 1373 – in particular those related to the prohibition of financing terrorism and providing services to terrorists or terrorist organizations and the prosecution of alleged terrorists – without clear guidance as to what constitutes terrorism has allowed states to abuse the use of anti-terrorist legislation to unduly restrict the right to freedom of association of those who object to government policies or political views.[124] Of particular concern is the flexibility permitted to states to label a particular organization as 'terrorist' and, consequently, criminalize membership or association with that organization as terrorism.[125] The Special Rapporteur on Counter-Terrorism has concluded that only organizations that engage in or call for the use of deadly or other serious violence against persons may be characterized as terrorist organizations.[126] Moreover, characterization of an organization as terrorist has to be made on a case-by-case analysis, on the basis of evidence of its activities, and by an independent judicial body in a process that provides for an appeal of the decision proscribing the organization.[127] In a report on Egypt, for example, the Special Rapporteur cautioned against the plans of Egyptian authorities to define

Division Directorate General of Human Rights and Legal Affairs, Council of Europe, November 2008.

122 HRC, General Comment No. 34, Article 19: Freedom of Opinion and Expression (UN Doc. CCPR/C/GC/34 (2011), para. 46).

123 *Ibid.*

124 Report of the Special Rapporteur on the promotion and protection of human rights and fundamental freedoms while countering terrorism (UN Doc. A/61/267 (2006), paras. 18–19). The resolution requires states *inter alia* to: '"prohibit" their nationals or any persons and entities within their territories from making any funds, financial assets or economic resources or financial or other related services available, directly or indirectly, for the benefit of persons [involved in] terrorist acts or of entities controlled by such persons [. . . and also to . . .] refrain from providing any form of support active or passive, to entities or persons involved in terrorists acts.'

125 *Assessing Damage, Urging Action*, 133–6.

126 Report of the Special Rapporteur on the promotion and protection of human rights and fundamental freedoms while countering terrorism, para. 24.

127 *Ibid.*, para. 26.

an organization as terrorist on the basis of its aim to commit acts legally characterized as terrorist, rather than on the commission of the specific acts. In that respect, the Rapporteur recommended Egypt not to criminalize an organization on the basis of its goals because that 'would risk targeting legitimate associations, including human rights organizations and opposition groups that should not fall within the ambit of any counter-terrorism law.'[128] Similar concerns have been expressed by the Special Rapporteur on human rights defenders pointing out the risk faced by human rights organizations and human rights defenders of being labelled as terrorist, particularly in situations of armed conflict, such as the one existing in Colombia.[129]

Furthermore, the scope of 'material support' to a terrorist organization has also being considered as problematic given the ambiguity of this term.[130] This issue was discussed in a recent judgment of the Supreme Court of the United States in the case of *Holder* v. *Humanitarian Law Project*.[131] At issue was whether domestic US anti-terrorist legislation[132] criminalizing the provision of any 'training', 'expert advice or assistance', 'service', or 'personnel' to an organization designated as terrorist by the Secretary of State was too vague and violated the right to freedom of speech and association. Plaintiffs in this case were members of civil society organizations and other activists who were willing to engage in political speech, promoting lawful and non-violent activity, including teaching and advocating the use of international law and other non-violent means to reduce conflict, advance human rights, and promote peace to members of the Kurdistan Workers' Party and the Liberation Tigers of Tamil Eelam (LTTE). Plaintiffs used to carry out that work until the material support statute was enacted. Afterwards, the plaintiffs challenged the constitutionality of that statute out of fear that they could be prosecuted if they continued to carry out their activities. The Supreme Court rejected all counts of unconstitutionality claimed by the plaintiffs. First, the Court concluded that the statute was not vague because it

[128] Report of the Special Rapporteur on the promotion and protection of human rights and fundamental freedoms while countering terrorism, Martin Scheinin, Mission to Egypt (UN Doc. A/HRC/13/37/Add.2 (2009)).

[129] Report of the Special Rapporteur on the situation of human rights defenders, Margaret Sekaggya, Addendum Mission to Colombia (UN Doc. A/HRC/13/22/Add. 3 (2010)).

[130] *Assessing Damage, Urging Action*, 134.

[131] *Holder* v. *Humanitarian Law Project*, 561 US ___ (2010); 130 S.Ct 2705 (2010).

[132] 18 USC § 2339B(a)(1). The US federal legislation makes it a crime to 'knowingly provide material support or resources to a foreign terrorist organization'.

clearly stated that the prohibited conduct involved the activities that the petitioners sought to carry out, namely providing any type of 'training' and 'expert advice or assistance' to the proscribed organizations.[133] The Court, however, distinguished that the plaintiffs were not prohibited under this statute for making independent advocacy on behalf of the terrorist organizations; notwithstanding, they were prohibited from coordinating the advocacy with those organizations.[134] Next, the Court relying on the position expressed by the Executive Branch concluded that plaintiffs' rights to freedom of speech and association were not violated in the present case given the deference that the political branch has when assessing the policies to fight terrorism.[135] The Executive Branch had argued that given the sensitive issues of national security at stake, the government's interests in preventing terrorism required that all forms of support to a foreign terrorist organization, even non-violent ones, had to be prohibited.[136] In contrast, the dissenting opinion found that the application of the statute as interpreted by the government would gravely and without justification breach the rights protected by the First Amendment of the US Constitution.[137]

Also, the broad scope of the notions of 'support or services provided to terrorists organizations', coupled with the designation as terrorist organizations of the non-state armed groups in non-international armed conflicts, has been identified by the ICRC as problematic for the humanitarian organizations or other actors carrying out assistance in war zones.[138] In light of the duties arising out of Resolution 1373, states have criminalized conduct to punish the provision of support or services to terrorist organizations without excluding from the prohibited conduct acts related to humanitarian action. Thus, the core activities of humanitarian organizations and their personnel aimed at assisting victims of armed conflict could fall within the prohibited activities and therefore expose members of humanitarian organizations to criminal prosecution.[139] Furthermore, the ICRC has concluded that potential

[133] *Holder* v. *Humanitarian Law Project.* [134] *Ibid.*, 2722. [135] *Ibid.*, 2728.

[136] *Ibid.*, 2727.

[137] *Ibid.* (Justice Breyer, with whom Justices Ginsburg and Sotomayor join, dissenting). Interesting to note is Justice Breyer's conclusion suggesting that the law would be constitutional if the scope of the statute were read as prohibiting pure speech and association only 'when the defendant knows or intents that those activities will assist the organization's unlawful terrorist aims'.

[138] *International Humanitarian Law and the Challenges of Contemporary Armed Conflict*, 51–2.

[139] *Ibid.*

criminalization of its own humanitarian assistance to non-state armed groups would be incompatible with the letter and spirit of well-established principles of international humanitarian law protecting the notion of neutrality and independent humanitarian action.[140]

Finally, another issue that requires consideration when analyzing the interplay between the international and domestic notions of terrorism relates to the issue of international judicial cooperation for the prosecution of alleged terrorists. Most of the 'sectoral' anti-terrorist-terrorist conventions recognize a broad jurisdiction to prosecute suspected terrorists, including jurisdiction based on the principles of territoriality, the nationality of the offender and the victim, and of 'universal jurisdiction'.[141] Also, the anti-terrorist conventions enshrined the principle *aut dedere aut punire* that requires a state party in the territory of which an alleged offender is present to either prosecute the suspect or extradite him or her, regardless of whether the acts of terrorism have occurred or not in the territory of that state.[142] To ensure judicial cooperation between states, some of the anti-terrorist conventions also provide that none of the offences proscribed by those treaties can be characterized as political offences for purposes of extradition.[143] The Draft Terrorism Convention follows a similar approach.[144]

UN Security Council Resolutions have also called upon states to cooperate in the prosecution and/or extradition of suspected terrorists. Resolution 1373 provides that states shall afford each other 'the greatest measure of assistance in connection with criminal investigations or criminal proceedings relating to the financing or support of terrorist acts'.[145] Also, it calls upon states to ensure that the political offence

[140] *Ibid.*

[141] See, *inter alia*, International Convention against the Taking of Hostages, Art. 5; International Convention for the Suppression of Terrorists Bombings, Art. 6; and International Convention for the Suppression on the Financing of Terrorism, Art. 6.

[142] See, *inter alia*, International Convention against the Taking of Hostages, Art. 8; International Convention for the Suppression of Terrorists Bombings, Art. 8; and International Convention for the Suppression on the Financing of Terrorism, Art. 10. Also, for a more detailed examination of the issue of the duty of *au dedere au judicare*, see Chapter 3 in this volume.

[143] See, for example, International Convention for the Suppression of Terrorists Bombings, Art. 12; International Convention for the Suppression on the Financing of Terrorism, Art. 14; and International Convention for the Suppression of Acts of Nuclear Terrorism, Art. 15.

[144] See Report of the Ad Hoc Committee established by General Assembly resolution 51/120 of 17 December 1996.

[145] UN Doc. S/Res./1373 (2001), para. 2.

principle is not recognized as a ground for refusing extradition of alleged terrorists.[146] Furthermore, Resolution 1566 calls upon states to ensure that those responsible for supporting, facilitating or participating in the financing, planning or perpetration of acts of terrorism are brought to justice on the basis of the principle to extradite or prosecute.[147] Both resolutions urge states to ratify the anti-terrorist treaties as a matter of urgency.[148]

Despite the existence of clear provisions regarding judicial cooperation in the anti-terrorist conventions and the UN Security Council resolutions, international assistance to prosecute alleged terrorists has been hampered by a number of reasons. First, ratification of the anti-terrorist treaties is fragmented. Second, even in regard to treaties that have been widely ratified, not all states have enacted laws on mutual assistance and extradition incorporating the obligations enshrined in those instruments.[149] Finally, and most importantly for purposes of our analysis in this section, lack of a common definition of international terrorism has impeded in practice that states cooperate effectively in ensuring that alleged terrorists are brought to justice.[150] The fragmented approach in the domestic counter-terrorist legislation has not facilitated prosecution of certain violent acts because there is no consistency as to what conduct is characterized as terrorism in the different jurisdictions. Moreover, diverging domestic definitions on terrorism also pose difficulties for purposes of extradition. First, the principle of double criminality requires that the conduct for which a person is sought in extradition must be criminalized in both the requesting and the requested state. Second, for purposes of overcoming the political offence exception, it is essential that states agree that certain acts of violence constitute terrorism and are not justified on the basis of political reasons. A recent example of this disagreement is reflected in the judgment of the Supreme Court of Brazil where it ruled that the decision of former President Lula granting refugee status to an Italian national wanted by Italy following his conviction *in absentia* for terrorist acts constituted a sovereign act of the president which could not be subjected to review. At stake was whether the acts characterized by Italy as terrorist acts were

[146] *Ibid.*, para. 3. [147] UN Doc. S/Res./1566 (2004), para. 2.

[148] UN Doc. S/Res./1373 (2001), para. 3; UN Doc. S/Res./1566 (2004), para. 4.

[149] *Global Survey of Implementation of Security Council Resolution 1373 (2001) by Member States*, para. 16.

[150] Report of the Special Rapporteur on the promotion and protection of human rights and fundamental freedoms while countering terrorism, para. 26.

political acts that prevented the extradition of the foreign national on the basis of the potential persecution he would suffer as a result of his political views.[151]

In conclusion, the interplay between the international and domestic jurisdictions for purposes of prosecuting suspected terrorist has been constantly affected by the lack of an internationally agreed definition of terrorism. First, blurring the notions of international and domestic terrorism and bringing the regulation of this offence within the purview of international law without defining its scope has had adverse consequences for the protection of certain human rights. Second, the inexistence of a definition of terrorism has hampered international judicial cooperation to ensure prosecution of alleged terrorists.

4 Conclusions

Overall, this chapter explored two issues that remain unresolved as a result of the lack of a definition of terrorism at the international level and that have become either an obstacle for combating this crime or adversely impacted the respect of other rules of international law, especially human rights and humanitarian law principles. The first section explores the relationship between international terrorism and armed conflict and concludes that those notions should not be conflated. Efforts at the international level to agree on a comprehensive definition on international terrorism should focus on considering as such only illegal acts of violence that occur in peacetime. In contrast, acts that transpired in an international or non-international armed conflict should be regulated in their entirety by the principles of international humanitarian law. Moreover, an exploration of the existing rules appears to show that blurring terrorism and acts of warfare does not bring any benefit to the punishment of that crime. First, violent acts directed against civilians and civilian objects in an armed conflict are already considered war crimes under treaty and customary international humanitarian law. As such they entail the individual criminal responsibility of the perpetrators who may be prosecuted by national and international courts under different bases of jurisdiction, including universal jurisdiction if they constitute grave breaches. Second, designating certain parties in a conflict as 'terrorist' despite the fact that their acts of warfare

[151] Noticias STF, STF concede libertade a Cesare Battisti, 8 June 2011 at http://www.stf.jus.br/portal/cms/verNoticiaDetalhe.asp?idConteudo=181559&caixaBusca=N.

are lawful under international humanitarian law could contribute to a process of eroding compliance with these rules by all parties in a conflict. Also, it may endanger the peaceful solution of armed conflicts, particularly at the domestic level, by restricting states' power to grant a broad amnesty to those who participated in the conflict and were not involved in the perpetration of genocide, war crimes or crimes against humanity.

The second section considers the relationship between international and domestic notions of terrorism and concludes that the interplay between the international and domestic jurisdictions for purposes of prosecuting suspected terrorists has been constantly affected by the lack of an internationally agreed definition of terrorism. First, state practice and the work of international human rights monitoring organizations demonstrate that blurring the notions of international and domestic terrorism and bringing the regulation of this offence within the purview of international law without defining its scope has had adverse consequences for the protection of certain human rights, including the principle of legality, freedom of expression and freedom of association. Likewise, the inexistence of a definition of terrorism has hampered international judicial cooperation from ensuring prosecution of alleged terrorists.

Ultimately, despite the recent judgment of the Special Tribunal of Lebanon asserting that an international crime of terrorism in times of peace has crystallized into a rule of customary international law or the efforts done at different levels of the United Nations or other regional organizations to define the scope of this crime, it seems that reaching agreement on a comprehensive definition of terrorism in an international instrument appears to be the next unavoidable step forward, if states become serious about implementing a successful approach to fighting this crime.

21

All necessary measures? Reconciling international legal regimes governing peace and security, and the protection of persons, in the realm of counter-terrorism

KARIMA BENNOUNE

1 Introduction

Where action against terrorism is mandated or authorized by UN Security Council (SC) resolutions adopted under Chapter VII of the UN Charter, do member states' obligations under international human rights law and international humanitarian law still apply as they would otherwise? Alternatively, in such situations, are human rights and IHL obligations instead subordinate to state obligations to implement the resolutions of the SC? Examples might include an SC resolution that requires freezing the funds of suspected supporters of al-Qaeda without necessarily affording the due process required by human rights law, or SC resolutions authorizing the use of force (or otherwise necessitating the presence of member states' armed forces) in circumstances that may give rise to violations of those states' human rights and humanitarian law commitments.

The interplay of these legal regimes has vexed numerous judicial and quasi-judicial bodies in recent years, leading them to produce a disparate jurisprudence. While scholars of international organizations have devoted much ink to this problem of late, human rights scholars (especially outside of Europe) have not yet fully engaged with it. This chapter

The author would like to acknowledge the research assistance of Natalae Anderson, Jennifer Berman, Moraa Onyonka, Mary Orsini and Chris Royal. She would also like to thank Kristen Boon, E. J. Flynn, Claus Kress and Nigel Rodley for their helpful comments. Remaining shortcomings are the sole responsibility of the author.

hopes to encourage that much-needed engagement by synthesizing the debate, and bringing together the international organizations and human rights issues. However, the topic presents a complex puzzle and this chapter cannot fully address all of its pieces.

Indeed, the question of the relationship between state obligations regarding international peace and security under the UN Charter and obligations regarding the protection of persons leads to other questions. Are there legal parameters to Security Council action under Chapter VII, and if so, what human rights and humanitarian norms constrain the Council? What are the consequences of putatively *ultra vires* resolutions? If states act in furtherance of their obligations under the Charter, who is responsible for any human rights violations that may result? How do we empower states to effectively combat international terrorism as mandated by both fundamental international human rights norms and Council decisions, but not create a global architecture of impunity for counter-terrorism measures that violate rights?

In confronting this conundrum as manifested in the early phases of the *Kadi* case, Jan Klabbers asked: 'Should human rights be respected even at the (possible) expense of effective governance? Or should effectiveness of governance be preferred, even at the (possible) expense of the protection of individual human rights?'[1] These are the kind of questions often asked about the trade-offs between liberty and security. The real challenge today is to find ways to move beyond these binary oppositions between human rights and effectiveness, and between liberty and peace/security. Instead, the contemporary moment requires a holistic understanding of both security and rights on the part of governments, international organizations and human rights advocates. Such an approach requires reconciling the international legal regimes that govern peace and security on the one hand, and the protection of persons on the other.

2 Current legal position

2.1 The UN Charter

The UN Charter undoubtedly represents the starting point for this discussion. While Article 103 is particularly relevant, that article must

[1] J. Klabbers, 'Kadi Justice at the Security Council' (2007) 4 *International Organizations Law Review* 1.

be understood in the context of the Charter's other provisions.[2] A number of articles spell out the remit of the Security Council. According to Article 24, the Security Council has 'primary responsibility for the maintenance of international peace and security'.[3] Chapter VII elaborates on 'the specific powers granted to the Security Council for the discharge of these duties'.[4] According to its articles, the Security Council can make the threshold determination of 'the existence of any threat to the peace, breach of the peace, or act of aggression'.[5] Subsequently, Chapter VII enables the SC to decide what measures shall be taken to restore international peace and security. According to the authoritative Simma *Commentary* on the UN Charter, Chapter VII makes the UNSC the most powerful international organ in history,[6] giving it what Pierre-Marie Dupuy has called the role of an 'executive of the international community'.[7]

The toolbox of the SC under Chapter VII includes measures not involving the use of armed force (*inter alia* interruption of economic relations, and the severance of diplomatic relations).[8] If those are inadequate, measures involving the use of force (*inter alia* blockades and other operations by air, sea or land forces)[9] may be authorized. Note that according to the Appeals Chamber of the International Criminal Tribunal for the former Yugoslavia (ICTY) in the *Tadić* case, the SC

[2] How one interprets the Charter shapes one's view of these issues. Some scholars receive the Charter not as just another treaty, but as a constitution of sorts for the international community, giving it primacy. See, e.g., B. Fassbender, 'Review Essay: *Quis judicabit?* The Security Council, Its Powers and Its Legal Control' (2002) 11 *European Journal of International Law* 227. Other scholars reject this position, seeing the Charter as one multilateral treaty among others to be interpreted using international law. See, e.g., J. Herbst, *Rechtskontrolle des UN-Sicherheitsrates* (1999), as cited by Fassbender, '*Quis judicabit?*', 226.

[3] The Charter of the United Nations, San Francisco, 26 June 1945, in force 24 October 1945, Art. 24(1).

[4] UN Charter, Art. 24(2). According to this article, the specific powers of the SC are also laid down in Chapters VI (pacific settlement of disputes), VIII (regional arrangements) and XII (international trusteeship system).

[5] *Ibid.*, Art. 39.

[6] Bruno Simma (ed.), *The Charter of the United Nations: A Commentary* (Oxford: Oxford University Press, 2002), 702.

[7] P. Dupuy, 'The Constitutional Dimension of the Charter of the United Nations Revisited' (1997) 1 *Max Planck Yearbook of United Nations Law* 21–4, cited in Simma, *Commentary*, 702.

[8] UN Charter, Art. 41. [9] *Ibid.*, Art. 42.

has a 'wide margin of discretion in choosing its course of action' once it determines the existence of a threat to or breach of the peace.[10]

In light of the failure to implement Article 43 of the Charter (calling on members to make arrangements to make armed forces available to the SC), forcible measures must rely on so-called decentralized enforcement by member states acting alone or in coalition.[11] Put simply, in the real world the SC cannot act, for the most part, except through member states. This makes their obligations to comply with the decisions of the SC especially critical. Under Article 25, '[t]he Members of the United Nations agree to accept and carry out the decisions of the Security Council in accordance with the present Charter.'[12]

Given that the SC must act effectively to fulfil its mission to guarantee international peace and security and that states must comply with the resolutions of the SC to make this happen, what is to become of states' other obligations under international law? The Charter seeks to facilitate compliance with its provisions by minimizing other international legal constraints on member state action. As Article 103 stipulates, '[i]n the event of a conflict between the obligations of the Members of the United Nations under the present Charter and their obligations under any other international agreement, their obligations under the present Charter shall prevail.'[13] Article 103 is not explicit on its face as to the exact fate of treaty provisions that conflict with obligations under the Charter. Experts have debated whether they are void, voidable, suspended or simply unenforceable.[14] However, the Study Group of the International Law Commission on the fragmentation of international law (ILS Study Group) suggests that the majority view holds the question to be one of priority of obligations, not of validity.[15]

Dapo Akande argues that Article 103 is overplayed in these debates, though he notes conversely that many have actually criticized the ECJ in *Kadi* and the Human Rights Committee in *Sayadi* for giving insufficient

[10] *Prosecutor* v. *Tadić*, Decision on the Defence Motion for Interlocutory Appeal on Jurisdiction, Case No. IT-94-1-AR72, A.Ch., 2 October 1995, para. 31.

[11] See, e.g., T. Franck, *Recourse to Force: State Action against Threats and Armed Attacks* (Cambridge: Cambridge University Press, 2002), 22–31.

[12] UN Charter, Art. 25. [13] *Ibid.*, Art. 103. [14] Simma, *Commentary*, 1295.

[15] *Fragmentation of International Law: Difficulties Arising From the Diversification and Expansion of International law*, Report of the Study Group of the International Law Commission, Finalized by Martti Koskenniemi, UN Doc. A/CN.4/L.682, 13 April 2006, para. 333 [hereafter: *Fragmentation of International Law*]. See the lengthy discussion of Art. 103 (*ibid.*, 166–81).

consideration to this Article.[16] Interpretation of Article 103 depends, of course, on how one understands the meaning of 'obligation'. Does this include only that which the SC mandates under the Charter or also that which it authorizes but which might be seen as discretionary action? This is the subject of some academic debate. Also, in the view of the ILC study group, 'non-binding resolutions' adopted by the SC are not covered by Article 103.[17] Does it exclude resolutions of the SC which are *ultra vires* or in violation of international law in some way? The ILC study group argued that *ultra vires* decisions, including by the SC, 'do not give rise to any obligations to begin with . . . [and] [h]ence no conflict exists'.[18]

Of course, human rights norms are not just found in treaty form but also in customary international law and general principles of law. Article 103 on its face makes reference only to treaty law. Hence, some experts have argued that this article cannot be read to undermine state obligations under customary international law.[19] However, the ILC study group, while noting that a literal reading of Article 103 cannot encompass customary international law obligations, nods to what it sees as SC practice and ultimately 'affirms that charter obligations prevail also over United Nations Member States' customary law obligations'.[20]

In any case, Article 103 is not the end of the story but instead raises further questions. If member states *must* do the bidding of the SC as if it were the alpha in a wolf pack, the question is, are there legal limits on what the alpha may order? The UN Charter easily answers part of the limits question. According to Article 24(2), in fulfilling its responsibility for maintaining international peace and security, 'the Security Council shall act in accordance with the Purposes and Principles of the United Nations'.[21] In the *Certain Expenses of the United Nations* case, the

16 D. Akande, 'The Security Council and Human Rights: What Is the Role of Art. 103 of the Charter?' (2009), EJIL: Talk!, at www.ejiltalk.org/the-security-council-and-human-rights-what-is-the-role-of-art-103.

17 *Fragmentation of International Law*, para. 331, citing R. Kolb, 'Does Article 103 of the Charter of the United Nations Apply Only to Decisions or also to Authorizations Adopted by the Security Council?' (2004) 64 *Zeitschrift für ausländisches öffentliches Recht und Völkerrecht* 21.

18 *Fragmentation of International Law*, para. 331.

19 See, e.g., Christian Tomuschat, 'Case Note *R* (*On the Application of Al-Jedda*) v. *Secretary of State for Defence*: Human Rights in a Multi-Level System of Governance and the Internment of Suspected Terrorists' (2008) 9 *Melbourne Journal of International Law*, 402.

20 *Fragmentation of International Law*, para. 345.

21 UN Charter, Art. 24, para. 2. The Simma *Commentary* labels these 'guidelines rather than concrete limits for SC action' (Simma, *Commentary*, 710).

International Court of Justice (ICJ) held that 'when the Organization takes action which warrants the assertion that it was appropriate for the fulfillment of one of the stated purposes of the United Nations, the presumption is that such action is not ultra vires the Organization.'[22]

The Purposes and Principles of the United Nations are, according to Article 1: (1) to maintain international peace and security, including by taking 'effective collective measures for the prevention and removal of threats to the peace, and for the suppression of acts of aggression or other breaches of the peace';[23] (2) to develop friendly relations among nations; (3) 'to achieve international co-operation in solving international problems of an economic, social, cultural or humanitarian character, and in promoting and encouraging respect for human rights and for fundamental freedoms for all without distinction as to race, sex, language, or religion';[24] and (4) to coordinate international action towards all of these ends. If the SC must operate so as to be in accordance with all of these purposes, which has primacy if they are seen to conflict?

In assessing Article 1 of the Charter, the ICJ in *Certain Expenses* theorized further that 'The *primary place* ascribed to international peace and security is natural, since the fulfillment of the other purposes will be dependent upon the attainment of that basic condition.'[25] For some academic experts as well, Article 1(1) represents the touchstone of both the UN system and the SC's role. As Frowein and Krisch have phrased it, 'the drafters' *primordial goal* of ensuring rapid and effective action to maintain international peace and security'[26] means that 'the powers of the SC under Chapter VII of the Charter are extremely far-reaching and subject to very few express limitations'.[27] In fact, they claim (citing Kelson, Claude and Koskenniemi for support) that 'under the Charter, peace takes precedence over justice'.[28]

As the sterile debates about the International Criminal Court's impact in places like Uganda have made clear, we need to get beyond a thin conception of peace that pits peace versus justice or human rights.[29]

22 *Certain Expenses of the United Nations (Article 17, paragraph 2 of the Charter)*, Advisory Opinion of 20 July 1962 [1962] ICJ Rep. 151.

23 UN Charter, Art. 1(1). 24 *Ibid.*, Art. 1(3).

25 *Certain Expenses*, 167 (emphasis added).

26 Simma, *Commentary*, 705 (emphasis added). Elsewhere, they have labelled it 'the most important goal of the UN' (*ibid.*, 719).

27 *Ibid.*, 705, 719. 28 *Ibid.*, 711.

29 A convincing case for moving beyond the narrow confines of this debate is made in P. Castillo Diaz, 'The International Criminal Court in Central and Eastern Africa: between the possible and the desirable', Ph.D. dissertation, Rutgers University-Newark (May 2010) (on file with the author).

Rather, we need an understanding that justice and rights are integral to meaningful and lasting peace and security.[30] Moreover, the Simma *Commentary*'s interpretation of Article 1 indicates that 'peace is more than the absence of war' but also includes 'the diminution of those issues likely to cause war'.[31] However, too often human rights voices have conversely downplayed the centrality of peace and security to the protection of human rights and this pitfall is to be avoided also.[32]

Even if we accord equal weight to peace and human rights, what exactly are the human rights obligations entailed by the language of Article 1(3) of the Charter and its other human rights provisions?[33] Wolfrum has labelled the human rights language in the preamble to the UN Charter a 'mini human rights charter'.[34] However, some see Article 1(3)'s commitment 'to achieve cooperation in . . . promoting and encouraging respect' for human rights as 'a rather attenuated obligation'.[35] Nevertheless, human rights have been, in practice, a core part of the work of the United Nations (especially since the tenure of Kofi Annan as Secretary-General – and subsequently Ban Ki-Moon).[36] In fact, human rights have become every bit as central to the work of the United Nations as the protection of peace and security. Whether one interprets the notion of achieving cooperation in promoting rights broadly or not, it is hardly reconcilable with the sanctioning of human rights abuses.

Following this overview of the UN's purposes as the guiding principles of the SC, we return to the question of enforcement action under Chapter VII. Once it determines the existence of a threat to the peace or breach of the peace, how creative can the SC be in its response? Following the atrocities of September 11, 2001, the SC established far-reaching obligations for states in the field of combating terrorism, beginning with the

[30] See, e.g., L. Keller, 'The False Dichotomy of Peace Versus Justice and the International Criminal Court' (2008) 3 *Hague Justice Journal* 12.

[31] Wolfrum, in Simma, *Commentary*, 41.

[32] For greater discussion of this problem, see K. Bennoune, 'Terror/Torture' (2008) 26 *Berkeley Journal of International Law* 1.

[33] These include Arts. 55 and 56, as well as the preamble.

[34] Wolfrum, in Simma, *Commentary*, 35.

[35] Posting of N. Bhuta, 1 April 2009, EJIL: Talk!, at www.ejiltalk.org/the-security-council-and-human-rights-what-is-the-role-of-art-103-of-the-charter.

[36] See *Renewing the UN: A Programme for Reform*, Report of the Secretary-General (A/51/1954), 14 July 1997; and Florian Hoffman, 'Human rights mainstreaming in the United Nations', paper presented at the annual meeting of the ISA's 49th Annual Convention, 26 March 2008, at www.allacademic.com/meta/p_mla_apa_research_citation/2/5/1/7/3/p251738_index.html.

adoption of Resolution 1373.[37] Deeming international terrorism to constitute a threat to international peace and security, the SC incorporated provisions from earlier counter-terrorism treaties, thereby binding non-parties; and it has applied these provisions generally to the problem of international terrorism. Though this view is controversial, according to Frederick Kirgis, Chapter VII of the Charter actually gives the SC the power to legislate and create new law, making recent SC action in this realm in keeping with Chapter VII.[38] On the contrary, others have argued that it is difficult to justify under the Charter, because it makes law beyond a concrete case.[39] Nevertheless, these measures have been taken by a unanimous SC, and states have not objected to them.

In addition, human rights lawyers should think carefully about arguing for a strict interpretation of the SC's ambit. It is only an evolutionary creativity which has allowed the body to directly address a range of human rights matters, deeming them threats to international peace and designing innovative responses. In the *Tadić* case, the Appeals Chamber, in justifying the creation of the ICTY, explained that it is up to the SC to 'evaluate the suitability of the measures chosen, as well as their potential contribution to the restoration or maintenance of peace'.[40] The Chamber was willing to accept the novel creation of an international court despite such a measure not being explicitly listed in Chapter VII. The measures listed in Articles 41 and 42 of the Charter, in the Chamber's opinion, are merely illustrative and not exhaustive.[41] Nevertheless, the breadth of SC action on terrorism since September 11, 2001 complicates the question of the relationship between states' Charter-based obligations and their human rights/IHL obligations.

In assessing this relationship, one must determine whether or not the SC, when acting under Chapter VII, must respect international law beyond the Charter. The Appeals Chamber of the ICTY noted in the *Tadić* case that 'neither the text nor the spirit of the Charter conceives of the Security Council as *legibus solutus* (unbound by law)'.[42] However, the

[37] UN Doc. S/Res./1373 (2001).

[38] F. Kirgis, 'The Security Council's First Fifty Years' (1995) 89 *American Journal of International Law* 520. See also S. Talmon, 'The Security Council as World Legislature' (2005) 99 *American Journal of International Law* 175. Not all scholars accept this view. It is especially controversial with regard to democratic legitimacy because SC resolutions reflect the views of only fifteen UN members. G. Nolte, cited in Simma, *Commentary*, 709.

[39] See, e.g., M. Happold, 'Security Council Resolution 1373 and the Constitution of the United Nations' (2003) 16 *Leiden Journal of International Law* 593.

[40] *Tadić*, para. 32. [41] *Ibid*., para. 35. [42] *Ibid*., para. 28.

question remains as to what law exactly binds it, and in particular when it acts under Chapter VII of the Charter. One may discern a range of positions on the answer to these questions in the academic literature and case law: (1) the SC is not bound by law outside of the Charter; (2) the SC is, in general, not obligated to respect international law when acting under Chapter VII, except that it may not act in contravention of *jus cogens* norms; (3) the SC should be presumed to act in accordance with international law; (4) the SC must respect international law, even when acting under Chapter VII of the Charter. As these different positions have a direct impact on problems that may arise in the interplay of the legal regimes governing international peace and security and those governing the protection of persons under international law, they will be reviewed in turn.

2.1.1 When acting under Chapter VII, the Security Council is not bound by law outside of the Charter

Strikingly, Frowein and Krisch argue in the Simma *Commentary* that the Charter's drafters decided 'to allow the SC to disregard international law when taking enforcement action'[43] and that this decision is not one that should be easily set aside. They view the Charter's approach to peace enforcement as political rather than legal, and as such human rights norms and IHL are simply guidelines that do not establish precise limits for enforcement actions.[44] Bardo Fassbender elaborates further on the purist approach to this question when he suggests that:

> [t]here is no room for a category of 'general international law' existing independently beside the Charter. Instead, the Charter is the supporting frame of all international law existing today and, at the same time, the highest layer in a hierarchy of norms of international law. Norms of *jus cogens*, which rest on the foundation of the Charter and could not be imagined without it, cannot be set against Charter provisions. From this it follows that the Security Council is bound by the law of the Charter alone.[45]

The advantage of this approach is that it can facilitate enforcement by granting the SC freedom of action to protect the core values of international peace and security. The significant downside is that it can marginalize human rights and humanitarian law norms in the institution at the heart of the global order, undermining the legitimacy of both the Council

[43] Frowein and Krish, in Simma, *Commentary*, 711. [44] *Ibid.*

[45] Fassbender, '*Quis judicabit*?', 227.

and the norms as a result, and legalizing human suffering at the highest international levels.

While many international organizations specialists may take the position that the SC is not bound by international law outside the Charter, many other international lawyers dispute it. Note, for example, that in the decision on provisional measures in *Lockerbie*, both Judges Weeramantry and Jennings argued that the SC must operate within the bounds of international law. For Jennings, '[i]t is not logically possible to claim to represent the power and authority of the law, and at the same time, claim to be above the law.'[46]

2.1.2 The Security Council may not act in contravention of *jus cogens* norms

Another position holds that the SC is not obligated to respect general international law when acting under Chapter VII *except* that it cannot act contrary to peremptory norms of international law. This position was taken by the Court of First Instance in *Kadi*.[47] In terms of treaty law, it coheres with the notion that no international treaty, not even the Charter, can violate peremptory norms.[48] Some suggest that this applies through the vehicle of state requirements vis-à-vis *jus cogens*. Others go so far as to suggest that the UN itself must be seen as directly bound by *jus cogens* norms.[49]

In his separate opinion in the *Application of the Genocide Convention* case, Judge Ad Hoc Lauterpacht opines that the SC cannot contravene *jus cogens*:

> The relief which Article 103 of the Charter may give the Security Council in case of conflict between one of its decisions and an operative treaty obligation cannot – as a matter of simple hierarchy of norms – extend to a conflict between a Security Council resolution and jus cogens.[50]

[46] *Questions of Interpretation and Application of the 1971 Montreal Convention Arising from the Aerial Incident at Lockerbie* (*Libya* v. *United States*), Provisional Measures, Order of 14 April 1992 [1998] ICJ Rep. 110 (Dissenting Opinion of Judge Sir Robert Jennings, 110).

[47] Case T-315/01, *Kadi* v. *Council and the Commission of the European Communities*, para. 5, 2005 ECR 11-3649 (2008).

[48] 1969 VCLT, 1155 UNTS 131, Art. 64. [49] Simma, *Commentary*, 711.

[50] *Application of the Convention on the Prevention and Punishment of the Crime of Genocide* (*Bosnia and Herzegovina* v. *Serbia and Montenegro*), Order of 13 September 1993 [1993] ICJ 325, para. 100 (Separate Opinion of Judge Lauterpacht) [hereafter *Prevention and Punishment of Genocide*, Opinion of Judge Lauterpacht]. See also the discussion of this issue in S. Lamb, 'Legal Limits to United Nations Security Council

He points out that it is unlikely that the SC would ever deliberately seek to pass a resolution counter to a *jus cogens* norm or mandating a human rights violation, but expresses fear that a resolution could inadvertently lead to such a result.[51] While Judge Lauterpacht is vague as to the action necessary to redress such a situation, he indicates that one possibility is that the resolution 'cease[s] . . . to be valid and binding' in whole or in relevant part.[52] This could protect those human rights and IHL norms that rise to the level of *jus cogens*.

This intermediate approach (of seeing the SC as only bound by the Charter and by *jus cogens* norms when acting under Chapter VII) has the benefit of freeing the SC from most legal limits when it acts to secure the basic goal of international peace, while still maintaining a red line beyond which it cannot go. Even an expert like Fassbender, who sees the Charter as the only legal constraint on the SC when it acts in the ambit of Chapter VII, understands there to be an overlap such that some *jus cogens* norms (he lists prohibitions of genocide, aggression, slavery and the right to self-determination) are relevant to the SC because they are also protected by the Charter. Nevertheless, he does suggest that the Charter itself may allow for departure from *jus cogens*, in particular under Chapter VII. Similarly, Gregory Fox reads the deliberations of the International Law Commission on the matter to 'dictate that Council decisions not be subject to the trumping authority of jus cogens'.[53]

While such a suggestion is jarring to human rights lawyers, it would solve certain legal difficulties. For example, Article 2(4) of the UN Charter has been labelled as rising to the level of *jus cogens* by the ICJ in the *Nicaragua* case.[54] Does this mean that when authorizing the use of force under Chapter VII of the Charter, the SC must assess whether or not this action comports with Article 2(4)? Fassbender argues that such an assertion does not accord with either the language of the Charter or its object and purpose.[55] Moreover, by the very terms of the Charter, even

Powers', in G. Goodwin-Gill and S. Talmon (eds.), *The Reality of International Law: Essays in Honour of Ian Brownlie* (Oxford: Oxford University Press, 1999), 361, 373.

51 *Prevention and Punishment of Genocide*, Opinion of Judge Lauterpacht, para. 102.

52 *Ibid.*, para. 103.

53 See the lengthy discussion of this issue in G. H. Fox, *Humanitarian Occupation* (Cambridge: Cambridge University Press, 2008), 211–13, 213. Note, on the other hand, the position taken on these questions in E. de Wet, *The Chapter VII Powers of the United Nations Security Council* (Oxford: Hart, 2004), 189.

54 *Military and Paramilitary Activities in and against Nicaragua* (*Nicaragua* v. *United States*), Judgment of 27 June 1986 [1986] ICJ 14, para. 190.

55 Fassbender, '*Quis judicabit?*', 226.

the fundamental principle of sovereignty is vitiated by the application of Chapter VII, indicating just how extraordinary action under this part of the Charter is understood to be.[56]

2.1.3 The Security Council should be presumed to act in accordance with international law

This position was taken by Nigel Rodley in his concurrence in *Sayadi* v. *Belgium*.[57] Not wanting to assert that the SC *cannot* act so as to require disregard for human rights, Rodley instead claims that 'there should be a presumption that the Security Council did not intend that actions taken pursuant to its resolutions should violate human rights'.[58] This would seem to be a logical conclusion of Article 24(2) of the Charter, discussed above.

Rodley's approach is analogous to the Charming Betsy presumption in US foreign relations law, which holds that a federal statute should never be presumed to violate international law if any other interpretation is possible.[59] The positive consequences of such approaches are that they serve as 'an antidote to possible legislative inadvertence' (responding to Lauterpacht's fear of accidental results) and require 'a high level of political resolve ... to conflict with international law'.[60] In other words, the SC would have to explicitly authorize any violations of international law.

On the contrary, the SC (and other UN bodies) often 'reaffirm[s] the need to combat by all means, *in accordance with the Charter of the United Nations and international law, including applicable international human rights, refugee and humanitarian law,* threats to international peace and security caused by terrorist acts'.[61]

[56] UN Charter, Art. 2, para. 7.

[57] *Sayadi* v. *Belgium*, Human Rights Committee, UN Doc. CCPR/C/94/D/1472/2006 (29 December 2008), 36.

[58] *Sayadi* v. *Belgium*, 36. This presumption was underscored in Amnesty International and the Human Rights Law Resource Centre, Human Rights and Human Security: Joint Submission to the Commonwealth Attorney-General's Department Regarding National Security Legislation 42 (2009). As of 2011, it has also been adopted by the ECtHR. See discussion at text to nn. 176–7 below.

[59] See, e.g., discussion in D. Bederman, *International Law Frameworks* (New York: Foundation Press, 2006), 174.

[60] *Ibid.*

[61] It most recently used this formula in the preamble of S/Res./1989 (2011), preambular para. 3 (emphasis added). Similar prior references include S/Res./1373 (2001), preambular para. 5; S/Res./1455 (2003), preambular para. 3; and S/Res./1624 (2005), preambular para. 2 and operative paras. 1 and 4. See A. Conte, *Handbook on Human Rights Compliance while*

World leaders themselves confirmed the importance of these legal obligations in the 2005 World Summit Outcome Document which declared that:

> international cooperation to fight terrorism must be conducted in conformity with international law, including the Charter and relevant international conventions and protocols. States must ensure that any measures taken to combat terrorism comply with their obligations under . . . human rights law, refugee law and international humanitarian law.[62]

They did not include an escape clause for action under the Charter in this regard.

Moreover, it would make no sense if the SC could depart from the UN's own Global Counter-Terrorism Strategy which centres the protection of human rights as an integral part of any effective counter-terrorism effort.[63] In fact, the current High Commissioner for Human Rights (HCHR) in 2009 exhorted the Security Council's counter-terrorism bodies to more clearly signal acceptance of this strategy by considering the human rights implications of any counter-terrorism measures.[64] According to the HCHR, the Counter-Terrorism Committee's Executive Directorate has already moved in this direction by committing to consider relevant human rights issues when reviewing state compliance with SC Resolutions 1373 and 1624.[65] Furthermore, the Counter-Terrorism Committee has, in fact, raised such concerns in its dialogues with states.[66]

The Rodley approach is then a logical and sensible reflection of such policy and practice. Further development of the presumption's contours and implications will be necessary. It can be an important interpretative

Countering Terrorism (New York: Center on Global Counterterrorism Cooperation, 2008), fn. 13.

62 UN General Assembly, *2005 World Summit Outcome* (UN Doc. A/Res./60/1 (2005), para. 85.

63 See 'The UN Global Counter-Terrorism Strategy', annexed to UN Doc. A/Res./60/2008, 8 Sept. 2006, preambular para. 3 and section IV.

64 Address by Ms. Navanethem Pillay to the Counter-Terrorism Committee of the Security Council, New York, 29 October 2009, 3, at www.un.org/sc/ctc/pdf/HC_statement_to_CTC_29_Oct_09.pdf [hereafter Pillay Address].

65 *Ibid.*, 4.

66 In its global surveys of the implementation of SC Res. 1373 by member states, the Counter-Terrorism Committee has referred extensively to relevant human rights concerns. See, e.g., *Survey of the Implementation of Security Council Resolution 1373* (2001) *by Member States* (UN Doc. S/2009/620 (13 November 2009)), at www.un.org/sc/ctc/pdf/GIS2009.pdf.

tool in situations where states maintain discretion in how to implement SC resolutions, a point underscored by Baroness Hale when *Al-Jedda* was considered in the House of Lords.[67] However, this presumption can only resolve these dilemmas where the relevant SC resolution(s) afford discretion to states in how to implement them, such as when they authorize states to use 'all necessary measures' to do so.[68] Hence, even if this presumption is accepted, additional approaches may still be needed to solve those parts of the problem beyond its reach.

2.1.4 The Security Council must respect international law, even when acting under Chapter VII of the Charter

This position might be the one most hoped for by international human rights lawyers. A number of international experts and bodies have taken this view. In approaching the general question of the applicability of human rights norms to the United Nations, Fréderic Mégret and Florian Hoffman have argued that radical changes in the UN's mandate over time justify the applicability of human rights standards to the UN itself.[69] More specifically, Dapo Akande believes that the SC itself is bound by human rights law because it has to act in accordance with the purposes and principles of the UN, and these explicitly include the promotion of human rights.[70]

For Akande, there is a genuine question as to *which* human rights norms bind the SC, but not a foundational question as to whether they are relevant at all.[71] He asserts that the SC is bound by rights contained in human rights instruments adopted within the UN system which he argues to be elaborations of the UN Charter itself.[72] Similarly, Jordan Paust argues that Article 55 (c) of the Charter 'condition(s) the authority of [UN] entities, such as the Security Council' not to violate human rights or authorize the violation of human rights, including human rights obligations under customary international law.[73] In

[67] *Al-Jedda* v. *Secretary of State for Defence*, para. 129 (Opinion of Baroness Hale).

[68] M. Milanović, 'The Human Rights Committee's Views in *Sayadi* v. *Belgium*: A Missed Opportunity' (2009), 3 *Goettingen Journal of International Law* 534.

[69] F. Mégret and F. Hoffman, 'The UN as a Human Rights Violator? Some Reflections on the United Nations Changing Human Rights Responsibilities' (2003) 25 *Human Rights Quarterly* 314. See also A. Reinisch, 'Developing Human Rights and Humanitarian Law Accountability of the Security Council for the Imposition of Economic Sanctions' (2001) 95 *American Journal of International Law* 851.

[70] Akande, 'Security Council and Human Rights'. [71] *Ibid.* [72] *Ibid.*

[73] J. Paust, 'The UN Is Bound by Human Rights: Understanding the Full Reach of Human Rights, Remedies and Nonimmunity: Responding to Tom Dannenbaum, Translating the Standard of Effective Control into a System of Effective Accountability' (2010) 51

complementary fashion, Article 56 conditions the related conduct of member states of the United Nations in the same way.[74] Similarly, Fraas takes the view that the SC has to act in accordance not only with the Charter, but also with *jus cogens* norms and the non-derogable human rights listed in Article 4 ICCPR.[75] However, just as states may derogate from certain rights in the face of an emergency threatening the life of the nation, Akande suggests that the SC may do the same when acting under Chapter VII.[76]

What are the consequences when the SC acts beyond these limits? Akande goes so far as to assert that since the SC is bound by human rights law, if it acts in contravention of such norms, it is acting *ultra vires*. Thus, those decisions are a nullity and do not give rise to 'obligations' within the meaning of Article 103. Another approach has been to suggest that the clause at the end of Article 25 ('in accordance with the present Charter') means that states do not have to carry out resolutions that contravene the Charter, including its purpose of promoting human rights. Even the European Commission took the view in *Kadi* that 'an act adopted by [the Security Council] in breach of human rights . . . might be regarded as having been adopted ultra vires and therefore, as not binding on the Community.'[77]

The argument that the SC is bound by international human rights law is compelling in many regards, not the least of which is that it will be extremely difficult to convince states that they must respect international human rights norms in the face of the exigencies of combating terrorism if the central organ of the international security apparatus – the SC – is not required to do so as well. Making this argument could be an important interpretative strategy for human rights lawyers in this domain and could contribute to the progressive development of international law in this area. However, as indicated above, one should be careful not to overstate the language of Article 1(3) of the Charter which after all speaks only of 'achiev[ing] cooperation in . . . promoting and encouraging respect' for human rights. Additionally, in so doing, one must not downplay the significant human rights values also

Harvard International Law Journal 301, at www.harvardilj.org/articles/51_Online_Paust_4_6_10.pdf, 2–3.

74 *Ibid.*, 3. 75 See Fassbender, '*Quis judicabit?*', 221–2. 76 *Ibid.*

77 *Kadi and Al Barakaat International Foundation* v. *Council*, Joined Cases C-402/05 P and C-415/05 P, 3 CMLR 41 (2008), para. 270. Nevertheless, the Commission felt that the ECJ was not empowered to review whether a particular SC resolution fell into this category (*ibid.*, para. 271).

protected by enabling the SC to act effectively to deal with threats to and breaches of the peace, as human rights discourse sometimes does in the counter-terrorism area.[78]

Beyond the question of any human rights requirements on the Council itself, there is also the related question of whether or not states must respect IHL/human rights when implementing Council resolutions under Chapter VII. There is clear support for the position that they must do so in international law and in recent statements by the SC itself. The 2003 Declaration of the SC meeting with Ministers of Foreign Affairs adopted under Resolution 1456 specifically requires that:

> States must ensure that any measure [sic] taken to combat terrorism comply with all their obligations under international law, and should adopt such measures in accordance with international law, in particular international human rights, refugee, and humanitarian law.[79]

Of course, as Alex Conte notes, this statement is most likely hortatory rather than binding within the meaning of Article 25 of the Charter.[80] However, when requiring states to take measures to prohibit incitement of terrorism, the SC has specifically reminded states in an operative paragraph to comply with human rights and IHL obligations when so doing.[81] In addition, the Counter-Terrorism Committee of the Security Council, created under SC Resolution 1373, has stressed that states have to make sure that their implementation of counter-terrorism measures accords with other international law obligations, including those under human rights law and IHL.[82] Its report to this effect was endorsed by the SC.[83] Moreover, the Commission on Human Rights in 2004 '[u]rge[d] states 'to fulfill their obligations under the Charter of the United Nations in strict conformity with international law, including human rights standards and obligations'.[84]

78 See Bennoune, 'Terror/Torture', 39. 79 UN Doc. S/Res./1456 (2003), para. 6.

80 Conte, *Handbook*, 2–3. See also UN Doc. S/Res./1805 (2008), preamble.

81 UN Doc. S/Res./1624 (2005), para. 4.

82 UN Counter-Terrorism Committee, *Report of the Counter-Terrorism Committee to the Security Council for Its Consideration as Part of Its Comprehensive Review of the Counter-Terrorism Committee Executive Directorate* (UN Doc. S/2005/800 (2005)); UN Counter-Terrorism Committee, *Reports of the Counter-Terrorism Committee to the Security Council for Its Consideration as Part of Its Comprehensive Review of the Counter-Terrorism Committee Executive Directorate* (UN Doc. S/2006/289 (2006)).

83 Conte, *Handbook*, 3.

84 See Human Rights and Terrorism, Commission on Human Rights Resolutions 2004/44 (UN Doc. E/CN.4/Res./2004/44 (2004), para. 7).

One of the sources of confusion in this area is the use of broad language like 'all necessary means' or 'all necessary measures' in some resolutions authorizing state action to implement SC resolutions under Chapter VII of the UN Charter.[85] Leading international lawyers have insisted that such language be seen not to require measures that would contravene international human rights law obligations.[86] In any case, even if measures that negatively impact human rights are to be justified on the grounds of action authorized by the SC, states must find the most rights-friendly means of effectively complying with the resolution. The fact of SC resolutions does not justify *any* action claimed to be taken to implement them.

Moreover, the mere citation of the SC or Article 103 of the Charter should not end any legal inquiry regarding the action in question as in the *Behrami–Saramati* approach discussed below. In her House of Lords' opinion in *Al-Jedda*, Baroness Hale underscored this issue.[87] Judges Bedjaoui, Ranjeva and Koroma's joint declaration in the *Lockerbie* case did as well. They strongly endorsed the ICJ's decision to allow the case to proceed to the merits phase, noting that, 'it is not sufficient to invoke the provisions of Chapter VII of the Charter so as to bring to an end *ipso facto* and with immediate effect all judicial argument on the Security Council's decisions.'[88]

2.2 *Treaty law*

In addition to the UN Charter, the corpus of treaty law should also be considered when reconciling international legal regimes governing peace and security and the protection of persons. Treaty law shapes how we should understand both the Charter and the human rights covenants and IHL treaties in question, and their interrelationship.

[85] See, e.g., UN Doc. S/Res./1863 (2009), para. 2 (authorizing member states of the African Union to take 'all necessary measures' to carry out the AMISOM mission in Somalia).

[86] See, e.g., S. Farrior, 'Introductory Note to *R (Al-Jedda)* v. *Secretary of State for Defence*, UKHL', Vermont Law School Legal Studies Research Paper Series, Research Paper No. 09-26 (2009), 4.

[87] *Al-Jedda* v. *Secretary of State for Defence*, para. 129 (Opinion of Baroness Hale).

[88] *Questions of Interpretation and Application of the 1971 Montreal Convention Arising from the Aerial Incident at Lockerbie* (*Libya* v. *United States*), Preliminary Objections, Judgment of 27 February 1998 [1998] ICJ Rep. 115 (Joint Declaration of Judges Bedjaoui, Ranjeva and Koroma).

The primordial principle of *pacta sunt servanda* requires states to implement their treaty obligations in good faith.[89] A departure from doing so, even in accordance with Article 103, is a significant derogation from general international law. Note that under the Vienna Convention on the Law of Treaties, even in the face of a material breach, rules allowing a resultant suspension of the treaty in question do not apply to 'provisions relating to the protection of the human person contained in treaties of a humanitarian character'.[90]

Moreover, the UN Charter itself stipulates that another of the UN's purposes is indeed 'to establish conditions under which justice and *respect for the obligations arising from treaties* and other sources of international law can be maintained'.[91] Reading this language in light of the comments of some delegations to Dumbarton Oaks, Wolfrum suggests that it indicates an intention on the part of the drafters of the UN Charter that the United Nations should not be just a political organization, but one that is also 'committed to international law'.[92] This would make the power of the SC to act beyond or against international law or to authorize such action a fundamental departure from the UN project itself.

However, even the Vienna Convention on the Law of Treaties nods to Article 103. Its Article 30, which governs the application of successive treaties relating to the same subject matter, specifically stipulates that its rules are '[s]ubject to Article 103 of the Charter of the United Nations'.[93] VCLT Article 30(2) also establishes that when a treaty indicates that it is subject to, or not to be considered as incompatible with another treaty, the provisions of that other treaty apply.[94]

In fact, the ICCPR in its Article 46 concedes that 'Nothing in the present Covenant shall be interpreted as impairing the provisions of the Charter of the United Nations'.[95] The International Covenant on Economic, Social and Cultural Rights (ICESCR) contains precisely the same language in its Article 24. This appears to confirm the preclusive effect of obligations under the Charter. It is interesting, however, that the HRC has found that Article 46 ICCPR does not preclude consideration of whether or not measures taken by states pursuant to SC resolutions violate the Covenant when considering a case under the Optional Protocol.[96] Manfred Nowak's commentary to the ICCPR explains that Article 46 serves 'merely [as] an interpretational

[89] VCLT, Art. 26. [90] *Ibid.*, Art. 60(3). [91] UN Charter, preamble (emphasis added).
[92] Wolfrum, in Simma, *Commentary*, 36. [93] VCLT, Art. 30(1). [94] *Ibid.*, Art. 30(2).
[95] 1966 ICCPR, 999 UNTS 171, Art. 46. [96] *Sayadi*, para. 10.3.

rule'[97] which 'regulates only the relationship of the Covenant to the "UN family"'[98] and 'merely expresses that the functions of the UN organs entrusted with civil and political rights (particularly, the GA, ECOSOC, the HRComm, the Sub-Commission, the Commission on the Status of Women and the Commission on Crime Prevention and Criminal Justice) . . . were not impaired by entry into force of the Covenant'.[99]

2.3 *Recent jurisprudence*

The recent jurisprudence on these issues is somewhat conflicting. It is a product both of the renewed vigour of the SC since the end of the Cold War, and also especially of the robust action taken by the SC since September 11, 2001, which has had some well-documented human rights fallout.[100] These cases have been especially notable in the European context given the vitality of supranational judicial bodies in the region. Many of the decisions have sparked considerable controversy among academics, and there has often been a worryingly wide gap between the positions taken on the litigation by states and those taken by human rights actors, a disconnect that needs to be addressed. The cases will be discussed in chronological order below.

2.3.1 *Behrami/Saramati* – 2007 (ECtHR)

It was *Behrami/Saramati*[101] perhaps more than any other case which put the topic of this chapter on the human rights agenda. In *Behrami*, the European Court of Human Rights (ECtHR) considered a case brought against individual states for action taken as part of KFOR in Kosovo after the end of NATO's air campaign against the Federal Republic of Yugoslavia. Mr Behrami sought justice for the death of his son due to cluster-bomb units that had not been removed.[102] Meanwhile, Mr Saramati complained of his detention from April to June of 2001.[103] Ultimately, in a much maligned decision, the ECtHR decided that it was

97 M. Nowak, *UN Covenant on Civil and Political Rights: CCPR Commentary* (Kehl: Engel, 1993) 627.

98 *Ibid.*, 625. 99 *Ibid.*, 626.

100 See, e.g., José Alvarez, 'The "Dark Side" of the UN's War on Terrorism', in A. Sajó (ed.) *Abuse: The Dark Side of Fundamental Rights* (Amsterdam: Eleven International Publishing, 2006), 163.

101 This refers to the joined cases of *Behrami and Behrami* v. *France* and *Saramati* v. *France, Germany and Norway*, 45 EHRR SE10 (2007).

102 *Ibid.*, paras. 5–7. 103 *Ibid.*, paras. 8–9.

incompetent *ratione personae* to review the actions in question and found the cases inadmissible.[104] The reasoning for the Court's decision is perhaps most clearly spelled out in its paragraph 149:

> Since operations established by UNSC Resolutions under Chapter VII of the UN Charter are fundamental to the mission of the UN to secure international peace and security and since they rely for their effectiveness on support from member states, the Convention cannot be interpreted in a manner which would subject the acts and omissions of Contracting Parties which are covered by UNSC Resolutions and occur prior to or in the course of such missions, to the scrutiny of the Court. To do so would be to interfere with the fulfillment of the UN's key mission in this field including . . . with the effective conduct of its operations.[105]

For the ECtHR, the SC retained ultimate authority for the operation and thus the conduct of KFOR was to be attributed to the UN rather than to states. This position on the issue of attribution is hotly disputed.[106] Sari, citing a 1996 report of the UN Secretary-General, argues that the UN denies that its responsibility is engaged by internationally wrongful acts and omissions of peace support operations authorized under Chapter VII but carried out under national or multinational command and control.[107] Moreover, the Secretary-General responded to the *Behrami* decision by explicitly limiting the international responsibility of the UN for violations of international law under its 'effective operational control' when endorsing the reconfiguration of UNMIK.[108] (Some have labelled this as a rejection of the *Behrami* decision.)[109]

Many international lawyers have been especially critical of this ECtHR decision. Milanović says that 'it is so utterly wrong that it is . . . one of the worst decisions of the European Court in recent memory'.[110] Tobias Thienel has written that it was 'wrongly decided, or at least wrongly reasoned'.[111]

[104] *Ibid.*, para. 152. [105] *Ibid.*, para. 149.

[106] A. Sari, 'Jurisdiction and International Responsibility in Peace Support Operations: The *Behrami* and *Saramati* Cases' (2008) 8 *Human Rights Law Review* 162.

[107] *Ibid.*, 165.

[108] See E. de Wet, 'The Governance of Kosovo: Security Council Resolution 1244 and the Establishment and Functioning of Eulex' (2009) 103 *American Journal of International Law* 83, fn. 79 (discussing *Report of the Secretary-General on the United Nations Interim Administration Mission in Kosovo*, UN Doc. S/2008/354 (2008)).

[109] de Wet, 'Governance of Kosovo', fn. 84.

[110] M. Milanović, posting, 14 January 2008, *Opinio Juris*, at http://opiniojuris.org/2008/01/14/is-the-us-army-in-iraq-acting-for-the-un.

[111] T. Thienel, 'Is the US Army in Iraq acting for the UN?', 14 January 2008, *Opinio Juris*, at http://opiniojuris.org/2008/01/14/is-the-us-army-in-iraq-acting-for-the-un.

He argues that it is an example of result-oriented jurisprudence, decided regardless of the law because the ECtHR did not want to interfere with the Chapter VII system.[112]

After the ECtHR issued the judgment, many feared it would have major repercussions for attempts to hold states accountable when they participate in internationally mandated peace operations.[113] In fact, the ECtHR employed *Behrami/Saramati* to find other complaints about KFOR inadmissible.[114] Moreover, the ghost of *Behrami* also haunted the UK House of Lords' subsequent judgment in *Al Jedda* v. *Secretary of State for Defence*.

2.3.2 *Al-Jedda* – 2007 (UK HL)

In 2004, Mr Al-Jedda,[115] a British national, was detained without trial by British troops in Iraq for allegedly being a member of a terrorist group that carried out bomb attacks, and for recruiting terrorists outside of Iraq to participate in attacks there.[116] He challenged his detention before British courts on the grounds that it contravened the prohibition on arbitrary detention found in Article 5 European Convention on Human Rights (ECHR) and Article 78 Fourth Geneva Convention.[117]

At the level of the House of Lords, the Secretary of State's line of argument on attributability drew substantially from *Behrami*. (*Behrami* was decided by the ECtHR after the Court of Appeal issued its judgment in *Al-Jedda*, but before the House of Lords heard the matter.)[118] The House of Lords departed from the view of the Secretary of State and factually distinguished the situation of national contingents operating in Kosovo under KFOR mandate from that of UK forces in Iraq which it saw as not acting under effective command and control of the UN.[119] In

[112] *Ibid.* Similar suggestions have been made about *Banković and others* v. *Belgium and 16 Other Contracting States*, ECtHR, App. No. 52207/99, 41 ILM 517 (2001).

[113] See Sari, 'Jurisdiction and International Responsibility', 151.

[114] *Ibid.* (citing *Ilaz Kasumaj* v. *Greece*, Decision of 5 July 2007, App. No. 6974/05; *Slavisa Gajic* v. *Germany*, Decision of 28 August 2007, App. No. 31445/02; *Dušan Berić and others* v. *Bosnia and Herzegovina*, Decision of 16 October 2007, App. No. 36357/04 and others). An analogous use of *Behrami* was made in *Stephens* v. *Cyprus, Turkey and the United Nations*, App. No. 45267/06, Decision of 11 December 2008.

[115] *R (On the Application of Al-Jedda) (FC)* v. *Secretary of State for Defence* [2007] HL 58, at www.publications.parliament.U.K./pa/ld/ldjudgmt.htm (decided by the HL Appellate Committee, 12 December 2007).

[116] *Al-Jedda* v. *Secretary of State for Defence* (Opinion of Lord Bingham), paras. 1–2.

[117] *Al-Jedda* v. *Secretary of State for Defence*, para. 3.

[118] A. Orakhelashvili, 'Case Note: *R (On the Application of Al-Jedda) (FC)* v. *Secretary of State for Defence*' (2008) 102 *American Journal of International Law* 339.

[119] *Al-Jedda* v. *Secretary of State for Defence* (Opinion of Lord Bingham), paras. 7–19.

other words, the detention of Mr Al-Jedda was attributed to the UK. Still, the Law Lords found that SC resolutions with the backing of Article 103 did authorize the detention of individuals such as Mr Al-Jedda.[120] These SC resolutions superseded any conflicting treaty obligations which could not be overridden save by *jus cogens*. Lord Bingham explained that deferring Article 5 ECHR to Article 103 UN Charter was consistent with the jurisprudence of the ECtHR.[121] Hence, though the UK was responsible for the detention it was absolved for holding Mr Al-Jedda because it was simply following SC resolutions that prevail over the ECHR.

According to Alexander Orakhelashvili, the House of Lords failed to consider how it should interpret SC resolutions.[122] He was not convinced that the SC resolution in question (Resolution 1546) actually authorized detentions in the manner of Al-Jedda's,[123] and he pointed for support to Baroness Hale's complaint that the judgment

> devoted little attention to the precise scope of the authorization [under Resolution 1546]. There must still be room for argument about what precisely is covered by the resolution and whether it applies on the facts of this case.[124]

Christian Tomuschat concurs, suggesting that Resolution 1546 manifests no intention to depart from IHL or human rights norms (in fact it specifically affirms IHL).[125] He underscores the fact that the term 'internment' does not appear in the relevant clause of Resolution 1546.[126] Thus, Article 103 simply does not end the matter.

Many human rights lawyers shared the following negative appraisal of the judgment:

> The central conclusions of the *Al-Jedda* decision [in the House of Lords] – concerning the impact of Security Council resolutions – rest on questionable presumptions and on incomplete, partial analyses of the overarching legal framework and available evidence, thereby compromising the potential of *Al-Jedda* judgment [sic] to contribute to the development of international law.[127]

[120] Orakhelashvili, 'Case Note', 339–40.
[121] *Al-Jedda* v. *Secretary of State for Defence* (Opinion of Lord Bingham), para. 36.
[122] Orakhelashvili, 'Case Note', 342. [123] *Ibid.*, 343.
[124] *Al-Jedda* v. *Secretary of State for Defence* (Opinion of Baroness Hale), para. 129.
[125] Tomuschat, 'Case Note', 401.
[126] *Ibid.* He does note that internment is listed as a necessary measure in Colin Powell's 5 June 2004 letter which was attached to the resolution.
[127] Orakhelashvili, 'Case Note', 345.

Tomuschat says that the House of Lords 'interpretation of art 103 ... runs counter to the underlying philosophy of the human rights system'[128] and warns that it 'would have disastrous results for international human rights law if applied in the future'.[129]

However, the UK House of Lords was not alone in taking such a position in 2007 and 2008. A similar decision was reached by the District Court in the Hague in a 2008 civil case regarding responsibility for failures to prevent atrocities in Srebrenica.[130] The conduct of Dutch troops was attributed to the United Nations and the court then rejected the notion that it would still need to test whether the Netherlands complied with human rights and humanitarian law, focusing on the fact that the UN is not a contracting party to the ECHR. Likewise, in its November 2007 holding in *Nada*, the Swiss Supreme Court dismissed a case filed by Youssef Nada and a number of organizations seeking removal from the Swiss Decree of 2 October 2000 which implemented UN sanctions on entities associated with bin Laden, al-Qaeda and the Taliban.[131] The Supreme Court argued that according to Article 103 UN Charter those provisions prevailed over conflicting obligations under human rights treaties.[132] Otherwise

> the global uniform application of UN sanctions would be jeopardized if the courts of individual member states could amend or reverse sanctions against individuals or entities because of possible violations of fundamental rights under the European Convention of Human Rights and the UN International Covenant on Civil and Political Rights.[133]

The Swiss Supreme Court argued that only *jus cogens* could override the binding effect of SC decisions and found that the rights at stake in the case (right to fair trial and to an effective remedy) did not rise to that level.

In light of this jurisprudence of auto-absolution that was proliferating in 2007–8, it was significant that the *Al-Jedda* case subsequently went to the ECtHR. In 2011, the ECtHR issued a judgment in the case discussed

[128] Tomuschat, 'Case Note', 399. [129] *Ibid.*, 403.

[130] *H.N.* v. *the State of the Netherlands* (*Ministry of Defense and Ministry of Foreign Affairs*), Rechtbank's – Gravenhage, Case Number 265615/HA ZA 06-1671 (Neth.), 10 September 2008 (English translation).

[131] See J. Brisard, 'Swiss Supreme Court keeps Youssef Nada on the Terrorist List' (30 November 2007), at http://jcb.blogs.com/jcb_blog/2007/11/swiss-supreme-c.html. The Swiss Supreme Court ruling is available in the original German version at http://jcb.blogs.com/jcb_blog/files/tf_youssef_nada.pdf.

[132] *Ibid.* [133] *Ibid.*

below which came to a very different conclusion.[134] Note, moreover, that in the interim the Supreme Court of the United Kingdom itself quashed the Terrorism Order (United Nations Measures) 2009 on the grounds that it went beyond the requirements imposed by relevant SC resolutions.[135] Less than a month before the ECtHR ruling in *Al-Jedda* in 2011, a Dutch Appeals Court also reversed the district court's ruling, finding instead that the Dutch authorities did have 'effective control' when Bosnian Muslim men were sent out of DutchBat headquarters to their deaths at the hands of the Bosnian Serbs in Srebrenica, and could therefore be held responsible.[136] These later results mitigated the impact of the House of Lords' decision in *Al-Jedda*. This subsequent turn toward accountability could be argued to begin with the next case under consideration: *Kadi*.

2.3.3 *Kadi* – 2008 (ECJ)

The European Court of Justice took a decidedly different approach to that taken in the *Behrami* decision in the *Kadi*[137] case, handed down in 2008. Here the ECJ found that the European Community regulation implementing an SC resolution was indeed subject to question under European Community fundamental rights standards. It annulled the regulation in question. Nothing in the UN Charter, in the view of the Court, mandated the EC to give primacy to an international agreement within the EC legal order. UN measures could not supersede primary treaty rules or fundamental rights. The Court could indeed assess the compatibility of the EC implementing regulation with EC fundamental rights law, while not challenging the SC resolution itself.[138] Since member states may comply with SC resolutions in different ways, with no particular method being mandated, judicial review of the selected methodology was deemed completely appropriate.[139]

[134] See Statement of Facts and Questions to the Parties, App. No. 27021/08 by Hilal Abdul-Razzaq Ali Al-Jedda, lodged 3 June 2008 ECtHR, Fourth Section.

[135] *Her Majesty's Treasury* v. *Mohammed Jabar Ahmad* [2010] UKSC 2 (decided by the UKSC, 27 January 2010).

[136] *Hasan Nuhanovic* v. *The Netherlands*, Gerechtshof's-Gravenhage, Case Number 200.020.174/01, July 5, 2011 (Neth.) (English translation). See also, 'Dutch state "responsible for three Srebrenica deaths"', BBC News, 5 July 2011, at www.bbc.co.U.K./news/world-europe-14026218.

[137] *Kadi and Al Barakaat International Foundation*, para. 270.

[138] See Angus Johnston, 'Case and Comment: Frozen in Time? The ECJ Finally Rules on the *Kadi* Appeal' (2008) 68 *Cambridge Law Journal* 1; *Kadi and Al Barakaat International Foundation*, paras. 294–310.

[139] *Kadi and Al Barakaat International Foundation*, paras. 298–9.

Mr Kadi and the Al Barakaat International Foundation had been listed as persons or entities connected to Osama bin Laden whose assets must be frozen in accordance with SC Resolution 1333 and EC Regulation 881/2002.[140] In this regard, the ECJ found that the rights of defence, especially the right to be heard and to effective judicial review of those rights, were not respected.[141] The ECJ opined that the European Communities were bound to make sure that any implementing legislation for SC resolutions had to respect at least 'the minimum criteria in the field of human rights'.[142] Here the court distinguished *Kadi* from *Behrami* because in the instant case the actions in question were not directly attributable to the United Nations.[143] Moreover, according to the ECJ, in *Behrami* the actions in question did not take place on the territory of the defendant states or even due to decisions taken by their national authorities.[144] None of this was deemed true in *Kadi* as regards the EC.

In 2009, the SC responded to the judgment in *Kadi* by providing some recourse for individuals who claim to have been erroneously listed, including by creating an ombudsperson who can hear complaints.[145] This was seen as a response to criticism of the listing system generally,[146] but in particular to *Kadi* and other cases.[147]

Angus Johnston argues that *Kadi* is 'one of the ECJ's most significant judgments to date', that solidifies the role of fundamental rights protection at the heart of the EC legal order.[148] While the case is grounded in the particular dynamics of EC law, the approach of the ECJ to centring rights protection is undoubtedly something for human rights lawyers to seek to replicate elsewhere. However, Johnston also warns that 'its [*Kadi*'s] implications for the future operation of the legal regimes for terrorist asset freezing . . . will be substantial'.[149] Given that the pursuit of terrorist financing is one of the most important and effective means of

[140] A. Posch, 'The *Kadi* Case: Rethinking the Relationship Between European Union Law and International Law' (2009) 15 *Columbia Journal of European Law Online* 1.

[141] *Kadi and Al Barakaat International Foundation*, para. 334. [142] *Ibid.*, para. 279.

[143] *Ibid.*, para. 311. [144] *Ibid.*, para. 312.

[145] UN Doc. S/Res./1904 (2009) (adopted unanimously under Chapter VII). This mandate was extended and further elaborated in 2011 (UN Doc. S/Res./1989 (2011), para. 21 and Annex II).

[146] See, e.g., Alvarez, '"Dark Side" of UN's War on Terrorism'.

[147] See, e.g., N. MacFarquhar, 'UN measure offers recourse to blacklisted', *New York Times*, 17 December 2009, at www.nytimes.com/2009/12/18/world/18nations.html?_r=1&ref=world.

[148] Johnston, 'Frozen in Time', 3. [149] *Ibid.*, 4.

combating international terrorism,[150] a form of violence that gravely impacts human rights, rights advocates should not overlook this aspect of *Kadi*'s fallout either.

The challenge is to develop methods of suppressing the financing of terrorism that are the least rights restrictive as possible. They must be necessary and proportional, and non-discriminatory, but also effective notwithstanding the creativity and subterfuge often involved in funding terrorism.[151] Governments must take this task very seriously. At the same time, human rights advocates may need to stomach some justifiable and transparent derogations from derogable human rights norms in this regard (when carried out in accordance with international law), and lawful limitations on rights that are subject to them, to protect the rights of others by combating the financing of terrorism.

2.3.4 *Sayadi* – 2008 (UNHRC)

The same year the ECJ ruled in *Kadi*, the Human Rights Committee issued its view in *Sayadi* v. *Belgium*,[152] which adopted a similarly critical posture of state implementation of international counter-terrorism obligations. Two married Belgian nationals, Nabil Sayadi and Patricia Vinck, claimed they were wrongfully placed on the lists of associates of Osama bin Laden pursuant to SC resolutions and the EU regulation designed to implement them. Consequently, all of their financial assets were frozen despite the fact that they were not convicted of a crime.[153] They argued that this constituted a violation of a range of their rights under the ICCPR. Sayadi and Vinck were the director and secretary of an NGO called Fondation Secours International, purportedly the European wing of the Global Relief Foundation in the US which had been on the sanctions list since 2002 due to being suspected of financing al-Qaeda.[154] However, a Belgian judicial investigation 'confirmed the plaintiffs' innocence'.[155]

[150] See, e.g., Center for Defense Information, 'Combating Terrorist Financing: A Key Aspect of the War on Terrorism' (20 May 2005), at www.cdi.org/friendlyversion/printversion.cfm?documentID=3024. Combating the financing of terrorism is often seen as a more rights-friendly way of dealing with the problem than resort to the use of force or arbitrary detention or other measures.

[151] See, e.g., Vardi, 'Al Qaeda's new business model', *Forbes*, 18 December 2009, 153.

[152] *Sayadi* v. *Belgium*, Human Rights Committee, UN Doc. CCPR/C/94/D/1472/2006 (29 December 2008).

[153] All of these facts are drawn from the Committee's view (*ibid.*).

[154] *Ibid.*, para. 4.2.

[155] *Ibid.*, para. 2.6.

Unlike the ECtHR in *Behrami*, the Human Rights Committee (HRC) found that it could hear the case because it concerned an allegation of a violation of the ICCPR by a state party, though it would not be able the entertain challenges to UN counter-terrorism rules themselves.[156] On the merits, the Committee found that Belgium had violated Articles 12[157] and 17[158] of the Covenant, as the individuals were prevented from travelling and there had been an unlawful attack on their names and reputations.[159] (It found no violation of Articles 14[160] or 15[161] because it deemed the measures in question not to be of a criminal nature.)[162] The HRC attributed the violative actions to Belgium because, while the Belgian government did not maintain the list, it was responsible for the inclusion of their names.[163] Similar to the view of the ECJ in *Kadi*, the HRC emphasized that, notwithstanding the Charter, it had a duty 'to consider to what extent the obligations imposed on the State party by the SC resolutions may justify the infringement' of rights.[164] The view of the majority of the HRC does not engage in a thorough discussion of the impact of Article 103 of the Charter. While agreeing with the result, Milanović sharply criticizes the HRC's methodology for 'sidestep[ping] Article 103 . . . as if it was not even there'.[165]

In fact, concurring HRC members Yuji Iwasawa and Nigel Rodley both faulted the HRC for failing to address the UN Charter issues. Iwasawa nevertheless concludes that 'state parties to the Covenant are obliged to comply with the obligations under it to the maximum extent possible, even when they implement a resolution of the United Nations Security Council.'[166] Echoing the Bedjaoui/Ranjeva/Koroma declaration in *Lockerbie*,[167] Iwasawa opines that Article 103 does not bar the HRC from issuing a view. Significantly, he believes that Belgium could indeed have complied with the SC resolutions while still conducting itself in a different manner.

156 *Ibid.*, para. 7.2.
157 Art. 12 guarantees freedom of movement, and the right to leave one's country.
158 Art. 17 guarantees the right to privacy, and guards against unlawful attacks on honour and reputation.
159 *Sayadi* v. *Belgium*, paras. 10.8 and 10.13.
160 Art. 14 guarantees fair trial rights.
161 Art. 15 prohibits ex post facto convictions.
162 *Sayadi* v. *Belgium*, para. 10.11.
163 *Ibid.*, para. 10.13.
164 *Ibid.*, para. 10.6.
165 Milanović, 'The Human Rights Committee's Views in *Sayadi* v. *Belgium*', 526.
166 *Sayadi* v. *Belgium* (individual opinion of Yuji Iwasawa).
167 *Questions of Interpretation and Application of the 1971 Montreal Convention Arising from the Aerial Incident at Lockerbie*, at Joint Declaration of Judges Bedjaoui, Ranjeva and Koroma.

Rodley's initial take on the subject was that Article 103 would decide the matter in favour of SC-mandated action. He also felt that the HRC was 'not well placed to assess the legal validity'[168] of the decisions in question. However, on further reflection he decided that the HRC can take a prima facie view as to the existence of a conflict between the state party's obligations under Article 25 of the Charter and under the Covenant. He suggested criteria that could be applied to interpret the resolutions for these purposes. These include the presumption discussed above that the SC does not intend that actions taken pursuant to its resolutions should violate rights (now ratified by the ECtHR in *Al-Jedda*), that there should be a presumption of no intention to violate *jus cogens*, that there should be a presumption of no intent to violate non-derogable rights and that any derogations would be shaped by necessity and proportionality.

Ruth Wedgwood dissented from the HRC view in *Sayadi*. For her, as for the justices of the ECtHR in *Behrami*, the complaint was inadmissible because 'it pleads no cognizable violation by the State party. The authors are complaining about the actions and decisions of the United Nations Security Council, not the acts of Belgium.'[169] Citing Charter Articles 48 (2), 25 and 103, she admonishes the HRC that it cannot use a pleading against a state as a ruse for reviewing the decisions of the SC nor can it penalize a state for complying with those decisions. Here her view recalls both the losing position taken by the US on jurisdiction and admissibility in *Lockerbie*,[170] and the dissent by Judge Schwebel in that case.[171]

In Wedgwood's view, the HRC 'cannot take a blinkered account of what is at stake here. Human rights and the enforcement decisions of the Security Council share a common concern for the lives of innocent people.'[172] While one may disagree with Wedgwood on the admissibility issue, this last point is a vital one that needs to be borne in mind by human rights advocates whenever addressing this question. In other words, just as SC resolutions should not operate to defeat human rights, a satisfactory outcome is not one in which human rights measures defeat the implementation of SC resolutions seeking to prevent terrorism. The

[168] *Sayadi* v. *Belgium* (individual opinion of Nigel Rodley).
[169] *Ibid.* (dissenting opinion of Ruth Wedgwood).
[170] *Questions of Interpretation and Application of the 1971 Montreal Convention Arising from the Aerial Incident at Lockerbie*, paras. 36–40.
[171] *Lockerbie* (dissenting opinion of President Schwebel).
[172] *Sayadi* v. *Belgium* (dissenting opinion of Ruth Wedgwood), para. 30.

successful approach entails effectively reconciling the two sets of obligations.

2.3.5 *Al-Jedda* – 2011 (ECtHR)

On 7 July 2011, the ECtHR issued a long-awaited decision in the case of *Al-Jedda* v. *United Kingdom*,[173] based on the same facts that had been considered by the UK House of Lords. In contradistinction to the House of Lords, the Court ruled here that the nearly forty-month detention of Mr Al-Jedda – a person suspected of recruiting terrorists but never charged or tried – in a facility run by UK forces in Iraq, was a violation of his human rights under the ECHR. A unanimous European Court found the detention clearly attributable to UK forces, just as the House of Lords itself had determined. However, according to sixteen out of seventeen European Court judges, the UK authorities were not absolved of responsibility by SC Resolution 1511 as the Law Lords had reasoned. The UK government was ordered to pay substantial costs and damages in the order of €65,000.

Marko Milanović has interpreted this judgment as the European Court 'effectively overrul[ing] the House of Lords on a number of points'.[174] The case has been interpreted to mean that governments' human rights duties 'cannot easily be displaced by rulings of the UN Security Council'.[175] Read closely, the opinion distinguishes the Court's own ruling in *Behrami* due to the factual situation in Iraq being rather different than in Kosovo in the Court's view, rather than explicitly overruling the earlier decision. Accepting the 'effective control test', it found that the UK and not the UN had effective control over the place where Al-Jedda was detained, hence the action could be attributed to it. The UN's role in Iraq was to provide relief and support reconstruction, not in the realm of security. Moreover, a number of UN officials actually protested the use of detention without trial.

Perhaps most significantly, the Court here ratified Nigel Rodley's approach in *Sayadi*, an innovative stance that was endorsed by the *Leiden Policy Recommendations on Counter-Terrorism and International Law* as well in 2010. To wit, 'in interpreting its resolutions,

[173] *Al-Jedda* v. *United Kingdom* [2011] ECHR 27021/08.

[174] M. Milanović, 'European Court Decides *Al-Skeini* and *Al-Jedda*', 7 July 2011, EJIL Talk!.

[175] O. Bowcott, 'Iraq Abuse ruling by European court says UK failed human rights role', *Guardian*, 7 July 2011, at www.guardian.co.U.K./world/2011/jul/07/iraq-abuse-european-court-ruling.

there must be a presumption that the Security Council does not intend to impose any obligation on member states to breach fundamental principles of human rights. In the event of any ambiguity in the terms of a Security Council Resolution, the Court must therefore choose the interpretation which is most in harmony with the requirements of the Convention and which avoids any conflict of obligations.'[176]

Human rights lawyers across Europe celebrated while reading these passages. They recognized that 'the presumption can prove to be an absolutely key tool for human rights compliance in the future with respect to UNSC decisions'.[177] However, on a more sober note, they also expressed concern about an implication of the Court's reasoning, i.e. that the SC could enable or require states to violate their human rights obligations if it expressly chose to do so. As the Court phrased this, 'it is to be expected that clear and explicit language would be used if the Security Council intended States to take particular measures that would conflict with their obligations under international human rights law.'[178] Amnesty International retorted that, 'no Security Council resolution purporting to authorize, let alone oblige, states to act in contravention of fundamental principles of human rights could ever in that respect be valid under international law.'[179] The final outcome of that debate remains outstanding. Moreover, the question of the impact of Article 103 UN Charter may be revisited by the ECtHR. It avoided that aspect of the issue here because it found that the SC resolutions did not *oblige* the state conduct in question, hence there was no legal conflict at play.[180]

2.4 Overview

What seems clear, if anything, taking all of these cases together is that international adjudicative bodies have sometimes been more comfortable holding states responsible for action that is perceived to take place within their own territory (*Sayadi*, *Kadi*) than for extraterritorial conduct (*Behrami*). Moreover, they have sometimes been more comfortable addressing the human rights impact of listing and asset freezes (*Kadi*,

[176] *Al-Jedda*, ECtHR, para. 102. [177] Milanović, 'European Court Decides', 5.

[178] *Al-Jedda*, ECtHR, para. 102.

[179] Amnesty International, 'European Court Criticizes UK for Violating Human Rights in Iraq', 8 July 2011, AI Index: EUR 45/009/2011.

[180] *Al-Jedda*, ECtHR, para. 109.

Sayadi), than that related to action in and around a field of armed conflict (*Behrami*). Some national courts (*Al-Jedda* – House of Lords, *Nada*, Srebrenica – District Court) seem to be searching for ways to absolve states for action in these areas, or simply to be able to refrain from engaging with this complex interface of national human rights obligations with transnationally mandated action. Though not always a prerequisite, one of the most convenient strategies for doing the latter is to shift responsibility to another actor, often an international organization. This process risks transforming the complex relationship between the laws on state responsibility and those on the responsibility of international organizations, into a recipe for impunity. Four years after *Behrami*, the ECtHR now appears to be pushing back, seeking to avoid that result where possible (*Al-Jedda* – ECtHR). In addition, some domestic courts also now appear uncomfortable with this outcome, even as it concerns actions in a field of conflict (Srebrenica – Appeals Court).

The pendulum has clearly begun to swing towards greater accountability, beginning with the ECJ's bold move in *Kadi* in 2008 which signalled that deference was not the only appropriate judicial posture. Nevertheless, we still do not have a definitive answer to the question of what should occur when SC resolutions may be read to *oblige* states to act in specific ways that contravene their human rights commitments. Some governments still see Article 103 as a trump card, while human rights groups reject this entirely. Clearer resolution may come through cases pending in the ECtHR in the aftermath of *Al-Jedda*, such as the follow-up to the Swiss *Nada* case, where the *Al-Jedda*–Rodley presumption may not cure the problem.[181] At present this remains a largely European-focused jurisprudence whose global impact is not yet certain.

2.5 The law of responsibility: states and international organizations

As noted, the topic at hand clearly implicates both the law of state responsibility and the law on the responsibility of international organizations. Given that both of those bodies of law represent broader topics

[181] *Nada* v. *Switzerland*, ECtHR, Application No. 10593/08. The Grand Chamber held its hearing in the case on 23 March 2011. See discussion in Marko Milanović, 'More on *Nada* v. *Switzerland*', EJIL: Talk!, 23 December 2010, at www.ejiltalk.org/more-on-nada-v-switzerland.

beyond the scope of this paper, they will only be addressed briefly and in relevant part here.[182] Though not yet crystallized in treaty form, the law of state responsibility is currently further evolved than that on the responsibility of international organizations, which is even more controversial.[183] However, state responsibility law is a state-centric body of law in which the central paradigm is one state injuring another and then making reparation to that injured state. Hence, it is not entirely apposite to the matters discussed here since the relevant actors may also include international organizations and the injury may even be to an individual who is a national of the breaching state.

What is most often at stake in the cases summarized in the section above is whether or not a state can be held *responsible* for violations of human rights and IHL it claims were required or authorized by SC action and thus were attributable to the United Nations or some other international organization. *Behrami* uses attribution to the UN as a way to avoid the responsibility of the states implicated and to vitiate jurisdiction. The House of Lords' decision in *Al-Jedda* attributes the action in question to the UK, yet absolves the UK government for its actions due to the presumed SC authorization. In *Kadi* and *Sayadi*, the relevant adjudicators clearly distinguish between the decisions of the SC and the responsibility for national action to implement those resolutions. Therefore, the ECJ and the HRC find it entirely acceptable in those cases to judge whether or not the state has complied with its own international obligations in the process.

Ordinarily, a state incurs international responsibility for its breaches of international obligations. The state is then responsible for the consequences of that breach.[184] The two principal questions that arise here

[182] For further discussion of each set of issues, see, e.g., D. Bodansky and J. R. Crook, 'Symposium: The ILC's State Responsibility Articles' (2002) 96 *American Journal of International Law* 773; J. Alvarez, 'International Organizations: Accountability or Responsibility' (27 October 2006), address to the Canadian Council of International Law, at www.asil.org/aboutasil/documents/CCILspeech061102.pdf; Gregory Fox, 'Responsibility of International Organizations: The Problem of Attribution', *Opinio Juris*, 16 November 2009, at http://opiniojuris.org/2009/11/16/responsibility-of-international-organizations-the-problem-of-attribution; J. Crawford, A. Pellet, S. N. Olleson (eds.), *The Law of International Responsibility* (Oxford: Oxford University Press, 2010).

[183] The ILC adopted the articles in 2011. See *Responsibility of International Organizations* (UN Doc. A/CN.4/L.778, 30 May 2011).

[184] *Corfu Channel* (*United Kingdom of Great Britain and Northern Ireland* v. *Albania*), Judgment on the Merits of 9 April 1949 [1949] ICJ 4, 23; *Factory at Chorzów* (*Germany* v. *Poland*), Judgment on the Merits of 26 July 1927 [1927] PCIJ (Ser. A) No. 9.

for our purposes are (1) whether or not the conduct can be attributed to the state and, if so, (2) whether or not SC resolutions give rise to a circumstance precluding wrongfulness. States face a double-edged sword of responsibility at the intersection of their responsibilities for peace and security and for the protection of persons. In the *Sayadi* approach, they may be held responsible for the human rights results of complying with SC resolutions. On the other hand, states may also incur international legal responsibility for failing to implement SC resolutions on terrorism, if harm results from such an omission.[185] Perhaps this is why the ECtHR and the House of Lords tried to resolve this dilemma by using Article 103 in *Behrami* and *Al-Jedda*, respectively, an approach the ECtHR subsequently declined to apply in its *Al-Jedda* ruling.

As to the question of attribution, usually, 'the conduct of any State organ shall be considered an act of that State under international law'.[186] In the *Nicaragua* case, the ICJ used an effective control test to decide whether or not to attribute conduct to a state.[187] The ICTY rejected the *Nicaragua* test for actors in organized military or paramilitary groups, using instead an 'overall control' approach that entailed a 'lower degree of control'.[188] However, the ICJ declined to follow this approach in *Bosnia* v. *Serbia*.[189] Needless to say, this dissonant jurisprudence has resulted in some confusion about the exact international law standard, and that has hampered a clear resolution of the problems discussed here.[190]

Critics have suggested that part of the problem with *Behrami* was that the ECtHR employed a distorted view of the effective control test when attributing action to the UN, rather than to sending states.[191] Experts

[185] See V. Gowlland-Debbas, 'Security Council Enforcement Action and Issues of State Responsibility' (1994) 43 *International & Comparative Law Quarterly* 90.

[186] Articles on Responsibility of States for Internationally Wrongful Acts, in Report of International Law Commission, 53rd Session (UN Doc. A/56/10, 59 (2001), Art. 4).

[187] *Nicaragua*, para. 109. [188] *Tadić*, paras. 115, 124.

[189] *Application of the Convention on the Prevention and Punishment of the Crime of Genocide*, paras. 385–407.

[190] For a recent attempt to clarify the relevant standards with regard to peacekeepers, see T. Dannenbaum, 'Translating the Standard of Effective Control into a System of Effective Accountability: How Liability Should be Apportioned for Violations of Human Rights by Member State Troop Contingents Serving as United Nations Peacekeepers' (2010) 51 *Harvard International Law Journal* 113.

[191] See ILC Commentary in UN Doc. No. A/64/10, 62–70; and M. Milanović & T. Papić, 'As Bad as It Gets: The European Court of Human Rights' *Behrami* and *Saramati* Decision and General International Law' (2009) 58 *International & Comparative Law Quarterly* 282.

read the ILC Commentary on the Draft Articles on Responsibility of International Organizations as a rejection of this aspect of *Behrami*.[192]

Even if states are found to be the authors of the conduct in question, they may also be seen to be excused from responsibility for harms that result from their good faith implementation of SC resolutions (the House of Lords' *Al-Jedda* approach). Vera Gowlland-Debbas reminds us that Article 103 of the UN Charter serves not only to elaborate the 'principle of the predominance of Charter obligations' but also as a ground for precluding wrongfulness within the framework of the International Law Commission's Draft Articles on State Responsibility.[193] Certainly, not all international lawyers would agree with that result in all circumstances, as the *Kadi* and *Sayadi* cases make clear. Gowlland-Debbas herself worries that the powerful states that dominate the SC may simply use the 'corporate veil' of the SC to enable themselves to 'escape conditions placed on unilateral countermeasures by current (as well as evolving) general international law'.[194]

As to the direct responsibility of international organizations, while the SC possesses a remit to act to advance human rights, it is not understood by some international lawyers to be directly bound by international human rights law in the classical sense. As Fox notes, '[t]he Security Council is an odd duck in the international order. It is charged with upholding the core rights of states and individuals reflected in the Charter, but it does not clearly owe reciprocal obligations under those same norms.'[195] In fact, some experts have expressed concern about holding international organizations, rather than state members, accountable. However, other experts on international organizations have called for the development of mechanisms and norms to directly circumscribe the actions of international organizations.[196] While many articulate a need to hold international organizations responsible, some international lawyers have expressed scepticism about whether or not the ILC Draft Articles on Responsibility of International Organizations, adopted in 2011, will be helpful in achieving that goal.[197] Yet, other

[192] Fox, 'Responsibility of International Organizations'. See also ILC Commentary in UN Doc. No. A/64/10, 62–70.

[193] Gowlland-Debbas, 'Security Council Enforcement Action', 90. [194] *Ibid.*, 91.

[195] Fox, 'Responsibility of International Organizations', 303.

[196] A. Reinisch, 'Securing the Accountability of International Organizations' (2001) 7 *Global Governance* 143.

[197] See Alvarez, 'International Organizations'.

experts like Kristen Boon see that these draft articles could be a significant step in addressing what they see as 'the accountability deficit'.[198]

According to Article 7, 'The conduct of an organ of a State . . . that is placed at the disposal of an . . . international organization shall be considered under international law an act of the . . . organization if the organization exercises effective control over that conduct.'[199] This is adapted from Article 6 of the Articles on State Responsibility. Questions have been raised as to whether or not this article is adequate to deal with the specific situation of peacekeeping. The precursor to this article was cited by the ECtHR in *Behrami*.[200] However, Milanović and Papić argue that the Court misinterpreted the ILC's test. In their view, reading the ILC's discussion of the article, what matters is 'effective control of the conduct in question. In other words, who is giving the orders – the State or the organization'.[201] Moreover, they argue that the Court conflated the questions of attribution and responsibility.[202]

Some international lawyers posit that these problems could be solved by a sort of dual attribution, that is to say in a peacekeeping operation, both the state and the international organization could be held responsible for wrongful acts.[203] This avoids what was called the *Behrami* fallacy, the idea that just because something is attributable to an international organization it is not also attributable to a state. The wider the accountability[204] net is cast, the more likely a remedy will be available.

Given the positions taken by many governments and by some national courts in the cases summarized above, dual attribution might be a hard sell but it could solve problems of the *Behrami* ilk. Moreover, the ECtHR left open the possibility of such an approach when it noted in its version

198 See K. Boon, 'Responsibility of international organizations II: where is the internationally wrongful act?', 11 November 2009, posted on *Opinio Juris*, at http://opiniojuris.org/author/kristen-boon/.

199 See UN Doc. No. A/64/10, 62 (Art. 7). 200 *Behrami*, para. 30.

201 Milanović and Papić, 'As Bad as It Gets', 282. 202 *Ibid*., 285.

203 Indeed, Alain Pellet suggested in 2002 that there was no universal answer to the question of responsibility in cases of multinational action, and that such analysis must be done on a case-by-case basis, in light of the particular circumstances ('L'imputablilité d'éventuels actes illicites: Responsabilité de l'OTAN ou des États membres', in C. Tomuschat (ed.), *Kosovo and the International Community: A Legal Assessment* (The Hague: Kluwer Law International, 2002), 201). This remains a valid methodological concern.

204 '"Accountability" does not have a settled meaning in international law. It is understood as a broader concept than the narrower, more legalistic notion of "responsibility"' (J. Brunnée, 'International Legal Accountability through the Lens of the Law of State Responsibility' (2005) 36 *Netherlands Year Book of International Law* 3–7).

of *Al-Jedda* that it did 'not consider that, as a result of the authorization contained in Resolution 1511, the acts of soldiers within the Multi-National Force became attributable to the United Nations – or more importantly, for the purposes of this case – ceased to be attributable to the troop-contributing nations'.[205] This 'essentially admit[s] the possibility of dual or multiple attribution of the same conduct to the UN and to a state, a possibility that the Court did not entertain in Behrami'.[206] Generally speaking, greater clarity on the responsibility of international organizations under international law, and its interface with the law of state responsibility, will be crucial to resolving difficulties in this area.

3 Practical challenges and outstanding issues

The post-9/11 decade has brought the need for reconciling state obligations for peace and security with their obligations for human rights into stark relief. Time and again we have seen the disastrous consequences when states do not fulfil their obligations to prevent terrorism or conversely when they do so but without regard to legal norms.

Placing responsibility for conduct by states implementing UN resolutions on the United Nations can perpetuate a significant accountability gap. The United Nations benefits from immunity under the Convention on the Privileges and Immunities of the UN. As Tomuschat notes:

> There ought to be a high threshold for excluding the jurisdiction of states, which are more likely to have a comprehensive human rights system than international organizations; sufferers of human rights abuses should not be denied a remedy merely because of the number of actors bearing potential responsibility for a particular situation ... If accountability can be shifted from the state of nationality of the wrongdoer to an international organization too readily, many victims will be denied reparation simply because of the lack of appropriate remedies available.[207]

Kristen Boon's analysis suggests that even the Draft Articles on the Responsibility of International Organizations will not cure this problem any time soon in the absence of an available forum, and in light of the immunities involved.[208]

[205] *Al-Jedda*, ECtHR, para. 80. [206] Milanović, 'European Court Decides'.

[207] Tomuschat, 'Case Note', 396.

[208] K. Boon, 'New Directions in Responsibility: Assessing the International Law Commission's Draft Articles on the Responsibility of International Organizations' (2011) 37 *Yale Journal of International Law Online* 1.

Human rights NGOs often recommend internationalized responses to grave human rights abuses.[209] Such international responses may be desperately needed to mitigate human rights tragedies. However, the paradox becomes that under a *Behrami* approach, such responses may then also become a recipe for impunity. Indeed, one of the arguments made by the ECJ in *Kadi* to justify its willingness to afford a remedy was precisely that the UN system did not offer sufficient judicial protection.[210] Given that the UN Charter does not provide for judicial review of the actions of the SC by the ICJ,[211] we are left with a predicament in which the central institution of global order may otherwise be seen to operate almost entirely outside the law. This is not good for international law or for the SC's own legitimacy. Indeed, if we take the success of counter-terrorism seriously, the SC should see that it has an interest in the perceived justice of its counter-terrorism resolutions.

There are tricky methodological pitfalls here. National and supranational courts and adjudicative bodies should be encouraged to hear cases involving the interplay of state obligations for peace and security with obligations for the protection of persons, following the reasoning of the *Kadi* case. However, this should not eclipse the importance of collective action for peace and security. One needs to be careful of pushing too far the argument that implementation of UN Charter rules should be limited by regional or national rules, as the primacy of such rules over international law is a double-edged sword in the arena of human rights implementation. However, the *Kadi* jurisprudence was critical in light of the reaction it provoked in the SC. The call and response between adjudicative bodies and the SC can help to fill the lacunae in the responsibility of international organizations discussed above.[212] This

[209] See, e.g., 'Human Rights Watch, DR Congo: Increase Peacekeepers in Eastern Congo', 11 November 2008, at www.hrw.org/news/2008/11/11/dr-congo-increase-peacekeepers-eastern-congo.

[210] *Kadi and Al Barakaat International Foundation*, paras. 321–3.

[211] J. Alvarez, 'Judging the Security Council' (1996) 90 *American Journal of International Law* 14–21.

[212] See discussion in L. van den Herik and N. Schrijver, 'Delisting Challenges in the Context of UN Targeted Sanctions Regimes: A Legal Perspective', in T. Biersteker and S. Eckert (eds.), *Addressing Challenges to Targeted Sanctions: An Update of the 'Watson Report'*, 45, at www.watsoninstitute.org/pub/2009_10_targeted_sanctions.pdf (accessed 23 May 2012); M. Milanović, 'The Human Rights Committee's Views in *Sayadi* v. *Belgium*', 537. Milanović argues that decisions such as *Kadi* and *Sayadi*, 'have exerted significant pressure on the Security Council ... and its member states ... to show more respect for ... due process' (*ibid.*, 537). For example, the Committee's view

process may be carried forward further still by the ECtHR ruling in *Al-Jedda* which will make states even more aware of the potential costs of their actions.

Still, we must also consider whether or not Fassbender's assertion made at the end of the twentieth century remains correct, that 'the world clearly requires an exercise of more, not less authority on a global level . . . and international lawyers . . . should encourage this development rather than warn against it'.[213] As Susan Lamb notes, historically the concern has been that the SC is too weak, not that it is too strong.[214] Hence, it is important that the growing and laudable move towards accountability of states when participating in international enforcement efforts or acting pursuant to UN resolutions be carefully considered so as not to undermine states' willingness or ability to implement those resolutions. Though it should not be bought at the price of impunity and gross abuses, such implementation may be vital to effective counter-terrorism or other enforcement action and thus can itself have a massive impact on human rights. As Tim Daniel reminds us in this volume, the motivation behind SC Resolution 1373 was to combat 'inertia' around the issue of terrorist financing.[215] A return to such inertia is not a desirable outcome either. This factor must be carefully considered even while correctly working against impunity. The real challenge is to actualize counter-terrorism enforcement that is both rights respecting and effective.

In light of this need, the SC should be encouraged to think proactively about the rights implications of its own resolutions so as not to put member states in lose-lose situations, like that of Belgium in *Sayadi*. As Rodley excoriated the Council in that case:

> it is not easy to see why nearly a decade after the first resolution 1267 (1999) and seven years after 9/11 the Council could not have evolved procedures more consistent with the human rights values of transparency, accountability and impartial independent assessment of facts. It may be hoped that it will not too much longer delay adjusting the procedures in line with these values. This would avoid putting States . . . when determining the . . . action to be taken, in the unenviable position of having to engage in difficult exercises in interpretation of or even challenges to the validity of provisions of Security Council resolutions.[216]

in *Sayadi* led directly to the applicants' de-listing by the SC Sanctions Committee in July 2009.

213 Fassbender, '*Quis judicabit?*', 220. 214 Lamb, 'Legal Limits', 361.

215 See Chapter 8 in this volume.

216 *Sayadi* v. *Belgium* (individual opinion of Nigel Rodley, 37).

One possible remedy could be a measure endorsed by the *Leiden Policy Recommendations*, namely that draft counter-terrorism resolutions be the object of human rights impact assessments.

Meanwhile, human rights lawyers cannot afford to take a naïve stance towards terrorism or the necessity of law-abiding counter-terrorism measures.[217] This sometimes manifests, for example, as an impulse to defend virtually any charity accused of involvement in terrorist financing. Of course, most charity groups are entirely legitimate. However, some terrorist groups have systematically used charities as a cover for fundraising activities, a difficult reality that also has to be tackled, however inconvenient.[218] Ruth Wedgwood was quite right to remind human rights lawyers in *Sayadi* that '[t]he sanctions of the Security Council were undertaken to protect the foremost human right, namely, the right to life'.[219] Governments and human rights advocates alike have much at stake here.

As this chapter has demonstrated, we are in a transitional moment with regard to the nexus of questions concerning the interplay of legal regimes governing international peace and security and the protection of persons. Many outstanding issues remain. Bhuta has argued that in this period 'the role of scholars and scholarly debate will be very significant'.[220] This role can only be fulfilled if international lawyers of differing specialties – security, counter-terrorism, international finance, international organizations, responsibility, human rights, IHL – work together to fashion a truly integrated approach.

217 For further discussion of this issue, see K. Bennoune, 'Remembering the Other's Others: Theorizing the Approach of International Law to Muslim Fundamentalism' (2010) 41 *Columbia Human Rights Law Review* 635.

218 See M. Nawaz, 'Charity or extremist group?', *Guardian*, 31 March 2009, at www.guardian.co.U.K./commentisfree/belief/2009/mar/30/religion-islam-green-crescent-bangladesh; Center for Defense Information, 'Combating Terrorist Financing: A Key Aspect of the War on Terrorism'.

219 *Sayadi* v. *Belgium* (dissenting opinion of Ruth Wedgwood, 30).

220 Posting of Bhuta, 1 April 2009.

ANNEX

LEIDEN POLICY RECOMMENDATIONS ON COUNTER-TERRORISM AND INTERNATIONAL LAW

1 INTRODUCTION

1. This set of policy recommendations emanates from a consultative process which was concluded on 1 April 2010. Its basic aims are to address the challenges that combating international terrorism poses to international law and to contribute to the international debate on selected contemporary issues in the struggle against international terrorism. It involved approximately thirty experts from a variety of professional and geographical backgrounds, taking part in their personal capacity.
2. The process started with the Oud-Poelgeest conference, which was convened on 10 to 13 April 2007 by the Grotius Centre for International Legal Studies of Leiden University and Campus The Hague. This conference of eminent persons at the Oud-Poelgeest estate, close to the city of Leiden, was organized with the full support of the Netherlands Ministry of Foreign Affairs. The 2007 conference resulted in a report addressing a variety of challenges to current international law resulting from the struggle against terrorism and providing suggestions for a follow-up process.[1] The report addressed the need to agree on a definition of terrorism; the use of force in self-defence against terrorist acts; the interrelationship between human rights law and international humanitarian law; the need for closer cooperation between states in criminal matters; the issue of law enforcement in fragile states; and the need for a preventive and integrated approach.
3. A follow-up project was launched in 2008 with a three-fold focus. First, it examined questions relating to law enforcement and criminal justice outside the context of armed conflict and the need to improve international cooperation in the investigation and prosecution of terrorist acts. Secondly, it studied operations that include the transboundary use of

[1] The final report of the Poelgeest Seminar was submitted to Parliament by Minister of Foreign Affairs Verhagen by letter of 25 June 2007, parliamentary document 27 925 No. 255; the report was also published in the *Netherlands International Law Review* 54(3) (2007), 571–87. The current set of the *Leiden Policy Recommendations* has also been published in the *Netherlands International Law Review* 57(3) (2010), 531–51.

force, and in particular the use of force in self-defence against non-state actors. Once armed force is used, the question regarding the applicability of international humanitarian law arises including its relationship to human rights law. The third object of study concerned the specific relationship between international humanitarian law and human rights law. Three working groups were established, with two co-chairs each. The co-chairs were respectively Anton du Plessis and Michael Newton (working group 1), Andrea Bianchi and Sir Michael Wood (working group 2), and Helen Duffy and Jelena Pejic (working group 3). The project was coordinated by Nico Schrijver and Larissa van den Herik of the Grotius Centre of Leiden University.

4. On 1 April 2010, the combined recommendations resulting from the three working groups were offered to the Netherlands Minister of Foreign Affairs, Maxime Verhagen. As stated above, this set of interrelated and policy-relevant recommendations is the product of a group process. The recommendations are not attributable to any particular expert. They do not necessarily reflect the individual views of all experts. The individual experts concentrated their efforts on the work of their own respective groups and endorsed the specific recommendations of their own group only. The background papers, to be published in an edited volume, contain further pertinent recommendations of the individual authors of the respective working groups.
5. These recommendations aim to contribute to the debate on the role of international law in countering terrorism. They provide expert perspectives on areas in which greater consensus needs to be pursued.

PART I

IMPROVING INTERNATIONAL COOPERATION IN THE INVESTIGATION & PROSECUTION OF TERRORIST ACTS

Aim and scope of the Policy Recommendations

6. Improving inter-state cooperation in the investigation and prosecution of terrorist acts is vital for a well functioning universal criminal justice approach towards terrorism. States must work towards comprehensive implementation of the relevant international and regional counter-terrorism legal instruments and compliance with relevant UN Security Council resolutions. Terrorist cases involve complex intersections of human rights principles, executive discretion, national security interests, and the larger imperatives of human security. Justice is a moral imperative in its own right, but is also an essential obligation for governments that

seek to preserve human dignity and strengthen the social contract with their citizenry.

7. Contemporary terrorist acts often implicate the citizens of one state, but may involve the complicity of nationals of other nations, or assistance in the form of funding and training originating from outside sovereign boundaries. The need for enhanced international criminal justice cooperation in terrorist cases is therefore a vital component of any effective and sustainable global response to terrorism. The discussions largely avoided reference to the body of norms regulating the conduct of hostilities or consideration of the possible enforcement of the *jus in bello* using forums or principles derived from international humanitarian law. In light of international obligations, however, the improvement of regional and bilateral mechanisms that facilitate domestic criminal and civil justice enforcement efforts is the *sine qua non* of progress towards an integrated system that promotes fair and human rights-compliant criminal justice responses to terrorism. These recommendations are aimed at developing workable and pragmatic approaches and suggestions.

Sufficiency of the existing framework

8. Despite the challenges in reaching a comprehensive multilateral definition of terrorism, the existing framework of multilateral instruments provides sufficient legal basis for domestic prosecution of terrorist crimes (defined in the 16 UN instruments and relevant regional counter-terrorism instruments) and international cooperation. The importance of domestic prosecutions and international cooperation is highlighted by the fact that there currently exists no international forum for prosecuting acts of terrorism[2] and it is unlikely, and undesirable, that the Rome Statute of the International Criminal Court will be amended to include terrorism as a specifically articulated crime. Domestic states should cooperate to eradicate terrorism to the fullest extent possible based on the unequivocal condemnation of all acts, methods, and practices of terrorism as criminal and unjustifiable committed wherever and by whoever.

Strengthen the domestic capacity for investigation and prosecution of terrorist cases

9. Effective international cooperation requires respect for human rights. Criminal justice response to terrorism (which includes the investigation, prosecution, and adjudication of terrorist crimes) forms the cornerstone of any sustainable

[2] The Working Group recognizes the limited mandate of the Lebanon Tribunal that may include prosecution of terrorist acts.

counter-terrorism effort that respects the principles of the rule of law, human rights, and due process. The recent record demonstrates that the reliance on extrajudicial methods has undermined respect for and protection of human rights. In particular, the extrajudicial transfer of terrorist suspects (known as extraordinary rendition) has become emblematic of this problem. The disregard for fundamental human rights norms also has the demonstrable effect of undermining international cooperation in the struggle against suspected terrorists, as well as eroding the available channels for assisting investigations and prosecutions related to transnational terrorist acts, particularly those that cross regional boundaries. The absence of an effective and efficient regime for international cooperation can result in frustration among law enforcement and security officials that in turn leads to human rights violations. This is particularly important when dealing with fragile states.

10. For the purposes of international cooperation, there is no compelling need for renewed diplomatic efforts to be expended on developing new multilateral instruments. There is an existing network of bilateral and multilateral treaties as well as domestic law that is sufficient for criminalization and effective and efficient international cooperation, especially in counter-terrorism.
11. The central challenge, however, is the lack of adoption, ratification, accession, and most significantly, implementation of the existing instruments and mechanisms. There are striking gaps across regions in state practice in this regard, and there is a need for increased domestic criminal justice capability as part of an overarching and integrated development agenda in order to achieve the goals of the respective multilateral instruments.
12. In addition, widespread, consistent, and appropriately defined domestic criminalization of terrorist acts will facilitate effective international cooperation. This would enhance the ability of states to comply with their obligations to 'prosecute or extradite' as mandated by the international and regional counter-terrorism regimes. There is a pressing need for more states to embed prohibitions on terrorist acts within their domestic legislation along with comprehensive cooperative regimes. Extensive reliance on special anti-terrorism legislation that creates extended administrative detention regimes should be avoided.

Reinforced domestic systems depend on improved and appropriate international cooperation

13. Despite discernible islands of cooperation, the overall cooperative regime is being implemented in an uneven manner. There is a need across all regions for legislation which adopts a more flexible approach to international cooperation in criminal matters. On the operational level, a strengthened and

knowledgeable central authority is essential to improving international cooperation. At present, the proliferation of multiple central authorities with overlapping mandates hinders effective international and inter-agency cooperation. In addition, the poor quality and clarity of many requests for international assistance is a critical barrier to effective cooperation. In this regard, there are available tools that are, at present, underutilized. One specific example is the UNODC Mutual Legal Assistance Request writer tool.

14. The default approach by which many domestic bureaucracies and regulations commingle the extradition regime with that applicable to information sharing and evidence gathering must be re-evaluated and redesigned. The principles and restrictions that govern extradition practice have been inappropriately (and unnecessarily) fused into the practice of mutual legal assistance, with the predictable effect of hindering investigations and the free flow of information. This is a radical but much needed shift because of the deeply ingrained habits of approaching extradition and evidence gathering as nearly identical processes with the same procedural requirements and the same need for protections. The practice must be reframed to approach evidence gathering as a distinct process which should move much more rapidly and be effectively synthesized into ongoing investigations.
15. One key approach to improving international cooperation is to dramatically expand the establishment of national joint investigation teams which has the collateral benefit of eliminating the barriers to information sharing that are commonly encountered when information has been derived through intelligence channels and classified as such by domestic authorities. Such joint investigative teams should be interdisciplinary and operated on the basis of agreed upon procedures and practices. An additional benefit of this approach is to integrate prosecutorial expertise in a more visible and vibrant role at an earlier stage.

Sharing sensitive information

16. The transnational character of modern terrorism means that intelligence and law enforcement agencies must increasingly share information with their foreign counterparts. This cooperation often involves working with states that have few domestic human rights safeguards, or, worse still, with foreign intelligence agencies that have long histories of involvement in systematic human rights violations. States should ensure that national intelligence services have clear guidance and appropriate oversight mechanisms that do not hinder the free flow of timely intelligence among nations. Information should be declassified and disseminated as rapidly as possible when needed to disrupt terrorist operations.

17. In addition, the roles and responsibilities of intelligence officials and law enforcement authorities should be clearly defined. There are processes that can and should be replicated across domestic jurisdictions that provide workable methods for protecting sources and methods, while still complying with the human rights of defendants facing trial for specific acts.

The importance of regional organizations

18. Regional organizations play an important role in promoting cooperation and information sharing in counter-terrorism matters. They also facilitate capacity building to states in various areas of counter-terrorism, including intelligence gathering, financial cooperation, and mutual legal assistance. Informal mechanisms often provide the impetus and opportunity for improved cooperation. Regional organizations are an irreplaceable venue for establishing and enforcing the legal and procedural frameworks for counter-terrorism cooperation. Regional mechanisms supplement but do not replace the framework of cooperation from international multilateral instruments and UN channels.
19. Terrorist organizations have become adept at exploiting regional animosities and finding the rifts in bilateral relations to conduct operations. Regional organizations can play the decisive role in building trust between national actors that leads to more effective and timely cooperation that can produce notable improvements in the common effort to prevent and/or punish terrorist acts.
20. Successful practices of regional organizations, such as the European Arrest Warrant and EUROJUST, should inform practices in other regions. One key lesson from EUROJUST and the European Arrest Warrant is that mutual trust is the cornerstone of more efficient and streamlined cooperation procedures. In particular, building mutual trust contributes to more effective international cooperation such as the elimination of barriers created by dual criminality, transnational recognition of search warrants, and wider recognition of asset freezing and confiscation orders.

Increased use of multidisciplinary fusion centres

21. Multidisciplinary fusion centres are a critical tool to facilitate the earlier involvement of prosecutorial expertise in terrorism investigations. Integration of experts from a number of nations and professional disciplines would also provide an integrated forum for enhancing international cooperation in relation to fragile states. States should re-examine their national laws in this regard to ensure that progress can be made in assisting transregional investigations. Multidisciplinary fusion centres

can also provide available staff and integrated operational framework for rapid movement into areas affected by terrorist acts following a request by the sovereign government.

International cooperation in countering the financing of terrorism

22. Stemming the flow of terrorist finances is a crucial component of the fight against terrorism. Following the flow of terrorist finances may lead to invaluable information that can assist investigators in uncovering terrorist activities. The financing of terrorism was an early target of the international effort to combat terrorism. Security Council resolutions 1267 and 1373 were designed to promote international cooperation in the pursuit and freezing of assets believed to be connected with terrorists or terrorist organizations. Legislation to implement those resolutions has been the subject of numerous challenges, especially in relation to the due process concerns associated with the 1267 regime. On the other hand, the Convention on the Suppression of the Financing of Terrorism does provide another important tool in the fight against terrorist financing. It requires States Parties to implement specific measures, including innovative asset freezing and confiscation regimes.
23. Global implementation of this regime is inconsistent. For example, many EU states have not implemented some of the basic measures to give effect to these obligations. For example, an EU – US Agreement on mutual legal assistance which includes important provisions on access to bank accounts is not in force. At the regional level, a number of states have not signed and ratified the 2005 Warsaw Convention on Money Laundering and Terrorist Financing. Under the Warsaw Convention, States Parties are required to 'co-operate to the widest extent possible under their domestic law with those Parties which request the execution of measures equivalent to confiscation leading to the deprivation of property, which are not criminal sanctions, in so far as such measures are ordered by a judicial authority of the requesting Party in relation to a criminal offence'.
24. There should be a greater emphasis on non-conviction based forfeiture of assets. This does not imply agreement with the expanded use of the Security Council Resolution 1267 regime. On the contrary, in keeping with the earlier focus on the protection of fundamental human rights, a revitalized regime for freezing and/or confiscation of the proceeds or instrumentalities of terrorist crimes should be based on direct enforcement with judicial oversight and safeguards designed to prevent misuse of the regime for politicized purposes.
25. Unlike criminal forfeiture, which requires a criminal trial and conviction, civil forfeiture is an action *in rem* against the asset itself, not the

individual. The World Bank, under its Stolen Asset Recovery (StAR) initiative, produced a 'Good Practices Guide' for non-conviction based asset forfeiture which encourages those states which do not already provide for such forfeiture to introduce the necessary measures. In addition, widespread ratification of the Warsaw Convention noted above could create more opportunities to enforce civil confiscation orders in other countries.

26. EU states should seek a new agreement with the United States on the processing and transfer of financial messaging data. The interdiction of funding streams is a vital tool in protecting society and preserving human rights. Tracking the flow of terrorist financing is also an essential component of many successful prosecutions and hence must be a high priority for the future of transnational cooperative efforts.

Specific policy recommendations

- Effective and sustainable transnational cooperation to prevent or counter terrorist acts should respect human rights and due process standards.
- There is no compelling need for new multilateral international cooperation treaties. There is, however, an urgent need for increased ratification and implementation of existing agreements.
- More states should criminalize the terrorist acts defined by the relevant multilateral and regional treaties in order to eliminate existing barriers to their obligation to prosecute or extradite terrorist suspects.
- Proliferation of national Central Authorities with overlapping mandates and unclear authority should be avoided.
- As distinct from the policy and practice applicable to extradition, the practice of mutual legal assistance must be reframed to ensure timely and flexible international cooperation.
- National intelligence agencies should have clear guidance and oversight mechanisms that appropriately complement the roles and responsibilities of law enforcement authorities.
- Regional organizations have an irreplaceable role supporting the development of policy and practice on international cooperation, and should be used when possible to build capacity in domestic judicial and investigative systems.
- Multidisciplinary fusion centres should be used where possible as an integrated forum to enhance international cooperation and provide specialized prosecutorial expertise at an early point in investigations.
- States should increase their ability to interdict the flow of terrorist financing, and in particular should expand the processes available for non-conviction based forfeitures of assets under judicial oversight.

PART II

THE USE OF FORCE AGAINST TERRORISTS

27. As stated in the conclusions of Part I, terrorism should be primarily dealt with at the level of national criminal justice systems. Force should be used only as a last resort.

Aim and scope of the Policy Recommendations

28. There is no need for new rules of general international law to deal with the use of force in relation to international terrorism. The framework laid down in the UN Charter is the cornerstone of the international legal regime on the use of force and states are deeply committed to it. However, the Charter is not a static instrument and needs to be interpreted in the light of contemporary practice and taking states' expectations into account. States are encouraged to express their views promptly and openly, in all available fora, on the legality (or lack thereof) of any instance in which force is used. This will contribute to establishing or consolidating international consensus over the applicable rules.
29. The aim of the following policy recommendations is twofold. On the one hand, they aim at clarifying the state of international law on the use of force against terrorists against the backdrop of recent practice. On the other, they intend to highlight areas in which greater consensus needs to be pursued at the international level. The recommendations focus on the issues most relevant to the use of force against terrorists, ranging from the role of the Security Council and the notion of armed attack, to the requirements for the exercise of self-defence and, particularly, of anticipatory self-defence. Finally due heed is paid to the specific issue of the use of force against terrorist groups operating from the territory of fragile states.

Use of force as measure of last resort

30. All efforts should be made to exhaust means other than force to prevent and repress terrorist activities. States and the Security Council should give priority, wherever possible, to law enforcement measures and recognize that the use of force is a measure of last resort, to be employed only where absolutely necessary.
31. Article 2(4) of the Charter prohibits states from using force, or threatening to do so, against the territorial integrity or political independence of any state or in any other manner inconsistent with the Purposes of the United Nations. This core provision of contemporary international law bans coercive military action by a state against another state, meaning any such action on the latter's territory, and in some circumstances action

against its assets abroad. This prohibition includes coercive military action against other states as a response to terrorist acts. The two exceptions to this prohibition are: (a) Security Council authorization for a state to use force, and (b) the use of force in self-defence in response to an armed attack, or an imminent threat thereof, in accordance with Article 51 of the Charter.

32. It should be emphasized that states considering the use of force against terrorists must take due account of the exceptional nature of military action on foreign territory. The territorial state's consent to military action is required, except where the territorial state is unable or unwilling itself to deal with the terrorist attacks.
33. In any use of military force states must comply with applicable rules of international humanitarian law and human rights law.

The role of the Security Council

34. According to the UN Charter, the Security Council has primary responsibility for the maintenance of international peace and security. States should consider enhancing the Security Council's role in respect of the use of force against terrorists, so as to develop multilateral approaches to the matter wherever possible. This is best done case-by-case, not by way of a general declaration in a resolution or Presidential statement.
35. Security Council authorization under Chapter VII is legally necessary for the deployment of force against terrorists in another state without that state's consent, except when the requirements for self-defence are met; even in the case of self-defence the Council has a role under the Charter.
36. Security Council endorsement should be seen as politically desirable, even in cases of self-defence (and need not affect the right of self-defence). Measures taken with Security Council endorsement will have stronger domestic and international support, and for that reason should be more effective than if taken without such endorsement. A state contemplating the use of force in self-defence against terrorists should therefore normally first go to the Security Council, except when there is no time, or where the Security Council is manifestly unable to act. Any action taken in self-defence has to be notified to the Security Council and appropriate justification, in light of all relevant circumstances, should be provided.
37. Regional and sub-regional organizations, such as NATO, the African Union and ECOWAS, when playing a role in respect of the use of force against terrorist groups, should not undermine the Security Council's primary responsibility under the Charter.

Armed attack

38. The recognition in Article 51 of the inherent right of individual or collective self-defence in the event of an armed attack makes no reference

to the source of the armed attack. It is now well accepted that attacks by non-state actors, even when not acting on behalf of a state, can trigger a state's right of individual and collective (upon request of the victim state) self-defence. A state that is the victim of an armed attack by terrorists may thus take action against those non-state actors operating from another state, although the scope of that response will depend upon a variety of factors and requirements discussed below.

39. Article 51 does not include a scale requirement for an armed attack, and there is disagreement on the existence and contours of such a requirement in the case of an attack by one state on another. In the case of an attack by terrorists that is not attributable to a state, Article 51 should be read to require that the attack be large-scale in order to trigger the right of self-defence; in assessing the scale, account may be taken of a series of attacks emanating from the same territory and the same terrorist group. The heightened threshold stems from the critical role of the state(s) on whose territory terrorists operate and the primary responsibility of such state(s) for the prevention and suppression of such acts. It recognizes that such a state or states would be affected by the force used in self-defence and ensures that self-defence and the consequences for that state or states that flow from a military response are not triggered too soon.

Self-defence requirements

40. A state exercising self-defence must respect the limits of necessity and proportionality. Both conditions are fully applicable to self-defence against terrorist attacks emanating from the territory of another state. Where the terrorist attacks emanate from more than one state those conditions must be assessed in relation to each state.
41. The use of force in self-defence is justified only when force is necessary to bring an attack to an end, or to avert an imminent attack (under the conditions discussed below). Force is not necessary, for example, if the terrorist acts can be dealt with by measures of law enforcement.
42. The requirement of necessity must first be assessed in the light of the actions of the state from the territory of which the terrorist acts emanate. Where a state is itself supporting or encouraging the actions of terrorists on its territory, it may well be unwilling to avert or repel the attack and action in self-defence may be necessary. Self-defence may also be necessary if the armed attack *cannot* be repelled or averted by the territorial state. States relying on self-defence therefore must show that the territorial state's action is not effective in countering the terrorist threat. Whether this is the case depends on circumstances such as the nature and gravity of the threat, including the territorial state's attitude vis-à-vis the group operating on its territory. Being an inherent right to repel or

avert attacks, self-defence does not require that armed attacks by terrorists be attributable to the territorial state under the rules of state responsibility.

43. In order to be proportionate, measures of self-defence must be limited to what is required to repel or avert the armed attack. Proportionality in this sense requires states regularly to monitor ongoing measures of self-defence and ensure that they remain defensive in character. This may entail limitations on the intensity and duration of force employed and on the theatre and target of operations. In particular, it will normally mean that measures of self-defence against suspected terrorists must be directed primarily against the terrorist groups responsible for the armed attack in question or their facilities. Only in exceptional circumstances will self-defence justify the use of force against the armed forces or facilities of the territorial state, for example, in circumstances where the territorial state is supporting suspected terrorists, as in Afghanistan in 2001.
44. Unnecessary or disproportionate use of force cannot be justified as a measure of self-defence under international law. As the application of both factors is heavily fact-dependent, states using force in self-defence should be prepared to make publicly available information and data that will support the necessity and proportionality of their conduct. International law does not prevent third states from scrutinizing the necessity and proportionality of self-defence operations or from requesting further evidence.

Anticipatory self-defence

45. States have a right of self-defence against a threatened attack, but only if the attack is imminent and if the armed action in self-defence is necessary to avert the attack and is proportionate to it. Action to avert a threatened attack is best termed anticipatory self-defence and must be distinguished from the use of so-called 'pre-emptive' or 'preventive' force before a threat has crystallized, which could only be lawful if authorized by the Security Council.
46. Whether an attack may be regarded as imminent falls to be assessed by reference to the immediacy of the attack, its nature and gravity. There must be a reasonable and objective basis for concluding that an attack will be launched, while bearing in mind that terrorists typically rely on the unpredictability of attacks in order to spread terror among civilians. Armed force may be used only when it is anticipated that delay would result in an inability by the threatened state effectively to avert the attack.

47. As indicated above, it is only exceptionally that the threatened state may take armed action in self-defence against a non-state actor in the territory of another state without first seeking the consent of that state. It will thus be only in the most compelling emergency that there will be necessity for the threatened state itself to take military action before an attack is launched.
48. Any use of force in anticipatory self-defence should be justified publicly by reference to the evidence available to the state concerned; the facts do not speak for themselves, and the state should explain, as fully as it is able to do, the nature of the threat and the necessity for anticipatory military action.

Use of force and fragile states

49. The rules on the use of force, set out above, apply equally to non-state actors launching cross-border attacks from a failed state (a state without a functioning government), or from a failing state (a state with a particularly weak government).
50. Even the complete absence of a government does not per se lead to a loss of statehood. Instead, state practice suggests that a fragile state will generally continue to exist as a state under international law over a considerable time. The territory and the population of that state will continue to be protected by the prohibition of the use of force. It follows that the use of force on the territory of a failed or failing state carried out by another state requires legal justification. In the absence of a Security Council authorization under Chapter VII of the UN Charter, the right to self-defence is the only possible legal basis for another state to respond forcibly to a non-state armed attack emanating from a failed or (absent consent) failing state.
51. A fragile state lacks an organ to express its consent to the use of force carried out by another state on the former state's territory. Conversely, the expression of such consent is conceivable in the case of a failing state. State practice suggests that even a government unable to deal with the non-state actors in its own territory can express an internationally valid consent, unless such government lacks international recognition. A failing state unable to avert or halt a non-state armed attack ought to consent to forcible action by other states to act in its place. If it does not do so, action may be taken in self-defence.
52. In the case of a fragile state and, where its government is unable to deal with the non-state actors, in the case of a failing state, the non-state armed attack cannot be attributed to the state. Nor will the state necessarily incur responsibility for a failure to exercise due diligence to prevent the armed attack. This does not, however, exclude the victim state's right to

self-defence because this right can be exercised against non-state armed attacks and does not presuppose the territorial state's responsibility for internationally wrongful conduct.

PART III

INTERSECTION BETWEEN INTERNATIONAL HUMAN RIGHTS LAW AND INTERNATIONAL HUMANITARIAN LAW IN THE FIGHT AGAINST TERRORISM

Aim and scope of the Policy Recommendations

53. States are obliged to take effective measures to prevent terrorist acts and to protect the human rights of their citizens. In so doing, states must act consistently with their obligations under international law, including international human rights law and international humanitarian law. This injunction recognizes that upholding human rights and protecting the public from terrorist acts are not antithetical, but complementary responsibilities of states. The legitimacy of any measure taken by states to combat terrorism will depend upon compliance with the full range of applicable international law.
54. As pointed out in the Poelgeest Report there is no single answer to the question of which legal regime – human rights law or international humanitarian law – applies in the fight against terrorism. The applicable legal regime and the necessary concurrent application of several legal regimes can only be determined on a case-by-case basis. While the relationship between IHRL and IHL remains an evolving issue, every effort should be made by human rights and humanitarian law experts, whether belonging to governments, international organizations, non-governmental organizations or other actors to get better acquainted with each others' legal and policy perspectives, as well as with the realities of the application of the different bodies of law on the ground.
55. The aim of the recommendations in this Part is to highlight several areas central to defining the relationship between human rights and humanitarian law as a matter of law, policy and practice. The topics are grouped around three headings related to the applicability of the two bodies of law, their interplay on certain specific issues and their interface with other legal frameworks. The recommendations strive to restate existing law on some issues, to provide a reading of what developments in the law might be in others, and to suggest topics for further discussion and follow up by experts and policy-makers at the international level on yet others. The recommendations do not purport to address the broad array of IHRL or IHL issues raised by the fight against terrorism.

SECTION 1

APPLICABILITY OF IHRL AND IHL

Applicability of international human rights law

56. International human rights law applies at all times and is the body of international law most commonly applicable to counter-terrorist activity, whether at home or abroad. The application of human rights law in situations of armed conflict, alongside IHL, is now beyond reasonable debate.
57. The Human Rights Committee, the European Court of Human Rights and the former European Commission on Human Rights, as well as the Inter-American Commission on Human Rights have all found their respective instruments to apply extraterritorially, even in situations of armed conflict. Clearly, the fact that a state acts beyond its borders does not give rise to the applicability of the full range of positive human rights obligations binding on a state within its own territory. However, obligations do arise in respect of, and commensurate with, the exercise of the state's authority and control abroad. Where the state exercises direct control over individuals, IHRL is in principle applicable. This is of course distinct from the question of the interplay between IHRL and IHL addressed below.
58. An issue on which greater consideration is due is the derogability of human rights treaty obligations by states engaged in military operations in the territory of a third state, whether individually or collectively. Consideration should be given to whether extraterritorial derogability is or should be possible by an intervening state. This issue remains unresolved both in law and practice and should be the subject of further expert debate at the international level.

Applicability of international humanitarian law

59. Acts of terrorism in themselves do not automatically amount to 'armed conflict'. The majority of terrorist acts that take place around the world fall outside armed conflict and should be dealt with under a law enforcement paradigm. This means that the applicable legal regimes are domestic law, human rights law and international criminal law.
60. The threshold for the application of international humanitarian law is the existence of an armed conflict or occupation. It is thus necessary to exercise particular rigour in classifying a situation as an armed conflict so as not to extend IHL application to situations that, objectively, do not amount to armed conflict and where the exclusive application of human rights law is warranted.
61. While international armed conflict involves hostilities between states only, it is more difficult to determine when the threshold of non-international

armed conflict under Common Article 3 to the 1949 Geneva Conventions has been reached. A Common Article 3 conflict is one waged between one or more states and one or more organized non-state armed groups or between such groups themselves. It is generally accepted that there are two basic criteria for determining that a situation of violence may be classified as a Common Article 3 conflict: the intensity of the violence involved and the level of organization of the non-state party to such a conflict.

62. In so far as intensity of violence is concerned, it would include protracted violence meaning that acts are not perpetrated in isolation but as part of an ongoing campaign. It is immaterial whether the acts of violence perpetrated may or may not be characterized as terrorist in nature. With regard to the organization of the non-state party, an organized group would, *inter alia*, require a command structure and a leadership with a capacity to exert authority over its members.

63. It is possible for an armed conflict involving non-state actors to extend to the territory of more than one state, without necessarily qualifying as an international armed conflict. Such 'transnational' armed conflicts would be subject to IHL applicable to non-international armed conflicts. This will, however, depend on whether, within any particular state, the factual conditions are met for an armed conflict to exist. The application of IHL in one country does not mean that there is a global armed conflict and law enforcement will remain the principal means of dealing with acts of terrorism in countries/places where the armed conflict threshold has not been crossed.

SECTION 2

INTERPLAY OF IHRL AND IHL ON SPECIFIC ISSUES RELATED TO THE PROTECTION OF PERSONS

64. Where IHRL and IHL are both applicable, they should, where possible, be interpreted harmoniously. A harmonious approach to interpretation is possible where both bodies of rules have parallel purposes and principles that enable apparent conflicts to be resolved through consistent interpretation. The substantive coherence between the content of IHRL and IHL is extensive, notably in relation to the treatment of persons, fair trial and accountability.

65. However, the complexity of harmonious interpretation must also be recognized. The operation of the *lex specialis* rule is relevant when there are norms of IHL directed to the particular situation that are at variance with those of IHRL, which arises most obviously in relation to rules on the

right to life and detention in armed conflict. A context sensitive application of IHRL and a human rights informed application of IHL may not lead to greatly divergent standards on the vast majority of issues.

66. Attention should be paid to ensuring that all those charged with the implementation of IHRL and IHL understand and apply the relevant bodies of law. Emphasis should be placed on the duties of states to provide guidelines to those on the ground to clarify applicable law, including the interrelationship of IHRL and IHL in relation to particular situations and norms.
67. Human rights courts and treaty bodies have become increasingly engaged in the adjudication or assessment of human rights violations arising in armed conflict, providing victims with the prospect of a remedy, which may otherwise be elusive. However, these bodies have not always had due regard to IHL in their determinations of human rights issues in armed conflict situations.
68. Accountability for crimes committed in the name of counter-terrorism should be seen as a legal imperative under IHRL and IHL, not a policy alternative. Investigation of serious violations of either IHRL or IHL should be thorough and independent in line with established international standards. The right to reparation of victims of terrorism or of victims of violations committed in the name of fighting international terrorism should be recognized.

Treatment and procedural guarantees for persons detained in the fight against terrorism

69. Torture or cruel, inhuman or degrading treatment or punishment are absolutely prohibited by both international human rights and international humanitarian law. Calibrating standards of treatment to different categories of detainees, based on the reasons or circumstances of their detention is clearly unlawful. Every effort must be made to ensure that the prohibition of torture or cruel, inhuman and degrading treatment is observed in all places of detention and that persons responsible for possible violations are held to account. 'Ticking time-bomb' scenarios do not afford any exception to the prohibition of torture or cruel, inhuman or degrading treatment and should be categorically rejected.
70. Interrogation methods must be in conformity with the prohibition of torture or cruel, inhuman and degrading treatment and must be constantly reviewed to ensure that these prohibitions are respected in practice. While certain forms of treatment (such as mutilation, rape, electric shocks, etc.) per se amount to torture or cruel, inhuman and degrading treatment and are prohibited at all times, it is not possible to draw up finite lists of authorized interrogation methods.

71. Under international law, the use of statements and other evidence obtained by torture or cruel, inhuman and degrading treatment must be excluded from any criminal or other judicial proceedings, except in cases specifically provided for in Article 15 of the Convention against Torture.
72. While humanitarian and human rights law are essentially the same as regards fair trial rights, procedural safeguards for persons detained for posing a serious security threat differ depending on whether detention is governed by international humanitarian or human rights law. The latter mandates court supervision of any type of detention, including security detention, a requirement that may be derogated from only in the exceptional circumstances of a public emergency threatening the life of the nation. There is also a growing body of opinion according to which court supervision of detention can never be derogated from.
73. Humanitarian law deals with a different reality in which there might not be a functioning court system, in which detainee numbers might be significant and in which there may be a range of other obstacles to judicial review arising from the battlefield context. Thus, IHL in international armed conflict provides for review of internment based on imperative reasons of security (PoW detention is excluded), either by a court or administrative board. There are in certain circumstances particular challenges in implementing procedural safeguards for internment in non-international armed conflicts, which constitute the majority of armed conflicts today. This is an issue which merits further discussion at the international level and, if possible, the elaboration of specific rules or guidelines. In the interim, existing principles and safeguards, such as those proposed by the ICRC in 2005,[3] may be relied on as minimum standards of due process in any type of detention for security reasons.
74. A significant subset of non-international armed conflicts are those in which a coalition of states detains nationals of a 'host' state in its territory. The legal and practical problems involved in ensuring procedural safeguards in this type of detention are considerable and as yet not fully understood or explored.

[3] See J. Pejic, 'Procedural Principles and Safeguards for Internment/Administrative Detention in Armed Conflict and Other Situations of Violence' (June 2005) *International Review of the Red Cross* 87(858). It was published as Annex 1 to the ICRC report *International Humanitarian Law and the Challenges of Contemporary Armed Conflicts* presented to the 30th International Conference of the Red Cross and Red Crescent held in Geneva in 2007 and reflects the ICRC's institutional position (see www.icrc.org/Web/Eng/siteeng0.nsf/htmlall/p0892/$File/ICRC_002_0892.PDF).

The use of lethal force in the fight against terrorism

75. The issue of whether the use of lethal force against a person suspected of acts of terrorism is lawful depends on two separate questions: a) whether use of force in a territory which is not under the jurisdiction of the state whose agents employ the force violates the affected state's territorial integrity, and b) whether it involves an arbitrary deprivation of life of the targeted person.
76. Whether use of lethal force against a person is lawful may be judged according to two legal regimes: the law enforcement regime, governed by international human rights law, and rules on the conduct of hostilities governed by the law of armed conflict. IHL is *lex specialis*, which applies only when there is an ongoing armed conflict and the targeting has a nexus to the hostilities connected with that conflict.
77. Under the law enforcement regime governed by human rights law, a person may be targeted only when use of lethal force is absolutely necessary to protect others from unlawful violence. This is generally taken to mean that the unlawful violence is imminent, leaving no room or time for the employment of non-lethal methods of law enforcement. In IHL the use of lethal force is regulated by rules on the conduct of hostilities, which include provisions on the protection of civilians against direct attack unless and for such time as they take a direct part in hostilities.

Transfer of persons in the fight against terrorism

78. Human rights, refugee law, and humanitarian law protect individuals when they are transferred from the custody of one state to another. A minimum baseline standard which should be applied as regards transfers pertains to: threshold principles, substantive guarantees of *non-refoulement* and procedural guarantees. At least two threshold principles should be observed. The first is that formal procedures for transfer, such as extradition or deportation, may not be intentionally bypassed, and the second is that the transferring state should have a valid legal basis for apprehending the individual in contemplation of transfer.
79. It is generally accepted that there may be no transfers to a real risk: of torture or cruel, inhuman or degrading treatment; of persecution; of enforced disappearance; or of arbitrary deprivation of life.
80. The relevant procedural guarantees include the ability of the affected person to challenge the basis for his or her apprehension/detention and his or her ability to challenge transfer based on the grounds provided for in international law. Procedural safeguards also include a person's ability to challenge transfer before it takes place, before an independent decision-maker. Resort to diplomatic assurances can never per se obviate

the risk of serious violations referred to above. Where diplomatic assurances are used, as one element in the assessment of risk, they should be accompanied by rigorous safeguards such as judicial review and effective post-return monitoring by the transferring state.

81. The legal, practical and policy implications relating to the transfer of persons in the fight against terrorism are believed to require further expert discussion at the international level.

SECTION 3

INTERSECTIONS WITH OTHER LEGAL FRAMEWORKS

Obligations regarding peace and security and the protection of persons

82. Problems have arisen for the application of IHRL and IHL in relation to Security Council resolutions and their implementation. Examples include issues relating to the detention of persons and the freezing of assets.
83. States have a responsibility to implement Security Council resolutions. In the exercise of their discretion in the choice of methods of implementation, they should ensure conformity with human rights, international humanitarian law and other relevant bodies of international law. Lack of accountability for violations of IHRL and IHL arising in the implementation of counter-terrorism resolutions leads to a denial of access to justice for victims and should be avoided.
84. The Security Council cannot authorize violations of human rights and IHL norms that rise to the level of *jus cogens*. The Security Council should, moreover, take full account of the UN's own Global Counter-Terrorism Strategy, which centres on the protection and promotion of human rights as an integral part of any effective and sustainable counter-terrorism approach. Where Security Council resolutions are unclear, there should be a presumption that the Security Council does not intend that actions taken pursuant to its resolutions should violate international human rights and international humanitarian law.
85. The Security Council should avoid placing states in situations where their obligations regarding peace and security and under IHRL and IHL cannot be simultaneously respected. The human rights impact of all draft counter-terrorism resolutions should be thoroughly considered. Consideration should also be given to ongoing monitoring and conducting human rights impact assessments of all counter-terrorism resolutions.
86. The relationship between states' obligations regarding international peace and security and states' obligations for the protection of persons deserves further attention by experts at the international level.

Terrorism and criminal justice

87. Acts of violence carried out in the context of an international or non-international armed conflict are governed by the rules of international humanitarian law and should remain excluded from the notion of international terrorism under the criminal justice regime. Deliberate attacks against civilians and civilian objects are considered war crimes under international humanitarian law; consequently, the perpetrators of these acts may be prosecuted in domestic and international courts.
88. Consistent efforts should be made to ensure that legislation enacted to criminalize acts of terrorism in a State's domestic jurisdiction respects the non-derogable principle *nullum crimen sine lege* (the principle of legality). Counter-terrorism legislation should not jeopardize the rights to freedom of expression and association nor unduly restrict the due process rights of those accused of committing acts of terrorism.
89. Violations of fundamental human rights such as the right not to be subject to torture or other forms of ill treatment may hamper the criminal prosecution of suspected terrorists and have a negative impact on international cooperation in criminal matters. States must abide by the fundamental principles of due process in the collection of evidence in order to preserve the integrity of the judicial process and ensure successful domestic prosecution and inter-state cooperation.

INDEX